LNG Markets in Transition:
The Great Reconfiguration

LNG Markets in Transition:
The Great Reconfiguration

Edited by
ANNE-SOPHIE CORBEAU and DAVID LEDESMA

Contributors
CHRISTOPHER CASWELL
SYLVIE D'APOTE
ANDY FLOWER
JAMES HENDERSON
ANOUK HONORE
JAMES T JENSEN
KEN KOYAMA
CHRIS LE FEVRE
HOWARD ROGERS
BRIAN SONGHURST
JONATHAN STERN

Published by the Oxford University Press
for the Oxford Institute for Energy Studies and the
King Abdullah Petroleum Studies and Research Center
2016

OXFORD
UNIVERSITY PRESS

Great Clarendon Street, Oxford OX2 6DP
United Kingdom

Oxford University Press is a department of the University of Oxford.
It furthers the University's objective of excellence in research, scholarship
and education by publishing worldwide.
Oxford is a registered trade mark of Oxford University Press
in the UK and in certain other countries

© Oxford Institute for Energy Studies Studies and the
King Abdullah Petroleum Studies and Research Center
2016

The moral rights of the author have been asserted
Database right Oxford Institute for Energy Studies (maker)

First Edition published 2016

All rights reserved. No part of this publication may be reproduced,
stored in a retrieval system, or transmitted, in any form or by any means,
without the prior permission in writing of the Oxford Institute for Energy
Studies, or as expressly permitted by law, or under terms agreed with
the appropriate reprographics rights organization. Enquiries concerning
reproduction outside the scope of the above should be sent to Oxford
Institute for Energy Studies, 57 Woodstock Road, Oxford OX2 6FA

You must not circulate this book in any other binding or cover
and you must impose this same condition on any acquirer

Published in the United States of America by Oxford University Press
198 Madison Avenue, New York, NY 10016, United States of America

British Library Cataloguing in Publication Data
Data available

Library of Congress Control Number 2016943469

Cover designed by COX Design Limited
Typeset by Davidson Publishing Solutions, Glasgow
Printed by Hobbs the Printer, Southampton

ISBN 978-0-19-878326-8

The contents of this book are the sole responsibility of the authors.
They do not necessarily represent the views of the
Oxford Institute for Energy Studies or any of its members.

1 3 7 9 10 8 6 4 2

CONTENTS

Preface		*vii*
Acknowledgements		*ix*
Notes on Contributors		*x*
List of Figures		*xv*
List of Tables		*xxii*
List of Maps		*xxvi*
Glossary		*xxvii*
	Introduction Anne-Sophie Corbeau	1
1	Looking Back at History: the early development of LNG supplies and markets Jonathan Stern and Ken Koyama	10
2	The Maturing of the LNG Business Anne-Sophie Corbeau and Andy Flower	44
3	The Changing Commercial Structure of the Upstream and Midstream LNG Business David Ledesma	96
4	Facilities, Infrastructure, and Costs	131
	Liquefaction costs Brian Songhurst	132
	Changes in the LNG shipping business James T Jensen	160
	Regasification terminals: adapting to a new environment Chris Le Fevre	181
5	Future LNG Supply: looking ahead, who will be the main potential LNG suppliers?	209
	Outlook for Australian LNG: the limits of expansion James Henderson	215
	North America enters the LNG export race James T Jensen	230

		The outlook for Russian LNG: current delays, long-term upside *James Henderson*	255
		Eastern Africa: beyond 2020 *Anne-Sophie Corbeau*	273
		Other potential LNG supplies *James Henderson*	290
6		LNG Demand Potential	307
		What role for Europe in the global LNG market? *Anouk Honoré*	308
		Mature Asian markets: limited growth potential *Howard Rogers*	327
		More recent and emerging Asian LNG markets *Howard Rogers*	349
		LNG demand perspectives in Latin America and the Caribbean *Sylvie D'Apote*	385
		The Middle East and Africa region *Anne-Sophie Corbeau*	422
7		LNG as a Transport Fuel *Chris Le Fevre*	442
8		LNG Pricing: challenges in the late 2010s *Jonathan Stern*	468
9		LNG Contracts and Flexibility *Anne-Sophie Corbeau*	502
10		Conclusion: LNG markets – the great reconfiguration *Anne-Sophie Corbeau*	554
		Technical Appendix: introduction to LNG and LNG technologies *Christopher Caswell*	578
		Data Appendix	613
		Index	639

PREFACE

The King Abdullah Petroleum Studies and Research Center and the Oxford Institute for Energy Studies have assembled a group of leading experts to address the drivers and anatomy of LNG's great reconfiguration, at a time when the industry faces a larger number of possible futures than may have ever previously existed. This book sets out to provide a framework for understanding these futures and navigating the path that will begin to crystallize over the coming years.

From a business that was founded in a paradigm of pipelines (but with liquefaction, shipping, and regas standing in for the pipes), the LNG industry finds itself shaped by challenges that could not have been foreseen just a few years ago. In the past decade, Qatar doubled the size of the LNG market. This decade sees a further doubling, with a supply surge from two very different market and regulatory environments – North America and Australia – that appears to have overwhelmed demand in the short term. The LNG industry has matured, not only in terms of numbers of sellers and buyers, but also with new technologies such as floating liquefaction, smaller scale liquefaction and transportation of LNG, and the entry of new companies who are challenging the existing structure of the business. This has put pressure on the mechanisms of price formation and contract flexibility at a time of downward pressure on oil-linked pricing, for reasons quite unconnected with the fundamentals of LNG development. A key question is whether North American spot prices will set a cap on global LNG prices, or will demand for new, more flexible, LNG introduce international netbacks into North America?

The long-term bullish case for investment in supply was underpinned by the *Golden Age of Natural Gas* narrative; that the 'low-carbon hydrocarbon' would be the fuel of choice for reliable power generation and, furthermore, would encroach into the territory of high-priced liquid fuels. An alternative story is that natural gas may be entering a *New Dark Age*; caught between decarbonization and the rise of renewables and cheap coal, not to mention cheap oil. Customers in growth markets, particularly in Asia, that were once seen as the anchors for future LNG developments now question whether they can afford to pay the prices needed to precipitate the next wave of supply investment.

The lack of new final investment decisions last year may lead to the next price spike and drive the continuing cycles of boom after bust, confirming the traditional view of LNG markets. In this view, the old rules bend to accommodate the current imbalances but do not break to create a discontinuity. But there is another view. New business models among LNG players and new energy policies in gas importing countries lead to a switch to flexible, spot prices. These prices link the major price discovery hubs, albeit imperfectly, to create a more global gas market than has ever existed.

Adherents of the first view maintain that capital for infrastructure investment depends on long-term contracts and relationships, mostly funded by the aggregated balance sheets of captive end-use customers. This business model underpinned the first 50 years of the industry's growth. But perhaps the necessity-driven efficiencies demanded in a less certain market environment will prove to be precisely the spur needed to shift to a paradigm where flexible, hub-priced LNG can be financed and developed. The resulting gas prices could be low enough to compete with coal (when air quality and carbon reduction targets are taken into account), and support the continued growth of LNG, while fundamentally changing the industry's structure and business model in the future.

David Hobbs and Bassam Fattouh
June 2016

ACKNOWLEDGEMENTS

No work of this size and complexity can be brought together without the efforts of many people. We would like to particularly thank all of our fellow authors, not just for all the effort that they have put into their chapters, but also for their self-discipline in meeting the agreed deadlines throughout the preparation of this book. Their hard work and dedication has enabled us together to author such an extensive book on LNG. We would also like to thank our friends at GIIGNL, the International Group of Liquefied Natural Gas Importers, for letting us use their data. Anne-Sophie Corbeau would like to express her gratitude to her KAPSARC colleagues, in particular to David Hobbs and Samantha Gross, for their continuous support over two years. David Ledesma would like to thank his colleagues at the Oxford Institute for Energy Studies, in particular Bassam Fattouh, Jonathan Stern, and Howard Rogers, for their help and support in the drafting of this book. Sylvie D'Apote would like to thank Edmar Almeida for valuable insights and comments and Yanna Clara for substantial help in data research and modelling.

Thanks too to Dave Samson who prepared the maps, diagrams, and graphs; Catherine Gaunt, our copy editor, and Christopher Riches for his help with graphics and preparing the index, and who have both helped us pull together contributions from such a wide number of authors; and Evelyn Sword and Margaret Walker for typesetting. The Oxford Institute for Energy Studies would also like to thank the sponsors to the Oxford Institute for Energy Studies Natural Gas Research Programme for their continuous support, without which this book would not have been written; Kate Teasdale, the administrator at the OIES, and Jo Ilott, the administrator of the Natural Gas Research Programme.

Anne-Sophie and David would like to thank their families (Jacob and Marie; Fiona and Catherine) for all their support in the preparation of this book. David would also like to remember Ian and thank him for all his support and guidance over the years.

Anne-Sophie Corbeau and David Ledesma
June 2016

NOTES ON CONTRIBUTORS

Christopher Caswell joined the MW Kellogg Company (now KBR) in 1991. He has 25 years of experience in the engineering and construction industry with an exclusive focus on LNG since the year 2000. His areas of responsibility include liquefaction, regasification terminals, and offshore LNG. Chris leads the Houston LNG Technology Development Team, which has technical oversight responsibility for KBR's worldwide LNG projects, while maintaining KBR's technical know-how and execution consistency. He has led and co-authored several papers on LNG with a focus on communicating technical issues to a commercial audience. Chris is an instructor for two of the Gas Technology Institute's training courses on the LNG industry and sits on the governing body of Gastech and the Program Committee for the LNG-X conference series. Chris is a mechanical engineering graduate of Cornell University (NY, USA) and a registered Professional Engineer in the State of Texas.

Anne-Sophie Corbeau has been working in the energy industry for 15 years with a particular focus on gas markets. She joined KAPSARC as Research Fellow in 2014 to head its gas research. Before this, she worked as senior gas expert at the International Energy Agency. She was responsible for the research on short- to medium-term developments in global gas markets, and energy security. She developed a new publication – *the Medium Term Gas Market Report* – and also authored or co-authored several publications on trading hubs, Asian markets, China, and India. Prior to this assignment, Anne-Sophie worked at CERA as Associate Director in the European gas team, as a specialist in gas market fundamentals and demand forecasting. She also worked on fuel cells and hydrogen in her early career. Anne-Sophie holds an MSc from the Ecole Centrale Paris and from the University of Stuttgart.

Sylvie D'Apote has 20 years' experience as an international energy consultant, largely focusing on natural gas in Latin America. Based in Brazil since 2003, she has a deep expertise in regional gas supply and demand, regulatory issues, market integration, gas and LNG trade, and gas-to-power. Since 2013 she has been Managing Partner of Prysma E&T Consultores, in Rio de Janeiro, after acting as Gas Energy's Managing Partner and HIS-CERA's Southern Cone Director for Gas. Prior to moving to Brazil, she headed the Latin American Program at the International

Energy Agency (IEA) in Paris and was senior economist for WEFA Energy, in London. She authored *South American Gas: Daring to Tap the Bounty* (IEA, 2003), and has written several papers and contributed chapters to a number of books. She has an MSc in economics from La Sapienza University, Rome, Italy, and an MSc in energy technology from Imperial College, London.

Andy Flower has been working as an Independent Consultant since May 2001, specializing in the LNG business where his areas of expertise include strategy, marketing, project structures, shipping, pricing, supply and demand, and project economics. He retired from BP in 2001 after 32 years of service, including 22 years working in the company's LNG and natural gas business units, where his roles included managing BP's interests in LNG projects in Abu Dhabi, Nigeria, Australia, and Qatar, and developing new investment opportunities. He led the negotiation of the first Qatargas sales and purchase contract and has negotiated LNG sales and purchase agreements with buyers in Asia, Europe, and the USA. He has authored many articles on LNG and contributed chapters to a number of books on LNG and natural gas. He has an MA in mathematics from Oxford University and an MSc in mathematical statistics from Birmingham University.

Dr James Henderson is a Senior Research Fellow at the Oxford Institute for Energy Studies, working for the Gas and Oil Programmes covering Russia and CIS issues as well as global energy matters that affect the region. He is a BP Professor of Energy at the Skolkovo Management School in Moscow and lectures on energy issues at a number of universities in Europe and the USA. He has worked in the oil sector for US company Amerada Hess, as well as spending time as a consultant and investment banker, most notably working on the Novatek IPO and BP's investment in and exit from TNK-BP. His publications include numerous papers on the Russian oil and gas sector, including most recently work on the future of Russian gas exports and the outlook for Russian oil production. He has also published in 2010 *Non-Gazprom Gas Producers in Russia*, co-edited *The Russian Gas Matrix: How Markets are Driving Change* for OIES (2014), and recently published *International Partnership in Russia* with Palgrave Macmillan (2014).

Anouk Honoré is a Senior Research Fellow at the Oxford Institute for Energy Studies, a recognized independent centre of the University of Oxford. Her research focuses mainly on gas market fundamentals (supply, demand, and policies) and power generation. Her main areas of expertise include the European region (35 countries) and South America. She is the author and co-author of several chapters, papers, and shorter works on natural gas in these regions and speaks frequently on the subject at academic and industry conferences. She published *European Natural Gas Demand, Supply and Pricing: cycles, seasons and the impact of LNG arbitrage* (Oxford University Press) in December 2010. Before joining the Institute, Dr Honoré worked at the International Energy Agency in Paris. Her work focused mainly on natural gas policies in the 26 IEA member countries, but also on China and on South America.

James T Jensen has been President of Jensen Associates, a consulting firm in Weston, Massachusetts, specializing in international energy economics. He received the 2001 Award for Outstanding Contributions to the Profession of Energy Economics and its Literature from the International Association for Energy Economics. He has been an Advisory Committee Member of the Interdisciplinary MIT Study, 'The Future of Natural Gas', and a member of the Brookings Institution Natural Gas Task Force. He has studied LNG prospects for projects involving Algeria, Indonesia, Nigeria, Norway, Qatar, and Trinidad. He has also evaluated various pipeline projects in North America, the Caspian region, and eastern Asia. He is a past President of the Boston Economic Club, a member of the International Association for Energy Economics, the National Association of Petroleum Investment Analysts, the Paris Energy Club, and the Society of Petroleum Engineers. He has a BS in chemical engineering from MIT and an MBA from Harvard Business School.

Dr Ken Koyama is Chief Economist and Managing Director at the Institute of Energy Economics, Japan (IEEJ). He also takes a position of Visiting Professor at Graduate School of Public Policy at the University of Tokyo. He was awarded a BA in economics in 1982 from Waseda University, Tokyo, Japan; an MA in economics in 1986 from Waseda University; and a PhD in 2001 from University of Dundee, Dundee, Scotland. His specialized field of research is energy security and the geopolitics of energy; and analysis for the global energy market and policy, with emphasis on the Asia–Pacific region. He has served as a member of energy policy related advisory councils and committees of the Japanese government on many occasions. He also plays a role as a member of the International Advisory Board, Energy Academy Europe (the Netherlands) and International Advisor at the Energy Commission of Tenaga National University (Malaysia). He was awarded the BrandLaureate's 'Brand Personality Award 2016'.

David Ledesma is a Research Fellow at the Oxford Institute for Energy Studies and an independent energy and strategy consultant specializing in LNG and gas. In his 32 years of experience in the energy and utility sector in Shell and other companies, David worked on the development of complex integrated energy projects, negotiations at government level, and in the management of joint ventures. David has been the co-author of *Gas in Asia* (2008), *Natural Gas Markets in the Middle East and North Africa* (2011), *The Price of Internationally Traded Gas* (2012), and *The Principles of Project Finance* (2012). He has also authored several papers for the Institute; 'The Changing relationship between NOCs and IOCs in the LNG chain' (2009), 'East Africa – Potential for Export' (2013), and 'The Future of Australian LNG Exports: Will domestic challenges limit the development of future LNG export capacity?' (2014).

Chris Le Fevre is a Senior Visiting Research Fellow at the Oxford Institute for Energy Studies and an independent consultant specializing in strategic, commercial, regulatory, and operational issues in the natural gas sector. He has over 30 years' experience in the energy sector including roles with Transco (now National Grid Gas), British Gas, and Shell. At Transco he was the director responsible for implementing the Network Code and the introduction of domestic competition. His roles in British Gas included managing operations in Spain, the former GDR, Hungary, and the Czech Republic. Before British Gas he worked for Shell in exploration and production companies in the Netherlands and Malaysia. Chris also served on the Board of the Northern Ireland Utility Regulator. He has published studies on UK Gas Storage (2013), *The Prospects for Natural Gas as a Transportation Fuel in Europe* (2014), and *The Role of Natural Gas in UK Energy Policy* (2015).

Howard Rogers is the Director of the Natural Gas Research Programme at the Oxford Institute for Energy Studies. Prior to OIES, Howard was with BP for 29 years, mostly in business development, strategy, planning, mergers and acquisitions, and negotiation roles in upstream oil and gas in European, North American, Middle Eastern, and FSU locations. In 2003 he became Head of Global Gas Fundamental Analysis. He has a degree in chemical engineering and is a Fellow of the Institution of Chemical Engineers. Howard has published research papers and authored book chapters on LNG price arbitrage between the regional markets of Asia, Europe, and North America, and on shale gas in the USA and the UK. More recently Howard and Jonathan Stern have jointly written papers on the transition to hub-based pricing in Europe and the changing roles and risks of key players, and also on the challenges to JCC pricing in Asian LNG markets.

Brian Songhurst has an honours degree in chemical engineering from Imperial College, London, is a Fellow of the Institution of Chemical Engineers, and a Research Associate with the Oxford Institute of Energy Studies. He has had 48 years' experience in the oil and gas industry, working for engineering contractors, energy companies, and specialist consultants. He was Manager of Facilities Engineering at J Ray McDermott, one of the leading offshore contractors, and Engineering Manager of the LNG Import Terminal Group at MW Kellogg, one of the world's leading LNG contractors. This combination of offshore and LNG design and project experience has enabled him to play an active role in the design and execution of floating LNG projects. Brian is past chairman of the Institution of Chemical Engineers Subject Oil & Natural Gas group which provides technical networking between its members to deliver best practices within the chemical engineering community.

Professor Jonathan Stern founded the OIES Natural Gas Research Programme in 2003 and was its Director until October 2011 when he became its Chairman and a Senior Research Fellow. He is Honorary Professor at the Centre for Energy, Petroleum & Mineral Law & Policy, University of Dundee; Visiting Professor at Imperial College's Centre for Environmental Policy in London; and Fellow of the Energy Delta Institute at Groningen in the Netherlands. He also teaches at the Environmental Change Institute in Oxford and Sciences Po University in Paris. Since 2011 he has been the EU speaker for the EU–Russia Gas Advisory Council. He is the author of several books and many shorter works on energy and natural gas issues in the UK, Europe (western and eastern), the former Soviet Union, and Asia.

LIST OF FIGURES

Chapter 1
Figure 1.1	LNG exporters, 1964–2000	12
Figure 1.2	LNG imports by region, 1964–2000	17
Figure 1.3	European LNG imports, 1964–2000	18
Figure 1.4	Japan's LNG imports by source	22
Figure 1.5	LNG use in the power sector	24
Figure 1.6	LNG use in the city gas sector	28
Figure 1.7	Energy import dependence of Japan, Korea, and Taiwan	29
Figure 1.8	Korean LNG imports by source, 1986–2000	31
Figure 1.9	Taiwanese LNG imports by source, 1990–2000	32
Figure 1.10	LNG import source diversification of Japan, Korea, and Taiwan in 2000	34
Figure 1.11	Shares of Japan, Korea, and Taiwan in global LNG imports	38

Chapter 2
Figure 2.1	FID activity and liquefaction capacity additions	45
Figure 2.2	A limited diversification away from Asia: regions importing LNG	46
Figure 2.3	Pipeline and LNG compete to supply Europe	49
Figure 2.4	US LNG import forecasts differ markedly from actual LNG imports	54
Figure 2.5	Chinese LNG contracts against actual imports and capacity	60
Figure 2.6	LNG exports from new LNG exporters compared with Qatar, 1999–2015	64
Figure 2.7	Qatar LNG exports by region, 1997–2015	79
Figure 2.8	LNG supplies diverted away from Europe	80
Figure 2.9	Regional gas prices, 2007–16	81
Figure 2.10	Japan's sourcing additional LNG supplies, difference between 2010 and 2014	85

Chapter 3

Figure 3.1	LNG value chain – gas use, capital cost, and unit costs (based on an 8 mtpa plant)	98
Figure 3.2	Integrated project structure	106
Figure 3.3	Transfer pricing project structure	107
Figure 3.4	Tolling project structure	108
Figure 3.5	Tolling project structure example	109
Figure 3.6	FLNG example project structure	110
Figure 3.7	LNG project structures, by start-up year and capacity, for projects in operation and under construction	112
Figure 3.8	Typical financing structure for the liquefaction portion of the LNG chain	117
Figure 3.9	LNG project structures – key commercial agreements	119
Figure 3.10	LNG aggregator structure of the business	121
Figure 3.11	Sabine Pass tolling structure	125
Figure 3.12	Cameron LNG tolling structure	127

Chapter 4

Figure 4.1	CAPEX by year (unit liquefaction costs by year of production start)	132
Figure 4.2	Plant production capacity (train size) by year (liquefaction plant capacity growth)	133
Figure 4.3	Cost components (cost breakdown by category)	134
Figure 4.4	Equipment count vs processing (equipment count increase vs scope)	136
Figure 4.5	LNG escalation excluding Australian projects	142
Figure 4.6	Average size of LNG tankers by launch year (excluding tankers of less than 25,000 m^3)	162
Figure 4.7	Tanker transportation cost as a function of size	163
Figure 4.8	Length of long-term contract commitments written in a given year	167
Figure 4.9	Long-term contract commitments written in a given year by contract type	169
Figure 4.10	Age distribution of tankers when they are scrapped or converted to other service	170
Figure 4.11	History of operable tanker capacity since first orders were delivered for Algeria to the UK and France in 1965	171
Figure 4.12	Tanker ownership by type for selected periods, 1970–2014	172

Figure 4.13	Short-term LNG trade as a percentage of total trade	175
Figure 4.14	LNG spot tanker rates as a percentage of the estimated rate required to justify a newbuild 145,000 m^3 tanker	176
Figure 4.15	Regasification terminal capacity by region	182
Figure 4.16	Global terminal capacity and LNG throughput	183
Figure 4.17	Regasification plant utilization levels by region, 1969–2014	184
Figure 4.18	Indicative evolution of the terminal business model	186
Figure 4.19	Capacity availability in a multi-user terminal (dependent rights)	194
Figure 4.20	Allocation of spare berthing slots at Grain LNG	201

Chapter 5

Figure 5.1	New capacity coming on line, 2010–20	210
Figure 5.2	LNG contracted by region versus planned capacity	212
Figure 5.3	Outlook for Australian LNG capacity to 2020	218
Figure 5.4	Australian dollar versus US dollar, 2011–15	223
Figure 5.5	Capacity of proposed US export projects by regulatory and contract status	238
Figure 5.6	Capacity of proposed British Columbia LNG export project by sponsor	242
Figure 5.7	Illustration of the incentive that the Asian Premium created	247
Figure 5.8	Illustration of the price risk in delivering LNG to Europe from the US Gulf coast	248
Figure 5.9	Illustration of the Asian spot price 'safety net'	249
Figure 5.10	Tanker rates to Japan	252
Figure 5.11	Percentage of expanded Panama Canal capacity needed to accommodate potential shipments from the US Gulf to Japan in 170,000 m^3 vessels	253
Figure 5.12	Spot LNG volumes traded by Gazprom Marketing and Trading	257
Figure 5.13	Possible outlook for Russian LNG production	272
Figure 5.14	Different scenarios for LNG developments in Eastern Africa	278
Figure 5.15	Asian companies' shareholding in relevant LNG projects	282
Figure 5.16	Transport costs to various markets at different oil prices from Eastern Africa	283

Figure 5.17	Tanzania's plans to increase power capacity	288
Figure 5.18	LNG exports scenarios	290

Chapter 6

Figure 6.1	European LNG imports per month by country of destination, 2004–16 (bcm)	309
Figure 6.2	European regasification capacity (existing and projects) as of 31 December 2015 vs LNG imports in 2015 (bcm)	310
Figure 6.3	Natural gas demand in OECD Europe, by sectors, 1970–2015 (bcm)	315
Figure 6.4	Relationship between gas prices ($/MMBtu), coal prices ($/mt), and EU ETS prices (€/tCO2) in Europe in 2015	318
Figure 6.5	Scenarios for natural gas demand and indigenous production in Europe, 2015–30 (bcm)	320
Figure 6.6	Scenarios for natural gas demand, indigenous production (high and low), and pipeline imports, in Europe, 2015–30 (bcm)	321
Figure 6.7	Scenarios for natural gas demand, indigenous production (high and low) and pipeline imports in Europe, 2015–30 (bcm)	323
Figure 6.8	Fuel consumption for electricity generation (general electric utilities)	330
Figure 6.9	Japanese nuclear restart scenarios	333
Figure 6.10	Future power generation gas consumption for six cases	334
Figure 6.11	Historical and future Japanese gas demand	334
Figure 6.12	Japan's LNG supply outlook and demand uncertainty, 2010–30	336
Figure 6.13	South Korea fuel consumption for power generation, 2000–14	339
Figure 6.14	Historic and illustrative future South Korean gas demand	341
Figure 6.15	South Korea's LNG supply outlook and demand uncertainty, 2010–30	342
Figure 6.16	A possible future generation outlook to 2030 for Taiwan	345
Figure 6.17	Taiwan gas demand outlook to 2030	346

Figure 6.18	Taiwan future LNG demand and contractual position	346
Figure 6.19	Primary energy mix of China, 1995–2014	349
Figure 6.20	Chinese historical and future natural gas demand from various sources	353
Figure 6.21	Historical and future Chinese domestic natural gas production	354
Figure 6.22	China supply and demand on base-case demand assumptions, 2000–30	355
Figure 6.23	China supply and demand – high demand assumption, 2000–30	356
Figure 6.24	China's LNG import requirements on base and high future demand cases and contractual commitments	357
Figure 6.25	Primary energy mix of India, 1995–2014	359
Figure 6.26	Indian demand outlooks and domestic gas production, 2005–30	362
Figure 6.27	India's future LNG import requirements and contractual commitments	363
Figure 6.28	Outlook for Singapore gas demand and supply	365
Figure 6.29	Thailand gas supply and demand outlook, 2009–30	367
Figure 6.30	Indonesia primary energy mix, 1995–2014	369
Figure 6.31	Indonesia production and consumption of natural gas, 2000–13	370
Figure 6.32	Natural gas balance, 2000–30	371
Figure 6.33	Malaysia energy balance, 1995–2014	372
Figure 6.34	Malaysia LNG contract ACQs, 2010–30	373
Figure 6.35	Malaysian supply outlook to 2030	374
Figure 6.36	Malaysian demand and export outlook to 2030	375
Figure 6.37	Pakistan gas supply and demand outlook, 1995–2030	378
Figure 6.38	Bangladesh potential gas supply and demand to 2030	379
Figure 6.39	Asian LNG imports, 2010–30: low case	383
Figure 6.40	Asian LNG imports, 2010–30: high case	383
Figure 6.41	Asian LNG imports, 2010–30: differences between low and high cases	384
Figure 6.42	Natural gas reserves, dry gas production, and consumption by country, 2014	388
Figure 6.43	Natural gas demand by sector of use in Latin America, 2013	389

Figure 6.44	Historical growth of LNG imports in Latin America by country of destination	392
Figure 6.45	Argentina's natural gas consumption	395
Figure 6.46	Argentina's domestic natural gas production and imports	396
Figure 6.47	Brazil's natural gas consumption	400
Figure 6.48	Brazil's domestic natural gas production and imports	401
Figure 6.49	Brazil's LNG import scenarios (bcm/year): Lower LNG Demand Scenario	404
Figure 6.50	Brazil's LNG import scenarios (bcm/year): Higher LNG Demand Scenario	405
Figure 6.51	Projected supply–demand balance in Colombia, 2016–30	410
Figure 6.52	Power generation mix in selected Caribbean and Central American countries, 2013	413
Figure 6.53	Pipeline and LNG imports in Mexico (bcm/year)	420
Figure 6.54	Sectoral gas use in selected MENA countries (2013)	423
Figure 6.55	LNG imports from MENA countries	424

Chapter 7

Figure 7.1	Existing and possible new emission control areas (ECAs)	448
Figure 7.2	Marine fuel price comparisons with regional gas prices	449
Figure 7.3	Marine fuel price differentials with regional gas prices (negative differential means gas is cheaper)	450
Figure 7.4	EU Blue Corridors – main routes	459

Chapter 8

Figure 8.1	Regional gas prices, 2008–15	471
Figure 8.2	Average monthly LNG import prices in Japan, China, Korea, Taiwan and China, 2000–10 ($/MMBtu)	474
Figure 8.3	Average monthly Asian LNG import prices in Japan, Korea, Taiwan China, and India, 2010–15	477
Figure 8.4	Illustrative prices of LNG in Asia indexed to JCC and Henry Hub at different price levels	480
Figure 8.5	JKM, NBP, and JOE Prices, July 2009–December 2015	483

Chapter 9

Figure 9.1	Spot and short-term LNG exports, 1996–2015	509
Figure 9.2	Spot and short-term trade against countries' LNG exports	509
Figure 9.3	Short-term against spot trade, 2000–15	511
Figure 9.4	Portfolio LNG as a source of spot LNG	515
Figure 9.5	Spot LNG imports, 2006–15	517
Figure 9.6	Surplus regasification capacity rises	519
Figure 9.7	Destination flexibility in long-term contracts as of 2015	521
Figure 9.8	Third-party access (TPA) to LNG terminals in different regions, 2015	522
Figure 9.9	Number of LNG terminals by size of maximum cargo allowed	524
Figure 9.10	Japan's contracted LNG quantities against import needs	528
Figure 9.11	Estimated uncommitted LNG supply, 2015–25	530
Figure 9.12	LNG contract expiry dates	531
Figure 9.13	Destinations of contracts expiring over 2015–25	531
Figure 9.14	Quantities potentially available if selected contracts are not extended (excludes Qatar)	532
Figure 9.15	Qatar's LNG in 2015: spot trade, LNG exports, and long-term contracts	534
Figure 9.16	Qatar's potential spot and short-term LNG trade	536
Figure 9.17	Future spot and short-term LNG trade	539
Figure 9.18	Interregional LNG flows by 2020	546

Chapter 10

Figure 10.1	Supply scenarios, 2014–20	565
Figure 10.2	Key suppliers' strengths and weaknesses	568
Figure 10.3	The steps towards a price war in Europe between US LNG and Russian pipeline gas	571

Technical Appendix

Figure A.1	Example of a refrigeration cycle used for natural gas liquefaction	579
Figure A.2	LNG as one of many products from natural gas	580
Figure A.3	Simplified block flow diagram for a liquefaction plant	581
Figure A.4	Defining LPG, NGL, and LNG from natural gas	583
Figure A.5	The AP-C3MR™ liquefaction process	588

Figure A.6	Coil-wound heat exchanger by APCI	589
Figure A.7	The ConocoPhillips Optimized Cascade© liquefaction process	590
Figure A.8	Examples of a cold box and a plate fin heat exchanger from Chart Industries	591
Figure A.9	Growth in LNG train size over time	592
Figure A.10	Cross-section of LNG ship types	595
Figure A.11	Example of a Moss LNG carrier and a membrane LNG carrier	596
Figure A.12	Percentage of LNG carrier fleet by containment type	598
Figure A.13	Process flow diagram for an LNG regasification terminal	599
Figure A.14	The full floating LNG value chain	605

LIST OF TABLES

Chapter 2

Table 2.1	Drivers behind the construction of LNG terminals in Europe, 2000–15	47
Table 2.2	Why small importers turned to LNG	89
Table 2.3	FSRUs as of January 2016	91

Chapter 3

| Table 3.1 | Number of vessels required to move 1 mtpa LNG | 100 |
| Table 3.2 | LNG project structures, by start-up year and capacity, for projects in operation and under construction | 113 |

Chapter 4

Table 4.1	Cost comparison summary (costs 2014 basis)	138
Table 4.2	Operating cost breakdown	139
Table 4.3	Liquefaction costs (CAPEX + OPEX)	140
Table 4.4	FLNG projects currently under construction	147
Table 4.5	SWOT analysis of FLNG	148
Table 4.6	OPEX cost estimate for a 2.5 mtpa FLNG	157
Table 4.7	Proposed design and construction schedules of current FLNG projects	158
Table 4.8	Current planned FLNG projects and prospects	159
Table 4.9	Largest independent ship owners	173

Table 4.10	Comparison of netbacks to Nigeria and Algeria from Japan and Spain, February 2011: pre-Fukushima	178
Table 4.11	Comparison of netbacks to Nigeria and Algeria from Japan and Spain, July 2012: peak charter rates	178
Table 4.12	Comparison of netbacks to Nigeria and Algeria from Japan and Spain, March 2015: post price collapse	179
Table 4.13	LNG terminals by region	182
Table 4.14	Terminal utilization levels for selected plant in NW Europe in 2014	185

Chapter 5

Table 5.1	Pricing mechanisms for different future LNG suppliers	213
Table 5.2	IOCs' planned projects	214
Table 5.3	Asian investment in Australian LNG projects	219
Table 5.4	Contracted gas from Australian LNG projects	226
Table 5.5	Australia's LNG projects	228
Table 5.6	North American LNG projects by region and status (as of January 2016)	236
Table 5.7	US projects under construction	239
Table 5.8	Approved BC projects (as of December 2015)	242
Table 5.9	Eastern Canadian projects	245
Table 5.10	Balance of SPAs in US LNG projects under construction	246
Table 5.11	Assessment of current state of Russian LNG projects	260
Table 5.12	LNG contracts signed by Yamal LNG and Novatek	268
Table 5.13	Contracts for LNG supply from Far East LNG	269
Table 5.14	Key indicators for Mozambique and Tanzania	273
Table 5.15	Shareholdings in licences with significant discoveries	275
Table 5.16	Fiscal terms	286
Table 5.17	LNG liquefaction capacity and LNG production (2014)	291

Chapter 6

Table 6.1	Assumptions used in this section for natural gas demand and supply balances in Europe, 2015–30 (bcm)	326
Table 6.2	Japanese low and high LNG import cases	337
Table 6.3	South Korea LNG imports – low and high cases	343
Table 6.4	Taiwan LNG import outlook – low and high cases	347
Table 6.5	China supply and demand on base case demand assumptions (bcm/year)	356

Table 6.6	China supply and demand on high case demand assumptions (bcm/year)	357
Table 6.7	China LNG import cases	358
Table 6.8	India LNG import requirements	364
Table 6.9	Singapore LNG import outlook	366
Table 6.10	Thailand LNG import outlook	368
Table 6.11	Indonesia net LNG import outlook	371
Table 6.12	Malaysia LNG import outlook	375
Table 6.13	Pakistan LNG import outlook	378
Table 6.14	Bangladesh LNG import outlook	380
Table 6.15	Vietnam LNG import outlook	381
Table 6.16	Low and high LNG import cases to 2030 (mtpa)	385
Table 6.17	Comparative demographic, economic, and energy indicators	386
Table 6.18	Latin America's existing regasification terminals and under construction	390
Table 6.19	Latin America's proposed regasification terminals	391
Table 6.20	Argentina's LNG import outlook range (bcm/year)	398
Table 6.21	Brazil's LNG import outlook range (bcm/year)	405
Table 6.22	Chile's LNG import outlook range (bcm/year)	406
Table 6.23	Uruguay's LNG import outlook range (bcm/year)	408
Table 6.24	Colombia's LNG import outlook range (bcm/year)	411
Table 6.25	LNG import outlook range for the Caribbean and Central America (bcm/year)	418
Table 6.26	Latin America LNG import outlook range (bcm/year)	422
Table 6.27	Middle East and Africa LNG demand (mtpa)	431

Chapter 7

Table 7.1	One hundred year GWP for the main GHGs (Fifth assessment from IPCC)	444
Table 7.2	Comparison of natural gas consumption for different types of vessels and vehicles	445
Table 7.3	Main stakeholders in marine transport	447
Table 7.4	Comparison of emissions by fuel type	448
Table 7.5	Top ten bunkering ports and LNG terminal locations	452
Table 7.6	Estimated commercial vehicle populations (thousands) and 2013 sales	453
Table 7.7	Main stakeholders in road freight transport	453
Table 7.8	Retail and wholesale natural gas prices and retail diesel, in $/MMBtu for Q4 2015	454

Table 7.9	Global oil demand in transportation, in million b/d	456
Table 7.10	LNG infrastructure in Europe	460
Table 7.11	Selected forecast for global LNG consumption in transport (mtpa)	462

Chapter 9

| Table 9.1 | The origins of spot cargoes: analysis of contracts, 2015 | 512 |

Chapter 10

| Table 10.1 | LNG demand ranges (mtpa) | 562 |

Technical Appendix

Table A.1	Simplified process technology matrix	587
Table A.2	LNG process technology providers/licensors	609
Table A.3	AGRU process technology providers/licensors	610
Table A.4	Liquefaction engineering, procurement, and construction (EPC)	610
Table A.5	Regasification terminal EPC companies	610
Table A.6	LNG storage tank technology providers and constructors	611
Table A.7	Offshore classification societies	611

Data Appendix

Table D.1	LNG export data by year and by country (mtpa)	614
Table D.2	LNG import data by year and by country (mtpa)	616
Table D.3	Liquefaction plants	620
Table D.4	Regasification terminals	627

LIST OF MAPS

Chapter 2
Map 2.1	European LNG terminals	50
Map 2.2	China's import infrastructure	58
Map 2.3	Middle East gas infrastructure	62

Chapter 5
Map 5.1	Australia's gas market and LNG export projects	217
Map 5.2	US projects under construction (as of end 2015)	234
Map 5.3	US projects proposed to FERC or MARAD (as of end 2015)	235
Map 5.4	Schematic of Russia's existing and potential LNG projects	261
Map 5.5	Eastern Africa's gas resources	276

Chapter 6
Map 6.1	Latin America's four sub-regions	387
Map 6.2	South America's main pipelines, existing and proposed LNG terminals	393
Map 6.3	Main pipelines, existing and proposed LNG terminals in Mexico, Central America, and the Caribbean	412

GLOSSARY

°C	degrees Celsius
°F	degrees Fahrenheit
/d	per day
ACQ	Annual Contract Quantity
ADB	Asian Development Bank
AECO	Alberta hub
aggregator	A company that purchases LNG from several sources, supplies LNG to several buyers, and uses its LNG supply and shipping portfolio to its commercial advantage
AGRU	Acid Gas Removal Unit
ANEA	Argus north-east Asia price
APLNG	Australia–Pacific LNG (Australia)
APM	Administered Price Mechanism
arbitrage	Where a cargo is moved from one trading region or country to another in order to enjoy an upside financial gain
Aus$	Australian dollar
b/d	Barrels per day
BAFA	Average price for all German gas imports
basis differential	Difference between the price at a particular market point and the marker reference price
BBL	Balgzand Bacton Line (pipeline)
bbl	Barrel
bcf	Billion cubic feet
bcf/d	billion cubic feet per day
bcm	Billion cubic metres
bcm/year	Billion cubic metres per year
biogas	Gas produced from the anaerobic digestion of organic matter such as animal manure, sewage, and municipal solid waste
biomethane	Biogas which is upgraded to grid fuel quality. Biomethane can be liquefied and is referred to as BLNG or LBM
BLNG	See biomethane
bn	Billion meaning 1000 million or 10^9

BOG	Boil-Off Gas. When LNG is at boiling point, small quantities will continue to boil off during shipping and storage. Not emitted to atmosphere, the gas is used as ship's fuel and in regasification terminals
brownfield plant	New LNG facilities added to an existing LNG facility
CIF	Carriage, insurance, and freight
Can$	Canadian dollar
CAPEX	Capital expenditure
C3/MR	The Propane Pre-cooled Mixed Refrigerant Liquefaction Process offered by Air Products & Chemicals Inc
CBM	Coal bed methane (also known as CSG)
CCGT	Combined-Cycle Gas Turbine
CEER	Council of European Energy Regulators
CFE	Comisión Federal de Electricidad (Mexico's state power company)
CH_4	Methane
CN	Confirmation Notice
CNG	Compressed natural gas. Usually used as a fossil fuel substitute for gasoline (petrol), diesel, or propane/LPG
CPC Corporation	a state-owned Taiwanese oil and gas company
CO_2	Carbon dioxide (the principal greenhouse gas)
CSG	Coal seam gas (also known as CBM)
CWHE	Coil Wound Heat Exchanger
debottlenecking	Identifying those parts of a plant (such as gas compressor plant) that are constraining production, and then removing the constraint
$	All $ in this book are US dollars unless otherwise stated
$/tpa	LNG plant cost metric, expressed as $ per tonne per annum produced
$/MMBtu	Value of LNG expressed as $ per million Btu
dark spread	The theoretical gross margin of a coal-fired power plant resulting from selling a unit of electricity, having bought the coal required to produce this unit of electricity
demurrage	The charges paid by a vessel charterer to the ship owner for any extra use of the vessel not agreed at the time of charter. Demurrage is a form of liquidated damages for breaching the laytime allowance as stated

	in the vessel charter party (contract); it increases the total freight cost
DES	Delivered Ex-Ship. LNG is sold to the buyer at the discharge port and title and risk passes at the flange at the discharge port. The LNG sales price includes freight.
destination clause	A clause in the LNG SPA that limits the buyer's market to a named destination
DFDE	Dual Fuel Diesel–Electric (tanker propulsion)
diversion rights	Right of a buyer to divert cargoes to another market
DMO	Domestic Market Obligation
DMR	Dual Mixed Refrigerant (used in liquefaction process)
DOE	US Department of Energy
DQT	Downward Quantity Tolerance
Dusup	Dubai Supply Authority
E&P	Exploration and Production
EAX	East Asia Index (spot LNG price published by ICIS Heren)
EC	European Commission
ECA	Emission Control Area
ECA	Export Credit Agency – government-funded bodies which advance funds and provide risk cover, in return for selling their country's goods and services
EGLNG	Equatorial Guinea LNG
EA	Environmental Assessment
EIA	US Energy Information Administration
EIB	European Investment Bank
EIS	Environmental Impact Statement
EMGME	ExxonMobil Gas Marketing Europe
Enecan	Energy and Environment Council (Japan)
ENH	Empresa Nacional de Hidrocarbonetos, the state energy company in Mozambique
EPC	Engineering, Procurement, and Construction (contract)
EUR	Estimated Ultimate Recovery (of a gas discovery)
EWC	Energy World Corporation (Australia)
FO	Fuel oil
FOB	Free on board. The LNG is sold to the buyer at the load port and title and risk passes at the flange at the load port. The LNG sales price does not include freight

FEED	Front End Engineering & Design (the design process that defines a plant)
FERC	US Federal Energy Regulatory Commission
FID	Final Investment Decision
FLNG	Floating Liquefaction Unit
FPSO	Floating Production Storage and Offloading unit (also referred to as FLNG)
FSRU	Floating Storage and Regasification Unit
FSU	Former Soviet Union
FTA	Free Trade Agreement (usually applied to countries with which the USA has a bilateral trade treaty)
FY	Fiscal Year
GAIL	Gas Authority of India Limited
gas storage	The storage of natural gas in either underground structures (such as depleted oil or gas reservoirs, salt caverns, or aquifers) or as LNG (either in storage tanks at regasification terminals or in LNG Peak Shaving facilities)
GBS	Gravity Based Structures (in relation to offshore LNG)
GECF	Gas Exporting Countries Forum
GHG	Greenhouse gas (primarily CO_2, methane, and N_2O)
GIIGNL	Groupe International des Importateurs de Gaz Naturel Liquéfié (International Group of Liquefied Natural Gas Importers)
GLNG	Gladstone LNG (Australia)
GLW	Gross Laden Weight
GMT	Gazprom Marketing and Trading
GNF	Gas Natural Fenosa
GNPC	Ghana National Petroleum Corporation
GOG	Gas-on-gas competition
greenfield plant	A completely new LNG plant built on a clean site
GSA	Gas Supply Agreement/Gas Sales Agreement
GTL	Gas-To-Liquids
GW	Gigawatt
GWP	Global Warming Potential
HFO	Heavy Fuel Oil
HGV	Heavy Goods Vehicle
HH	Henry Hub. The pricing point for natural gas futures contracts traded on NYMEX. It is a point on the natural gas pipeline system in Erath, Louisiana

	where nine interstate and four intrastate pipelines interconnect. Spot and future prices set at Henry Hub are denominated in $/MMBtu and are generally seen to be the primary price set for the North American natural gas market
HHC	Heavy Hydrocarbon
HoA	Heads of Agreement
HP	Horsepower
hub	The location, physical or virtual, where a traded market for gas is established
ICE	Intercontinental Exchange
IEA	International Energy Agency
IEC	Israel Electricity Corporation
IED	Industrial Emissions Directive
IGU	International Gas Union
IMO	International Maritime Organization
IOC	International Oil Company
IPCC	International Panel on Climate Change
IPP	Independent Power Producer
IRR	Internal Rate of Return
IUK	UK to Europe natural gas interconnector
JAIF	Japan Atomic Industrial Forum
JBIC	Japan Bank for International Co-operation
JCC	Japan Customs-cleared Crude oil price (the average price of customs-cleared crude oil imports into Japan). It is the commonly used price formation mechanism in long-term LNG contracts in Japan, Korea, and Taiwan. (The JCC was formerly obtained by taking the average of the top 20 crude oils by volume as reported in customs statistics, and it was nicknamed the 'Japanese Crude Cocktail'.)
JDA	Joint Development Area (offshore gas fields between Thailand and Malaysia)
JKM	Japan Korea Marker (spot LNG price published by Platts)
JLC	Japanese LNG Cocktail (average price of Japanese LNG imports)
JNOC	Japan National Oil Corporation
JOA	Joint Operating Agreement
JOGMEC	Japan Oil, Gas and Metal Corporation

JV	Joint Venture
JVA	Joint Venture Agreement
KEPCO	Korea Electric Power Corporation
KOGAS	Korea Gas Corporation
kWh	Kilowatt hour
laytime	The time allowance included in a vessel charter party (contract) to load (or discharge) the vessel
LBM	See biomethane
LCPD	Large Combustion Plant Directive
LDC	Local Distribution Company
liquefaction plant	A large-scale processing plant in which natural gas is cryogenically cooled to −161 °C, at which point it becomes a liquid at atmospheric pressure
LNG	Liquefied Natural Gas
LOI	Letter of Intent
LPG	Liquid Petroleum Gas
m^3	cubic metre
M&NE	Maritimes and Northeast System (Canadian pipeline)
MARPOL	International Convention for the Prevention of Pollution from ships
mboe	Million barrels of oil equivalent
MENA	Middle East and North Africa
methane slip	Methane emissions from the dispensing, or incomplete combustion, of natural gas in transportation
METI	Ministry of Economy, Trade and Industry (Japan)
MGO	Marine gasoil
MITI	Ministry of International Trade and Industry (Japan)
mmcm	Million cubic metres
mcm	Thousand cubic metres
MMBtu	Million British thermal units
mmcf	Million standard cubic feet
mmcm	Million cubic metres
MOTIE	Ministry Of Trade, Industry and Energy (Korea)
MOU	Memorandum Of Understanding
MR	Mixed Refrigerant (used in liquefaction process)
MSA	Master Sales Agreement
MSEB	Maharashtra State Electricity Board
mt	Million tonnes
mtoe	Million tonnes of oil equivalent
mtpa	Million tonnes per annum

MW	Megawatts
MWh	Megawatt hours
N_2O	Nitrous Oxide (a very potent greenhouse gas)
NMV	Netback Market Value
NBP	National Balancing Point (a virtual point hub in the UK's national transmission system where gas trades are deemed to occur; it is also used as shorthand for the UK spot gas price)
NDRC	National Development and Reform Commission (China)
NEPA	National Environmental Policy Act (USA)
netback	The value of LNG at a market, less transportation costs
NGA	Natural Gas Act (USA)
NGLs	Natural Gas Liquids
NGV	Natural Gas Vehicle
nm	Nautical mile
non-FTA	Non Free Trade Agreement countries (normally defined as 'countries outside US Free Trade areas')
NO_x	A mixture of various nitrogen oxides emitted by combustion sources
NRA	Nuclear Regulation Authority (Japan)
NWE	North-West Europe
NWS	North West Shelf (Australia)
NYMEX	New York Mercantile Exchange
oil-indexed gas prices	Gas prices within long-term contracts which are determined by formulae containing rolling averages of crude oil or defined oil product prices
OPEC	Organization of Petroleum Exporting Countries
OPEX	Operating Cost
ORV	Open Rack Vaporizer
OTC	Over the counter
Optimized Cascade	The Optimized Cascade Liquefaction Process offered by ConocoPhillips
p/th	Pence per therm (UK)
PCI	Project of Common Interest
PFHE	Plate Fin Heat Exchanger
PM	Particulate Matter (microscopic emissions from diesel engines that have been shown to cause breathing difficulties and to have a carcinogenic effect)

portfolio LNG	LNG sold from an IOC or aggregator
PPA	Power Purchase Agreement
PRICO	The Liquefaction Process offered by the Black & Veatch Company
PSA	Purchase and Sale Agreements
PSC	Production Sharing Contract
PSM	Profit Sharing Mechanism
QCLNG	Queensland Curtis LNG (Australia)
Q-Flex	Qatari LNG tanker with cargo capacity of 210,000–217,000 m^3
Q-Max	Qatari LNG tanker with cargo capacity of 263,000–266,000 m^3
R&C	Residential and Commercial
regasification (REGAS)	The process of reinstating LNG to a gaseous state (for injection into a distribution system for end-user consumption)
reserves	The amount of gas underground that can be commercially recovered
RR	Russian rouble
SCOTA	Standard Coal Trading Agreement
S curve	An LNG pricing formula (the relationship of prices varies above and below certain oil prices to lessen the impact of high oil prices on the LNG buyer/low oil prices on the seller, in $/MMBtu terms)
SCV	Submerged Combustion Vaporizer
SEC	US Securities and Exchange Commission
SEIC	Sakhalin Energy Investment Company
shale gas	Natural gas formed in fine-grained shale rock (gas shales) with low permeability in which gas has been adsorbed by clay particles or is held within minute pores and micro fractures
short-term LNG	An LNG cargo (or series of cargoes) sold under contract(s) of less than four years' duration
SMR	Single Mixed Refrigerant (used in liquefaction process)
SO$_x$	Sulphur oxides
SPA	Sales and Purchase Agreement
spark spread	The theoretical gross margin of a gas-fired power plant resulting from selling a unit of electricity, having bought the gas required to produce this unit of electricity

SPB	Self-supported Prismatic shape International Maritime Organization type-B carrier
SPEC	Sociedad Portuaria El Cayao (Colombia)
Sponsons	Sponsons are projections extending from the sides of LNG tankers to facilitate the location of process facilities on an FLNG vessel
spot LNG	Single cargo of LNG sold outside of a term contract
spot price	Price of gas determined through trading (determined by supply and demand and/or gas-on-gas competition). Usually referred to as 'prompt' price
ST	Steam Turbine tanker propulsion
TAPI	Turkmenistan–Afghanistan–Pakistan–India pipeline project
TFDE	Triple Fuel Diesel–Electric (tanker propulsion)
tcf	Trillion cubic feet
tcm	Trillion cubic metres
TCPL	TransCanada Pipeline system
TEPCO	Tokyo Electric Power Company
toe	tonnes of oil equivalent
tonne-km	The transport of 1 tonne over 1 km
TOCOM	Tokyo Commodity Exchange
TOP	Take-or-pay (or 'minimum bill', the quantity of gas which, during a gas contract year, the buyer is obliged to pay for, regardless of whether it physically takes the gas)
TPA	Third-party access
tpa	tonne per annum
TPES	Total primary energy supply
train	A facility for the liquefaction of a specific quantity of LNG (plants typically comprise two or more trains built in stages)
TSO	Transmission System Operator
TTF	Title Transfer Facility (the Dutch gas hub)
TTW	Tank To Wheel/Wake (usually used in relation to fuel emissions from a vehicle/vessel)
TUA	Terminal Use Agreement
UAE	United Arab Emirates
UIOLI	Use-It-Or-Lose It
UKCS	UK Continental Shelf
ULCC	Ultra Large Crude Carrier

upstream	Facilities (including drilling, well completion, and gas gathering) required to supply feed gas for a liquefaction plant
value chain	Combination of the liquefaction, shipping, and regas parts of the LNG business
VLCC	Very Large Crude Carrier
WCSB	Western Canadian Sedimentary Basin
Wobbe index (or Wobbe number)	A measure of the rate at which gas will deliver heat on combustion, and hence of the compatibility of a gas with gas burning equipment
WTI	West Texas Intermediate (US crude oil price)
WTO	World Trade Organization
WTT	Well To Tank (usually used in relation to fuel emission calculations)
WTW	Well To Wheel/Wake (total emissions associated with the production, treatment, and transportation of a fuel – from the primary energy source to its use in a vehicle/vessel), it combines WTT and TTW
YLNG	Yemen LNG
ZEE	Zeebrugge gas hub (the Belgian gas hub)

INTRODUCTION

Anne-Sophie Corbeau

Natural gas may be the cleanest of all combustible fuels, but its physical properties make the transportation and storage of gas more complex and expensive than that of other fossil fuels. These challenges would not matter if gas could be consumed where it is produced, but gas resources are often found far from demand centres and markets. Roughly one-third of global gas supply has to cross borders, and it may be piped over thousands of kilometres in large countries such as Russia, the USA, Canada, and China.

The LNG industry came into being to get around an inconvenient physical property of natural gas – its energy density is 1,000 times lower than that of oil (at normal atmospheric conditions). Liquefying natural gas at roughly −160 °C reduces its volume 600 fold, making it possible for the gas to supply distant markets, such as Japan, across oceans that it could never have crossed otherwise. This advance in transport, together with the desire to avoid transiting countries by pipeline for political reasons, has made LNG a key element in gas markets worldwide, contributing to the increased role and market share of natural gas in the global energy mix.

Purpose of the book

The primary rationale for this book is the perception that the LNG industry is now facing a cliff. It is up to the reader to decide whether it is standing at the bottom looking at ways to overcome the current difficulties, or at the top fearing an abrupt downsizing of future business opportunities. The sector has now embarked on an expansion in LNG export capacity of such a size that it is likely to emerge substantially changed four years from now. The question is not just one of LNG supply and demand, but also of whether the LNG industry's pricing and contractual frameworks could be fundamentally reconfigured. To better grasp the potential future of the LNG industry, it is useful to look at the accomplishments in its past. This book offers, therefore, a comprehensive analysis of developments since the birth of the LNG industry, as well as perspectives on how it could evolve.

Over its 50 year lifetime, the LNG industry has changed in many ways, constantly adapting itself. LNG began as the 'little brother' of the pipeline business: a point-to-point business where the seller's liquefaction plant was linked to a few buyers' regasification terminals – sometimes even just one – by dedicated ships and a long-term, inflexible gas purchasing contract. Since then, the countries and players involved, the technology, and the business models have changed so much that the current industry bears very little resemblance to the original one. Most of these changes took place in a relatively smooth way – at least until 2010 when it became obvious that LNG demand in North America would not grow as expected and that North America itself would become a large source of LNG. The 'little brother' has now grown up, reinvented itself with more variety and flexibility on both the buyer and seller sides, and loosened the chains of inflexibility quite significantly. LNG is now ready to challenge its elder brother.

Why does LNG matter?

LNG plays a crucial role in the gas industry. The future of global gas IS clearly in the hands of LNG. The industry's success or failure in bringing additional LNG supplies to the market will directly impact future global gas demand because of the increasing distance and continental separation between discovered gas resources and future demand centres. Most forecasts anticipate at least a doubling of LNG trade over the next 20 years. While very few large inter-regional pipeline projects are moving ahead anywhere in the world, around 150 mtpa of LNG export capacity will come online over 2015–20 (an increase of 50 per cent). The list of proposed LNG export projects, with a total capacity of around 1,000 mtpa, is even more impressive. Though only some of these plants will move ahead, LNG is clearly poised to take an increasing role in the global gas trade.

The battle is taking place on different fronts. The growth of LNG demand depends on the future role of gas in the energy mix. Arguably, economics play a large role – with inter-fuel competition, notably with coal, as a backdrop – as do environmental and geopolitical considerations. LNG has to be competitive to be considered as a viable alternative, notably in developing countries. Additionally gas pipelines are ready to defend their territories and could represent a threat to LNG growth. The regions where the 'pipeline versus LNG' battle rages – Europe, China, and potentially India – are, or will become, significant importing regions. Against this backdrop, China appears as the next prize for both LNG and pipeline gas. While LNG did manage to set foot on Chinese territory first, pipeline supplies to China currently exceed LNG supplies. The proposed Russian pipelines – Power of Siberia and Altai – could challenge the LNG import story there.

A backward glance

Chapter 1 follows the early steps of the LNG industry as we know it – with a liquefaction plant linked to a regasification plant through shipping – from its early inception until the late 1990s. The concept of liquefying natural gas (and other gases) was developed in the nineteenth century. The very first LNG plant was built in West Virginia in 1912 and the first commercial liquefaction plant started operations in Cleveland in 1941. However, the element of transporting LNG across oceans was still missing.

As often happens, a few determined individuals drove the emergence of a new technology. In this case, it took three decisive elements: the idea of an industrial user from Chicago, the emergence of a new market for natural gas – the United Kingdom – together with the gas resources waiting to be exploited in Algeria.

In 1951, William Wood-Prince, president of Chicago's Union Stock Yard and Transit Company, faced a price hike from his local gas supplier (Corkhill, 2014a). Rather than accepting it, he came up with a potential alternative: liquefying cheaper volumes from Texas and shipping them by barge to Chicago. With input from engineers, the concept of transporting liquefied gas by barge became technically possible. But when those involved sought advice from the gas industry's professionals, in particular from Continental Oil, those experts concluded that transporting gas by barge might not make economic sense. However, shipping natural gas in LNG form across the oceans could be a very interesting option.

The technology enabling the transport of gas between continents was still nothing, however, without a supply source and a market. The UK was looking for cleaner fuels including natural gas after the Great Smog of December 1952 and the 1956 Clean Air Act. Meanwhile, the discovery of large gas resources in Algeria that the country wanted to commercialize led to the construction of the Camel liquefaction plant at Arzew. All the factors came together: on 26 September 1964, the Camel plant started loading LNG on to the *Methane Princess*, which delivered LNG to a regasification plant on Canvey Island in the Thames Estuary, not far from London. The LNG industry was born.

Concentration has characterized the first decades of the history of LNG. In the beginning, LNG was a rather exclusive club made up of a few buyers and sellers, as highlighted in Chapter 1. After 15 years of LNG history there were still only six buyers and six exporters. Some tend to think that Asia has always dominated the LNG markets, but until the mid-1970s Europe was the main market for LNG. However, starting in the 1970s, Japan began to build a dominating position within the industry, not only as a buyer, but also with Japanese trading houses taking shares in projects, banks offering preferential loans to projects, and Japanese engineering companies building the LNG plants.

The subsequent developments from 2000 onwards (described in Chapter 2) show the evolution from this exclusive club to a global industry. As of early 2016, LNG has truly connected all regions, with 20 countries exporting to 35 importing countries. Step by step, LNG began to reach other countries in a more significant manner during the 2000s. Discoveries in the North Sea distanced north-western European countries from LNG for a few decades, but as European domestic gas production started to dwindle in the early 2000s, LNG started to penetrate European markets in a significant way. LNG leaped into Latin America, the Middle East and, in 2015, made its way to Africa. These regions, which on the whole are gas exporters, import LNG either due to failures in the development of regional networks, or as a result of political decisions which have led to insufficient domestic production. However, despite attempts to introduce diversification during the 2000s, the LNG markets are back in the hands of the very same region which has dominated the industry since the 1970s: as of 2015, Asia still attracts 72 per cent of LNG supplies.

Meanwhile, LNG supply has experienced some concentration. Between 1980 and 2000, this was mainly in the hands of three south-east Asian countries, which represented more than 50 per cent of global LNG output. While the emergence of new suppliers in the early 2000s reduced their share to 20 per cent in 2015, the supply side has again been experiencing some concentration, with Qatar alone accounting for one-third of LNG supply since 2011. But this won't last.

Business models, strategies, and the way in which players position themselves, have changed. This applies to liquefaction (Chapter 3) as well as to shipping and regasification (Chapter 4). Gone are the days when the sellers, often a mix of national oil companies (NOCs) and international oil companies (IOCs), negotiated with monopsony, state-owned, vertically integrated buyers. The LNG business is now full of smaller players, new entrants, traders, brokers, and banks. Buyers have also become increasingly keen on being involved as stakeholders in upstream gas supply and liquefaction projects. On the shipping side, Japanese and Korean shipping lines used to play a major role in the LNG projects, where cargoes were purchased on a FOB basis. But in the early 2000s many companies with LNG shipping, LPG carrier, and oil tanker experience entered the market; they were followed later by Greek shipowners who now control 20 per cent of the world's tonnage (Corkhill, 2014b). Regasification plants are now being built for a variety of purposes: not only to supply a final market, but also for arbitrage or risk-spreading, or to be leased on a long-term basis (Chapter 4).

The global LNG business has evolved from one which was as inflexible as fixed pipelines, into a much more flexible business where the product can be redirected, serve two or three destinations during one journey, or be re-exported, depending on price differentials. Flexibility and diversity of supply and demand are now the key trademarks of the LNG business. More contractual flexibility for buyers and FOB contracts, together with aggregators taking advantage of arbitrage opportunities, have led to a position where some 28 per cent of the LNG traded is on spot and short-term contracts. These factors have influenced the projects' business structures.

Chapter 4 and the technical appendices review the technology side. The LNG industry started 'small', then for a few decades it was constantly aiming at building larger and larger infrastructure before, recently, showing interest in the small scale. Remember that in the 1960s the Arzew Camel plant's capacity was only 1.2 mtpa. The race to build bigger processing units seems to have stopped with Qatar's 7.8 mtpa mega liquefaction trains in the late 2000s. Most trains in the projects currently under construction are around 4.5 to 6 mtpa. But the industry has continued to build mega complexes with four or six trains while gas resources remain available. Ships have also gotten bigger. The capacity of the *Methane Princess* (27,000 m^3) was almost exactly one-tenth that of the Q-Max, the world's largest LNG cargo ship (266,000 m^3) built for Qatar's mega-trains. Here, too, the race to build still larger ships seems to have stopped: the need to adapt port infrastructure, both at the liquefaction and regasification points, and the ability to use the expanded Panama Canal, have set size limits. Finally, recent technical developments may yet fundamentally change the LNG business, even though their impact is still unquantified. The advent of floating storage and regasification units (FSRUs) in the 2000s quickly made these the favourite option of developing markets. The Floating Liquefied Natural Gas unit (FLNG), designed to develop stranded gas fields, is the latest technical evolution. Finally, breaking away from the race to always build bigger infrastructure, small-scale LNG, onshore and offshore, could also bring major changes to the LNG markets.

Another of LNG's qualities is its perceived positive role in terms of gas supply security. Because of its flexibility, LNG could replace missing supplies from other sources for importing regions. This obviously requires three things: the relevant market must have LNG import capacity as well as the transmission infrastructure to bring gas supplies where they are needed; LNG must be available on global gas markets; and the end users must be ready to pay a high enough price to attract the LNG to its market. Due to the lack of historical major disruptions to LNG supplies, it tends to be considered as a solution rather than as a potential problem. Only a few analyses have considered the impact of an LNG disruption (IEA, 2012; Growitsch et al., 2013).

At the crossroads

Until 2014, the gas industry was looking proudly at the new wave of LNG supply set to hit markets through 2020. This supply expansion was seen as an indispensable tool for greater gas penetration in the energy mix, notably in Asia. That sentiment had changed by 2016: with every passing day the expected incremental LNG supply looked larger than previously expected. It kept growing as new Final Investment Decisions (FIDs) were taken in 2015. Chapter 5 reviews this unprecedented wave of LNG projects coming on line between 2015 and 2020 (around 150 mtpa, a 50 per cent increase) and the implications for proposed projects, notably in North America, Russia, Australia, and Eastern Africa.

The gas industry's feelings towards LNG have changed from pride to apprehension. The forthcoming wave of LNG supply will have far-reaching implications for global gas markets – and these may be quite different from what was originally expected. The coming new deliveries are remarkable not only for their total size, but also for their origin. Around 40 per cent of new LNG export capacity will originate from the USA, which had been predicted to become a larger LNG importer than Japan only 10 years ago. Investors in US LNG have tended to move like a herd, following on behind the first bold mover (US LNG terminal developer Cheniere), and questions remain as to how much US LNG will really be exported over the long term.

The industry may have created a significant boom-and-bust cycle. Even if a few suppliers such as Egypt and Yemen default, and projects such as Angola have start-up delays, it will do little to change the impression of a massive LNG oversupply. Given the weak demand in Asia in 2015 and the low oil and LNG spot price environment since late 2014, there are worries that these conditions will create a dearth of FIDs over the coming years, as sponsors wait for better times or address the issue of sky-rocketing capital costs.

Faced with ample supply on its way, the gas industry's concerns swing back to the uncertain demand prospects analysed in Chapter 6. Asia has always been regarded as a bottomless sink for LNG, but it now seems set to confound expectations. The World Gas Conference of 2015 highlighted a growing anxiety that the rest of the world could start looking like Europe, where gas is squeezed by renewable energy and coal in the power sector. Still, Europe may attract more LNG than previously thought, while developing markets in Latin America, Africa, and the Middle East have potential. Additionally, Chapter 7 investigates how using LNG as a fuel in road and maritime transportation has also started to attract interest in recent years. While the technology is not new, environmental concerns and regulations could trigger a fundamentally new market.

Pricing and costs are at the centre of a fierce debate (Chapter 8). From 2011 through 2014, LNG prices were above $15/MMBtu in key importing markets, making new LNG capacity seem like a terrific investment. This opportunity attracted the incredible quantities of LNG capacity that are under construction as we write. China crystallized appetites for LNG investment, even though analysts failed to agree when forecasting its LNG needs. The gas industry realized that Asia may not be ready to accept LNG if prices are too high, even if the only alternative that would give access to power to hundreds of millions in south-east Asia is 'dirty' coal. Gas is a clear loser against coal at $15/MMBtu, the average Japanese import price in 2014. In contrast, markets could see another dash for gas – and LNG – at $4–$5/MMBtu, the level of Asian LNG spot prices in early 2016. But investors were counting on higher prices to guarantee that their new LNG plants would be economical. Most new LNG importers have low wholesale gas prices, while prices observed in Europe and Asia in early 2016 are below the level required to justify FID. This likely price squeeze creates a strong imperative to keep costs under control or to wait until the price environment improves so the LNG boom can prosper.

Key to this change is US LNG, as buyers become more selective about what terms they are ready to accept. Oil indexation is under attack, with US LNG selling at Henry Hub-indexed prices (plus costs), while other sellers have been pressured to adopt different pricing policies and secure more flexibility in their LNG contracts. However, sellers facing high costs are reluctant to abandon a business model in which they have confidence. While LNG has helped gas markets to become more global, complete globalization is still an elusive prospect in the absence of a global gas price.

One important element currently remains untouched in the LNG business: long-term contracts. Conventional wisdom is that LNG export plants must be supported by long-term contracts covering most of their capacity. Due to the huge capital costs, financing the construction of an LNG plant would be next to impossible without the assurance of a long-term contract. Chapter 9 describes how current market conditions, and the increasing amount of gas that is likely to be traded on a short-term basis because of oversupply, may challenge the dominance of long-term contracts. Absorbing this new supply will affect trade-flow patterns, competition with other gas supply channels and other fuels (notably in the power sector), as well as pricing mechanisms.

As this book goes to press in June 2016, half of the Australian LNG plants have started, while the first LNG cargo from Sabine Pass has been sent to Latin America – a sign of the profound changes in the markets' dynamics. Spot prices in Europe and Asia have settled around $4–5/MMBtu for most of 2016. The LNG 18 conference which took place in April 2016 highlighted the concerns of sellers about finding new markets, but also the realization that only cost-competitive projects will move forward. Cost is king. 'Collaboration', 'standardization of engineering, design, and construction' and 'learning from the past' have become the new motto of the LNG industry, highlighting the fact that companies have to adapt to the new business environment. However, the stance of buyers is getting tougher: existing projects will have to accept more flexible contract structures. The largest buyer – JERA – has taken the lead by asking for an introduction of spot indexes and a move away from oil indexation in Asian long-term contracts. The contractual framework for new projects is therefore in flux: buyers want shorter contracts and different pricing terms. Let us hope that this will not create a major hiatus in LNG supply post 2020.

BIBLIOGRAPHY

Corkhill, M. (2014a). *'Methane Pioneer* sets the scene', *LNG shipping at 50*, SIGTTO/GIIGNL, 10–11. www.giignl.org/sites/default/files/PUBLIC_AREA/Publications/lng-shipping-at-50compressed.pdf.

Corkhill, M. (2014b). 'New players make the LNG leap', *LNG shipping at 50*, SIGTTO/GIIGNL, 96–7. www.giignl.org/sites/default/files/PUBLIC_AREA/Publications/lng-shipping-at-50compressed.pdf.

Growitsch, C., Hecking, H., and Panke, T. (2013). 'Supply disruptions and regional price effects in a spatial oligopoly', EWI Working Paper No. 13/08, Institute of Energy Economics at the University of Cologne. www.ewi.uni-koeln.de/fileadmin/user_upload/Publikationen/Working_Paper/EWI_WP__13-08_Supply_disruptions_and_regional_price_effects.pdf.

IEA (2012). *Medium-Term Gas Market Report 2012, Market Trends and Projections to 2017*, Paris: OECD/International Energy Agency. https://www.iea.org/publications/freepublications/publication/MTGMR2012_web.pdf.

CHAPTER 1

LOOKING BACK AT HISTORY: THE EARLY DEVELOPMENT OF LNG SUPPLIES AND MARKETS

Jonathan Stern and Ken Koyama

Introduction

The first accounts of gas liquefaction date back to the nineteenth century and the work of Linde and Faraday. Peebles attributes the first liquefaction of methane to the French chemist Cailletet in 1877, but Hrastar believes that Olszewski was the first to achieve this in Warsaw in 1886.[1] Development of LNG as a commercial fuel resulted in the first peak shaving plant in Cleveland, but this ended in disaster in 1944 with the collapse of one of the storage tanks; the resulting fire killed 130 people in a residential area.[2]

Despite this setback, LNG development was taken forward over the subsequent decade by US industrialists, in particular by William Wood-Prince, of Chicago's Union Stock Yard and Transit Company, who is regarded as the founder of the commercial LNG industry. In response to price increases by his local gas company, Wood-Prince attempted (unsuccessfully) to develop barge transportation of LNG up the Mississippi River from Louisiana.[3] Further work by Wood-Prince's company eventually led to much larger ship designs and to the development of a barge-mounted liquefaction plant on the Calcasieu River near Lake Charles (Louisiana). It was from here that the first international cargoes of LNG arrived at Canvey Island in the UK in 1959, in the *Methane Pioneer*, a converted World War II dry cargo ship (Williams, 1981, 145–6).

These trial cargoes totalled 12,000 tonnes and their success created momentum for the building of dedicated ships which delivered their first

---

[1] Peebles (1980, 187); Chapter 4 in Hrastar (2014) contains a history of liquefaction of the full range of gases.
[2] Hrastar (2014) devotes Chapters 5–7 to the Cleveland episode, describing in detail the technological, material, and planning failings which led to the accident and the lessons which were learned from it.
[3] The history of barge-mounted transportation in Louisiana and how this ultimately led to the development of commercial LNG shipping with the *Methane Pioneer* can be found in SIGTTO/GIIGNL (2014, 10–11).

cargoes of Algerian LNG to the UK (*Methane Princess* and *Methane Progress*) and France (*Jules Verne*) in 1964 and 1965 respectively.[4] However, more than 10 years then passed before global LNG trade reached double digits in million tonnes, with Algeria having been joined by three other exporters – the USA (Alaska), Libya, and Brunei. Exports from Abu Dhabi and Indonesia began in 1977, and these six countries should be considered the pioneers of LNG trade.[5] But it would require Malaysia (1983) and Australia (1989) to join their ranks before global trade exceeded 50 mt in 1990.

This chapter traces the development of commercial LNG trade from its beginnings to around the year 2000. We look first at the exporting countries, before considering the three different regional markets – the USA, Europe, and Asia – which imported LNG during this period, paying particular attention to Japan which was the dominant market at this time.

The pioneers of LNG exports

Algeria was, without doubt, the leader of the LNG pioneers – dominating most of the first 15 years of LNG trade before first being challenged by Brunei and then overtaken by Indonesia by the mid-1980s (Figure 1.1). Its dominance would have continued had the early trades with European customers reached contracted volumes on a consistent basis and been supplemented with exports to US customers, as had been contractually committed.[6] However, pricing disagreements, which became known as Algeria's 'gas battle', limited volumes in existing contracts (such as that with Enagas in Spain), resulting in facilities not being built for which contracts had been signed (Ruhrgas and Gasunie in Germany and the Netherlands respectively), and the cancellation of contracts only a few years after the start of deliveries (Trunkline and El Paso in the USA).[7] These price disagreements centred on a number of different issues:

---

[4] Hrastar (2014, 205); for a detailed account of the *Methane Princess* and the *Methane Progress* see SIGTTO/GIIGNL (2014, 10–16).

[5] See communal data.

[6] See Aissaoui (2001, 189), for Algeria's LNG contract portfolio; more details of the contracts can be found in Stern (1984, 93–4).

[7] For details of the gas battle and pricing policy see Aissaoui (2001) pages 91–3 and 184–195, and Hayes (2006). For details of the US contractual problems see Stern (1985, 94–111); an account of the El Paso project, in particular the shipping aspects, can be found in SIGTTO/GIIGNL (2014, 26–7).

12   LNG Markets in Transition

- the cost of facilities,
- the development of maritime pipeline technology (allowing gas to be delivered by pipeline to southern Europe more cheaply and in larger quantities), and
- the arrival of deregulation in the USA which rendered expensive imported LNG largely unsaleable.[8]
- These issues came together to complicate the first two decades of Algerian LNG exports.

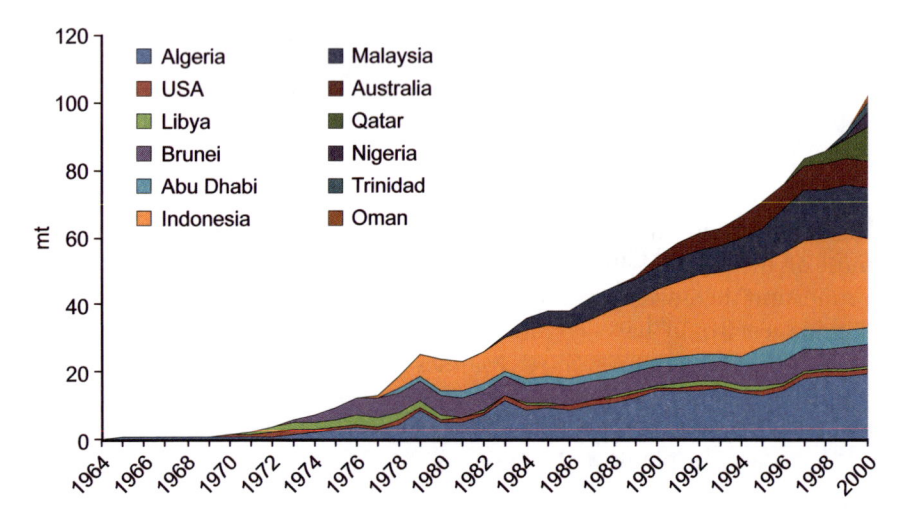

Figure 1.1: LNG exporters, 1964–2000
Source: Communal data.

But if Algeria's LNG experience had some unhappy aspects, Libya's was significantly more problematic. Colonel Gaddafi had seized power in a coup a few months before deliveries were due to start in 1970 and the pricing arrangements which had been negotiated under the Idris government therefore required significant changes before the first cargo could be loaded (Gurney, 1996, 187–8). Almost continuous price renegotiations in the early years of the contract caused deliveries to Spain and Italy to be halted periodically. In addition, there were suggestions that Libya's Brega plant had unresolvable technical problems, although export statistics show that during 1972–9 it operated close to its 3.2 mtpa capacity.

---

[8]   With the exception of the Distrigas contract which, with only minor interruptions, has delivered Algerian LNG to the Boston area since 1971.

In 1980, Libyan price demands caused exports to Italy to be phased out (aside from spot cargoes) and shortly thereafter Esso (operator of the Brega plant) withdrew from the country (Gurney, 1996, 188–91). Although deliveries to Spain continued, the plant rarely operated above 50 per cent capacity in most years. Part of the problem was a need for refurbishment which was never carried out, largely due to international sanctions.

If the early experience of exports from the Atlantic Basin was somewhat mixed, the Pacific has an altogether happier story. The plant at Kenai in Alaska has been delivering small volumes (0.4 mtpa) of LNG to Tokyo Electric since 1969 to the present (with a short break in the early 2010s when it was mothballed), with extensions being negotiated well beyond the initial 15 year term of the contract (Sakmar, 2013, 59–60; SIGTTO/GIIGNL, 2014, 23). The Brunei plant at Lumut was the first large-scale (7.1 mtpa) export project in Asia and, like its Alaskan predecessor, it has run successfully since 1972, having run for more than double its initial 20 year term (SIGTTO/GIIGNL, 2014, 25; Jones, 1998, 49–51). The same can be said for Abu Dhabi's ADGAS project which commenced in 1977, was expanded in 1995, and delivered virtually the totality of its cargoes to Tokyo Electric and Chubu Electric in Japan.[9]

Indonesia exported its first cargo in the same year as Abu Dhabi and by the mid-1980s had become the world's largest LNG exporter, a status which it would maintain for more than 20 years until overtaken by Qatar. The first two liquefaction plants – at Bontang (Borneo) and Arun (Sumatra) – began exporting in the late 1970s and were supplemented, more than 30 years later, by plants at Tangguh (Papua) and Senoro (Sulawesi).[10] In the early 1990s, more than a decade after the start of LNG deliveries, sales to the domestic market still remained minor compared with exports.[11] However, domestic demand, fuelled by very low prices, began to increase under the twin pressures of population growth and industrialization, while production failed to respond (in part due to the same low prices); Indonesian LNG exports thus came under pressure and began to decline in the mid-2000s (a trend which would be experienced by a number of LNG exporters) (Ledesma, 2008, 285–96).

While Indonesia established itself relatively rapidly as an LNG exporter, development in Malaysia was very much slower, partly because of its rather more cautious and measured approach to foreign investment (Stern, 1985, 179–83). A decade after the start of deliveries in 1983, exports were still less than 10 mtpa, but the Bintulu LNG complex with its three projects – Satu,

---

[9] A full account of the project can be found in Dargin and Flower (2011, 453–62).
[10] Chapman (1985); for a detailed history of Arun LNG see Von Der Mehden and Lewis (2006).
[11] Barnes (1995), Chapter 4.

Dua, and Tiga, each with different foreign partners – steadily increased in size, surpassing Indonesia and becoming the leading Pacific exporter in 2007 (Ledesma, 2008, 296–305).

The next country to export LNG was Australia, whose first LNG deliveries took place in 1989 and the first three (of eventually five) trains were built prior to 2000, despite the discovery of the North West Shelf fields having taken place in the early 1970s.[12] The North West Shelf project established a number of precedents – in terms of developing a local market for gas and ensuring that labour and equipment were sourced from within the country – that would be followed elsewhere in succeeding decades. From an international perspective, it followed the trend set by Indonesia and Malaysia, selling LNG to a large number of buyers in Japan and Korea (and after 2000 also in China) (Ledesma et al., 2014, 11–12).

Four additional countries began to export LNG in the final few years prior to 2000. The development of the North Field in Qatar has assumed such a position of importance in global LNG trade that it will be dealt with in a separate section (see Chapter 2). Plans for LNG exports from Trinidad date back to the early 1980s, but discussions about the project (which eventually became Atlantic LNG) only began in 1992, with first deliveries in 1999, the same year as Nigeria LNG (see below).[13] In 2000, the 6.7 mtpa Oman LNG project delivered its first cargoes to (largely) Asian buyers. The project was expanded in 2005 through the construction of the 3.7 mtpa Qalhat LNG project; this was developed to supply European and North American markets, although cargoes were ultimately sold to Asia.[14]

LNG exporters: slow starters and (as yet) non-starters

One of the significant features of LNG history is that many trades required decades before finally getting under way, and some aspiring exporting countries have yet to see projects materialize despite decades of (sporadic) discussion and negotiation. Of the countries where LNG exports have

---

[12] Given its size and importance, there is comparatively little literature available in the public domain about the North West Shelf LNG project. Some early history can be found in Bambrick (1978); Murray (1991), based on interviews with the major protagonists, takes the story up to first deliveries, and a summary of the contractual position can be found in Ledesma (2008, 310–11). There is a wealth of detail in reports (North West Shelf Report) which were issued monthly, starting in 1980 by the project partners, but I have been unable to discover whether these are still in the public domain.

[13] For the history of Atlantic LNG see Shepherd and Ball (2006).

[14] The two projects merged in 2013. A comprehensive account of the development of the gas and LNG industries in Oman can be found in Ledesma (2011).

finally been launched, Nigeria and Russia are rivals for the title of hosting the longest-running projects (from first discussions to start-up).[15] The Nigerian LNG story started in the mid-1960s when a British Gas delegation visited Lagos. After more than 30 years of various different project configurations and negotiations, Nigeria's LNG partners took a final investment decision and the project delivered its first cargo in 1999, and by the end of 2007 six trains were operating.[16]

Hrastar suggests that a Venezuelan export proposal had been made as early as 1957, but the country's modern LNG history starts with the Cristobal Colon project which was announced in 1990 for export to the USA.[17] After various changes of name and partners, this became the Mariscal Sucre project in 2002 (SGS, 2004). By the late 2000s two additional projects (Plataforma Deltana and Blanquilla-Tortuga) had been proposed, as had the idea of a pipeline from Venezuelan fields to the Trinidad and Tobago liquefaction plants (EIA, 2009). Little progress has been made towards the realization of any of these plans and the fields are being developed for domestic consumption.

Some of the Canadian LNG export projects which are being developed in the 2010s are the successors of projects which were planned in the 1970s. Possibly the best known from that era is the Western LNG project – to export from a terminal near Prince Rupert to Japan.[18] Another project in which (around 1980) US and European importers were extremely interested was Arctic Pilot LNG, with a liquefaction terminal on Melville Island.[19] Nearly 40 years after the first discussions, however, we still await a final investment decision for the first Canadian LNG export project (see Chapter 5).

The history of Iranian LNG dates back to the 1970s, when negotiations on what were then known as the Kangan and Kalingas export projects (planned to deliver gas to Belgium, Japan, and the USA) reached an advanced stage (Adibi and Fesheraki, 2011, 294). However, many of these projects had been abandoned even before the Islamic Revolution, and discussions on a range of new projects started in the 1990s. Given the financial and technology sanctions which were imposed by the USA and

---

[15] The history of Russian LNG can be found in Chapter 2.

[16] For the early history see Stern (1984, 125–9). A project history from FID to 2015, which includes major milestones, can be found in NLNG (2015, 23–7).

[17] Hrastar (2014, 220); the history of Cristobal Colon can be found in Boué (1993, 105–9) and Shepherd and Ball (2006, 314–5).

[18] For details of the project, including a regulatory analysis of project economics and pricing, see NEB (1983, 59–66).

[19] Stern (1984, 133–4); Stern (1985, 46–8). An alternative project was considered by Ruhrgas based on the King Christian Island reserves with a terminal on Ellef Ringnes Island.

Europe (the source of most LNG technology and equipment), and questionable economic attractiveness from an Iranian perspective, it proved impossible to make progress; it still remains uncertain whether and when it will be possible to proceed with these projects, even following the lifting of sanctions (Adibi and Fesheraki, 294–9; Hassanzadeh, 2014, Chapters 3 and 6).

In the early 1980s, LNG exports from Cameroon seemed extremely likely, and 30 years later the project's main international sponsor was still claiming that its technical and economic viability had been demonstrated (Stern, 1984, 131–3; Nussbaum and Folo, 2013). Finally, in 2015, contracts were signed (with different partners from the original project) for a floating liquefaction terminal exporting 1.2 mtpa, starting in 2017.[20] Argentinian, Chilean, and Colombian export projects were first discussed in the 1980s; however, the first two countries subsequently became LNG importers and Colombia seems likely to follow their example – Chapters 2 and 5.

The point of recalling these various historical episodes is twofold. First, however their sponsors and the press may present them, there are very few truly 'new' LNG projects, unless they are based on a newly discovered resource. Second, a particularity of LNG projects is that they can require several decades to commercialize, and many never reach a final investment decision. Virtually all LNG projects have required at least 10 years between first discussions and start of deliveries, particularly in countries without an established gas industry. Even some of the countries which have become well-established exporters have required a long time scale. Qatar exported its first cargoes nearly 20 years after the start of discussions – and 25 years after the discovery of the North Field (Flower, 2011). This is not surprising considering the huge capital investment requirements (and therefore risks involved) and the lead times required to build the project; for example a minimum of four years to build a land-based liquefaction plant.[21]

The Atlantic and Pacific Basins LNG markets

Atlantic Basin LNG trade: why did it never recover from a bad start?

Figure 1.2 shows the development of LNG imports by region over 35 years from the start of trade in 1964 to 2000. Although trade started in the

---

[20] 'Golar, Perenco Reach Agreement on Commercial Terms of Cameroon FLNG Project', Press Release, Golar LNG Limited, 1 July 2015.
www.rigzone.com/news/oil_gas/a/139400/Golar_Perenco_Reach_Agreement_on_Commercial_Terms_of_Cameroon_FLNG_Project.

[21] This is the timescale for an onshore worldscale plant, a floating plant can be built and installed much more quickly.

Atlantic Basin, it remained at a low level for a decade; by the early 1980s, however, Asia, and specifically Japan (imports did not reach Korea until 1986), had become the dominant global LNG market, a position which would progressively strengthen. By 2000, Pacific Basin markets were importing more than twice as much LNG as those in the Atlantic Basin and, given that trade in the Pacific started later, it is important to understand the reasons behind this. (There was no trade outside these regions during this period.) In the Americas, Dominican Republic imports began in the early 2000s, followed by Mexico, and then by South American countries much later in the decade. In Asia, Indian and Chinese imports started in 2004 and 2006 respectively, and Middle Eastern countries only in the late 2000s (see Chapter 2).

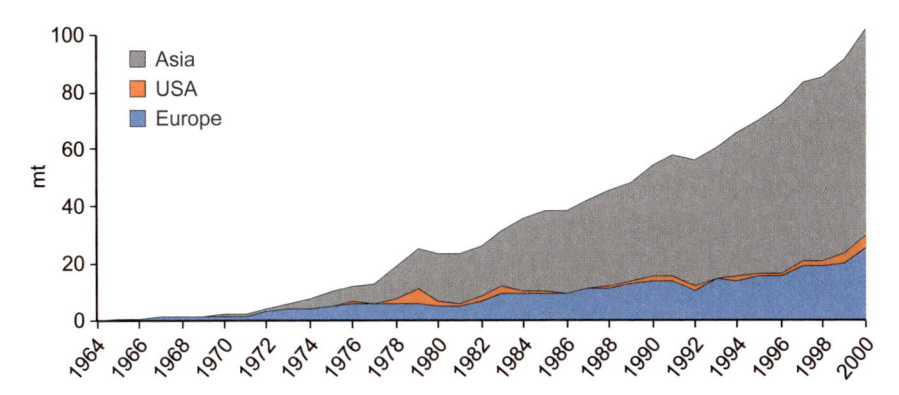

Figure 1.2: LNG imports by region, 1964–2000
Source: Communal data.

The US market

The loss of the US market was a very significant blow to the development of LNG in the Atlantic Basin from which, it could be argued, trade in the region never recovered. Algerian exports to the USA (which were contractually intended to reach 30 mtpa in the 1980s), only exceeded 1 mtpa for a few years in the late 1970s and early 1980s; indeed it was only in the late 1990s that imports exceeded this level on an ongoing basis, although they increased significantly in the 2000s (see Chapter 2).[22] The Natural Gas Policy Act of 1978, which launched the liberalization of the US industry, was largely responsible for halting the vast majority of US LNG imports. Liberalization of transportation, prices, and contracts

---
[22] For more details of the El Paso, Trunkline, Eascogas, and Tenneco (TAPCO) projects see Stern (1985, 109–11).

18 *LNG Markets in Transition*

created a huge surplus of supply over demand, which had fallen substantially due to the previous high price period. In 1986, US demand was 22 per cent below its 1979 peak and demand did not exceed 1979 levels for 20 years. The 'gas bubble' led to more than a decade of prices in the $2–$3/MMBtu range, which finished only at the end of the 1990s. During this period, the Federal Energy Regulatory Commission (and its predecessor the Federal Power Commission), which at that time defined and administered regulated gas prices, was not willing to tolerate import price levels which dramatically exceeded those of domestic US production, even if the volumes were insignificant in relation to the total market.[23] This made imported LNG at contract prices commercially untenable, a situation which was only (briefly) reversed in the 2000s.

The European market

Europe's experience was similar to that of the USA, as Algerian claims for parity with crude oil prices (which were increasing rapidly) meant that LNG (and pipeline gas) could not compete with domestic and other imported gas which was (generally) priced in relation to oil products. In the period up to 2000, France provided the majority of the market for European LNG supplies, a position which Spain (a slow starter in relation to imports) would assume thereafter (see Chapter 2 of this book and Chapter 3 of Stern, 1984).

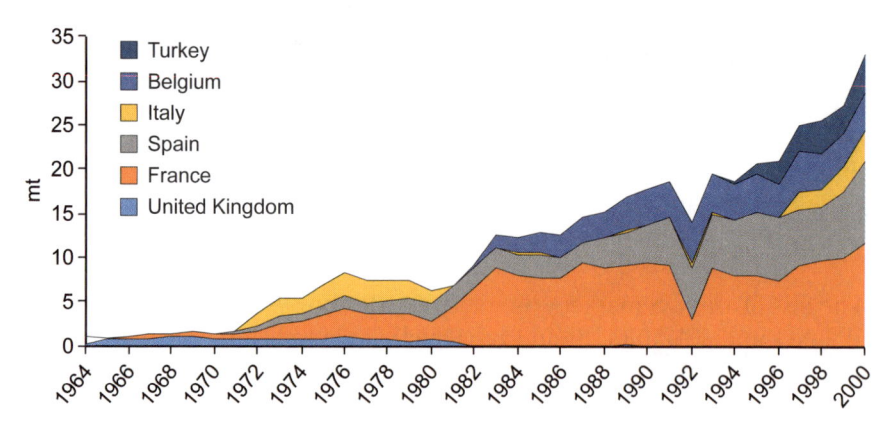

Figure 1.3: European LNG imports, 1964–2000
Source: Communal data.

UK imports never reached 1 mtpa and (aside from a couple of years) ceased after the expiry of the Algerian contract in 1981, restarting only in

---
[23] For an account of North American gas pricing in the 1980s see Stern (2012) especially 46–54.

the mid-2000s following the construction of new import terminals (see Chapter 2). The other early LNG importer was Italy where, for a relatively brief period in the 1970s, volumes exceeded those of all other countries (including, in some years, those of France) before being virtually eliminated after 1980 following a price dispute with Libya after which only spot cargos were purchased. Italian imports only recovered significantly in the late 1990s with the start of deliveries from, first, Algeria and then Nigeria. Belgium began importing significant volumes of LNG in the early 1980s, and continued doing so through 2000 and beyond. Two additional European countries – Turkey in 1994 and Greece in 2000 – started LNG imports in this timeframe with the former rapidly becoming the European continent's third largest importer (after France and Spain) by 2000.

But although six countries were importing LNG in 2000 (with Portugal soon to join, and the UK to rejoin, their ranks), total European imports amounted to less than 25 mt in that year and even with the addition of US volumes, the entire Atlantic Basin was importing less than 30 mt. This was much less than had been anticipated (with the majority of the volumes from what we have called above the 'slow starter' and 'non-starter' projects aimed at European and US markets), and relatively small compared with the more than 70 mt being delivered to just three countries in Asia (Japan, Korea, and Taiwan). The main reason for this was that European and US gas buyers could be somewhat relaxed about the timing of LNG projects because they had (both domestic and import) pipeline supply options: Canada, in the case of the USA; the Netherlands, and subsequently Norway and Russia (the USSR, prior to 1991), in the case of Europe. Spain was the only large European gas market with minimal domestic production and no significant pipeline imports. But this changed in the 1980s and 90s as advances in deepwater pipeline technology made possible the construction of the Trans-Mediterranean and GME pipelines from Algeria to Italy and Spain (through which deliveries started in 1983 and 1996 respectively), and after 2000 the Green Stream pipeline from Libya to Italy. At that time, exporters preferred pipeline gas to LNG exports because of the lower cost and therefore higher return.[24]

As a result of the alternative gas supply options enjoyed by Atlantic Basin importers, commercial (specifically price) disputes tended to be litigated by the international arbitration proceedings allowed for in the long-term contracts. If no mutually satisfactory solution could be found, projects were either abandoned (such as happened to all Algerian contracts with US buyers, with the exception of Distrigas) or reduced to marginal

---

[24] For an account of the Algerian pipeline projects see Hayes (2006). There is very little publicly available information on Libya's Green Stream pipeline even on the company's website: www.greenstreambv.com/en/pages/company/company.shtml.

levels (the Libyan contract with Italian buyers). Governments and companies allowed this to happen partly because they had pipeline alternatives and would not face an *acute* supply shortage in the absence of LNG. In 2000, LNG imports accounted for less than 6 per cent of total European gas demand.[25] But for individual countries the situation was different: aside from Spain which was near-totally dependent, LNG imports accounted for 25–30 per cent of gas demand in France, Belgium, Turkey, and Greece (although the figure was far less in Italy).

However, as is evident from Figure 1.2, from the early 1980s Asia progressively dominated LNG trade and for this reason the rest of this chapter is devoted to importers in that region.

The dominance of Japan and the Pacific market post-1975

The introduction of LNG in Japan

LNG was first introduced into Japan in 1969 when Tokyo Electric Power Company (TEPCO) and Tokyo Gas jointly imported LNG from Alaska. Since their first introduction, LNG imports continued to expand up to 2000, leading to Japan's position as the world's largest LNG importer, and LNG becoming a key part of the country's energy market. There were two key factors behind the 'success story' of LNG in Japan: its contribution to easing the widely shared perception of the country's energy security problem, and its contribution to environmental protection in relation to urban air quality.

The importance of LNG to Japan's energy security stemmed from the recognition by policy planners and the energy industry that the fuel provided a workable solution to the problem of needing to reduce oil import dependence and to diversify energy sources. In the 1960s and early 1970s energy demand, in particular oil demand, had continued to grow rapidly, backed by strong economic growth. Lacking domestic energy (fossil fuel) resources, this resulted in high energy import dependence. Under these circumstances, securing stable energy supplies became an essential task for both government and industry in Japan. In Fiscal Year (FY[26]) 1973, the share of oil in total primary energy supply reached a historical high at 77 per cent, with overall energy import dependence reaching 89 per cent. Furthermore, Japan became heavily dependent on Middle East crude oil,

---

[25] Demand data from 35 European countries including Baltic states and Turkey. BP (2011, 23).

[26] The Japanese fiscal year runs from April to March. All years quoted in this section related to Japan are fiscal years.

with more than 90 per cent of imports from that region during the early part of the 1970s.

Under these circumstances, the 1973 oil crisis had a grave impact on the Japanese economy and society, and energy security became a national top priority. After the first oil crisis, government and industry embarked on strenuous efforts – including efficiency improvements, diversification of energy supplies and import sources, and improving emergency preparedness – to enhance energy security. In this context, the promotion of LNG use in Japan was regarded as a key building block for energy security, because LNG could reduce oil dependency, diversify the energy mix, and thus reduce dependence on Middle East oil. Furthermore, LNG supply itself was regarded as inherently 'stable and reliable', backed by the contractual characteristics of long-term supply guarantees and accompanied by very close and stable relationships between sellers and buyers of LNG. In other words, LNG became a preferred option for contributing to Japan's energy security, which became a national priority.

However, when LNG was first introduced, its role as a clean fuel was arguably more important than its contribution to energy security. During the 1960s and early 1970s, when Japan's economy and energy consumption continued to grow rapidly, local and regional environmental problems – such as air pollution and water pollution caused by emissions from factories – created strong public concern. Rapid growth in fossil fuel (particularly oil) consumption had created health-hazardous air pollution problems in many urban and industrial regions in Japan. Air and water pollution had become national problems attracting very strong social and political attention (see IEEJ, 1986). One of the measures taken as a result was the promotion of cleaner oil (crude oil and oil products) use, particularly in the power generation sector. National and local government regulation became increasingly stringent; for example, both the Tokyo metropolitan and Osaka prefectural governments mandated the use of very low (less than 0.1 per cent) sulphur and low-nitrogen feedstock for oil-fired power generation in specific areas of their regions.

As LNG emits far less SO_x and NO_x than oil, its introduction as an energy option for urban and industrial areas made a significant contribution to the improvement of air quality. This was an important background factor influencing TEPCO and Tokyo Gas[27] in their decision to introduce LNG; other power and gas companies followed their example for similar reasons.

By the 1990s, climate change had become recognized as a worldwide problem, and the issue of how to manage or reduce the contribution of

---

[27] It is believed that Mr. Anzai, the then President of Tokyo Gas, and Mr. Kikawada, the then President of TEPCO, made the critical decision to introduce LNG in Japan, thus becoming 'the fathers of LNG in Japan'.

22 LNG Markets in Transition

CO_2 to greenhouse gas (GHG) emissions became a serious energy and environment policy agenda item in many countries, including Japan. Particularly after the Kyoto Protocol agreement of 1997, which included concrete targets to reduce GHG emissions for the period 2008–12 for Annex 1 countries (including Japan), the de-carbonization of Japan's primary energy supply structure was made a priority in its national energy policy. Given its advantage as the least CO_2-intensive of fossil fuels, expanded use of LNG was expected to contribute to Japan's GHG reductions.

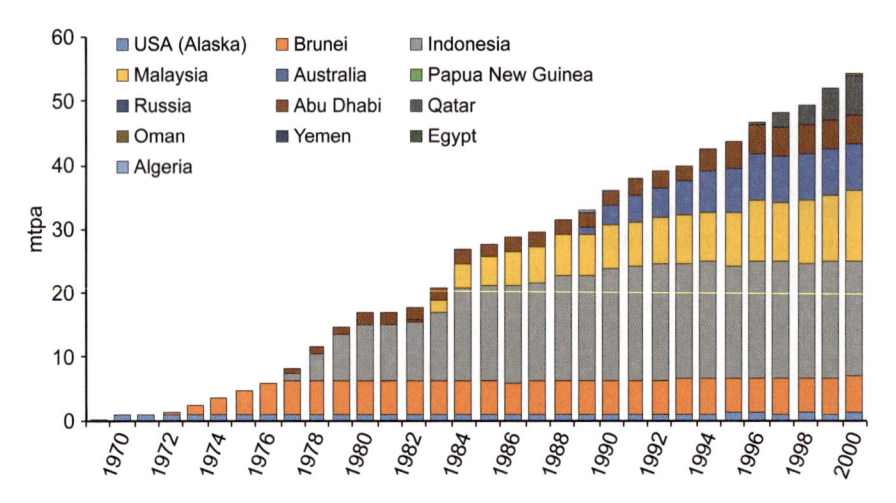

Figure 1.4: Japan's LNG imports by source
Source: IEEJ/EDMC (2015).

These factors led to the expansion of LNG imports from 0.05 mtpa in 1969 to 53.3 mtpa in 2000 (Figure 1.4). In the early 1970s, the country became the world largest LNG importer, and by 2000, it accounted for 52 per cent of global LNG trade. The share of natural gas in Japan's primary supply increased from 1.0 per cent in 1969 to 13.1 per cent in 2000 and the next sections discuss in detail the development of LNG in the power and city gas sectors.

The power sector
As mentioned earlier, Japan's power industry had to cope with the task of building baseload power stations, as well as diversifying sources of electricity generation, when energy (particularly electricity) demand was growing rapidly during the 1960s.[28] The perceived stability of LNG supply and its

---
[28] Electricity demand in Japan increased at an annual average growth rate of 12.4% during the 1960s.

merits as a 'clean' fuel were important factors underpinning the introduction of LNG to the power sector.[29] The fact that natural gas is a more geographically diversified resource than oil was also a very important consideration. And the size and very long-term nature of the investment required for LNG projects were recognized as factors likely to result in stable and reliable supply.[30]

LNG liquefaction projects require huge investments (often tens of billions of dollars) and long lead times, due to their technical complexity and capital intensity. Long-term supply contracts (often more than 20 years) with a 'take-or-pay' clause that obligates the user to pay for the contracted volume of LNG are crucial to determining the economic viability of the project (see Chapter 2). Although the long-term nature of these contracts contributed to a stable supply of energy to users in Japan, the inflexibility of 'take-or-pay' and 'destination clauses' subsequently became problematic (see below). However, the fact that the country's major LNG import sources were in the Asia–Pacific region and not in the Middle East contributed to the perception of LNG as a stable source of energy.[31]

As already noted, the introduction of LNG for power generation was partly promoted to allow compliance with stringent air pollution controls, particularly in urban areas, as pollution caused by emissions of SO_2 had become a serious social problem. To deal with this problem, in 1969 Japan's Advisory Council on Energy made a recommendation to the Ministry of International Trade and Industry (MITI)[32] to substantially reduce the sulphur content of fuels used in urban areas.[33] Therefore, LNG as a fuel for power generation, particularly in urban areas, was regarded as extremely beneficial with respect to air quality, as LNG has virtually no sulphur content.

As a result, the import and consumption of LNG in Japan's power industry increased rapidly, especially in the Tokyo and Osaka areas. From 1969 to 1973, LNG consumption in Japan's power industry sharply increased from 0.09 to 1.38 mtpa.

---

[29] See MITI (1975, 86) for the energy policy planners' perception on this issue.

[30] See MITI (1973) and MITI (1975) about its perception and recognition.

[31] In FY 2000, LNG imports from Asia–Pacific region accounted for 80% of Japan's total LNG import.

[32] In 2001, the name of the ministry was changed to Ministry of Economy, Trade and Industry (METI).

[33] Pressed to cope with the problem, the government established a series of pollution control regulations, as follows: 1) Enactment of the Soot and Smoke Regulation Law in 1962; 2) The designation of Tokyo, Kanagawa, Osaka, etc. as areas in need of anti-air pollution measures, based on amendment of the enforcement regulations under the above law in 1963; 3) Enforcement of the Anti-Pollution Basic Law in 1967; and 4) Enforcement of the Air Pollution Control Law in 1968.

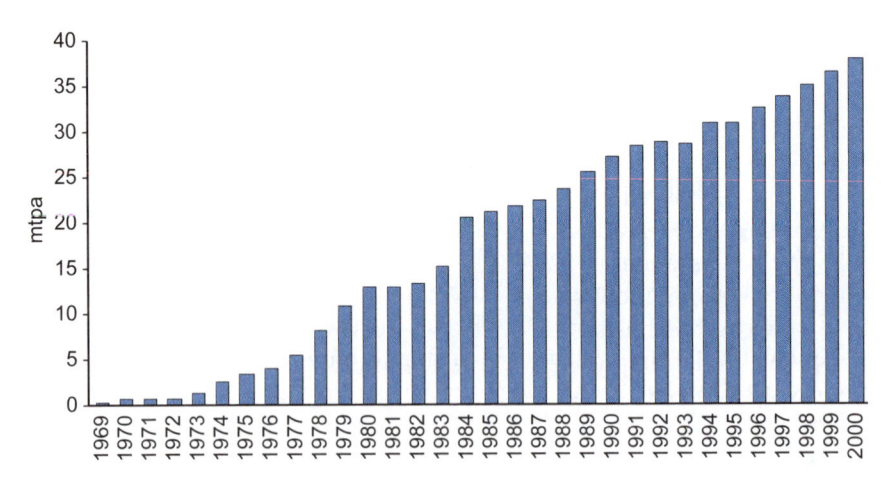

Figure 1.5: LNG use in the power sector
Source: IEEJ/EDMC (2015).

LNG development was further promoted after the first oil crisis, as its security advantages were greatly valued by MITI[34] because nuclear development, another important element for enhancing energy security, had started to encounter powerful opposition as early as 1970.[35] For these reasons, government-backed financial support was given to LNG development in the power sector from 'Special Accounts for Electric Power Development Acceleration Measures' and 'Special Accounts for Electric Power Diversification'.[36] To encourage LNG/natural gas utilization, long-term finance at favourable interest rates from the Development Bank of Japan became available.[37] The Export–Import Bank of Japan[38] provided finance for the second LNG import project from Brunei. In addition, following a revision of the 'Japan National Oil Corporation (JNOC) Law', finance from JNOC[39] to support LNG projects also became available in

---

[34] See MITI (1975) for more detail about its views.

[35] For example, in 1972, Kumano city (Mie prefecture) officially refused the proposal of the Chubu Electric Power Company for a new plant, residents of Arahama in Kashiwazaki city (Niigata pref.) voted against a Tokyo Electric Power plan, and litigation began to halt construction of the Shikoku Power Electric Ikata power station.

[36] The special laws were enacted in 1974 to establish these special accounts.

[37] The soft loans amounted to 881.1 bn yen for FYs 1974 to 1990.

[38] In April 1999, Export–Import Bank of Japan (EIBJ) and Overseas Economic Cooperation Fund (OECF) were merged in a new organization, Japan Bank for International Cooperation (JBIC).

[39] JNOC was later reorganized and renamed as Japan Oil, Gas and Metal Corporation (JOGMEC).

1994. With this financial support from the government, LNG consumption in Japan's power sector increased substantially in the 1970s and early 1980s, reaching 21.3 mtpa in 1985 (Figure 1.5).

In addition to government support, the trading houses (sogo shosha) of Japan – such as Mitsubishi Corporation, Mitsui & Company, and Sumitomo Corporation – played a unique role in promoting LNG development in the Japanese market. Trading houses have traditionally played a role as a 'middleman' between suppliers (NOC and IOC) of crude oil and Japanese energy companies (power and oil refining companies). As Japanese utility companies had no business experience in the area of LNG (which required large-scale initial supply side investment), the role of the 'middleman' was appreciated by both buyers and sellers of LNG. For example, in 1969, Mitsubishi Corporation decided to invest in Cold Gas Trading (the trading arm of the Brunei LNG project) on a 50:50 basis with Shell, Mitsubishi also invested in Brunei LNG (the LNG manufacturing arm of the project) with a 45 per cent participation. Shell also held 45 per cent, the remaining 10 per cent being held by the government of Brunei. Mitsubishi then played an important role in finding and securing LNG sales outlets in Japan.

During the early 1980s, however, concern over 'take-or-pay' provisions in LNG contracts arose,[40] especially as the economics of LNG-fired power generation were regarded as being inferior to those of nuclear and coal, with the cost of power generation estimated at 17 yen (7.0 US cent[41])/kWh for LNG, 12.5 yen (5.1 US cent)/kWh for nuclear, and 14 yen (5.7 US cent)/kWh for coal (See MITI, 1984, 161). Based on these considerations, LNG-fired power generation started to be positioned as middle-load capacity (which requires flexible operation to follow daily and/or seasonal fluctuations in electricity demand), with nuclear and coal-fired power generation as baseload capacity.

By the 1990s, however, the introduction of more advanced technology, particularly in the form of combined-cycle gas turbines (CCGT), improved the economics of LNG-fired power generation; MITI then revised its estimate of the cost of LNG-fired power generation to 10 yen (9.3 US cent[42])/kWh, slightly higher than that of nuclear at 9 yen/kWh (8.3 US cent) but comparable to that of coal (MITI, 1993, 393). Furthermore, as global warming became a serious policy issue in the late 1980s, at the same time as the anti-nuclear movement was becoming powerful again (after the Chernobyl accident), the promotion of LNG in

---

[40] See MITI (1984, 65) for more detail about this concern.

[41] The power generation cost in Japanese yen here is converted to US cents, based on the actual exchange rate of 243.9 yen/$ in FY 1984.

[42] The conversion from Japanese yen to US cent here is based on the actual exchange rate of 107.8 yen/$ in FY 1993.

the power industry was once again considered very important. As a result, LNG consumption in power generation increased from 21.3 to 38.4 mtpa over the period 1985–2000.

The city gas sector

Gas demand in the city gas sector increased rapidly after the 1950s as growth in income per capita resulted in sharp increases in both the numbers of households using city gas, and in the unit consumption per household, backed by the penetration of gas appliances for cooking (IEEJ, 1986, 230–1). This resulted in a sharp increase in sales from 0.46 mtoe in 1950 to 1.58 mtoe in 1960. These trends continued, and accelerated in the 1960s, as the population density increased in urban areas and a boom in housing construction greatly contributed to an increased demand for gas appliances.[43] In 1970, city gas sales were about three times greater than in 1960, with 9.42 million customers using 5.23 mtoe (this figure includes losses in the manufacturing process).

On the supply side, the city gas industry depended heavily on domestic coal as a feedstock after the end of World War II. Oil-based feedstock was introduced after the 1950s due to concern over the stability of coal supplies which was triggered by the large-scale coal miners' strike in 1952 (which lasted for 63 days), and the abundant availability of imported oil at a lower cost than coal.

In 1955 coal-based feedstock still accounted for 90.8 per cent of total city gas supply, followed by oil-based feedstock (6.9 per cent), and domestic natural gas (2.1 per cent). However, by 1968, consumption of largely naphtha-based feedstock had increased rapidly, to 2.04 mtoe (from 0.75 mtoe in 1955). Oil thus became the dominant (48.6 per cent of total) feedstock, with coal the second-most important source (41.8 per cent), and domestic natural gas (9.4 per cent) a minor contributor due to the limited domestic resources (as was the case for crude oil). Faced with sharply increasing dependence on oil, the city gas industry started to consider (as did the power sector) diversification of feedstocks.

The introduction of LNG as a city gas feedstock was – as in the power sector – regarded as beneficial because of perceived supply security and its merits as a 'clean' fuel. However, specific characteristics of LNG, such as its calorific value, were also very favourable for the city gas industry and its users. As the calorific value of LNG (0.0013 toe/kg) is more than double that of other feedstocks, a switch to LNG allowed twice as much energy to be delivered through the existing transportation network (IEEJ, 1986, 243).

---

[43] The share of population in the Tokyo area increased from 17.2% in 1955 to 24.2% in 1975, and new housing construction reached a historical peak of 1.86 million houses in 1972.

It was also expected that this higher calorific value would result in 'new' demand for city gas from penetration of new and more convenient gas appliances, such as gas cookers.

Furthermore, the introduction of LNG was regarded as a means of increasing the efficiency of the gasification process. This is because almost 100 per cent of LNG is regasified, compared to 85–90 per cent gasification rates for gas manufacturing processes using oil or coal as feedstock (IEEJ, 1986, 243). Backed by these perceived benefits, LNG was first introduced for city gas use by Tokyo Gas in 1969; LNG consumption in the sector increased rapidly from 0.08 mtpa in FY 1969 to 0.96 mtpa in FY 1973.

The outbreak of the 1973 oil crisis also became a turning point for the development of LNG in Japan's city gas industry. LNG became recognized as an important alternative to oil, particularly because of the security of supply. The 'System of encouragement for LNG use in the industry sector' was adopted as policy, based on recommendation by a MITI advisory council in 1979; this promoted LNG as an alternative to oil in the city gas sector. Under this system, preferential pricing was applied to eligible users satisfying such conditions as specified rates of minimum LNG usage[44] based on long-term contracts, although pricing details were not available as this was regarded as confidential. To promote this system, long-term finance at favourable interest rates from the Development Bank of Japan became available.

With this support, demand in the industrial sector increased sharply from 0.89 mtoe (12.6 per cent share of total city gas sales) in 1975 to 2.33 mtoe (19.5 per cent share) in 1985. This in turn resulted in a rapid increase in LNG consumption in the city gas industry from 1.6 mtpa in 1975 to 5.8 mtpa in 1985 (Figure 1.6 overleaf). As a result, there was a structural change in city gas energy usage, with the share of LNG increasing from only 6.1 per cent in 1970 to 59.9 per cent in 1985, and that of oil declining from 47.5 per cent to 24.6 per cent over the same period.

Thus in the 1980s, LNG became the dominant feedstock for city gas. This dominance was brought about mainly by the introduction of LNG into the three largest city gas companies, namely: Tokyo Gas, Osaka Gas, and Toho Gas, although, with a few exceptions, 200 small- and medium-sized local city gas companies continued to use oil, coal, or domestic natural gas as feedstock because the investment required to introduce LNG was too high to justify the expense (MITI, 1993). However, it appeared that growth in LNG consumption in Japan's city gas industry might slow during the second half of the 1980s as the switchover to LNG by the three major companies came close to completion.

---

[44] Two categories of eligible users were established: those using over 4 million cubic metres of LNG per year, and those using over 1 million cubic metres per year.

28   *LNG Markets in Transition*

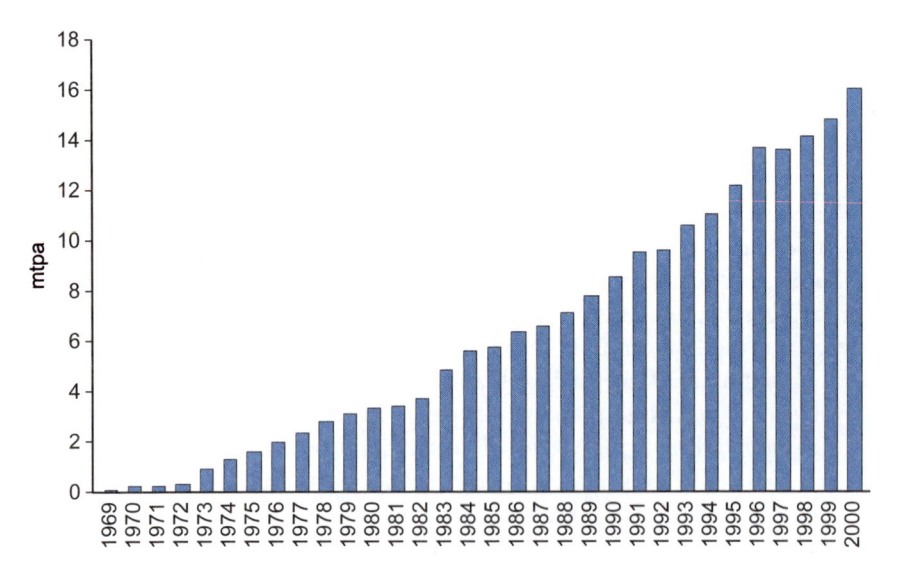

Figure 1.6: LNG use in the city gas sector
Source: IEEJ/EDMC (2015).

Given this situation, the promotion of LNG to local city gas companies became the next target of the Japanese government. In order to do this, the government decided to provide a variety of supports such as: subsidies to promote LNG use in local city gas companies, long-term finance at favourable interest rates from the Development Bank of Japan, and tax incentives through the law 'Tax system to promote investment for economic, social and energy infrastructure'. To implement these measures, the Centre for Promotion of Introduction of Natural Gas was established in 1985 as an extra department of MITI. In addition, MITI then started to emphasize the development of 'new' demand for city gas, such as: co-generation, district heating, and air conditioning (MITI, 1993, 166–7). This led to the number of city gas companies using LNG as a feedstock (including those dependent on the three principal city gas companies as original importers for their LNG supply) increasing to 45 in 1993 (MITI, 1994). Furthermore, city gas companies started to develop new demand by persuading large industrial users to switch from oil products to natural gas. As a result of all these measures, city gas LNG consumption increased steadily from 5.8–16.0 mtpa between 1985 and 2000 (Figure 1.6).

The combined effect of these developments meant that by 2000, the Japanese LNG industry was dominated by the power generation (69 per cent) and city gas (29 per cent) sectors.[45] In addition, starting in the early 1990s, MITI

---

[45] A small amount of LNG is also consumed by the steel industry in Japan. For example, LNG consumption in the industry was 0.67 mtpa in 2000.

emphasized the promotion of LNG as an effective climate change measure. This is because increased LNG use in the fossil fuel mix implies lower CO_2 emissions, due to the lower carbon intensity of LNG compared to coal and oil (MITI, 1994). For example, the carbon intensity of LNG is 40 per cent lower than that of coal and about 25 per cent lower than that of oil.[46]

Between 1970 and 2000, LNG consumption increased from 2.1 mtpa to 53.3 mtpa and the share of natural gas[47] in Japan's total primary energy supply increased from 1.2 to 13.1 per cent. Backed by the conditions mentioned above, both government planners and industry expected LNG demand in Japan to continue to grow. For example, in MITI's 1998 'Long Term Outlook for Energy Supply and Demand', demand for natural gas (LNG and domestic natural gas combined) was projected to increase from 48.2 mtpa in 1996, to 57.1–60.9 mtpa in 2010.

The emergence of new LNG importers in Asia: Korea and Taiwan

Korea started to import LNG in 1986 and, with Taiwan following in 1991, these countries became the second and third largest importers respectively in Asia. The reasons behind the introduction of LNG in these two countries were similar to those relating to Japan, namely the need to enhance energy security and to promote a cleaner energy source.

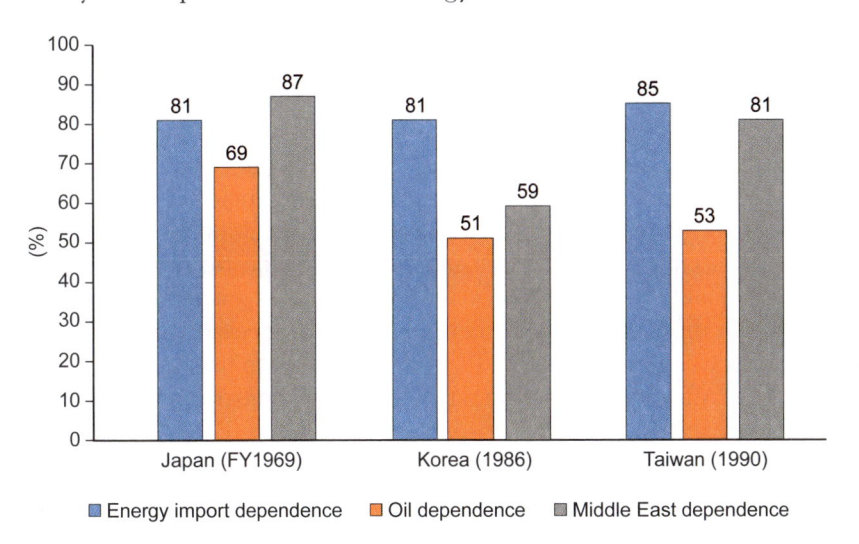

Figure 1.7: Energy import dependence of Japan, Korea, and Taiwan
Sources: IEEJ/EDMC (2015); APEC (1995); KEEI; MITIE (2014); and BoE (Taiwan).

---

[46] Yoon and Yamada (2000) pointed out that the lower carbon intensity of LNG could contribute lower carbon emission, at a life cycle level, than coal and oil.
[47] LNG accounted for 97% of total natural gas supply in Japan in 2000.

30   *LNG Markets in Transition*

Both Korea and Taiwan are, like Japan, highly energy import-dependent, oil-dependent, and Middle East-dependent (Figure 1.7). For them, LNG imports (in particular from Asia–Pacific countries) were regarded as an effective tool to diversify energy sources and reduce dependence on the Middle East. Korea and Taiwan were two of the 'Four Asian Tigers' of the 1980s which all recorded sustained high economic growth rates. This rapid economic growth and industrialization resulted in growing environmental problems, including air pollution and other problems similar to those faced by Japan. As the climate change issue started to attract the attention of policy planners in the early 1990s, the need to cap GHG emissions played a role from the early period of LNG introduction in these two countries, particularly in the case of Taiwan (although the latter is not an UN member). This summarizes the main reasons why LNG became a preferred option in these two countries and led to them becoming major importers.

The Korean market
As a country with a very similar energy supply–demand structure to that of Japan, Korea also developed an energy security strategy in the 1970s, having suffered from two oil crises. Its policy components were thus very similar to those in Japan: improving energy efficiency, diversifying energy and import sources, and enhancing emergency preparedness. In this context, the introduction of LNG was discussed and decided in the early 1980s.

Nevertheless, in 1980, oil dependency was still 64 per cent and Middle East oil dependency 99 per cent. Thus LNG was planned to play a key role in reducing both oil and Middle East import dependence. The expected stability of LNG supply was also regarded as enhancing energy security. Another specific reason was the replacement of traditional coal use in the residential sector, which made a major contribution to improvements in urban air quality.[48]

In 1983, the Korean government took a policy decision to establish the Korea Gas Corporation (KOGAS) as a state entity to promote natural gas and LNG. After the establishment of KOGAS, construction of the first LNG receiving terminal at Pyeongtaek started in 1983, and the first national trunk pipelines in the following year. With the completion of the terminal in 1986, KOGAS received its first LNG from Indonesia. The roles of KOGAS were: sole importer of LNG in Korea; supplier of LNG (natural gas) to large-scale gas users including Korea Electric Power Corporation (KEPCO) and city gas companies; and constructor and operator of the LNG receiving terminal and national pipeline network.

---

[48] Coal consumption accounted for 64% of Korea's residential sector final energy consumption in 1980.

Looking Back at History 31

In the early 1990s, KOGAS and the Ministry of Trade, Industry and Energy (MOTIE) published strategic plans for the promotion of natural gas use and pipeline development in a two phase pipeline development programme: the first phase, completion of a 1,500 km high-pressure pipeline network by 1997; the second phase, construction of branch pipelines to connect major cities to the high-pressure network. In the 1990s, KOGAS also embarked on an expansion of Pyeongtaek and construction of a new receiving terminal at Incheon.

Backed by infrastructure development and government financial support, natural gas demand in the city gas sector increased from 0.91 mtoe to 11.31 mtoe between 1990 and 2000, while consumption in the power sector increased from 2.03 mtoe to 5.25 mtoe over the same period. As a result, the share of natural gas in primary energy supply rose from 3.0 per cent in 1990 to 9.1 per cent in 2000, and LNG imports increased correspondingly from 2.3 mtpa to 14.3 mtpa (Figure 1.8). Thus Korea became the second largest LNG importer in the world after Japan, accounting for 14 per cent of global LNG imports in 2000.

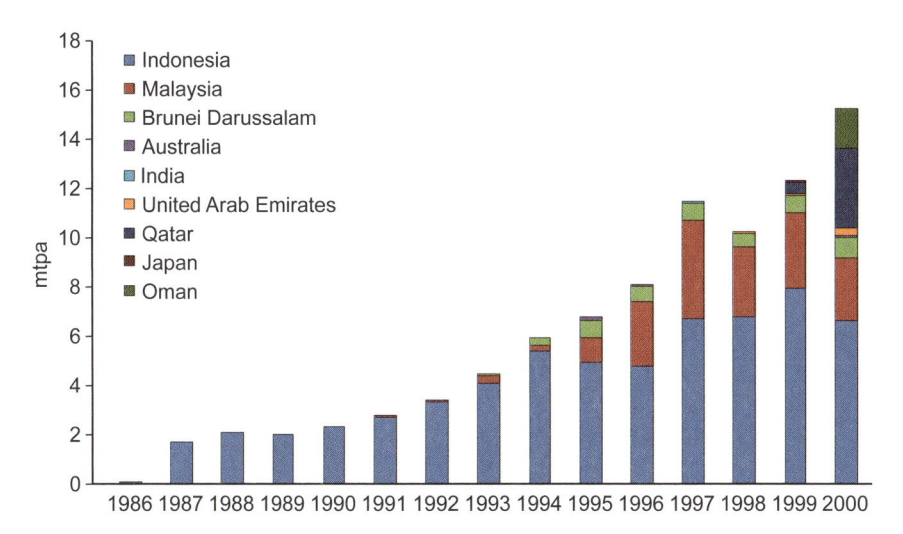

Figure 1.8: Korean LNG imports by source, 1986–2000
Source: KOGAS Annual Report.

The Taiwanese market
Taiwan's energy security and environmental challenges were similar to those facing Japan and Korea. After the oil crises in the 1970s, Taiwan continued its efforts to reduce dependence on oil in total primary energy supply, and specifically on Middle East oil. Taiwan started to develop nuclear power as

32 LNG Markets in Transition

a means of reducing oil and Middle East dependency as early as the 1970s. Nuclear power generation started in 1977 and grew steadily to 33.1 TWh in 1987 (18 per cent of total primary energy supply). But the country's anti-nuclear movement became influential in the 1980s, and the government and the state-owned Taiwan Power Company encountered opposition to construction of the fourth nuclear power plant. Under these circumstances, the government was required to promote natural gas in order to diversify the energy mix and reduce Middle East dependency, and also to combat air pollution (and later CO_2 emission) problems.[49]

Taiwan has small-scale domestic natural gas production, but because of limited reserve availability, domestic natural gas production peaked at 2 bcm in 1980 and declined to below 1 bcm/year in the early 1990s. The government started preparations for LNG imports in the 1980s; these included construction of the Yung-An receiving terminal (which was completed in 1989) and a 310 kilometre national trunk pipeline to connect the LNG terminal (in the south) with the major gas consuming regions in the north. The completion of this infrastructure, expansion of Yung-An, the construction of an additional LNG terminal (Taichung in 2009), as well as major additions to the pipeline network, facilitated a substantial increase in natural gas demand.

Natural gas and LNG-related infrastructure was constructed and operated by CPC Corporation, a state-owned Taiwanese oil and gas company, which is responsible for LNG imports and for supplying natural gas to domestic users such as the Taiwan Power Company, industrial users, and city gas companies.

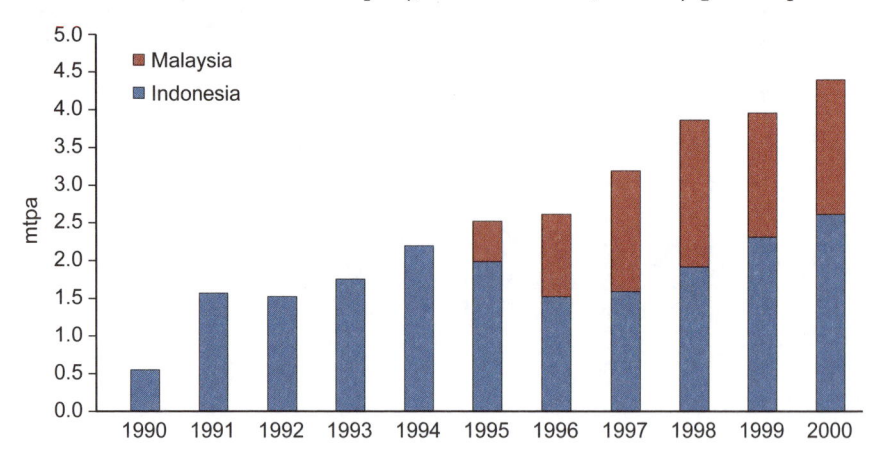

Figure 1.9: Taiwanese LNG imports by source, 1990–2000
Source: BoE (Taiwan).

---

[49] Interestingly, Taiwan is not a United Nation member, and is thus officially outside the UNFCCC framework, but the country is nevertheless very positive about voluntary participation in GHG emission reduction initiatives.

Before the introduction of LNG, natural gas was mainly used in the residential sector (the share in total final gas consumption was 59 per cent in 1989). Natural gas had previously not been used in power generation, but after the start of LNG imports, the demand for power generation grew rapidly, reaching 4.08 mtpa in 2001 (68 per cent of national gas consumption). With LNG use in the power sector as a main driver, Taiwan's LNG imports, which had started in 1990 from Indonesia, reached 4.4 mtpa in 2000 (Figure 1.9). This figure was the third largest in Asia (after Japan and Korea) and the sixth largest in the world, and made Taiwan (and CPC) a major player in the LNG market.

LNG issues and challenges for Asian buyers

Security of supply

As noted above, the introduction of LNG in Japan, Korea, and Taiwan was seen as a way of enhancing energy security – by diversifying the energy mix and reducing Middle East oil dependence. But subsequently, the security of gas and LNG supply itself became an important issue for policy makers and buyers. These countries have very limited domestic natural gas resources and, with rising natural gas demand, all were highly dependent on LNG imports. In contrast to most Atlantic Basin countries, LNG importers in Japan, Korea, and Taiwan had no commercially viable or politically acceptable pipeline gas import options,[50] no other gas supply, and limited alternative energy options. Many more Asian LNG projects thus reached a final investment decision even if, in some cases, this took a considerable period of time.

As discussed earlier, however, there was recognition in the three countries that LNG supply had inherent security 'advantages', including the fact that the main suppliers were from the Asia–Pacific region, which implied reduced dependence on Middle East energy supplies. Long-term contracts and stable supply characteristics were also perceived as making a contribution to security of supply.

Under these circumstances, and with these advantages in mind, Asian LNG buyers placed emphasis on diversification of LNG import sources to enhance the security of LNG supply. This is particularly the case for large buyers, because the scale of their import requirements allows them to procure from a number of different sources. Large buyers such as TEPCO, Tokyo Gas, Chubu Electric Company, Osaka Gas, KOGAS, and others thus embarked on LNG import source diversification.

---

[50] Japanese imports of Soviet pipeline gas were considered as far back as the 1960s (i.e. predating the LNG era) but not only was this politically unacceptable during the Cold War, but the lack of domestic pipeline networks in Japan, and the unwillingness of the electric utilities to cooperate, were additional barriers.

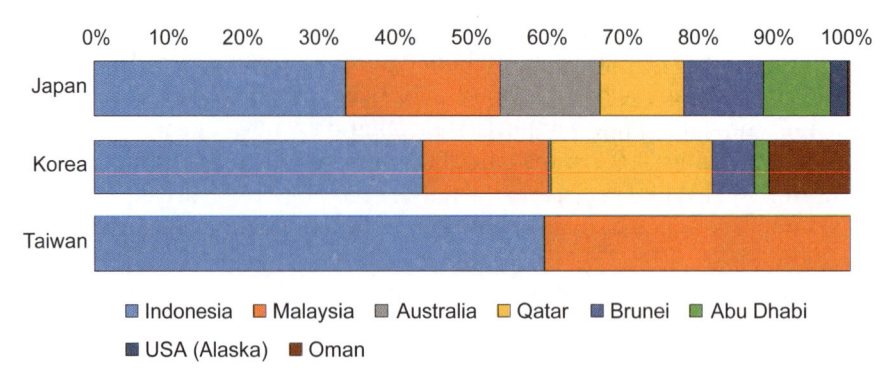

Figure 1.10: LNG import source diversification of Japan, Korea, and Taiwan in 2000
Source: IEEJ/EDMC (2015); KOGAS Annual Report; and BoE (Taiwan).

As a result, by 2000, Japan was importing LNG from eight countries, and Korea and Taiwan from seven and two countries respectively (Figure 1.10).[51] It should also be noted that LNG imports were more diversified in terms of the number of LNG supply projects than the number of source countries.

In the 1990s, a new trend emerged in Asian buyers, with regard to additional measures to enhance security of LNG supply. These companies had traditionally been 'pure buyers', not involved in other parts of the LNG supply chain. But they subsequently became interested in participating in the upstream, namely gas field development providing feed gas to LNG liquefaction plants.[52] They also became interested in getting involved in liquefaction[53] and in tanker transportation of LNG.[54] Participation in other parts of the supply chain was motivated by a recognition of the fact that it would enhance access to supply and make the buyers more integrated market players. In addition, it was also argued that in order to gain a better understanding of the cost and profit structure of the overall LNG supply chain, buyers needed to participate in the upstream and midstream sectors.

The final element of supply security relates to the issue of emergency

---

[51] In the case of Taiwan, the number of import sources was two in 2000, but by 2006 this had increased to eight.

[52] In 1990 Osaka Gas became the first player to acquire an interest in the Sanga Sanga PSC that supplied gas to the Bontang LNG plant. (The company holds 33.4% in Universe Gas and Oil which in turn has 4.4% of the PSC.)

[53] In 2003 TEPCO and Tokyo Gas became the first to join the Darwin LNG project (TEPCO acquired 6.72% and Tokyo Gas 3.36% of the equity in the project at that time).

[54] In 1993 the first attempt in the area of LNG transportation was the tanker *LNG Flora*, with Osaka Gas owning 35% and Tokyo Gas owning 10%.

preparedness. In the case of oil supply, Japan, Korea, and Taiwan made serious efforts to enhance emergency preparedness by creating oil stockpiles. But in the case of LNG, stockpiling is much more difficult both physically and commercially. Thus, LNG inventories held by Asian buyers have been at a 'minimum' level for commercial and operational purposes, at around 15–20 days cover, which is far below the corresponding levels for oil.[55] Emergency preparedness remains as a challenging issue for security of LNG supply.

Long-term contract stability versus supply flexibility
As discussed earlier, Asian LNG buyers continued to rely on long-term (20–25 year) contracts as a preferred option because of the perceived contribution to supply security; the long-term contract has therefore remained the dominant commercial framework. Spot and short/medium-term (less than four years) contract-based LNG supply accounted for less than 5 per cent of total global LNG trade up to the early 2000s (see Chapter 9).

While long-term contracts remained dominant, the necessity for greater supply flexibility for buyers gradually emerged. LNG-fired power generation (the dominant sector for LNG consumption) has a position of 'middle-peak' load which requires more flexible operation than coal-fired and nuclear stations, which provide baseload power. Because of temperature changes, the daily and seasonal LNG demand fluctuations were so large that flexible procurement became essential to accommodate demand fluctuations.

Electricity and gas market liberalization, which started in Japan in the 1990s, has gradually resulted in uncertainty over future power and gas demand. This has increased the value of flexibility (see Chapter 9).

Under these circumstances, Asian LNG buyers have made efforts to improve supply flexibility by: increasing upward and downward quantity tolerances in their long-term contracts; agreeing cargo swap arrangements (where destination restrictions permitted); and increasing purchases of spot, short-, and medium-term supply. This increase in flexibility, while maintaining stability of supply based on the dominance of long-term contracts, has contributed to strengthening the position of LNG as a reliable and attractive energy option in Japan, Korea, and Taiwan.

---

[55] No official data is available on LNG inventory in Asian countries, but industry sources suggest that the 15–20 days cover for LNG inventory applies both to the past (around 2000) as well as to the present day.

The creation of JCC pricing and ability to overcome commercial problems

Like their Atlantic Basin counterparts, the early pioneers of Pacific LNG export contracts (Alaska and Brunei) also had problems over pricing and had to change the original terms from fixed to crude oil-related prices.[56] This was not a straightforward process, but in complete contrast to what happened in the Atlantic Basin, Japanese buyers (until 1986 Japan was the sole importer of LNG in the Pacific) were able to cope with this change without disrupting the trade, because they were replacing crude oil with LNG in their power plants. They were therefore able to agree a crude oil-related price formula, of a type which was impossible for their Atlantic Basin counterparts. Early crude oil-related pricing in the Indonesian contracts was based on official government selling prices.[57] The subsequent change to a crude oil-related formula, the JCC (officially: the Japan Customs-cleared Crude oil price mechanism, also known as the Japan Crude Cocktail), according to which the gas price was set and related to an average of the prices of a number of crude oils imported into Japan, is believed to have been created in the Malaysian LNG contract signed with TEPCO and Tokyo Gas in 1983.[58] The other major element of JCC is known as 'the slope' (in the Atlantic Basin this is known as 'the index') which determines how the gas price changes in response to changes in oil prices. The most common slope in the early contracts was 14.85 (this dates back to the 1973 Indonesian contract with six Japanese buyers) which resulted in a premium over crude oil parity at low oil prices and a discount when the crude oil price rose above $26/bbl.[59]

By the early 1990s, two further elements were added to Japanese LNG contracts (with the exception of those with Indonesia): sellers were seeking increased protection against low oil prices and buyers against sudden increases in oil prices. This resulted in the introduction of the 'S-curve',

---

[56] Details of how these prices changed can be found in Stern (2012, 68–73) and Flower and Liao (2012).

[57] Indonesia continued the practice of basing LNG prices on its crude oil export price (rather than the crude oil import price of the buyers) into the 1980s and 90s, but official government selling prices were replaced by actual (ICP) prices.

[58] This stemmed from the fact that the Malaysian sellers were unwilling to accept Indonesian Official Government Selling Prices as their price benchmark. Starting in 1988, the Japanese Ministry of Finance began to publish monthly statistics of customs-cleared crude oil prices in its so-called 'Yellow Book' – a practice which continues today on its website.

[59] Parity with crude oil is reached with a slope of 17.1. For a detailed explanation of how the slope operates at different oil price levels see Appendix 2.2 in Stern (2012, 78–9); Flower and Liao (2012, 339–40).

which limited the exposure of both sides by limiting the impact on gas prices of oil price movements within a certain range. The second element was the 'applicable range' within which the S-curve would operate. This was set at $11 to $29/bbl (for more details see Chapter 8).[60]

The Japanese government and Japanese companies supported projects even when they began to fail because of disagreements over price (for example in the case of Indonesia's insistence on using government selling prices) not only with policy, but also financially.[61] Where there were disagreements over pricing in Asia, projects were not litigated. A good example of this is the ADGAS project, where disagreements on pricing led to long periods of time (as long as seven years) where funds were paid into an escrow account by the buyers pending a final agreement, but deliveries continued to flow (Dargin and Flower, 2011; Flower and Liao, 2012, 352–3). Part of the reason for this consensual resolution of commercial problems has been the very strong Japanese financial support for all the early Asian LNG projects, with the Japanese Export–Import Bank providing loans at attractive interest rates (Greenwald, 1998, 248–56). Indeed as far as is known, no Pacific LNG contract has ever been taken to international arbitration – in contrast to the Atlantic Basin, where arbitration has been used as a method of resolving long-term contract LNG disputes since the early years of the trade.

Summary and conclusions: the early development of LNG supplies and markets

The LNG industry overcame the 1944 Cleveland disaster, but it was to be 20 years before the start of commercial LNG trade – an indication (and a warning) of the potential impact of any major accident on the development of an industry. LNG trade began in Europe in the mid-1960s and, for the first few years, was dominated by exports from Algeria to the UK and France. Atlantic Basin trade was intended to expand rapidly in the 1970s, with the USA becoming a major importer from Algeria and a range of other countries. But reality proved to be entirely different; the USA and Europe developed alternative domestic and imported sources of pipeline gas, which proved to be less expensive and easier to organize than LNG imports.

---

[60] Flower and Liao (2012, 340–1). An S-curve was introduced into some Indonesian contracts in the early 2000s; Korea and Taiwan did not introduce S-curves until after 2000 and then only in one or two contracts.

[61] Indonesian refunds to Japanese buyers over a period of five years in the 1980s are described in Barnes (1995, 114–7).

38 *LNG Markets in Transition*

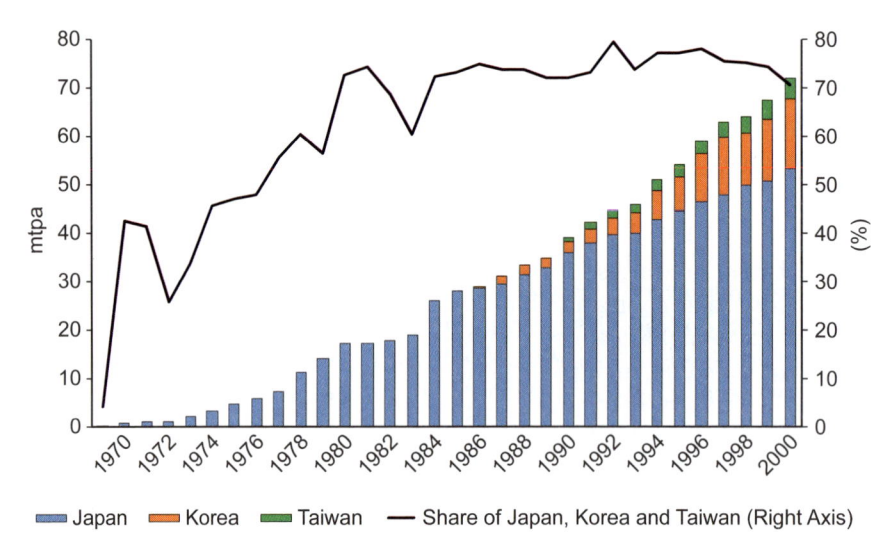

Figure 1.11: Shares of Japan, Korea, and Taiwan in global LNG imports

In the Pacific Basin, by contrast, a combination of concern about security of imported Middle East oil and deteriorating urban air quality led the Japanese government and utilities to develop substantial LNG imports, initially from Alaska. By 1975, somewhat against initial expectations, Japan (with no alternative domestic or imported gas options) had become the world's leading LNG importer. Atlantic Basin LNG trade never fully recovered from this early setback and Japan – joined by Korea in 1986 and Taiwan in 1991 – progressively dominated global LNG trade, accounting for 60–80 per cent of global imports from the late 1970s to the year 2000 (Figure 1.11). On the supply side, Alaska was joined by Brunei, Libya, Abu Dhabi, and Indonesia in the 1970s; Malaysia and Australia in the 1980s; and Qatar, Nigeria, and Trinidad in the 1990s.

Algeria was the pioneer of LNG exports and retained its position as the largest global exporter for 10 years, when it was overtaken by Brunei in 1974 and then by Indonesia in 1980; Indonesia itself was then overtaken, 25 years later, by Qatar. Problems with Atlantic Basin markets meant that although Libya exported small quantities sporadically from 1970, there was no other large-scale supply to the Atlantic Basin until the first deliveries from Nigeria and Trinidad in 1999. This was not for lack of planning – Nigerian LNG had first been proposed in the 1960s – but along with Venezuela, Iran, Canada, and other potential exporters, no other projects progressed beyond the planning stage, and in relation to the Atlantic Basin none would do so prior to (and for many years after) 2000.[62]

A small club with a 'relationship culture'

Up to (and indeed beyond) 2000, the LNG community was a very small club. In 1971, six countries were importing LNG from three exporting countries; by 2000 the 11 importing countries were facing 12 exporters.[63] This led, especially in Asia, to what has been termed a 'relationship culture', where very long contractual commitments, together with strong shared interests in a highly capital intensive business, resulted in considerable commercial rigidity. In other words, should a trade break down, it would be very difficult to find any alternative supply or any alternative use for the assets.[64] In Asia, this relationship culture was intimately related to a view of security of supply – because of the lack of alternative pipeline gas supplies – which caused governments to become major participants, thereby preventing LNG trades from failing in the face of commercial problems.

By 2000, Asia was importing 72 mt from eight suppliers, compared with a total of 30 mt of imports in the Atlantic Basin (25 mt to Europe and 5 mt to the USA and Puerto Rico) from four suppliers. At just under 100 mt, LNG trade was well and truly launched and a 'global market' was already being anticipated; nevertheless LNG still accounted for a relatively small part of international gas trade and energy balances outside Asia.[65] But this very small world was destined to become significantly larger over the subsequent two decades, and this caused stresses and changes which will be examined in the following chapters.

---

[62] With the exception of Qatar, discussed in Chapter 2.
[63] In 1971, GIIGNL (the association of LNG importing companies) had 19 members, most of which were Japanese (see the GIIGNL website: www.giignl.org/about-giignl/history). The UK was no longer importing LNG in 2000.
[64] For reflections on inflexibility, relationship culture, and LNG 'club rules', see Tusiani and Shearer (2006, 200–19).
[65] For an early assessment of the potential for a global LNG market see Jensen (2004).

BIBLIOGRAPHY

Adibi, S, and Fesheraki, F. (2011). 'The Iranian Gas Industry', Chapter 8 in Fattouh, B. and Stern, J.P. (eds.), *Natural Gas Markets in the Middle East and North Africa*, Oxford: OUP/OIES.

Aissaoui, A. (2001). *Algeria: The Political Economy of Oil and Gas*, Oxford: OUP/OIES.

APEC (1995). *APEC Historical Energy Statistics 1980–1992*, Asia–Pacific Economic Cooperation Regional Energy Cooperation Working Group.

Bambrick, S. (1978). 'Development of Australia's North West Shelf gas reserves', *Resources Policy*, December 1978, 279–86.

Barnes, P. (1995). *Indonesia: The Political Economy of Energy*, Oxford: OUP/OIES.

BoE (Taiwan) Bureau of Energy, Ministry of Economic Affairs (Taiwan), *Energy Statistics Database System*, https://web3.moeaboe.gov.tw/wesnq/Views/A01/wFrmA0103.aspx.

Boué, J.C. (1993). *Venezuela: The Political Economy of Oil*, Oxford: OUP/OIES.

BP (2011). *BP Statistical Review of World Energy*, June 2011.

Chapman, J. L. (1985). *Hands Across the Sea: the story of Indonesian LNG*, Jakarta: Pertamina.

Dargin, J. and Flower, A. (2011). 'The UAE Gas Sector', Chapter 13 in Fattouh, B. and Stern, J.P. (eds.), *Natural Gas Markets in the Middle East and North Africa*, Oxford: OUP/OIES.

EIA (2009). *Venezuela*, US Energy Information Administration www.eia.doe.gov:80/emeu/cabs/Venezuela/NaturalGas.html. Last accessed 27 January 2009.

Flower, A. (2011). 'LNG in Qatar', Chapter 10 in Fattouh, B. and Stern, J.P. (eds.), *Natural Gas Markets in the Middle East and North Africa*, Oxford: OUP/OIES.

Flower, A. and Liao, J. (2012). 'LNG pricing in Asia', Chapter 11 in Stern, J.P. ed. (2012). *The Pricing of Internationally Traded Gas*, Oxford: OUP/OIES.

Greenwald, G.B. (1998). 'LNG Project Finance: sharing risks with project lenders', Chapter 6 in Greenwald, G.B., (ed.), *Liquefied Natural Gas: developing and financing international energy projects*, The Hague: Kluwer.

Gurney, J. (1996). *Libya: The Political Economy of Oil*, Oxford: OUP/OIES.

Hassanzadeh, E. (2014). *Iran's Natural Gas Industry in the Post-Revolutionary Period: Optimism, Scepticism, and Potential*, Oxford: OUP/OIES.

Hayes, M.H. (2006). 'The Transmed and Maghreb projects: gas to Europe from North Africa', in Victor, D.G, Jaffe, A.M, and Hayes, M.H., (eds.), *Natural Gas and Geopolitics: from 1970–2040*, Cambridge: CUP, Chapter 3.

Hrastar, J. (2014). *Liquid Natural Gas in the United States: a history*, Jefferson North Carolina: McFarland & Co.

IEEJ (1986). 'Sengo Enerugi Sangyo Shi' ('The Postwar history of energy industry in Japan'), Toyo Keizai Shinpo, Tokyo, Institute of Energy Economics, Japan.

IEEJ (2000, 2001, 2002, 2003, 2004, 2005). 'Asia Taiheiyo oyobi Taisei Sijo no Tennen Gas Jukyu Doko Tyosa Houkokusho', (Research Report on Natural Gas Supply–Demand in Asia–Pacific and Atlantic Markets)', Institute of Energy Economics, Japan Tokyo.

IEEJ/EDMC (2015). 'EDMC Handbook of Japan's & World Energy & Economic Statistics 2015'.

Jensen, J.T. (2004). 'The Development of a Global LNG Markets: Is it likely? If so by when?', OIES Working Paper NG 5, Oxford Institute for Energy Studies.

JNOC (1995). 'Kankoku oyobi Taiwan no Tennen Gas Dounyu Keikaku ni Kansuru Tyosa', ('Research on Natural Gas Introduction Plan in Korea and Taiwan'), JNOC, Sekiyu no Kaihastu to Bitiku (June 1995).

Jones, R. J. E. (1998). 'LNG Markets: Historical Development and Future Trends', Chapter 2 in Greenwald, G.B., (ed.), *Liquefied Natural Gas: developing and financing international energy projects*, The Hague: Kluwer.

KEEI 'Yearbook of Energy Statistics', Korea Energy Economics Institute.

KOGAS *Annual Report*, www.kogas.or.kr/en/main.action.

Koyama, K. (2000). *Oil supply security policy initiatives taken by the Asian APEC economies*, The Institute of Energy Economics, Japan. (IEEJ website homepage http://eneken.ieej.or.jp/).

Ledesma, D. (2008). 'South East Asian and Australian Gas Supply to Asia', Chapter 7 in Stern, J. (ed.), *Natural Gas in Asia: the challenges of growth in China, India, Japan and Korea*, Oxford: OUP/OIES.

Ledesma, D. (2011). 'Natural Gas in Oman', Chapter 12 in Fattouh, B. and Stern, J.P. (eds.), *Natural Gas Markets in the Middle East and North Africa*, Oxford: OUP/OIES.

Ledesma, D., Henderson, J., and Palmer, N. (2014). 'The Future of Australian LNG Exports: will domestic challenges limit the development of future

LNG export capacity?', OIES Working Paper NG 90, Oxford Institute for Energy Studies.

Matsui, K. ed. (1995). 'Enerugi sengo 50 nen no kensho', ('Japan's energy policy in postwar 50 years'), Denryoku Shinpo. Tokyo.

MITI (1973). 'Nippon no enerugi mondai', ('Energy problems in Japan'), Tsusho Sangyo Chosa Kai, Tokyo, (Ministry of International Trade and Industry).

MITI (1975). 'Showa 50 nendai no enerugi: Antei kyokyu no tame no sentaku', ('Energy in 1975–1985: The choice to secure stable supply'), Tsusho Sangyo Chosa Kai, Tokyo, (Ministry of International Trade and Industry).

MITI (1984). '21 seiki heno enerugi jukyu tenbo: Choki enerugi jukyu mitooshi no kaitei to enerugi seisaku no so-tenken', ('The outlook for energy demand and supply toward the 21st century: The revision of the long term outlook for energy demand and supply and overall examination on energy policy'), Tsusho Sangyo Chosa Kai, Tokyo (Ministry of International Trade and Industry).

MITI (1993). 'Enerugi seisaku no ayumi to tenbo', ('Development of and outlook for energy policy'), Tsusho Sangyo Chosa Kai, Tokyo, (Ministry of International Trade and Industry).

MITI (1994). 'Kyojin katsu shinayaka na Enerugi vision', ('A strong and flexible energy vision'), Tsusho Sangyo Chosa Kai, Tokyo Ministry of International Trade and Industry.

MITIE (Korea) (2014). *Industry Main Statistics*, Ministry of Trade, Industry and Energy, Korea.

Murray, R. (1991). *From the Edge of a Timeless Land: a history of the North West Shelf Gas Project*, Australia: Allen and Unwin.

NEB (1983). *Reasons for Decisions in the Matter of: Phase II the License Phase and Phase III – the Surplus Phase of the Gas Export Omnibus Hearing, 1982*, National Energy Board, Canada, Ottawa, January.

NLNG (2015). *Facts and Figures on NLNG 2015*, Nigerian LNG, www.nigerialng.com/Media-Center/Publications/Facts_and_figures_2015.pdf.

Nussbaum, M. and Folo, M. (2013). *Design Selection of the Cameroon LNG Project*, paper for 17th International Conference & Exhibition on Liquefied Natural Gas (LNG 17), Houston.

Peebles, M.W.H. (1980). *Evolution of the Gas Industry*, London: Macmillan.

Sakmar, S.L. (2013). *Energy for the 21st Century: opportunities and challenges for liquefied natural gas (LNG)*, Cheltenham: Edward Elgar.

SGS (2004). *Mariscal Sucre LNG Project – a downstream perspective*, Shell Global Solutions www.venezuelagas.net/documents/2004-ST-08-eng.pdf.

Shepherd, R. and Ball, J. (2006). 'Liquefied natural gas from Trinidad & Tobago: the Atlantic LNG project', Chapter 9 in Victor, D.G., Jaffe, A.M., and Hayes, M.H., (eds.), *Natural Gas and Geopolitics: From 1970 to 2040*, Cambridge: CUP.

SIGTTO/GIIGNL (2014). *LNG Shipping at 50 (SIGTTO at 35 and GIIGNL at 43)*, SIGTTO (The Society of International Gas Tanker and Terminal Operators): London, GIIGNL: Neuilly Sur Seine. www.giignl.org/sites/default/files/PUBLIC_AREA/Publications/lng-shipping-at-50compressed.pdf.

Stern, J.P. (1984). *International Gas Trade in Europe: the policies of exporting and importing countries*, London: RIIA.

Stern, J.P. (1985). *Natural Gas Trade in North America and Asia*, London: RIIA.

Stern, J.P. (2012). 'The Pricing of Gas in International Trade – an historical survey', Chapter 2 in Stern, J.P., (ed.), *The Pricing of Internationally Traded Gas*, Oxford: OUP/OIES.

TEPCO (1983). *'Tokyo Denryoku 30 nenshi' ('The history of Tokyo Power Electric for the 30 years')*, Tokyo Electric Power Company.

Tusiani, M.D. and Shearer, G. (2006). *LNG: a nontechnical guide*, Tulsa: PenWell.

Von der Mehden, F. and Lewis, S.W. (2006). 'Liquefied natural gas from Indonesia: the Arun LNG project', Chapter 4 in Victor, D.G., Jaffe, A.M., and Hayes, M.H., (eds.) *Natural Gas and Geopolitics: from 1970–2040*, Cambridge: CUP.

Williams, T.I. (1981). *A History of the British Gas Industry*, Oxford: OUP.

Yoon, S. Y. and Yamada, T. (2000). *Life cycle inventory analysis of fossil energies in Japan*, IEEJ. IEEJ website homepage (http://eneken.ieej.or.jp/). January.

CHAPTER 2

THE MATURING OF THE LNG BUSINESS

*Anne-Sophie Corbeau and Andy Flower**

Introduction

On entering the new millennium, the LNG industry was neither as global nor as flexible as it has become in 2016. With only nine LNG importers[1] and 11 LNG exporters as of January 2000, only a few regions were connected. Among them, Asia dominated both demand and supply (see Chapter 1). With the exception of the Atlantic-based liquefaction plants, all the LNG liquefaction projects had been supported by Japanese trading houses along with IOCs and (where relevant) the countries' NOCs or governments. Japanese, Korean, and Taiwanese buyers had contracted the majority of LNG volumes. Markets were, however, beginning to globalize. A diversification of LNG buyers and sellers was already in sight, while the LNG industry was taking measured steps to introduce more flexibility to LNG deliveries by allowing arbitrage between markets. Middle East LNG supply grew five-fold during 2000–15, allowing access to both basins at the same cost.

The LNG trade has expanded faster over the period 2000–15 than it did over the first 35 years of its history. LNG has become the bright spot of the gas industry: a way to penetrate new markets, develop new resources, and seize the opportunity of regional price divergences. After crossing the 100 mtpa mark in 2000 (5 per cent of total gas demand), LNG trade jumped to 245 mtpa in 2015 (9 per cent of total gas demand). This evolution was far from homogeneous, with alternating periods of 'fast forward', 'play', and 'pause', both in terms of final investment decisions (FIDs) and of capacity becoming operational (Figure 2.1). After a rapid expansion of liquefaction capacity during 2004–7 and 2009–11, LNG trade growth abruptly switched to a 'pause' mode during 2011–14 as a result of lower export capacity additions and gas shortages in a few LNG exporters. The 2009–15 period has been a 'fast forward' time for FIDs. We now stand at the dawn of a new capacity addition cycle (2014–20), the first results of

---

* Andy Flower contributed the section on Qatar (pages 68–79)
[1] Not including the UK which had stopped importing LNG in the early 1980s.

which were already visible in the LNG markets in 2015 as LNG trade grew by 2.5 per cent. However, new LNG supply is coming to markets precisely when Asia, and especially China, is losing steam, leading to a collapse of spot prices. With a potential lack of additional FIDs in sight, this truly feels like a boom-and-bust cycle.

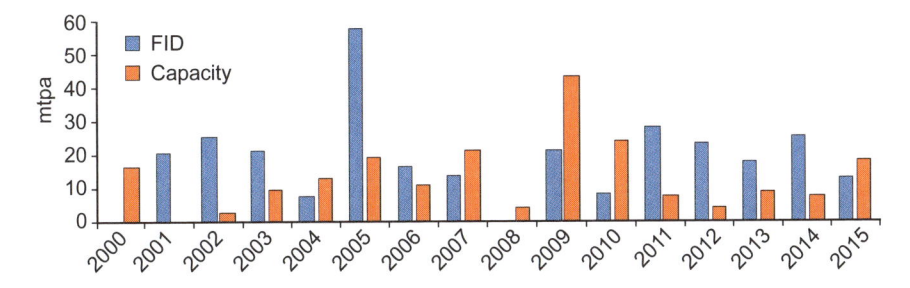

Figure 2.1: FID activity and liquefaction capacity additions
Source: GIIGNL, author's research.

The small club of LNG exporters has expanded substantially. As of late 2015, the number of LNG exporting countries had doubled since early 2000,[2] contributing greatly to supply diversification and giving LNG a reputation for flexibility and security of supply. Qatar's presence has become so overwhelming in the LNG market of 2015 that we tend to forget that the first LNG from Qatar only dates from end-1996. Many new LNG exporters – Trinidad and Tobago, Nigeria, and Oman – made their debut in the years 1999–2000; these were followed by Egypt, Equatorial Guinea, and Norway during 2005–7. Russia, Peru, and Yemen began exporting in 2009–11, and Angola and Papua New Guinea during 2013–14. In some cases the fairy tale halted abruptly: Egypt, Libya, and Yemen no longer export as of early 2016, while Angola is taking a halting path towards LNG exports as a result of technical problems at its plant.

LNG imports are also globalizing (Figure 2.2). Europe was the first region to import LNG in 1964, but from 1980 until the late 1990s it took a back seat while Japan, Korea, and Taiwan dominated the scene (Chapter 1). After a false start in the late 1970s, the USA retreated from the LNG scene for 20 years. However, by 2000, both Europe and the USA had re-entered the market, and the mid-2000s saw a period of Atlantic Basin market arbitrage as LNG moved between the markets attracted by price. Up to 2010, Europe managed to attract increasing LNG supplies: the proximity

---

[2] This includes Yemen, Angola, and Egypt even though the plants were not operational as of late 2015.

of new LNG suppliers such as Egypt, Norway, Nigeria, Equatorial Guinea, and Qatar boosted the build-up of LNG imports in Europe. The emergence of Trinidad and Tobago influenced the return of the USA as an LNG importer in the early 2000s but growing gas production in North America considerably reduced that region's LNG imports after 2010. The largest energy consumers (along with the USA) – China and India – had entered the LNG scene by the mid-2000s. Other regions – Latin America, the Middle East, and south-east Asia – followed a few years later. Once Africa had joined the group of LNG importing regions, in 2015, all areas of the world (apart from the Former Soviet Union) now import LNG. Nevertheless, the period 2000–15 has shown that LNG remains stubbornly attracted to Asia, which investors appear to view as a bottomless sink for LNG.

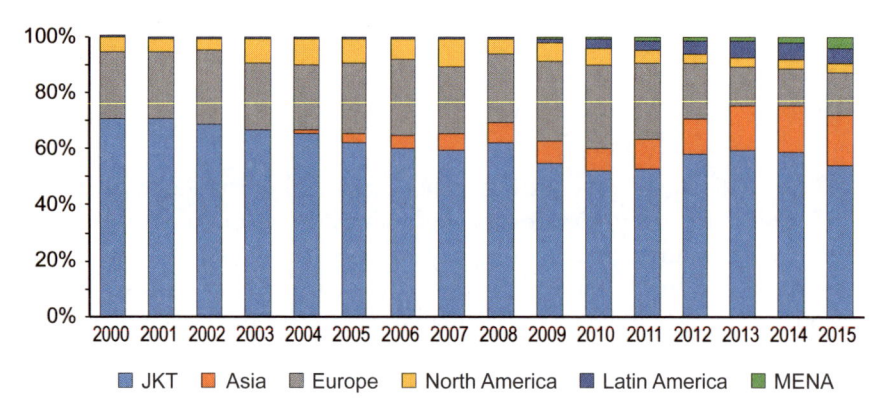

Figure 2.2: A limited diversification away from Asia: regions importing LNG
Source: GIIGNL.

The 2000s: diversifying LNG demand away from Japan, Korea, and Taiwan

Europe: a major new LNG market?

European LNG imports jumped from 25 mtpa (34 bcm) in 2000 to 65 mtpa (88 bcm) in 2010, with Spain and the UK accounting for 70 per cent of that growth. The increase in LNG import capacity was even larger (+86 mtpa). Other than the emergence of neighbouring LNG suppliers, there were four main reasons for this increase of LNG demand in Europe: increasing power sector gas demand, decreasing local gas production, diversification of gas supply, and liberalization of gas markets (Table 2.1).

Table 2.1: Drivers behind the construction of LNG terminals in Europe, 2000–15

	Additional demand	Declining production	Diversification	New entrant's strategy
Belgium	X			
France	X			X
Greece	X		X	
Italy	X		X	X
Lithuania			X	
Netherlands		X (long term)	X	X (Europe)
Poland			X	
Portugal	X		X	
Spain	X		X	X
Turkey	X		X	X
United Kingdom	X	X	X	X

Source: Author's research.

Increasing power sector gas demand

The dash for natural gas, notably in the power sector, was the main reason for increased LNG imports in most countries. In the early 2000s, investors expected robust European gas demand growth. Gas-fired plants had become popular with power generators because of their flexibility and low capital costs, triggering a 50 per cent increase in gas demand from the power generation sector between 2000 and 2010. The IEA's *World Energy Outlook 2002* (IEA, 2002) forecast that OECD Europe's gas demand would grow from 475 bcm in 2000 to around 900 bcm by 2030.

Individual countries were equally bullish. Among the most optimistic was Turkey, with consumption projections for natural gas rising to 82 bcm in 2020.[3] In 2003 the UK's National Grid predicted that gas demand would rise by 14 per cent to 129 bcm by 2011 (from 113 bcm in 2002), compared with the figure of 83 bcm effectively consumed that year.[4] Even in 2010, Spanish gas use was still expected to grow by 2.3 per cent per

---

[3] 'Turkey Determined to Remain at the Center of East–West Energy Corridor', *Oil & Gas Journal*, 14 January 2002. www.ogj.com/articles/print/volume-100/issue-2/transportation/turkey-determined-to-remain-at-the-center-of-east-west-energy-corridor.html.

[4] 'Securing Britain's gas supply', Ofgem factsheet 37, 5 December 2003, http://news.bbc.co.uk/nol/shared/bsp/hi/pdfs/03_03_04securinggasupply.pdf. According to the IEA, gas consumption in 2000 was 100 bcm (IEA, 2015b).

year until 2020 (from 35 bcm in 2010), while in fact demand has fallen by 25 per cent over 2010–14.[5]

The 900 bcm of European gas demand forecast by the IEA in 2002 would have been met by around 625 bcm of imports, calling for different sources of supply and the construction of LNG import terminals. However, that demand is now unlikely to materialize: reality struck the European gas markets with the 2008 financial crisis, the rapid growth of renewables, and accrued competition from coal-fired plants. The IEA's 2015 *World Energy Outlook* (IEA, 2015) predicted that OECD Europe gas demand would reach 526 bcm by 2030, against 452 bcm in 2014.

Gas production decline
From 2000 onwards, gas production started to dwindle in most OECD Europe countries. The only notable exception was Norway, where production more than doubled to 110 bcm by 2010, allowing total European gas production to continue to increase until the mid-2000s (IEA, 2015b). But production from the rest of Europe peaked in 2000; in particular, UK output plummeted from 115 bcm to 60 bcm between 2000 and 2010.

After having been the first country to import LNG in 1964, the UK had stopped importing in the early 1980s as its North Sea gas production built up. But by the early 2000s the country was again becoming import dependent. The alarm rang loudly in November 2005, when a cold spell sent UK gas prices soaring to over 150 p/th ($26/MMBtu) in a market accustomed to 30 p/th ($5.2/MMBtu).[6] New infrastructure was required sooner than expected. Some was already under construction, but would only be available in one or two years' time. Between 2005 and 2008, three gas pipelines, in addition to an expansion of the existing UK–Belgium Interconnector by 17 bcm/year (from 8.5 bcm/year to 25.5 bcm/year),[7] brought 47 bcm/year of new capacity, while four LNG terminals, representing 39.3 mtpa (53.6 bcm/year), came on line.

Diversification of gas supply sources
With gas demand expected to grow and domestic production falling, Europe needed more import infrastructure (Figure 2.3). This introduced the issue of diversification, not only in terms of security of supply but also

---

[5] Boletín Oficial De las Cortes Generales, Congreso de los Diputados, IX Legislatura, 30 de diciembre de 2010, Núm. 501, www.congreso.es/public_oficiales/L9/CONG/BOCG/D/D_501.

[6] 'Wholesale gas prices, rises explained', Ofgem factsheet 54, 28 November 2005. https://www.ofgem.gov.uk/sites/default/files/docs/2005/11/12141-wholesalegaspricesexplained_0.pdf.

[7] Interconnector (UK) Limited, company timeline: www.interconnector.com/about-us/how-we-got-here/company-timeline/.

in terms of costs. Pipeline suppliers had proved quite reliable and Europe was in the process of expanding piped gas supplies not only from Russia, but also from Algeria, Libya, Iran, and Azerbaijan. In the early 2000s worries regarding security of supply centred on the concentration of supplies in one specific route. The Yamal Nenets corridor transported 90 per cent of Russian gas; Algeria and Russia had no clear gas upstream or transport regulation; and consumers were concerned that investments in these countries might fall short of expectations (Cornot-Gandolphe and Dickel, 2004). Additional pipeline supplies from Russia's Yamal Peninsula, the Shtokman field, Iran, and the Caspian region could have met part of Europe's need for imports, but these projects appeared to be expensive options.

LNG looked like a good solution in terms of diversification, since it was available from different sources via different routes and did not have to cross any country where political risk was a concern. In the early 2000s the industry was growing quickly with the arrival of new players such as Nigeria, Oman, and Trinidad and Tobago and total LNG trade jumped by 40 mtpa from 2000 to 2005 (from 102 mtpa to 142 mtpa). More importantly, LNG was becoming cheaper, through substantial reductions in capital and shipping costs that enabled price competition with pipeline gas (see Chapter 4). Finally, for reasons of volume and diversification, many resource-owning countries were keen to develop LNG as an export solution.

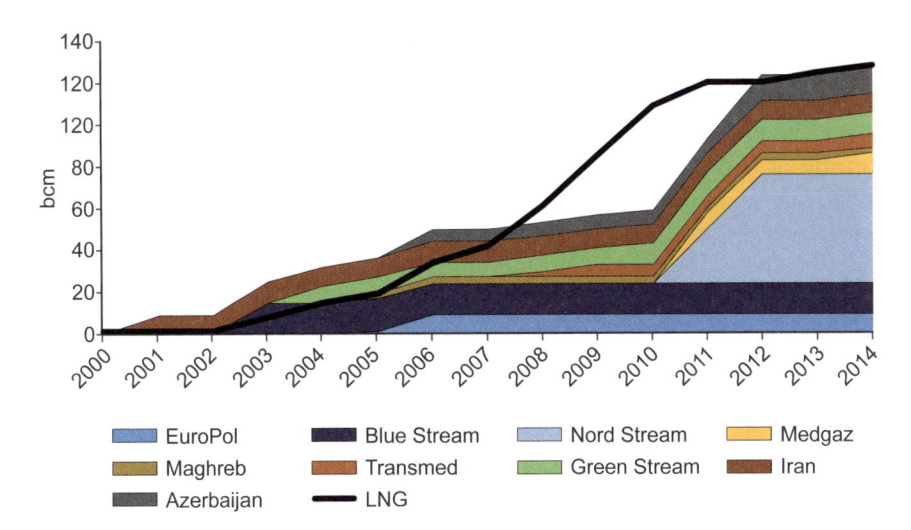

Figure 2.3: Pipeline and LNG compete to supply Europe
Source: GIIGNL, author's research.

50   *LNG Markets in Transition*

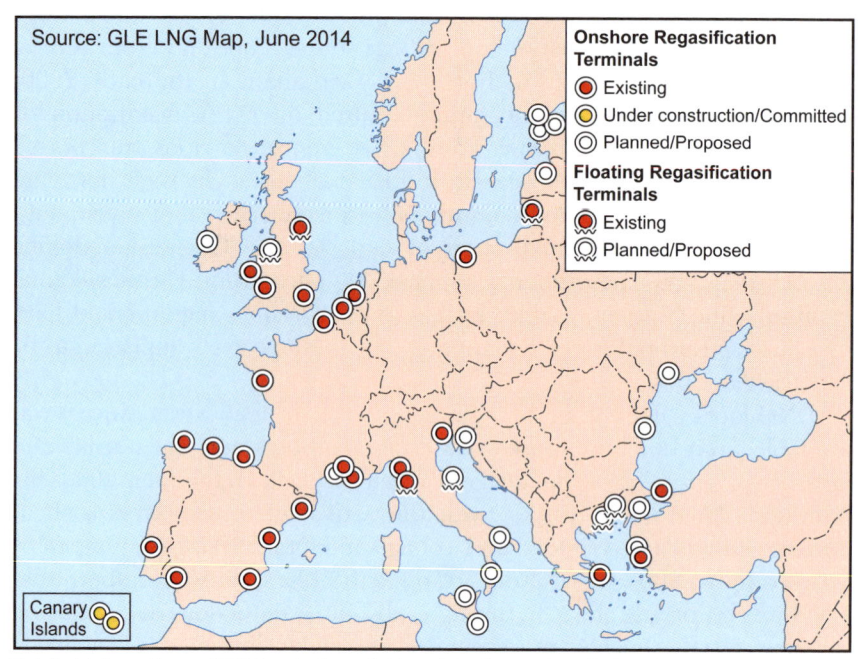

Detailed information on LNG terminals available at http://www.gie.eu/index.php/maps-data/lng-map
*El Musel completed but mothballed as at April 2016.

Map 2.1: European LNG terminals

Diversification was thus an important driver of new LNG terminals, even before tensions appeared between Russia and Europe, or the Arab Spring of 2011. The European Commission (EC) has always considered LNG as 'a source of diversification that contributes to competition in the gas market and security of supply'.[8] Spain, for example, has a regulation on the diversification of gas supplies which sets a maximum figure of 50 per cent of annual supplies to come from a single country.[9] This was mostly intended to limit the dominance of Algeria, but because of the difficulty of building pipeline interconnections with France, LNG has been the only alternative. Lithuania and Poland, the last European countries to begin importing LNG, aim to diversify their sources away from Russia.

---

[8] 'Gas and oil supply routes', European Commission, https://ec.europa.eu/energy/en/topics/imports-and-secure-supplies/gas-and-oil-supply-routes.

[9] 'Emergency response systems of individual IEA countries', Chapter 4, *Energy Supply Security 2014*, IEA, https://www.iea.org/media/freepublications/security/EnergySupplySecurity2014_Spain.pdf.

Gas markets' liberalization

The liberalization of European gas markets in the 2000s was another key element in the expansion of Europe's LNG import capacity. The UK was the front runner in liberalizing its gas markets in the 1990s; the opening of continental European markets happened at a later stage and a much slower pace. Historically, gas infrastructure was built on a national basis by vertically integrated companies. In the early 2000s the European gas industry was still dominated by these incumbents. Liberalization gave new entrants the chance to gain market share.

Two major changes made that possible: industrial companies and power generators were enabled to choose their supplier, while access to pipelines for third parties became more transparent and effective, with the EC's First and Second Gas Directives in 1998 and 2003. LNG offered advantages in open markets – such as flexibility and smaller size – compared with gas from long-distance pipelines. However, access to LNG terminals was often on a negotiated basis, so new entrants opted to build their own LNG terminals.

Market liberalization triggered something of a herd effect in terms of new LNG terminals, notably in the UK, Italy, and Spain. Despite the risk of overcapacity, the UK market attracted four separate terminals, each with a totally different strategy, representing an import capacity of around 54 bcm/year. This, in addition to new pipelines, gave a total import capacity of over 130 bcm/year, which was too much for a market that never consumed more than 103 bcm annually.[10]

There was clearly a strategy to use the UK as an entry point to the wider European market via the UK to Europe natural gas interconnector (IUK).

- The *South Hook regasification terminal*, supported by Qatar Petroleum and ExxonMobil, was designed to receive part of the new Qatari LNG supplies from trains under construction at that time.

- The *Dragon LNG Terminal* provided BG with an outlet for its Atlantic Basin production, and Petronas with an outlet in the Atlantic basin.

- The *Isle of Grain terminal* was built on a quite different model: the UK Transmission System Operator (TSO) National Grid leased capacity on a long-term basis to companies such as Sonatrach, BP, and GDF Suez (now Engie).

---

[10] 'Gas supplies', Energy UK, www.energy-uk.org.uk/energy-industry/gas-generation/gas-supplies.html.

All three terminals were given exemptions from third-party access (TPA), accommodated by use-it-or-lose it (UIOLI) rules.[11]

- Finally, the *Teesside GasPort terminal* was the first floating storage and regasification unit (FSRU) ever built in Europe. Its construction was a direct consequence of the 2005 crisis mentioned above. Driven by the need to bring import capacity quickly on line, the Excelerate Energy project was moved forward. Only 12 months passed from the site selection to online service in early 2007, a record at that time. The plant was decommissioned in 2015, but it proved that FSRUs could be brought online rapidly to meet urgent needs.

At one point, Italy had no fewer than 11 proposed regasification terminals, equivalent to 57 mtpa proposed LNG import capacity, as much as its own demand – a European record. The saying '*all roads lead to Rome*' had never seemed so true. Sponsors included IOCs, large European gas players, and consortia of new entrants, all aiming to enter the Italian market and benefit from the country's dash for gas in the power generation sector. In the end, only two terminals have been built since 2000.

Meanwhile, Spain had three new terminals developed by new entrants – BP, Repsol, Endesa, and Union Fenosa – looking for volumes for their gas-fired power plants.

New entrants sometimes failed, as illustrated by the Izmir terminal in Turkey. Built by new entrant EgeGaz on its own land, the terminal remained for a long time without a connection to the Turkish gas network, despite being fully functional, because the incumbent (BOTAS) refused to build the necessary pipeline interconnections.[12] Though Turkey's liberalization process officially started in 2001, BOTAS still effectively dominated the market. The Izmir terminal came into service to import LNG for BOTAS following significant gas supply problems with Iran during winter 2006/7 (IEA, 2007).

When the Netherlands developed the 'Dutch roundabout' (which included the GATE terminal) it was targeting a symbiotic relationship between production, LNG, and pipeline imports that would create a

---

[11] The rule requires transport capacity booked but not used by energy companies to be made available to other network users.

[12] 'First independent enters Turkish LNG import market', ICIS, 9 April 2009. www.icis.com/resources/news/2009/04/09/9310902/first-independent-enters-turkish-lng-import-market/ and 'LNG Terminal Import Profile', Marmara Ereglisi and Aliaga LNG, Izmir, Turkey, 1 May 2005, http://member.zeusintel.com/ZLNGR/show_image.aspx?id=1149.

large hub and access to new gas sources for the north-western European region.[13]

North America returns ... for less than a decade

US LNG imports have a chequered history. Back in the 1970s four LNG terminals (Lake Charles, Everett, Elba Island, and Cove Point) were developed. But as domestic supply increased following gas market liberalization, two were mothballed and their supply contracts (with Algeria) were cancelled due to price disputes. In the early 2000s, interest in LNG imports surged again, first through increasing demand in the power generation sector, and then because Trinidad and Tobago started to export LNG. However, reviving the LNG business in the USA was a public relations battle, given the disastrous explosion in Cleveland in 1944 and the previous contract issues with Algeria (See Chapter 1).

History would have probably taken a different turn had it not been for the efforts of a few individuals. In the 1990s, the Everett LNG terminal in Massachusetts was suffering from low utilization. Its owner, Cabot, tasked one of its employees, Gordon Shearer, with reviving its LNG business.[14] After looking without success for supplies in Nigeria and Venezuela, he became aware of Trinidad's potential at a lunch with Cliff Davis, an industry veteran who was trying to develop LNG exports from the island. With the help of Kenneth Julien, the former chairman of Trinidad's national gas company, Gordon Shearer managed to convince Trinidad's authorities. Negotiations dragged over 1993–6, while the majors, Amoco and BG, remained doubtful about the plan and were concerned about the US appetite for LNG. (Though these concerns proved correct in the long term, it is doubtful that those companies anticipated the future shale gas surge.) In Trinidad, the LNG plant's small size, in comparison with industry standards of the time, enabled lower capital costs ($1 billion). The short shipping distance (2,200 miles) also allowed for reduced transport costs, while the involvement of Amoco dampened fears of political risks. First LNG was successfully shipped in 1999.

The arrival in the USA of these LNG imports was very timely. Gas supplies had been tight over winter 2000/1, sending Henry Hub prices to $8.9/MMBtu in December 2000, against an average of $2.3/MMBtu in 1999. California was experiencing an unprecedented energy crisis. In addition, gas demand prospects seemed bright, with the majority of the power plants under construction being gas-fired. Meanwhile, most forecasts

---

[13] 'Gas roundabout', definitions, Gasunie website, www.gasunie.nl/en/definitions/gas-roundabout.

[14] 'How Trinidad Became a Big Supplier Of Liquefied Natural Gas to the U.S.', Alexei Barrionuevo, *The Wall Street Journal*, 13 March 2001. www.wsj.com/articles/SB98443474293628576.

predicted slightly increasing domestic gas supplies. Prospects for importing gas from Canada looked limited due to the depletion of conventional resources in the Western Sedimentary Basin, while prospects for production additions in eastern offshore Canada, or of coal bed methane production in western Canada, appeared uncertain (EIA, 2004).

In the early 2000s the US EIA's long-term forecasts were decidedly bullish on LNG imports. Its *Annual Energy Outlook 2005* (EIA, 2005) even predicted net LNG imports of up to 180 bcm by 2025, a mouth-watering prospect for many companies (Figure 2.4). Subsequent LNG import forecasts were progressively revised downwards, reaching negligible amounts in the *Annual Energy Outlook 2011* (EIA, 2011) as domestic supplies surged and actual imports of LNG declined; by 2012 the USA was expected to become an LNG exporter.

However, in the early 2000s both policy makers and government officials had actively encouraged the construction of LNG import infrastructure, while the Federal Energy Regulatory Commission (FERC) and the US Department of Energy had streamlined the authorization process for new LNG import terminals. With the Natural Gas Act of 2005, FERC became exclusively responsible for approving or rejecting an application for the siting, construction, expansion, and operation of an LNG terminal.[15] In response to these incentives, investors developed many LNG import projects and contracted LNG supplies from various sources. An interesting feature of these planned imports of LNG was their destination flexibility: marketers would deliver LNG if the price were right, though they were not subject to any binding agreement, an element which proved useful in subsequent years (IEA, 2007).

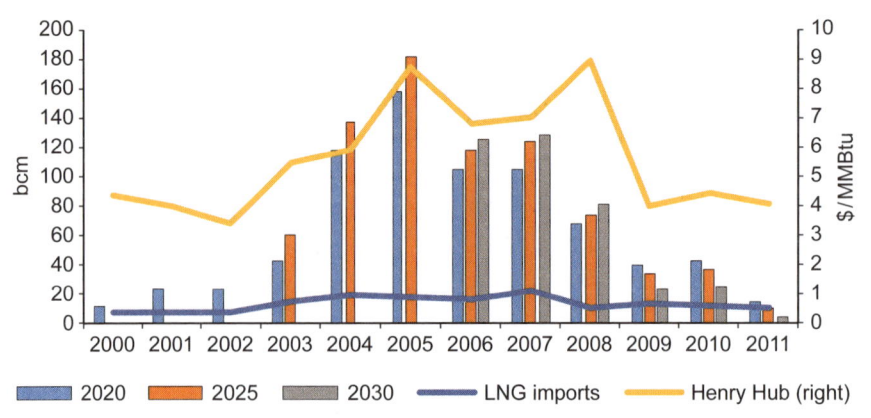

Figure 2.4: US LNG import forecasts differ markedly from actual LNG imports
Source: EIA.

---

[15] 'Liquefied Natural Gas (LNG) Litigation after the Energy Policy Act of 2005: State Powers in LNG Terminal Siting, Dweck, J., Wochner, D., & Brooks, M. *Energy Law Journal*, Vol. 27:473, 30 October 2006. http://eba-net.org/sites/default/files/docs/473-498.pdf.

Building the US LNG terminals did not go smoothly: most terminal projects on the east and west coasts attracted strong local opposition. Not a single LNG terminal was built on the US west coast, despite the attractive Californian market (Sakmar, 2013), although Sempra constructed a terminal in Baja California, in Mexico. The only projects on the east coast beyond the 1970s terminals were offshore terminals located near Boston – Excelerate Energy's Northeast Gateway and GDF Suez's Neptune. In addition, federal agencies, notably the FERC, could be at odds with local and state agencies, especially before the Natural Gas Act of 2005 consolidated FERC's powers. Subsequently, not only were state agencies required to comply with FERC scheduling, but they also faced court action if they denied a required permit. Individual states now retain very little power to obstruct an LNG project except under the Coastal Zone Management Act, the Clean Air Act, or the Federal Water Pollution Control Act.[16] In the end, despite many challenges, some 132 mtpa of LNG import capacity was built in the USA. Although a further 164 mtpa of LNG import capacity was still proposed in 2011, it has all now been shelved, and replaced by the new trend of the day – building LNG export plants (IEA, 2011).

Mexico and Canada also contributed to the region's LNG import capacity expansion, but faced diametrically different fates. Mexico has commissioned three LNG import terminals since 2006: Energia Costa Azul, Altamira, and Manzanillo. These plants were developed to feed growing power generation needs and supplement indigenous gas production, but also to reduce the country's dependence on US pipeline gas (IEA, 2007). As of 2015, Mexico imported four times as much US pipeline gas as LNG, with its pipeline imports having tripled since 2006.[17] Both Altamira and Manzanillo are owned by foreign companies with no downstream assets in the Mexican market. Altamira (developed by Shell, Mitsui, and Total) has been sold to Vopak and Enagas (with Shell and Total keeping the capacity). Initially, Shell also had capacity in the Baja California terminal, giving the company LNG assets on both sides of Mexico, complemented by capacity rights at two existing US LNG terminals (Elba Island and Cove Point).[18] Despite its proximity to California, 92 per cent of

---

[16] The 2005 Energy Policy Act: Analysis of the Jurisdictional Basis for Federal Siting Of LNG Facilities, Rachel Clingman and Audrey Cumming. www.tjogel.org/archive/Vol2No1/clingman_12_2_final.pdf.

[17] IEF JODI gas data and EIA data.

[18] 'Sempra Energy LNG and Shell International Gas Limited Announce New Capacity Agreement for Mexican LNG Receipt Terminal', PR Newswire, 14 October 2004. www.prnewswire.co.uk/news-releases/sempra-energy-lng-and-shell-international-gas-limited-announce-new-capacity-agreement-for-mexican-lng-receipt-terminal-156123635.html.

the gas from Sempra's Costa Azul terminal is consumed in the Mexican state of Baja California.[19]

Canada was a latecomer to the LNG race. Only one LNG import facility, the 7.7 mtpa Canaport terminal on the east coast at New Brunswick, was commissioned, in 2009. Ironically, it was built to supply both the Canadian and US markets. While most US LNG terminals were used somewhat during the 2000s, Canaport arrived precisely as the rise of shale gas was starting to make its mark on the Canadian gas market. With the prolific Marcellus shale on the other side of the border, Canaport is no longer needed. In 2009, there were still proposals for five further LNG import terminals in Canada.[20] They faced difficulties in securing long-term supplies. Eventually concerns over excess regas capacity in North America, coupled with rising regional production, made the projects redundant. Meanwhile, Galveston LNG's Kitimat, in British Columbia, switched from being an import to an export project in 2008. After many shareholding changes, that project is now in the hands of Chevron and Woodside.

China and India – Asian giants enter the LNG scene

In 2004 India became the first of the two Asian energy giants to import LNG. Due to insufficient domestic supplies, India has been constantly short of gas, with a large gap between forecasts of theoretical demand and actual consumption. While pipeline projects from Iran, Turkmenistan, and Myanmar failed to materialize, two LNG import terminals were commissioned, in 2004 and 2005, respectively. The first, Dahej, was promoted by Petronet LNG, a joint venture of Indian companies (ONGC, GAIL, IOCL, Bahrat Petroleum), GDF Suez (now Engie), and the Asian Development Bank (ADB). The second, Hazira, is a merchant terminal owned by Shell and Total. Another two terminals, Dabhol and Kochi, were commissioned in 2013, but have never operated at capacity.

Two years before the start of LNG imports, the Krishna Godavari K6-D6 field was discovered on India's east coast. Despite a promising start in 2009, the field's production collapsed shortly afterwards: the level of 4 bcm as of 2015 being far below previous expectations of 30 bcm.[21] More than ever India needed gas to feed the power generation sector, so both pipeline

---

[19] Strategic Location of Energía Costa Azul: 15 miles north of Ensenada, Baja California, Mexico. http://energiacostaazul.com.mx/english/about-us-location.html.

[20] Canada, 2009 Review, Energy Policies of IEA Countries. https://www.iea.org/publications/freepublications/publication/canada2009.pdf.

[21] 'KG-D6 output to stay static for at least 4 years', *The Financial Express*, 8 May 2015. www.financialexpress.com/article/industry/companies/kg-d6-output-to-stay-static-for-at-least-4-years/70416/.

and LNG projects were investigated. One fundamental issue is the price sensitivity of the Indian market, notably that of the power producers. The administrative price mechanism (APM) for some domestic production was set at $1.9/MMBtu until mid-2010, before rising to $4.2/MMBtu (Corbeau, 2010). This was initially comparable to the cost of LNG acquired on long-term contracts: the Qatari contract linked to Dahej began by being based on a fixed price indexed to a Japan Crude Cocktail (JCC) price of $20/bbl ($2.53/MMBtu) for the first five years until December 2008. The price was then linked to the average of JCC prices over the previous 12 months, with a floor and a cap based on JCC prices averaged over the previous 60 months. Given the subsequent evolution of oil prices, India has therefore been paying much higher prices for LNG – around $13/MMBtu in 2014 – than for domestic gas. This was something that protected customers, such as power plants and fertilizer manufacturers, were unwilling to accept; many gas-fired plants have thus been idle since 2011, leading to India seeking a price review of the contract with Qatar, together with domestic policies to increase the use of gas in power. Petronet successfully obtained a change in the price formulae at the end of 2015. Despite these difficulties, India has been routinely importing some 12–14 mtpa since 2010.

China came to the LNG scene relatively late. When it started importing LNG in 2006, its gas consumption amounted to 'only' 60 bcm. By 2012 it was already the world's third-largest LNG importer (with 15 mtpa). As of end-2015, China had 13 operational LNG terminals, representing 41 mtpa capacity. CNOOC built China's first three LNG terminals during the period 2006–10. CNOOC had also successfully concluded some LNG contracts, notably a historically cheap contract with Australia at $3.2/MMBtu (as a result of a $25/bbl cap in the oil-related pricing formula). These terminals were all in the southern half of China, far from the competition of the first West–East pipeline. CNOOC later extended its geographical coverage with a first FSRU in Tianjin; this gave a warning to CNPC and Gazprom, which for 10 years had failed to complete an agreement for Russian pipeline gas supplies. CNPC, which controls most of China's domestic production and pipeline imports, entered the LNG market in 2011 with three terminals in the north of the country. The third major NOC, Sinopec, commissioned its first LNG plant in 2014. The NOCs occasionally partnered with other Chinese organizations, or even IOCs: the Guangdong LNG company was formed by BP and seven other Chinese companies.

From 2010 onwards, new LNG terminals have been keeping pace with the ambitious forecasts of Chinese gas demand (Map 2.2). While the big three NOCs own most LNG terminals, JOVO Group owns the Dongguan

58   *LNG Markets in Transition*

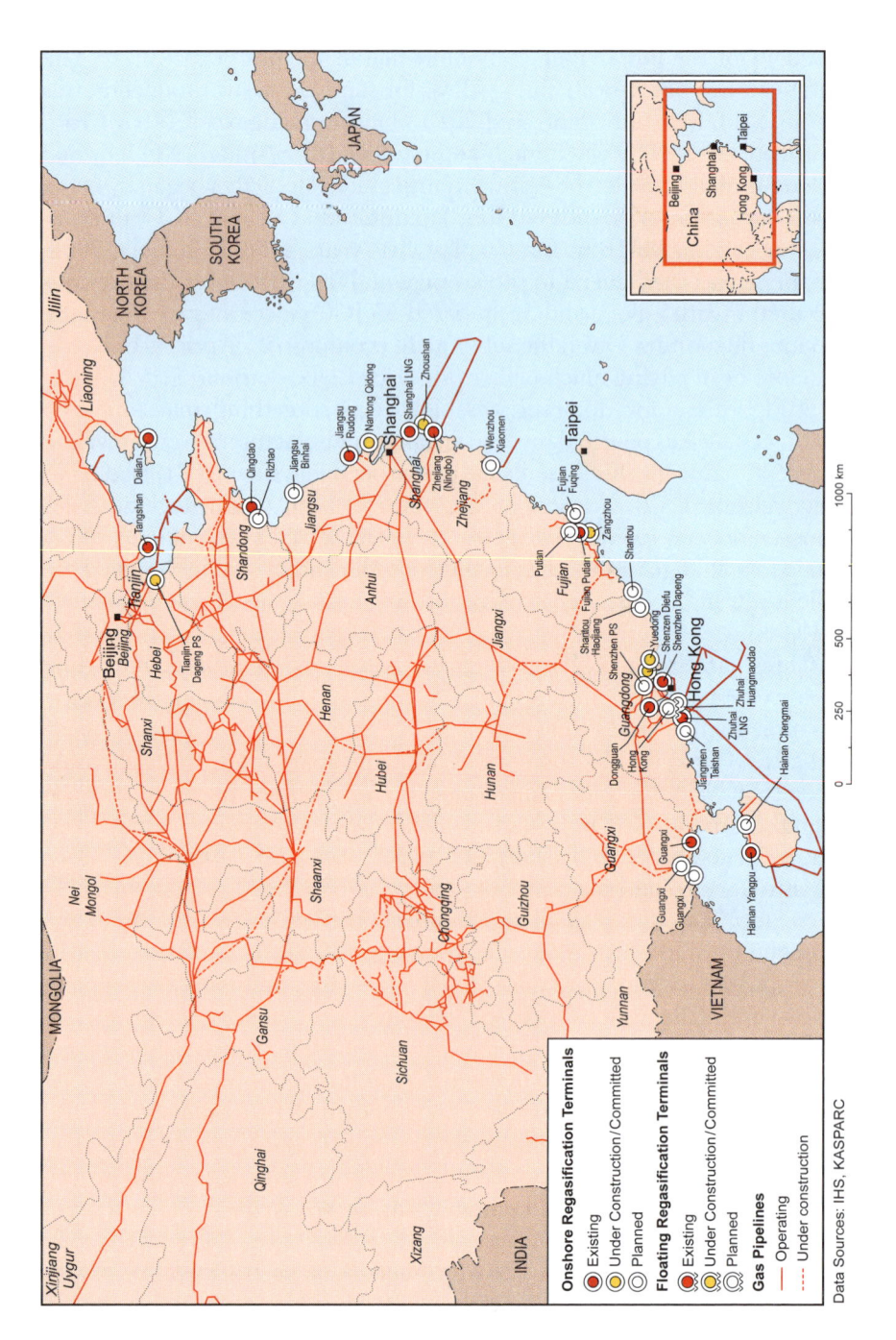

Map 2.2: China's import infrastructure

plant in Guangdong province. In 2014 China's National Development and Reform Commission (NDRC) issued guidelines to boost private investment in LNG and provided for TPA in existing LNG terminals owned by the NOCs. Although CNOOC has been reluctant to comply, PetroChina signed contracts with ENN Energy to use two of its terminals (Rudong and Dalian).[22] The NDRC initially specified that any LNG import project should be covered by a contract, but utilization has been going down nonetheless: in 2014, import terminals were half utilized, though this was still higher than the average global utilization figure. A substantial change occurred in 2015 as, for the first time, LNG imports dropped due to the combination of slow gas demand growth, rising domestic production, and relatively high oil-linked LNG contract prices in the early part of the year.

Since China started importing pipeline gas from Turkmenistan in 2010 and from Myanmar in 2013, there has been competition between pipeline and LNG supplies. Neither is cheap, but some of China's LNG sources were quite expensive in the period 2012–14. While average LNG prices reached $13/MMBtu in 2014, some LNG prices had regularly peaked at around $18–$19/MMBtu in early 2014 (according to Argus LNG). In contrast, the average delivered price of pipeline imports was $9.70/MMBtu in 2014, with gas imports from Myanmar at $11.56/MMBtu and Turkmen volumes at $9.69/MMBtu (without taking into account a non-negligible transport component[23]). On the whole, LNG imports seem to have matched contracted volumes until 2014 (Figure 2.5), but they dropped in 2015 despite a decline of the average LNG import price to $8.7/MMBtu and stood well below the contracted quantities.[24] It remains to be seen how the situation will evolve in 2016 as new LNG liquefaction projects, with contracts with Chinese buyers, start. LNG import prices stood at around $7/MMBtu as of early 2016.

Similar to companies in Japan, Korea, or Taiwan, Chinese and Indian companies have been eager to invest in the liquefaction part of the gas value chain, as demonstrated by Chinese shareholdings in operating Australian plants, as well as Chinese acquisitions in projects in Australia, Mozambique, Russia, and Canada. Indian companies have been less aggressive, targeting projects in Mozambique and Canada.

---

[22] 'Opportunities emerge for private firms to enter China's LNG market', *South China Morning Post*, 19 April 2015. www.scmp.com/business/china-business/article/1771510/opportunities-emerge-private-firms-enter-chinas-lng-market.

[23] 'China's December Gas Pipeline Imports Hit Record High 3.41 bcm', Singapore (Platts), 26 January 2015. www.platts.com/latest-news/natural-gas/singapore/chinas-december-gas-pipeline-imports-hit-record-26991967.

[24] GIIGNL reports an increase in Chinese LNG imports in 2015, but this is in contradiction with other sources.

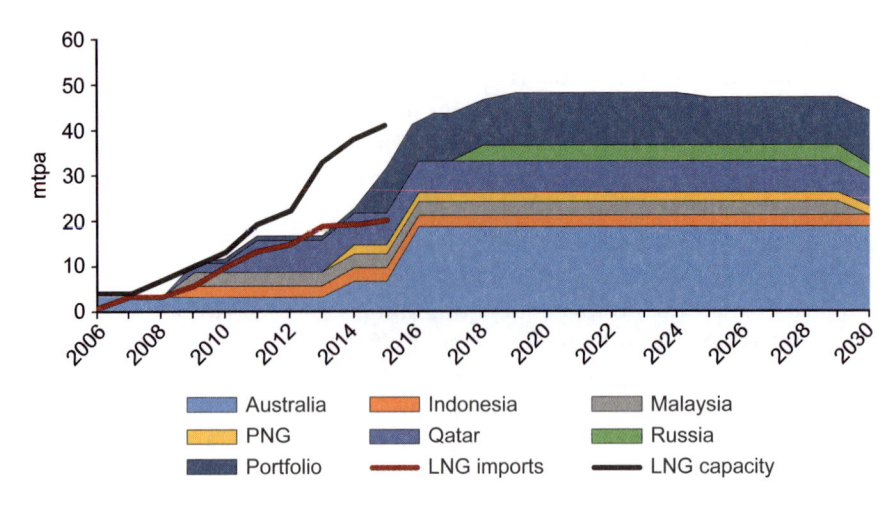

Figure 2.5: Chinese LNG contracts against actual imports and capacity
Source: GIIGNL.

Latin America, the Middle East: the failure of regional integration

Both Latin America and the Middle East are net gas exporters, on the whole. But difficult relationships between producers and importers, together with political decisions hampering the development of domestic gas production, or production not growing fast enough, have driven Argentina, Brazil, Chile, Kuwait, and Dubai to become LNG importers since 2008. They are relatively small importers (totalling 16.9 mtpa in 2015).

In Latin America, gas shortages have become endemic in Argentina and Chile;[25] this has resulted in a move away from the regional integration trend of the 2000s. Surging resource nationalism and unsound economic policies in key producing countries, together with intermittent gas demand due to extensive use of hydro for power generation, has led to a move towards LNG.

Argentina's deep economic crisis that began in 2001 is particularly illustrative of the region's difficulties; it had dire consequences for the country's domestic gas production. Tariffs were capped at $0.80/MMBtu[26]

---

[25] 'The Chilean Search for Energy Security', Nelson Altamirano, Center for Strategic and International Studies-CSIS, Washington D.C., 24 March 2007. http://csis.org/images/stories/Americas/070316_altamirano_chile.pdf.

[26] 'Chile – Gas, Politics, and New LNG port' https://wikileaks.org/gifiles/attach/170/170638_Chile_politics per cent20 per cent20gas per cent20 per cent20and per cent20a per cent20new per cent20LNG per cent20port.doc.

causing upstream investments to suffer, and in 2004 production started to fall, while demand was increasing by 50 per cent over 2002–8. Argentina had to pay Bolivia $3/MMBtu to import gas, creating a huge deficit. The quantities available for pipeline exports fell considerably. Supplies to Chile, where the two main power systems (necessary because of the country's complex geography) depended entirely on Argentina for gas, plummeted. This caused shutdowns at power plants and forced consumers to switch to other fuels, such as diesel. In addition to cutting volumes, Argentina also increased prices, so that export prices reached $20/MMBtu in 2008 (IEA, 2008), which led Chile to turn to other fuels such as coal, and to LNG for its gas. Ironically, Peru, which became an LNG exporter in 2010, has only exported a few cargoes to Brazil (in 2010), and not a single one to Argentina or Chile. (Chile and Peru have a long-standing border dispute dating from the Pacific War of 1879.)

In the Middle East, both Dubai and Kuwait turned to LNG supplies to solve their energy crises (Map 2.3). In 2013, the total gas deficit for the United Arab Emirates (UAE) was around 13 bcm, or 19 per cent of the country's gas demand (Dargin and Flower, 2011). The region's large gas resources are centred in Abu Dhabi, leaving Dubai and the Northern Emirates with only 7 per cent of total gas reserves. Gas demand has doubled since 2000, inflated by gas prices at $1/MMBtu. Most of the UAE's gas is associated, and hence subject to the production limitations imposed by OPEC quotas. Gas in non-associated fields is sour. No additional long-term pipeline imports can be expected from Qatar as the initial supplies from the Dolphin Gas pipeline were delivered at extremely low gas prices – around $1.3/MMBtu. Qatar has put in place a moratorium on the development of additional gas from the North Field, and is not keen to sell more gas to the UAE at subsidized prices when it could sell LNG at much higher prices on global markets. Dubai opted for a FSRU as the country's gas requirement is largely related to summer air conditioning. The Golar Freeze FSRU, chartered by Dubai Supply Authority (Dusup) from Bermuda-based Golar LNG, began operations in 2010. In 2015 a newer and higher capacity FSRU replaced the original FSRU, and will be able to receive twice the number of cargoes than the original design.[27] The UAE plans to build a larger LNG import facility (9 mtpa) at Fujairah.

In summer 2007 a critical gas shortage led to power cuts in Kuwait. As industrial users were ordered to redirect gas supplies towards the power sector, the search for an import solution became urgent. A year later, an FSRU built by Excelerate Energy went into operation, enabling Kuwait to

---

[27] Website of Dubai Supply Authority, www.dusup.ae/lng; baseload capacity is 500 mmcf/d.

62 *LNG Markets in Transition*

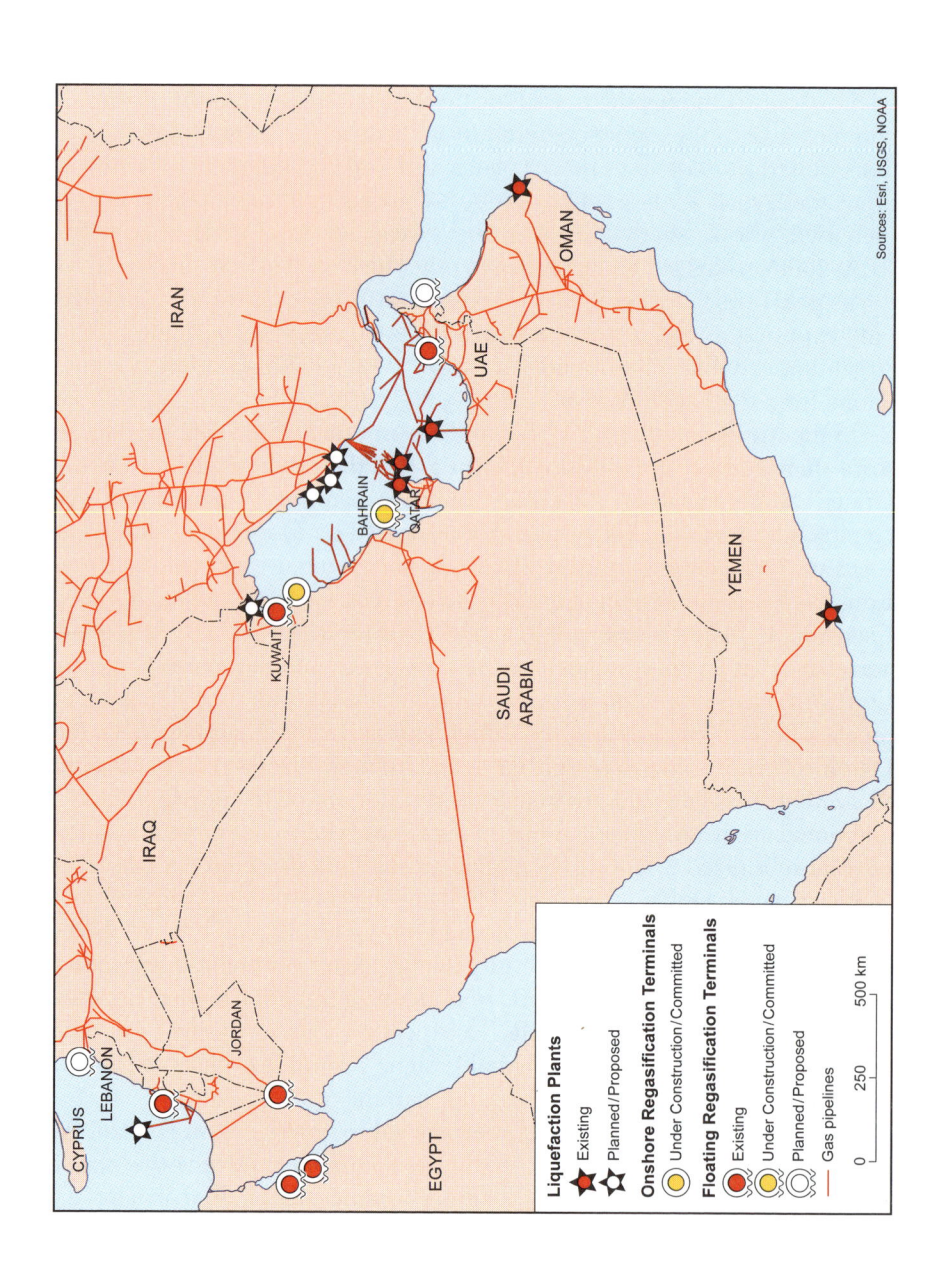

Map 2.3: Middle East gas infrastructure

import 600 mmcf/d during the peak summer months.[28] Gas demand from power generators has been increasing sharply, with the share of gas in the power mix increasing to 40 per cent in 2014. Associated gas production is limited by OPEC quotas, while the development of Jurassic gas fields has proved challenging. In 2014, a larger FSRU, the Golar Igloo, was installed and Kuwait's LNG imports were reported as being on the rise by 17 per cent, to 3 mtpa in 2015. Facing a sharp gas consumption rise in the power sector, Kuwait is keen to build a new land-based terminal that would be operational by 2020.

Regional cooperation has been working much better in the Middle East than in Latin America, as both Dubai and Kuwait have sourced LNG from Qatar. This, however, has been at higher prices than those in the historical agreement between Qatar and the UAE for Dolphin gas.

A new generation of LNG suppliers

Qatar's six mega-trains dwarf many other developments. However, 11 new LNG export countries have come to the market since early 1999, bringing the number of LNG exporters to 20 by end-2015 and diversifying LNG supply sources and routes considerably. Nonetheless, the combined liquefaction capacity of these 11 new producers totals 97 mtpa, only 25 per cent above that of Qatar. And these suppliers have only added an incremental 70 mtpa of LNG exports, less than Qatar's exports in 2015. For the first time in history, LNG liquefaction brought on line was not being as highly utilized as had previously been the norm, since some countries' output was failing to meet expectations. In fact, as of end-2015, three countries – Egypt, Angola, and Yemen – were not exporting LNG, though Angola is expected to be operational again by 2016. On the brighter side, four countries – Algeria, Australia, Indonesia, and Malaysia – made significant comebacks by adding new LNG export capacity. Prior to this, Algeria had not built a single new LNG train since 1981 and Indonesia's last LNG project dates from 1998.

The 1999–2014 period can be divided into three distinct parts: a smooth growth in LNG trade by 50 mtpa over 1999–2005, a tremendous inflation by 100 mtpa over 2005–11 (due largely to Qatar), and then a slight drop in LNG trade over 2011–14 (Figure 2.6). This latter period includes fewer capacity additions as well as the under-performance mentioned above. The year 2015 marks the beginning of a new increase in LNG supply as LNG trade grew from 239 mtpa in 2014 to 245 mtpa in 2015.

---

[28] Mina Al-Ahmadi GasPort, Kuwait's first LNG receiving facility, Excelerate Energy website. http://excelerateenergy.com/project/mina-al-ahmadi-gasport/.

LNG supply is a game of patience (Chapter 1). Decades can pass from discovery until the first LNG cargo is commissioned. It also involves the implementation of technical innovations to meet challenging conditions.

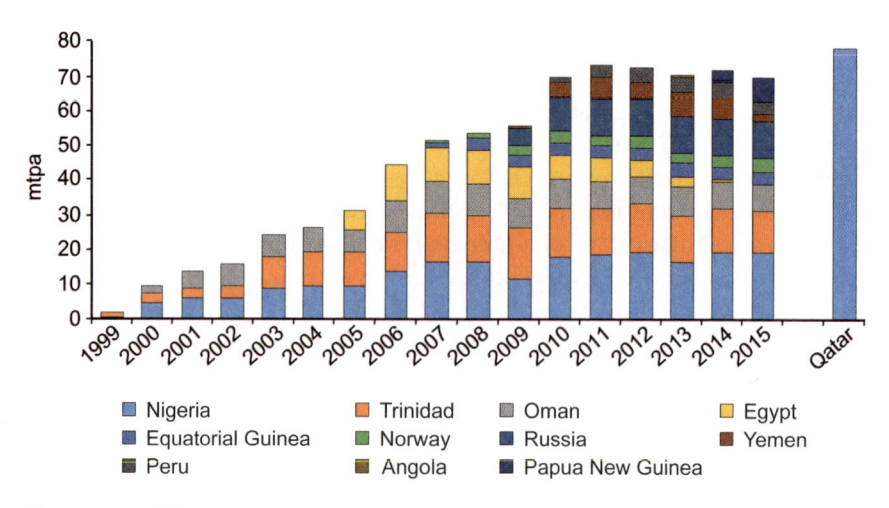

Figure 2.6: LNG exports from new LNG exporters compared with Qatar, 1999–2015
Source: GIIGNL.

As described in Chapter 1, it took Nigeria 40 years from the first idea to the first LNG. Similarly, Russia's Sakhalin 2 LNG was also a long time coming. The Piltun-Astokhskoye oil field and the Lunskoye gas field were discovered in the mid-1980s, although exploration activities had started some 30 years previously. The gas purchase and sale agreements (PSAs) between the Russian Federation, the Sakhalin Oblast Administration, and the Sakhalin Energy Investment Company (SEIC) (comprising Shell, Mitsui, and Mitsubishi)[29] were signed a decade later when Russia was in a precarious economic situation. Their terms have consequently been considered advantageous for the foreign partners. However, the project faced substantial delays and cost increases – $10 billion by 2005. One key challenge for the project was that the fields are located in a difficult environment that required the building of an 800 km onshore pipeline across the whole island to reach a loading point that would not be frozen year-round, though it still required ice-strenghtened ships. Facing pressure from the Russian Federal Environmental Agency, the SEIC partners handed over a controlling 50 per cent plus 1 share to Russia's Gazprom for

---

[29] 'The Sakhalin II PSA – a Production "Non-Sharing" Agreement, Analysis of Revenue Distribution', Ian Rutledge of Sheffield Energy & Resources Information Services. www.foe.co.uk/sites/default/files/downloads/sakhalin_psa.pdf.

$7.45 billion in December 2006. The project started in February 2009, marking the advent of Russia not just as an LNG exporter but as an LNG supplier in the Asian region, and thus fulfilling the Russian Government's ambitions. LNG exports have been running smoothly since then and the plant regularly exports above its nominal capacity.

Both Equatorial Guinea LNG and PNG LNG in Papua New Guinea were completed on time and on budget – a remarkable feat for LNG plants. The $1.5 billion Equatorial Guinea LNG project started in May 2007, six months ahead of its original schedule. Sponsored by Marathon (60 per cent) and Sonagas (25 per cent), together with the Japanese trading houses Marubeni and Mitsui, the project contracted 3.4 mtpa to BG for 17 years, with pricing linked to Henry Hub.[30] The project earned the distinction of being 'the fastest LNG project from initial concept in 2002 to FID' in June 2004. It was also expected to be one of the lowest-cost LNG operations in the Atlantic basin, with an LNG cost of about $1/MMBtu at the loading point and capital costs amounting to $1.4 billion.[31] This plant did face one construction challenge: the work site is 60 metres above the ocean, which required the construction of a suspension bridge with one onshore and one marine tower. The project has been running smoothly since its start. The USA was to have been the principal market for LNG supplies, but the agreement provided BG with flexibility on the destination. Taking advantage of a few portfolio contracts in Chile and Korea, LNG supplies have been shipped mostly to Asia and Chile and occasionally to Europe and the USA.

The fact that PNG LNG started ahead of schedule – the first train was commissioned in May 2014 – and on budget was remarkable for a project built in such difficult conditions. The inland Hides field that supports the LNG plant was discovered in 1987 by BP.[32] The initial plan – to locate the LNG project on the southern coast – did not proceed and BP sold all its PNG assets to Exxon in 1998. A competing project, a 4,000 km pipeline to Australia, was considered by Chevron, but this proposal did not go ahead. Another concept emerged: a 750 km pipeline was built, linking the field to an LNG plant near Port Moresby. ExxonMobil and Oil Search are the project's main sponsors and Sinopec, Osaka Gas, TEPCO, and CPC

---

[30] 'Equatorial Guinea LNG Project, Bioko Island, Punta Europa, Equatorial Guinea', hydrocarbons-technology.com. www.hydrocarbons-technology.com/projects/bioko-lng/.
[31] 'Mitsui, Marubeni Join Marathon's Equatorial Guinea LNG Export Project', NGI Daily Gas Price Index, 7 June 2005, www.naturalgasintel.com/articles/68865-mitsui-marubeni-join-marathon-s-equatorial-guinea-lng-export-project.
[32] 'PNG Gas Finds Push LNG Plans', Michael McWalter, American Association of Petroleum Geologists, July 2011. www.aapg.org/Publications/News/Explorer/Column/ArticleID/2257/PNG-Gas-Finds-Push-LNG-Plans.

contracted for its output. Since its start-up, the plant has ramped up rapidly to plateau production and it was a major contributor to spot LNG in 2014.

In four countries – Trinidad, Oman, Egypt, and Peru – LNG exports face a steady drain from domestic demand. LNG exports from Trinidad and Oman have been on a slightly downward path while, in the most extreme case, Egypt stopped exporting LNG only a decade after its first exports. Egypt once had dreams of being a large LNG exporter and its Damietta and Idku LNG plants were successfully developed by Segas (Union Fenosa, ENI, EGAS, and EGPC) and a consortium of BG, GDF Suez, Petronas, EGAS, and EGPC, respectively. Damietta has operated under a tolling scheme, where the plant liquefies the gas on a merchant basis, receiving a liquefaction fee. Both projects were looking at adding another train, but these plans failed due to the absence of adequate reserves, increasing domestic demand, and Egypt's strict restrictions on exports. The situation worsened dramatically in 2013, with a combination of abrupt production decline and gas demand rise. Despite halting pipeline exports, Egypt still had insufficient gas for its domestic market; it therefore closed Damietta in December 2012 and Idku in early 2014. Using Israeli gas to feed the plants has been discussed, but this is stymied by the geopolitical situation. The discovery in Egypt by ENI of the large Zohr gas field in August 2015 could change the picture considerably, by providing a new potential source of gas supply for these plants. However, expectations are that this gas will be allocated to the domestic market and that LNG imports could continue for a while.

Peru's LNG project consists of a 408 km pipeline and a 4.45 mtpa train in Pampa Melchorita, which became operational in 2010. The project was challenging due to high seismic activity and it experienced a force 8.0 (Richter scale) earthquake during construction (Sakmar, 2013). Sponsored by Hunt Oil, SK Corporation, Repsol, and Marubeni, the project's output was contracted by Repsol for 18 years, to serve the company's contract with CFE at Mexico's Manzanillo plant. Shell's buyout of Repsol's LNG assets means that it has also acquired the Peru LNG offtake contract and the equity stake in Peru LNG. These deliveries are priced at 91 per cent of the HH month-ahead price, much lower than Asian spot prices. Still, Peru LNG is able to pass on these low prices to upstream producers, as the LNG sale price is based on the cost of the final cargo. This has sparked some controversy, given the rapid increase in domestic demand, and there have been calls for the diversion of LNG exports to satisfy domestic demand instead.

Three liquefaction plants (in Norway, Angola, and Yemen) have been beset by technical or geopolitical difficulties.

Norway's Snøvhit utilization rate over the period 2008–14 was 65 per cent, against the usual 90 per cent. The first Arctic LNG project, Snøvhit started up in October 2007, exported two cargoes, and then shut down due to technical issues until February 2008. Output has been halted regularly since then. Due to the remote location and hostile conditions, prefabrication and modularization were chosen for the plant. It is the world's most energy-efficient LNG plant, with a liquefaction process efficiency of 243 kWh per ton of LNG.[33]

The Angola LNG plant was built to use associated gas and reduce gas flaring. After a delayed start in July 2013, it exported a few cargoes before being shut down for repairs in mid-2014. One explanation for this is the difficulty of handling the compositional changes of associated gas from different fields against the original plant design. As exports targeted the US gas market (through a specially built regasification terminal at Pascagoula), the project sponsors have not seen much need to find alternative LNG supplies. The plant restarted in 2016 after a super heater had been installed and other modifications had been made.

The 6.7 mtpa Yemen LNG, contracted by Total, GDF Suez, and KOGAS, started up in 2009. However, the rapid deterioration of the country's political climate in 2015 resulted in the plant being closed only five years after its start. It is not known when it will be able to restart but it is theoretically operational. Built to develop the 260 bcm field in Block 18 in the Marib region, the liquefaction plant is linked to the field by a 325 km pipeline. The biggest industrial project in Yemen's history, the plant would have diversified revenues away from oil. Since the beginning of the Arab Spring, the pipeline has been bombed several times, notably in 2012, and has been subject to force majeure.

In 2015, three new projects started operating worldwide: BG's Queensland Curtis and Santos' Gladstone LNG projects on the east coast of Australia, as well as Donggi-Senoro in Indonesia. This is actually much less than had been expected. The Gorgon project was initially expected to start in 2014, but only became operational in late March 2016. Similarly, Cheniere's Sabine Pass had been expected to deliver its first cargo in late 2015, but its start was postponed to February 2016. The project certainly started in a much more challenging context than the point at which it took FID. NBP prices stood at around $4.3/MMBtu in February 2016, which means that it would not cover the cost of gas, the liquefaction fee, and the shipping and regasification costs despite a much lower level of HH gas prices (around $1.9/MMBtu).

Meanwhile, LNG dreams have not come true for some countries which, based on their reserves, could have become LNG exporters. Iran is probably

---

[33] 'Technical and Operational Innovation for Onshore and Floating LNG', Jostein Pettersen et al., Paper presented to LNG 17, 19 April 2013, www.gastechnology.org/Training/Documents/LNG17-proceedings/12-2-Jostein_Pettersen.pdf.

the most notable example. The holder of the second-largest reserves in the world, Iran had many LNG export plans. Non-binding deals had been signed, mostly with Asian offtakers, while IOCs such as Total and NOCs such as CNPC, Petronas, and CNOOC were involved in liquefaction projects. Those projects, however, have fallen victim to international sanctions, which led to withdrawals of international partners and potential technology providers. Venezuela has also been discussing LNG exports for 25 years, but offshore gas fields have been developed either to supply the domestic market, or not at all. In Myanmar, Korea's KOGAS and India's ONGC and GAIL looked into a project based on the resources in the Rakhine basin, but a competing pipeline project to China was built instead. Even landlocked Bolivia was planning LNG exports in the early 2000s, based on the Pacific LNG project supported by Repsol, BG, Pan American Energy, and Sempra Energy. However, Bolivia never managed to get access to the Pacific Ocean and is still trying to do so by appealing to the International Court of Justice.[34]

The rise of Qatar

Qatar has made remarkable progress as an LNG exporter. Within 10 years of starting production at the end of 1996, it had overtaken Indonesia as the world's largest producer. In 2015 it produced 78.4 mtpa, three times the figure of its nearest competitor, Australia. Its success as an LNG producer is based on the North Field, which has estimated proven natural gas reserves of nearly 25.5 tcm (900 tcf) and 10 billion barrels of condensate. When the field was discovered in 1971 it was classed as a stranded resource, since domestic demand was too small to support development and there were no immediate opportunities for LNG or pipeline exports. It took 25 years for the LNG export potential to be realized, opening the way for the development of 14 liquefaction trains.

The development of the LNG option

The non-associated natural gas in the North Field, which has a high condensate content, lies in four independent reservoir structures. The field extends into Iranian waters, where it is estimated that there are 13 tcm (460 tcf) of recoverable reserves. The total reserves of 38.5 tcm represent

---

[34] President Abraham presiding, in the case concerning Obligation to Negotiate Access to the Pacific Ocean (Bolivia v. Chile) Preliminary Objection, Public sitting, 4 May 2015, International Court of Justice, the Hague. www.icj-cij.org/docket/files/153/18628.pdf#view=FitH&pagemode=none&search= per cent22Chile per cent22.

just over 20 per cent of the world's proved conventional natural gas reserves.

In the early 1970s, Qatar was a nation of less than 200,000 inhabitants with an annual energy consumption of around 1 million tonnes oil equivalent (mtoe). There were no gas pipeline systems in the Gulf region for the export of gas, while the limited demand for gas in neighbouring countries made the construction of export pipelines uneconomic. The LNG industry was in its infancy in the 1970s – global production, at the end of the decade, was 25 mtpa. Qatar's location in the Middle East put it at a disadvantage to other LNG producers that were closer to the main demand centres in north-east Asia and Europe.

By the early 1980s, Qatar Petroleum (QP) was actively planning development of gas production for the domestic market, followed by LNG exports.[35] It invited proposals from international oil companies to participate in the development of the North Field.[36] The government's plan was for QP to own and operate the upstream development, while a 30 per cent share in the proposed liquefaction plant was to be allocated to foreign companies.

BP and Total were initially selected as partners in the liquefaction company, to be known as Qatargas.[37] A Joint Venture Agreement (JVA) was signed in 1984 under which BP and Total each had a 7.5 per cent share in the liquefaction company.[38] In September 1985, the Japanese trading house, Marubeni, became the third foreign participant, with a 7.5 per cent share.[39] Securing buyers for the output was difficult in the mid-1980s. Japan was the main target market, but its medium-term demand was largely satisfied following the start of imports from Malaysia in 1983 and the signing of a contract to import 5.8 mtpa from Australia's North West Shelf project commencing in 1989. Korea, which started importing LNG in 1986, was only likely to commit to a small share of the planned output, at best. In Europe, Qatar faced strong competition from pipeline gas, while US demand for LNG had collapsed in 1980. The breakthrough for Qatargas came with the entry of the Japanese trading house, Mitsui, as the

---

[35] 'Liquefied Natural Gas from Qatar – the Qatargas Project', Kohei Hashimoto, James Elass, and Stacy Eller. Part of: Geopolitics of Natural Gas (working paper series), a joint project of the Program on Energy and Sustainable Development at Stanford University and the James Baker III Institute for Public Policy at Rice University, published in December 2004.

[36] 'CFP seeks Qatar LNG partnership', *World Gas Report*, 20 July 1981, 6.

[37] 'The Qatar government has signed a memorandum with BP and Française des Petroles' subsidiary, Total', Lloyd's List International, 22 June 1983.

[38] 'Qatar concludes deal to develop world's biggest known gas field', Dixon, A. and Lawson, D., *Financial Times*, 28 June 1984.

[39] 'Marubeni of Japan is to have a 7.5% stake in a gas project offshore the state of Qatar', *Financial Times*, 6 September 1985.

fourth foreign partner, in May 1989[40] bringing with it the Japanese power company, Chubu Electric, as a buyer.

The economics for the project were based on an oil price of $20/bbl in real terms, which translated into an LNG price of $3.45/MMBtu on a crude oil parity basis. However, the project was not economically viable with the tax regime included in the JVA. The Government of Qatar recognized that Chubu's interest in committing to the output from the first two trains meant that, nearly two decades after the North Field was discovered, Qatar was positioned to export its gas. It therefore agreed to a tax rate of 35 per cent on Qatargas profits (the JVA had set a rate of 55 per cent), a rate that has since been applied to all of Qatar's LNG developments. In addition, the government offered a 10 year tax holiday and it was agreed that the price for gas supplied to the plant by QP would be $0.50/MMBtu, indexed to the LNG price. However, in order to increase early cash flows for the project, part of the payment was to be deferred until the cash flows from the project reached a level that would generate a real after-tax rate of return of 12.8 per cent.

In January 1991, Qatargas and Chubu Electric signed a Letter of Intent (LOI) for the sale and purchase of the entire 4 mtpa output from the first two liquefaction trains, with an option for Chubu to purchase an additional 2 mtpa from train 3. The LNG was to be sold on a Delivered Ex-Ship (DES) basis for 25 years.

The restructuring of the upstream phase

Shortly after the LOI was finalized, QP advised its shareholders that it had negotiated an agreement with the French company, Elf, for the latter to develop upstream production facilities in Qatar in return for a share of the condensate production. QP proposed to implement the agreement with Elf to provide gas supply to the project. But Qatargas shareholders wanted to be involved themselves, since it would allow a closer integration between the two phases of the project, simplifying the structure and reducing the risks. They were also concerned that Elf's proposed upstream development was low cost and technically risky.

BP, Mitsui, and Marubeni favoured a joint proposal by the Qatargas shareholders to take responsibility for the upstream development, but Total, decided to approach QP separately and offer the same deal as had been agreed with Elf. QP accepted Total's proposal in mid-1991.[41] Total invited BP, Mitsui, and Marubeni to participate in the Production Sharing Contract it had signed with QP. The other three foreign partners were

---

[40] 'Mitsui buys 7.5 pct share in Qatargas', Reuters News, 18 May 1989.
[41] 'Total-Compagnie Française in Pact for Qatar Project', Dow Jones Newswires, 29 May 1991.

concerned that Total was proposing the same low-cost development as Elf, which they saw as involving unacceptable technical risks, especially when a multi-billion dollar investment in the liquefaction plant and ships depended on its performance. However, enhancing the design to reduce the risk would involve extra costs and lower the rate of return on the upstream investment to an unacceptable level.

BP's withdrawal from Qatargas

Despite the progress that the Qatargas project was making by mid-1991, BP was beginning to review its continued involvement in the project. Its doubts about the investment in Qatargas were triggered by a combination of its own need to reduce capital investments and concerns about the direction the project was taking. The Qatargas project had lower returns than other projects in its portfolio and BP did not give high priority strategically to LNG, especially in a country like Qatar, where it did not believe there would be an opportunity for either follow-on LNG investments or to participate in upstream exploration and production. In January 1992, BP informed the Government of Qatar, its partners in Qatargas, and Chubu Electric of its decision to withdraw from the project.

Qatargas was left in a position where it was progressing towards making a FID around the end of 1992 or early in 1993. The Sales and Purchase Agreement (SPA) with Chubu Electric was close to completion, the award of the FEED contract was imminent, and the agreements for tax and gas payments had been finalized. The withdrawal of BP raised doubts about the viability of the project and Qatar needed a major player with LNG experience to replace BP.

The Qatar Government cast around for a new partner and found several companies were interested. The company that stood out was Mobil, an experienced LNG player through its involvement in the Arun project in Indonesia. It would also bring a US company into the development of Qatari LNG, an important consideration for the government in the aftermath of the first Gulf War. Mobil was looking for a new LNG investment to replace its involvement in the Arun project, which was entering into a long-term decline as the reserves supplying the plant depleted.

Mobil's starting position in the negotiations with the Government of Qatar was similar to the objectives of BP before its withdrawal. It wanted the upstream development to be more closely integrated with the liquefaction phase, a more robust technical design for the upstream facilities, clear leadership by a single partner, and guarantees that the fiscal and gas payment agreements would not be changed. It also sought a larger share in the project than the 7.5 per cent on offer.

The Qatari authorities were prepared to make some concessions to meet Mobil's requirements, but they were unwilling to unwind the arrangements that were already in place for Qatargas. They offered Mobil participation in a second project, which would be developed in a way that would largely meet its objectives. As a result, RasGas was born as a second Qatari project.[42]

Qatargas restructuring and FID 1992–3

The Qatargas project underwent some restructuring when Mobil joined. The shares of Mobil and Total in Qatargas were increased from 7.5 per cent to 10 per cent each and QP's share reduced to 65 per cent, while the shares of Marubeni and Mitsui remained at 7.5 per cent each. The other partners agreed to participate in Total's upstream PSC. QP took a 65 per cent share and Mobil a 10 per cent share, in line with their respective holdings in Qatargas. However, the Japanese participants were only willing to take a share of 2.5 per cent each, leaving Total with a 20 per cent share. The upstream facilities were redesigned to meet the requirements of the liquefaction project, resulting in an increase in the capital cost. However, the Government of Qatar agreed to reduce its shares of the condensate revenues to improve the economics.

Ras Laffan industrial city

The Government of Qatar decided in 1990 that Ras Laffan, in the north of the country, would be the location for industries – which would include Qatargas and any future LNG developments – using gas from the North Field. It also planned the development of a port – for the export of LNG, condensate, and other products – at an estimated cost of around $1 billion. Construction work on the port was substantially completed by September 1996, three months before the first LNG cargo was exported.

The development of Ras Laffan Industrial City and Port proved to be an inspired decision of the government, since it provided the space needed to support the expansion of LNG capacity and other gas-based industries; this would not have been possible at the originally proposed LNG site at Umm Said south of the capital Doha. The port now covers an area of 56 square kilometres. It has six LNG berths capable of loading ships with capacities of up to 267,000 m^3 and a shipyard for the repair and maintenance of LNG ships.[43]

---

[42] 'Total-Compagnie Française in Pact for Qatar Project', Dow Jones Newswires, 29 May 1991.

[43] 'A successful investment', Rasgas, www.rasgas.com/Operations/RLICPort.html.

Construction and start-up of Qatargas

With Mobil on board as a replacement for BP and the project restructured, Qatargas progressed to a FID in May 1993. The SPA with Chubu Electric for 4 mtpa, with an option for a further 2 mtpa, was signed on 13 May 1992.[44] The Engineering, Procurement, and Construction (EPC) contract was awarded to the Japanese company, Chiyoda.[45]

Qatargas chartered seven ships from a consortium of Japanese shipping companies (Mitsui OSK Line, NYK, and K-Line) to deliver the output from the first two trains, with a further three ordered subsequently for the output of train 3. The ships were constructed in Japan and were delivered into service between 1996 and 2000.[46] Financing for the onshore liquefaction plant came from commercial banks in Japan and the Japan Bank for International Co-operation (JBIC), and was finalized in late 1993.[47] The upstream phase was financed separately. The total cost of the first phase of the project was around $6 billion, divided approximately into $1 billion for the upstream, $3 billion for the two-train plant, and $2 billion for the seven ships.

Chubu Electric decided in 1994 that it did not have the demand to justify committing to the output from the 2 mtpa third train and it brought together a consortium of six other Japanese utilities to purchase the LNG on the same terms as had been agreed with Qatargas for the first two trains. The SPA for the train 3 volumes was signed on 31 December 1994 and commitment to the construction of the train was made in 1995 by exercising the option in the original EPC contract with Chiyoda. The timing allowed the construction of the first three trains to take place as a single project.[48]

The first cargo was loaded at the end of December 1996[49] and it arrived at Chubu's newly constructed receiving terminal in Nagoya in early January 1997. Train 2 was commissioned in the second half of 1997 with train 3 following in 1999.

The commissioning and build-up from the three trains went relatively smoothly and, by mid-2001, the capacity of the three-train plant was 7.5 mtpa, some 25 per cent above Qatargas's contractual commitments with its Japanese buyers. The capacity of the plant was further enhanced

---

[44] 'Chubu signs up Qatar LNG', *Financial Times*, 15 May 1992.
[45] 'Chiyoda lands $1.4bn Qatar Contract', *International Gas Report*, 11 June 1993, 4.
[46] 'Qatargas signs vessel chartering agreement', *MEED*, 25 October 1993.
[47] 'Finance fixed for Qatargas downstream works', *MEED*, 20 December 1993.
[48] 'Japan to sign up for Qatargas supplies', *MEED*, 12 December 1994; Special Report: 'Japan shares big LNG deal', Lloyd's List International, 27 December 1994.
[49] 'Qatar ships first LNG to Japan, signs accord', *Oil and Gas Journal*, Vol. 94, No. 53, 30 December 1996, 28; and *Oil and Gas Journal*, Vol. 94, No. 53, 24 January 1997, 28.

by debottlenecking, which increased it to around 10 mtpa. This increase allowed Qatargas to diversify the markets for its output, with Spain's Gas Natural Fenosa becoming a long-term buyer and BP entering into a medium-term contract. Diversifying the outlets for Qatar's LNG projects became an important marketing strategy.

RasGas 1

A key part of the agreement between the Government of Qatar and Mobil in 1992 was the establishment of a second liquefaction company, Ras Laffan Liquefied Natural Gas Company Limited (RasGas).[50] The joint venture agreement was signed in 1993 under which QP took a 70 per cent share and Mobil 30 per cent. RasGas was given the right to drill for and produce gas from the North Field and to export up to 10 mtpa of LNG. It is structured as an integrated project, with RasGas owning and operating the upstream production facilities, the pipeline to shore, and the liquefaction plant. It pays a royalty on the natural gas supplied to the liquefaction plant and on the condensate sales. The same structure has been used for the expansions of the RasGas and the Qatargas projects.

The target markets for RasGas 1 output were Korea and Japan, since natural gas prices in Europe were too low to remunerate the investment. In 1996, the Japanese companies, Itochu and LNG Japan purchased 4 per cent and 3 per cent respectively in RasGas 1.[51] They agreed to assist the project's marketing in Japan and to provide QP with a loan facility to assist the funding of its equity share of the investment. In the event, the output from the first two trains was committed to Korea Gas and as part of the deal a consortium of Korean companies (under the name of KORAS – Korea RasGas LNG) was given the right to purchase a 5 per cent share in RasGas 1. KOGAS eventually secured its position in RasGas 1 in September 2005.[52] In October 1995, Korea Gas committed to 2.4 mtpa from the first of the planned two trains for 25 years. The agreement was unique at that time in having a floor price, but in June 1997 Korea Gas increased the contract volumes to 4.8 mtpa and the floor price was dropped.[53]

The estimated cost of the project was $2.5 billion for a single train development and $3.4 billion for two trains. The project successfully raised

---

[50] 'Qatar General Petroleum Corp establishes Ras Laffan Liquefied Natural Gas Co', *MEED*, 16 July 1993.

[51] 'Trading companies to take equity in Ras Laffan', *Gas Matters*, December 1996, 31; 'Itochu, Nissho Iwai Buy Shares In Qatar Firm', *Energy Alert*, 10 December 1996, Vol. 28, No. 50.

[52] 'Korea Gas Takes RasGas Stake', *Energy Argus Gas and Power*, Vol. V, No. 19, 28 September 2005.

[53] 'Qatar, South Korea sign deal to double gas supply', Reuters News, 30 June 1997.

$2.55 billion of finance in December 1996; this consisted of $1.2 billion of bond financing (a first for an LNG project), $0.9 billion from Export Credit Agencies, and $0.45 billion from commercial banks.[54]

RasGas 1 entered into a lump sum contract with a joint venture of JGC and Kellogg for the construction of a single train liquefaction plant with a nameplate capacity of 2.6 mtpa. An option for a second train of the same design and capacity was exercised when KOGAS doubled its contracted volumes. Production from train 1 commenced in April 1999 and from train 2 in March 2000. Output from each train reached 3.3 mtpa, 27 per cent above their nameplate capacity, soon after start-up.

By the end of 2001, Qatar had five LNG trains in operation with a total capacity of around 14 mtpa. The enormous proven natural gas reserves and the infrastructure developed at Ras Laffan put Qatar in a good position to expand its liquefaction capacity.

RasGas 2

The first phase of the expansion was the establishment of RasGas 2; this involved the construction and operation of three additional trains at RasGas, each with a capacity of 4.7 mtpa. The shareholdings in RasGas 2 were the same as those for RasGas 1 when it was originally established in 1993: QP 70 per cent and Mobil (now ExxonMobil) 30 per cent.[55]

The output from the first of the RasGas 2 trains was contracted to the Indian company Petronet. The initial contract was for 5 mtpa of LNG,[56] with the option for the volume to be increased to 7.5 mtpa. The sales were on an FOB basis and Petronet chartered two ships to transport the LNG. After several rounds of negotiation and various proposals on price, RasGas 2 agreed to a fixed FOB price of $2.53/MMBtu for five years from the start of deliveries. The period of fixed prices ended in December 2008 and the following month a five-year transition to a linkage with crude oil prices commenced. A combination of falling LNG construction costs, the lower unit costs of an expansion compared with a greenfield development, and the economies of scale through constructing larger LNG trains, helped underpin the economics of sales to India, despite the low price for the first five years of operation.

The output from the second RasGas 2 train was committed to Edison in Italy,[57] under a DES contract for 4.6 mtpa. RasGas 2's marketing efforts continued to show positive results through agreements with CPC in Taiwan

---

[54] 'Qatar's Rasgas raises $1.2 billion via two bonds', Reuters News, 12 December 1996; 'Qatar's Rasgas Secures $2.25 Bln Financing', *Energy Alert*, 30 December 1996.

[55] 'Qatar's USD2bn third LNG JV', *Middle East Daily Financial News*, 27 March 2001.

[56] 'Qatar's RasGas seals Indian Petronet deal', *International Gas Report*, 6 August 1999, 4.

[57] 'Edison Gas', *Oil and Gas Journal*, 2 July 2001, 9.

for 3 mtpa from 2008,[58] with Endesa in Spain for 0.8 mtpa,[59] and with Distrigas in Belgium for 2.1 mtpa from 2007.[60] In addition, RasGas 2 committed to 3.4 mtpa of capacity in the expansion of Fluxys LNG's terminal, at Zeebrugge in Belgium.[61] In June 2007, the capacity rights at Zeebrugge were transferred to EDF Trading, and RasGas 2 signed an interruptible contract to deliver up to 3.3 mtpa of LNG to EDF Trading.[62] The agreement, which was originally for four and a half years but was extended in 2011, gives RasGas 2 the right, but not the obligation, to deliver LNG to the Zeebrugge terminal – effectively providing a flexible outlet in Europe for LNG cargoes that are surplus to the needs of long-term buyers.

The RasGas 2 trains came into operation between January 2004 and December 2006, taking Qatar's total capacity to over 30 mtpa. The RasGas 2 trains are designed for LPGs (propane and butane) to be extracted from the natural gas and exported as separate products. This was necessary since some of the output was expected to be sold to markets which require LNG with a lower heating value than those in Japan and Korea, the original markets for Qatargas 1 and RasGas 1.

Qatar's LNG mega-trains

Qatargas 1 and RasGas 1 and 2 were developed using the conventional business model, in which most of the output is sold on a long-term take-or-pay basis to gas and power utilities, mainly in Asia but with some sales to Europe. The only exception was RasGas's contract with EDF Trading, which gave it the right but not the obligation to deliver LNG cargoes to the Zeebrugge terminal. All three projects used proven technology and conventionally sized LNG ships. The next phase of the expansion (which involved the development of six 'mega-trains', each with a capacity of 7.8 mtpa) broke new ground in terms of the capacities of the trains and the ships, and in the marketing of the LNG.

In October 2002,[63] QP and ExxonMobil announced plans for the Qatargas 2 project; this was to have two mega-trains and would use ships

---

[58] 'A Story we're Proud of': the 'About RasGas' page on the RasGas website (www.rasgas.com), link to 'Milestones'.
[59] 'Endesa Goes Shopping', *World Gas Intelligence*, 6 August 2003.
[60] 'Qatar to sign final LNG supply deal with Distrigas', Reuters News, 28 February 2005.
[61] 'Fluxys agrees LNG supply', *Oil and Gas Journal*, 12 July 2004, 9.
[62] 'EDF Trading Takes RasGas Volume and Capacity at Zeebrugge', ICIS Heren, 22 June 2007.
[63] 'Qatar LNG's Mega Growth', *World Gas Intelligence*, Vol. XII, No. 42 1, 16 October 2002.

belonging to two classes of LNG tankers, Q-Flex (210,000 m^3 to 217,000 m^3 capacity) and Q-Max (263,000 m^3 to 267,000 m^3 capacity). The LNG was to be supplied to the UK through a terminal at South Hook, near Milford Haven in south-west Wales, which would be owned and operated by ExxonMobil and QP. ExxonMobil Gas Marketing Europe (EMGME) would be the buyer of the regasified LNG, at a price netted back from the UK's National Balancing Point (NBP) price (which is set by the supply of and demand for natural gas in the UK market). Producers selling into this type of market need to ensure that unit production costs are kept as low as possible to minimize the risk of making losses if prices fall. QP and ExxonMobil used economies of scale to achieve this objective.

Raising finance for the project, which was successfully completed in 2004, involved major challenges; one of these was that, for the first time, three phases (the upstream production facilities, the liquefaction plant, and the regasification terminal) of an LNG project were to be financed together. The total estimated cost was $10.15 billion: $9.4 billion for the facilities in Qatar and $0.75 billion for the receiving terminal in the UK. The entire output was to be sold in the UK, where it represented around 20 per cent of market demand. The price was linked to the NBP price, the first time that an LNG project had been financed on the basis of hub-based pricing rather than on an oil-linked price formula. The liquefaction trains were the largest ever built and used many items of equipment that had never been used before in a liquefaction plant. Although the ships were financed separately, the fact that they would be the largest ever built was another risk factor for financiers. FID on Qatargas 2 was taken in December 2004.

FID on RasGas 3 (the addition of two mega-trains to the RasGas plant), followed in September 2005[64] and FID on the last two mega-trains, Qatargas 3 and 4, was taken in December 2005. This took the total capacity Qatar had under construction and in operation to 77.5 mtpa. The output from Qatargas 3 and 4 and from RasGas 3 was originally targeted for delivery to the US market, where QP and ExxonMobil were developing the Golden Pass receiving terminal.

ExxonMobil, with a 30 per cent share, is QP's only foreign partner in three of the mega-trains (Qatargas 2 train 1 and RasGas 3). Total acquired a 16.7 per cent share in the second train of the Qatargas 2 project, with ExxonMobil's share reduced to 18.3 per cent and QP's to 65 per cent. Total committed to take delivery of 5.2 mtpa from the output of Qatargas 2 train 2 at terminals in the UK, France, Mexico, and the USA.[65]

The government of Qatar decided to introduce new partners into

---

[64] 'Qatar Contracts Flow', *World Gas Intelligence*, Vol. XVI, No. 39, 28 September 2005.
[65] 'Total Buys 5.2mtpa from Qatargas II and Takes a 16.7% Stake', *Gas Matters Today*, 28 February 2005.

Qatargas 3 and 4. ConocoPhillips was the chosen partner for Qatargas 3 and Shell was the chosen partner for Qatargas 4. They each had a 30 per cent share, with QP retaining the other 70 per cent, although in the case of Qatargas 3 QP reduced its share to 68.5 per cent, through an agreement for Mitsui to take a 1.5 per cent share. The six mega-trains came into operation between March 2009 and February 2011.

Qatar's changing marketing strategy

In the 1980s and early 1990s, when LNG exports from Qatar were first planned, the country's location in the Middle East put it at a competitive disadvantage since it is further from the main LNG markets than projects in Australia, south-east Asia, North Africa, and the Atlantic Basin. Today its location gives it an advantage, since it is well placed to switch cargoes between markets in response to changes in the global LNG market.

The initial marketing of Qatar's LNG output was largely concentrated in Asia. In 2008, the year before the start-up of the first Qatargas megatrain, 79.4 per cent of the country's output was delivered to Asia and 20.2 per cent to Europe, while two cargoes were shipped to North America. By targeting the UK and the USA for the output from the six mega-trains, Qatar appeared to be moving towards a position where approximately one-third of its output would be delivered to each of Asia, Europe, and the Americas. However, between taking FID on Qatargas 2, 3, 4, and RasGas 3, and the start of production in 2009, the global LNG market changed. The USA no longer needed LNG imports, because of the growth in its shale gas production (which few had forecast), so Qatar had to look for alternative markets for the output from four of its mega-trains.

Europe was the main alternative market. Its LNG import terminals were under-utilized and Qatar had positioned itself to access the market through its ownership of the South Hook terminal in the UK, the Adriatic LNG terminal in Italy, its agreements to supply LNG to the Zeebrugge terminal in Belgium, and its contracts with buyers in Spain. Its deliveries to Europe more than doubled and in 2010 they were marginally greater than those it made to Asia (Figure 2.7). Japan's Fukushima crisis (triggered by the Great East Japan earthquake and tsunami on 11 March 2011) resulted in another change in the global LNG market. Japan needed more LNG as its nuclear power plants were taken off line. Qatar responded by diverting cargoes from Europe. Further new opportunities in Asia emerged after 2011 as China's LNG demand increased and Thailand, Singapore, and Malaysia began to import LNG. In addition, Qatar's exports to South America increased, and it also began to supply new markets in the Middle East in 2010 and in North Africa in 2015. In 2014, Asia accounted for 71 per cent of Qatar's exports, with Europe's share having halved to 22.8 per cent

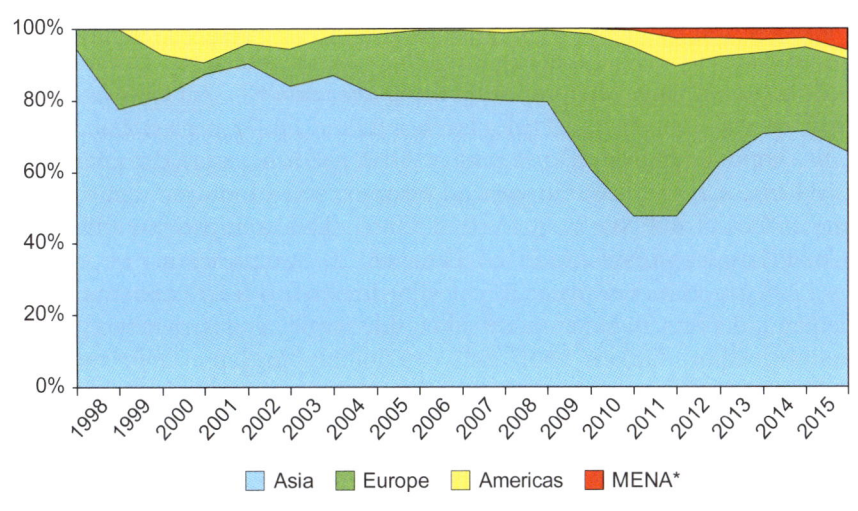

Figure 2.7: Qatar LNG exports by region, 1997–2015
Source: Cedigaz and GIIGNL.

The year of 2015 has seen further change in the market. LNG demand in Asia has dropped by 2 per cent because of competition from nuclear and coal in the power sector and slower economic growth in some countries. At the same time LNG production in the Pacific basin has increased, with the commissioning of new liquefaction trains in Papua New Guinea, Australia, and Indonesia. Qatar has had to switch cargoes from Asia to Europe and to new markets in the Middle East and North Africa. Asia's share of Qatar's exports has once again declined.

Qatar has delivered LNG to 25 out of the 35 countries that were importing LNG in 2015. Qatar has created new opportunities for its output by providing the first cargoes for new importers (including Egypt, Jordan, Pakistan, Dubai, Malaysia, and Singapore since 2011) and it delivered the first cargo to Poland in December 2015.

A reversal of 'fortunes' in the 2010s: shale gas and Fukushima

LNG supplies are diverted away from Europe

The LNG industry has had to deal with significant supply and demand shocks over the 2010–15 period. North America progressively withdrew from LNG imports and prepared itself to become an LNG exporter.[66]

---
[66] Not taking into account LNG exports from Alaska.

Europe's role in the LNG market eroded as LNG was progressively diverted to the more attractive Asian markets. This was not good news for European politicians at a time when reducing dependence on Russian gas was top of their energy agenda. By 2014, Asia accounted for 75 per cent of global LNG imports, up from 61 per cent in 2010, restoring Asia's dominance of LNG imports. In 2007 Europe had been expected to attract between 80 and 160 bcm of LNG by 2015 (IEA, 2007). This contrasts painfully with actual European LNG imports of 44 bcm in 2014, representing 14 per cent of LNG trade, down from 29 per cent in 2010 (Figure 2.8). European demand decreased by one-fifth alongside growing gas demand in the mature Asian markets (+30 bcm) – notably in Japan following the Fukushima accident. Other Asian countries also become major markets for LNG, with demand rising by 86 bcm. By 2014 China had become the third-largest LNG importer and was taking more than any European country. In that year China alone imported 60 per cent of Europe's total 2014 imports.

Prices played a determining role in driving LNG away from Europe between 2011 and 2014 (Figure 2.9). Asian LNG import prices increased substantially after 2011 and occasionally peaked at $18/MMBtu. Japan's LNG import prices were the highest, averaging $16–$17/MMBtu over 2012–14, while Korea and Taiwan paid on average $14–$15/MMBtu. China was not immune from the price increases. Average LNG prices there climbed from $4.5/MMBtu in 2009 to almost $13/MMBtu in 2014. The historic cheap Australian LNG contract (at around $3/MMBtu), as well as relatively low prices from Indonesia's Tangguh and Malaysia's LNG Tiga

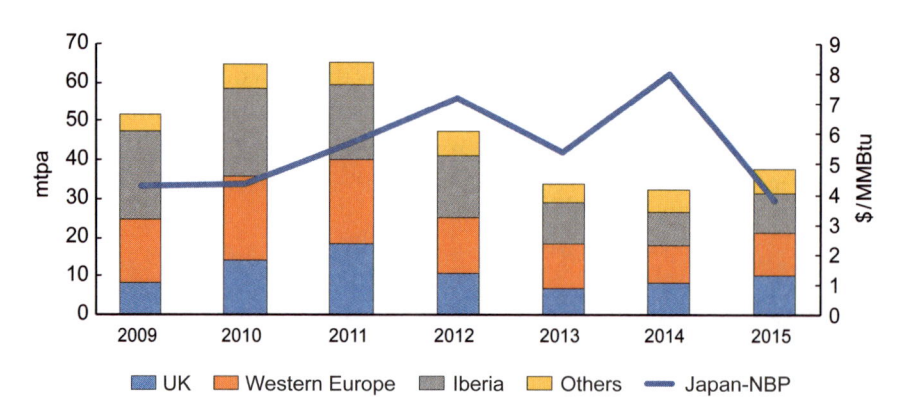

Figure 2.8: LNG supplies diverted away from Europe

Note: 'Japan–NBP' represents the difference between the average LNG import price in Japan and the UK NBP spot price.

Source: GIIGNL, Japanese customs, Bloomberg.

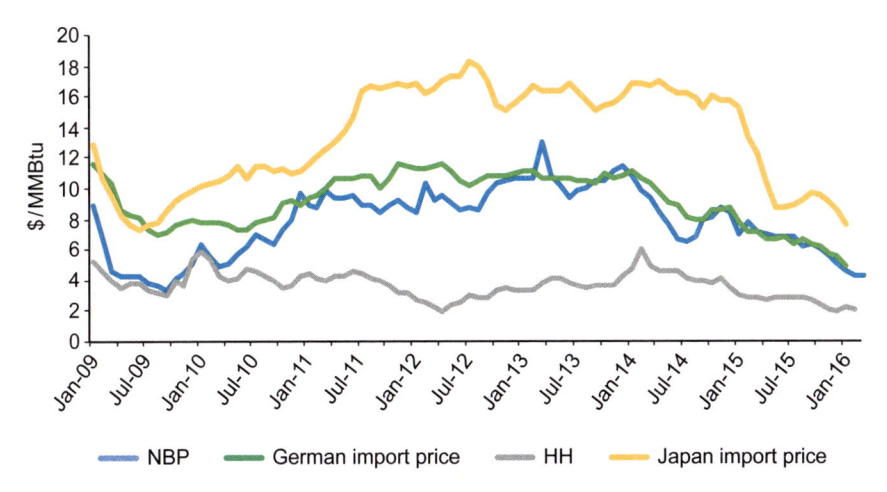

Figure 2.9: Regional gas prices, 2007–16
Sources: Japanese customs, German ministry of economics, Bloomberg, EIA.

(which were later revised upward), could not prevent this dramatic increase in the average LNG import price. Malaysian LNG has a 'slope' of around 7–10 per cent, while that of Qatari LNG is 17 per cent.[67] With a contract from Qatar linked to oil prices, even new importers such as Thailand paid around $15.5/MMBtu 2014.[68] In contrast, European gas prices stayed relatively low at $9.4/MMBtu over 2012–14. The large price gap between regions also led to re-exports, mostly from Spain and Belgium to Asia and Latin America. However, 2015 has proved to be different, as European and Asian prices have converged somehow, amid decreasing LNG imports in Japan, Korea, and China. Consequently Europe has become the market of last resort, able to absorb the surplus of LNG on global gas markets. European LNG imports increased to 37.6 mtpa in 2015 from 32.5 mtpa in 2014.

Although Belgium had been one of the pioneers in terms of re-exports (GIIGNL, 2008), the phenomenon really started to take off in the USA in 2009. Re-exporting LNG was a way in which the pressure from an oversupplied North American gas market could be relieved. Unlike exports of 'US-made' LNG, which were subject to some restrictions, re-exports were allowed as this was 'foreign-made' LNG (IEA, 2012), but this

---

[67] Chen (2014), and 'China imported LNG from 17 countries in 2014', Alaska Natural Gas Transportation Projects, Office of the Federal Coordinator, 5 February 2015. www.arcticgas.gov/2015/china-imported-lng-17-countries-2014.

[68] 'Thai LNG price remains high at $15.5/MMBtu in 2014', Robert Sullivan, Interfax Global Energy, 20 February 2015. http://interfaxenergy.com/gasdaily/article/15323/thai-lng-price-remains-high-at-155mmbtu-in-2014.

phenomenon was short-lived. While global LNG re-exports expanded from 1.9 mtpa in 2011 to 6.4 mtpa in 2014, the share of US LNG re-exports then declined and in 2014, the USA only re-exported around 0.1 mtpa. Meanwhile, many import terminals around the world were adapted in order to provide re-loading services. The oversupplied European gas market became a key source of LNG re-exports – 6 mtpa in 2014, with Spain representing 3.8 mtpa followed by Belgium with 1.1 mtpa. Among the key drivers was the price differential between the Asian and Latin American markets on the one side and the European market on the other side. Besides, Europe – especially Spain – had contracted too much LNG to be able to absorb it all. However, the tide turned again in 2015 as the price gap between the Asian and European markets reduced. This has resulted in a significant reduction in LNG re-exports to 4.4 mtpa, notably from Spain.[69]

North America's LNG import U-turn

The USA is one of the few countries where, due to its size, changes in the energy spectrum can produce ripples across the world. The shale gas revolution was unanticipated and passed unnoticed in its very early stages. Shale gas was often considered too costly to produce and was not economic at a gas price of $4/MMBtu. However, when gas prices increased to $7–$8/MMBtu in 2006, shale became good value. Driven by entrepreneurs, the rise in its production has been unstoppable since then, and it has taken established LNG players and IOCs by surprise. From 20 bcm in 2005, US shale gas production rose to 381 bcm in 2014.[70] The size of this surge took most analysts by surprise. In 2010 many were still predicting that the shale gas revolution would not survive an extended period of low gas prices (at or below $4/MMBtu). It did. Also wrong was the assumption that the abrupt drop in the number of gas rigs drilling would result in at least a slowdown in US gas production growth. While the number of gas rigs at end-2015 is almost one-tenth of what it was at its peak in 2008, US gas production has jumped by more than 196 bcm over 2008–15.

The North American LNG import story was coming to an end by the early 2010s. Over the subsequent period (2010–14) US imports declined dramatically from 15.7 mtpa in 2007 to 1.7 mtpa in 2014 (21.3 bcm to 2.3 bcm). The implications for the US gas market took time to sink in. An intermediate solution emerged for those LNG terminals that were still running: LNG re-exports, a clever answer to the oversupply in the

---

[69] 'Gas price convergence stalls Spanish LNG exports', Oleg Vukmanovic, Reuters, 29April 2015,
http://uk.reuters.com/article/uk-spain-lng-global-gas-idUKKBN0NK2BU20150429.

[70] Shale Gas Production, EIA data: www.eia.gov/dnav/ng/ng_prod_shalegas_s1_a.htm.

North American market. LNG terminal operators could receive LNG and thus keep the tanks cold. They could also re-export the LNG to more profitable markets. Cheniere was the first to apply for a re-export licence, in early 2009.[71] However, re-exports did not last long since most of the LNG intended for the US market was on flexible terms and could be diverted to other destinations without landing, which proved quite useful after Fukushima.

The idea of US LNG exports emerged in 2010. A decisive factor was the realization that the USA has considerably larger recoverable natural gas resources than previously thought, meaning that it would be able to feed its domestic market and still export. Before the rise of US shale gas, the country's import dependence on sometimes unstable foreign countries had looked set to increase. Suddenly, it could not only become self-sufficient but also supply LNG to other countries, especially if the country had a Free Trade Agreement (FTA) with the USA,[72] which is an interesting tool in future free trade negotiations.

The massive growth in shale gas transformed the USA within a decade from a massive prospective LNG importer into one of the three largest future LNG exporters. In 2005, the USA was expected to import more LNG than Japan by 2030. A whole series of LNG projects, such as those in Trinidad and Tobago, Qatar, and Angola, were built to serve the US market and were later forced to find alternative customers. A large number of prospective projects had also aimed at the North American LNG market, some of which (such as Russia's Arctic Shtokman) may never get the go ahead.

The growth in US production also affected Canada and Mexico. Deprived of its only export market, Canada was prompted towards LNG exports, while Mexico became a keen importer of US pipeline gas and reduced its LNG imports to 4.9 mtpa in 2015 (from 6.6 mtpa in 2014). Mexico now represents 70 per cent of the region's LNG imports. The ongoing liberalization of Mexico's upstream sector could have positive consequences for domestic gas supply, notably shale gas, while the country enjoys increasing US pipeline gas supplies, at Henry Hub prices, that could eventually displace LNG imports (Chapter 6). Finally, US LNG could also

---

[71] Sabine Pass LNG Export Project, Environmental Assessment, FERC and U.S. Department of Energy, February 2009. http://energy.gov/sites/prod/files/nepapub/nepa_documents/RedDont/EA-1649-FEA-2009.pdf.

[72] The USA has free trade agreements in force with 20 countries. These are Australia, Bahrain, Canada, Chile, Colombia, Costa Rica, Dominican Republic, El Salvador, Guatemala, Honduras, Israel, Jordan, Korea, Mexico, Morocco, Nicaragua, Oman, Panama, Peru, and Singapore. FTAs aim at reducing trade barriers and creating a more stable and transparent trading and investment environment.

impact the Caribbean region, potentially offering a cheaper source of regional LNG supply.

Fukushima: reverberations in global gas markets

On 11 March 2011 an earthquake and tsunami stuck Japan. Around 40 GW of nuclear and thermal power capacity in the areas supplied by TEPCO and the Tohoku Electric Power Company were hit. The most damage was at the Fukushima Daiichi power plant, where a nuclear meltdown took place in three of its six reactors, while other plants shut down automatically. Over the following year most Japanese nuclear power plants were shut down, some for regular maintenance, and never restarted (with the exception of two units in Ohi which passed stress tests and operated from July 2012 to September 2013). Afterwards, Japan had no nuclear generation until August 2015, though nuclear had accounted for around 29 per cent of its power in 2010. Replacing 1 GW of nuclear capacity requires around 1 mtpa of LNG imports. According to Japan Atomic Industrial Forum (JAIF), 43 reactors are now operable, but as of May 2016, only four had restarted – Sendai 1 and 2 and Takahama 3 and 4.[73]

To replace the missing 280 TWh of nuclear generation, Japan used mostly diesel, gas, and to a lesser extent coal, in addition to an energy-saving campaign. The share of fossil fuels in total power generation jumped from 61 per cent in 2010 to almost 90 per cent in 2014. Meanwhile LNG imports leaped from 70.9 mtpa to 89.2 mtpa in 2014; incremental LNG supplies came from neighbouring suppliers, new suppliers, or were diverted away from Europe (Figure 2.10). For Japan, the economic consequences were dramatic: its trade surplus of 5.3 trillion Yen in FY 2010 became a deficit of 13.8 trillion Yen in FY 2013. The LNG and oil import volume increase coincided with rising oil prices, making LNG more expensive. Japan's foreign exchange rate played an important role, and it started to make a contribution in 2013 under the Abenomics economy policy. The exchange rate became the largest contributor to the LNG import value expansion in 2015 (Yanagisawa, 2015). As nuclear restarted and LNG remained expensive against coal, LNG imports dropped to 85.1 mtpa in 2015

The rising cost of importing LNG brought about a radical change of attitude for Japan, with buyers looking for more affordable and flexible LNG sources. This double strategy led many Japanese companies to source US LNG, either directly through securing liquefaction capacity, or though secondary purchases from other companies. However, the decline in oil prices since late 2014 brought Asian spot prices and Japan's average

---

[73] Nuclear Power Plants in Japan, JAIF website. www.jaif.or.jp/en/npps-in-japan/.

LNG import prices to levels below $10/MMBtu, bringing into question the urgent need to move away from oil-indexed prices (Chapter 8). Due to the lag in the formulae, oil-linked contract gas prices only started to drop in early 2015 and were still at around $9/MMBtu in November 2015. The impact of oil prices at or below $50/bbl appeared in early 2016, with Japan's average import price standing at $7.6/MMBtu in January 2016.

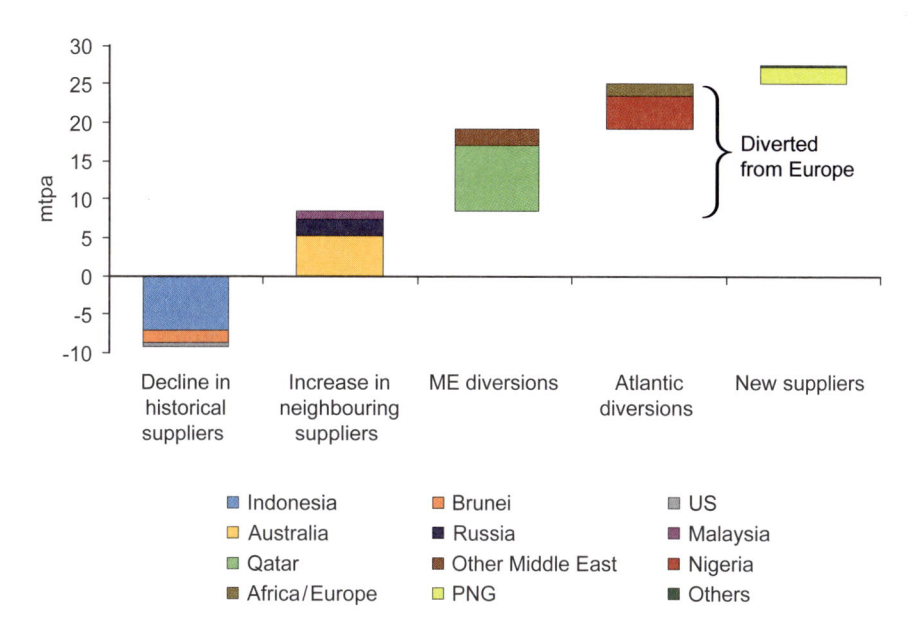

Figure 2.10: Japan's sourcing additional LNG supplies, difference between 2010 and 2014
Source: GIIGNL.

The emergence of south-east Asia

While both China and India have attracted increasing amounts of LNG since 2004, south-east Asia only joined them in 2010 when Thailand, Singapore, Malaysia, and Indonesia all became LNG importers. As of 2015, these south-east Asian countries imported 8.5 mtpa, up from 6.3 mtpa in 2014. Though this is only 3.5 per cent of global LNG demand, the region's entry into the LNG world could prove quite crucial.

The south-east Asian gas market is integrated, and the prospects of the countries in the region are linked. Both Malaysia and Indonesia were among the first LNG exporters and have dominated LNG supply for decades (Chapter 1). With domestic production dwindling and demand centres distant from gas resources, both countries chose to build LNG terminals, though their approach and strategy were different. Malaysia's Petronas has been active in contracting LNG supplies from international markets. It will receive LNG from Australia's Gladstone LNG, in which it is a partner. It is also involved in Canada's Pacific Northwest project, which announced a conditional FID in 2015, though as of May 2016 it is yet to start construction. At the same time, the company is actively developing its own LNG export capacity with a ninth train at the Bintulu facility as well as two small FLNGs. Petronas is planning to sustain output to supply its long-term customers and has developed a portfolio approach for the latest capacity additions, which are not attached to any specific customer. There is no sign that domestic LNG would end up in Malaysia, but it will be part of its wider supply portfolio.

In contrast, Indonesia has been inward looking: its LNG supply originates exclusively from the country's own plants at Bontang and Tangguh. Pertamina's activities in the global LNG markets have been limited to two long-term contracts with Cheniere for Corpus Christi gas. Unlike Malaysia, which has increased its output since 2000, Indonesia's LNG exports have been falling rapidly, from 27 mtpa in 2000 to 18 mtpa in 2015. Clear proof of this is the conversion in 2014 of the Arun LNG plant from an export to an import terminal. Although gas demand is expected to increase, price is a major issue. LNG is thought to be too expensive for the domestic market. Indonesia is contemplating a radical overhaul of its gas sector by establishing one or several aggregators to sell gas from production and LNG imports at government-approved prices, rather than having producers selling gas directly to end-users. A new LNG export plant, Donggi-Senoro, started in 2015.

Thailand was considered as a potential LNG market by Oman and Qatar in the 1990s, but this failed due to pipeline competition and Thailand's insistence on coal indexation. More recently (since 2004), LNG imports have featured on the government's agenda. PTT concluded an oil-linked contract with Qatar for 1 mtpa in 2008, when it started building the 5 mtpa Map Ta Phut terminal. That terminal is being expanded, and a third phase is under consideration for purposes of national energy security. As the country's power mix is 60 per cent dependent on gas, Thailand has been seeking additional supplies and has signed another 2 mtpa contract with Qatar.

The last new south-east Asian LNG market, Singapore, comes from a different background. With no gas production, the country had relied exclusively on piped natural gas imports from Indonesia and Malaysia. The government then decided to reduce its dependence on pipeline gas from these countries and turned to LNG, even though it was more expensive. In addition, Singapore created demand for LNG by requiring power generators to use it. The country declared a moratorium on pipeline gas imports, which proved insightful, considering the rapid deterioration of Indonesian export potential. Singapore's LNG import strategy is also interesting: as the country does not have a 'national' gas company, its Energy Marketing Authority appointed BG as its exclusive supplier and aggregator for the first 3 mtpa of LNG supply. It is using the same tranche-by-tranche process to select future LNG suppliers. Singapore has been aggressively expanding its LNG terminal on Jurong Island with the aim of reaching 9 mtpa and it plans to build a second receiving terminal as it pursues a strategy of becoming Asia's LNG trading hub. This is consistent with the emergence of companies such as Pavilion Energy, a subsidiary of Sovereign Wealth Fund Temasek, which has the ambition of becoming a regional LNG player. Pavilion Energy has acquired a stake in Tanzania's upstream gas reserves and in the country's proposed liquefaction project, and has signed long-term supply contracts for LNG from several companies.

Is small beautiful? The emergence of smaller LNG importers (2010–16)

Up to 2010, most non-OECD LNG importers have been relatively large countries (or large gas users), such as China and India. Since then a different breed of LNG importers has appeared. This group includes countries as diverse as Lithuania, Uruguay, Israel, Jordan, the Philippines, Colombia, Pakistan, Ghana, and Egypt. Excluding Egypt and Pakistan, these markets share one trait: they are quite small, with annual LNG import demand below 10 bcm or even 5 bcm. Most are facing the same challenge: a dire energy crisis for which LNG is the only rapid solution (especially if they can make use of FSRUs). However, a few do not plan to keep these facilities on a long-term basis. This is certainly the case for Israel, and potentially now also for Egypt since its recent large Zohr find. For other countries, LNG is here to stay unless the fuel mix changes in such a way that gas imports are no longer necessary.

The gas shortages in Israel, Jordan, and Egypt all have the same origin: Egypt's increasingly tight gas supply and demand situation. Egypt's gas demand has been increasing much faster than its production since 2005, mostly due to relatively low wholesale gas prices and payment arrears in the upstream sector. After the Arab Spring in 2011, Egyptian pipeline exports to Israel were cut because of political tensions and growing domestic gas demand. Egypt has changed from being an exporter of 18 bcm in 2009 into an LNG importer in 2015; the transition accelerated after the collapse of its domestic production in 2013. Despite a complete halt of all pipeline and LNG exports, the country still needed more gas supplies and consequently experienced power blackouts. Negotiations to get an FSRU and LNG supplies have been ongoing since late 2012.[74] In November 2014 EGAS concluded a contract with Höegh of Norway; the resulting FSRU started operating in April 2015. Rather than contracting significant amounts from one supplier, Egypt has been organizing tenders for a specified number of cargoes over short periods and imported 2.6 mtpa in 2015. A second FSRU was contracted from BW shipping and started operations in October 2015. It is uncertain whether recent gas discoveries will be enough to make Egypt self-sufficient post-2020.

Egypt's disruptions have particularly affected Jordan, which used to import 80 per cent of its gas from Egypt through the Arab Gas Pipeline. Plans to build an LNG terminal date from the original crisis in 2011, and after lengthy negotiations, Jordan's new terminal was finally commissioned in May 2015 and the country imported 1.9 mtpa in 2015. Egypt's supply cuts have also affected Israel to a lesser extent, though Israel has been able to count on its growing gas production from the Tamar field. The LNG supply deal won by BP with Israel Electric Corporation (IEC) was said to involve delivery of two cargoes per month from December 2012 until May 2013, but in practice Israel still received LNG (0.12 mtpa) in 2015.[75] The Public Utilities Authority has approved the continued use by IEC of the FSRU to import LNG until 2019.[76]

Pakistan is also experiencing gas shortages (Gomes, 2013). It has been trying for a long time to get pipeline supplies from either Iran or Turkmenistan, with no success so far. Pakistan began considering LNG in 2007.[77] GDF Suez won a tender to build a 3.5 mtpa FSRU in 2010, but the Court of Justice cancelled the tender. Consequently, it took another five years to commission the FSRU. Pakistan started importing LNG through tenders (1.1 mtpa in 2015), but negotiated a 15-year supply contract with Qatar. The price was reported to be initially based on a slope of 13.9 per cent, but Qatar agreed to lower it to 13.7 per cent following tenders won by Gunvor in late 2015.

---

[74] 'Egypt revisits FSRU import plan', ICIS, 24 October 2013. www.icis.com/resources/news/2013/10/24/9718630/egypt-revisits-fsru-import-plan/.

[75] 'BP wins Tender to Supply Israel with LNG', *Haaretz*, 25 July, 2012. www.haaretz.com/business/bp-wins-tender-to-supply-israel-with-lng-1.453454 and GIIGNL (2014).

[76] 'IEC extends LNG floating tanker contract', Hedy Cohen, Globes, 3 November 2015. www.globes.co.il/en/article-iec-extends-lng-ship-contract-1001078472.

[77] 'ESIA of LNG Terminal, Jetty & Extraction Facility – Pakistan Gasport Limited', Environmental and Social Impact Assessment Report prepared by Environmental Management Consultants (EMC). https://www3.opic.gov/environment/eia/pakistangasport/Chapter per cent201-Introduction.pdf

Table 2.2: Why small importers turned to LNG

Country	Capacity (mtpa)	Online date	Supplier(s)	Issues faced
Colombia	2.6	late 2016	Under negotiation	Expected gas shortages; droughts due to El Niño
Egypt	3.5	2015	Gazprom, Vitol, Noble, Sonatrach, Trafigura, BP	Demand outstripping domestic production
Israel	3.5	2013	BP (portfolio)	Shortage due to Egypt stopping pipeline supplies
Jordan	3.5	2015	Shell (portfolio) for 5 years	Shortage due to Egypt stopping pipeline supplies
Lithuania	3	2014	Statoil (portfolio) for 5 years	Dependence on Russia and the wish to diversify gas supplies
Philippines	3	2016	None	Drop in domestic gas supply
Uruguay	2.7	2017	Under negotiation	High dependence on hydro

Source: Author's research.

Lithuania's gas imports have not been cut, but it relies on Russia as its sole supplier, and relations have been tense. According to EC reports, Lithuania pays the highest wholesale gas prices in Europe.[78] The country has been keen to reduce this dependence on its neighbour and named its FSRU, commissioned in October 2014, Independence. One objective – getting more affordable gas – was reached, as Gazprom cut prices by 20 per cent to keep its market share. Ironically, with the drop in oil prices, Russian gas is no longer so expensive, while Lithuania is committed to paying LNG operational costs – $189,000 per day for the FSRU and jetty lease over 10 years. In early 2016, the contract with Statoil was renegotiated. The price was lowered, while the contract has been extended from five to 10 years, and total contracted volumes increased from 2.7 bcm to 3.7 bcm. However, annual contracted volumes will drop.[79]

Four other small importers expect LNG supplies to start in 2016–18, as this book goes to press. Uruguay is the smallest gas market among all the countries considered – around 0.1 bcm. It receives its gas from Argentina

---

[78] Market analysis, Gas and electricity market reports, European Commission. https://ec.europa.eu/energy/en/statistics/market-analysis.

[79] 'Lithuania negotiates LNG price cut with Statoil', *LNG World News*, 25 January, 2016. www.lngworldnews.com/lithuania-negotiates-lng-price-cut-with-statoil/.

by pipeline. Following the crisis in Argentina in 2001, exports to Uruguay never took off, though they were not fully disrupted. Uruguay is largely dependent on hydro and is keen to diversify to improve the security of its power supplies. Mitsui OSK Lines will build, own, and operate an FSRU, expected to be operational mid-2017 (Chapter 6).

The story is different in Colombia, which is a natural gas producer (unlike Uruguay) and does not import gas. In fact Colombia exports gas to Venezuela through a pipeline that was supposed to be reversed in 2012, but was not, due to continued gas shortages in Venezuela. Colombia will need to import LNG to offset its own gas shortages. In addition, the country is subject to droughts as a result of El Niño (every three to five years), that require additional gas supplies for gas-fired power plants. The FSRU Höegh Challenger has been chartered for 20 years by Sociedad Portuaria El Cayao (SPEC) and will be moored off Cartagena, on the Atlantic coast of Colombia, which will enable Colombia to take advantage of the proximity of US LNG exports.[80] It is expected to start by mid-2017–8 (Chapter 6). However, no supply deal had been signed as of early 2016.

A relative newcomer in the LNG import scene is Ghana. In early 2016, Ghana National Petroleum Corporation (GNPC) and Quantum Power signed heads of terms to build for the 3.4 mtpa Tema FSRU. The Tema LNG project will be implemented on a build–own–operate–transfer basis with the assets transferring to GNPC after 20 years. LNG imports are due to start in early 2017.

Finally, the Philippines has been experiencing severe gas and power shortages. With a population of 100 million, the country has only 20 GW of power capacity. The Philippines' one gas field, Malampaya, is expected to be depleted in a decade and accounts for 34 per cent of the 55 TWh generated in Luzon, the main island. The Australian company Energy World Corporation (EWC) is constructing a regasification plant that is expected on stream by 2016, even though supply has yet to be contracted. This will be the only LNG facility in this group of countries that is not an FSRU. A key challenge for LNG is that coal-fired power is still much cheaper than LNG-based power generation and already accounts for almost half of the Philippines' total power generation.[81]

---

[80] 'Hoegh LNG strikes Colombia FSRU deal', *LNG World News*, 3 November 2014. www.lngworldnews.com/hoegh-lng-strikes-colombia-fsru-deal/.

[81] 'Supply shortages lead to rolling power outages in the Philippines', Today in Energy, EIA, 6 March 2015. www.eia.gov/todayinenergy/detail.cfm?id=20252.

Table 2.3: FSRUs as of January 2016

Project	Country	Start-up	FSRU Contractor
Gulf Gateway	US	2005	Excelerate Energy
Teesside	UK	2007	Excelerate Energy
Bahia Blanca	Argentina	2008	Excelerate Energy
North East Gateway	US	2008	Excelerate Energy
Pecem	Brazil	2008	Golar LNG
Guanabara Bay	Brazil	2009	Excelerate Energy
Mina Al-Ahmadi	Kuwait	2009	Golar LNG
Dubai Supply Authority	UAE	2010	Excelerate Energy
Neptune	US	2010	Höegh LNG
GNL Escobar	Argentina	2011	Excelerate Energy
Livorno OLT	Italy	2011	Owned by OLT
Hadera	Israel	2012	Excelerate Energy
West Java	Indonesia	2012	Golar LNG
All Saints Bay	Brazil	2013	Golar LNG
Tianjin	China	2013	Höegh LNG
PGN Lampung	Indonesia	2014	Höegh LNG
Klaipedos Nafta	Lithuania	2014	Höegh LNG
EGAS – Ain Sokhna	Egypt	2015	Höegh LNG
Engro – Port Qasim	Pakistan	2015	Excelerate Energy
Aqaba LNG Terminal	Jordan	2015	Golar LNG
EGAS – Ain Sokhna	Egypt	2015	BW Group

Source: Author's research.

Conclusion

During the period 2000–15, the LNG industry has grown from infancy into adulthood, with a large variety of suppliers and markets spread over the world. The industry has expanded from a relatively restricted and cosy club dominated by Japanese, Korean, and Taiwanese players along with NOCs and IOCs, to encompass a wider diversity of players and regions. LNG has become global as all the regions export LNG (as of end 2015), and all areas of the world (but the Former Soviet Union) import it. The Middle East region has become the centre of LNG exports, with Qatar representing around 32 per cent of global LNG exports in 2015. Despite many attempts at diversification away from Japan, Korea, and Taiwan, LNG has remained stubbornly attracted to Asia, now extending to China,

India, and south-east Asian countries. The post 2015 picture may again be different as LNG oversupply realigns European and Asian prices.

Overall, the LNG industry has coped relatively well with supply and demand shocks using one of its key assets: flexibility. Despite many successes, there have been some false starts – the U-turn in the USA will probably go down in LNG history as one of the all-time worst assessments of future LNG demand. This may prove that big markets are not always the most reliable. Small markets facing acute import needs can also be attractive, even though they require a different mindset in terms of infrastructure size and procurement.

The size of LNG assets has also undergone transition. After 2000, the trend was towards larger capacity in all elements in the LNG value chain, from liquefaction plants to ships and regasification plants, culminating with Qatar's mega-trains in 2009–11. Since then, the industry has come to see the advantages of mid-size projects (2–3 mtpa) such as FSRUs, which have become quite popular in the non-OECD region to support small LNG importers. Meanwhile, the first floating liquefaction (FLNG) unit will start operating in Malaysia in 2016.

Gas markets are globalizing, but a truly global price has not emerged from these improved linkages between regions. LNG is often described as the glue between regional gas markets, but true price convergence has yet to occur. Gas markets have certainly become more connected: the Fukushima nuclear plant disaster illustrated how events in Japan can directly impact countries from Europe to Latin America. Nonetheless, in April 2012 the ratio between US and Japanese prices hit a record high of eight, clearly a failed price convergence. During 2007/8, regional prices in North America, Europe, and Japan moved in concert, which seemed to reflect coming gas price globalization, but this fell apart in 2009 when US spot gas prices started to reflect North America's increasing self sufficiency instead. Japanese prices remained linked to oil prices while European prices hovered somewhere between, reflecting a mix of regional supply/demand balance and oil indexation. Since late-2014 there seems again to be some price convergence between Asian and European spot prices, largely driven by LNG oversupply.

The nature of LNG trade has also changed considerably over the period 2000–15. The traditional point-to-point business started to fade away as aggregators appeared, buying the total output of LNG plants and marketing it themselves via multiple LNG import terminals in different regions. While still based on long-term contracts, LNG has been increasingly sold under FOB offtake commitments, giving traders the possibility to arbitrage between different consuming markets. Spot and short-term[82] trading have

---

[82] Short-term LNG trade is defined as LNG contracts with a duration below 4 years.

become key features of the LNG industry, reaching 28 per cent of LNG trade in 2015 (GIIGNL, 2015). The rise of Qatar, strategically positioned to supply both the Pacific and the Atlantic basin, has provided the main boost for short-term and spot trading.

Finally, the period 2009–15 saw a significant number of FIDs being taken. These will support the new and unprecedented wave of LNG supply which started reaching the markets in 2014, with the PNG plant. Despite a limited growth of LNG supply in 2015 (+6 mtpa) global LNG markets already reflect an oversupply situation, as spot prices in Asia and Europe have declined significantly. The mature markets in Japan and Korea, as well as those in China and India – once the drivers for LNG demand growth – have stalled while new LNG markets emerge in the Middle East, Africa, and other parts of Asia. The LNG industry still seems to have set itself in a boom-and-bust situation. The outlook for supply and demand, which are analysed in Chapters 5 and 6, respectively, are crucial for the understanding of how the situation will unfold for global LNG and gas markets.

BIBLIOGRAPHY

Chen, M. (2014). 'The Development of Chinese Gas Pricing: Drivers, Challenges and Implications for Demand', OIES Working Paper NG89, Oxford Institute for Energy Studies.

Corbeau, A.-S. (2010). 'Natural gas in India', International Energy Working Paper, Paris: OECD/IEA.

Cornot-Gandolphe, S. and Dickel, R. (2004). *Security of Gas Supply in Open Markets – LNG and Power at a Turning Point*, Paris: OECD/International Energy Agency.

Dargin, J. and Flower, A. (2011). 'The UAE Gas Sector', Chapter 13 in Fattouh, B. and Stern, J.P. (eds.), *Natural Gas Markets in the Middle East and North Africa*, Oxford: OUP/OIES.

EIA (2005). *Annual Energy Outlook 2005 with Projections to 2025*, US Energy Information Administration, DOE/EIA-0383(2005).

EIA (2011). *Annual Energy Outlook 2011 with Projections to 2035*, US Energy Information Administration, DOE/EIA-0383(2011), April 2011.

EIA (2014). *Annual Energy Outlook*, Washington D.C.: EIA.

GIIGNL (2008). *The LNG Industry in 2008*, International Group of Liquefied Natural Gas Importers. (GIIGNL Annual Report)

GIIGNL (2015). *The LNG Industry in 2015*, International Group of Liquefied Natural Gas Importers. (GIIGNL Annual Report)

Gomes, I. (2013). 'Natural gas in Pakistan and Bangladesh: current issues and trends', OIES Working Paper NG77, Oxford Institute for Energy Studies.

IEA (2002). *World Energy Outlook 2002*, Paris: OECD/International Energy Agency.

IEA (2007). *Natural Gas Market Review 2007*, Paris: OECD/International Energy Agency.

IEA (2008). *Natural Gas Market Review 2008*, Paris: OECD/International Energy Agency.

IEA (2011). *Medium-Term Oil & Gas Markets 2011*, Paris: OECD/International Energy Agency.

IEA (2012). *Medium-Term Gas Market Report 2012, Market Trends and Projections to 2017*, Paris: OECD/International Energy Agency.

IEA (2015a). *World Energy Outlook 2015*, Paris: OECD/International Energy Agency, November.

IEA (2015b). *Natural gas information 2015*, Paris: OECD/IEA.

Sakmar, S. L. (2013). *Energy for the 21st Century, opportunities and challenges for Liquefied Natural Gas (LNG)*, Cheltenham: Edward Elgar.

Yanagisawa, A. (2015). *LNG became Japan's largest import item*, The Institute of Energy Economics, Japan. http://eneken.ieej.or.jp/data/6070.pdf.

CHAPTER 3

THE CHANGING COMMERCIAL STRUCTURE OF THE UPSTREAM AND MIDSTREAM LNG BUSINESS

David Ledesma

Introduction

The LNG project chain is made up of various elements, each with different risk factors and drivers that, though separate, need to work together to ensure smooth delivery of gas from the wellhead (where the gas comes out of the ground) to the end buyer (where the gas is consumed). Commercial structures have been developed over time that bind these different elements of the chain together and establish a fair allocation of risk between the upstream, midstream, and downstream.[1]

Since the first commercial delivery of LNG was made in 1964, the chain has seemingly become increasingly diversified and 'disaggregated' (dividing up into its component parts). That said, LNG projects still require structures that have clear revenue and liability flows to enable third-party lenders and shareholders to lend money to develop new projects. The question, in relation to these revenue flows, of who bears the risks and receives the rewards has been based on three principal models: the integrated project structure, the transfer pricing project structure, and the tolling or throughput structure. This chapter will explain these structures, why they have changed over time, the risks and rewards affecting the different players and, as the LNG industry may be reaching a crossroads, give an opinion as to the key project drivers and what future project structures could look like.

---

[1] The LNG value chain is usually divided into different stages:
Upstream: The exploration for gas and, when found, the production of gas.
Midstream: The liquefaction process where gas is cooled to −161 °C (at which point it turns into a liquid) and the shipping of the LNG in specialized tankers.
Downstream: The regasification of the LNG where the LNG is converted back to gas (through the addition of heat) and the downstream market.

Overview of the LNG value chain

The LNG chain consists of four interlinked activities that connect upstream gas production to the end gas user:

i) development of the upstream gas supply system;
ii) design and construction of the liquefaction plant;
iii) building and operation of the shipping;
iv) construction of the regasification facilities.

The LNG chain can be looked at as a pipeline. If one part fails to perform, it could mean that other parts have to cease operations as well. That said, as we see a rise in trading of LNG – which has the effect of increasing flexibility in different parts of the chain – problems in one part of the chain are becoming less of an issue for other elements in it. In the case of LNG supply disruptions, replacement cargoes are becoming more readily available, so where one part of the LNG value chain fails, alternative LNG supply, or markets, can be secured. Excluding the upstream and end-user market parts of the chain, the liquefaction portion represents the largest investment (See Figure 3.1), with the cost of shipping being dependent on the number of ships required to move the LNG to market – the further that the liquefaction plant is from the market, if LNG supply is made direct, the more ships are required.[2]

Different elements of the value chain

This section will examine the different parts of the LNG value chain; see the Technical Appendix for a technical overview.

Upstream
LNG projects usually require in excess of 10 tcf (270 bcm) gas that can be produced at a stable level for at least 20 years.[3] The upstream facilities must be delivered on time to supply gas to the liquefaction plant, because if there is no gas there will be no LNG, and therefore no revenues. This gas must also be of a consistent quality, as the liquefaction plant will be designed around a particular gas specification. If the gas contains natural gas liquids (propane, butane, and higher fractions[4]) then these will provide additional

---

[2] Each ship of 170–180,000 m^3 size costs approximately $220–250 million, depending on design.
[3] For an 8 mtpa LNG plant.
[4] C5 and higher.

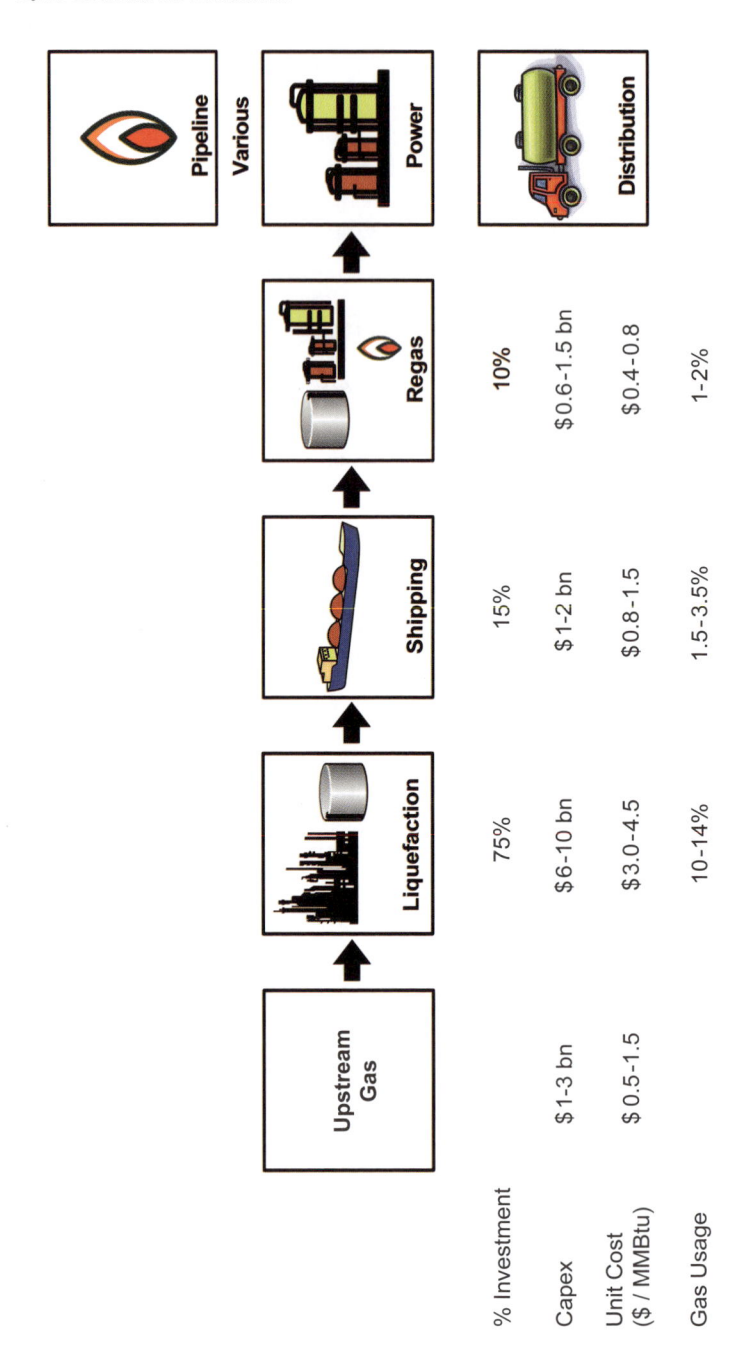

	Upstream Gas	Liquefaction	Shipping	Regas	
% Investment		75%	15%	10%	
Capex	$1-3 bn	$6-10 bn	$1-2 bn	$0.6-1.5 bn	
Unit Cost ($ / MMBtu)	$0.5-1.5	$3.0-4.5	$0.8-1.5	$0.4-0.8	
Gas Usage		10-14%	1.5-3.5%	1-2%	

Downstream: Pipeline / Various / Power / Distribution

Figure 3.1: LNG value chain – gas use, capital cost, and unit costs (based on an 8 mtpa plant)

Source: Author's research and assumptions, based on an 8 mtpa plant.

revenue for the development of the project. Often this 'liquids credit' is kept by the upstream (in some cases the liquids revenue can pay for the upstream development, as it did for Oman LNG and the initial RasGas project in Qatar). However, if the gas contains impurities (such as hydrogen sulphide and mercury) then this can result in additional costs, as they will have to be removed before liquefaction. Gas reserves were traditionally dedicated to a specific LNG project; this was normally a requirement of buyers and financiers, to ensure that sufficient gas was available to cover the long-term sales agreements. The size of gas reserves was also assessed by independent expert advisers as part of the buyer and lender due diligence process. In some of the later project structures, buyers have relied on purchasing from a company rather than a project, so the need for dedicated gas reserves has been less relevant. Reserves are not an issue in the case of the more recent US projects, due to the size of the US gas resource base and the readily available gas supply direct from the market. Gas is usually sourced from several fields (causing some gas quality and cost issues), but some countries, such as Qatar, have the benefit of producing gas from a single field with a common specification and set of facilities.

Liquefaction
This part of the chain normally includes all the plant facilities that take the feed gas from the gas supply source to the liquefaction plant. Title to (ownership of), and risks relating to, the gas normally pass at the inlet to the plant (although under an integrated project structure, title may not need to pass at this point as the shareholders of the upstream and midstream parts of the chain would be the same). The plant cools the gas to −161 °C, stores the LNG in cryogenic tanks, and loads the LNG onto ships in the port through specialist cryogenic loading facilities. The plant includes all the utilities, such as power and water, but in some projects (for example the US Freeport LNG project) the power is sourced from the grid or elsewhere. The plant has to be constructed and delivered on time to ensure no delay in start-up and flow of revenues from sales. Delays in construction, or to the start-up of the facilities, are a major risk to the sponsors and any third-party lenders. They will therefore try to pass that risk on to the engineering contractor through a fixed price 'turnkey' construction contract with clear performance guarantees.

Shipping
Whether the LNG is sold FOB[5] or DES,[6] the details of who will be

---
[5] FOB – Free on board. The LNG is sold to the buyer at the load port and title and risk passes at the flange at the load port. The LNG sales price does not included freight.
[6] Delivered Ex-Ship, or DES – LNG is sold to the buyer at the discharge port and title and risk passes at the flange at the discharge port. The LNG sales price includes freight.

arranging and operating the shipping (and, potentially, details of the particular ships to be used) will need to be determined to ensure that the LNG produced by the plant can be transported to market (though with the increase in volumes of short-term LNG, the definition of specific vessels against a supply contract is not as important as it used to be). The LNG buyer (in the case of an FOB LNG sale) or LNG seller (in the case of a DES LNG sale) will need to construct or charter vessels (see Chapter 4). The number of these vessels will depend on the volume of LNG, the size of the ships, and the distance from the supply point to the intended buyer. Table 3.1 shows the number of ships required to move 1 mtpa from different supply points to Japan. It can be seen that the number varies from 0.8 (for a 180,000 m³ vessel from Australia) to 2.2 for the number of 145,000 m³ vessels from the US Gulf (via the Panama Canal).

Table 3.1: Number of vessels required to move 1 mtpa LNG

		Vessel size	
Route	Distance (nm)	145,000 m³	180,000 m³
US Gulf to Japan	9,220	2.2	1.8
Middle East to Japan	6,530	1.6	1.3
Australia to Japan	3,850	1.0	0.8

Note: It is assumed that vessels travel at 19 knots, operational for 350 days p.a., it takes one day to load, and one day to discharge. It is assumed that the Panama Canal is used for US Gulf–Japan trade.

The contracting structure for the LNG vessels will depend on the type of sale and, often, on political factors. For example, it was a requirement of the LNG purchase agreement for the Guangdong LNG import terminal project from the Australian North West Shelf project that BP and Shell assist in helping the Chinese develop shipbuilding and operations skills (Ledesma et al., 2014). Likewise in 1994, KOGAS sought to buy FOB from both Oman LNG and RasGas as it wanted to construct the LNG vessels in order to develop its own LNG shipbuilding business.

Regasification and market
The performance of the buyer is a key element of the LNG chain, as the revenue from sales forms the main security for income flows into the project to service third-party or corporate debt and operational costs. Shareholders and lenders will focus considerable attention on the buyers of the LNG, their market, their import facilities and other gas infrastructure, and

whether they can perform the contract and pay the required revenues. If new import facilities are being built, the seller will want to know what guarantees are in place in case the building of the facilities is delayed – meaning that the LNG cannot be received at the start-up of the supply contract. Or alternatively whether there is another market into which the LNG could be sold. Given the high costs of the LNG chain, it is important for the shareholders to ensure that performance liabilities are clearly set out in the project's structure and the project agreements.

Changing ownership structures in the chain
The 'traditional' model
Traditionally, the roles of the LNG seller and buyer were quite distinct. The seller developed the gas supply, owned and operated the liquefaction plant, marketed the LNG, and sold it to the LNG buyer (taking the price risk), and often controlling the ships to deliver the LNG. The buyer contracted for the LNG on a take-or-pay[7] basis (taking the volume offtake risk), owned and operated the receiving terminal, and developed the gas market in the buying country. This traditional structure had real advantages – the buyers and sellers each had clear roles, gas and LNG supplies were 'dedicated' to the buyer. This direct link between gas in the ground, liquefaction, shipping, and delivery to the regasification terminal, gave security of supply for the buyer and security of demand for the seller. Under this model, a consortium company developed the reserves, constructed the plant, and usually sold the LNG (Malaysia LNG and Brunei LNG are examples of this type of company). However, with multiple shareholders, projects took time to develop and could be delayed, as a consortium can only move as fast as the slowest partner. Also, the sellers of the LNG were the consortium company, not the individual shareholders; if there was a supply disruption then the buyers could not look to the individual shareholders to make up any cargo shortfall, as their contract was with the joint-venture LNG sales company.

Changes to the 'traditional' model
The late 1990s and early 2000s saw the traditional model beginning to change, with sellers (LNG producers such as Shell and Total) starting to

---

[7] Take-or-Pay (TOP) is a common provision in gas contracts under which, if the buyer's annual purchased volume is less than the Annual Contract Quantity minus any shortfall in the seller's deliveries, minus any Downward Quantity Tolerance, then the Buyer pays for such a shortfall as if the gas had been received. The buyer may have the right in subsequent years to take the gas paid for but not received, either free or for an amount reflecting changes in indexed prices (called Make-Up Gas). TOP commitments are a critical element supporting the financing of LNG projects as they provide a guaranteed cash flow to the LNG project.

move downstream into the markets. These companies developed the Hazira LNG regasification terminal that started operations in India in 2005 (Shell 74 per cent, Total 26 per cent) (Petroleum Economist, 2013). Likewise, BG and Petronas developed the Dragon regasification terminal in the UK (BG 50 per cent, Petronas 50 per cent) that started operations in 2009, while Qatar Petroleum (67.5 per cent), ExxonMobil (24.15 per cent), and Total (8.35 per cent) invested in the South Hook Terminal in the UK that started receiving cargoes from Qatargas in 2009/10. This vertical integration move into regasification terminals enabled LNG sellers, and selling companies, to have direct access to end-users of gas rather than through an intermediary.

Likewise buyers have moved upstream to secure positions in the gas fields, production facilities, and liquefaction plant (see Chapters 1 and 2). This move was driven by the wish of buyers to diversify their portfolios and secure economic returns that could be counter cyclical to their normal business. It also gives buyers a 'seat at the table' in the production and liquefaction processes so they could gain experience, with the aim of eventually developing their own projects. In the author's opinion, the experience gained by Japan's Mitsubishi, as a partner in the Brunei, Malaysia, and Oman projects, was critical in developing its own Indonesian Donggi-Senoro project in 2013–15 that exported its first cargo in August 2015.[8] During the buyers' market of the mid-1990s and mid-2000s, buyers saw equity in the upstream or midstream as a prerequisite for signing long-term LNG offtake contracts. Examples of buyers moving upstream are numerous and include (Flower, 2004):

- Korean Consortium (including KOGAS): 5 per cent in RasGas I and 5 per cent in Oman LNG. Korea Gas: 6 per cent in Yemen LNG.
- Tokyo Electric/Tokyo Gas: 9.2 per cent in Darwin LNG, Australia (jointly).
- CNOOC: 13.9 per cent in Tangguh (Indonesia) project and 5 per cent in Australia's NWS reserves.
- Union Fenosa Gas (7.68 per cent), Osaka Gas (3 per cent): Qalhat LNG (Oman). Union Fenosa Gas: 80 per cent in Segas/Damietta LNG (Egypt).
- Sinopec: 25 per cent share in Australia Pacific LNG (APLNG).

---

[8] 'First Shipment of LNG from Donggi-Senoro Project in Indonesia', Mitsubishi press release, 2 August 2015. www.mitsubishicorp.com/jp/en/pr/archive/2015/html/0000028212.html.

- KOGAS (10 per cent), CPC (5 per cent) in the Prelude floating liquefaction unit.
- Tokyo Gas, Toho Gas, Osaka Gas, and Chubu Electric are partners in the Australian Inpex sponsored Ichthys project

Factors that determine project structure

The structure of a project reflects the roles and responsibilities of the different stakeholders along the whole LNG value chain. There is a range of factors that determine the final structure of an LNG project, some of these are listed here.

Shareholder requirements and interests of the host government or state company
The structure must set out a clear alignment of shareholder interests along the whole LNG chain and clearly define the flow through of liabilities along the chain, such that the party who takes the risk is the best party to control it. There must be equitable sharing of risk and rent along the chain over time, reflecting the roles of each of the shareholders in the chain. This flow of risk and liabilities will be set out in key commercial agreements, which need to be drafted in parallel.

Project shareholders may seek to develop a structure that meets their own internal strategic requirements. This could include how the LNG will be marketed – by a joint venture company or by the companies themselves. Where shareholders seek to market the LNG and the government (which may lack LNG expertise) has a shareholding, this raises the question of how the government can effectively market its share. Often the government will be keen to develop skills within the country and therefore will be keen to establish its own LNG marketing organization. This was the case for Malaysia in 1983 when MLNG Satu, the country's first export project, started production. The Malaysian government, through the State Energy company Petronas, was keen for the LNG to be marketed through a Malaysian joint venture company, staffed initially by a mixture of Malaysian and expatriate secondees from the shareholders. The clearly defined policy of 'Malaysianization' increased the skills of Malaysians in the energy sector.[9]

Fiscal terms
There may be a specific domestic and export fiscal regime that leads in the direction of a particular project structure. Large capital investment requirements mean that LNG project developers will look to the government

---

[9] 'Malaysia Goes Deeper And Further Afield', *Oil & Gas Financial Journal*, 20 July 2010. www.ogfj.com/articles/print/volume-7/issue-7/special-report/malaysia-goes_deeper.html.

to provide fiscal incentives. These may be in the form of lower tax rates, tax holidays, accelerated depreciation, or even immunity from certain taxes. It has been reported that the $27 bn Yamal LNG project pays zero mineral extraction tax and export duty from the fields, and also enjoys tax holidays[10] (see Chapter 5). Also, the development of LNG export projects from western Canada has shown the importance of fiscal support. In October 2014, in response to requests from project developers, the British Columbian Government introduced a two-tier 'LNG tax'. The tier-one tax rate is 1.5 per cent and the tier-two rate is 3.5 per cent (it was originally set at 7 per cent, but was reduced after project developers lobbied for lower levels) (Gomes, 2015).

The role of the buyer
This raises several questions that need to be addressed by the original shareholders – in particular whether the buyers want to take equity in the liquefaction plant and the upstream and, if they do, whether the original shareholders will want their involvement. The shareholders' decision is often determined by the importance of individual buyers and whether they are able to arrange access to low-cost financing.[11] This leads to questions such as: which project structure will enable the buyer to be involved in development of the project; will buyers will pay an 'entry fee' to join a project later in its development; will buyers see the signing of a long-term offtake agreement as their entry fee?

Construction contracting strategy
This can also have an impact on project structure. If there is a need for a project to access a specific source of finance, then this may result in the inclusion of a specific shareholder in the project structure. Where a project is seeking to secure Export Credit Agency (ECA)[12] support, it may need to include companies from that country in the project structure, to agree to sell LNG to the country, or to award engineering contracts to companies within it.

Financing requirements
The source of finance is the critical element in developing a project. It could drive the project structure, and shareholders will ask some

---

[10] 'Russia's Putin offers more tax incentives for Yamal LNG', Reuters, 21 October 2013. www.reuters.com/article/2013/10/21/russia-gas-tax-idUSL5N0IB0DJ20131021.

[11] Often projects are keen to secure Japanese and Korean buyers in order to attract lower-cost finance from Japanese or Korean Exim banks.

[12] Export Credit Agencies are government-funded bodies which advance funds and provide risk cover, in return for selling their country's goods and services (e.g. USA Exim, Japan Exim, Italy SACE).

fundamental questions: how is the project being financed; if third-party finance is being used, can all the shareholders pay their equity share; what project structure will facilitate the easiest way to raise finance? These questions will be discussed further in the section 'Financing' on page 116.

The importance of sound project structuring

LNG projects are capital intensive and this has led to projects being developed as long-term investments underpinned by long-term contracts, which normally last for 20–25 years. Even US LNG projects launched in the 2010s are still underpinned by long-term offtake commitments. All structures are designed for a specific project but, although each offtake or capacity is slightly different, they can be grouped into three different types: integrated, transfer pricing, and tolling structures. In each case, the structure has been specifically designed and adapted to meet the specific requirements of the project stakeholders.[13] The structure must ensure that the gas flows from the wellhead to the end buyer, and that the income flows back from the LNG buyer to the different parts of the chain in a manner that gives an equitable sharing of the project revenues between the different parts of the chain. Any weak link in the chain that can cause the non-supply of LNG, or non-payment for the LNG, could result in the project not being developed, or stopping once in operation (as happened, for example when Egypt's two LNG projects ceased LNG production in 2012 and 2014, due to shortage of feed gas). Shipping can be structured to be FOB, DES, or CIF, with the vessels owned by the project, the shareholders, or third-party companies. The function of LNG sales and LNG shipping are so inextricably linked that they should really be considered as a single component (Kay and Roberts, 2012).

Integrated project structure

The integrated project structure has common ownership and shareholding in the upstream and liquefaction parts of the chain. This means that there is equal sharing of economic rent in both parts of the chain, so there is no need to have a transfer price between the upstream and liquefaction stages, thereby avoiding contentious negotiations to agree a gas Into Plant Price. (That said, there might be a need for different pricing structures to apply to the upstream and midstream segments of the chain for fiscal purposes.)

---

[13] Project stakeholders can include the governments of buying and selling countries, the buying and selling companies themselves, as well as the LNG export project shareholders.

106　*LNG Markets in Transition*

Figure 3.2 shows the integrated structure for Qatargas 2.

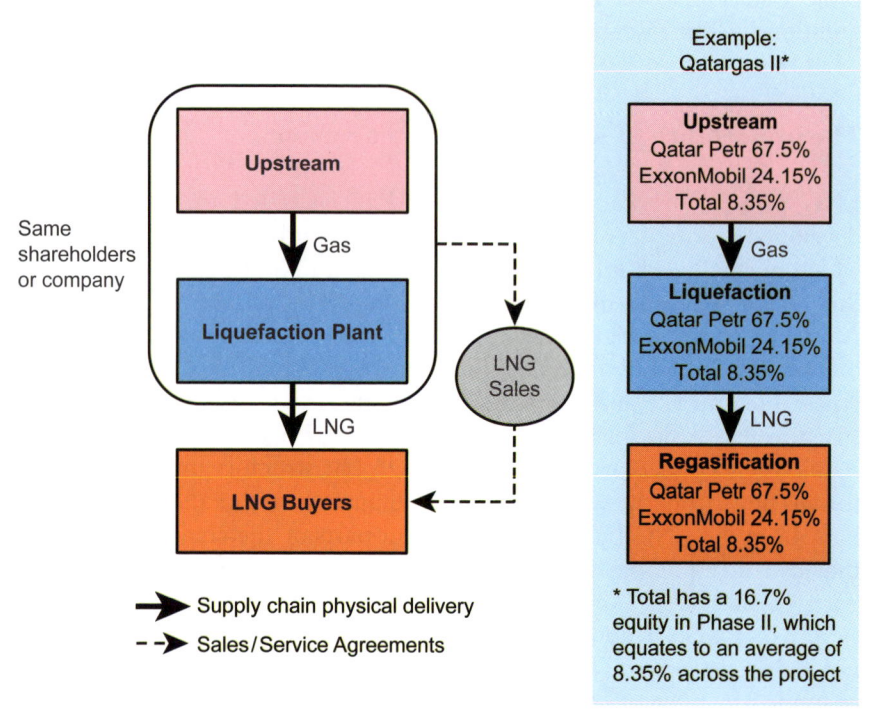

Figure 3.2: Integrated project structure
Source: Author research.

The upstream and liquefaction parts of the chain can, therefore, be developed by the same company, which can often lead to efficiencies in timing and to the employment of common contractors. This structure can increase the size of the project, and it often means that only large international oil and gas companies, or national oil and gas companies, can develop projects using this structure. It can also make expansion difficult since, if new reserves are held by third parties (not involved in the original project), they would have to negotiate their way into the existing project, and this may be opposed by the original shareholders. Under this structure the LNG can be sold by the joint venture company (made up of the common shareholders in a scheme such as: Indonesia's Tangguh LNG project, Angola LNG Project, or Australia's Gorgon Project) where each shareholder is selling its own equity LNG.

Transfer pricing project structure

Under the transfer pricing structure, the shareholders in the upstream and liquefaction plant parts of the chain are different. (Figure 3.3 shows the transfer pricing structure for Qatargas 1.) The plant feed gas would therefore need to be sold by the upstream producers to the liquefaction plant company, usually a joint venture company, with transfer price agreed, as set out in a GSA (Gas Supply Agreement, also known as a Gas Sales Agreement). The liquefaction plant company then sells to the LNG buyers. The transfer price agreed between the upstream and the liquefaction plant owners is the key factor in determining the rates of return in the upstream and the plant, and therefore can take considerable time to agree. By breaking up these two capital intensive parts of the chain, smaller companies and governments with tight budgets are enabled to operate in

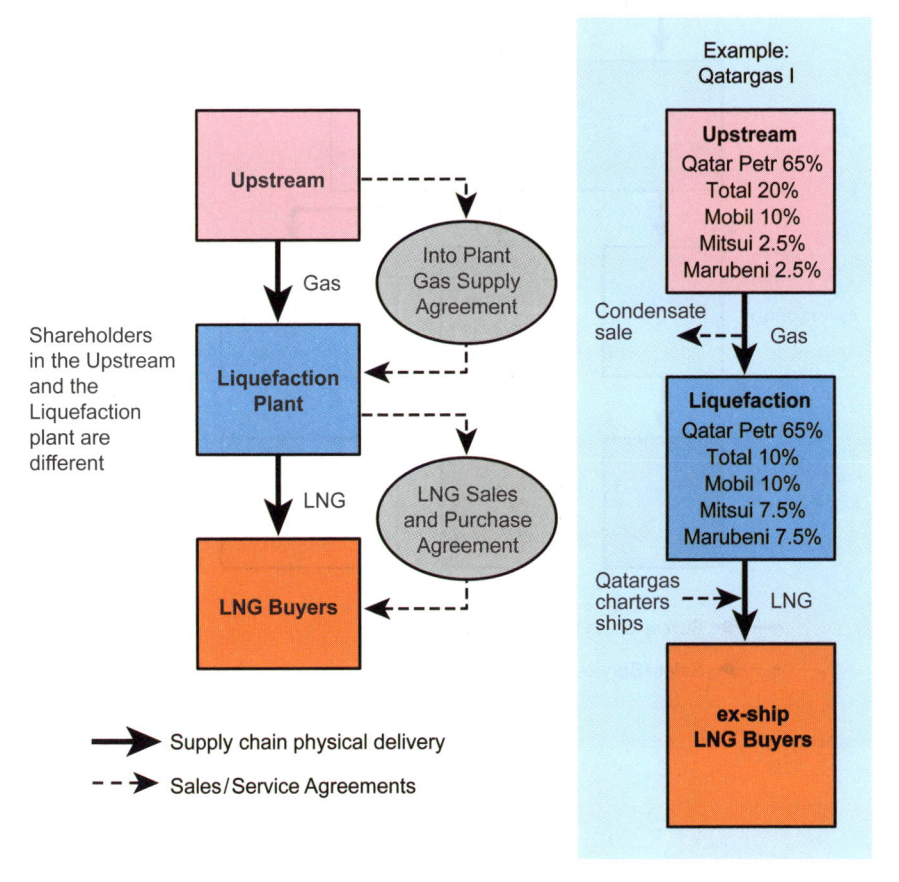

Figure 3.3: Transfer pricing project structure
Source: Author's research.

the different parts with a smaller shareholding. This structure also allows additional partners to be brought into the project, and it is often used when the upstream, or gas supply, is solely owned by the government – such as in Oman or Yemen LNG – where the liquefaction company purchases the gas from the government. Having different shareholdings in various parts of the chain can cause some contention and potential conflicts of interest, as a range of economic rents is earned in separate parts of the chain.

Tolling or throughput structure

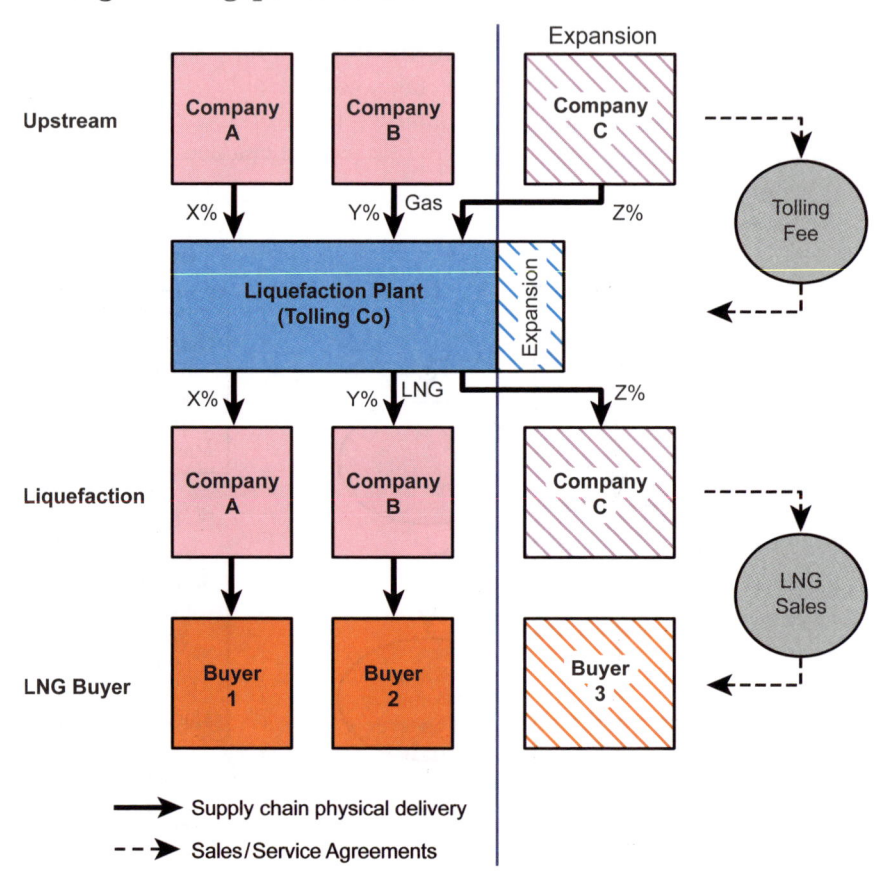

Figure 3.4: Tolling project structure
Source: Author's research.

Under this structure the upstream producers pay the liquefaction plant owners (who may not be involved in the upstream or marketing activities) a tolling fee to use the plant to liquefy their gas, and then sell the LNG to the buyers. This structure is gaining in popularity for two reasons: firstly it enables companies to secure 'branded LNG' (LNG is sold in the name of the upstream companies rather than the joint venture company), secondly, it makes it easier for the project to be expanded if new gas is found. Figure 3.4 sets out an example of a project structure, with 'Companies A & B' being the initial companies that toll their gas through the liquefaction plant, and subsequently receive LNG in the same proportions as they put the gas into the plant. Then, at a later date, 'Company C' negotiates to toll its gas through the same facility, which is expanded by 'Tolling Co'. Egypt's ELNG and Segas projects, designed to allow for expansion at a future date, used this structure.

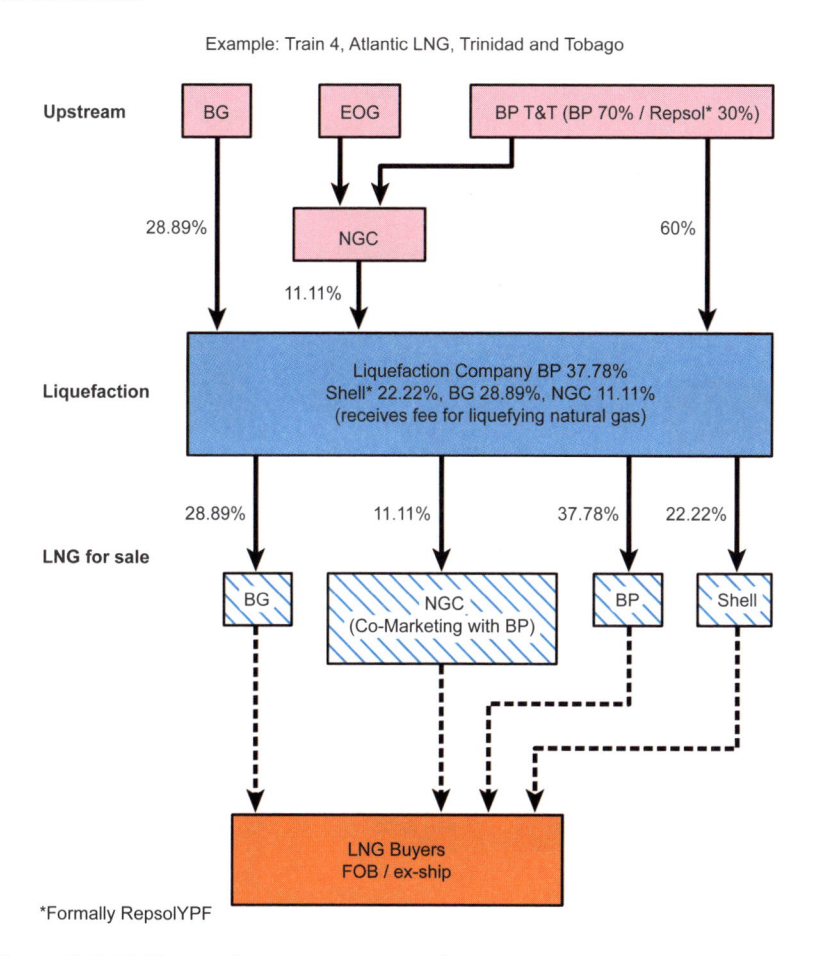

Figure 3.5: Tolling project structure example
Source: Author's research.

110   *LNG Markets in Transition*

The tolling structure was first used by two Indonesian LNG projects (Arun and Bontang) but, rather than the LNG being marketed by the upstream production sharing contractors (PSC), the state company Pertamina marketed the LNG and the PSC received its share of the LNG revenues after the costs of liquefaction and shipping had been deducted. This adaption of the tolling structure by Pertamina shows how LNG project developers can take the three basic structures (integrated, transfer pricing, and tolling), and adapt them for their own projects. Figure 3.5 shows the tolling structure for Trinidad's Atlantic LNG train 4.

In most cases, the business models adopted by floating liquefaction (FLNG) projects have been adapted from the business structure used by Floating Storage and Regasification Units (FSRU) and from the tolling model. Different models are being used; in one, the upstream partners, who control the resource, charter the FLNG facility (usually paying a $/day 'charter' rate) and are responsible for marketing the LNG. In another model (such as that used for the Australian Prelude project), the same parties

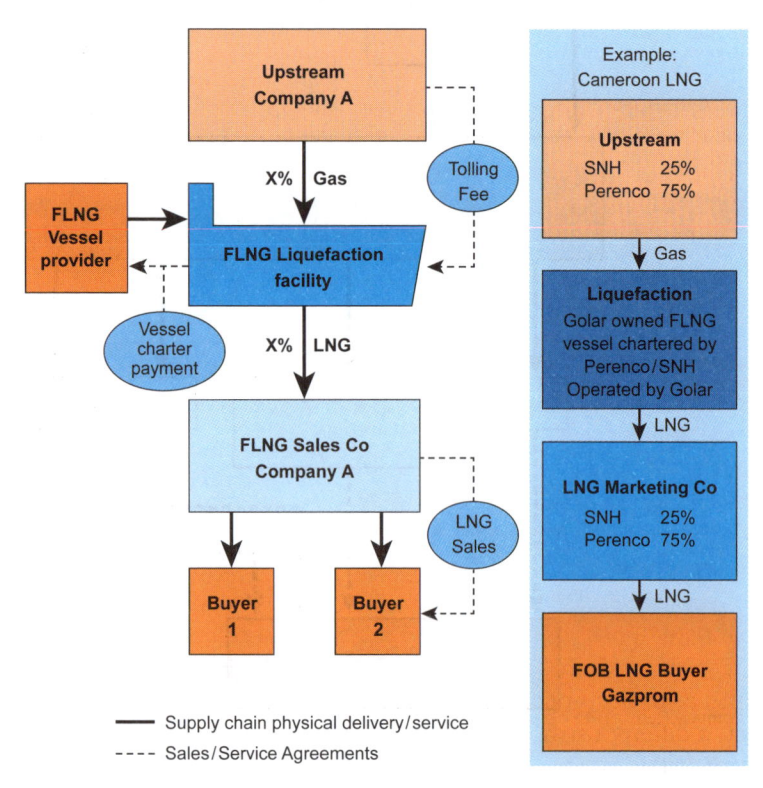

Figure 3.6: FLNG example project structure
Source: Author's research.

are in the upstream and the midstream, while the FLNG facility is an asset held under, and in accordance with, the general project joint operating agreement (JOA). This means that some of the smaller exploration companies, such as Ophir, which is developing the Fortuna FLNG project in Equatorial Guinea, will be taking on the role of marketing the LNG, and this is a new activity for the company. Taking on this role adds additional risk to the project, in addition to the technological risk that FLNG carries – in the eyes of the financiers. Ownership of the technology, together with the guarantees that it will operate effectively, could also add complications to the project structure. Figure 3.6 shows an example of an FLNG tolling structure, with an example of the Cameroon FLNG project, where Perenco/SNH charter an FLNG unit from Golar paying a day rate, tolling their gas through the 2.2 mtpa capacity facility, and marketing the LNG. The allocated reserves only support 1.2 mtpa LNG production, and this has been sold to Gazprom under an eight year LNG sales agreement.[14] The balance of the capacity should be utilized, and marketed separately, once additional reserves have been allocated to the project.

Evolution of project structures over time

Different structures have been used over time and Figure 3.7 and Table 3.2 set out the development of various project structures. Prior to 2000, the use of the different structures was fairly balanced, with the type used being determined by the international company that was sponsoring the project. For example, Shell tended to prefer the transfer pricing model, Sonatrach the integrated, and Pertamina/VICO the tolling structure. The period 2000–10 has seen an increase in integrated projects, (driven by Qatar and also by Australia), while the recent developments of US LNG export projects have all been based on tolling structures, some having been adapted by the developing company (see the section 'US LNG exports – adapting the LNG tolling structure', page 124).

There is a trend towards a single model being dominant in a country; a possible explanation for this could be that each company tends to prefer a specific project structure, and a single company has tended to have a dominant presence in a specific country. The company is familiar with that type of project, and if it has worked successfully in the past, it means that the company tends to prefer to use the same structure on future projects. This is not, however, always the case. In Indonesia and Trinidad, for example, as project sponsors changed the specific requirements of the new project, a different structure was required. In Trinidad, the first train was

---

[14] 'Gazprom to buy all LNG from Cameroon export plant – sources', Reuters, 26 November 2015.
www.reuters.com/article/gazprom-lng-cameroon-idUSL8N13L2BQ20151126.

112 *LNG Markets in Transition*

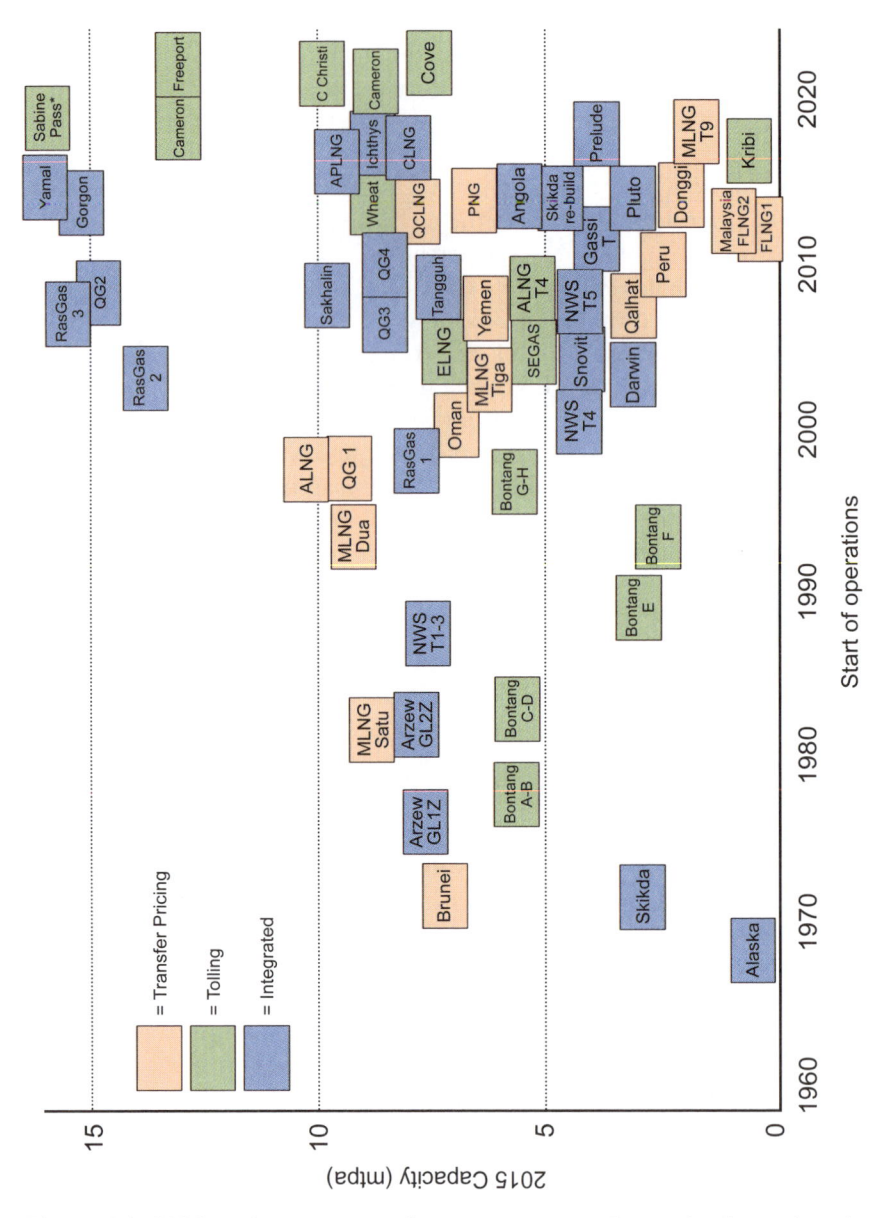

Figure 3.7: LNG project structures, by start-up year and capacity, for projects in operation and under construction

* Sabine Pass trains 1–3, classed as a tolling structure, Cheniere also sources the gas and delivers the LNG FOB to the tolling companies so it is an 'adapted tolling' model.

Source: GIIGNL (2014), IGU (2015), Petroleum Economist (2013), and author's research.

developed using the transfer pricing model, but trains 2 and 3 were based on a quasi transfer and tolling pricing structure (with BP and BG supplying gas to the two trains in different percentages), while the fourth train was on a tolling structure in order to include all of the shareholders in the liquefaction company.

Table 3.2: LNG project structures, by start-up year and capacity, for projects in operation and under construction

Country	LNG project	Status	Date first project	Capacity in 2015	Project structure
Abu Dhabi	ADGAS	Operational	1977	5.8	Transfer pricing
Algeria	Arzew GL1Z	Operational	1978	7.9	Integrated
	Arzew GL2Z	Operational	1981	8.2	Integrated
	Arzew (Gassi Touil)	Operational	2014	4.7	Integrated
	Skikda	Operational	1972	3.2	Integrated
	Skikda GL1K re-build	Operational	2013	4.5	Integrated
Angola	Angola LNG	Re-starting (June 2016)	2013	5.2	Integrated
Australia	North West Shelf T1–3 (NWS)	Operational	1989	7.5	Integrated
	North West Shelf T4	Operational	2004	4.4	Integrated
	North West Shelf T5	Operational	2008	4.3	Integrated
	Darwin	Operational	2006	3.4	Integrated
	Pluto	Operational	2012	4.3	Integrated
	Gorgon	In start-up (June 2016)	2015/16	15.6	Integrated
	Wheatstone	Under construction	2016/17	8.9	Tolling
	Ichthys	Under construction	2017/18	8.4	Integrated
	Prelude	Under construction	2017	3.6	Integrated
	Queensland Curtis (QCLNG)	Operational T1 Operational T2	2015/16	8.5	Transfer pricing

114 *LNG Markets in Transition*

Country	LNG project	Status	Date first project	Capacity in 2015	Project structure
	Gladstone (GLNG)	Operational	2015/16	7.8	Integrated, with gas purchase from third parties
	Australian Pacific (APLNG)	Operational	2015/16	9.0	Integrated
Brunei	Brunei	Operational	1972	7.2	Transfer pricing
Cameroon	Kribi FLNG	Under construction	2017	1.2	Tolling
Egypt	Damietta (Segas)	Operational/ temporarily suspended due to feedgas shortages	2005	5.0	Tolling
	Egypt LNG (Idku)	Operational/ temporarily suspended due to feedgas shortages	2005	7.2	Tolling
Equatorial Guinea	EG LNG	Operational	2007	3.7	Transfer pricing
Indonesia	Arun	Closed	1978	0.0	Tolling
	Bontang (Trains A–B)	Operational	1978	5.4	Tolling
	Bontang (Trains C–D)	Operational	1983	5.4	Tolling
	Bontang (Train E)	Operational	1990	2.9	Tolling
	Bontang (Train F)	Operational	1994	2.7	Tolling
	Bontang (Trains G–H)	Operational	1998	5.9	Tolling
	Tangguh	Operational	2009	7.6	Integrated
	Donggi-Senoro	Operational	2015/16	2.0	Transfer pricing

The Changing Commercial Structure   115

Country	LNG project	Status	Date first project	Capacity in 2015	Project structure
Malaysia	MLNG Satu	Operational	1983	8.1	Transfer pricing
	MLNG Dua	Operational	1995	9.3	Transfer pricing
	MLNG Tiga	Operational	2003	6.8	Transfer pricing
	MLNG Train 9	Under construction	2017	3.6	Transfer pricing
	FLNG 1 (Kanowit)	Under construction	2016	1.2	Believed to be transfer pricing
	FLNG 2 (Rotan)	Under construction	2016/17	1.5	Believed to be transfer pricing
Nigeria	Nigeria LNG	Operational	1999	21.9	Transfer pricing
Norway	Snøvhit	Operational	2007	4.3	Integrated
Oman	Oman LNG	Operational	2000	7.1	Transfer pricing
	Qalhat LNG	Operational	2006	3.6	Transfer pricing
Papua New Guinea	PNG LNG	Operational	2014	6.9	Transfer pricing
Peru	Peru LNG	Operational	2010	4.5	Transfer pricing
Qatar	Qatargas 1	Operational	1997	9.6	Transfer pricing
	Qatargas 2	Operational	2009	15.6	Integrated
	Qatargas 3	Operational	2010	7.8	Integrated
	Qatargas 4	Operational	2011	7.8	Integrated
	RasGas 1	Operational	1999	6.6	Integrated
	RasGas 2	Operational	2004	14.1	Integrated
	RasGas 3	Operational	2009	15.6	Integrated
Russia	Sakhalin	Operational	2009	9.6	Integrated
	Yamal	Under construction	2017/18	16.5	Integrated

Country	LNG project	Status	Date first project	Capacity in 2015	Project structure
Trinidad & Tobago	Atlantic LNG Trains 1–3	Operational	1999	10.3	Transfer pricing
	Atlantic LNG Train 4	Operational	2007	5.2	Tolling
USA	Alaska	Operational	1969	0.4	Integrated
	Sabine Pass	Train 1 Operational Trains 2 & 3 Under construction	2016	18.0	Tolling. Adapted to source feedgas and supply LNG ex-plant
	Cameron	Under construction	2017	13.5	Tolling
	Cove Point	Under construction	2018/19	7.8	Tolling
	Freeport (Trains 1–3)	Under construction	2018/19	13.3	Tolling
	Corpus Christi	Under construction	2018/19	10.0	Tolling
Yemen	Yemen LNG	Operational	2009	6.8	Transfer pricing

Source: GIIGNL (2014), IGU (2015), *Petroleum Economist* (2013), and author's research.

Financing

The high capital cost of the LNG chain means that shareholders are frequently unable to finance an entire project; consequently there is a need to use third-party finance to provide part of the funding. Prior to the 1990s, shareholders used their own equity or corporate debt. Since 1994 third-party financing, using limited recourse project financing, has become the major funding source for new LNG projects, as the equity holders do not have the necessary available funds. In the mid-2000s, Qatar additionally used corporate bonds as well as project finance debt, while in 2013/14 some US LNG export projects tapped into new sources of funds, such as insurance funds and US private equity. Some projects also seek ECA finance. All these funding sources require the project to have a secure structure that clearly defines the cost, revenue, and liability flows along the chain.

The Changing Commercial Structure   117

The Japanese ECA – the Japan Bank for International Cooperation (JBIC) – has played a considerable role in supporting Japanese policy to secure long-term LNG, which is part of Japan's energy strategy. Through discounted loans and political risk cover support, JBIC has assisted Japanese companies to secure long-term LNG supply from projects in countries with relatively challenging political, economic, and credit conditions – such as Sakhalin 2 LNG (Russia) and Papua New Guinea LNG – as well as in more credit-worthy countries such as Australia (the Gorgon and Ichthys projects) and the USA (the Cameron and Freeport projects).

A typical project structure for the liquefaction part of the LNG chain is set out in Figure 3.8. In this structure the joint venture project company is funded through a portion of equity and debt (usually 60–80 per cent of the project cost, depending on the project's risk level). Lenders to the project (often a mix of commercial banks, ECAs, and other financial institutions) rely on the revenue stream from the LNG buyers as financial security for the debt. As such, a project structure must be established that will guarantee this revenue flow, while providing sufficient funds to pay for the costs of construction, feed gas, and the operating costs of the plant. If the project structure does not guarantee a specific allocation of the revenues, then lenders will be less likely to make funds available for the project. However, even though a project may raise debt to fund its development, the shareholders will still have to fund the equity, and this may be difficult for some companies and governments. For example, Empresa Nacional de

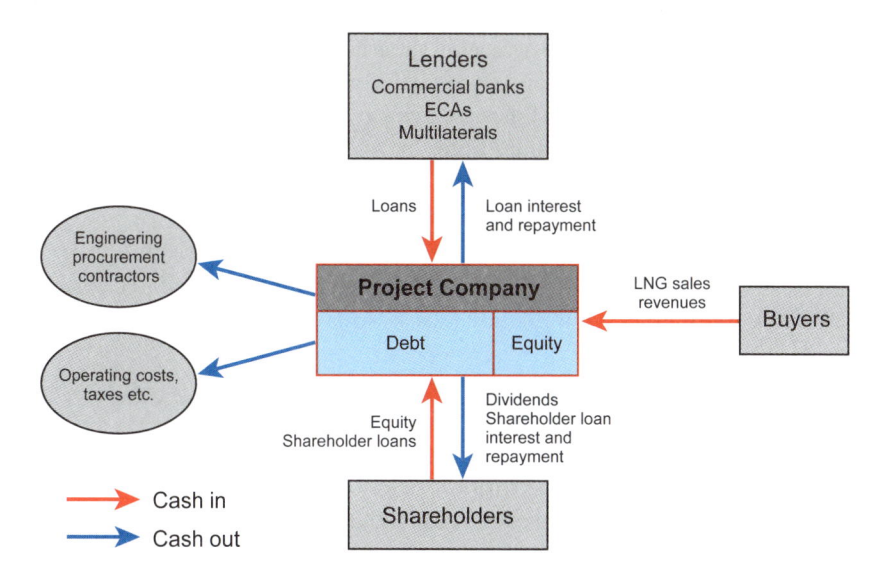

Figure 3.8: Typical financing structure for the liquefaction portion of the LNG chain
Source: Ledesma (2012).

Hidrocarbonetos (ENH), the state energy company in Mozambique, has a 15 per cent shareholding in the upstream and liquefaction parts of the proposed LNG project 'Mozambique LNG'. If total capital costs are around $20 bn, and the project achieves 70 per cent gearing, ENH will still have to invest $900 million equity, which may be difficult to raise (Ledesma, 2013).

A primary risk to a project is the technical start-up of the plant and LNG chain. Lenders, therefore, will usually expect shareholders to give pre-completion guarantees prior to completion of the plant and for completion tests to be carried out. Lenders will also want to ensure that other parts of the chain – parts that may not be directly part of the financing – are available and operating effectively, or that alternative capacity is available to ensure that the LNG from the liquefaction plant can be moved to market.

Lenders will be particularly concerned if the facility is using new technology (such as larger LNG processing trains, a new process, or floating LNG). In this case lenders will probably seek assurances and guarantees from the provider and the shareholders, until the facility has a proven operational track record. Guarantees may be an issue if the project shareholders have different credit ratings, or if a shareholder cannot give sufficient financial guarantees. In this case, lenders could seek ECA support or insurance cover. Lenders may insist on using an experienced plant operator and on putting in place training schemes for local staff. They will also want to understand how the LNG is being shipped to the market, even in the case of FOB sales, and to understand the market itself, since no revenues will flow back to the project if the market is not established. In the case of financing regasification terminals, a structure has to be developed that ensures a guaranteed flow of revenue from high credit capacity holders, unless it is to be funded by a state utility.

Lenders will seek to understand the political risks to the LNG chain and how these could change over the period of the contract.

Even in the case of shareholders funding the debt directly on their own balance sheets, the shareholders will also need to understand these risks to ensure that planned revenues will flow to the project.

Key commercial agreements

All project structures are bound together by a series of commercial agreements that set out the terms linking the different parts of the chain. It is critical that the obligations and liabilities of the parties 'flow through' the agreement, such that the risks and rewards are correctly located. Figure 3.9 shows the key agreements that are required in developing an LNG project.

The Changing Commercial Structure 119

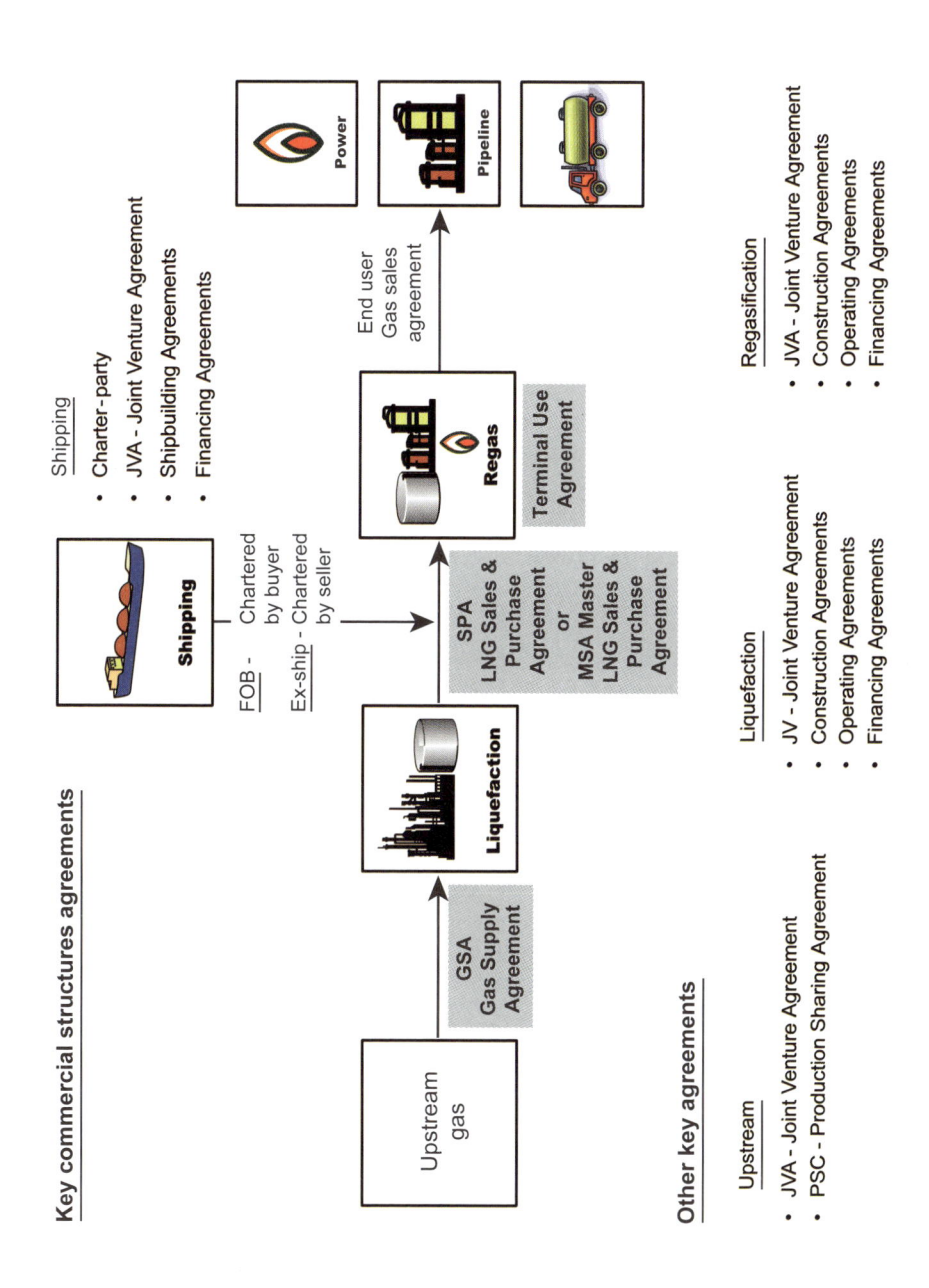

Figure 3.9: LNG Project structures – key commercial agreements
Source: Author's research.

The main agreements that hold the LNG project structure and chain together are:

Gas Supply Agreement (GSA) – This agreement sets out the rights and obligations between the upstream suppliers and the liquefaction plant (required for a transfer pricing structure) relating to the sale of feed gas.

LNG Sales & Purchase Agreement (SPA) – This agreement sets out the rights and obligations between the liquefaction plant joint venture or LNG-supplying company, and the LNG buyer, relating to the sale of LNG. The sale of LNG can be on an FOB or DES basis and the SPAs will reflect the different title and transfer point, together with the obligations of the buyer or seller to provide shipping. Key terms that would apply to the SPA (and the GSA) include:

a) delivery terms & transfer of risk and title,

b) terms of the agreement,

c) quality of the feed gas/LNG,

d) quantities and flexibilities of the volume of gas/LNG to be supplied/taken,

e) take-or-pay obligation on the buyer (the buyer's liabilities for non-take of gas/LNG),

f) price and payment,

g) price review,

h) invoicing,

i) annual delivery programme of the gas/LNG to the buyer,

j) transportation (who is responsible for arranging),

k) destination flexibility,

l) governing law & arbitration,

m) liabilities for non-supply of gas/LNG,

n) termination,

o) force majeure.

Master Sales Agreement (MSA) – With the increasing volume of LNG sold on a short-term/spot basis, buyers and sellers are entering into MSAs that set out the main terms of an LNG sale that will apply to any cargoes that are sold. The MSA is agreed ahead of any LNG sales and, when a cargo is sold, then the terms specific to that sale are set out in a Confirmation Notice (CN) that is appended to the MSA.

Terminal Use Agreement (TUA) – This agreement sets out the terms under which a company takes capacity in a regasification terminal, on a short- or long-term basis.

Developments in the value chain

Growth of the aggregator

LNG project structures have always been flexible and have adapted to meet the changing LNG environment. One significant change has been in the development of the aggregator model. Under this model, shown in Figure 3.10, there is no direct physical and contractual linkage between the gas and LNG supply and the LNG buyer. An aggregator company sources its LNG from a variety of places (for example supply projects A–E) and sells the LNG to a variety of buyers (buyers V–Z), using its own or chartered vessels and buying and selling LNG in a way that reduces costs and optimizes

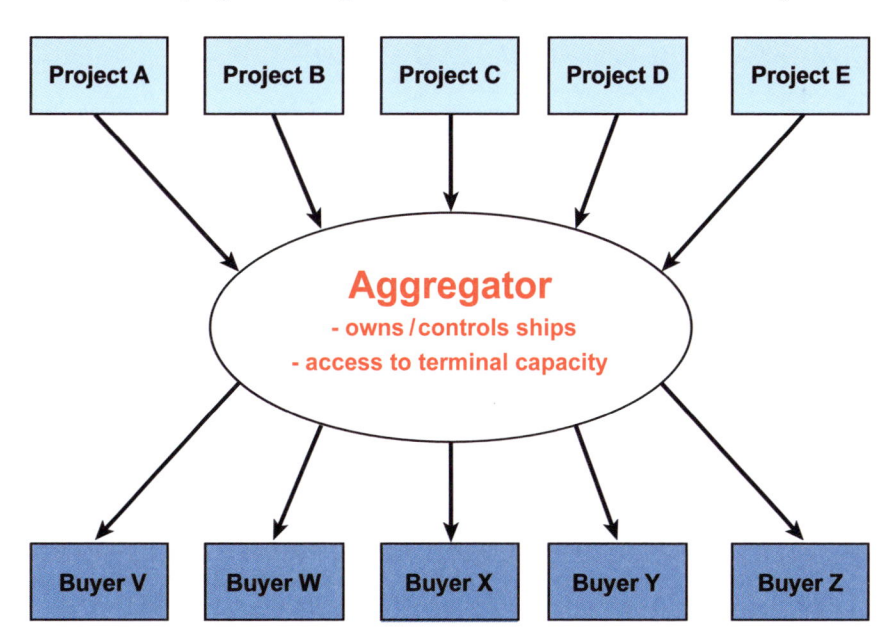

Figure 3.10: LNG aggregator structure of the business
Source: Flower LNG.

its overall portfolio. Under the aggregator model, the supply chain is driven by cost optimization, minimization, and the optionality to capture price differentials, rather than relying on a fixed supply from one point to a specific market point. This is expected to give economic benefits to the LNG buyer, the seller, and the aggregator. The LNG is sold as 'branded LNG' – for example 'BP' or 'Shell' LNG – not as LNG from a specific country or project.

Under this model, the aggregator uses its own credit rating to source the LNG and takes a margin for doing this (thereby adding costs to the end-buyer as the aggregator will want to make a margin). The buyers are happy to pay this margin as it give them access to a larger number of LNG sources, while placing the risk of supply on the aggregator. The growing volumes of LNG available from aggregators have enabled more buyers to get into the LNG market, as they do not need to enter into long-term offtake agreements directly with LNG producers, and the aggregator provides greater contractual flexibility. The buyer, however, loses the direct link between the gas reserves and the market – an important element of LNG security of supply – and will look to the aggregator to give that security through diversity of its supply portfolio. The number of aggregators has grown and, as at May 2016, include, for example the larger international energy companies: BP, Shell/BG, Total, and Gas Natural Fenosa (GNF).

Greater flexibility to access the LNG market

The structure of the regasification portion of the LNG value chain has also changed. Under the traditional model, ownership of a land-based regasification terminal was part of the buyer utility, with access controlled by that utility for the purpose of supplying its market. This is still the case in Japan, Korea, and Taiwan.

However, in Europe and the USA, LNG terminals have been constructed as standalone businesses, with the owner not directly linked to a domestic consumer. These infrastructure owners construct the land-based facility and sell the capacity rights to companies on a long-term basis; payments for the capacity are used to underpin the capital costs. In Europe and the USA, since the Hackberry Decision[15] made by FERC (the US regulator) in December 2002, terminals have been developed as non-open access facilities (under open access rules, the owner of the terminal must give access to third-party users, unless they have received a waiver or exemption from the national or regional regulator). In its decision FERC acknowledged that LNG import

---

[15] 'FERC Hackberry Decision will Spur More US LNG Terminal Development', Oil and Gas Journal, 10 November 2003, www.ogj.com/articles/print/volume-101/issue-43/transportation/ferc-hackberry-decision-will-spur-more-us-lng-terminal-development.html.

terminals are actually part of the upstream LNG supply chain, not the starting point of the US pipeline infrastructure. This ruling enabled new terminals to be developed, charging market-based regasification rates, thus enabling the development of new regasification capacity as commercial businesses. This structure has applied to the new, and expanded, LNG terminals in the UK.

The regulatory approvals which allow non-open access are often accompanied by an obligation on the terminal capacity holder to offer unused capacity to third parties.[16] This sale of spare capacity, through a secondary market, has lowered the barriers to entry for accessing LNG markets and has enabled entry for new companies, thereby bringing increased competition to LNG importing countries such as the UK, the Netherlands, and France. Ownership of the regasification capacity also enables the capacity holders to potentially re-load LNG cargoes back onto vessels as part of the global trading of LNG.

FSRUs also give faster access to the market; they are described in Chapter 4.

New players/new models

Changes such as: greater volumes of LNG being available outside of long-term contracts, the increased ability to access markets, and different pricing and contracting structures, have all attracted new companies into the LNG business, throughout the whole value chain. These new players have brought with them new ideas and ways of doing business and have challenged the norms of the LNG sector. Most noticeable are the companies that have started trading LNG. The 2000s saw banks – such as Morgan Stanley, Merrill Lynch, and Citigroup – enter the LNG business, although the financial crisis of 2008–10 also saw many exit it. Those remaining still trade LNG but are also developing liquidity in the paper market, trading small lots of JKM futures contracts over the counter.[17]

In addition to the aggregator companies that buy, sell, and trade LNG as part of their wider energy portfolio, the 2010s have seen different companies getting involved. Traditional oil, and also non-energy, trading companies such as Vitol, Gunvor, Mercuria, Trafigura, and Glencore-Xstrata have begun to trade LNG. LNG buyers (such as Engie – formerly GDF Suez, and also Gas Natural and Iberdrola) as well as some Asian end users (such as JERA – a joint venture of Tokyo Electric and Chubu Electric, and also KOGAS and PetroChina, to name just a few) are also trading as a

---

[16] In Europe this is known as 'use it or lose it' and can involve auctioning, or selling, surplus 'time slots' at the terminal.

[17] For details of the ICE contract see 'JKM LNG Future Contract Specifications', ICE Futures Europe, https://www.theice.com/api/productguide/spec/6753280/pdf.

means of optimizing their portfolios and they are positioning themselves to take on the role of trader. The Japanese trading houses Mitsui, Mitsubishi, Marubeni, Itochu and LNG Japan have also taken on a trading role.

All these new companies are increasing the liquidity of LNG trading, to the extent that in 2015 28 per cent of total LNG trade was on a spot or short-term basis (see Chapter 9).[18]

US LNG exports – adapting the LNG tolling structure

US LNG projects, that started exporting in February 2016 with the first cargo from Sabine Pass,[19] will, in the view of the author, have a huge impact on the LNG business (see Chapter 5). These exports are based on the successful development of huge volumes of shale gas. These reserves, linked to the US domestic market by a mature and flexible domestic pipeline network, have meant that gas of a uniform quality (it has to meet a standard pipeline specification) can be delivered to the coast for liquefaction at low cost. The abundance of shale gas reserves[20] has also led to an expectation that US gas prices will remain below $4/MMBtu over the coming years; this figure is rather lower than global gas and LNG prices. When Asian prices were above $12/MMBtu, there was an incentive to export cheap US gas to these premium markets; however, recent Asian price falls have challenged the economics of selling US LNG into the Asian market (see Chapter 8).

The development of shale gas has also meant that the regasification terminals that were developed in the mid-2000s to import LNG into North America became redundant (see Chapter 2). Companies such as Cheniere have converted these facilities into LNG export plants, through the addition of liquefaction trains, while utilizing the existing tankage and port infrastructure. This can be achieved with a roughly 40 per cent capital cost saving when compared with building a new greenfield liquefaction plant in other countries. US LNG plants also benefit from lower-cost skilled labour and a favourable planning regime, when compared with similar expansion projects in Australia. Is the conversion of LNG import facilities to export operations an example of a 'correction of a mistake', or does it show the adaptability of the LNG business to changing market circumstances?

The combination of abundant low-cost gas and low plant capital costs

---

[18] GIIGNL (2015) defined spot and short-term LNG trading as volumes delivered under contracts of four years or less. See Chapter 9.

[19] 'US LNG to Brazil as Cheniere offers more DES spot volumes', ICIS Heren Global LNG Markets, 25 February 2016.

[20] 'National Oil and Gas Assessment', Energy Resources Program, USGS, http://energy.usgs.gov/OilGas/AssessmentsData/NationalOilGasAssessment.aspx.

has therefore led to new companies entering the business to develop LNG export capacity, using adapted LNG business models which are suited to the US gas and LNG market. Two such companies are Cheniere and Sempra.

Example – Cheniere Energy's Sabine Pass

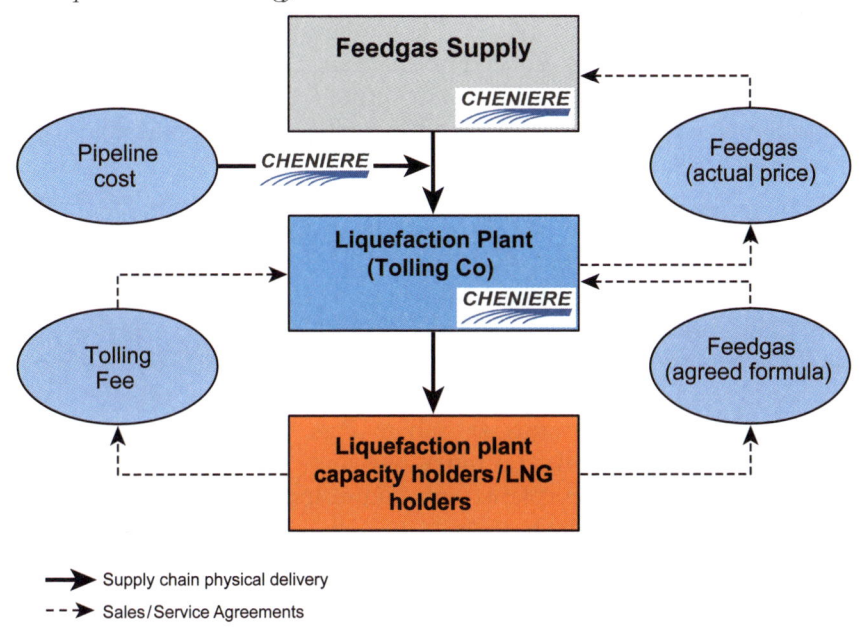

Figure 3.11: Sabine Pass tolling structure
Source: Author research.

Cheniere is an LNG industry innovator which developed the Sabine Pass regasification terminal in 2007 to meet the growing US gas import requirements. By 2010, however, market conditions had changed, leaving the company in a very weak financial position. To rectify that situation, it became the first company to convert a US LNG import facility to liquefy shale gas for export. Due to its tight financial position, Cheniere sought to develop a liquefaction project structure that resulted in minimal financial exposure. It had no need to invest in the upstream as it could buy gas from existing shale gas suppliers and from the liquid Henry Hub market.

Cheniere took the established tolling model (used before in Indonesia, Trinidad, and Egypt) and, based on the LNG produced from trains 1–5, sold long-term, 20 year, processing capacity to high credit quality companies: BG (5.0 mtpa), Gas Natural Fenosa (3.5 mtpa), GAIL (3.5 mtpa), Total (2.0 mtpa), and Centrica (1.75 mtpa), retaining 2.25 mtpa for its own trading activities. Based on these long-term capacity agreements (where the tolling companies pay an average tolling fee of around $3.0/MMBtu, equivalent to around $500 million per annum for each 3.5 mtpa capacity agreement, regardless of whether the LNG is lifted) Cheniere was able to raise third-party non-recourse finance, as well as corporate debt and bond finance, to cover its equity payments.

Cheniere, however, adapted the basic tolling model (see Figure 3.11), sourcing the plant feed gas on behalf of the capacity holders and supplying the LNG to the plant. They did this to ensure a consistent supply of feed gas to the plant (to assist it in the plant operations) and also as a business opportunity, to gain additional revenue through trading gas in the USA. Cheniere has used the same structure for Corpus Christi, its second liquefaction project, that took FID on the first two trains in May 2015. The pricing formula states that the capacity holders will buy the gas at 115 per cent of the Henry Hub price. The 15 per cent premium over the Henry Hub price was to cover gas used in LNG processing, pipeline feed gas usage, and transportation of gas to the plant; if it could secure the gas at a lower cost Cheniere would make a margin. Cheniere will eventually buy gas for five LNG trains at Sabine Pass, two at Corpus Christi (representing a capacity of 31.5 mtpa, plus any expansions), and possibly for additional trains at these plants in the future and for other gas processing facilities. Once they are all on stream, Cheniere will become the largest gas purchaser in North America and could, therefore, secure lower prices and make an additional trading margin.

Example – Sempra's Cameron
Sempra sought to develop an LNG export project at Cameron. It also opted for the tolling model (as did Freeport LNG), but used the more traditional structure whereby the capacity holders – Mitsubishi (4 mtpa), Mitsui (4 mtpa), Engie (4 mtpa) – would source the feed gas themselves and toll it through the plant.

Cheniere, Sempra, and Freeport LNG have all been able to raise third-party finance through the tolling structure, on the basis of securing high quality capacity holders under long-term tolling agreements. The companies have also been creative, in that they have secured finance of different tenures and structures (traditional project finance, corporate guaranteed debt, and bonds) and taken advantage of the depth of finance liquidity in North America. They have also seen the entry of new financing players (hedge funds, insurance and pension funds) as well as project finance from established commercial banks. In the future it is likely that these entities will lend to other LNG projects outside North America, thereby increasing lending liquidity and reducing financing costs.

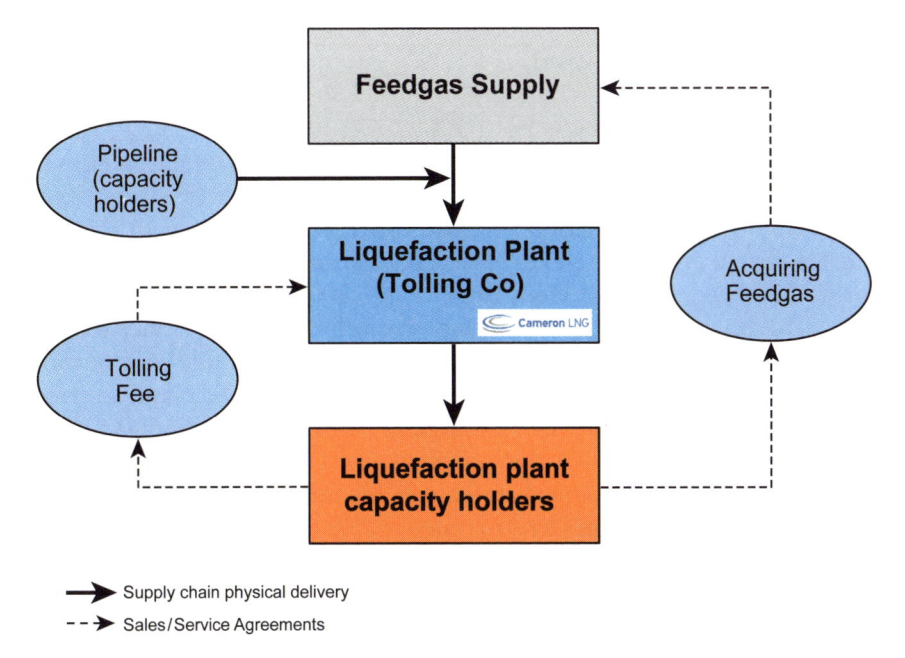

Figure 3.12: Cameron LNG tolling structure
Source: Author research.

Where are we headed?

Over the past 50 years, LNG project structures have proven to be adaptable and capable of meeting the changing needs of the industry and, specifically, of both the requirements of the sponsors to develop LNG projects, and of financiers to lend money to the LNG sector. When the first tolling model was created in Indonesia in 1978, enabling Pertamina to market all the LNG from the gas suppliers, it could not have been foreseen that, 35 years later, the same tolling model would be used as the basis for a US LNG export plant. The LNG sector has proven itself to be resilient in the face of changes. The need of buyers to secure gas to meet their growing markets (which in many cases have no alternative source of supply), together with the wish of governments and companies to sell their (often stranded) gas reserves, has driven cooperation and creativity to develop workable commercial LNG structures.

As buyers seek to secure more LNG on a short-term basis, the concept of long-term offtake may be undermined, thus affecting the ability of companies to develop new LNG export capacity. Without an equitable sharing of risk and economic rent between buyers and sellers, new LNG capacity will not be developed.

The LNG industry is going through a step change and will see unprecedented growth over 2015–20 as 150 mtpa new capacity starts production. The challenge to the industry is how to structure the additional LNG growth that will be required in the next wave. While new capacity is required to come on stream post 2020, the environment of early 2016 is challenging, as Asian spot prices have collapsed and oil prices have reduced term contract prices to levels that, potentially, will not support the anticipated costs of new LNG capacity. Projects can only be sanctioned if there is an economic arbitrage between supply sources and end buyers. To achieve this, supply costs will need to fall (through lower plant and feed gas supply costs) (see Chapter 4) and gas/LNG prices in the markets will need to be restored to levels which support project economics (see Chapter 8). Assuming this economic barrier can be surmounted, which in the author's view it will be, project structures will be developed using the three basic structures – integrated, transfer pricing, and tolling – as a foundation, but with adaptations to meet the specific market requirements of a project. Each structure will need to be underpinned by certain requirements that are fundamental for the development of an LNG project – available gas reserves, acceptable project economics, sales of LNG, supportive government and geopolitical factors, and access to finance. In the challenging economic environment of 2015/16 where global LNG prices are weak and capital costs still remain high, such arrangements will be painful as governments, LNG project developers, LNG buyers, and LNG sellers will all need to agree on a structure that works for them and for the project, in order for it to proceed. This will mean compromise by all players, as well as opportunities, as new companies take up different roles in the LNG value chain. Also, there must be clear project coordination to ensure that the different elements of the chain are developed in parallel, to ensure that no single element is developed too quickly, thus creating surplus capacity that could lead to lower value.[21]

The recent trend towards tolling structures is likely to continue for any additional US capacity, by the nature of the market, and it may be adapted. In other countries where new LNG export projects are likely to be

---

[21] For example, if the LNG ships are delivered ahead of the upstream and liquefaction portions being ready, then the ships would need something else to do in the meantime. This would have the disadvantage of giving the impression that the shipping market is oversupplied and would drive down charter rates. Such a position would change when the liquefaction finally comes on stream and calls the ships back to their original intended duty – creating a reduction in the availability of short-term charter vessels.

developed, such as in East Africa, Russia, and Australia, it is likely that transfer pricing or integrated project structures will be used, as they are more applicable to the project requirements. That said, the industry goes through phases, and each phase tends to utilize a different type of project structure at any particular point in time. FLNG projects that are being developed in West Africa (such as by Perenco/SNH and Golar in Cameroon, and Ophir and Golar in Equatorial Guinea), are using an 'adapted tolling' structure where the gas owner is chartering the FLNG facility and tolling its gas through the facility before selling the LNG in its own name. This structure could set the basis for future FLNG projects.

Experience has shown that project structuring will not hold back the development of new capacity. The 'favoured' structure changes over time; currently the tolling model, as used in US LNG projects, is favoured, but it could again revert to either the transfer pricing or integrated structure to meet the specific requirements of a project. The only cases where LNG project structures have had problems have been either where there are so many shareholders in a project that it takes time to finalize the project structure in order to meet the aspirations of all the companies, or where, during the period of the project's operations, a party in one part of the chain feels that it is not being treated fairly and it should be earning more economic rent. This was the case in Abu Dhabi and Oman, in relation to the sales of gas by the government to the LNG plant.[22] It is important, therefore, that long-term agreements along the chain should reflect a reasonable sharing of risk and profit.

Future project structures will always adapt, as they have in the past, to the changing market. However, as experience has shown, it is either the stakeholders or market circumstances that slow down new projects (or stop them proceeding) rather than the specific structure itself.

---

[22] Source: Author research and interviews.

BIBLIOGRAPHY

Flower, A. (2004). *LNG Today (2004 Edition)*, Andy Flower, The Energy Publishing Network in cooperation with Gas Strategies.

GIIGNL (2014). *The LNG Industry in 2014*, International Group of Liquefied Natural Gas Importers. (GIIGNL Annual Report)

GIIGNL (2015). *The LNG Industry in 2015*, International Group of Liquefied Natural Gas Importers. (GIIGNL Annual Report)

Gomes, I. (2015). 'Natural Gas in Canada: what are the options going forward?', OIES Working Paper NG 98, Oxford Institute for Energy Studies. https://www.oxfordenergy.org/2015/05/natural-gas-in-canada-what-are-the-options-going-forward/.

Heren LNG. ICIS Heren Global LNG Markets (subscription service).

IGU (2015). *World LNG Report – 2015 Edition*, International Gas Union.

Kay, J. and Roberts, P. (2012) 'Structuring LNG projects – evolution or revolution in the LNG supply value chain?', in Griffin, P. (ed.), *Liquefied Natural Gas*, Second Edition, Globe Law and Business.

Ledesma, D. (2012). 'Project Financing LNG Projects', Chapter 16 in Morrison, R. (ed.), *The Principles of Project Finance*, Farnham, Surrey, UK. Gower Publishing Company.

Ledesma, D. (2013). 'East Africa Gas – Potential for Export', OIES Working Paper NG 74, Oxford Institute for Energy Studies. www.oxfordenergy.org/2013/03/east-africa-gas-the-potential-for-export/.

Ledesma, D., Henderson, J., and Palmer, N. (2014). 'The Future of Australian LNG Exports: will domestic challenges limit the development of future LNG export capacity?', OIES Working Paper NG 90, Oxford Institute for Energy Studies. www.oxfordenergy.org/wpcms/wp-content/uploads/2014/09/NG-90.pdf.

Petroleum Economist (2013). *World LNG Factbook, 2013 Edition*, in association with BG Group.

CHAPTER 4

FACILITIES, INFRASTRUCTURE, AND COSTS

Brian Songhurst, James T Jensen, and Chris Le Fevre

Introduction

Chapter 3 looked at the commercial structures of the upstream and midstream businesses, analysing how they have evolved since 1964. Different structures have been advanced to determine the risks and rewards in developing the upstream and liquefaction plants as these represent the most expensive parts of the total LNG value chain – liquefaction represents roughly 75 per cent of the total investment. The evolution of the costs of liquefaction plants, therefore, deserves special attention. The first part of this chapter will start by exploring how and why the costs of liquefaction plants have increased over the past decade and what the strategies for cost reduction could be. In particular, a great deal of attention is currently being given to floating liquefaction of natural gas as the year 2016 is expected to see the start of the first FLNG operation, in Malaysia. One key question is whether FLNG could contribute to a cost reduction.

The other two parts of the LNG value chain – shipping and regasification – are explored next. These processes are less costly but are equal in importance to the upstream and midstream businesses. Shipping is an essential part of the LNG business, enabling gas to be moved across the oceans and to reach markets which otherwise would never have consumed significant amounts of gas. While the technical characteristics of the shipping business have evolved over 50 years, business practices have also changed and have contributed to increased flexibility in the LNG business; this is visible through the rise of spot and short-term trading. LNG terminals have also become more flexible over time, because of the need to adapt to a changing business and regulatory environment. They are now present in most regions in the world. Over the past 10 years, a number of LNG carriers have been converted into floating storage and regasification units (FSRUs) and new build vessels have also been completed; these have enabled quicker access to developing markets in the Middle East, Africa, Latin America, and Asia. The evolution of the business models and technical aspects of regasification terminals are analysed in the final part of this chapter.

Liquefaction costs

The cost of liquefaction plants has almost quadrupled over the past 10 years – this rate being twice that experienced by the oil and gas sector generally. Particular reasons for these increases in capital costs include project scope, location, and execution strategy. While plants currently under construction in the USA benefit from lower costs due to their brownfield nature, it can be questioned whether this signals a return to more normal costs. As the industry looks at the next wave of LNG plants to come online (beyond 2020) the question of whether these costs will continue at their recent level, rise, or whether strategies for cost reduction will be successful, is crucial for the future of the LNG industry. A range of cost reduction strategies – including new processes and plant construction methods, as well as the application of new floating liquefaction units – will be analysed in more detail in this section.

Evolution of plant costs

Recent experience

LNG plant capital costs (CAPEX) have increased by a factor of three to four over the period 2000–15, as shown in Figure 4.1. However the CAPEX of upstream oil and gas plants generally only increased by a factor of two to three in the same period, implying that LNG plant costs increased at twice that rate. The plant's CAPEX is shown as a metric of cost in US$ per tonne produced per year ($/tpa) to enable comparisons to be made between

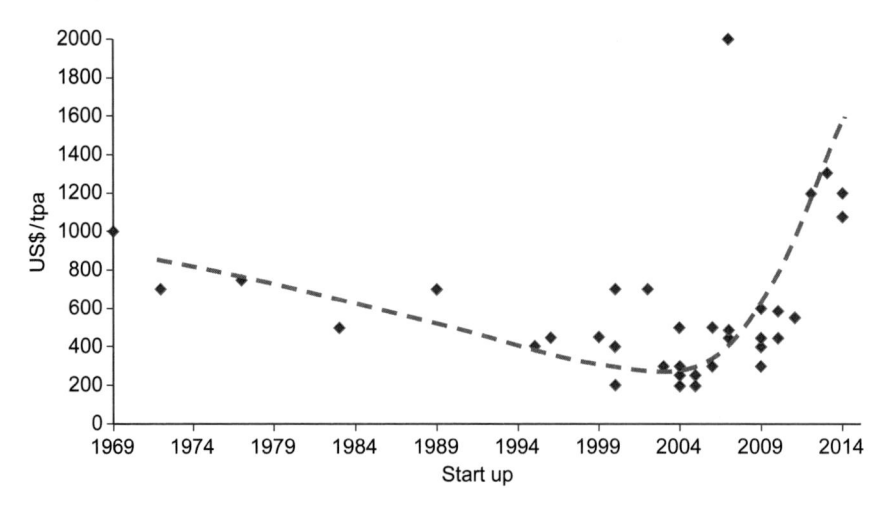

Figure 4.1: CAPEX by year (unit liquefaction costs by year of production start)
Source: IHS CERA Upstream Capital Costs Index (UCCI) www.ihs.com/info/cera/ihsindexes/index.aspx.

plants of different capacity. It should be noted that this metric is a broad tool (shown by the data points being both above and below the curve) due to the fact that the costs are also driven by the physical plant scope, plant location, and local construction costs not just by capacity (as discussed later in this chapter).

Costs reduced during the period 1980–2000 as the industry became more efficient at designing and building the plants, and also due to economies of scale as production train capacities became larger: the early plants' size was typically 1 mtpa, and this increased to 3 mtpa by 2000 (see Figure 4.2).

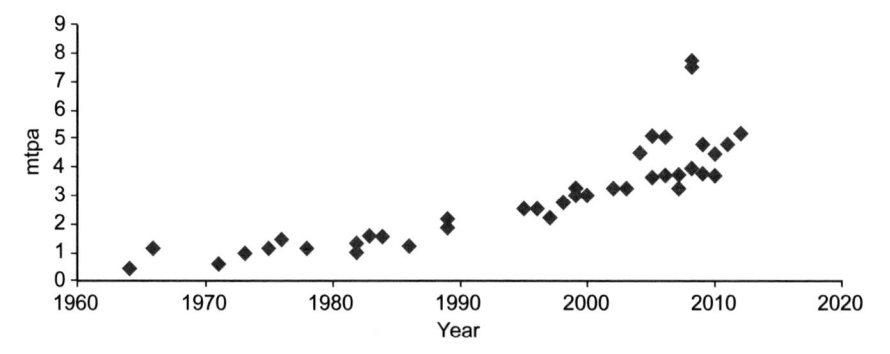

Figure 4.2: Plant production capacity (train size) by year (liquefaction plant capacity growth)

Source: Author from published data.

Cost components
The main cost components for LNG liquefaction plants are similar to those of most process plants:

- **Owner's costs** typically cover the owner's project teams (located in the home office, design contractor's office, and on site during construction), permitting costs, specialist consultants, land purchase, and insurance.
- **Engineering and project management** covers the costs borne by the contractor in undertaking the design, procurement of the equipment (not the equipment cost), managing the project overall, and supervising the site construction and commissioning.
- **Equipment supply and logistics** covers the purchasing and transportation of the specific items of equipment to the plant site. These

134   *LNG Markets in Transition*

items are procured on a worldwide basis from specialist manufacturers. For much of the major equipment (such as: turbo compressors and cryogenic heat exchangers), there is a very limited number of manufacturers. Transportation costs are very significant for projects in remote locations.

- **Bulk material supply** represents the procurement and transportation of the non-specific equipment (such as: piping, steelwork, cabling, electrical equipment, instrumentation, and control systems). The quantities are determined from the design and layout drawings.

- **Construction** costs represent the largest cost and cover the site construction activities required to assemble the plant and prepare it for operation. These include: site preparation and equipment foundations, equipment erection, and interconnection with piping, electrical, and control systems. Preparation for start-up, often referred to as 'commissioning', includes mechanical testing, flushing to remove debris, and purging with nitrogen prior to introducing hydrocarbons. It can also include the cost of temporary and permanent construction facilities (such as: accommodation facilities, offloading dock, and in some cases an airstrip) especially for remote locations with limited infrastructure.

The typical distribution of these costs is shown in Figure 4.3.

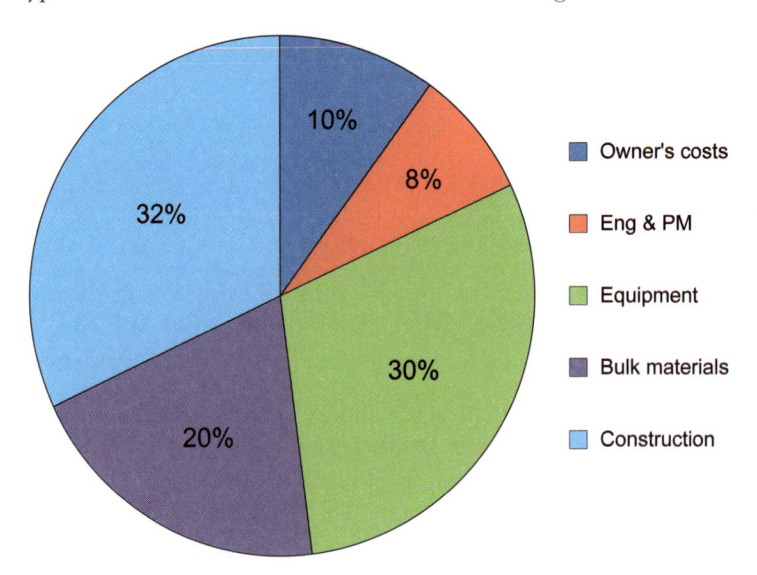

Figure 4.3: Cost components (cost breakdown by category)
Source: Author's research.

Drivers behind the recent cost increase
There are two major factors that drive liquefaction plant costs:

- The **physical scope of the project** (capacity, complexity, and infrastructure).
- The **location and construction costs** (including temporary facilities).

The physical scope of the project. It must be stressed that whilst the scope of basic liquefaction plants are generally the same (cryogenic refrigeration to condense the natural gas – mainly methane and ethane – into LNG) the rest of the plant can vary significantly for the following reasons:

Processing capacity and complexity: A plant's 'capacity' is the rate at which LNG is produced; the larger the capacity the larger the size of equipment required (when the maximum equipment size has been reached, the number of production trains is increased).

The complexity will depend on whether the plant is built as an expansion of an existing one (brownfield) or is built from scratch (greenfield), and on the composition of the feed gas.

- A brownfield development just involves the adding of gas treatment and liquefaction train(s). In this case, much of the existing infrastructure (such as tanks and a jetty) can be used. Many of the US export plants which are being converted from import terminals already had the jetty and tankage and just needed the addition of a liquefaction plant.
- A greenfield development is a completely new plant comprising: gas pre-treatment, liquefaction plant, storage, export jetty, and utility systems. These can have very different levels of complexity due the composition of feed gas source, for example:
  - The processing of a very lean or pipeline quality gas requires minimal gas processing and no condensate or LPG facilities.
  - The processing of a rich gas (such as associated gas) requires major gas pre-treatment, condensate and LPG recovery, storage and export, and possibly CO_2 reinjection and sulphur recovery.

A greenfield plant processing a rich sour gas can have up to four times more equipment than a simple brownfield (base liquefaction plant) site (Figure 4.4).

136 *LNG Markets in Transition*

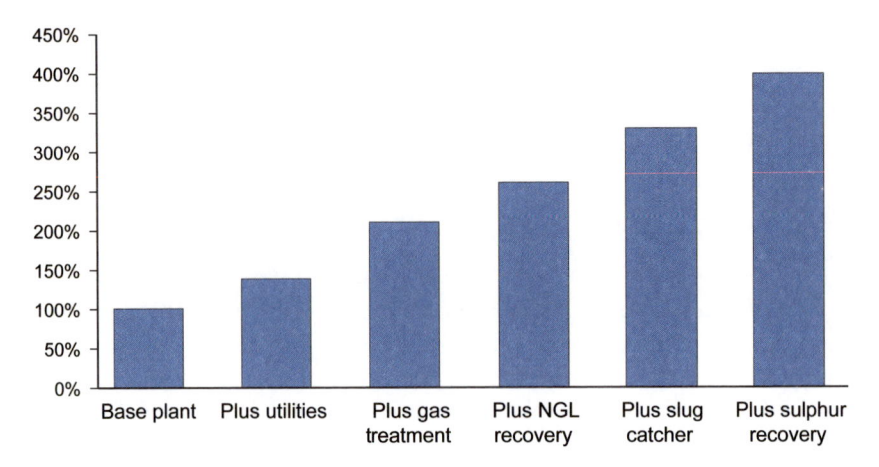

Figure 4.4: Equipment count vs processing (equipment count increase vs scope)
Source: Kotzot et al., 2007.

Available infrastructure: Another item that has a major cost impact on the physical scope of the project is the extent of existing infrastructure that is available to support the plant. A plant built in a highly developed industrial location is likely to have local facilities such as: housing, schools, medical services, airport, and roads. However, for remote locations such facilities have to be included and this will have a major impact on the capital cost. Indonesia's Tangguh project[1] required the relocation of the existing residents and the development of major new infrastructure, including an airfield.

The location and construction costs. The major cost components of engineering, equipment, and bulk materials are generally independent of plant location, as they are required regardless of location. However, construction costs are totally location-driven due to several factors:

- site terrain,
- local labour costs,
- construction productivity,
- construction infrastructure.

---

[1] 'Tangguh LNG Project in Indonesia', Summary Environmental Impact Assessment, June 2005. www.adb.org/sites/default/files/project-document/69276/ino-tangguh-lng-project.pdf.

It is far easier to build a liquefaction plant (in fact any plant) in a highly developed industrial area such as the US Gulf Coast or Qatar than in a remote location such as North West Australia or Papua New Guinea.

Site terrain: Difficult soil conditions (including land reclamation, soil improvement, or rock blasting) can add major costs and time to a project. The Nigerian LNG plant located in the swamp of the Niger Delta required major land preparation and Hammerfest LNG plant at Melkøya, Norway required rock blasting and an access tunnel to the mainland. Other high-cost items also include dredging or long jetties to provide the 13 metres of water depth required for an LNG tanker. In the case of Equatorial Guinea, a major bridge was required to carry the offloading lines from the plant located on the cliff to the berth. Dredging can also be an environmental issue as well as a high-cost issue.

Local labour costs: Recent Australian projects quoted labour rates of $200,000 per year for a welder, which is double the global average.[2] These high rates were the result of restrictions on imported labour at a time when Australia was constructing simultaneously six major LNG projects worth $180 billion. These projects were competing for limited resources and driving labour rates to an unprecedented high level, leading to major cost overruns and LNG liquefaction plant costs of a size not previously experienced.

Construction productivity: The productivity of construction staff varies significantly from location to location. This is often measured by the contracting industry's Lang factor.[3] The base figure for the US Gulf Coast is 1.0, but it can drop to 0.5 or even less for some locations. The values of this factor are regarded as proprietary information by LNG plant contractors as they affect their price competitiveness. One method of managing construction costs in high-cost locations is to modularize plant, build the modules in a highly efficient environment (such as a Korean shipyard), and ship to site. This not only helps manage the construction costs but also the construction schedule, due the higher confidence of shipyard delivery dates. This method has been extensively used in Australia, but not in the USA where traditional 'stick building' is generally cheaper as the productivity is higher.

---

[2] 'Highest-Paid Workers Driving Shell Off Australian Shores', James Paton, Bloomberg Business, 26 April 2013. www.bloomberg.com/news/articles/2013-04-25/highest-paid-workers-driving-shell-gas-terminal-offshore.

[3] The Lang factor is a measure of the total cost of installing a process in a plant compared to the cost of its major technical components.

Construction infrastructure: It is far cheaper (and quicker) to build a liquefaction plant in an established industrialized area where there are many oil and gas facilities. Established areas such as the USA and Qatar have ready access to plant construction equipment, ports to bring in equipment and materials, as well as resources and a familiarity with the oil and gas process plant business. Contrast this with a remote location such as Yemen where very few such facilities exist, major construction plant will need to be imported, and local staff trained. Whilst this will benefit the nation overall in the long term, it adds significantly to the cost of that project. The lack of infrastructure in Tanzania and Mozambique will increase the costs of planned LNG projects significantly and will lengthen the schedule. For remote locations this infrastructure can include extensive accommodation facilities such as a new township, an offloading port, and even an airstrip. In some cases this infrastructure is only temporary but it is often permanent and seen as part of a plan to improve the infrastructure for the local community (the Tangguh LNG project is an example of this).

Cost comparisons: Whilst it is relatively easy to compare plant costs using the $/tpa metric, great care must be taken as to whether the comparison is on a like for like basis – and in most cases it will not be! The OIES paper 'LNG Plant Cost Escalation' (Songhurst, 2014) compares costs in considerable detail and produced the outline guide shown in Table 4.1 which compares costs relating to physical scope and location.

Table 4.1: Cost comparison summary (costs 2014 basis)

Scope			
	Complete facility	$1,000–$1,200/tpa	$1,400–$1,800/tpa
	Liquefaction only	$600–$800/tpa	$1,000–$1,200/tpa
		Normal cost	High cost
		Location	

Source: Songhurst (2014).

The lowest cost metric range ($600–$800) relates to liquefaction train(s) added as an expansion to an existing LNG plant in a normal cost area. An example of this is the Sabine Pass plant being developed by Cheniere, where the existing import terminal is being converted into a 22.5 mtpa export facility by the addition of five 4.5 mtpa trains processing pipeline quality gas but retaining the LNG tanks, export jetties and utility systems, and infrastructure. A sixth train is planned. The cost of the initial four train 18 mtpa development has been quoted as $10 billion, resulting in a cost metric of $556/tpa ($10 billion/18 mtpa). This figure includes the four liquefaction trains and minor modifications to the existing facility (tank export pumps, some new buildings, and roads). However, it should be noted that this low cost is, in part, also due to processing pipeline quality gas that requires less pre-treatment than natural gas from a reservoir.

At the other extreme is the range of $1400–$1800 which covers a complete greenfield facility built in a high-cost area. Examples of these would be the recent projects in Australia and the planned projects for Mozambique, Tanzania, and western Canada.

Operating costs (OPEX)

OPEX cover the running of the plant and are usually expressed as a percentage of CAPEX for comparison purposes. Table 4.2 lists the main OPEX components for a 9.2 mtpa liquefaction plant (two trains of 4.6 mtpa) in Australia with a CAPEX of around $13 billion. The following should be noted:

- The figures are based on a recent conceptual design study using the C3/MR process and are indicative only. Each project requires a definitive study based on the specifics of that project.
- Fuel gas consumption has been charged at the feed gas rate at the plant gate of $5/MMBtu.
- Manning is based on 200 personnel including shift workers.
- Power generation is by open cycle gas turbines.

Table 4.2: Operating cost breakdown

Production: 9.2 mtpa

Item	$m/year	% CAPEX
Manning	58	0.4%
Fuel gas (liquefaction)	165	1.1%
Fuel gas (power generation)	55	0.4%
General and administration	23	0.2%
Consumables	13	0.1%
Plant maintenance	150	1.2%
Maintenance dredging	8	0.1%
Sewage and waste disposal	6	0.0%
Insurance	22	0.2%
Total	499	3.6%

Source: Author.

OPEX figures can also be expressed in $/MMBtu. For this example, the production of 9.2 mtpa represents an export of 450×10^6 MMBtu/y giving an OPEX metric of 499/450 = $1.1/MMBtu. These OPEX figures include fuel consumption, which is the largest single element at 1.5–1.7 per cent. If the fuel consumption is excluded, the OPEX is approximately 2.2 per cent or $0.6/MMBtu.

Value chain

For the purposes of the value chain calculation, the liquefaction cost is taken as the total of the CAPEX and the OPEX costs. Assuming a greenfield plant constructed in a normal-cost location with a CAPEX of $1100/tpa, the liquefaction cost CAPEX component is $3.85/MMBtu.[4] To this, the OPEX of around $1.1/MMBtu is added giving a total liquefaction cost metric of $4.95/MMBtu. However, it must be stressed that this is a midpoint figure and used purely as an example.

For a brownfield expansion in the US Gulf Coast area with a CAPEX of $700/tpa, the CAPEX component is only $2.5/MMBtu, whereas a high-cost case such as Australia with a CAPEX of $1100/tpa would result in a CAPEX component of $3.9/MMBtu. Table 4.3 below summarizes both cases. Each project's costs must be calculated based on its specifics. It should be noted that the industry typically quotes the contractor's project cost (EPC cost) as the CAPEX and it excludes the owner's costs which are typically of the order of 10 per cent – as well as other items that may not be included in the EPC scope.

Table 4.3: Liquefaction costs (CAPEX + OPEX)

	CAPEX $/tpa	CAPEX $/MMBtu	OPEX $/MMBtu	Total $/MMBtu
Brownfield expansion (liquefaction only)				
Normal cost area	700	2.5	**1.0**	**3.5**
High cost area	1100	3.9	**1.2**	**5.1**
Greenfield plant (full scope)				
Normal cost area	900	3.2	**1.0**	**4.2**
High cost area	1600	5.6	**1.2**	**6.8**

Source: Author.

---

[4] Using a conversion factor of $/tpa to $/MMBtu of 0.35 per cent. This factor of 0.35 per cent CAPEX is a typical industry figure and is calculated by spreading the project capital cost, including interest, over an agreed production period.

As shown in Table 4.3 the US brownfield projects could liquefy at a cost of $3.5/MMBtu and greenfield projects at $4.2/MMBtu. It should be noted that these are costs and not tolling prices, which will include a profit for the plant operators. Assuming a Henry Hub price of $3/MMBtu and a shipping cost to Europe of $1/MMBtu, then 'delivered Europe' costs would be $7.5/MMBtu and $8.2/MMBtu respectively. By contrast, the liquefaction costs of the high-cost area plants would be higher, at $5.1/MMBtu and $6.8/MMBtu, to which the feed gas costs and shipping would need to be added to calculate the delivered price.

Future LNG costs

As referenced in the LNG Plant Cost Escalation paper (Songhurst, 2014) the very large cost increases since 2009 have been mainly due to the high Australian labour costs, as discussed earlier. Based on the reported costs of current US projects under construction, liquefaction plant cost escalation is currently in line with other oil and gas plant cost escalation at 10 per cent per year (see Figure 4.5). The industry is currently looking at 'game changer' technologies and execution strategies to reduce costs; these are discussed in the next section ('Strategies for cost reduction').

However, the cost escalation figure of 10 per cent per annum is based on the USA, which enjoys a highly efficient construction industry located in an area that is very familiar with major oil and gas facilities, close to the major equipment manufacturers. Many of the future projects will be located in remote areas where there is limited, or even no, oil and gas experience. This will both delay the projects (due to permitting issues and a lack of understanding of the local decision making processes) and add costs (as construction equipment will need to be imported and the local workforce trained and supervised by expensive expatriate personnel).

High costs are also likely for future Australian projects, even though the US$/Aus$ exchange has normalized and construction costs from the previous rush for resources are not likely to occur again. Arctic projects are also likely to experience high costs due to their remote location and high costs of winterization – which include specialized ice-breaking tankers.

Another item that can add high costs to a project is the long pipelines that may be required to transport the gas from the gas field to the liquefaction plant located on the coast. Recent examples are the QCLNG project in Queensland which requires 540 km of buried 42 inch pipeline[5] and the Ichthys 980 km offshore pipeline to the plant located in Darwin.[6] Looking

---

[5] CCC Capability Presentation slide 7 –
 http://iploca.com/platform/content/element/14390/4Kawash.pdf.

[6] 'Gas export pipeline', Ichthys in detail, Ichthys LNG Project. www.inpex.com.au/our-projects/ichthys-lng-project/ichthys-in-detail/project-facilities/gas-export-pipeline/.

142 *LNG Markets in Transition*

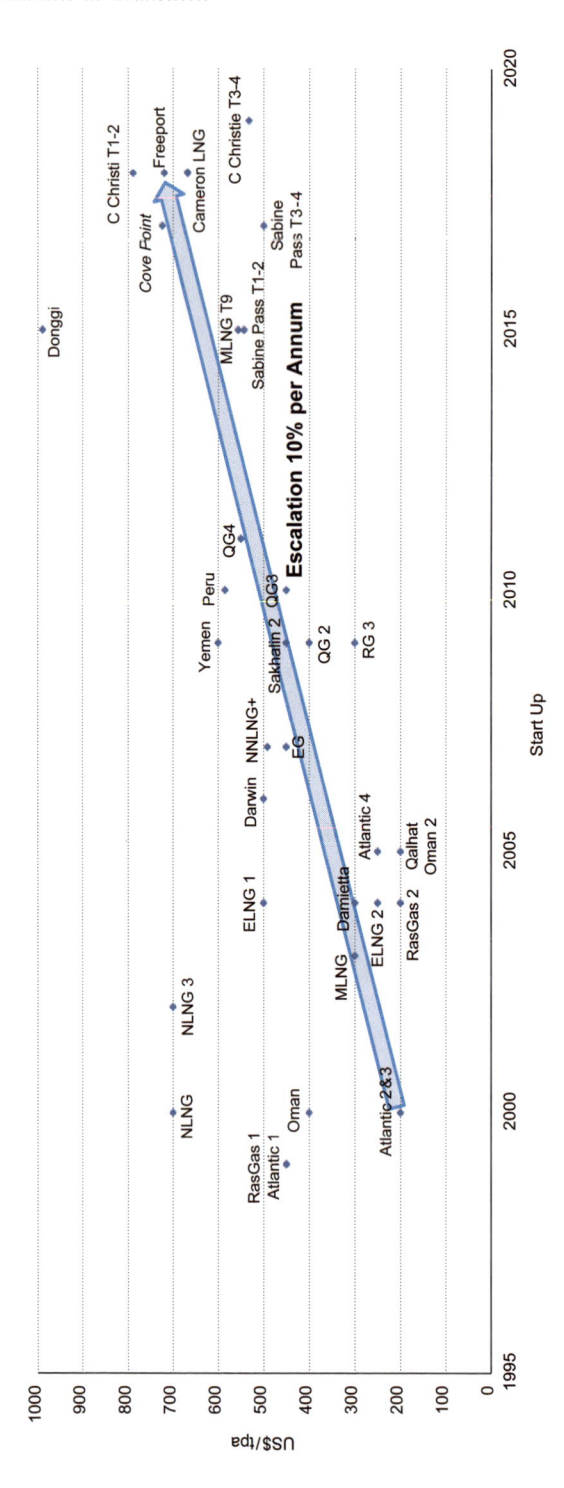

Figure 4.5: LNG escalation excluding Australian projects
Source: Author.

to future projects, the costs of pipelines in Canada to transport gas to plants at the coast are extremely high due to their lengths of 500–900 km through difficult terrain; together with other local permitting issues this will represent a major cost challenge.[7]

Again it must be emphasized that each project is unique in terms of gas source and composition. Plant location and costs must therefore be calculated on the basis of the specifics of that project. Metric costs need to handle with great care!

Strategies for cost reduction

Whilst the costs of US LNG plants are returning liquefaction costs to more normal figures, there is still an interest in reducing them further, as costs in other locations are still expected to be high.

Increasing competition
Contractors and processes: This market has traditionally been dominated by Bechtel and KBR for projects in the USA, Africa, Australia, and the Middle East – Bechtel offering the ConocoPhillips Optimized Cascade process and KBR the Air Products C3/MR process. In south-east Asia the market has been dominated by Chiyoda and JGC based in Japan and often working in partnership, as KBR/JGC, for example.

Looking at recent awards in the USA, the EPC contractor market has been dominated by Bechtel (Sabine Pass and Corpus Christi projects). However, CB&I, a relatively new player in liquefaction (previously only operating in Peru) have recently been awarded the Cameron LNG project, jointly with Chiyoda. IHI is also a new player and has been awarded the Cove Point project. Hence it can be concluded that competition is increasing in the worldscale LNG plant market.

Further competition could be brought into the business by using other contractors and processes that have served the smaller LNG plant market such as: Black & Veatch, Chart Industries, and Linde. B&V's PRICO process is well proven and uses standard industry equipment, but it is limited to a train size of around 1.2 mtpa, in contrast to the norm of 4–5 mtpa for the Optimized Cascade and C3/MR processes. This means that three trains would be required, resulting in loss of economy of scale. However the simple PRICO process scheme of using just one single mixed refrigerant circuit could offer cost benefits and may be worth considering. Their process is being used in many of the FLNG vessels under construction.

Another new entrant is Liquefied Natural Gas Limited which is offering

---

[7] 'Map shows multiple proposed oil, gas pipelines in BC's carbon corridor', The Commmonsense Canadian, 13 November 2013. http://commonsensecanadian.ca/map-shows-multiple-proposed-oil-gas-pipelines-bcs-carbon-corridor/.

its OSMR process for the Magnolia LNG project. This uses the MR (mixed refrigerant) process with ammonia pre-cooling instead of propane. LNG Ltd is working with a contractor consortium of KBR and SK to deliver an 8 mtpa plant. Cost estimation is still underway, but a production cost of just $2.5/MMBtu and a fuel consumption of just 8 per cent have been mentioned.[8] This compares to $3.5/MMBtu for Sabine Pass plus 15 per cent Henry Hub, so it would be significantly cheaper. The same consortium is also working on the proposed Bear Head plant in Canada.

For technical aspects relating to LNG liquefaction, see the Technical Appendix.

Equipment supply: Another area where competition would be helpful is in the supply of gas turbines and refrigeration compressors, which has been dominated by GE. Many other major gas turbine manufacturers – such as Rolls Royce/Siemens – are trying to break into this market. GE's success has been its ability to provide, shop test, and guarantee the performance of the complete string of gas turbine driver and compressor, which is critical to the performance of the plant. The competition needs to offer the same shop testing and performance guarantee for the entire gas turbine compressor string, and the acquisition of Rolls Royce industrial gas turbines by Siemens does offer that competition, as seen by the fact that it has recently been awarded the Magnolia LNG turbines and compressors. Siemens has also recently acquired Dresser Rand, which will also enhance their capability as a competitor.

Modularization
The high cost of construction in Australia has led to the modularization of LNG plants, with the modules constructed in Asian offshore construction yards (in, for example, Korea, the Philippines, Indonesia, and China). The first project to use this approach was NWS Train 5, which was designed as a stick built plant and then divided into modular sections. This method has since advanced into a more offshore approach of integrated decks, where each module comprises a process system to avoid excessive interconnections. The Gorgon and Ichthys projects also used this heavily modular approach.

The conclusion reached by the industry is that while modular construction does not reduce the overall project cost, it does provide a higher level of confidence in meeting the project cost and schedule, by reducing site construction delays due to labour disputes and bad weather; it also minimizes cost overruns. The main reason why cost savings have not materialized is largely because of the added structural steel needed for

---

[8] 'Magnolia LNG Status Update', ASX/Media Release, LNG The Energy Link, 14 September 2015 www.lnglimited.com.au/IRM/Company/ShowPage.aspx/PDFs/3590-10000000/MagnoliaLNGStatusUpdate.

transportation (typically 50 per cent of the module weight) and the transportation cost. It is interesting to note that the current plants in the USA are stick built, demonstrating that this execution strategy is a cheaper overall approach for projects constructed in well-resourced industrial areas which have oil and gas experience.

Contracting strategy
The traditional contract execution strategy for the delivery of LNG plants was to develop the project in three key stages:

- Define: this stage involves the feasibility and conceptual design studies to specify the basis of the project.
- Refine: this stage takes the specification and engineers it to a stage that allows EPC contractors to bid. This is commonly referred to as the FEED stage (front end engineering and design).
- Execute: this stage covers the detailed design, procurement, and construction (EPC) of the plant by the selected contractor.

This step-by-step process ensures that each stage is approved before moving to the next. Whilst this process is very precise, it is time consuming, which delays project start-up and LNG sales revenue.

A far quicker approach is for the energy company to select the EPC contractor at the outset, based on agreed criteria, and work with that contractor on a sole sourced basis to define, refine, and execute the plant. This approach can reduce the schedule by two years, and the earlier LNG sales revenue can easily offset the cost savings possible by the traditional step-by-step process with competitive bidding. The sole sourced process is not generally accepted by NOCs, who require competitive bidding at all stages of project execution.

A midway solution that has recently been adopted is to select two to three contractors and undertake a paid design competition whereby they undertake the conceptual and FEED stages and put in their price for the execution stage (EPC). Although this is quicker than the full step-by-step process, it is very expensive due to making payments for the same work two or three times (for each contractor), supervising all the contractors, and ensuring there is a balance between conforming to the basic specification while also allowing for innovation – a challenging environment! It has been reported that the cost of undertaking the pre-FID stage using this approach for complex multi-train greenfield developments costing around $10–$20 billion can be of the order of $1 billion.

Can floating liquefaction contribute to the cost reduction?
FLNG is a new and enabling technology and there are currently seven units under construction ranging from 0.7 to 3.6 mtpa. FLNG units offer many advantages over traditional onshore plants, namely the elimination of an offshore pipeline to bring offshore gas onshore, shipyard fabrication methods that give a higher confidence in the construction schedule, and the ability to lease the units rather than invest capital. Eliminating the pipeline is particularly important where the underlying gas reserves are small or short-lived. In that case, the vessel can be moved to a new location, provided its design is flexible enough to accommodate a different feedstock. Environmental issues can play a role and were one factor in the decision by Browse LNG to abandon an onshore site at James Price Point in Western Australia and consider FLNG.

This new technology has enabled the LNG shipping companies to enter into the liquefaction business; it was these companies who pioneered the highly successful business of Floating Storage and Regasification Units (FSRUs). Their involvement has introduced a more functional low-cost repeat design approach to projects, with the intention of significantly reducing costs. This is particularly attractive to the smaller independent oil companies who lack the balance sheet for high-cost capital projects and who do not have to comply with highly developed in-house standards. Current examples are the Fortuna project (Equatorial Guinea) being developed by Ophir and Kribi (Cameroon) by SNH/Perenco.

FLNG design is a much greater challenge than FSRU design. Since liquefaction is a much more complex process than regasification, the natural footprint of the process units which must be fitted on the deck of a vessel is much larger. This can be compounded by the quality characteristics of the gas feed. A feed gas that contains impurities (such as acid gas), or has a high liquids content, will require even more complex processing. While a liquids-rich gas will increase the cost of the vessel, this may be offset by the coproduct credits from liquids sale.

Floating liquefaction

FLNG has been studied for the past 40 years but, until recently, has remained on the drawing board. However, since Shell took FID on its Prelude FLNG project in 2011, a number of operators and FLNG solution providers have followed suit. There are now seven units under construction (Table 4.4).

Facilities, Infrastructure, and Costs 147

Table 4.4: FLNG projects currently under construction

Project	mtpa	Start-up	Location	Operator	Contractors
Caribbean FLNG	0.5	TBA	TBA	EXMAR	EXMAR/Wison/B&V
Kanowit (PFLNG-1)	1.2	2016	Sarawak, Malaysia	Petronas	Technip/DSME
Prelude	3.6	2017	Timor Sea, Australia	Shell	Technip/Samsung
Kribi (GoFLNG Hilli)	1.2	2017	Cameroon	SNH/Perenco	Golar/Keppel/B&V
Speculative	0.6	2018	TBA	TBA	EXMAR/Wison
Rotan (PFLNG-2)	1.5	2018	Sabah, Malaysia	Petronas	JGC/Samsung
Fortuna (GoFLNG Gandria)	2.2	2019	Equatorial Guinea	Ophir Energy	Golar/Keppel/B&V

Source: Author.

The configuration of FLNG units can be divided into two major groups: offshore and nearshore.

- Offshore units must operate in open ocean conditions and take reservoir gas directly from subsea wells.
- Nearshore units operate in relatively benign, inshore waters and typically take treated or partially treated gas from an onshore pipeline system.

In assessing the market opportunities for FLNG, it is interesting to look at the dramatic expansion of the FSRU market, with 20 projects having been developed in just 10 years, and many more under construction or planned. This is an amazing achievement in the LNG industry, which is historically very conservative, and FSRUs can be regarded as a game changer in the regas sector.

Most FSRUs are located close to land and may benefit from comparatively calm sea conditions. The FLNG projects that are under consideration, on the other hand, are often selected to save the cost of a long-distance pipeline to shore. They are thus more likely to be located in the open ocean, where the vessel must withstand extremes in weather conditions. There can thus be wide variations in cost. A vessel designed to handle complex gas feed that will be anchored in rough seas (such as Prelude) will be costly while another one, handling a clean feed gas, anchored in a bay or harbour, can be relatively cheap by comparison. But the economics are challenging in a world of lower oil prices and weakened Asian LNG prices. Two of the most advanced proposals – Browse in Australia and Abadi in Indonesia – have been put on hold in the changed pricing environment. Both of these projects, like many in Australia and south-east Asia, are rich in liquids and thus especially vulnerable to weaker oil prices.

SWOT analysis of FLNG

The strengths, weaknesses, opportunities, and threats of FLNG projects are summarized in Table 4.5 and discussed in this section.

Table 4.5: SWOT analysis of FLNG

Strengths	Weaknesses
Wide range production: 0.5–6.0 mtpa	Availability (uptime) of berthing and transfer
Option to lease	
Lower CAPEX for high-cost locations	Unproven offshore experience
Avoids costly gas pipeline from field to shore	Tanker conversions have a limited design life
Likely quicker schedule – fast track	High OPEX, high maintenance cost
Higher confidence in schedule and cost	Perception that it is too difficult
No NIMBY	Congested layout
Technology backed by IOCs	Minimal local content
Onshore site (land) is not required	

Opportunities	Threats
Relocation so not a sunk cost as onshore	Low LNG prices due to lower oil prices
Monetize stranded offshore gas fields	
No land for onshore	Low-cost onshore shale gas LNG from USA
Little infrastructure for onshore	
When onshore permitting is difficult	Lack of finance from commercial banks
Early monetization (EPF)	
Opening to smaller energy companies	Shipyard capacity or willingness to bid
Convert retired LNG tankers, adding value	Unproven contractors enter the market
Meeting increasing demand for gas	
Financing by banks	

Source: Author.

Strengths: Worldscale onshore plants tend to be designed as multiple 4–5 mtpa trains, whereas FLNG offers a wider range – from Caribbean FLNG's 0.5 mtpa up to Prelude's 3.6 mtpa, or even more. Further FLNG units can be leased, improving cash flow for the energy company, such as Ophir's Fortuna.

The other major cost advantage is avoiding the need for a subsea pipeline to shore. An example of this is the Ichthys project where the 890 km, 42 inch pipeline to Darwin required 700,000 tonnes of steel. Such pipelines cost in excess of $1 billion and can be avoided by using FLNG.

Small to mid-scale FLNG can typically be delivered quicker, due to shipyard manufacturing techniques, and typically with a higher schedule confidence than onshore plants. Traditional onshore plants can often be delayed due to local labour problems, or take longer due to the need to build the required infrastructure.

FLNG, with the possibility of lower capital costs, the opportunity to lease, and a faster schedule, should enable earlier monetization of the gas assets and improved cash flow.

FLNG also provides a solution where land onshore is either not available or difficult to develop due to permitting issues. An example of this is the possible development of the gas fields just 80 km offshore Israel, where space is not readily available along the highly developed coastline.

Weaknesses: FLNGs are currently not suitable for harsh environments where tandem offloading (as used for oil FPSOs) is required, as current offloading technology relies on the use of hard arms – offloading to LNG carriers in a side-by-side configuration. This limits offloading operations to a significant wave height of approximately 2.5 metres, and may negatively impact availability. Cryogenic tandem transfer systems are under development, but the technology has not yet been proven in service. This technology will likely be applied in the next few years, but it will require dedicated LNG carriers with bow loading manifolds and dynamic positioning capability.

FLNGs are not suitable for very large developments, due to shipyard limitations in the size of hull that can be built. Developments of up to 7.5 mtpa (against the current 4 mtpa) are being considered, for example Abadi, 7.5 mtpa and Scarborough 6–7 mtpa. In addition, whereas onshore plants may add additional liquefaction trains, incremental expansion of FLNG units is not possible without taking the entire facility out of service for a considerable period of time. However, it is possible to add multiple repeat FLNG units, but this will not offer any economy of scale, as would be the case for onshore plants.

Low local content is another potential drawback, as construction is almost exclusively out of country. Many developing countries view LNG projects as a major opportunity for local employment, with thousands of people being employed during the construction of an onshore plant. FLNG limits local employment opportunities to the operational phase, which will not meet the required expectations of many developing or developed countries which promote their capabilities (such as Brazil, Indonesia, and Nigeria).

Offshore OPEX will be higher than onshore, due to increased logistics costs and the requirement for various support vessels to service the facility. Potential CAPEX savings will be offset by the higher OPEX over the life cycle of the project. However, CAPEX is very often 'king' when FIDs are made.

The banks are still reluctant to finance FLNG due to the perceived risks of 'first of a kind' developments, but this appears to be changing. The Caribbean FLNG was in part financed with US Exim and Sinosure support, and Golar LNG has recently announced financing arrangements for the Hilli and Gimi conversions. This is a positive step, and financing is likely to become easier when the operating experience of the first units becomes available from 2016 onwards.

Concerns have been expressed over the field life expectancy of FLNGs developed as conversions of LNG tankers. However, it has been pointed out by the contractor offering this solution that the tanks are in excellent condition and the hull will be reinforced. Further, the processing plant will be new and be located on new sponsons.

Finally, many have regarded the liquefaction process as being too complicated for offshore application. These vessels are certainly more complicated than major FPSOs, but following many years of major studies (including physical equipment modelling and pilot unit testing) the companies with the seven vessels now under construction feel these issues have been solved. However, the industry is waiting to see how they perform in practice.

Opportunities: The major opportunity for FLNG is the monetization of offshore gas fields that cannot be developed otherwise, due to the high cost of a pipeline to shore, or the lack of a suitable onshore location due to land issues, permitting issues, or lack of infrastructure. Also FLNG can offer the possibility of lower production costs and of earlier production (which improves the project economics). The option to lease will enable smaller independent energy companies with limited capital to enter the market and meet the increasing worldwide demand for gas. FLNG also provides the opportunity to convert retired Moss LNG carriers into small to mid-scale floating liquefaction units. Moss tanks are ideal for offshore application due to the lack of sloshing issues, and process plant can be added by way of sponsons – as proposed by Golar LNG for the GoFLNG concept. Finally, FLNG provides financing opportunities for the banks, albeit they have been somewhat reluctant to date due to FLNG being new unproven technology, but this concern appears to be easing.

Threats: Low oil-indexed gas prices are a major threat for both FLNG and onshore plants. Assuming future higher prices, there is an opportunity to place an order now with a competitive shipyard, recognizing that a small-scale FLNG will likely take 48 months to construct (Table 4.7).

Shipyard capacity is a possible threat for larger FLNGs, due to the limited number of large dry docks available, but China is keen to enter the market and existing shipyards are likely to add larger dry docks if there is a market opportunity. There is also the threat of other shipbuilding and module construction work becoming more profitable and less risky.

FLNG requires a combination of cryogenic process, plant engineering, and marine engineering and only a limited number of contractors have that combined skill set in-house. There are many very capable onshore cryogenic contractors, but they will need to ensure their designs reflect the knowledge of offshore plant operation and maintenance, as has been learnt by the major FPSO contractors over many years. This knowledge must be incorporated into the design to ensure that the vessels work efficiently and, more importantly, safely; a poorly executed project would likely set back the FLNG business and would not be helpful in increasing the confidence of the banks to provide finance.

Small to mid-scale solution providers
In addition to the FLNG projects developed by Shell and Petronas on a traditional engineering, procurement, and construction (EPC) basis, the FSRU solution providers are now aggressively pursuing the FLNG market. The main companies are EXMAR, Golar LNG, Höegh LNG, and Excelerate Energy. (Although Excelerate Energy and Höegh LNG have recently stated that they will no longer pursue the FLNG market and focus their resources on FSRUs, they have been included for completeness.) EXMAR is headquartered in Belgium, Golar LNG and Höegh LNG in Norway, and Excelerate Energy in the USA. Companies such as SBM and Sevan Marine have also developed concepts. The majority of the solution providers are using the single mixed refrigerant process, with the exception of SBM and Sevan Marine who are using the nitrogen cycle.

EXMAR,[9] a specialized maritime logistics company, offers energy solutions to the oil and gas industry. It owns five LNG tankers, 10 FSRUs,

---
[9] 'Activities of the company', EXMAR LNG website (www.exmar.be/en/activities/exmar-lng).

and the 0.5 mtpa Caribbean FLNG. A second prospective 0.6 mtpa FLNG vessel is under construction. EXMAR's FLNG strategy is the same as for the FSRU market – build, own, and operate and focus on newbuild FLNG vessel of smaller capacities (0.5–0.6 mtpa).

Golar LNG[10] operates 20 LNG tankers (of which nine have been added to the fleet in the last two years) and four FSRU vessels, with three more in construction. It is currently converting three of its LNG tankers into FLNG vessels – Hilli, Gimi, and Gandria, and is discussing the conversion of a fourth vessel. Their strategy is conversion of their existing vessels by installing sponsons on the side of the tanker for the installation of the liquefaction plant. To date, three vessels have been based on four liquefaction units of 0.7 mtpa each, providing a nominal production capacity of 2.5 mtpa. Their approach is a standard design based on functional equipment rather than being project specific.

Höegh LNG[11] operates five LNG tankers and five FSRUs. Three further vessels are under construction. They were one of the earliest to pursue the FLNG market and have undertaken a generic design; they have been in discussion with energy companies but have not yet secured an order. Their concept is based on a newbuild vessel and originally was to use the novel and unproven Niche liquefaction process, which is a dual gaseous refrigerant scheme using nitrogen and methane. This has now changed to the proven SMR and DMR options, in line with other FLNG developers. Höegh LNG has recently decided not to pursue floating liquefaction, and focus its resources on the FSRU business.

Excelerate Energy[12] Excelerate were pioneers of the FSRU concept with the Gulf Gateway project offshore the Gulf of Mexico. They currently operate 10 vessels operating either as LNG tankers or FSRUs. A further eight vessels are under construction by DSME with a capacity of 173,000 m^3 and a regas capacity in the range of 3–4 mtpa. Excelerate developed their FLSO liquefaction concept for both inshore (Port Lavaca) and offshore. The inshore concept located the gas treatment onshore, freeing up deck space for 4 mtpa liquefaction, whereas offshore was 3 mtpa. Excelerate Energy, like Höegh, have also decided not to pursue floating liquefaction and focus on the FSRU business.

In addition to the FSRU solution providers, the oil FPSO contractors are also trying to enter the market. These contractors currently include:

---

[10] 'Our Business, Floating Liquefaction (FLNG)', Golar LNG website (www.golarlng.com/index.php?name=Our_Business%2FFloating_Liquefaction.html).

[11] 'Our Business', Höegh LNG website (www.hoeghlng.com/Pages/OurBusiness.aspx#FloatingLiquefactionTerminals-1).

[12] 'Floating Liquefaction (FLNG)', Excelerate Energy website (http://excelerateenergy.com/flng/).

SBM Offshore, BW Offshore, Bumi Armada, and Modec as summarized below:

SBM Offshore[13] – based in the Netherlands – provides FPSO solutions to the offshore energy industry, over the full product life-cycle and has multiple units in operation. The Company's main activities are the design, supply, installation, operation, and the life extension of FPSO vessels. These are either owned and operated by SBM Offshore and leased to its clients, or supplied on a turnkey sale basis. For the FLNG market, they are offering a mid-sized (1.5–2.0 mtpa) twin-hull FLNG using converted Moss tankers.

BW Offshore[14] – based in Norway – is one of the major FPSO contractors. They have 25 years of experience and have delivered 13 FPSO projects and 50 turrets and offshore terminals. They are currently working with Pangea LNG and are pursuing the Noble King project in Israel.

Bumi Armada Berhad[15] – ('Bumi Armada') based in Malaysia – is an international offshore oil and gas services provider and has a fleet of six oil FPSOs. They have recently entered the LNG market with the award of the Malta LNG FSU project. They have been working with Keppel and IHI on possible FLNG concepts.

MODEC[16] – based in Japan – currently operates 17 FPSOs with four more in construction. They have teamed up with Toyo Engineering and IHI to design a 2 mtpa FLNG vessel called *LiBro*. The refrigeration cycle will use lithium bromide as a pre-cooling refrigerant, followed by a nitrogen cycle using the AP-N process. IHI will provide the SPB tank design.

Costs

CAPEX. Accurate information for the FLNGs currently under construction is difficult to obtain due to client confidentiality and scope differences, making comparison on a like-for-like basis very difficult. Based on data available, the projects can be divided into two distinct cost groups: those developed by major energy companies as traditional EPC projects and those offered by solution providers on a more functional design basis.

Major energy company projects: Industry sources indicate Prelude and Kanowit are over budget. The 3.6 mtpa Prelude project is generally reported to have costs of $12 billion, resulting in a CAPEX metric of

---

[13] SBM company profile (www.sbmoffshore.com/who-we-are/company-profile/).
[14] 'Pangea LNG and BW Offshore to partner in Israel Noble King FLNG', 2B1st Consulting, 7 March 2013. (www.2b1stconsulting.com/pangea-lng-and-bw-offshore-to-partner-in-israel-noble-king-flng/).
[15] 'Bumi Armada eyes FLNG, FSRU market segments', *Borneo Post*, 1 April 2014. (www.theborneopost.com/2014/04/01/bumi-armada-eyes-flng-fsru-market-segments/).
[16] 'Modec eyes Floating LNG Market', IHS Fairplay, (http://fairplay.ihs.com/ship-construction/article/4048021/modec-eyes-floating-lng-market/).

$3,300/tpa ($11.6/MMBtu). Taking the total fluids production of 5.4 mtpa (LNG + LPG + condensate) gives $2,200/tpa ($7.7/MMBtu).

The value of the contract to DSME for the construction of the Kanowit vessel is stated as $771 million, against an overall project cost of $2.0 billion. Allowing for some cost overruns and the moorings, a cost of $1 billion translates in a metric of $833/tpa ($3.8/MMBtu). For the overall project cost (including drilling and subsea systems) of $2.0 billion the metrics are $1670/tpa and $7.5/MMBtu.

Solution providers: These companies are far more forthcoming on their costs. Indeed, they are selling their offerings to the LNG industry and the costs are likely to be the first major consideration when comparing FLNG to an onshore plant option. However, care needs to be taken with these quoted costs, as this is a new technology.

Golar have stated that their costs for the Hilli and Gimi FLNG vessels are in the order of $600/tpa ($2.1/MMBtu). This cost will likely include the moorings but exclude the drilling, subsea wells, and risers. These will be project-specific and be installed by the operator as part of the offshore installation programme. EXMAR have stated that the cost of the Caribbean FLNG is $305 million for 0.5 mtpa, which gives the same figure of $600/tpa.

Excelerate Energy originally developed their concept as an inshore FLNG for Port Lavaca in Texas to produce 4 mtpa. They have quoted costs of $600/tpa for inshore and $700/tpa for offshore.

Cost differences: The cost difference between the major energy companies and the solution providers is typically a factor of two or even three. Without a detailed cost breakdown a comparison is difficult, but one possible reason for this difference include the scope of the solution providers being limited to the vessel and moorings only (in other words, it excludes the subsea scope of drilling, wells, templates, and risers). These costs can be very significant and similar to the cost of the FLNG vessel for deepwater locations.[17]

Their approach to projects is completely different. The energy companies' designs are project-specific and follow corporate design standards developed over years of operating LNG liquefaction facilities, whereas the solution providers are taking a functional specification approach and are not bespoke, in that they are intended to be reused. This is very similar to comparing a bespoke offshore oil production facility designed to an energy company specification, with a leased FPSO which is modified and relocated at the end of its field life. Further, the solution providers are primarily focused on the liquefaction vessel only, and not the wells and subsea completions as mentioned above, whereas the energy

---

[17] 'Technip awarded subsea contract for Shell's Prelude FLNG development', Technip press release, 29 June, 2012. www.technip.com/en/press/technip-awarded-subsea-contract-shell%E2%80%99s-prelude-flng-development.

companies focus on the complete system from reservoir to LNG export.

The energy companies typically award a pre-engineering contract to define the plant (FEED) and then negotiate and award the engineering and construction to a major contracting group. The contracting group will incorporate the energy company standards and procedures which reflect years of learning by the energy company. Vendors often have to modify their standard equipment to meet those specific requirements.

Solution providers have a different approach. They typically use a functional specification, and design and construct the plant in accordance with the manufacturer's standard product line. This is due partly to the fact that they and their clients (often smaller independent energy companies entering into the LNG business) lack experience in operating and maintaining liquefaction facilities. This approach by the solution providers also makes sense in that the facilities need to be flexible for reuse at other locations. They have successfully applied this model to the FSRU market and appear to be adopting the same approach for liquefaction. Time will tell if this approach is successful.

These two approaches are different and serve different markets. Many major energy companies will be looking at the lower-cost developments of the solution providers and ask if they are getting value for money with their bespoke approach, and they could well undertake a value engineering of their own projects.

The first FLNG vessel (Kanowit) is expected to start operations in 2016, and experience from its start-up and longer-term operation will help identify whether the more traditional approach, although conservative, adds value overall.

OPEX. Operating costs typically cover the following:

- personnel on board,
- fuel gas,
- consumables,
- maintenance,
- support vessel costs (such as tugs),
- supply base costs,
- insurance.

Personnel on board: The number of people on board depends on the complexity of the facility. On a highly complex facility similar to Prelude, with the addition of LPG and condensate production, this would be around 170 on a regular basis and increasing to 340 during start-up and maintenance. A middle-range 2 mtpa vessel is likely to have 100–140 people on board. For a simple nearshore facility such as EXMAR's Caribbean FLNG this will be lower.

Fuel gas: Fuel gas consumption is typically 10–12 per cent of the feed gas depending on the liquefaction process used. It should be noted that fuel consumption will be higher than for onshore plants, to power the marine systems. This consumption figure is often referred to as 'shrinkage', being the difference between the feed gas in and LNG produced. The main user will be gas compressor drivers (gas turbines or steam boilers for steam turbine drivers). In addition, gas will be used for power generation as well as for other small fuel gas uses. The cost of the gas is accounted for very differently by different energy companies. Some regard it as a zero-cost item, as it is owned by the energy company and if not used now would be produced in 20 years time at a very low discounted value. Others regard it as a lost opportunity cost and will charge it at the LNG cost. A cost of $5/MMBtu has been assumed, which could be higher at $7/MMBtu, for a deepwater development.

Consumables: This covers the make-up of refrigerant losses, lubricating oil, diesel oil, chemicals, and similar items. For some processes, some of the refrigerants may be produced from the feed gas, depending on the composition.

Maintenance: This includes the ongoing maintenance of the vessel and the subsea systems handled by the on-board team, plus the major overhauls expected every three to four years which will require additional personnel. It is not practical to return the FLNG to a shipyard, due to the high cost of decommissioning and downtime due to sailing to and from a shipyard.

Tug and support vessels: A minimum of two and likely three tugs will be required to manoeuvre the shuttle tanker alongside the FLNG vessel for offloading. These tugs would likely be dedicated to the project, as it may not be practical to return to port between offloading, depending on the offloading frequency. A production rate of 2.5 mtpa and offloading to a 140,000 m^3 tanker will require approximately 39 ships per year (three per month). Security and standby vessels will also be required.

Supply base costs including supply vessels and helicopters: This will cover the onshore supply base providing support to the offshore operation.

Insurance: Insurance rates for new technology are subject to negotiation. The rate for FLNG is likely to be higher than for onshore plant, which typically costs 0.03–0.07 per cent of the site value.

OPEX estimate. Recent proposals by solution providers for a 2.5 mtpa vessel indicated an OPEX of $250,000/day – in other words, approximately $90 million per year excluding fuel cost. The feed gas will be used as fuel: a 12 per cent shrinkage and a feed gas cost of $5/MMBtu add a further $69 million per year. This total OPEX of $159 million per year represents $1.3/MMBtu (Table 4.6).

Table 4.6: OPEX cost estimate for a 2.5 mtpa FLNG

Component	$m/year	
Manning (100 people)	10	$100,000/year per person
Maintenance	45	3% CAPEX
Consumables, refrigerant make-up, lubricants and chemicals	5	
Tugs, support, security vessels	10	3 tugs
Base support, helicopters	10	
Miscellaneous	10	
Sub-total excluding fuel	**90**	
Fuel gas (12% gas feed)	69	5.0 $/MMBtu
Total	**159**	
OPEX		**1.3 $/MMBtu**

Source: Author, based on proposals.

Production cost and value chain. Using the typical solution providers' CAPEX estimates of $600–$700/tpa ($2.1–$2.5/MMBtu) plus an OPEX of $1.3/MMBtu gives an estimated production cost of $3.4–$3.8/MMBtu. Adding a contingency of 40 per cent will increase this to $4.76–$5.32/MMBtu, but this excludes the drilling and subsea production costs. Pandora FLNG in PNG stated a CAPEX of $900–$1100/tpa and tolling charge of $4/MMBtu plus OPEX of $2/MMBtu giving a similar production cost of $6/MMBtu.[18]

Development schedule of FLNG

The design and construction schedules for FLNG projects currently under construction range from just 31 months to 86 months (Table 4.7). The schedule covers the execution stage from FID/award of EPC contract to vessel delivery.

---

[18] Feasibility study for Pandora FLNG – Wison Offshore and Marine – by Cott Oil and Gas. www.cottoilandgas.com.au/files/8714/0236/3949/Cott_Feasibility_Study_Presentation_Final_Issued.pdf.

Table 4.7: Proposed design and construction schedules of current FLNG projects

Project	Months
Caribbean FLNG	32
EXMAR 2	32
Golar Hilli	31
Golar Gimi	33
Golar Gandria	31
Petronas Kanowit	42
Petronas Rotan	48
Shell Prelude	86

Note: Caribbean FLNG is the actual schedule as the vessel has been completed.
Source: Author, based on published data.

The extent to which FLNG can offer a quicker schedule than an onshore plant is location-specific. The supply of a FLNG will likely be quicker than onshore for Mozambique, but the same for US Gulf Coast. However, the reduced schedule risk could be a significant factor in choosing a shipyard rather than onshore construction. The Korean shipyards have an excellent track record of delivering major projects on time and on budget, unlike many onshore projects (such as Gorgon in Australia) which may suffer from extreme weather conditions, limited infrastructure, limited resources, and poor industrial relations.

FLNG will likely offer significant schedule savings in obtaining the necessary consents and permits, which can be a lengthy process for greenfield onshore developments. An offshore-moored FLNG vessel has relatively little social and environmental impact when compared with an onshore plant.

Future market
In addition to the seven projects under construction, we have identified a further 18 potential FLNG developments worldwide, totalling some 56 mtpa and 19.6 mtpa are in the pre-engineering phase (see Table 4.8). These projects are unlikely to be feasible as onshore developments and should all go ahead. However, FLNG is set to change the development of small to medium offshore gas fields, or potential onshore plants where development is difficult or expensive.

Table 4.8: Current planned FLNG projects and prospects

Country	Developer	Project	mtpa	Start-up
Pre-Engineering				
Australia	ExxonMobil	Scarborough/Thebe	6.5	TBA
Australia	Woodside	Browse FLNG1	3.6	TBA
Cameroon	NewAge/Euroil/Lukoil	Etinde	1.0	TBA
Congo	NewAge/SNPC	BLNG	1.0	2019
Equatorial Guinea	Ophir	Fortuna	2.5	TBA
Indonesia	Inpex/Shell	Abadi	7.5	TBA
Mozambique	ENI	Coral South	2.5	2020
		Sub total	**19.6**	
Prospective				
Australia	Woodside	Browse FLNG	3.6	TBA
Australia	Woodside	Sunrise	4.0	TBA
Canada	Altagas/EDFT/Idemitsu	EXMAR Kitimat	0.6	2018
Canada	Orca LNG	Orca LNG	4.0	2020
Canada	Altagas	Triton	2.0	2020
Israel	Noble Energy	Tamar	3.4	TBA
Tanzania	Ophir/BG/Statoil	Mzia/Chaza/Jodari	2.5	TBA
USA	Excelerate Energy	Lavaca Bay	4.4	Shelved
USA	Delfin	Defin LNG	5.0	TBA
USA	McMoran Exploration	Main Pass Energy Hub	4.0	TBA
USA	Cambridge Energy	CE FLNG	2.5	TBA
		Sub total	**36.0**	
		Total	**55.6**	

Source: Author, based on published data.

Conclusions: liquefaction plant cost increases and strategies for cost reduction

The recent high cost increases are mainly due to the execution of too many major capital projects at the same time in one country (Australia) that has a high-cost base, restricts imported labour, and has experienced a rapid increase in the value of its currency (the Australian dollar) compared to the US dollar on which the original estimates were based. The projects currently under construction in the USA are far more in line with typical cost escalation figures in the oil and gas and petrochemical plant businesses, as they do not exhibit these high Australian cost factors. Also, the US plants benefit from being built on existing import terminal sites, using the existing jetty and storage tank infrastructure, which lowers costs further.

Looking forward to the next phase of projects likely to be constructed in East Africa and Canada, costs are likely to be high due to their remoteness and lack of infrastructure. In the case of Canada, this will be exacerbated by the high cost of the long gas supply pipelines through difficult terrain. Regarding Mozambique and Tanzania, they lack the experience of developing major projects which involve complex decision making processes; this will likely cause major delays and increased costs, as was the case with the first Nigerian LNG project.

Cost reduction strategies for onshore plants could include: the use of multiple smaller plants designed on a more functional and standardized design basis rather than project-specific designs. This approach is used in the small-scale LNG plant market, and China has been particularly successful in this area. This standardized approach is also being used by the floating liquefaction companies supplying leased facilities which are likely to be reused on other fields.

Floating liquefaction may offer lower costs for offshore field developments, particularly where long onshore pipelines to shore are required. Fabrication of these vessels in highly productive shipyards in the Far East should lower plant costs while also offering a higher confidence in delivery schedules, which will improve the project economics. The approach of those LNG shipping companies currently supplying and operating FSRUs on a leasing basis, who are now constructing floating liquefaction vessels, will utilize a more functional, standard design approach, offering economies of scale, lower costs, and (likely) shorter schedules. These lower costs could also apply to the development of onshore projects using onshore gas in high-cost and remote areas, where traditional onshore-constructed plant could be replaced by cheaper and quicker barge-mounted facilities, in just the same way that FSRUs are now frequently favoured over onshore import terminals.

Changes in the LNG shipping business

While shipping represents a relatively small part of the capital expenditure for an LNG chain, the ability to move gas by sea over long distances is the basis of its transition from a regional fuel to an internationally traded commodity. The basic vessel platform has spawned two innovations that have further enhanced the international development of gas – the floating storage and regasification unit (FSRU) and the floating liquefaction vessel

(FLNG). FSRUs are discussed in the next section of this chapter and FLNGs were discussed in the previous section of this chapter.

The evolution of the LNG vessel

Basic designs

The first ocean cargo of LNG was delivered from Louisiana to the UK in 1959 aboard the *Methane Pioneer*. The ship was owned by Constock International Methane – a joint venture of Continental Oil Company and Union Stockyards of Chicago – and the development activity was funded by the British Gas Council. Shortly after the demonstration voyage, Shell joined the partnership and the company was renamed Conch International Methane (Tusiani and Shearer, 2006, 138).

The containment system of the *Methane Pioneer* was a self-supporting Prismatic type B, commonly called the 'Conch' system. It consisted of an aluminium inner tank with balsa wood insulation and access space between it and the hull. Later versions utilized polyurethane foam as insulation (Greenwald, 1998, 195).

Although several later ships were built using the Conch system, the design experienced a major failure in 1979. Avondale Shipyard in New Orleans had been commissioned to build three tankers for El Paso's Algeria–USA trade. The polyurethane insulation failed in the vessels' sea trials and the ships were never utilized for LNG transportation. One was converted to other uses and the other two went into layup, later to be scrapped.

At the same time, two French firms, Gaztransport and Technigaz, were developing membrane containment systems. The Gaz Transport system is a dual membrane of Invar, a nickel steel alloy. Technigaz's design is a single waffled stainless steel membrane.

Meanwhile, the Norwegian shipyard, Kvaerner Moss, came up with a design utilizing self-supporting spherical tanks, now referred to as the Moss Rosenberg design. Tankers of this type can be readily identified by the spherical tanks which protrude above the deck of the tanker.

As the interest in LNG moved to Japan, the two French firms suffered financially as Japanese shipbuilders began to dominate construction and the French firms had been reluctant to license foreign ship builders. The two merged in 1994 to form GTT (Gaztransport et Technigaz). The combined firm still offers both of the membrane designs. Kvaerner Moss, which was willing to license foreign shipbuilders, managed to weather the transition to Asian shipbuilding successfully. More details on LNG shipping are contained in the Technical Appendix.

As of the end of 2015, the fleet consisted of 314 membrane vessels, 111 Moss Rosenberg, and 34 of other designs. The membrane design thus accounted for 75 per cent of the fleet. Ten years earlier, the fleet consisted of 191 tankers of which 100 were membrane, 86 were Moss Rosenberg,

162 *LNG Markets in Transition*

and five were other designs. Since the membrane tankers had comprised only 52 per cent of the fleet in 2005, the design had clearly increased its market share over the decade. Since all of Qatar's Q-Class tankers utilized membrane technology, it was a major factor in the growth of the membrane fleet. Membrane vessels also provide more efficient rectangular storage, a smaller hull for the same volume, and lower Suez Canal fees.

For many years, the favoured propulsion system for LNG tankers was the steam turbine. These could use either bunker fuel oil or boil-off gas from the cargo. But steam turbines are relatively inefficient. More recently companies have become interested in the more efficient dual fuel or triple fuel diesel–electric propulsion systems (DFDE or TFDE).

Trends in tanker size

The early tankers were comparatively small by today's standards. Not only was the industry still at an early point on its learning curve, but the distances between Mediterranean suppliers and European customers were relatively short and the average size did not exceed 75,000 m³ until 1976. But as more distant suppliers, such as Abu Dhabi and Indonesia, entered the market there was pressure for larger vessels, and around 1976 there was a rapid rise in tanker sizes; the average size rose quickly to about 125,000 m³, and stayed there for more than a decade. Some smaller vessels continue to be built. Harbour draft restrictions have occasionally limited sizes, and small town gas utilities in Japan have been served by specially built smaller vessels.

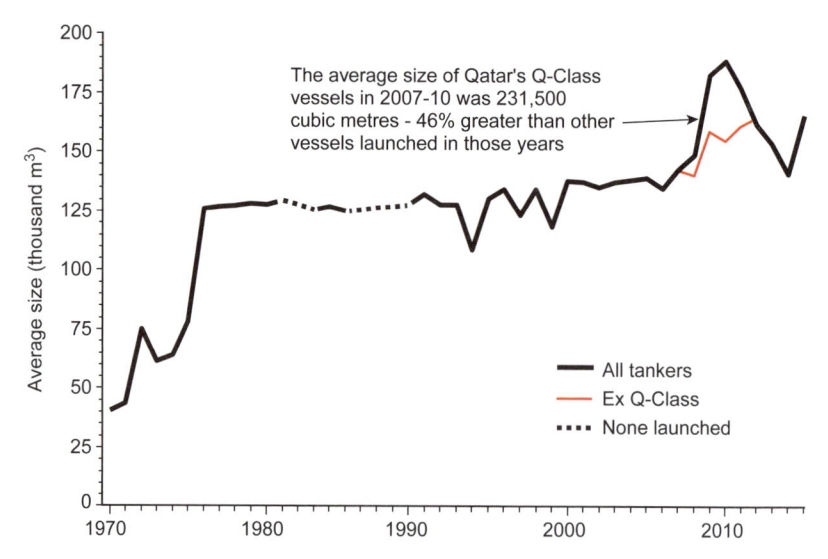

Figure 4.6: Average size of LNG tankers by launch year (excluding tankers of less than 25,000 m³)

Source: Estimates based on GIIGNL data.

The 125,000 m³ pattern began to creep up in the mid-1990s, reaching an average of 150,000 m³ for typical vessels by 2008. But 2007 saw the first deliveries of Qatar's very large Q-Class vessels, which sharply increased the average size of the overall fleet. But for non Q-Class ships, sizes continued to rise, reaching 165,000 m³ by 2014. The Q-Class ships were part of the construction of Qatar's six 'mega-trains'. The Q-Flex ships (210,000–217,000 m³ capacity) and the Q-Max ships (263,000–266,000 m³ capacity) were significantly larger than existing vessels.

There is little evidence that Qatar's leap to much larger sizes will set a general precedent for the future. As of year-end 2015, it seems more likely that the 170,000 m³ limitations on the expanded Panama Canal are establishing a new ceiling on typical sizes. Of the 38 tankers launched in 2014, 31 were larger than 160,000 m³, but only one exceeded 170,000 m³ and that was designed as an FSRU.

While there are certainly economies of scale in increasing the size of ships, these are not so great as to offset some of the flexibility disadvantages, such as those posed by receipt terminal sizes and harbour limitations.

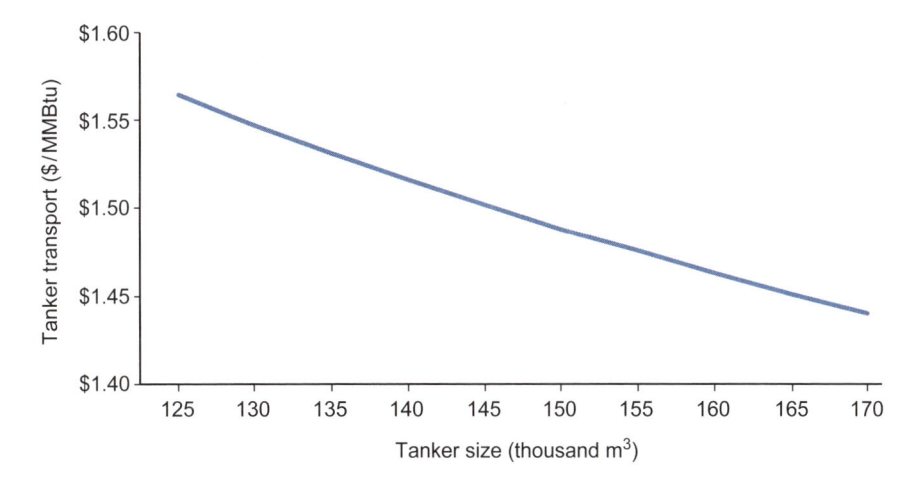

Figure 4.7: Tanker transportation cost as a function of size

Basis: 6,000 nautical miles, $5 gas into plant.
Source: Author's LNG economic model.

Figure 4.7 illustrates the reduction in tanker transportation costs as the tanker size increases from 125,000 m³ to 170,000 m³. The estimates assume a 6,000 nautical mile route and $5 feed gas to liquefaction. They are based on the author's model of LNG economics.

The emergence of the FSRU
The traditional LNG receiving terminal was a land-based facility, preferably in an urban location where it could be close to the centre of gas send out loads. Not only is it becoming increasingly difficult to find such sites, but public resistance to industrial development (the Not in My Back Yard, or NIMBY, effect) is often a problem. And the construction lead time can be longer than developers would choose. The answer to these problems is increasingly an FSRU.

The technology originated in the 'Energy Bridge' concept developed in 2000 by El Paso Natural Gas. It envisioned putting the regasification unit on the tankers themselves and then offloading the gas through a specially designed mooring buoy anchored at an offshore location. The initial concept assumed that the vessels' prime role was for transportation, with the benefit that they could deliver gas to market without the need for an expensive fixed terminal onshore. But the recognition that they could also be moored at market and supplied by other vessels gradually developed. In this role they became terminals first and tankers second. Thus the tanker became the FSRU.

The emerging interest in Arctic icebreaker designs
The growth of gas exploration in the Arctic, when combined with the shrinking of the Arctic ice cap, has generated interest in the 'Northern Sea Route' from Europe to Asia. This much shorter route across Northern Siberia is now partially open in the summer and early autumn. Interest has intensified with Novatek's proposed Yamal LNG project in the Russian Arctic.

The Russians and the Yamal partners have been actively pursuing tanker designs that might be used in summer and autumn months when the Arctic is most navigable. One major test occurred in November and December of 2012 when the LNG ship, *Ob River*, made the voyage from Snøvhit, in Norway to Japan via the Northern Sea Route.[19] The *Ob River*, a 145,700 m^3 tanker classed by Lloyds Register as Ice Class 1 A, was accompanied by a nuclear-powered icebreaker to clear the way.

But as the plans for Yamal LNG have proceeded, work has gone forward on icebreaking vessel designs that can make the run on their own without accompanying icebreakers. In July 2014, the Yamal project placed an order for nine such vessels with the Korean shipbuilder, Daewoo. They are rated as Ice Class ARC7 and can handle ice that is two metres thick.

For LNG ships, the design is unusual. Known as a 'double acting ship',

---

[19] 'Gazprom successfully completes world's first LNG supply via Northern Sea Route', Gazprom press release, 5 December 2012. www.gazprom/press/news/december/article150603.

the bow is shaped like a conventional bow (to enable it to make good headway in open water) while the stern has the icebreaking design. The vessel has reversible screws and when encountering ice it can go in reverse and break ice with the stern.

The tankers have a capacity of 170,000 m^3 and the order for the nine with Daewoo for Yamal is estimated at KRW2.8 trillion.[20] At year-end 2015 exchange rates, that would value each vessel at $265 million, approximately a 23 per cent premium over comparable regular tankers of that size. A subsequent order for five more tankers was placed with Daewoo in December 2015. The price quoted for this order in $US was equivalent to $318 million for each vessel.[21]

The Yamal project has sought a European transhipment terminal for periods when the shipments will be unable to use the Northern Sea Route, and has signed a contract with Zeebrugge in Belgium to play that role. Since the economics of Arctic shipping are sensitive to the effective speed of the tanker, and the ice thickness varies seasonally, the optimization of flows – using either the Northern Sea Route or making use of European transhipment – will prove to be a challenge.

The charterparty

Tankers are chartered to service a particular trade. The charterparty is a contract for the hire of an LNG vessel. It is entered into between a shipowner and a charterer who wants to deliver LNG to a particular market. Since the charterparty specifies the obligations of each party, it is also used internally, between the parent company and its subsidiaries.

Depending on the requirement, the shipowner can provide either a fully operational vessel or provide a bareboat charter in which the charterer is responsible for the crew and other costs. The charterer may choose to provide its own ship management or may hire a specialized independent ship management firm to do the job (Tusiani and Shearer, 2006, 157). The decision is usually based on economics and on the charterer's experience and skill level. More often than not, the shipowner provides a fully operational vessel.

Charters may be 'term charters' (covering a specified period of time) or 'voyage charters' (covering one or multiple voyages). While GIIGNL defines sales contracts of less than four years as 'short term', most of these short-term cargo movements are basically 'spot' sales.

While long-term charters are usually arranged by direct negotiation

---

[20] 'Daewoo to build Arctic LNG carriers for Yamal project', www.korea.net/NewsFocus/Business/view?artcleId=120754.

[21] 'China shipping firms, Dynagas in talks to build $1.6 bln Arctic LNG vessels', Reuters, http://af.reuters.com/article/energyOilNews/idAFLN11S08B2015099,

between charterer and shipowner, matching up the two parties for shorter-term charters is more complex. Since it depends on the availability of idle vessels to serve the proposed route, it is common to utilize intermediary shipping brokers for such deals.

There are a number of key provisions in the charterparty (Roberts, 2008, 246). The most important of these are the legal definitions of the shipowner and the charterer, charter duration, destination, rate of hire, crew description, vessel condition on delivery/redelivery, trading limits, maintenance, and key vessel performance characteristics. These performance characteristics must conform to classification society standards. And they must specify those items that control the economics of the charter – cargo capacity, speed, fuel consumption, boil-off rate, and cargo loading and discharge rates (Greenwald, 1998, 220).

Charter length

It is common to time charter enough tanker capacity to deliver LNG over the life of the project's Sales and Purchase Agreement (SPA). Thus for a new project with a 20 year SPA, the operator would typically charter capacity for a 20 year period. At the end of that initial period, buyer and seller might negotiate an extension of the SPA. The charterer would then have the option of also extending the charter of the original vessels, or instead charter in new capacity to cover the additional time period. One common time charter is known as a 20+5+5. It covers the initial 20 year period plus options on two additional five year periods.

Companies are less conservative about shipping coverage for expansion capacity than they are about that for start-up capacity. Thus as the industry matures, more capacity that does not require the initial 20 year commitment tends to come on the market. This has led to an increasing availability of LNG for shorter periods. Ship charters reflect this trend.

While some of the LNG tankers with expiring initial contracts will have their charters renewed, some will be replaced with new, probably larger, and more efficient vessels. Since the useful life of an LNG tanker considerably exceeds the 20 year period of the original SPA, there has been a growing inventory of second-hand tankers that are still trading. In 2015, short-term transactions accounted for 28 per cent of total trade (see Chapter 9). While some of this trade was performed on long-term chartered vessels, this is the part of the market where second-hand vessels compete for business.

The price and volume clauses in the original destination contract provided a means of sharing risks among buyer, seller, and the financing organization. The traditional contracts had take-or-pay clauses for the buyer, and price escalation clauses for the seller.

In this arrangement, the buyer's assumption of the volume risk guaranteed the seller an outlet for his LNG, but it also locked him into a regional market and a rigid price structure. With the greater flexibility provided by the growth of international LNG trade, many large companies have adopted a strategy of trading volume certainty for destination flexibility. They now choose to contract for LNG from various projects in order to assemble supply portfolios.

Since charterers tend to contract for capacity to cover the period of the SPA, it is possible to get some idea of trends in charter length by analysing trends in the length of new contracts. GIIGNL provides such information on an annual basis.

Unfortunately, GIIGNL does not seem to include information where the seller controls the receipt capacity and the transaction is essentially an internally integrated one. In its construction of six new mega-trains in 2009 and 2010 (Qatargas trains 4 to 7 and Rasgas 5 and 6), Qatar specifically chose to integrate downstream by building the South Hook receipt terminal in the UK and the Golden Pass terminal in the US Gulf Coast. Other venture partners controlled capacity in the USA and Belgium. Because of this approach, the very large capacity additions in Qatar in 2009 and 2010 are not included in GIIGNL's contract data. Figure 4.8 has included Qatar's expansion capacity, on the assumption that the implied capacity commitment would have been made five years before train start-up.

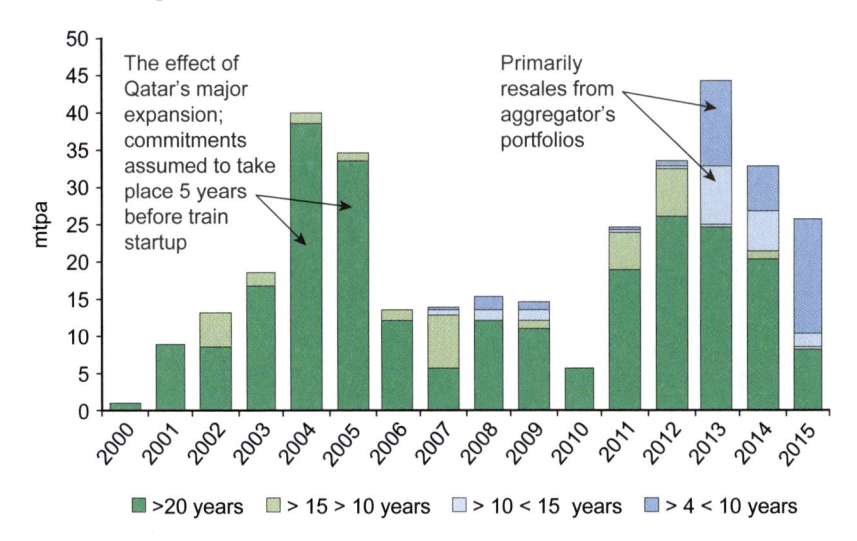

Figure 4.8: Length of long-term contract commitments written in a given year
Source: GIIGNL plus author's estimates of Qatar's integrated commitments.

New contract commitments are 'lumpy' in that they vary significantly from year to year. But the basic 20 year contracts still predominate. However, contracts of relatively short duration have begun to be a significant factor in recent years (see Chapter 9). Many of these appear to be resales out of portfolios where there is still an underlying long-term contract held by the portfolio aggregator.

Except for the emergence of shorter-term sales out of aggregators' portfolios, it is difficult to see a trend towards shorter contract lengths in the long-term LNG market. Perhaps a bigger factor in contract lengths is the nature of the contract. With few exceptions, new destination projects have sought 20 year contracts or better.

Qatar is a special case. The first eight trains in the Qatargas and Rasgas subsidiaries were implemented as typical destination contracts and utilized conventional tankers. But with the development of the mega-trains, Qatar changed its approach to emphasize scale, not only in the liquefaction trains but in its 'Q-class' vessels, as well. The basic design was the Q-Flex (210,000–217,000 m^3 capacity) which was designed to serve any customer whose harbour facilities could handle it. This was done at a time when new vessel sizes were closer to 150,000–160,000 m^3 in size.

But Qatar treated movements between Qatar, Golden Pass in the US Gulf, and South Hook in the UK as if they were integrated operations. For these designated runs, it designed 'Q-Max' vessels of 263,000–266,000 m^3 capacity. As of end 2015, the Q-Class fleet consisted of 14 Q-Max ships and 24 Q-Flex ships. Nakilat, a Qatari government company, has an ownership percentage in all of these vessels. Since they are dedicated to Qatar's trade, they – like new destination contracts – are considered as being committed long term.

The collapse of the US market as Qatar's new capacity was coming on stream posed serious market problems for Qatar. It had to redistribute the volumes originally intended for the US Gulf Coast to other markets. And weakness in the European LNG market posed additional problems, as well.

Much of the new capacity in Qatar was based on contracts with diversion rights. An estimated 32 mtpa[22] of Qatar's 77 mtpa capacity has such conditions, giving Qatar the flexibility to move the gas to other markets. Much of this diverted gas was placed in short-term markets, but some of the volumes were re-contracted on limited-length long-term contracts. It is these volumes that are included as 'Qatar Flexible' in Figure 4.9. But to the extent that these transactions – and the short-term sales – were delivered using the Nakilat Q-Class fleet, they had no effect of the length of Qatar's overall vessel commitments.

---

[22] 'Qatar targets Asia in "Flexible" LNG Strategy', *World Gas Intelligence*, 19 March 2008, Page 1.

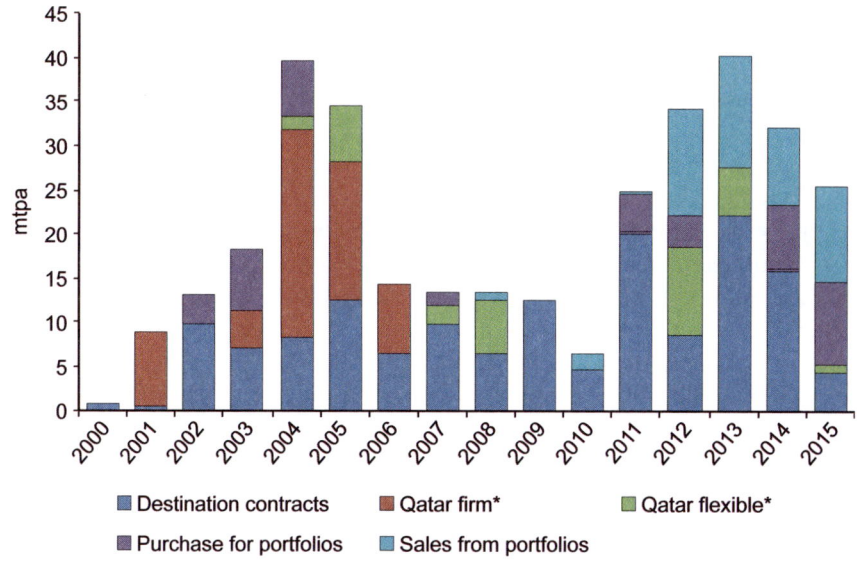

Figure 4.9: Long-term contract commitments written in a given year by contract type
Source: Author's estimate based on GIIGNL data.

Planning vessel capacity to meet demand

The tanker capacity required to meet demand from a new project is influenced not only by the size of the project, but also by the distance over which the LNG must be delivered. Thus, while new contract commitments are 'lumpy', tanker requirements are, if anything, even more so.

For example, for every tanker required to deliver LNG from Tangguh in Indonesia to Japan, it would take 2.8 tankers of an equivalent size to deliver the same amount from the US Gulf Coast via Panama. It would take 4.1 via Suez. And for each tanker required to deliver LNG from Qatar to western India, it would take 5.6 to deliver an equivalent amount from the US Gulf Coast.

Because the distances from North America to the major markets tend to be longer than those for traditional trades, North American participation in LNG can be a source of significant tanker market instability when there are unexpected changes in demand or supply. Two of the greatest upsets in tanker markets occurred in 1980 and again in 2008 when planned deliveries to the USA collapsed.

Ideally, the delivery schedule for the project's tankers is carefully coordinated with the start-up of the liquefaction facilities. But as is often the case, plant construction delays result in tanker capacity being available before the plant is ready. This capacity is available for trading in the spot market. Plant start-up then withdraws this capacity from the spot market, leading to some degree of market instability. But since tanker construction lead times are roughly half those of plant construction, it is easier to coordinate the scheduling with actual plant start-up.

The emergence of portfolio trading is a relatively new source of uncertainty in the demand for tanker capacity. Purchases for aggregators' portfolios are similar to destination contracts, in that they provide the seller with a long-term guarantee that they will cover debt service requirements. Thus, 20 year portfolio contracts are common. But the ship charter implications are quite different.

The matching of vessel capacity to the output of the plant is relatively straightforward in a destination contract. But that is not true of a portfolio resale which can be delivered anywhere, depending on market conditions. This argues for a flexible fleet portfolio in which owned, term-chartered, and spot-chartered vessels have a role to play. Each company will choose its own fleet strategy based on its supply and perceived market options.

The life cycle of a typical LNG vessel

While some speculative building may take place during periods when charter rates are high, most ships are commissioned for a specific trade and are chartered for the life of the SPA. Since the initial SPAs are most commonly 20 year contracts (occasionally longer), the early employment of the tanker is essentially committed. But the physical life of the vessel is considerably longer than 20 years. Therefore, the question of what to do with the ship after the initial charter becomes an important issue.

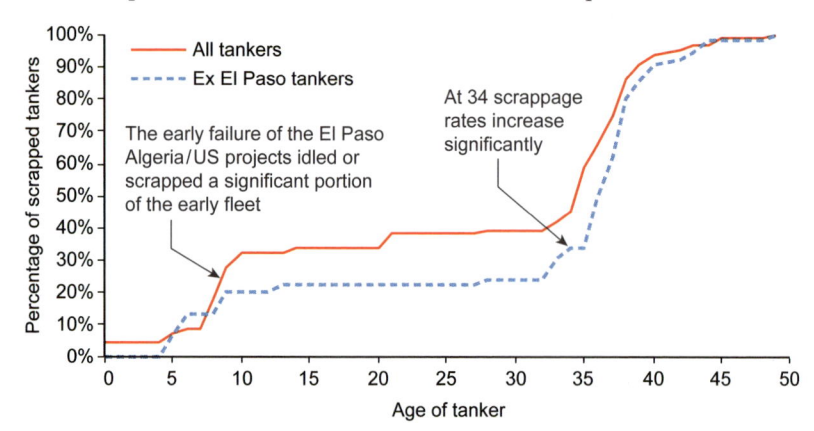

Figure 4.10: Age distribution of tankers when they are scrapped or converted to other service

Source: Author's estimate based on GIIGNL data.

Initial SPAs are frequently renewed (although not necessarily for the period of the initial contract) and often the ship charter is extended to match. But many vessels end up in the second-hand market where they are prime candidates for short-term trading or conversion to FSRUs and FLNGs.

A review of the age distribution of vessels that have been scrapped or converted to other service indicates that scrappage rates increase rapidly when the vessels reach 34 years old. That gives, on average, 14 extra years of utilization in their 'second career'. Figure 4.10 shows the age distribution of tankers when they have been scrapped or converted to other service. The historic age data is somewhat distorted by the early experience of El Paso's Algeria–USA trade. Because the project was both larger and at a greater distance from the supply source than previous projects, it required a substantial increase in the capacity of the world LNG fleet. The project ran in to difficulties almost from the start. Three of the new vessels failed their sea trials because of leaking containment, and they were never placed in LNG service. And when the USA liberalized its gas markets, the project was no longer economically viable. All in all, eight ships were converted to other uses or went into layup. While several of these were later refurbished for projects in Nigeria and Trinidad, the rest were scrapped. Figure 4.10 includes a curve for the fleet excluding the eight El Paso ships as well as one for all LNG vessels. Both because of the extended life of LNG ships and the rapid growth of the industry, relatively few vessels of the original fleet have been scrapped or converted. Figure 4.11 shows the growth of capacity as well as the accumulated tonnage actually scrapped.

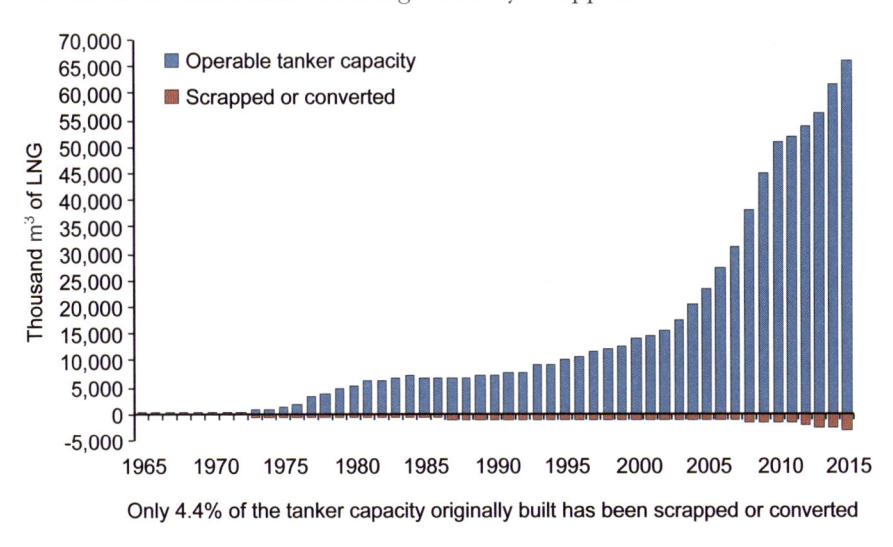

Only 4.4% of the tanker capacity originally built has been scrapped or converted

Figure 4.11: History of operable tanker capacity since first orders were delivered for Algeria to the UK and France in 1965

172   LNG Markets in Transition

Older vessels can be converted to FSRUs or to FLNG vessels. Because the flexibility of the older ships is limited by their age and size, conversion is likely to be a niche market rather than a broad market for older vessels.

Vessel ownership by type of owner

Operational control of a vessel is granted by the charter party and is the same whether the ship is owned by the operator or chartered from an independent shipowner. Thus the mere fact of merchant ownership does not indicate whether the vessel is dedicated to a long-term contract or is free for spot chartering.

Government-owned company suppliers often insist on using their own flagged vessels for their supply contracts. Examples include: MISC in Malaysia, Nakilat in Qatar, or Hyproc Shipping in Algeria.

It is possible to develop ownership information on tankers, but the information reflects current ownership. It may not represent the ownership status of the vessel when it was first committed into service.

Ships that are less than 20 years old are usually still on their initial charters and current ownership information is reasonably accurate. But many of the older vessels have changed hands, and it is from this 20 year plus group that nearly all of the scrappage has taken place.

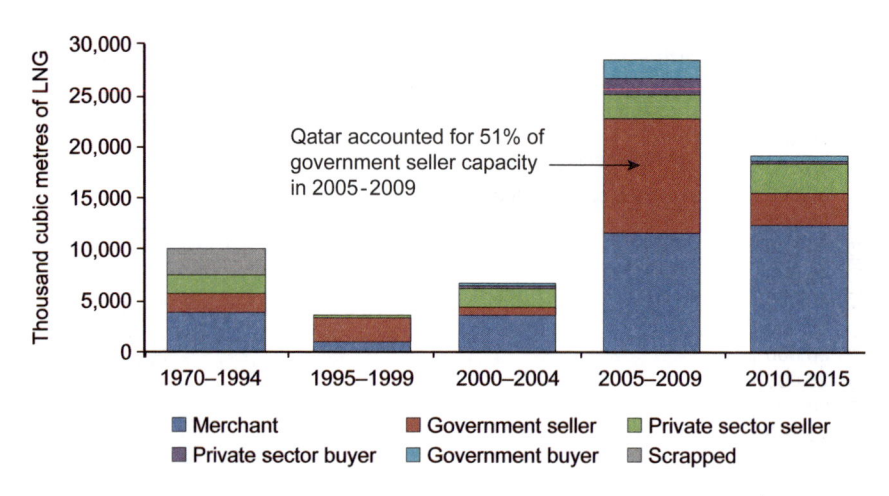

Figure 4.12: Tanker ownership by type for selected periods, 1970–2014
Source: Author's database based on GIIGNL and web tanker information.

Figure 4.12 summarizes the ownership status for vessels, dividing them into six categories. It includes all of the ships launched between 1970 and 1995 in one group, recognizing that many of them have new owners. It then subdivides the last 20 years into five-year periods. It is difficult to see a significant trend over the period. Ownership of vessels launched over the last 20 years is heavily in favour of merchant owners. The government seller figures are influenced by the addition of Qatar's Nakilat fleet in the period 2005–9, which accounted for more than half of the government commitments during the period

Until recently, buyers were seldom owners of tankers, but as some buyers have negotiated destination flexibility into their purchase contracts, they are now in a position to control some movements. And the contracting for US Gulf supplies – sold on an FOB basis – gives them full control of shipping. Private sector buyers, such as Kansai Electric, Osaka Gas, Tokyo Electric, and Tokyo Gas have ordered tankers of their own.

Government buyers have also emerged as ship owners as Chinese government companies have entered the market. During the early growth of Japanese trade, the companies were willing to let Japanese-flagged independent shippers handle the trade, but that is not the Chinese style.

Japan's private sector bias, together with its flag preference, created the three largest LNG merchant shippers – Mitsui O.S.K. Lines (MOL), K Line, and NYK. Table 4.9 lists the 10 largest independent ship owners ranked by number of LNG tankers (including FSRUs). It also lists their order books as of 31 December 2015. The data are from the author's database which has been developed from GIIGNL annual analyses and home page information on the internet for individual shippers.

Table 4.9: Largest independent ship owners

	Active vessels	*Vessels on order*
Mitsui O.S.K (MOL)	70	25
K Line	44	4
NYK	30	1
Teekay	29	4
Golar LNG	18	2
BW Group	20	
GasLog	14	8
Maran Gas Marine	16	14
Höegh	11	1
Excelerate Energy	10	

Source: Author's database.

Excelerate Energy is of interest since it pioneered on-board regasification technology (the 'Energy Bridge' concept). Some of its ships can be used to deliver regasified LNG to a special mooring buoy, as regular tankers, or as FSRUs. Golar has been active in converting (mostly) older vessels into FSRUs and FLNGs.

LNG vessel finance

While tankers are occasionally built speculatively, using equity funds, non-recourse lending is the usual method of financing. But it poses special problems and risks, since ships are movable assets operating in international waters, subject to maritime risks and Admiralty Law. It is common to place the tanker in a 'special purpose company' which isolates it and its special risks from other project activities (Greenwald, 1998, 242). Such a company would own the vessel, hold the charter, be responsible for debt service, and arrange for vessel management. Revenue is guaranteed by the long-term charter and lenders will take special care to assess any special risks that the proposed routing might entail.

Many of the same financial groups that provide financing for the liquefaction project will also lend for tankers. But export credit agencies (ECAs) often play a special role. In cases where governments are interested in promoting shipbuilding in their own yards, their ECAs often help to facilitate it through lending. In one recent deal, Korean ECAs financed the construction of six Golar vessels in the Samsung Shipyard without a charter in place.[23]

The short-term market

LNG trade originally developed around fairly rigid long-term destination contracts. As the system operated originally, there was little or no uncommitted tanker capacity available and little demand for short-term trade. That has changed dramatically in recent years. Short-term trade represented 29 per cent of total trade in 2014 (see Figure 4.13).

One of the reasons for this growth is the adoption of portfolio aggregation strategies by some of the major companies. They contract for supplies from a number of different sources, enabling them to move the LNG to the market that provides the best netback. This portion of the short-term trade got a substantial boost in 2009–11 when Qatar's elaborate plans to dedicate much of its expansion to the USA and the UK was upset by market developments. The flexibility to relocate these volumes to other markets contributed substantially to project economics but, at the same time, provided a big boost to the short-term market.

---

[23] 'Shipping Finance: A new model for a new market', *Global Trade Review*, March/April 2014, page 75,

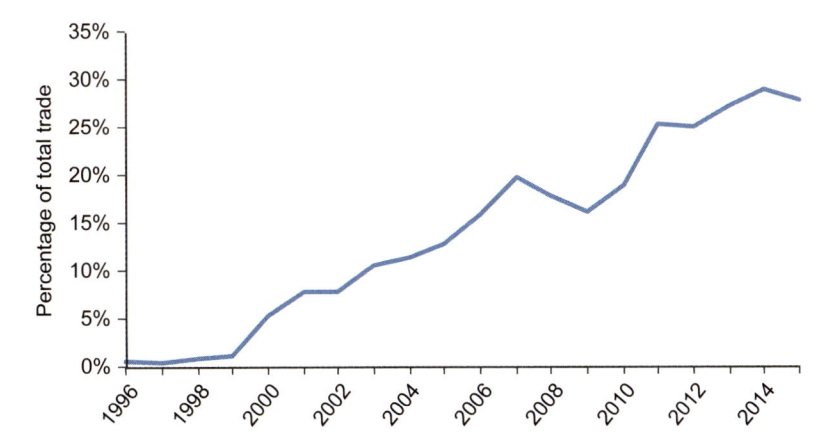

Figure 4.13: Short-term LNG trade as a percentage of total trade
Source: GIIGNL.

The traditional contract included a destination clause which prohibited the buyer from reselling into other markets. The justification for the practice was that sellers did not want to find themselves competing with themselves from buyers who had previously negotiated favourable long-term contract prices. But buyers have always valued flexibility, to balance occasional surpluses or deficits, and recently many have been successful in negotiating out the destination restrictions.

And finally, there is a growing pool of second-hand vessels that have outlived their original charters. They may be utilized by their owners in the short-term market or they may be sold to other operators – often smaller independents – at discounted prices where they can also be utilized in short-term markets.

Spot charter rates

Charter rates in the long-term market generally reflect the cost of building new vessels. The transportation rate typically is designed to allow the owners to recover costs and make a reasonable return on investment. But these rates are also influenced by the supply of newly built vessels coming on the market. Short-term tanker rates, on the other hand, are driven by the demand and supply of uncommitted capacity. Rates are quoted in $US/day and will vary both seasonally and with market conditions. The most common published rate series is for a 145,000 m^3 ST (steam turbine) vessel. This is representative of many of the older ships that come on the market after completing their original charters. But there are also rate quotations for the more modern 160,000 m^3 diesel–electric vessels, the so-called DFDE (dual fuel diesel–electric) and TFDE (triple fuel diesel–electric) vessels.

Spot charter rates can be volatile. Many factors will upset the normal market balance and induce substantial changes in charter rates. The business cycle is important. A European recession served to compound Qatar's problems, as it faced the loss of the US market in its 2008–10 expansion. Despite the potentially disrupting effects of redistributing the US-dedicated volumes, the recession tended initially to keep tankers in surplus and spot rates low.

Market psychology plays a role. Shipyards delivered 7,553,000 m^3 in 2009 and 4,097,000 m^3 in 2010 when spot rates were low. New orders dried up and only 308,000 m^3 were launched in 2012 after rates had tightened substantially.

A mismatch between the start-up of liquefaction and the delivery of its dedicated tankers will also affect markets. Plant start-up delays are common. Thus, dedicated vessels are often available before start-up, creating a short-term surplus. Similarly, unexpected shutdowns of liquefaction capacity can also idle ships.

But unexpected increases in demand can have the opposite effect. A good example is the behaviour of spot charter rates following the tsunami which destroyed the Fukushima Daiichi nuclear power plant in Japan in March 2011. As Japan shut down all of its nuclear plants, it was forced to increase its LNG and oil-fired generation.

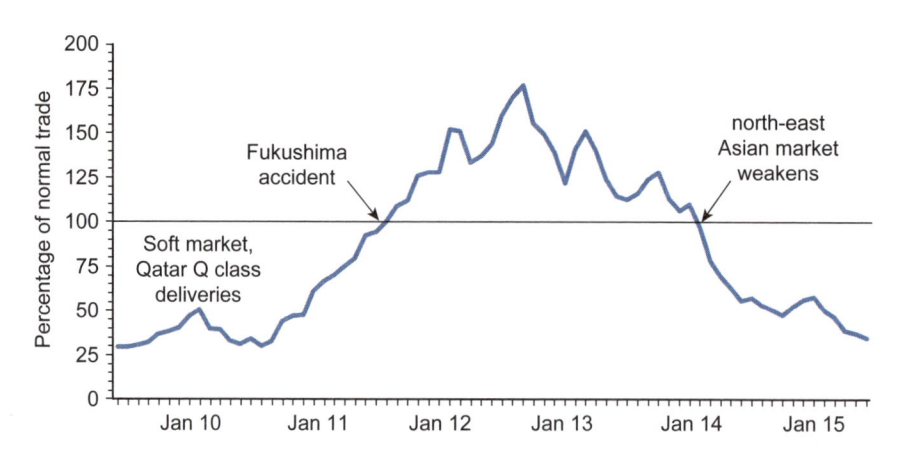

Figure 4.14: LNG spot tanker rates as a percentage of the estimated rate required to justify a newbuild 145,000 m^3 tanker

Source: Author's estimate based on proprietary tanker rate data.

Figure 4.14 shows spot tanker rates for 145,000 m³ vessels as a percentage of the estimated rate required to justify the order for a newbuild 145,000 m³ ST tanker. The weakness in rates when Qatar was adding new tankers at a time when LNG markets were soft is evident, as is the pressure on rates following the Fukushima accident, and the effect of reduced tanker launching in 2012.

A drop in short-term tanker rates has an additional effect on the market. Many of the older ships that are utilized for short-term trade are relatively inefficient; a fall in spot rates thus sends many of these older vessels to the ship recycling yards.

The combination of spot charter rates and spot cargo prices has proved to be effective in rebalancing regional variations in supply and demand. Neither exhibits the liquidity nor transparency desired in fully competitive commodity markets, and spot prices are influenced by oil-linked contract prices such as the Asian premium. But neither market is regulated, nor is it governed by external price clauses. LNG thus tends to flow to the market that provides the best netback, providing a semblance of a workable market to deliver cargoes where they are needed.

The period from 2008 (when the supply from Qatar's mega-trains first entered the market) through 2015 (following the oil price collapse) illustrates the interaction of spot prices and spot cargo rates in reacting to sharp changes in the market environment. In 2010, the market was soft as the supply from Qatar entered the market and a combination of recession and the collapse of US LNG demand led to surpluses. Spot charter rates were weak, reflecting surplus.

But Fukushima sharply changed the market dynamics. The surge in LNG requirements taxed the availability of LNG supply from traditional Pacific Basin and Middle East sources, creating a demand for Atlantic Basin LNG. In 2010, 2.5 per cent of Japanese LNG supply came from Atlantic Basin sources. By 2012, the share had risen to 11.3 per cent.

Because of the much longer distances, the Atlantic Basin shipments put pressure on spot charter rates. In February 2011, just before Fukushima, spot charter rates for 145,000 m³ STs were $64,625/day. By July 2012 they had reached $153,500/day. Spot cargo rates in Japan rose to accommodate the higher spot transportation costs. Fortunately, the European recession had depressed Atlantic Basin netbacks, or Japanese spot prices might have been forced even higher.

Tables 4.10 and 4.11 illustrate the netbacks to Nigeria and Algeria from Spain both in February 2011 before Fukushima and in July 2012 at the height of the spot charter market. Nigeria has usually been the largest source of Atlantic Basin shipments to Japan, attracted by the Asian premium in a time of weak European netbacks. The Algeria–Spain trade

178   *LNG Markets in Transition*

was selected because Spain is Algeria's closet market and should normally provide it with its best netbacks.

Table 4.10: Comparison of netbacks to Nigeria and Algeria from Japan and Spain, February 2011: pre-Fukushima

	Nigeria Japan	Nigeria Spain	Japanese advantage	Algeria Japan	Algeria Spain	Japanese advantage
Spot tanker rate ($/day)	$64,625	$64,625		$64,625	$64,625	
LNG ex-ship	$10.10	$8.65	$1.45	$10.10	$8.65	$1.45
less tanker	($2.14)	($0.91)	($1.23)	($2.09)	($0.39)	($1.70)
LNG netback	$7.96	$7.74	$0.22	$8.01	$8.26	($0.25)

Note: Japanese and Spanish spot cargo prices from weekly Spot LNG series in *World Gas Intelligence.*

In February 2011, the Japanese spot cargo price was $1.45 higher than that in Spain. But at the prevailing tanker rates, the transportation disadvantage was smaller for Nigeria but larger for Algeria. Thus Nigeria's preferred destination was Japan while Algeria's was Spain.

But by July 2012, spot cargo prices in Japan had risen so sharply that they more than offset the higher spot charter rates. Algeria, as well as Nigeria, found Japan a better market than Spain. The preferences are market-specific. If the choice were between Japan and north-west Europe, Nigeria would have still preferred Japan, while Algeria would have found north-west Europe the better destination.

Table 4.11: Comparison of netbacks to Nigeria and Algeria from Japan and Spain, July 2012: peak charter rates

	Nigeria Japan	Nigeria Spain	Japanese advantage	Algeria Japan	Algeria Spain	Japanese advantage
Spot tanker rate ($/day)	$153,500	$153,500		$153,500	$153,500	
LNG ex-ship	$14.53	$10.38	$4.15	$14.53	$10.38	$4.15
less tanker	($4.02)	($1.56)	($2.46)	($3.77)	($0.57)	($3.20)
LNG netback	$10.51	$8..82	$1.69	$10.76	$9.81	$0.95

Note: Japanese and Spanish spot cargo prices from weekly Spot LNG series in *World Gas Intelligence.*

The oil and LNG price collapse in 2015 burst the Asian shortage bubble and reordered both spot cargo prices and spot charter rates. While Nigeria's preference for Japan remained, Algeria reverted to Spain as its preferred market (Table 4.12).

Table 4.12: Comparison of netbacks to Nigeria and Algeria from Japan and Spain, March 2015: post price collapse

	Nigeria Japan	*Nigeria Spain*	*Japanese advantage*	*Algeria Japan*	*Algeria Spain*	*Japanese advantage*
Spot tanker rate ($/day)	$30,375	$30,375		$30,375	$30,375	
LNG ex-ship	$7.68	$7.06	$0.62	$7.68	$7.06	$0.62
less tanker	($0.85)	($0.61)	($0.23)	($1.40)	($0.30)	($1.11)
LNG netback	$6.83	$6.45	$0.39	$6.28	$6.76	($0.49)

Note: Japanese and Spanish spot cargo prices from weekly Spot LNG series in *World Gas Intelligence*.

Conclusion: the evolution in tanker markets and vessel designs

The ability to move gas by sea over long distances is the basis of the transition of gas from a regional fuel to an internationally traded commodity. Tanker employment for specific trades is based on the LNG charterparty. It defines the relationship between the ship owner and the charterer. It is usually utilized even when the charterer owns the vessel. Charters can be term charters for a specified period of time, or voyage charters for one or more voyages. The most common pattern is for independent ship owners to build the vessel against a long-term charter and supply both vessel and crew.

LNG trade originally developed on the basis of long-term contracts of 20 years or more that specified the locations of both buyer and seller. In this environment, tankers were commonly chartered for the life of the original SPA. But as world LNG markets have become more destination-flexible, the role of tankers has changed somewhat. There is now an active short-term market – 29 per cent in 2014 – and the expansion of existing LNG trains often does not require the 20 year SPA contract to be economically viable.

In addition, portfolio aggregators, and buyers with destination flexibility, are often no longer interested in predictable source and market pairings, where route certainty defines the tanker requirement. Shorter-term and voyage charters are becoming more common. But not all of the short-term trade is covered by voyage or short-term charters. Much of this trade, particularly that from Qatar or by portfolio aggregators, utilizes long-term chartered vessels in flexible trade.

Still, the pattern of chartering a tanker for the extended life of the initial SPA remains. The rapid growth of the industry indicates that much of the existing fleet is still operating on its initial charter. Since the life expectancy of the typical tanker is much longer than the length of the initial charters, tankers have a significant 'after life' – on average 14 years. It is these older tankers, still owned by their original owners or by independents that have purchased them, that form the basis of the flexible fleet.

In tight markets, there is some speculative tanker building. And while this speculative ordering dries up when charter rates soften, this is the period when older tankers are more likely to become surplus.

Long-term charter rates reflect the option of ordering a newbuild tanker from a shipyard, although they are also influenced by the supply of newbuild vessels entering the market. Short-term rates, however, reflect the short-term balance of tanker supply and demand. Thus spot charter rates can be very volatile.

But the combination of spot charter rates and spot cargo prices has proved to be effective in rebalancing regional variations in supply and demand. Neither is regulated nor is it governed by external pricing clauses. Thus they provide the semblance of a workable market that enables LNG to flow to the market that provides the best netback, and to deliver cargoes where they are needed.

The tanker capacity required to meet demand from a new project is influenced not only by the size of the project, but also by the distance over which the LNG must be delivered. Thus unanticipated changes in regional supply/demand balances can have a substantial impact on requirements for tanker capacity.

For example, the sharp increase in Japanese LNG imports following Fukushima created a demand for Atlantic Basin LNG to supplement traditional Pacific Basin and Middle East sources. The longer hauls necessary to meet this demand put upward pressure on spot charter rates. But the increase in spot cargo prices into Japan was sufficient to support the necessary trade.

LNG vessel sizes have been increasing: from the 125,000 m^3 size that predominated in the mid-1970s to the 170,000 m^3 tankers that are more common today. Qatar's expansion featured its unique Q-Class tankers – Q-Flex at 210,000 to 217,000 and Q-Max at 263,000 to 267,000 m^3. These were much larger than the existing fleet. It is not clear that these represent a precedent for future sizes. The limited benefits of economies of scale, and the difficulties of serving many ports with the larger vessels, argue against very large tankers. For the moment, the size limitation on the expanded Panama Canal – 170,000 m^3 – appears to have set a ceiling on sizes.

Three innovations have evolved from LNG ship design. The first is the FSRU, which has regasification on board. Although it was originally intended as an innovation in tanker design, it is increasingly being used as a floating receiving terminal. The second innovation is placing the liquefaction unit on the vessel – FLNG – where it can serve supplies that are far offshore from a potential onshore liquefaction site.

The third innovation is the ice-breaking tanker. The appeal of the Northern Sea Route from Europe to Asia is that the distances are much shorter. With the shrinking of the Arctic ice cap, it is possible to contemplate using the route for at least part of the year. The Russians have been actively working on the technology and now have a proposed ARC7 Arctic design. This does not require icebreaking escorts and can handle ice up to two metres thick. The Yamal LNG project has ordered 14 of these vessels from a Korean shipyard.

Regasification terminals – adapting to a new environment

Introduction

All LNG terminals perform the same broad function: to unload and store LNG and regasify it to supply end-users with natural gas. There is, however, a range of differences between terminals with regard to: initial investment drivers, levels of utilization, mode of operation, and ownership. Furthermore, the role of these terminals is changing as they have to become ever more flexible and customer orientated to reflect a new, multi-user environment. This section looks at this evolution in terms of scale, location, and business models. For technical aspects relating to LNG regasification, see the Technical Appendix.

Global overview of regasification terminals

At the end of 2015 there were 35 countries capable of importing LNG through some 113[24] regasification terminals. These terminals had a combined throughput capacity of over 1 tcm/year of gas and a total storage capacity of 56 bcm of LNG.

The pattern of growth in LNG terminals since 1969 is shown in Figure 4.15 by region. The dominance of Asia is particularly apparent. Japan (with over 25 terminals) accounts for almost 50 per cent of Asian import capacity; other major Asian importers are Korea (28 per cent), China (9 per cent), and India (5 per cent). North America is dominated by the USA, although since 2006 terminals have also been built in Mexico and Canada. In Europe the largest share of LNG import capacity is in Spain (30 per cent) and the UK (26 per cent), with France accounting for just over 11 per cent.

---

[24] This number includes ship-based regasification facilities but excludes expansion projects.

182 *LNG Markets in Transition*

The 'Other' category comprises terminals in South America and the Middle East; the breakdown (as at the end of 2015) is shown in Table 4.13. The recent growth in terminals includes a number of floating facilities[25] and there were 13 importing counties with 20 such facilities by the end of 2015, with a total throughput capacity of 96 bcm (GIIGNL, 2016).

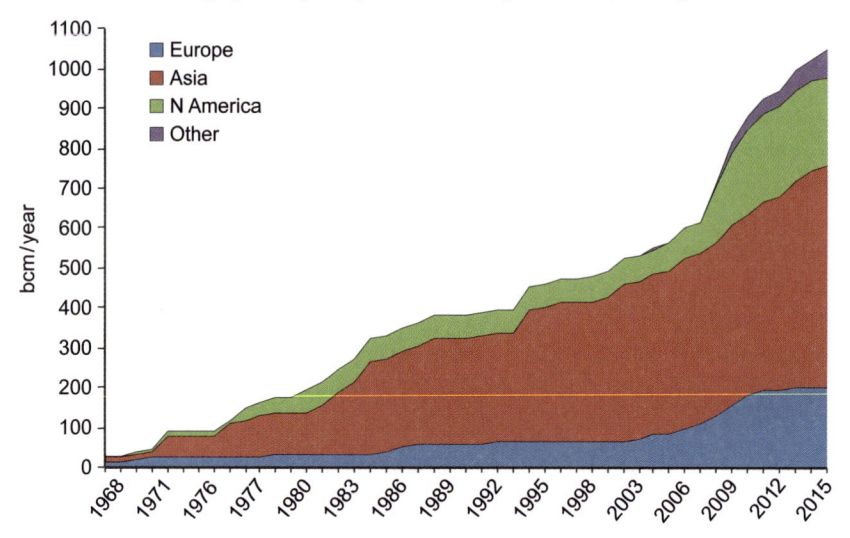

Figure 4.15: Regasification terminal capacity by region
Source: GIIGNL.

Table 4.13: LNG terminals by region

Location	Number of terminals	Throughput capacity (bcm/year)	Storage capacity (bcm)
North America	17	226	5.9
Europe	23	203	8.8
Japan/Korea/Taiwan	41	441	28.9
China and India	17	79	6.8
Asia (other)	6	32	1.6
Other (South America/ Middle East)	12	73	2.3
Total	**116**	**1,054**	**54.3**

Note: Terminal expansions are not counted separately in the number of terminals.
Source: GIIGNL.

---
[25] Referred to as floating storage and regasification units – FSRU.

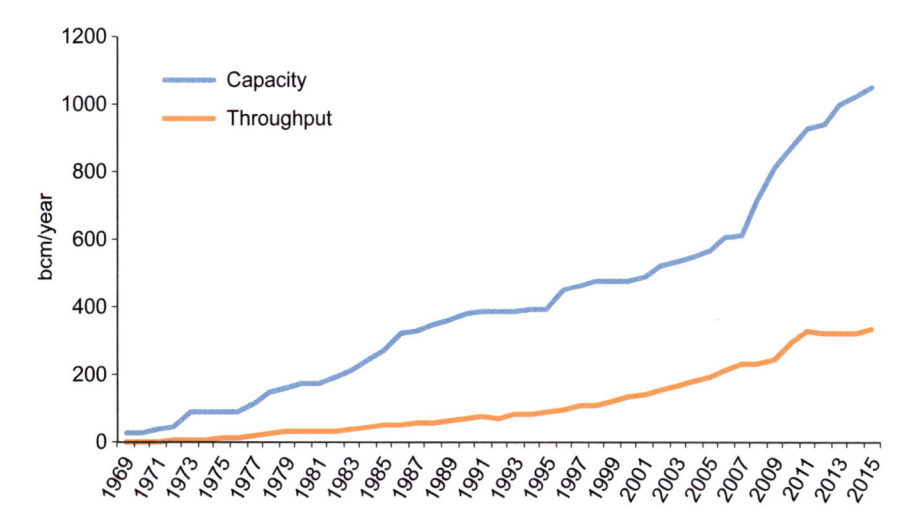

Figure 4.16: Global terminal capacity and LNG throughput
Source: GIIGNL.

Figure 4.16 shows the evolution of terminal capacity and actual LNG throughput over time. It is apparent that the global LNG market has always been characterized by a significant surplus of regasification capacity relative to liquefaction plant capacity. In 2000 total global liquefaction capacity was 138 bcm and regasification capacity was 480 bcm. By 2015 these figures had grown to 334 and 1036 respectively. Regasification terminal utilization rates were 28.9 per cent in 2000 and 32.2 per cent in 2015.

The tendency for an excess of regasification over liquefaction capacity is due to a number of reasons. Firstly the actual regasification unit is only a small part of the plant's total capital cost and there is little penalty associated with over-sizing it. Secondly some quoted capacities represent peak send outs that could not be sustained for any significant period. Thirdly receiving terminals will be designed to a minimum efficient size to be cost effective. Finally terminals are likely to be sized to reflect local demand requirements (including security of supply needs) as well as the configuration of supplies. So, for example, seasonal demand fluctuations may mean that terminal output is much higher during some months whilst LNG inputs remain fairly constant throughout the year. Frisch notes that factors such as shipping constraints, technical availability, and gas quality blending constraints make it difficult for terminals to match their nameplate capacity; these factors can be further exacerbated by the difficulties associated with multi-user terminal operations (Frisch, 2007). Another important influence has been the impact of changing gas market dynamics – most notably in the

USA and in Europe – where alternative supplies of gas have resulted in LNG imports being well below original expectations, leading to substantial surplus capacity with some terminals being closed or mothballed.

It is important to note that the relative cost of terminal construction and operation is low compared to other elements in the LNG chain. This means that terminals may be built in the clear recognition that they will not be fully utilized – though the issue of who will pay for this surplus capacity may arise. Regasification terminals, unlike liquefaction plant, can operate effectively at low levels of utilization (as long as there is sufficient 'heel' volume in the storage tank to keep the tanks cold) and if necessary the plant can be mothballed and re-instated relatively quickly. As a consequence, regasification capacity may exist, but not be immediately available.[26] Some terminals in Europe have introduced liquefaction of boil-off gas; this can be used if there are long periods when there is no send out.

Noting these caveats, regasification utilization can be calculated by taking LNG imports as a percentage of nameplate capacity. This shows that in global terms levels have fluctuated between 30 per cent and 38 per cent from 2000 to 2015. There has been a wide regional variation in utilization levels, as shown in Figure 4.17.

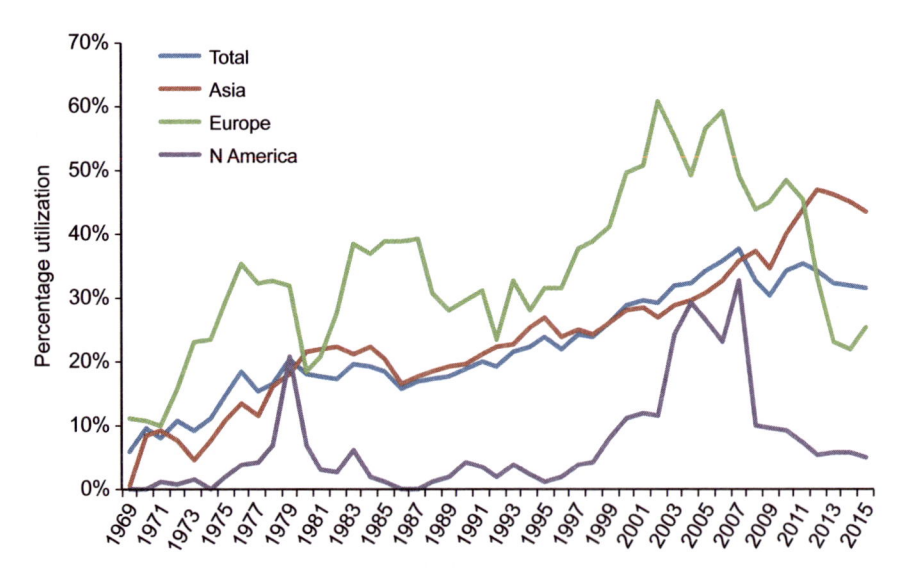

Figure 4.17: Regasification plant utilization levels by region, 1969–2014
Source: GIIGNL.

---

[26] This is primarily because some terminals might be warm and would need to be cooled down.

Utilization levels in Asia have grown from below 20 per cent in the mid-1980s to around 45 per cent in 2015, with a notable increase post 2011. In Japan this was a result of the Fukushima disaster, though other countries such as Taiwan and to a lesser extent Korea also increased utilization, due to growing gas demand. Utilization levels have fluctuated very widely in North America as a result of the huge growth in terminal capacity in the USA between 2005 and 2009. Imports peaked in 2007 at 22 bcm but fell to below 2 bcm by 2014 as a result of the growth in indigenous shale production. Utilization levels were comparatively high in Europe between 2002 and 2006, though they had fallen sharply by 2014, primarily due to declining demand. There is also a wide variation within regions, as shown in Table 4.14. The relatively high levels of utilization at South Hook and Zeebrugge reflect the presence of long-term LNG purchase agreements linked to these terminals.

Table 4.14: Terminal utilization levels for selected plant in NW Europe in 2014

Terminal	Nameplate capacity (bcm/year)	Throughput (bcm/year)	Utilization (%)
South Hook (GB)	20.4	8.9	44
Grain (GB)	19	1.3	7
Dragon (GB)	6.8	0.4	5
Zeebrugge (Belgium)	8.2	2.9	33
GATE (Netherlands)	10.9	1	9

Note: The numbers exclude re-loads.

Source: 'Aggregated LNG Storage Inventory (ALSI)', Publication of LNG inventory grouped by country area, Gas Infrastructure Europe (GIE) (http://lngdataplatform.gie.eu/).

Despite this pattern of under-utilization, a significant amount of new receiving terminal capacity is under construction. GIIGNL (2016) reports that 23 terminals (eight of which are FSRUs) plus five expansion projects, with a total capacity of 72 mtpa were under construction at the beginning of 2016. Over 70 per cent of this capacity is in Asia. During 2015 Egypt, Jordan, Poland, and Pakistan became importers of LNG for the first time.

As the number of receiving terminals has grown, terminal business models have also evolved. This feature is addressed in the following section.

Evolution of the regasification terminal business model

In the early stages of LNG market development in the late 1960s and 1970s, most regasification terminals were built as part of a single contract chain. There were, however, some exceptions where terminals were built independently of a specific LNG project, and the sector has evolved to a point where it is possible to distinguish between three broad categories of terminal (though in practice terminals may combine some or all of these elements). These categories, together with the broad scale of evolution, are shown in Figure 4.18 and discussed in more detail below.

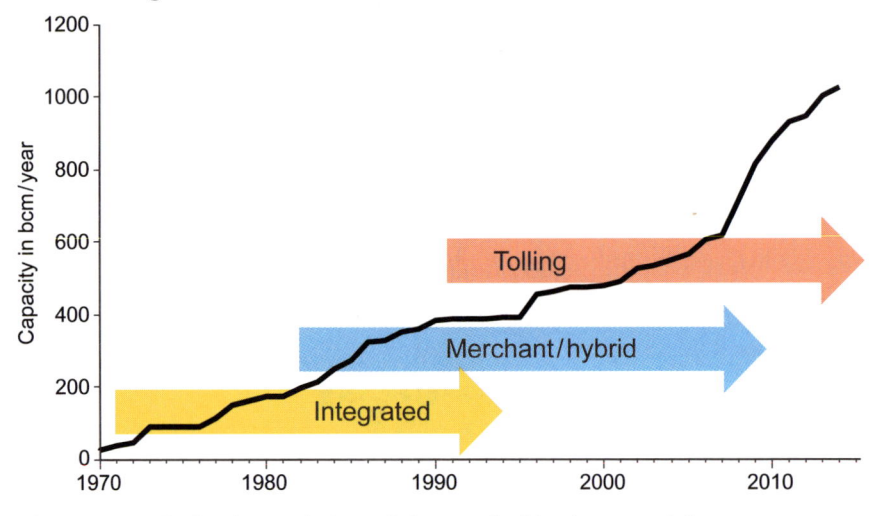

Figure 4.18: Indicative evolution of the terminal business model
Source: Author

Integrated or dedicated terminals
LNG regasification terminals that form part of an integrated LNG supply chain will typically involve a consortium of investors that includes both owners of gas reserves seeking monetization, and marketing companies with access to specific markets. The receiving terminal may be owned by the investing consortium or be constructed separately. The key feature is that the terminal is constructed and financed on the basis of exclusive access for a specific upstream development. This approach was evident in many of the early LNG projects such as the Alaska LNG project (Shaw Alaska, 2006) involving Phillips and Marathon in the upstream and Tokyo Gas's Negishi terminal.[27] Another example was the Fos Tonkin plant in

---

[27] This terminal started operation in May 1966 as a storage facility. Imports from Alaska started in 1969. 'Milestones', Tokyo Gas website (www.tokyo-gas.co.jp/Annai_e/mile_e.html).

France that opened in 1972 and was dedicated to receiving supplies from Algeria's Skikda plant.[28]

Many of these facilities were expanded over time, though again this was to serve specific sources of gas. The Negishi terminal was expanded in 1972 to accommodate imports from Brunei; the new, dedicated terminals at Sodegaura (Tokyo Gas) and Senboku (Osaka Gas) were also supplied by Brunei.[29]

Integrated projects in traditional LNG importing countries are now relatively rare as the amount of existing regasification capacity is such that projects are unlikely to need a specific outlet to secure an upstream project. Whilst some new markets are not large enough to underwrite a dedicated liquefaction project, some new terminals in larger markets have been linked to specific projects. Recent examples include the CNOOC/BP Guangdong Dapeng terminal in China, which is dedicated to receiving LNG from Australia's North West Shelf project[30] (first gas 2006). Another example is the Qatar Petroleum/ExxonMobil South Hook terminal in South Wales (first gas 2009), which is dedicated to the Qatargas 2 project.[31]

The advantage of the integrated model is that the sizing and timing of the facility can be precisely tailored to the needs of the overall project, while contractual linkages through the chain should make financing more straightforward. One drawback in some importing countries is that regulatory requirements regarding open access may require a higher degree of transparency. It should be noted that even though the South Hook shareholders[32] are present in every element of the Qatargas 2 value chain in structural terms, the terminal is a tolling plant (Tyler, 2007).

Tolling terminals

A combination of regulatory and financial drivers has led to an increase in the use of tolling models for fixed infrastructure such as regasification terminals. Under the tolling model, the terminal owner rents the capacity to third parties – usually the LNG seller or the gas buyer – on a long-term basis and does not take title to the gas at any stage of the operation. The owner will receive a fee (typically comprising fixed and variable elements) to cover unloading, storage, and regasification of LNG. Revenue streams

---

[28] '50 years of LNG – 1972: Fos Tonkin, an LNG terminal with an exemplary history', 11 May 2015. www.gdfsuez.com/en/news/50-years-lng-1972-fos-tonkin-lng-terminal-history/.

[29] 'Milestones', Brunei LNG website (www.bruneilng.com/milestone_70s.htm).

[30] BP and CNOOC hold 30% and 33% respectively.

[31] Though the South Hook terminal was structured as a tolling entity for regulatory reasons.

[32] Shareholdings are: Qatar Petroleum 67.5%, ExxonMobil 24.15%, and Total 8.35%. South Hook LNG Terminal Company – Our Shareholders. https://www.southhooklng.com/about-us/shareholders/.

188 *LNG Markets in Transition*

are guaranteed by a ship-or-pay provision in the agreements from companies with good credit ratings.

The nature of terminal promoters can vary quite widely. In the UK and the Netherlands infrastructure operators (National Grid and Gasunie) have developed terminals, as have oil storage companies such as Petroplus and Vopak. In the USA, the exploration company Cheniere promoted a number of tolling plants in the early 2000s. Some promoters may seek to combine merchant and tolling characteristics by reserving some capacity for their own use in order to import LNG when price arbitrage opportunities are attractive.

A typical example of a tolling terminal is the GATE facility in Rotterdam, which began operation in 2011. GATE was constructed on the basis of five primary capacity holders[33] taking 3 bcm/year capacities over a 20 year period. In the USA, the Cheniere terminal at Sabine Pass was underwritten by 20 year capacity contracts with Chevron and Total, though its marketing affiliate also reserved capacity in the terminal.[34]

One of the key advantages of the tolling model is that it enables terminals to be constructed independently of gas sales agreements and their associated price or volume risks. This was illustrated vividly in the case of Cheniere, whose decision to take capacity in its own US import terminals was exposed by the sudden growth in domestic gas production on the back of the US shale revolution. The company would almost certainly have disappeared if it were not for the fact that the rest of the capacity was underwritten by long-term capacity payments from Chevron and Total.[35]

Tolling facilities can provide smaller tranches of capacity to potential users, thus opening up the option of LNG purchases for smaller buyers such as regional gas marketing companies. This capacity can be relatively easily transferred or traded. Larger companies also like the tolling model, as it avoids upfront capital expenditure. Tolling plant can often be developed more quickly and should be easier to finance – it may attract a wider group of investors as the revenue stream and risks are easier to identify. A tolling structure may also be required for regulatory reasons.

The biggest challenge facing a tolling plant is that it is almost certainly going to operate on the basis of a number of unconnected users. Even terminals that have started with a single user may become multi-user, as

---

[33] These companies were German utilities E.ON and RWE, Dutch utility Eneco, Vienna-based Econgas, and DONG of Denmark.

[34] Cheniere, 2006 Annual Report. http://media.corporate-ir.net/media_files/irol/10/101667/2006%20Annual%20Report.pdf.

[35] 'How Cheniere Energy Got First In Line To Export America's Natural Gas', Christopher Helman, Forbes Energy, 17 April 2013. www.forbes.com/sites/christopherhelman/2013/04/17/first-mover-how-cheniere-energy-is-leading-americas-lng-revolution/.

capacity is expanded or is traded. These trends have led to the terminal's commercial and operational arrangements becoming subject to a series of contracts. The plant may also be exposed to risks arising in other parts of the LNG chain – for example force majeure events or the failure of users to ensure there is sufficient heel gas in the storage tanks.

Promoters of tolling projects may also offer a partial share in the equity in the terminal as part of the financing arrangements.

Merchant terminals
Whilst the definition of tolling and integrated terminals is relatively straightforward, it is less clear cut for merchant terminals. This group exhibits significant variation in terms of players and structures, and could be said to comprise 'all terminals that are not either tolling or integrated'. In broad terms, a merchant terminal is one that is not linked to a specific source of gas but is owned by parties who also own title to LNG and want control of the regasification facilities. The merchant terminal owner imports and markets the LNG and sits contractually between LNG producer and gas wholesaler or end-user. The cost of the regasification terminal is funded out of the margin achieved. In many cases merchant terminals are market driven, with gas buyers seeking new sources of supply and choosing LNG as an attractive option. Since the LNG buyers may have had to commit to long-term contracts with specific suppliers, these terminals can have features that are similar to those dedicated to specific projects; the key difference is that the terminal will have been developed independently of the supply source.

An early example of independent LNG regasification terminals is the USA, where US natural gas companies built four eastern seaboard terminals between 1971 and 1980.[36] These terminals were linked to long-term supply contracts, with six such contracts having been signed between October 1969 and October 1976.[37] One of the terminals was located in Boston Massachusetts, where Distrigas Corporation (a locally owned utility) built the LNG import facility as a key means of solving the energy shortages that were prevalent at the time. The terminal supplied LNG by truck to 46 utility-owned above ground LNG storage facilities around New England;[38]

---

[36] These were Lake Charles, La. (Trunkline), Everett, Mass. (Distrigas), Elba Island, Ga. (El Paso NG), and Cove Point, Md. (Dominion Energy). See 'Brief History of LNG', Center for Energy Economics. www.beg.utexas.edu/energyecon/lng/LNG_introduction_06.php.

[37] 'LNG TRADE: PAST, PRESENT, FUTURE (?)',Natural gas imports and exports, Third quarter report 1995, North American Gas Trade, *QUARTERLY FOCUS*. www.fe.doe.gov/programs/gasregulation/analyses/Focus/3rd95foc.pdf.

[38] 'LNG', GDF SUEZ/Engie (North America) website (www.gdfsuezna.com/lng-operations/).

this provided much needed flexibility in a region that was unsuitable for underground gas storage. In Europe, merchant terminals were developed in Spain by Union Fenosa at Sagunto[39] and by the Bahia de Bizkaia Group (a consortium including BP, Repsol, and Iberdrola) at Bilbao.[40] An example from Asia is the Hazira terminal in Gujarat, India, developed by Shell and Total.[41]

In another variation of the merchant model, an importing country may itself decide to promote the development of a terminal, together with the supply of LNG, in order to diversify energy supply. Under such arrangements a government entity may own the terminal, though operation might be outsourced to the LNG sellers or to a third party. Examples of this approach include Singapore, and the Quintero terminal in Chile.

In 2006 the Government of Chile invited bids from a number of LNG supply companies to participate in the construction and ownership of a LNG regasification terminal and an associated marketing joint venture. The successful bidder would also be obliged to supply two cargoes of LNG per month. The winning bidder was BG Group, which agreed to supply 1.7 mtpa of LNG from its portfolio and take 40 per cent ownership of the company that owns and operates the import terminal.[42] BG subsequently sold its terminal shareholding to Enagas.[43]

Singapore, through the state Energy Markets Authority, ran a process to appoint a demand aggregator to import LNG through a new terminal to be owned, financed, and built by the government of Singapore. In 2008, BG was appointed as the supplier and demand aggregator for the first 3 mtpa of LNG demand (Turner and Barker, 2013). The terminal arrangements had some tolling characteristics, as the aggregator was required to procure and manage terminal capacity though a Terminal Use Agreement (TUA), but it could not own equity in the terminal (this may be allowed in the future).

One of the major challenges of the merchant model is that because the terminal is not specifically linked to an upstream development, it may be difficult to synchronize the financing and construction of the terminal facilities with the gas supply contract. In the classic 'chicken and egg' dilemma facing many gas infrastructure projects, sellers may be unwilling to conclude a deal without clear evidence of the physical means for the

---

[39] Union Fenosa Gas website (https://www.unionfenosagas.com/en).
[40] 'Bahia de Bizkaia Regasification Plant, Bilbao, Spain', Hydrocarbons Technology website (www.hydrocarbons-technology.com/projects/bbg-plant/).
[41] 'Hazira LNG and port' website (www.haziralngandport.com/).
[42] 'Our History', GNL Quintero website (www.gnlquintero.cl/eng/about_us/history.htm).
[43] 'BG Group completes sale of interest in Chilean LNG terminal', BG Group press release, 5 September 2013. www.bg-group.com/~/tiles/?tiletype=pressrelease&id=464.

buyer to take delivery, whilst financing a terminal may be difficult without a gas supply contract in place.

Furthermore there is the risk that the terminal will not be ready in time for the start of contractual first gas delivery. A very graphic example of this occurred in 1996, when the Italian power company ENEL attempted to cancel a gas purchase contract with Nigeria LNG following permitting delays to its planned import facility on the coast of Tuscany. The $13 billion lawsuit was eventually settled out of court; the LNG supplies were diverted to France and the Italian terminal was never built.[44] More recently, delays to the Świnoujście terminal in Poland beyond the planned start date in 2014 led to gas buyer PGNiG incurring penalties on its gas contract with Qatar.[45] These risks can be mitigated to some extent by linking the terminal development with LNG supply through the services of an aggregator with access to a portfolio of LNG supplies, as in the case of Singapore. Terminal development can also be phased to ensure LNG cargoes can be received even if storage is not in place, through the use of ship-based regasification.

Merchant terminals may also be subject to some degree of price and volume risk, though how this is allocated in practice will vary. Other challenges include the credit risk associated with consumers, high working capital requirements, and possible local currency risk. One way of mitigating these risks may be to opt for a floating facility leased from a third party. This allows new players to invest in capacity ahead of a specific contract and it can be operated on a short-term basis simply floating away in the event of a default (see the following section on FSRUs).

In summary, there is a trend towards tolling models for terminals as gas markets become more transparent and liberalized and the liquidity of international LNG movements increases. This reflects the presence of regulatory pressures for open access, recognition that the benefits of terminal ownership are less important than owning capacity, and the relatively low cost of regasification capacity versus the potential arbitrage value from being able to switch cargoes quickly between markets. Nevertheless there may still be a need for project participants to own a terminal – at least in the start-up phase – to ensure that the project is financed and completed to a satisfactory level.

---

[44] See 'Greenfield LNG Import Terminal Approvals', Philip R. Weems and Kevin D. Keenan (King & Spalding, USA), *LNG Journal*, May/June 2002. www.kslaw.com/library/pdf/GreenfieldLNGTerminalApprovals.pdf.

[45] 'Start-up of Polish LNG terminal delayed to Q2 2016', Tom Marzec-Manser, ICIS, 23 July 2015. www.icis.com/resources/news/2015/07/23/9906118/start-up-of-polish-lng-terminal-delayed-to-q2-2016/.

Commercial and operational aspects

The evolution of LNG projects, together with the associated commercial relationships and regulatory environments, has led to an increasingly blurred distinction between types of terminal. For example merchant plant (and terminals that are part of integrated projects) are often structured so that the terminal company operates as a service provider with minimum liability. These terminals are effectively tolling operations embedded within a larger project.

The emergence of tolling terminals as a feature of many regasification facilities has led to a clear delineation of roles in the regasification arena:

- Terminal owner.
- Terminal operator (TO).
- Terminal user (TU).
- Agent.

The following sections explain how these roles relate to each other and the contractual arrangements that are necessary. The impact of FSRUs is also briefly considered.

Terminal user agreements

The most important distinction is that between the role of user and operator. This relationship is typically formalized through a Terminal Use Agreement[46] (TUA). The prime objectives of the TUA will be to facilitate the optimum and safe use of the terminal and to specify the duties and obligations of respective parties.

The main areas set out in a typical TUA are:

- Quantities to be processed. These are defined in a number of ways including annual capacity, hourly or daily send-out rates, and volume and duration of storage.
- Shipping sizes and ship scheduling arrangements.
- Charges or tariffs. These typically combine fixed and variable elements, with the latter linked to actual send-out.

---

[46] Other names include 'Throughput Agreement', 'Terminal Capacity Agreement', and 'Terminal Services Agreement'. There may also be a more detailed Terminal Access Code (Weems, 2005).

- Obligations and responsibilities of the two parties. For the operator this includes: the reception, storage and regasification of LNG, and the delivery of gas into the adjoining network. For the user: the delivery of LNG via approved vessels to agreed quality and performance standards.

- Liquidated damages. The costs arising from (for example) under-delivery by the TO; this is usually done through a reduction in charges.

- Other aspects will include: gas quality definitions, how to deal with off-spec gas, arrangements for handling unused berthing slots, force majeure events, and the provision of additional services such as nitrogen enrichment and ship re-fuelling.

The most important aspects of a TUA relate to capacity allocation, scheduling, and charging. These are explored in the following sections with particular reference to the challenges associated with multi-user terminals.

Terminal capacity allocation
Terminal capacity in a multi-user environment can be defined and allocated in various ways. These include: the number of berthing slots in a defined period, a defined input rate, a specific level of storage, and a defined maximum send-out capacity (or a combination of any of these). The most common approach is to allocate a proportion of annual throughput to each user and then determine the other elements (berthing slots, storage, and maximum send-out rates) as a consequence.

Weems notes that there are two basic options for a multi-user terminal configuration (Weems, 2005):

- Independent rights – each user is able to unload, store, and send-out gas independently of the other users.

- Dependent rights – some of the key terminal functions are shared between users.

Whilst the independent rights model is simpler to operate, it requires dedicated assets for each user. This can be a costly option as dedicated storage would be needed. LNG storage is the most expensive element of terminal construction costs[47] and in order to optimize the overall terminal configuration it is normally sized and allocated on the assumption of constant send-out and is provided to users on a shared basis (that is, under the dependent rights model). Users, on the other hand, will be seeking

---
[47] Typically 80 per cent of total capital expenditure.

194   *LNG Markets in Transition*

maximum flexibility in order to cater for different ship sizes and variations in send-out rates. In order to reconcile these conflicting objectives, each user would not be allocated a fixed amount of storage as the amount will vary day by day. Furthermore each user will be dependent on the other users acting in accordance with the TUA to ensure equitable access to capacity.

The issues are illustrated in simple terms in Figure 4.19; this shows the relationship between space and send-out for a terminal with three users under the dependent rights model. It is assumed that each user has a ship with a capacity of 150,000 m^3 of LNG berthing every six days. The terminal comprises a single LNG storage tank with a capacity of 300,000 m^3 and a minimum stock requirement of 20,000 m^3. User 1 will have a larger share of total storage just after one of its vessels has unloaded and this will be required to fall over time to ensure there is sufficient storage space to allow the ships of users 2 and 3 to unload. A terminal operating under the independent rights model would require three separate tanks of 150,000 m^3 each which would be much more costly, although more flexible for the individual user.

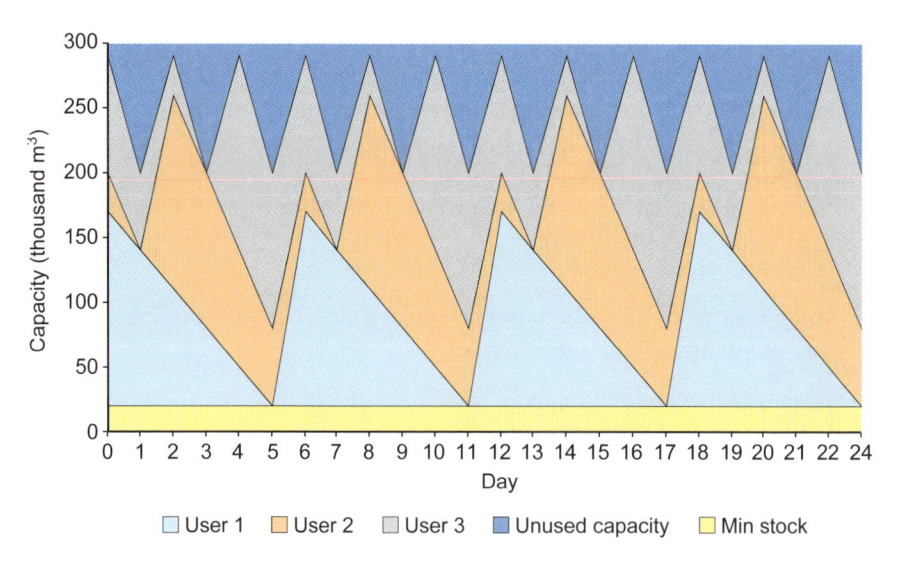

Figure 4.19: Capacity availability in a multi-user terminal (dependent rights)
Source: Author

There is thus a trade-off between cost and flexibility, with the dependent rights model being more prevalent where there is a multiplicity of users sourcing LNG from a range of locations, under differing contractual durations, and using a variety of tanker configurations. In the above example, this model also has the advantage of creating greater flexibility for handling larger ship sizes through temporary transfers of storage capacity between users. The terminal operator would normally prefer to comingle volumes, as this allows them to offer a lower throughput fee.

A further variation on the dependent rights model is to have tiered users who have different rights and obligations. Such arrangements might arise when a primary capacity holder or the terminal owner wishes to sell some of its capacity on a short-term interruptible basis. This can be useful when spare capacity is available, though it also adds a layer of complexity to the commercial and operational arrangements.

Dependent rights terminals can include the role of an agent[48] who will act as an independent interface between the operator and users, managing aspects such as nominations, allocation, and bulletin boards to advertise spare berthing slots.[49]

Terminal scheduling
A critical aspect of terminal operation is the arrangement for receiving and unloading LNG tankers. This is covered by the scheduling procedures in the TUA and usually involves agreeing an annual programme for the unloading of LNG (which is then followed up by a more detailed rolling programme, termed the '90 day schedule'). Under the programme, each user is allocated a number of berthing or delivery slots with a specified arrival time and laytime to allow unloading. Each arrival time will be allowed a degree of leeway (usually in the region of six hours) and delivery time would be around 30 hours; a vessel would thus have a 36 hour window to arrive, discharge, and depart.

Multi-user terminals with a single unloading jetty may need to enforce the times set out in the rolling programme. In some TUAs there is provision for a user to pay demurrage charges if, by overstaying, it causes delay to another user's ships.

Terminal charges
Charges for terminal use typically comprise two elements:

- a fixed monthly charge that covers the cost of booked capacity,

- a variable charge based on actual send-out. The variable charge might include the cost of additional services such as nitrogen enrichment.

---

[48] This role is often undertaken by a consulting or accounting organization.
[49] One such example is the BP/Sonatrach agent at the Grain LNG terminal. See 'BP / Sonatrach Phase 1 Isle of Grain Commercial Operations', LNG Grain Agency website (www.lngga.com/page.html).

The TUA may include options for higher send-outs or additional storage at a premium price. The treatment of fuel gas requirements can vary – in some cases this element may be deducted as a fixed percentage of the gas processed. Efficiency can also be improved by linkage with other facilities. The GATE terminal in Rotterdam utilizes residual heat from a nearby power station for regasification[50] whilst many terminals use the 'cold energy' from regasification for cryogenic applications (Sharratt, 2012).

The terminal operator will maintain a daily balance of LNG discharged into the facility and natural gas sent out for each user and this will include allocations for fuel gas and boil-off gas where appropriate. Arrangements for metering and reconciliation of each user's throughput are important and this is an area where an agent can play a key role.

Floating storage and regasification units (FSRUs)
The growth of Floating Storage and Regasification Units (FSRUs), in place of building new land-based facilities, has also created greater access to markets and increased buyer liquidity. These vessels, conversions of old vessels or newbuild vessels, are LNG ships with regasification facilities on-board. Moored at a jetty or out at sea, FSRUs receive deliveries of LNG from the delivery vessel (or in some cases the FSRU can itself collect the LNG from the supplier) and then regasify the LNG, which is pumped to sales gas pipeline pressure and then vaporized. The advantage of an FSRU is that it can be put in place faster and at a lower cost than a land-based facility. A land-based terminal can take from three to five years to build and cost $500–$1000 million; whereas an FSRU can, if it is a conversion of an old tanker and using existing facilities, take less than a year. Even in the case of a newbuild, an FSRU would only take around three years. An FSRU also avoids the problem of reduced availability of onshore sites and growing public opposition to industrial developments of this nature.

The technology employed originated in the 'Energy Bridge' concept developed in 2000 by El Paso Natural Gas. It envisaged putting the regasification unit on the tanker itself and then offloading the gas onto a specially designed mooring buoy anchored at an offshore location. El Paso abandoned the effort in 2002 and the venture was acquired by George Kaiser, a wealthy Oklahoma oilman who adopted the name Excelerate Energy.

Only three terminals have been built using the original mooring buoy approach: Excelerate's Gulf Gateway Deepwater Port (offshore Louisiana), its Northeast Gateway, and Engie's Neptune Deepwater Port (both offshore Massachusetts). Because of US gas market conditions, Gulf Gateway has

---

[50] 'Profile of Gate terminal: a storage and handling company', Gate (Gas Access To Europe) website (http://gate.nl/en/gate-terminal/profile.html).

been dismantled and the two Massachusetts terminals have seldom been utilized.

Excelerate can also utilize the technology by delivering to onshore gas receiving facilities where a buoy is not necessary. This is the approach utilized at Teesside in the UK – this plant was decommissioned in 2015.

The problem with the original concept is that it delivers gas only while the tanker is moored to the facility, but it is not able to provide the continuous flows required by most gas send out systems. Thus it only works where the intermittent supply is integrated with a variable onshore supply. Underground storage provided this 'replacement' capacity in Louisiana, while integration with complex seasonal peaking systems did so for Massachusetts.

The initial concept assumed that the vessels' prime role was transportation; this had the benefit that they could deliver gas to market without the need for an expensive fixed terminal onshore. But the recognition that they could also be moored at market and supplied by other vessels gradually developed. In this role they became terminals first and tankers second. Although used as terminals, they could be moved to other locations if needed. With the solution of technical issues relating to ship-to-ship transfer, this has now become the prime role of the FSRUs.

The ability to operate either as a terminal or as a trading ship has some distinct benefits. The Mina Al-Ahmadi terminal in Kuwait operates as a terminal during the summer air conditioning season, but then leaves and operates as a trading vessel during the northern hemisphere winter.

An existing FSRU can quickly be put into service as a holding operation while a more permanent solution – an onshore terminal or a specifically designed FSRU – is still under construction. The speed with which an FSRU can be put in place can be seen in Egypt. In mid-2014 the country issued a tender to secure an FSRU for a five-year charter; in November 2014 it signed an agreement with Höegh LNG, and in April 2015 Egypt received its first LNG cargo on an FSRU that Höegh LNG already had available.

FSRUs are typically developed by ship owning companies (Excelerate, Golar, and Höegh being the three main providers) and then chartered to the buying company (sometimes including the construction of the jetty facilities) on a daily hire rate basis. This means that the buyer will not have to make such large capital outlays, thereby enabling smaller companies to get involved in the business. Excelerate is the leader in FSRU ownership/operation with nine tanker-based FSRUs in operation. Golar has been a leader in converting used tankers to FSRUs, with four such conversions. But other companies are becoming active by ordering new FSRUs from the shipyards.

One of the disadvantages of using ships originally designed for transportation in the FSRU role is the sizing mismatch. In an ideal world, the capacity of the receiving storage should be double the capacity of any vessel that serves it (Tusiani and Shearer, 2006, 121). While this may be viewed today as too conservative, trying to utilize receiving vessels of a size similar to the delivering vessel provides no contingency for variations in scheduling or in gas send out, which makes it an inefficient way to operate.

There is a trend to order larger FSRUs to provide for such scheduling contingencies. Eight FSRUs were launched in 2014 and 2015, all of them 160,000 m^3 or above. But an interesting new vessel order in 2014 offers a possible glimpse of the future. Engie ordered a 263,000 m^3 FSRU for a new terminal in Uruguay. It is virtually the same size as Qatar's Q-Max tankers and could accommodate the increasingly common 170,000 m^3 tankers with a 55 per cent contingency margin. Engie and its partner Marubeni left the project in September 2015. MOL took over the build, own, and operate of the FSRU (see page 408).

The regulation of LNG regasification terminals

As we have already seen, many of the early LNG receiving terminals were built as utility assets that were integrated within the importing country's gas transportation infrastructure. The overall pace of market liberalization often, therefore, drives the treatment of LNG terminals from a regulatory perspective. The key factor shaping the degree of regulation of LNG regasification terminals is the extent to which the terminals are considered to be part of the downstream infrastructure. There are broadly two approaches (de la Flor et al., 2013):

1. The terminal is considered to be an element of the downstream infrastructure of the market to which it is linked. In these cases terminals will typically be subject to regulatory requirements for non-discrimination, transparency, unbundling, and market opening that will apply more generally. This is the approach adopted in the European Union for example, though as described below the regime has evolved over time and there are widespread exemptions.

2. The terminal is treated as an upstream asset and so is exempt from the application of regulatory requirements that might apply to downstream infrastructure. This is the approach adopted in the USA following FERC's decision regarding the Hackberry terminal in 2002.[51] It is also the *de facto* approach adopted in many other importing countries, such as China (ICLG, 2016; IEA, 2012, 33).

---

[51] See 'Legislation and Regulations: The Hackberry Decision', Annual Energy Outlook, Energy Information Administration, January 2004 (www.eia.gov/oiaf/archive/aeo04/leg_reg7.html). Prior to the Hackberry decision terminals were subject to open access obligations and this still applies to three original terminals.

Where terminals are regulated, rules are usually developed to avoid restrictions arising from contractual foreclosure or other measures that might result in the hoarding of capacity. On the other hand, there is the recognition that appropriate returns for investors are required if new terminals are to be built. Furthermore the effective regulation of terminals is only as good as the overall regulatory framework. In Japan, for example, third-party access (TPA) applies in theory, but the slow pace of market liberalization makes it very difficult to achieve in practice (de la Flor et al, 2013).

The European Union is probably more advanced than other regions in dealing with issues relating to the regulation of LNG terminals. The rest of this section focuses on the EU's treatment of LNG terminals and the issues that arise. The regulation of terminals has evolved over time and has focused primarily on the access regime that should apply. Under the First Gas directive of 1998[52] Member States could choose between:

- Negotiated third-party access rights ('nTPA') leading to a voluntary commercial agreement.

- Regulated third-party access rights ('rTPA') on the basis of published tariffs.

The Second Gas Directive[53] set rTPA as the default regime and this approach was confirmed by the European Gas Directive 2009/73/EC[54] which forms part of the EU's Third Energy Package.

The legislation[55] allows for exemptions to the requirements for TPA to be granted to a new terminal where:

- It will increase supply security.

- It would not be built unless an exemption was granted.

---

[52] DIRECTIVE 98/30/EC OF THE EUROPEAN PARLIAMENT AND OF THE COUNCIL of 22 June 1998 concerning common rules for the internal market in natural gas (the First Gas Directive). http://eur-lex.europa.eu/legal-content/EN/TXT/PDF/?uri=CELEX:31998L0030&from=EN.

[53] DIRECTIVE 2003/55/EC OF THE EUROPEAN PARLIAMENT AND OF THE COUNCIL of 26 June 2003 concerning common rules for the internal market in natural gas and repealing Directive 98/30/EC (the Second Gas Directive). http://eur-lex.europa.eu/legal-content/EN/TXT/PDF/?uri=CELEX:32003L0055&from=EN.

[54] DIRECTIVE 2009/73/EC OF THE EUROPEAN PARLIAMENT AND OF THE COUNCIL of 13 July 2009 concerning common rules for the internal market in natural gas and repealing Directive 2003/55/EC. http://eur-lex.europa.eu/LexUriServ/LexUriServ.do?uri=OJ:L:2009:211:0094:0136:en:PDF.

[55] Article 22 of Directive 2009/73/EC.

- It is not owned by a gas transporter.
- Terminal users pay charges.
- The exemption is not detrimental to competition.
- The European Commission is content with the exemption.

As a result of the evolution of arrangements and the availability of exemptions, different regimes apply to different terminals across the EU. Terminals built prior to 2003 are subject to some form of regulated TPA, whilst most new terminals have been granted exemption from TPA. In the UK, for example, all terminals have been exempted as long as the above criteria are met, there has been some form of open season, secondary trading of capacity is allowed, and 'use-it-or-lose-it' measures (UIOLI) are in place.[56] In Italy, only 20 per cent of capacity in the North Adriatic Terminal is subject to rTPA.

Exemption from TPA regulation does not mean that terminals are exempt from regulatory scrutiny. The opening of the Grain terminal in the UK coincided with a period of tightness in the global LNG market and as a result there was significant under-utilization of terminal capacity. There were also supply problems in the UK and Ofgem recorded specific concerns over transparency of terminal operation and the UIOLI arrangements.[57]

At the heart of the problem was the limited notice given to potential users of when slots would be available. Figure 4.20 shows that information on spare berthing slots only becomes available seven days before it has to be used. Given the lead times involved in procuring and re-routing cargoes, this means, in effect, that is not possible to utilize the slot. Ofgem was concerned this could have a material impact on UK gas supplies and threatened withdrawal of the TPA exemption.

Grain, along with most of the other terminals in Europe, has made major efforts to improve transparency; most terminals have websites with bulletin boards that advertise available berthing slots, although in many cases these are still subject to relatively short notice of availability. The present overhang of LNG import capacity has taken much of the heat out of the issue.

---

[56] See DTI (2003) for a detailed description of the criteria and Ofgem (2004) which illustrates the principles in the case of the South Hook Terminal.
[57] Letter from Sonia Brown to Ian Davis ('Use it or lose it (UIOLI) arrangements at Grain LNG', Ofgem, 21 November 2005, https://www.ofgem.gov.uk/ofgem-publications/41299/12165-25505.pdf).

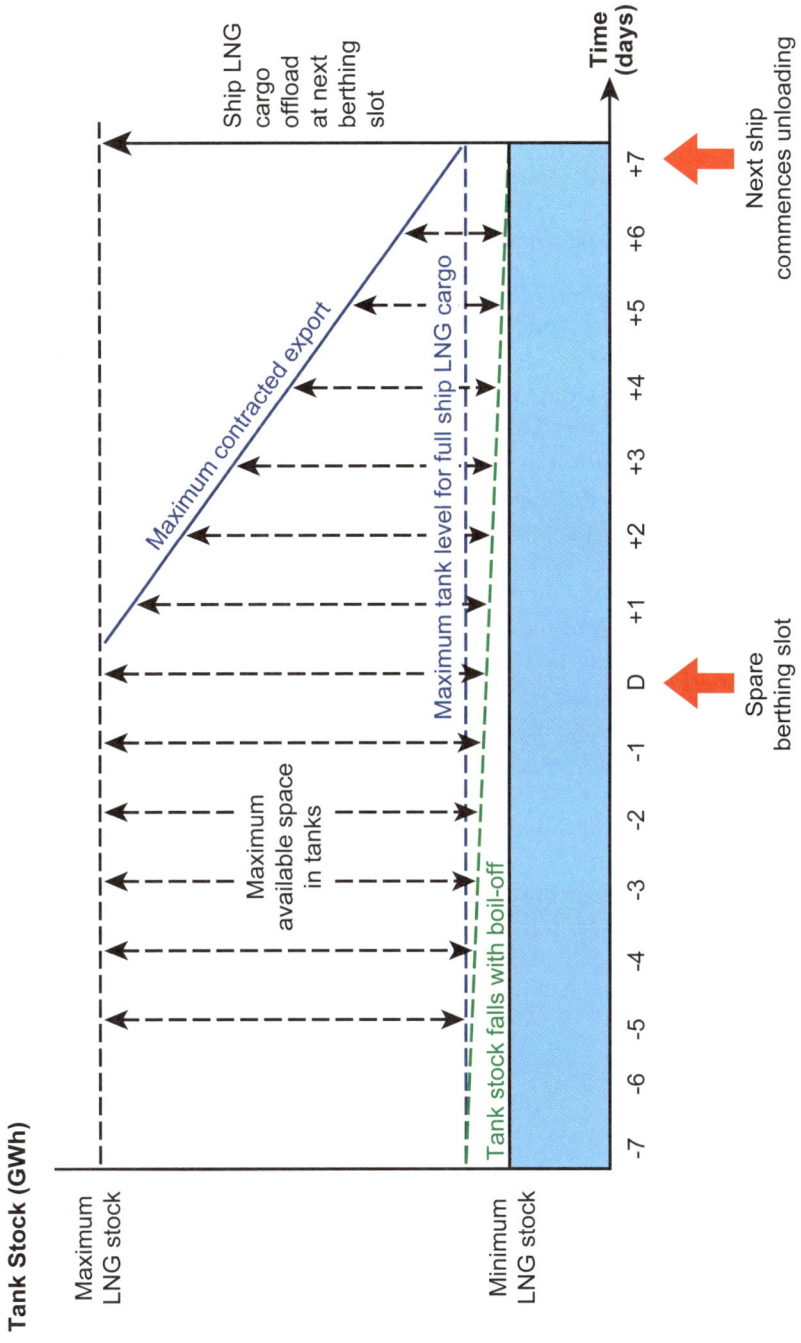

Figure 4.20: Allocation of spare berthing slots at Grain LNG
Source: Davis (2006).

Regulators may also become involved in approving terminal tariffs – or the mechanism by which they are calculated. In Spain, for example, LNG terminals fall under the same regime as that for regulating transportation assets. Revenue is based on tolling fees from users and a share of gas system income. In Belgium, the terminal operator Fluxys submits budget and tariff proposals to the Belgian regulator CREG for its Zeebrugge terminal.

Financing LNG regasification terminals[58]

With the increasing trend for terminals to be developed independently of other elements in the LNG chain, there is a growing requirement for these to be financed on a standalone basis. As for any investment, those companies that are able to self-finance will always be able to move forwards fastest – for example Shell and Sempra Energy's Costa Azul plant in Mexico.[59] Project financing can, however, have advantages – such as the opportunity to enhance returns on equity from higher leverage, creating a liability shield and allocating risk appropriately (Tyler, 2007).

Tolling terminals seeking finance will usually commence the process with an open season, inviting interested parties to bid for regasification capacity. Those prepared to subscribe would then negotiate a set of contracts based on agreed heads of terms. These agreements, once signed, would form the basis of commitment to financing and investment. Promoters will expect to be dealing with a number of bidding parties during the open season process, and so will be conducting a series of parallel negotiations. If the number of interested parties exceeds the available capacity, then this will normally be allocated on a first-come-first-served (FCFS) basis. The final agreements will normally need to be standardized, to ensure that regulatory requirements for non-discrimination are met. However, terms may vary on occasions, particularly if some of the capacity is allocated at a later stage.

Financial backers will require:

- Long-term capacity contracts in place, with substantive and credit worthy primary capacity holders.

- Clarity regarding construction strategy (with particular emphasis on the management of completion risk, see Noonan and Martin (2001)) and operating arrangements.

---

[58] For a detailed description of the issues see Ledesma (2014).

[59] This was subsequently restructured with Sempra owning and operating the terminal on a tolling basis for Shell's LNG supplies. See 'Financing LNG Terminals', Richard Nemec, *Oil & Gas Financial Journal*, 1 February 2005 (www.ogfj.com/articles/print/volume-2/issue-1/features/financing-lng-terminals.html).

- Sponsors with financial strength and credibility.

- Exemption from TPA regimes where applicable (for example, in Europe) and other regulatory approvals in place.

For merchant terminals, lenders will also want to understand whether the borrower is exposed to price and volume risk and to associated credit risk, and if so how this might be mitigated. For example, a merchant terminal may have to provide credit to upstream sellers as well as downstream buyers. In order to simplify and reduce the cost of financing terminals that are, in effect, merchant terminals, operators may opt for a tolling type structure. This was the case for South Hook.

Regasification terminals – both merchant and tolling models – will usually be structured similarly to other infrastructure projects for financing, with sponsors seeking a high level of project financing of around 80 per cent. Terms would be 20 years from start of construction, fixed interest, with repayments to start at project completion. Financing is non-recourse – in other words, the project sponsors are not liable for any failure either during construction or operation.

Lenders can include a mix of commercial banks and agencies such as the European Investment Bank[60] (EIB) and the Asian Development Bank[61] (ADB). These agencies will often act as anchor financer (and, as in the case of the ADB and the Dahej regasification terminal in India, equity investor), but will require longer to commit and this can extend timescales. They may also be reluctant to take completion risk and so some projects may be refinanced after construction and new equity partners (such as infrastructure funds and other private equity players) may become involved.

Some grant-based funding may also be available from state or supra-

---

[60] The EIB has provided loans to GATE and terminals in Lithuania and Poland amongst others: 'GATE LNG Terminal Expansion', EIB Reference: 20140236, 19 May 2014 (www.eib.org/projects/pipeline/2014/20140236.htm); 'EIB supports the construction of LNG terminal in Lithuania', EIB Reference: 2013-104-EN, 9 July 2013 (www.eib.org/infocentre/press/releases/all/2013/2013-104-eib-supports-the-construction-of-lng-terminal-in-lithuania.htm); and 'EIB supports Poland's transport and energy infrastructure', EIB Reference: 2011-199-EN, 15 December 2011 (www.eib.org/infocentre/press/releases/all/2011/2011-199-eib-supports-polands-transport-and-energy-infrastructure.htm).

[61] The ADB has provided loans to terminals in Pakistan and India amongst others: 'ADB to Help Fund Pakistan's First LNG Regasification Terminal', ADB News Release, 27 February 2015 (www.adb.org/news/adb-help-fund-pakistan-s-first-lng-regasification-terminal) and 'Dahej Liquefied Natural Gas Terminal Project (Equity Investment Number 7192-IND)', ADB Evaluation Document 30 November 2006 (www.adb.org/documents/dahej-liquefied-natural-gas-terminal-project-equity-investment-number-7192-ind).

national agencies, or governments may provide loan guarantees. The Government of Lithuania provided 100 per cent loan guarantees to underpin the financing of the Klaipedos regasification facility and it also levied an 'LNG supplement' on all gas users. These arrangements were unsuccessfully challenged as representing illegal state aid.[62]

Under-utilization and diversification opportunities for LNG regasification terminals

Earlier in this chapter we noted the global over-supply of regasification terminal capacity. Whilst operational factors account for this in part, longer-term shifts in supply dynamics can also have a dramatic impact.

There are a number of options facing under-utilized regasification facilities:

- In the USA, where domestic production has stranded a number of terminals, conversion to liquefaction and export is the most obvious possibility.

- Re-loading and re-exporting by transferring equivalent volumes from one ship to another – either directly or via the terminal. This activity occurs when prices make it attractive to re-load cargoes destined for the original receiving port to another country. This market has been dominated by Europe, where low demand has led to re-exports to the higher-priced markets in Latin America and Asia. In Spain, where pipeline export capacity is constrained, all six terminals have re-loading capabilities. There are, however, doubts over whether this activity will be curtailed, as excess LNG supplies erode regional price differentials, and regulatory concerns rise over re-export.

- Transfers of smaller volumes to bunkering vessels (referred to as break bulk) designed to serve smaller LNG receiving terminals or LNG fuelling points. Both GATE and Zeebrugge terminals are building second jetties typically capable of re-loading 2,000 m³ carriers, with over 200 small carrier berthing slots per year. GATE would appear to be transforming itself from a standard import facility to one that is equally focused on break bulk activity. LNG plant operators may need to get permission from regulatory agencies to provide re-load services. In Singapore, the Energy Market Authority agreed that SLNG could provide re-load

---

[62] 'State aid SA.36740 (2013/NN) – Lithuania: Aid to Klaipedos Nafta – LNG Terminal', European Commission, Brussels, 20.11.2013 C(2013) 7884 final (http://ec.europa.eu/competition/state_aid/cases/250416/250416_1542635_190_2.pdf). The challenge was unsuccessful, though the Commission deemed the LNG supplement to be in breach of Article 108.

services, though provisions were made to ensure that there was no interference with the security of supply needs of Singapore.[63]

- Road-loading (described in Chapter 7) – the development of LNG as a transport fuel could provide additional outlets for LNG terminal capacity. Recent examples include Fos Tonkin in France[64] (2014) and Grain LNG in the UK which opened in November 2015.[65]

Conclusions: regasification terminals

LNG regasification terminal capacity continues to grow as new countries join the LNG importers club and existing buyers seek new sources of gas. Three countries – Japan, Korea, and Taiwan – dominate with over 40 per cent of global regasification capacity, though capacity in China and India is growing quickly. Overall, Asia accounts for around 53 per cent of total capacity. Europe and North America are the other main regasification regions, though a number of South American countries have installed capacity and there are now over 30 LNG importing nations.

The global LNG market has always been characterized by a significant surplus of regasification capacity relative to liquefaction plant capacity, with utilization rates in the former averaging around 33 per cent in the period 2000 to 2015. There are significant variations in utilization rates between different regions, with levels in North America generally being well below those in Europe and Asia. There are a number of reasons for these relatively low utilization rates – not least the fact that regasification terminals are usually market facing and so act as a buffer between constant supply and variable demand. Owning spare terminal capacity also has the benefit of increased optionality for a relatively low cost compared to other elements in the LNG chain.

Despite this pattern of under-utilization, a number of new receiving terminals are under construction and new countries are joining the LNG importers club all the time. Terminal capacity will continue to grow even if there is spare capacity in adjacent markets. This might be due to constraints in the gas network or to a desire for supply diversification.

---

[63] Energy Market Authority Licence no. EMA/LNGTO/001; Type: LNG Terminal Operator; Licensee: Singapore LNG Corporation Pte Ltd. 9 June 2015. (https://www.ema.gov.sg/cmsmedia/Licensees/Gas_Licensing/LNG/SLNG%20Notification%206.pdf).

[64] 'LNG Tanker Truck Loading' information on Elengy (Engie) website (https://www.elengy.com/en/clients/lng-truck-loading.html).

[65] 'National Grid unveils new truck loading facility at Isle of Grain LNG terminal, GrainLNG, 11 November 2015. (http://grainlng.com/news/new-truck-reloading-facility.html).

LNG regasification terminals have adopted a range of business models, though many are having to become increasingly flexible. In general, the trends are towards a tolling model that minimizes risks, but this may require a more complex contractual and operational framework to deal with the challenges of multiple users. The financing and regulatory environments have also had to adapt to the increasing trend for terminals to operate as standalone entities.

Whilst the tolling model may predominate, it is likely that many smaller importers will still need to undertake merchant terminal construction. In this context, the option of FSRUs seems to be increasingly preferred as a speedy, low-cost route to establishing supplies. With new FSRUs achieving regasification capacities of up to 5 mtpa, with full boil-off gas management, it is quite possible that onshore regasification plant built on greenfield sites will become more the exception in future.

BIBLIOGRAPHY

Davis, I. (2006). *Grain LNG Terminal, Winter to date,* Presentation at Ofgem Seminar 24 January 2006. http://webarchive.nationalarchives.gov.uk/20130402174434/http://www.ofgem.gov.uk/Pages/MoreInformation.aspx?file=12740-winter%20to%20date%20agenda%20jan06.pdf&refer=Markets/WhlMkts/CustandIndustry/WinterOutlook.

de la Flor, F., Schlesinger, B., Gorospe, L., and de Vicente, M. (2013). *Current State and Prospects of LNG in the UNECE Region*, Economic Commission for Europe Committee on Sustainable Energy, 2013 https://www.unece.org/fileadmin/DAM/energy/se/pp/wpgas/23wpg_jan2013/8_Slesinger.pdf.

DTI (2003). *LNG facilities and interconnectors, EU legislation and regulatory regime, DTI/Ofgem final views,* DTI/Ofgem, November 2003. https://www.ofgem.gov.uk/ofgem-publications/41348/lng-facilities-and-interconnectors-25nov03.pdf.

Frisch M. (2007). 'LNG Liquefaction and Receiving Terminal Capacities: Is there a mismatch?', Presentation to Flame 2007 Conference in Amsterdam, The Netherlands on 12 March 2007. www.mfcgas.com/publications/4583467443.

Greenwald, G.B. (ed.) (1998). *Liquefied Natural Gas: Developing and Financing International Energy Projects*, Kluwer Law International.

ICLG (2016). *Oil & Gas Regulation 2016*, International Comparative Legal Guides. www.iclg.co.uk/practice-areas/oil-and-gas-regulation/oil-and-gas-regulation-2015.

IEA (2012). *Gas Pricing and Regulation – China's Challenges and IEA Experience*, IEA, 2012 https://www.iea.org/publications/freepublications/publication/ChinaGasReport_Final_WEB.pdf.

IGU (2015). *World LNG Report – 2015 Edition*, World Gas Conference Edition, International Gas Union. www.igu.org/sites/default/files/node-page-field_file/IGU-World%20LNG%20Report-2015%20Edition.pdf.

Kotzot, H., Durr, C., Coyle, D., and Caswell, C. (2007). 'LNG Liquefaction – Not All Plants Are Created Equal', KBR, LNG 15, (15th International Conference & Exhibition on Liquefied Natural Gas Barcelona, Spain, 24–27 April 2007). https://kbr.com/Documents/LNG%20White%20Papers/2007%20LNG%2015%20-%20Not%20All%20Plants%20Are%20Created%20Equal%20%5BPaper%5D.pdf.

Ledesma D, (2012). 'Project Financing LNG Projects', Chapter 16 in Morrison, R. *The Principles of Project Financing*, Gower Publishing, 2012. www.gpmfirst.com/books/principles-project-finance/project-financing-lng-projects.

Noonan, T. and Martin, M. (2001). 'Project Financing of a LNG import terminal as a tolling facility', LNG Conference, 2001. www.ivt.ntnu.no/ept/fag/tep4215/innhold/LNG%20Conferences/2001/Data/PAPERSVO/SESSION4/Ps4-4-ma.pdf.

Ofgem (2004) *Application by South Hook LNG Terminal Company Ltd (SHTCL) (owned by Qatar Petroleum and ExxonMobil) under section 19C of the Gas Act 1986 for an exemption from section 19D of the Gas Act 1986*, Ofgem final views, November 2004. https://www.ofgem.gov.uk/sites/default/files/docs/2004/11/267-04_0.pdf.

Roberts, P. (2008). *Gas Sales and Gas Transportation Agreements: Principles and Practice*, Second Edition, London: Sweet and Maxwell.

Sharratt, C. (2012) 'LNG terminal cold energy integration opportunities offered by contractors', in *LNG Journal*, March 2012, 22–4.

Shaw Alaska (2006). *Commercial future of the Kenai LNG Plant*, Report for ANGDA (Alaska Natural Gas Development Authority), April 2006. www.arlis.org/docs/vol1/AlaskaGas/Report2/Report_Shaw_2006_CommFutureKenai_LNG_Plant.pdf.

Songhurst, B. (2014). 'LNG Plant Cost Escalation', OIES Working Paper NG 83, Oxford Institute for Energy Studies, February. www.oxfordenergy.org/wpcms/wp-content/uploads/2014/02/NG-83.pdf.

Turner, P. and Barker, A. (2013). 'Singapore – Emergence of a new LNG market and the role of the aggregator', LNG-17, Houston, 16 April 2013. http://www.gastechnology.org/Training/Documents/LNG17-proceedings/1-1-Anthony_Barker.pdf.

Tusiani, M.D. and Shearer, G. (2006). *LNG: a nontechnical guide*, Tulsa: PenWell.

Tyler, R (2007). 'Structuring LNG Import Projects and Terminal User Agreements', FLAME LNG Summit, Amsterdam, 12 March 2007. http://www.cne.es/cgi-bin/BRSCGI.exe?CMD=VEROBJ&MLKOB=305459300909.

Weems, P. (2005). 'Agreements for LNG Terminal Services: Trends and Issues', Paper presented to CWC 6th Annual World LNG Summit, Rome, 30 November 2005. www.kslaw.com/library/publication/weemsagreements.pdf.

CHAPTER 5

FUTURE LNG SUPPLY: LOOKING AHEAD, WHO WILL BE THE MAIN POTENTIAL LNG SUPPLIERS?

James Henderson, James T Jensen, and Anne-Sophie Corbeau

Introduction

Over the past decade the LNG industry has demonstrated the classic trends of a capital intensive commodity business, with periods of high prices followed by major investment and a subsequent increase in production (see Chapter 2). Fewer Final Investment Decisions (FIDs) during 2007–9 led to a pause in the growth of LNG supply in 2011–14, with LNG trade hovering around 239–240 mtpa. The rise in oil prices since 2009, combined with high prices in Asia, prompted 19 projects to take FIDs between late 2009 and 2015, so that projects with total new capacity of 152 mtpa started to come online in 2015 and will reach full output before 2020 (IEA, 2015, 111). The scale of this export capacity addition is unprecedented.

In looking at which countries could supply significant volumes of LNG over the next 10 years (see Figure 5.1), four regions clearly stand out: Australia, North America (the USA and Canada), Russia, and Eastern Africa (Mozambique and Tanzania). The growth of LNG supply up to 2020 is mostly predetermined by the projects currently under construction. Supply growth is due to be most dramatic in Australia (+ 62 mtpa) and the USA (+ 64 mtpa), where the first new projects came online in late 2015 and early 2016, with each country set to bring to the markets the equivalent of approximately 135 per cent of the 2009–11 Qatari LNG expansion.

Beyond the capacity under construction, another 1,000 mtpa is at various planning stages; this includes around 90 mtpa in Australia, 666 mtpa in North America,[1] 70 mtpa in Eastern Africa, and 75 mtpa in Russia. Eighty per cent of the planned capacity is thus located in four regions.

However, low oil prices since mid-2014, combined with low contract and spot gas prices, and current anaemic demand for LNG in Asia, have undermined the commercial prospects of many projects that have not yet

---

[1] This includes 315 mtpa in the USA (including Alaska) and 352 mtpa in Canada – see North America section below.

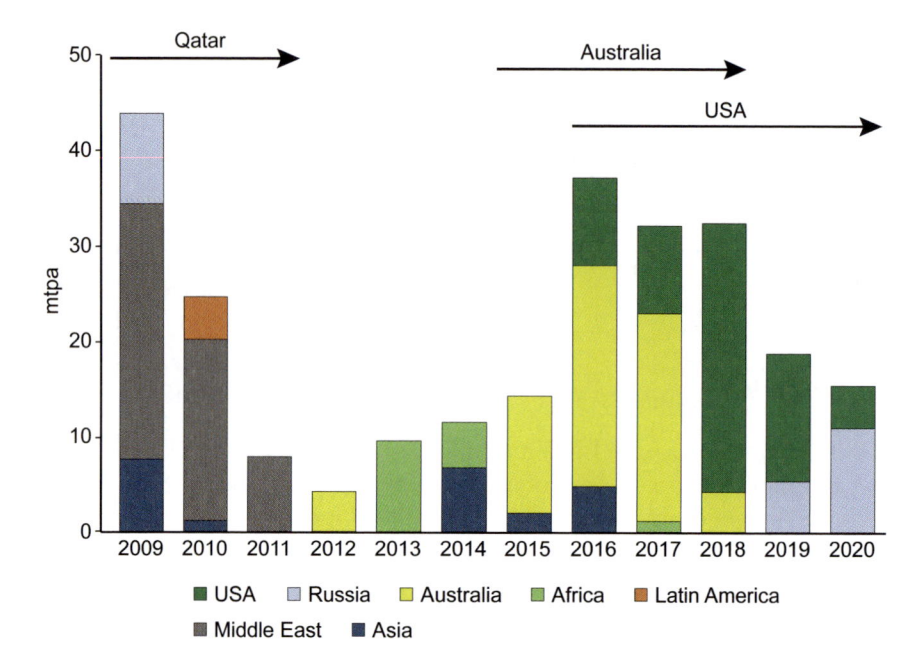

Figure 5.1: New capacity coming on line, 2010–20
Source: Author's research

taken FID. Consequently, companies may have to rein in their short-term ambitions and adjust their expectations towards a timetable that will bring their major projects online in the mid-2020s.

This chapter will analyse in detail the projects that will come online in Australia, Russia, and the USA, and assess the potential for additional supplies beyond 2020 in these countries and also in Canada and Eastern Africa. The next four sections analyse the comparative advantages and challenges for these regions by looking at the different projects, the issues they face, and their comparative advantages. Finally, in the last section, we consider other regions that could act as wild cards, and also at the prospects and main concerns facing the 20 countries where liquefaction facilities are already operating.

Comparing the four regions, we can find some overarching themes:

- Resources are not an issue in the four regions analysed, with the potential exception of Tanzania. The USA, Canada, Australia, and Russia have large proved reserves ranging from 2 to 32.6 tcm and even larger potential gas resources. Mozambique's estimated recoverable gas resources (3.7 tcm) are sufficient to support both LNG exports and domestic demand.

- The interaction of LNG with domestic demand will matter in the USA, Australia, and Eastern Africa as well as in many existing LNG exporters. In the USA, the industrial sector fears that LNG exports could cause an increase in domestic gas prices which would undermine its recovery, notably in petrochemicals. Australia's end users have faced a sharp increase in gas prices, but could also provide an outlet for gas resources if no further LNG expansion takes place. Eastern African countries are keen to use part of their gas domestically and to impose domestic market obligations. However, they face formidable challenges in developing the necessary pipeline infrastructure in nearly non-existent domestic gas markets. In North Africa, Nigeria, Indonesia, Malaysia, Trinidad and Tobago, Peru, Oman, and Abu Dhabi, rapidly increasing gas demand, combined with slow-growing gas production, is already resulting in an under-utilization of LNG plants.

- Meanwhile, local content is an important issue, notably for future projects in Eastern Africa and Canada. These countries are eager to see employment opportunities increase in many areas. The First Nations issue is also a major stumbling block in Canada, with a need to appease and compensate indigenous owners of land rights. Australia's restrictive laws on foreign employment were largely responsible for the sharp increase in salaries there (see Chapter 4), and there is a clear risk that similar cost pressures could emerge in other countries that are keen to maximize domestic employment.

- Due to the Asian gas price premium over 2011–14 and rising LNG demand, Asia has been considered as a key LNG market, although its attractiveness has been reduced since mid-2014 by the lower price environment. Nevertheless, Asian buyers have been keen to diversify their LNG supplies and to encourage multiple LNG developments. Asian customers are active in Australia, represent around 40 per cent of contracted gas supplies in the five US LNG projects under construction, and have massively invested in Mozambique. Petronas supports the most advanced Canadian project, while Japanese, Chinese, and Korean companies have invested in the Canadian upstream. Although they represent only a small portion of Yamal's contracts, Asian players are also beginning to be investors in the planned Russian LNG projects. In addition, they also have a small position in Tanzania. The countries with the strongest presence across the four regions through investments in upstream, LNG plants, and contracts are Japan, Korea, and China

(Corbeau et al., 2014). Meanwhile, Indonesia is the Asian country with the lowest investments in these four regions, having only signed contracts for US LNG. Finally, aggregators have strong positions in US, Canadian, and Russian LNG and can be expected to play a role in Tanzania.

- No project has been sanctioned without long-term contracts, but some projects have taken FID while having some uncommitted LNG, notably in Australia and in the USA (see Figure 5.2). In examining firm and preliminary contracts versus total capacity, some uncontracted LNG remains in Australian, US, and Russian projects under construction. However, potential projects that have not yet taken FID are still largely uncontracted in all countries, with the exception of the projects in Mozambique and a handful of US and Canadian projects.

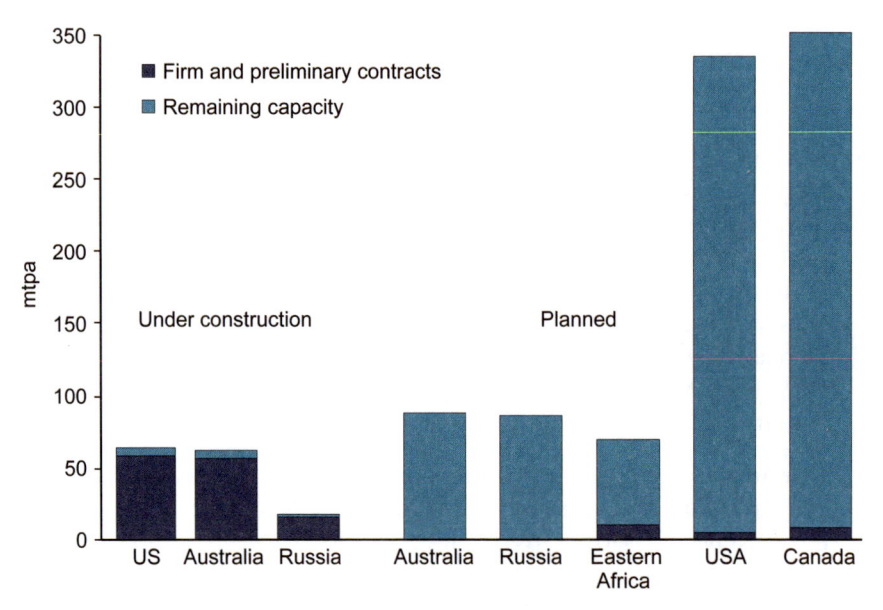

Figure 5.2: LNG contracted by region versus planned capacity
Source: Author's research.

- Investment costs reached record highs in Australia due to a rise in material costs, labour shortages, project complexity, and appreciation of the Australian dollar (see Chapter 4). Conversely, the fact that US LNG plants are mostly brownfield projects in a country with a plentiful and experienced workforce is resulting in much lower capital costs. High costs have plagued many Canadian projects due to the greenfield nature of projects, combined with the sheer size of infrastructure to be developed. Investment costs are also affecting a certain number of Russian projects, where the companies are also facing issues in raising finance due to sanctions. Oil prices at levels around $50/bbl and gas prices below $5/MMBtu are extremely challenging for all projects in the planning stage.[2] It remains to be seen whether lower prices translate into important cost reductions for some projects but if they do not, then the future of new LNG development must be in doubt.

- The pricing mechanisms offered by the different LNG projects vary widely (Table 5.1): US LNG is sold under Henry Hub (HH) indexation, Australian LNG under oil indexation, while Yamal LNG contracts are understood to be linked to some sort of oil indexation in Asia but to spot prices in Europe. Projects sponsors in Canada are offering oil-indexed prices despite Asian buyers' preference for gas-indexed pricing.

Table 5.1: Pricing mechanisms for different future LNG suppliers

Countries	Pricing mechanism prevailing as of October 2014
USA	Spot indexed (Henry Hub)
Canada	Oil indexation (could move to hybrid indexation)
Russia	Oil indexation in Asia, spot-indexed in Europe
Australia	Oil indexation
Mozambique	Oil indexation
Tanzania	n.a (probably follow Mozambique)

Source: Author's research.

- The involvement of IOCs in major LNG projects tends to be critical, given the high capital intensity of the projects and their technological complexity. As such, each LNG scheme needs not only to be internationally competitive, but also more attractive than other projects in the sponsors' portfolios (see Table 5.2). In a low oil and gas price environment, this presents another challenge to future LNG projects, and raises the question about which, if any, can justify the expenditure of future IOC investment funds.

---

[2] Prices as of early June 2016.

Table 5.2: IOCs' planned projects

	LNG projects	Capacity (mtpa)
BG	QC LNG (Australia)	8.5
	Prince Rupert LNG (Canada)	21
	Tanzanian LNG	10
	Total	**29.5**
Shell	Gorgon T1-3 (Australia)	15
	Prelude FLNG (Australia)	3.6
	Sakhalin 2 expansion (Russia)	5
	LNG Canada (Canada)	24
	Abadi (Indonesia)	2.5
	Crux LNG (Australia)	2
	Total	**52.1**
ExxonMobil	Gorgon T1-3 (Australia)	15
	Scarborough (Australia)	6
	Sakhalin 1 (Russia)	5–15
	WCC LNG (Canada)	30
	Golden Pass (USA)	15.6
	PNG T3	4.5
	Total	**76.1**
Total	Ichthys LNG (Australia)	8.4
	GLNG (Australia)	7.8
	Yamal LNG (Russia)	16.5
	NLNG (Nigeria)	8
	Brass LNG (Nigeria)	10
	Shotkman Phase 1	15
	Total	**65.7**
ENI	*FLNG (Mozambique)*	2.5
	Mamba LNG (Mozambique)	10+
	NLNG (Nigeria)	8
	Brass LNG (Nigeria)	10
	Delta Caribe Oriental LNG 3 (Venezuela)	4.7
	Total	**30.5**

Note: Projects in italics are planned, others are operating/under construction.

- A clear fiscal and regulatory environment is crucial for companies to take FIDs. Australia's open investment climate has been a strong catalyst behind the LNG projects and their high levels of foreign participation. The US system of regulatory approval, although lengthy for projects planning to export LNG to non FTA countries, is clear. So is NEB approval in Canada, but the process of making British Columbia's fiscal framework look attractive to companies took time, and may have made the province miss a window of opportunity. Eastern African countries have had to develop their regulatory and fiscal frameworks, and while this has been mostly achieved, IOC partners are still hesitant about committing to FIDs due to remaining uncertainties, in combination with low gas prices. In Russia, tax exemptions will be critical for some projects to move ahead, but legal and regulatory uncertainty (as well as the potential impact of sanctions) is leading to deferral of projects as foreign partners remain reluctant to participate.

With this broad context in mind, in the following sections we analyse the key drivers for the LNG industries in Australia, North America, Russia, and Eastern Africa, and assess potential constraints on future developments. We then review the existing LNG players, as well as a number of potential new entrants.

Outlook for Australian LNG – the limits of expansion

Introduction

The gas industry in Australia has much to be proud of. Australia is set to become the largest LNG exporter in the world by the end of this decade, moving up from its second position in 2015 to overtake Qatar. Seven new projects have been developed since 2009 and these have started to come on stream since early 2015, adding to the three projects already operating. Significant innovation has accompanied this surge in industrial activity, with the first coal seam gas (CSG)-to-LNG schemes under development in Queensland, the first floating LNG (FLNG) project set to come online offshore Western Australia, and the largest carbon dioxide (CO_2) sequestration plant being built at the Gorgon field on the North West Shelf. In addition, the intense levels of construction and the spill-over effects into the rest of the economy have significantly boosted Australian GDP (Cassidy and Kosev, 2015, 40). However, despite these successes, the intensity of the LNG expansion in Australia has also brought unique challenges, with demand for labour and equipment causing both sharp cost escalation and project delays. These factors, combined with a sharp appreciation of the Australian dollar during the period 2010–13, have challenged the economics of a number of the schemes that are now coming on stream, while the fall in the global oil price, and the consequent sharp decline in LNG prices in Asia, has further exacerbated the commercial challenges.

Ten projects will be online by 2019

Australia is endowed with 3.7 tcm of proved gas reserves with total gas resources including CSG, tight gas, and shale gas of 11.1 tcm (Ledesma et al., 2014, 4). Australia's first LNG scheme came online in 1989 when the North West Shelf (NWS) project sent its initial cargo to the Japanese market. It now has five trains and a total capacity of 16.3 million tonnes per annum (mtpa), and remains the country's largest gas producer and exporter. The relatively small 3.4 mtpa Darwin LNG followed in 2006, with the 4.3 mtpa Pluto project then coming online in 2012. These three projects made Australia the third-largest exporter of LNG in 2014, with total sales of just under 25 mt (around 35 bcm) targeted mainly at Japan but also sold to China, Korea, Taiwan, and Malaysia.[3] Map 5.1 below shows the location of these initial three developments as well as the country's new projects that have come online in 2015 or are under construction.

Although the growth in Australian LNG output in the 2000s was impressive, the foundation for the rapid jump that will occur in the rest of this decade was laid in the period 2009–12, when seven new projects took FID. This was an unprecedented level of activity for a single country in the hydrocarbons industry. The first of these projects came online at the end of 2014, when the first train of BG's Queensland Curtis (QCLNG) produced its initial cargo,[4] and the project's second train has since come online (in mid-2015). Subsequently the first trains at three other projects (Gladstone LNG (GLNG),[5] Australia–Pacific LNG (APLNG),[6] and Gorgon LNG) have also come online (although Gorgon exports have since been temporarily halted), bringing Australia's total annual LNG capacity to over 46 mt (63 bcm) as of May 2016. The remaining trains at these schemes are expected to be completed between 2016 and 2018, underlining the fact that the east coast projects are moving ahead on their original timetables. Over the next three years, production is also due from three other projects – Wheatstone, Ichthys, and Prelude – which will take overall LNG exports to 86 mt (117 bcm) by 2019. At this time, Australia's LNG output will exceed that of the current world leader Qatar, which has imposed a moratorium on its LNG output at 77 mtpa. Table 5.5 at the end of this section, provides details of all these projects, as well as Australia's possible new developments. Figure 5.3 demonstrates the growth in LNG exports that will be seen before 2020, assuming that the new developments continue to hit their production targets.

---

[3] GIIGNL Annual Report 2015.
[4] 'BG Group loads first LNG cargo from QCLNG project in Australia', BG Press Release, 29 December 2014.
[5] 'First cargo shipped from GLNG', Santos GLNG Press Release, 15 October 2015.
[6] 'Origin Energy sends first APLNG shipment', *The Australian*, 11 January 2016.

Future LNG Supply 217

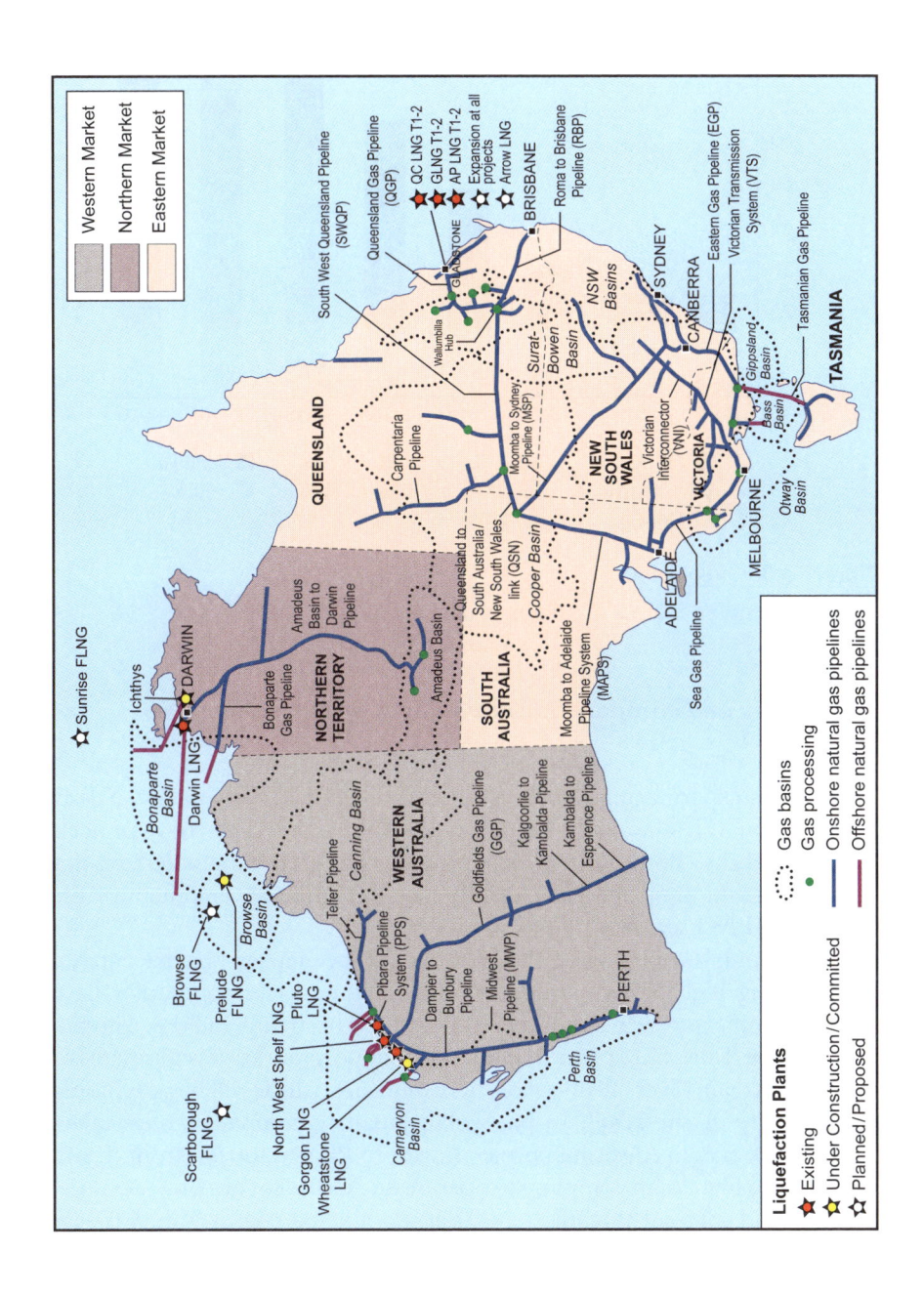

Map 5.1: Australia's gas market and LNG export projects
Source: Ledesma et al. (2014).

218   *LNG Markets in Transition*

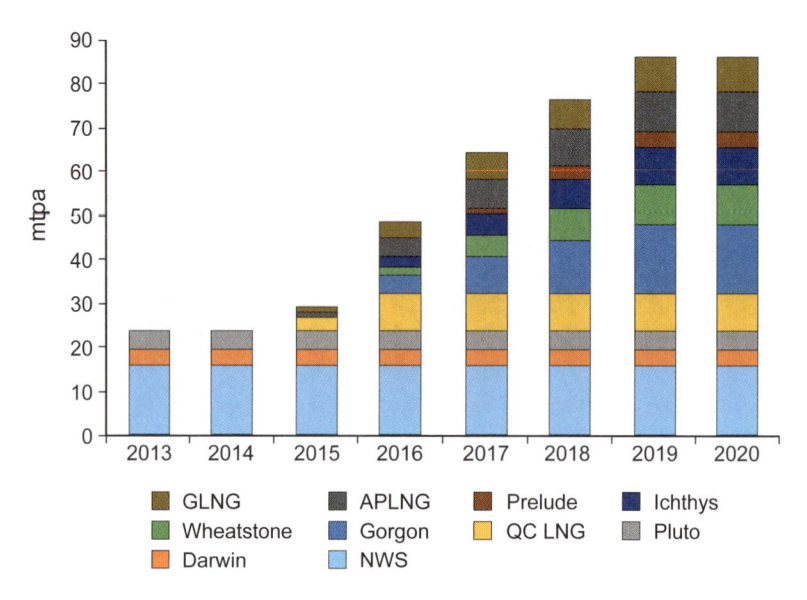

Figure 5.3: Outlook for Australian LNG capacity to 2020
Source: Author's analysis of company data and projections.

Challenges and comparative advantages of Australian LNG projects

Australia is experiencing unprecedented growth in LNG capacity. Nearly $200 billion will ultimately be spent developing the seven new projects discussed above. Both positive and negative issues have characterized this expansion, and these are likely to influence the future development of the Australian LNG sector.

The country's open investment climate has been a key positive catalyst encouraging high levels of foreign participation. Asian companies have taken a significant role in a number of the major upstream and downstream projects (see Table 5.3), providing financial support for the developments as well as upstream diversification for their countries, which will be purchasing the majority of the LNG. In particular, Japanese companies have taken numerous stakes in Australian projects, with INPEX at the forefront. It will become the first Asian company to operate an Australian gas project, at the Ichthys field where it is leading an Asian-dominated consortium. Chinese companies have also become major players, with CNOOC having acquired a 50 per cent stake in the first train at QCLNG and Sinopec owning 25 per cent of APLNG, while the Malaysian company Petronas has a 27.5 per cent interest in GLNG, the third CBM project in Queensland. This level of Asian involvement not only allows the companies involved to balance their upstream and downstream exposure but also provides a level of comfort that the projects will proceed, even in a lower-price environment. Most of the gas from these projects has not only been contracted to Asian buyers (see Table 5.4) but in many cases is also owned by them, providing an additional security of energy supply.

Table 5.3: Asian investment in Australian LNG projects

Project	Asian investors	Total Asian share
North West Shelf	Japan Australia LNG (20%)	20%
Darwin	INPEX, Tokyo Electric, Tokyo Gas	20.5%
Pluto	Tokyo Gas (5%), Kansai Electric (5%)	10%
Queensland Curtis LNG T1	CNOOC (50%)	50%
Queensland Curtis LNG T2	Tokyo Gas (2.5%)	2.5%
Gorgon	Osaka Gas (1.25%), Tokyo Gas (1%), Chubu Electric (0.4%)	2.7%
Wheatstone	PEW (8%), Kyushu Electric (1.5%)	9.5%
Ichthys LNG	INPEX (63.4%), CPC (2.6%), Tokyo Gas (1.6%) Osaka Gas (1.2%), Chubu Electric (0.7%), Toho Gas (0.4%)	70%
Prelude FLNG	INPEX (17.5%), KOGAS (10%), CPC (5%)	32.5%
Australia-Pacific LNG	Sinopec (25%)	25%
Gladstone LNG	Petronas (27.5%), KOGAS (15%)	42.5%

Source: Company data.

The QCLNG, APLNG, and GLNG liquefaction projects, located on Curtis Island on the coast of Queensland, are the first in the world to be based on the production of coal seam gas (CSG). These projects could set an example for the development of further CSG resources that might otherwise remain stranded assets. They are supplied by gas from coal seams in the Surat-Bowen and Cooper Basins that have previously been used for coal mining. Intensive drilling and water extraction release gas from these reservoirs.

However, the technology being used is very new, and in some states of Australia has caused controversy because of the alleged risks to the environment and especially to the country's sparse water resources.[7] This has caused some public relations issues for the projects,[8] but has also brought uncertainty over the exact rate of gas flow from new wells and the consequent speed of the ramp-up in production. As a result, all three project operators are purchasing gas from the domestic market to ensure that they can meet their export contract obligations.

Another issue involving public relations is the interaction of LNG projects with the domestic market. The start-up of so many projects over a short period of time has accelerated the move of Australia's domestic prices towards international levels on a netback basis as existing long-term contracts with end users expire; this has implications for domestic industry and power generation.[9] Calls for a gas reservation policy have been made in an attempt to undermine new export projects, but these have been largely ignored to date in the east of the country. Nevertheless, companies may be encouraged to develop new CSG resources for domestic use rather than solely for export projects. In Western Australia a gas reservation policy (known as the Domestic Market Obligation), which has been in place since the NWS project was developed, means that 15 per cent of all new gas must be supplied into the domestic market. However, this has not been a major problem for the three new projects located offshore, as they have been able to negotiate flexible arrangements with the regional government.

The cost inflation that has resulted from so many projects being constructed at one time is a more serious concern. For example, Gorgon has exceeded its original capital expenditure estimate by 46 per cent and now has a total cost of $54 billion.[10] Indeed, six of Australia's seven new projects have gone over budget by an average of 28 per cent, implying an increase in spending of over $40 billion (Ledesma et al., 2014, 19). A number of factors have driven this increase, including a rise in material costs (in particular steel, which was also in high demand during China's economic boom), inflated labour costs (not helped by the power of Australia's unions and restrictive laws on employing foreign workers), and a strong Australian dollar. Songhurst (2014) highlights the uniqueness of the situation in Australia over the past seven years, and shows that the average cost of projects in the country during this intense period of

---

[7] 'Anti-CSG protesters stage Australia's "longest ever" highway demonstration', *The Guardian*, 19 April 2015.

[8] 'The highways of NSW and Queensland were the big stage for an anti-coal seam gas protest', ABC News, 20 April 2015.

[9] 'Household, industrial gas prices to surge on LNG export boom', ABC News, 22 July 2015.

[10] 'Cost of Australia's Gorgon LNG project rises to $54bn', *The Financial Times*, 12 December 2013.

development has been almost twice as high as in other countries where LNG has been developed.[11] These pressures have now started to ease, as the main construction phase for the projects ends, but the high resulting costs are impacting the ability of companies to earn a reasonable rate of return on their investments, while the impact of tight labour and materials markets has also affected project timetables. Most of the developments have been delayed by up to a year from their originally planned start date (Ledesma et al., 2014, 19–23).

Shell's Prelude development, the world's first FLNG project, appears to have suffered least in terms of cost and timing. Indeed, the rising cost of onshore plants and the remoteness of the gas resource drove the field partners' decision to use an FLNG facility to develop the Prelude gas field and liquefy its output. Costs were further controlled by building what will be the world's largest vessel in a shipyard in Korea. The FLNG ship is expected to bring Prelude's 115 bcm of gas on stream in 2017, and will subsequently be available for use on other fields once Prelude is exhausted, enhancing its long-term economic returns (Ledesma et al., 2014, 25).

Meanwhile, the dramatic fall in oil and gas prices since the summer of 2014 has materially impacted project economics. Given that the bulk of the capital expenditure is already sunk, project developers will be keen to generate cash as soon as possible, meaning that production will continue even if the level of revenue is much lower than they had hoped for even a year ago – perhaps even below the worst-case assumptions when the project FIDs were taken. Furthermore, comments from a number of companies involved in the developments suggest that the schemes will be cash flow positive even at lower oil prices. For example, Origin Energy has stated that the breakeven oil price to generate positive free cash flow from its APLNG project at 'steady state operations'[12] is $40–45/bbl,[13] while Santos has also provided assurance that the company's GLNG project can generate cash at a price of $40/bbl.[14]

However, other projects do not appear so robust and will undoubtedly generate returns well below their investors' expectations in today's low-price environment (IEA, 2015, 117–18). Although BG has stated that the economics of its QCLNG project are 'sound and competitive across a wide

---

[11] Songhurst (2014, 22–3). Exceptions include the Snøvhit field in Norway, and Angola LNG, each of which had its own specific problems.

[12] 'Steady state operation' is defined as being the position after all opex, sustaining capex, project finance interest, and principal repayments and discretionary exploration and appraisal.

[13] 'Australian LNG projects can weather oil price of $45 per barrel', Platts, 11 March 2015.

[14] 'Fitch warns of pressures on Australian LNG investors', *Sydney Morning Herald*, 23 February 2015.

range of oil prices',[15] ratings agency Fitch estimates that the project requires an LNG price of $10/MMBtu to cover its cash costs,[16] compared with an April 2016 spot price in north-east Asia of just over $4/MMBtu.[17] Furthermore, in a 2014 study, the IEA estimated the average cost of supply for Australian LNG delivered to Japan at just below $10/MMBtu, with the country's high capital costs being offset by the low transport distance, which significantly reduces shipping costs (Corbeau et al., 2014, 52). However, various financial analysts have estimated the breakeven gas price on a full cost basis (including all capital expenditure) to be in a range of $12–14/MMBtu (with some even calculating a level above $19/MMBtu for some fields). This suggests that although the projects may cover their cash costs now that most of the major spending has been done, many of them will struggle to generate a return equivalent to their cost of capital if oil prices remain at their low 2015 levels for any length of time.[18]

Outlook for a further expansion of LNG capacity

The outlook for further growth in Australian LNG production beyond the capacity under construction is relatively bleak, at least in the short to medium term. Although the current projects can generate positive returns over the long term, a number of the project developers are struggling in the short term. Ratings agencies such as Moody's and Standard and Poor's have downgraded the credit ratings of Origin Energy (one of the operators of APLNG)[19] and Santos (GLNG),[20] with the latter having subsequently seen its CEO resign as a result of its financial difficulties.[21] Meanwhile, in early 2015, BG was acquired by Shell – arguably in part because of BG's financial difficulties with its QCLNG project.[22] Furthermore, the major LNG project operators have been dramatically cutting back their global

---

[15] 'Oil plunge dims outlook for LNG projects', *The Wall Street Journal*, 11 December 2014.

[16] 'Fitch warns of pressures on Australian LNG investors', *Sydney Morning Herald*, 23 February 2015.

[17] Data from *LNG Intelligence*, 20 April 2016.

[18] 'Oil plunge dims outlook for LNG projects', *The Wall Street Journal*, 11 December 2014.

[19] 'Origin Energy rating cut as oil price slides', *The Australian*, 22 April 2015.

[20] 'Santos suffers savage sell-off on Standard & Poor's ratings downgrade', ABC News, 9 December 2014.

[21] 'Santos chief David Knox to step down, interim profit drops', *Sydney Morning Herald*, 21 August 2015.

[22] 'Shell BG merger comes as LNG prices fall in main market', *The Wall Street Journal*, 10 April 2015.

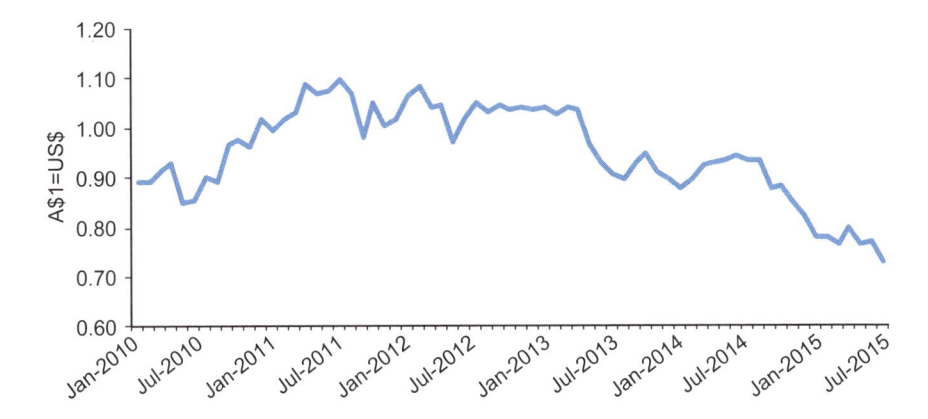

Figure 5.4: Australian dollar versus US dollar, 2011–15
Source: Reserve Bank of Australia.

capital expenditure.[23] Shell, for example, reduced its global spending by 20 per cent in 2015 compared to 2014,[24] while Chevron announced both a $10 billion reduction in capex and a $15 billion sale of assets to raise cash in a lower oil price environment.[25] In this worsening global environment, it is not surprising that Australia, which has seen the majority of spending in the LNG industry over the past five years, is no longer a major priority for the oil majors, at least until the current projects have demonstrated their viability.[26]

On a more positive note, the financial environment for producers in Australia is gradually improving. The weakening of the Australian dollar (see Figure 5.4), means that US dollar export revenues have greater value in local currency at a time when production is starting to ramp up. At the same time, cost inflation pressures have started to ease as the major construction phases of the new projects come to an end, with labour costs falling[27] and material costs declining as Chinese economic growth slows.[28]

---

[23] 'Energy groups take knife to $100bn of spending after oil rout', *The Financial Times*, 18 May 2015.
[24] 'Shell cuts 2015 capex again to face oil downturn', Reuters, 30 July 2015.
[25] 'Chevron to make $15bn in divestments and cut capex', *Pipeline Magazine*, 11 March 2015.
[26] 'Australia to lose out in US$259bn LNG capex spend', *Australian Financial Review*, 24 December 2014.
[27] 'Reserve Bank of Australia says falling labour costs are making Australia more competitive', ABC News, 15 June 2014.
[28] 'Iron ore drops as Chinese steel output slows', *The Financial Times*, 20 January 2015.

Although this improvement has come too late for the major offshore projects in Western Australia and the Northern Territories it could be vital to the economics of the CSG projects in Queensland, where the level of 'sustaining' capital expenditure is set to remain relatively high due to the need to drill new wells on a regular basis and tie them into the existing infrastructure (Ellis et al., 2013, 37). Furthermore, any rebound in the oil price from its lows under $40/bbl would clearly benefit LNG producers, albeit with a lag effect that is currently providing some protection from the decline. Over the longer term, companies with production coming online now may ultimately benefit from a supply shortage in the 2020s if current industry investment cuts continue.[29]

Table 5.5 identifies six possible brownfield expansions and ten potential new projects representing 44 and 44.6 mtpa of capacity respectively, that have been actively considered over the past few years. However, many of them are now either being shelved completely or at best deferred for some years. For example in January 2015 Shell cancelled Arrow LNG, a fourth proposed CSG to LNG project on Curtis Island.[30] It now seems more likely that the gas reserves could be allocated to a future expansion of the QCLNG project, in which the company has just acquired a 50 per cent interest via its purchase of BG. Even this plan is subject to the final closing of that deal and an improvement in the overall commercial environment.[31] Shell is also involved in the Browse LNG project with Woodside; this was originally planned to include an onshore liquefaction plant, but it was subsequently re-designed as a floating scheme to reduce costs. However, in December 2014 this plan was also deferred, and despite the announcement of the FEED (Front End Engineering and Design) process in the summer of 2015, the project is unlikely to start before 2020.[32] Meanwhile another potential FLNG project, Bonaparte, has been scrapped by its partners GDF Suez and Santos, due to concerns over poor economic returns,[33] and other planned schemes such as Sunrise, Crux, and Cash Maple also appear to have stalled.[34]

---

[29] 'Capex cuts trigger widespread FID delays', Interfax, 31 July 2015.

[30] 'Shell shelves Arrow LNG project in Queensland', *Sydney Morning Herald*, 30 January 2015.

[31] 'Shell's Simon Henry won't rule out write-down on Arrow LNG in Queensland', *Sydney Morning Herald*, 1 May 2015.

[32] 'Browse FLNG looks shaky despite Woodside optimism', Interfax, 10 July 2015.

[33] 'GDF Suez, Santos scrap Australian Bonaparte floating LNG project', Reuters, 19 June 2015.

[34] 'Australia's offshore gas mega-projects under threat?', *Hellenic Shipping News*, 30 April 2015.

Even the expansion plans for some existing projects (expected to perform better economically than greenfield projects given the synergy benefits of adding new trains to existing facilities) have been put on hold until a more certain price outlook emerges. The expansion of Pluto was deferred as early as 2013 and since then, plans to expand QCLNG have also been put back. Meanwhile, the schedules for expansion of the Gorgon, Wheatstone, and Ichthys projects have also been put in doubt by the 2015 market conditions (IEA, 2015, 117).

In addition, weaker than expected gas demand in Asia has raised another short-term concern for the Australian LNG operators, namely whether there will be a market for their uncontracted LNG – and indeed whether the customers for the contracted sales may attempt to reduce their offtake to minimum levels, again impacting the project economics. For example, reports have suggested that Japanese clients for Gorgon's LNG have decided not to buy the project's test shipments, preferring to buy LNG on the spot market.[35] This marketing issue, combined with project construction delays, has contributed to delaying the first LNG shipment from the project into 2016. Concern over the willingness of Asian buyers to take all their contracted volumes from other projects is also increasing, with Sinopec mentioned as being keen to renegotiate its contract to take 7.6 mtpa from APLNG.[36] Although this may not be legally possible, it nevertheless points to the pressure that Australia's LNG projects may feel from possible changes in contract terms or from continued low LNG prices, as buyers attempt to re-sell cargoes on the spot market.[37] With this in mind it is interesting to note (in Table 5.4) that around 9 per cent of LNG from the new Australian projects remains uncontracted, which will only add to the oversupply in the market. Irrespective of the impact of demand on projects with contracts in place, however, it is clear that demand for new Australian projects is minimal, again reinforcing the view that there is little scope for further expansion in the short to medium term.[38]

Concern relating to the fulfilment of gas sales contracts will clearly be a worry to the project sponsors, but may provide a boost to customers in the Australian domestic market, especially in the east of the country. Domestic gas prices have been rising rapidly towards international levels on a netback basis over the past year, as the operators of the CSG projects purchased gas to supplement their own reserves, either to act as feed gas during the ramp up phase of their projects or to provide insurance in case their upstream

---

[35] 'Test cargoes are a hard sell for Gorgon LNG', *Interfax*, 7 August 2015.
[36] 'Sinopec rattles Origin and ConocoPhillips', *Petroleum Economist*, 18 June 2015.
[37] 'Aussie LNG contracts under pressure', *Interfax*, 3 July 2015.
[38] 'Lack of demand to delay Australian LNG projects', *Sydney Morning Herald*, 22 June 2015.

Table 5.4: Contracted gas from Australian LNG projects

	Buyer	Volume		Buyer	Volume
Gorgon	Shell	1.4	**Ichthys**	Tepco	1.05
	BP	0.5		TG	1.05
	Tokyo Gas	1.25		Kansai Electric	0.8
	Chubu Electric	1.5		Osaka Gas	0.8
	Osaka Gas	1.6		Kyushu Electric	0.3
	Caltex	0.5		CPC	1.75
	Petronet	1.5		Toho Gas	0.3
	Petrochina	4.25		Chubu Electric	0.5
	SK Group	0.83		Inpex	1.1
	Uncommitted	*2.27*		*Uncommitted*	*0.75*
Wheatstone	Tepco	4.2	**QCLNG**	BG	3.6
	Kyushu Electric	0.8		CNOOC	3.6
	Tohoku Electric	0.9		TEPCO	0.9
	Chubu	1		Chubu Electric	0.4
	Shell	0.6		*Uncommitted*	*0*
	Uncommitted	*1.4*	**APLNG**	Sinopec	7.6
Prelude	KOGAS	3.6		Kansai Electric	1
	Uncommitted	*0*		*Uncommitted*	*0.4*
			GLNG	Petronas	3.5
				KOGAS	3.5
				Uncommitted	*0.8*
			Total uncommitted		**5.62**
			% capacity uncommitted		9%

Source: Ledesma et al. (2014, 18).

developments did not perform as expected (Ledesma et al., 2014, 48). This pressure may now start to ease, thanks to the fall in global LNG prices which will impact the netback price in eastern Australia, as will the possibility that there may now be extra gas for sale. Indeed, lower gas prices could encourage higher domestic demand and provide an outlet for future gas developments in Australia in preference to the export market, as the pipeline infrastructure in the east is already well-established (see Map 5.1) and domestic sales avoid the significant extra cost of liquefaction facilities.

One final point concerns the impact of the current depressed state of the LNG market on the federal and regional budgets in Australia. As late as 2014, the government expected that LNG revenues would provide a major boost to state income, and indeed that LNG exports would be the second-largest contributor to export revenues, behind iron ore. Although this may still be the case (given that, in a relative sense, the gas price has fallen in line with the prices of other commodities) the tax contribution is still expected to fall sharply as overall project revenues decline by as much as $20 billion in a $50 per barrel oil price world (IEA, 2015, 118). There has been some talk of government support for the industry to encourage new projects, in order to boost supply and revenue. The Queensland government, for example, has opened significant new areas of land for exploration in the hope of encouraging new investment.[39] This has included potential access to extensive shale gas resources, although it would appear that investors are sceptical about the commercial prospects for rapid development in the current low-price environment.[40] Meanwhile, other states such as Victoria and New South Wales continue to maintain fracking bans for gas development, which undermines both shale gas and coal seam gas development. Overall the Australian government appears to have little leeway for fiscal reform that that would allow it to boost the LNG industry in the face of the short-term global commodity market issues which it faces.

Conclusion

Australian LNG exports will rise to a record level of 86 mtpa by 2019, as the projects which have recently come online or are close to completion reach their peak output. Companies who have spent a combined total of over $200 billion are keen to generate any cash to start the process of recovering their costs, meaning that further extensive delays are unlikely. Indeed, the start-up of production at the three CSG projects on the east coast since late 2014 underlines the fact the progress that is being made. However, the industry is likely to stall thereafter as project developers struggle to generate sufficient cash to reinvest in new projects. Evidence for this is already clear in the number of project delays or cancellations that have been announced in 2014 and 2015. Even brownfield expansions, which would normally be an obvious way to generate synergy benefits from existing assets, are likely to be deferred until signs of an oil and gas price recovery emerge. Some good news can be found in the easing of cost and currency pressures on projects in production or under construction, but

---

[39] 'QLD looks for next wave of LNG projects', *Australian Financial Review*, 14 May 2015.
[40] 'Shale gas success still a decade away for Australia, says Santos', *The Australian*, 26 September 2014.

concerns are now emerging about the willingness of buyers to fulfil purchase obligations under current contracts. Although it seems unlikely that terms will be changed dramatically, it is clearly possible that if demand in Asia remains weaker than expected, the offtakers may be forced to sell any surplus gas on the spot market, further weakening prices and hindering the attempts of project developers to sell their own uncontracted gas. This potential marketing issue could further undermine project economics and act as an additional barrier to new projects, but it could benefit the Australian domestic market, where complaints over rising prices could be eased if spare gas becomes available. However, the federal and state budgets are set to suffer from lower tax revenues in a low-price environment, meaning that the Australian government is likely to have little opportunity to provide further investment incentives to LNG operators.

These factors suggest that we are reaching the end of the Australian LNG boom, although the extent of the country's gas resources offers the potential for further, more modest, expansion in the mid-2020s once the current global LNG oversupply has dissipated. Indeed, while the rather pessimistic tone of this section suggests that Australian LNG will plateau at 86 mtpa for some years (and indeed this would be the author's base case assumption), there is clearly the potential for further brownfield expansion at the current projects. While it is difficult to tell exactly which might take FIDs for new trains in the next five years, an upside case might see up to 20 mtpa of new capacity being approved by 2020, to come online before 2025 – as and when the oversupply situation in the global market looks to be coming to an end. It would therefore not be unreasonable to assume that Australia could be producing more than 100 mtpa of LNG by the middle of the next decade in a more positive investment scenario, given the lower cost of brownfield expansion compared to the recent greenfield developments that have dominated the Australian industry.

Table 5.5: Australia's LNG projects (as of end 2015)

	Operator	Capacity (mt)	Start-up	Total cost (US$bn)	Status at 31 Dec. 2015
Projects online					
North West Shelf T1–5	Woodside	16.3	1989	27	Online
Darwin	ConocoPhillips	3.4	2006	3.5	Online
Pluto	Woodside	4.3	2012	14.9	Online
Queensland Curtis LNG T1, T2	BG, QGC	8.5	2015	20.4	Online
Gladstone LNG T1	Santos	3.9	2015	9.25	Online
Total		**36.4**		**75.05**	

Future LNG Supply 229

	Operator	Capacity (mt)	Start-up	Total cost (US$bn)	Status at 31 Dec. 2015
Projects set to come online					
Gorgon T1, T2, T3	Chevron	15.6	2016	54	Under construction
Wheatstone T1, T2	Chevron	8.9	2017	29.7	Under construction
Ichthys LNG T1, T2	Inpex	8.4	2017	34	Under construction
Prelude FLNG	Shell	3.6	2017	12	Under construction
Australia-Pacific LNG T1, T2	Origin, ConocoPhillips	9	2016	22.5	Under construction
Gladstone LNG T2	Santos	3.9	2016	9.25	Under construction
Total		**49.4**		**161.45**	
Possible brownfield expansion projects					
Australia-Pacific LNG T3, T4	Origin, ConocoPhillips	9	NA		
Darwin T2	ConocoPhillips	3.6	NA		Pre-FID
Gorgon T4	Chevron	5.2	NA		Pre-FID
Pluto T2, T3	Woodside	8.6	NA		Pre-FID
Queensland Curtis LNG T3	BG, QGC	4.25	NA		Pre-FID
Wheatstone T3–5	Chevron	13.35			Pre-FID
Total		**44**			
Possible new projects					
Abbot Point LNG T1–T4	Energy World	2	2020		Pre-FID
Arrow LNG	Arrow Energy	8	NA		Shelved (as of Jan 2015)
Browse LNG	Woodside	10.8	2021		Pre-FID
Cash Maple FLNG	PTTEP Australia	2	NA		Pre-FID
Crux LNG	Shell	2	NA		Pre-FID
Fisherman's Landing	Gladstone LNG	3.8	NA		Pre-FID
Scarborough FLNG	ExxonMobil	6.5	2021		Pre-FID
Sunrise FLNG	Woodside	4	NA		Pre-FID
Timor Sea FLNG	PTT FLNG	2.5	NA		Pre-FID
Timor Sea LNG	MEO	3	NA		Pre-FID
Total		**44.6**			

Sources: IGU World LNG Report 2015, GIIGNL 2015 Annual Report.

North America enters the LNG export race

In 10 years, North American expectations have been transformed – from anticipating the future as a large LNG importer, into prospects of being one of the three largest future LNG exporters. This change was catalysed by the growing disequilibrium between North American gas prices, which fell with shale gas development and market oversupply, and Asian prices, which rose with rising world oil prices in the period 2011–14. This resulted in a large gap between North American gas prices (below $4/MMBtu) and Asian oil-linked contract prices (above $14/MMBtu), which provided a major incentive for North American LNG export projects. Asian buyers saw the potential not only for cheaper supply, but of a different pricing formula, indexed on Henry Hub (HH) spot prices, that could challenge the rigidity of the traditional Asian formula. For unaffiliated project developers in North America, the potential profitability of the Asian market was a major attraction. Meanwhile for portfolio aggregators, the existence of a potential Asian spot market with premium prices provided a form of safety net for protection from adverse market conditions elsewhere.

In addition to the price incentive, many forecasts have long considered Asia as a growing market for imported gas.[41] Equally, a growing confidence that North America has plentiful supplies of cheap gas which can ensure that the region should be able meet its own needs and be able to export LNG, has developed. US production jumped by almost 190 bcm over 2009–15 despite low gas prices. Canada's production has been dropping over the same period as exports to the USA are facing lower demand. The only outlet for Canada's gas resources is LNG exports. Meanwhile, tensions between Russia on one side and Europe and the USA on the other have also prompted the idea of decreasing Europe's dependency on Russian gas by sending shipments of US LNG.

As in other regions, the developers' FIDs determine which of the many proposed LNG projects are finally built. The regulatory framework, the financial feasibility, the costs of the projects, the adequacy of future supplies, and the existence of sales and purchase agreements will determine whether projects move ahead or not. In the following sections we analyse US and Canadian projects within this context, and assess the potential volume growth from projects under construction and proposed. Firstly, though, we review the essential regulatory processes in each country.

The North American project approval process

One of the most visible signs of progress towards a viable FID is the status of the regulatory applications.

---

[41] In 2015, the IEA predicted that Asia's imports would reach 565 bcm by 2040.

The regulatory framework in the USA
In the USA, the Natural Gas Act of 1938 establishes two responsibilities that are relevant to LNG exports.[42] First, exports of natural gas must obtain specific authorization from the Department of Energy (DOE).[43] Second, a 'certificate of convenience and necessity' from the Federal Energy Regulatory Commission (FERC) is required before a project sponsor can construct facilities. The relevant passage of the export authorization states that:

> The Commission shall grant such application, unless … it finds that the proposed importation or exportation will not be consistent with the public interest.[44]

This effectively places the burden of proof that the export is not in the public interest on those who object to it. The US Maritime Administration, rather than FERC, has certificate jurisdiction for deep water installations, such as offshore FLNG projects.

In the USA, the DOE approval process differs between countries that have Free Trade Agreements (FTA)[45] with the USA and those that do not. Free Trade Agreements are bilateral treaties that eliminate trade barriers. Since trade with such countries is deemed to be in the public interest, DOE approval is essentially automatic, but non-FTA countries must go through the full process. DOE approval is relatively simple and authorization can come quickly.

On the other hand, being granted a FERC Certificate can be a very long and costly process. Because the hearings are adversarial proceedings (in which the applicant must demonstrate that the construction of the LNG plant is in the public interest), the applicant must address the objections of the many interveners who want time to make their cases.

The requirements of the National Environmental Policy Act (NEPA) further complicate the process. NEPA requires an Environmental Assessment (EA) by government agencies to determine if there is a significant environmental impact and then an Environmental Impact

---

[42] When the Natural Gas Act of 1938 was passed, the Federal Power Commission (FPC) had responsibility for gas exports. In 1977, Congress created the Department of Energy, which assumed the FPC's export authorization responsibility, and a new agency, the Federal Energy Regulatory Commission, to assume the FPC's certificate responsibility.

[43] Department of Energy Organization Act.

[44] Section 3, Natural Gas Act of 1938.

[45] FTA countries include: Australia, Bahrain, Canada, Chile, Colombia, Costa Rica, Dominican Republic, El Salvador, Guatemala, Honduras, Israel, Jordan, Korea, Mexico, Morocco, Nicaragua, Oman, Panama, Peru, Singapore.

Statement (EIS) by the applicant if there is one. This can take as long as 20 months for the EA and 26 months for the EIS.[46]

Because of this disparity in the difficulty of the process, the DOE has approved far more projects than FERC. As of year-end 2015, the DOE had approved 45 FTA applications and ten non-FTA applications. FERC had only approved six projects. In August 2014, the DOE announced that it would not act on non-FTA applications until the requirements of NEPA had been met in a FERC proceeding. This was expected to weed out many marginal proposals.

State and local jurisdictional issues can also influence the approval process. These depend strongly on local conditions and can affect the ultimate location of successful projects. The two principal issues are state regulation of fracking and local objections to terminal siting and pipeline right-of-way. The fracking issue has been important in the north-east: New York, Pennsylvania, and West Virginia share the very large Marcellus shale resource. New York has banned fracking, while Pennsylvania has become the second-largest gas producing state. Environmental opposition to terminal siting and pipelines is much stronger on the east and west coasts than in the Gulf coast. Elba Island, Georgia and the two projects in Oregon have all encountered substantial local opposition.

The regulatory framework in Canada
The authority of Canada's National Energy Board (NEB) is similar to that of the USA's DOE/FERC. Part IV, Section 117 of the National Energy Board Act requires an export licence for an LNG export project. Part III, Sections 30 and 31 give certificate jurisdiction over inter provincial pipelines. The NEB is also responsible for an Environmental Assessment (EA). While it can initiate an EA on its own, it may be required to do so by the Canadian Environmental Assessment Agency.[47] Export projects using US feedgas will also need US FERC and DOE approval if the LNG is sent to non FTA countries. The NEB has been liberal in granting approvals for licence applications. As of the end of 2015, it had granted all but three of the 25 applications for LNG export projects.[48]

For LNG export projects, a facility permit may be required. In British Columbia (BC), the BC Oil and Gas Commission issues the permit. Tax policy is the most contentious issue involving provincial regulation, particularly in BC. The initial positions of the government and the project

---

[46] David L. Goldwyn, Brookings Task Force Session, 25 January 2013.
[47] Canadian Environmental Assessment Act 2012.
[48] Canada's National Energy Board – LNG Export and Import Licence Applications.

developers were far apart,[49] but BC has now fielded its 'Bill 6 – 2014' that spells out the tax regime.[50]

Overview of the North American LNG export projects

While their motives were similar, the USA and Canada have so far had rather different trajectories as future LNG exporters. As of end-2015, five projects with 64 mtpa are under construction in the USA. In contrast, no Canadian project is under construction, although Petronas has taken conditional FID on its project. Another 334 mtpa of possible capacity is in the planning stage in the USA, with a further 353 mtpa in Canada. It is clear that much of this proposed capacity will never be built; the challenge is therefore to understand those factors that will drive the LNG export expansion, and thus determine how much of the proposed capacity is realistic.

LNG projects are usually based on stranded gas reserves that have no market value without the construction of a downstream transportation system. In contrast, none of the North American projects are based on dedicated reserves, and with the exception of the larger British Columbia projects, most assume that regional supply will be available throughout the life of the project. However, although project developers can avoid the upstream investment in such cases, they cannot book the reserves on their balance sheets.

Many US projects – notably four of the five under construction – are based on existing LNG import capacity, implying lower investments costs (see Chapter 4). These projects have opted for a tolling structure, with LNG being sold FOB and based on HH indexation. The flexibility has attracted Asian and European companies usually planning to use the gas for their markets (destination buyers), as well as aggregators wishing to add US LNG to their portfolio. In Canada, projects are of a greenfield nature and most will require extensive upstream and pipeline infrastructure investments. As a result, project sponsors have seemed to favour oil indexation to cover higher capital costs, to date.

The following two maps show the location of the six US plants that have full approvals (five of them under construction) and those plants with active FERC filings as of year-end 2015.

---

[49] 'Jack M. Mintz: B.C.'s LNG tax could bomb', *Financial Post*, 18 March 2014. http://opinion.financialpost.com/2014/03/18/jack-m-mintz-b-c-s-lng-tax-could-bomb/.
[50] BC Parliament, Bill 6 – 2014 Liquefied Natural Gas Income Tax Act.

234 *LNG Markets in Transition*

FERC APPROVED - UNDER CONSTRUCTION

1. Sabine, LA — Sabine Pass LNG Cheniere, 27.00 mtpa
2. Hackberry, LA — Sempra Cameron LNG, 13.50 mtpa
3. Freeport, TX — Freeport LNG Development, 13.20 mtpa
4. Cove Point, MD — Dominion Cove Point LNG, 5.25 mtpa
5. Corpus Christi, TX — Cheniere Corpus Christi LNG, 13.50 mtpa

FERC APPROVED - NOT UNDER CONSTRUCTION

6. Lake Charles, LA — Southern Union Lake Charles LNG, 15.00 mtpa

US Jurisdiction
- FERC
- MARAD/USCG

As of January 6, 2016

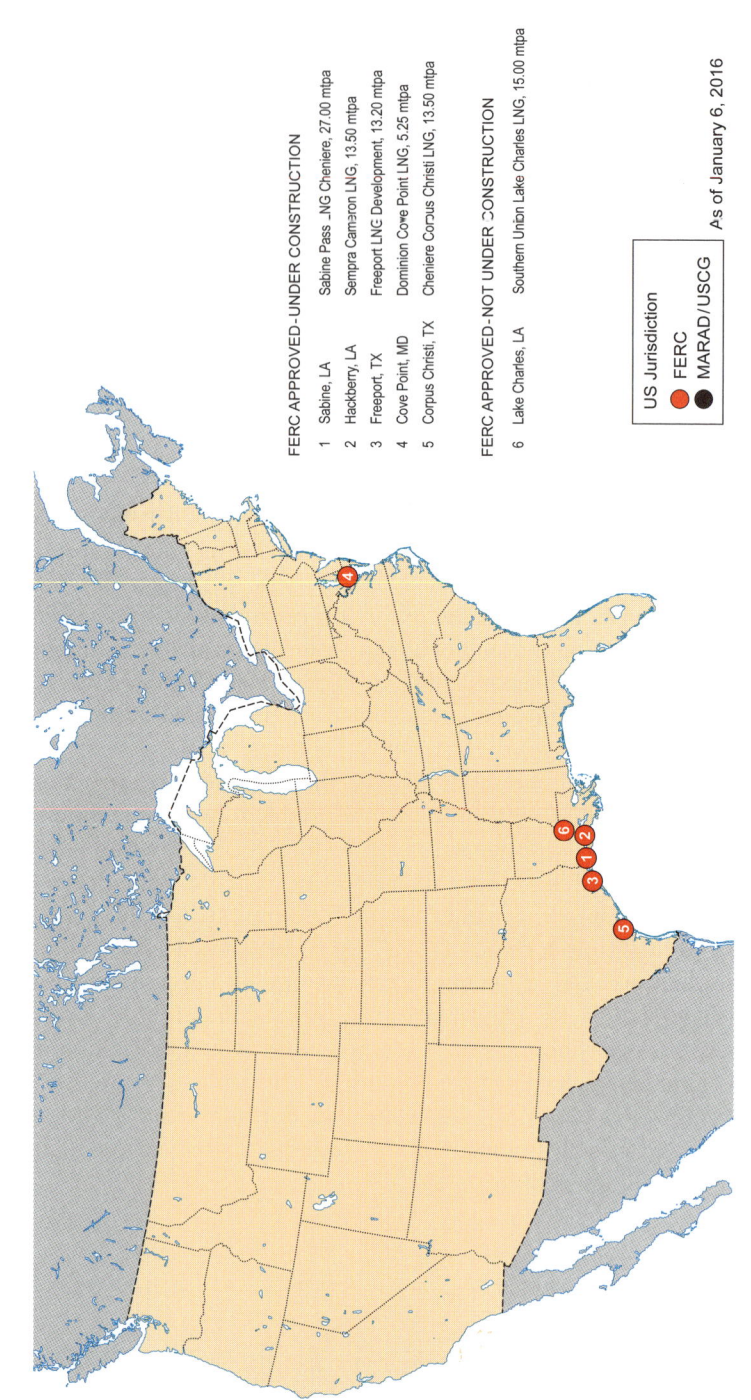

Map 5.2: US projects that are under construction (as of end 2015)

Future LNG Supply 235

FERC PROPOSED

1 Coos Bay, OR — Jordan Cove Energy Project, 7.00 mtpa
2 Astoria, OR — Oregon LNG, 9.60 mtpa
3 Elba Island, GA — Southern LNG Company, 2.50 mtpa
4 Lake Charles, LA — Magnolia LNG, 8.00 mtpa
5 Sabine Pass, TX — ExxonMobil Golden Pass, 15.60 mtpa
6 Pascagoula, MS — Gulf LNG Liquefaction, 10.00 mtpa
7 Freeport, TX — Freeport LNG Development, 5.00 mtpa
8 Cameron Parish, LA — Venture Global Calasieu Pass, 10.00 mtpa
9 Hackberry, LA — Sempra Cameron LNG, 9.97 mtpa
10 Plaqemines Parish LA — CE FLING, 8.00 mtpa
11 Plaqemines Parish, LA — Louisiana LNG, 2.00 mtpa
12 Robbinston, ME — Kestrel Energy - Downeast LNG, 3.45 mtpa
13 Jacksonville, FL — Eagle LNG Partners, 0.56 mtpa
14 Brownsville, TX — Texas LNG Brownsville, 4.00 mtpa
15 Brownsville, TX — Annova LNG Brownsville, 7.00 mtpa
16 Port Arthur, TX — Port Arthur LNG, 10.00 mtpa
17 Brownsville, TX — Rio Grande LNG - Next Decade, 27.00 mtpa
19 Corpus Christi, TX — Cheniere Corpus Christi LNG, 9.00 mtpa
20 Plaqemines Parish, LA — Venture Global LNG, 20.00 mtpa
21 Nikiski, AK — Alaska LNG Project, 18.00 mtpa
22 Cameron Parish, LA — G2 LNG, 13.49 mtpa

MARAD PROPOSED

23 Gulf of Mexico — Delfin FLNG, 8.00 mtpa

US Jurisdiction
● FERC
● MARAD/USCG

As of January 6, 2016

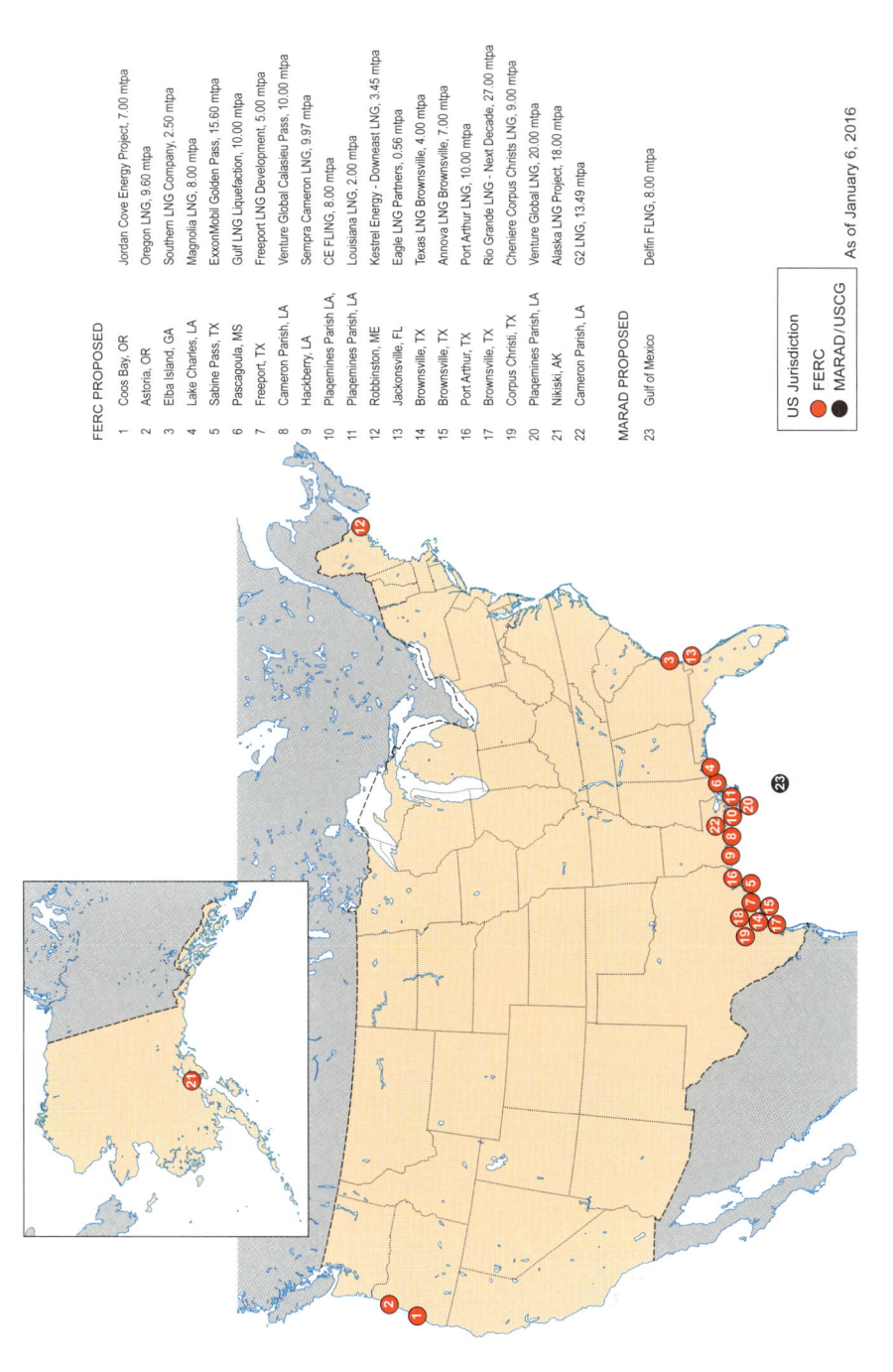

Map 5.3: US projects that that have been proposed to FERC or MARAD (as of end 2015)

There are many ways to categorize the North American projects, particularly the proposed projects. The region where they are located determines the regulatory and fiscal frameworks they depend upon, the markets they will be targeting preferentially, and also the sources of gas supply. Their regulatory status, the amount of LNG contracted, and the nature of each project's investors are other criteria enabling a differentiation between the projects.

Table 5.6: North American LNG projects by region and status (as of January 2016)

Region	Total number of projects	Total capacity including under construction (mtpa)	Number of projects under construction	Capacity (mtpa)
USA				
US Gulf and East Coasts	35	364	5	64
Oregon	2	16.6	0	0
Alaska	1	18	0	0
Canada				
British Columbia	18	301	0	0
Eastern Canada	5	52	0	0

Source: Author's database.

The proposed North American projects fall into five regional groupings (see Table 5.6).

- **Gulf coast and east coast projects represent the majority of US projects.** Four Gulf coast projects and one east coast project are already under construction. They are tolling projects that assume that commodity gas will always be available. Gulf coast projects rely primarily upon the US south-west producing region while the US east coast projects will source gas from Marcellus production in the north-east. In both cases, the volume of gas for the project over its life is not in question. The fact that no upstream investment is required and that some projects are brownfield sites will keep capital costs low. The major supply issue is how US prices will respond to demand growth over time. These projects have relatively low shipping costs to Europe and Latin America compared to competitors, but shipping costs to Asia (through the Panama Canal) are higher than those of Canadian, Australian, east Russian, and Eastern African projects (Corbeau et al., 2014). Meanwhile, the potential for Panama Canal congestion represents a risk for shipment to Asian markets. A significant question for east coast projects is the adequacy of pipeline infrastructure, whose bottlenecks at the moment have distorted regional basis differentials creating an unsettled price relationship to the Henry Hub marker.

- The two **Oregon projects** do not have substantial gas supply nearby and will have to rely on pipeline deliveries from BC, Alberta, or the Rockies. However, they will benefit from a closer distance to Asian markets. Their success will depend on how the project developers and potential buyers share the supply risk.

- The **Alaska project** uses stranded gas in the North Slope, transporting it across the region to an LNG plant in the south of Alaska. This is a greenfield project with high development costs, which targets Asian markets.

- **British Columbia (BC)** is a part of the Western Canadian Sedimentary Basin (WCSB). While small projects might rely on local production, the capacity of larger projects will be likely to exceed WCSB supply and will probably require pipeline access to the Horn River and Montney shales in northern BC. The BC projects have a transportation advantage to Asia over the US Gulf and east coast projects, but they will be greenfield projects. The pipeline cost, plus possible field development investment, will substantially increase the projects' capital expenditures.

- **Eastern Canada** has limited production offshore Nova Scotia. Any significant-sized project would rely on pipeline deliveries from the WCSB or imports from the Marcellus in the US north-east. The supply cost remains uncertain. The Eastern Canadian projects have a transportation advantage going east (to Europe).

US projects
As of the end of 2015, the DOE had 25 applications for new LNG export projects, totalling 311 mtpa of capacity. Another six projects (excluding Alaska) totalling 49 mtpa had been reported in the trade press but had not yet filed. Two of these projects, totalling 16.6 mtpa, were located in Oregon while the rest were on the Gulf and Atlantic coasts. The DOE has approved five Gulf/Atlantic projects and both Oregon projects. Figure 5.5 shows the potential export capacity broken down by regulatory and contract status.

238   *LNG Markets in Transition*

Figure 5.5: Capacity of proposed US export projects by regulatory and contract status (as of end 2015)

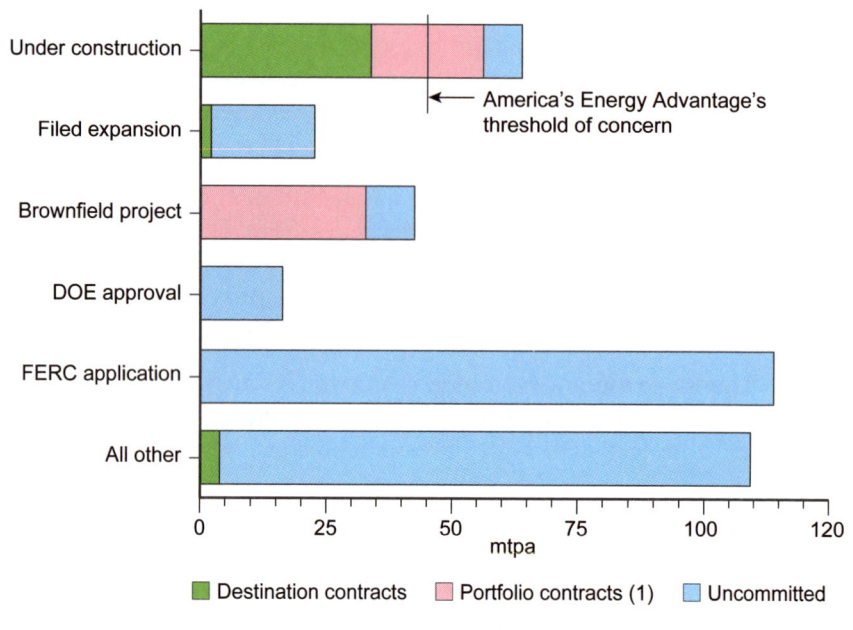

Source: Author's database.

'Destination contracts' are those where the buyer is expected to import the LNG into a specific market. 'Portfolio contracts' are those where the buyer is an aggregator who wants the flexibility to deliver the LNG to the market that provides him the best netback.

The largest group of projects in Figure 5.5 are those that have pre-filed applications before FERC. Although the odds of successful projects from this group are relatively low, it does include several experienced developers with LNG operating experience.

The US Gulf and Atlantic coast projects. The DOE lists 29 projects with 266 mtpa of capacity for this region. Five of the plants, totalling 63.95 mtpa, are already under construction and four have applied for expansion, totalling another 32.97 mtpa (see Table 5.7). All projects under construction so far, with the exception of Corpus Christi, are brownfield projects based on existing LNG import terminals. Corpus Christi, managed by Cheniere (the operator of Sabine Pass) had previously acquired a FERC authorization for an import terminal.

The collapse of LNG prices is providing a strong challenge to further FID approvals during this economic cycle. But among the more likely candidates that might still take FID are expansions of the projects under construction, as well as four brownfield projects supported by IOCs.

- The expansion projects have begun to assemble contracts but have not reached FID as of year-end 2015. If approved – and if they can sign enough additional contracts – their expansion should be relatively straightforward.

- Four potential brownfield projects that have applied to DOE but which have not yet reached FID are ExxonMobil/QP's Golden Pass, BG's Lake Charles, Shell/Kinder Morgan's Elba Island, and Kinder Morgan's Gulf LNG Liquefaction (Elba Island took its FID in June 2016). Of these, Lake Charles has also been granted a FERC certificate. Since a portfolio aggregator either owns, or has the rights to receive output, for the first three of these projects, the FID decision does not rely on third-party contracts, but would presumably reflect each company's assessment of its own portfolio options. ExxonMobil/QP have excellent economics for serving Asian markets. By shifting supply for their UK South Hook terminal to the USA, they can send Qatari LNG to Asia. BG and Shell must also go through a post-merger evaluation of their positions as a merged company.

Table 5.7: US projects under construction

Project	Capacity (mtpa)	Ownership	Destination contracts	Portfolio contracts	Un-committed	Proposed expansion
Sabine Pass	22.5	Cheniere	12.25	7.5	2.75	4.5
Freeport LNG	13.2	Michael Smith, Global Infrastructure Partners, Osaka Gas	8.8	4.4		5
Dominion Cove Point LNG	5.75	Dominion	4.5		1.25	
Cameron LNG	13.5	Sempra, Engie, Mitsui, Japan LNG Investment	2.99	9.01	1.5	9.97
Corpus Christi LNG	9	Cheniere	6.63	2.37		13.5
Total	**63.95**		**34.07**	**23.28**	**5.5**	**32.97**

Source: Author's database.

The Oregon projects. The two US Oregon projects, Jordan Cove and Oregon LNG, have DOE approvals, but as of the end of 2015 had neither the sales contracts necessary for financing, nor FERC approval. Jordan Cove's application was temporarily suspended in March 2016, but was subsequently reinstated. It has now signed tolling agreements with JERA and Itochu. Oregon LNG abandoned its project in April 2016. These projects are the closest US projects to Asian markets. Unlike the Gulf coast, Oregon has no regional gas supply. It must rely on pipeline supply from BC, Alberta, or from the Rockies. Both projects have NEB export licences for Canadian gas. Some gas might come from BC, but if the large BC projects go ahead they will have to compete for limited local supply and may need access to large diameter pipelines from the Horn River and Montney shales in northern BC. There is unused pipeline capacity from Alberta, enabling the projects to target supply from Alberta's Duvernay shales, and Jordan Cove has taken a 50 per cent interest in the Ruby Pipeline from Wyoming. But the challenge will be to convince customers that there will be reliable supply over the project's lifetime.

The Alaska LNG project. The Alaska LNG project is not a product of the shale gas revolution, but is based on the Prudhoe Bay field on the North Slope of Alaska, discovered in 1968. The field, with its initial proved reserves of 10 billion barrels of oil and 736 bcm of associated gas, was the largest hydrocarbon discovery in North America. A more recent gas condensate discovery, Point Thomson, has added another 227 bcm of gas reserves.

Initial ideas to develop a pipeline to the lower 48 states fell through when wellhead price deregulation turned gas shortages into surpluses. A subsequent LNG export plant, based on the field, to ship the gas to Asia emerged in 1982, but failed to move ahead as it did not line up enough customers. Interest in the pipeline to the lower 48 states was revived with the gas shortages of the early 2000s, but shale gas developments again discouraged the pipeline. Most recently, high Asian gas prices rekindled interest in developing the LNG project, which includes a treatment plant on the North Slope, a 1,300 km 42 inch pipeline to Nikiski (where the existing small Cook Inlet LNG project is located) and liquefaction capacity of 15–18 mtpa.

The current project, Alaska LNG, involves the three producers – BP, ConocoPhillips, and ExxonMobil – and includes an equity position for the State of Alaska. TransCanada Pipeline also previously held an equity position, but it has now been bought out by the state. Current cost estimates are around $45–65 billion. The Alaskan government is keen for the project to move ahead to bring additional revenues to replace falling oil revenues, create job opportunities, and bring gas supplies to its southern population centres.

Canadian LNG projects
Canada's gas production dropped from 188 bcm in 2006 to 162 bcm in 2014 as exports to the USA – its only export market – fell. Meanwhile, Canada is facing an invasion of low-cost US shale gas in its own markets. Canadian producers have no option other than LNG to export their gas resources, given the relatively limited prospects of the domestic gas market. Additionally, the provinces' revenues have been affected by lower gas production and exports and by falling gas spot prices since 2009.

Consequently, 25 projects with a capacity of 353 mtpa have been filed with NEB (3.5 times Canada's current production): 20 projects in BC totalling 301 mtpa, and five eastern Canadian projects totalling 51.5 mtpa. As of year-end 2015, none have achieved FID. Western Canadian LNG projects benefit from a relative proximity to Asia. Many IOCs and Asian companies have invested in BC since 2009, either by acquiring upstream assets that feed proposed LNG projects or by participating in the development of planned LNG projects.

The British Columbia projects. The BC LNG projects are located in three main areas: North BC, the Kitimat and Prince Rupert area, and the Campbell River and Delta area. Some projects (such as Kitimat, Canada LNG, WCC LNG, and PNWLNG) have dedicated gas resources, whereas others such as Prince Rupert LNG are not connected to specific upstream developments (Gomes, 2015).

The NEB has already approved projects totalling 295 mtpa, including those supported by aggregators with strong LNG development experience (115 mtpa), independent project developers(105 mtpa),[51] First Nations sponsors (30 mtpa), and destination buyers (30 mtpa)[52] (see Figure 5.6). Another 14.5 mtpa of First Nations applications have not been approved. The challenge of all the developers is to sign up customers to SPAs (sale and purchase agreements). This has been challenging due to the uncertainties over taxation, access to sites, rights-of-way, and reliable supply. Given these risks, and the relatively high costs of the projects, developers initially sought traditional oil-linked contracts (with some form of protection from low oil prices) for these projects rather than a Gulf coast or Canadian hub type formula. This has proved difficult to do and some projects, such as Pacific Northwest LNG and LNG Canada, have offered equity participation in the project as an incentive. Another problem for Canadian projects is that the portfolio aggregators, who do not need customer contracts, are still judging potential commitments in Canada against other options for their companies.

---

[51] Companies without previous experience in LNG.
[52] This treats Petronas, developer of Pacific NW LNG, as a destination buyer rather than a portfolio aggregator.

242   *LNG Markets in Transition*

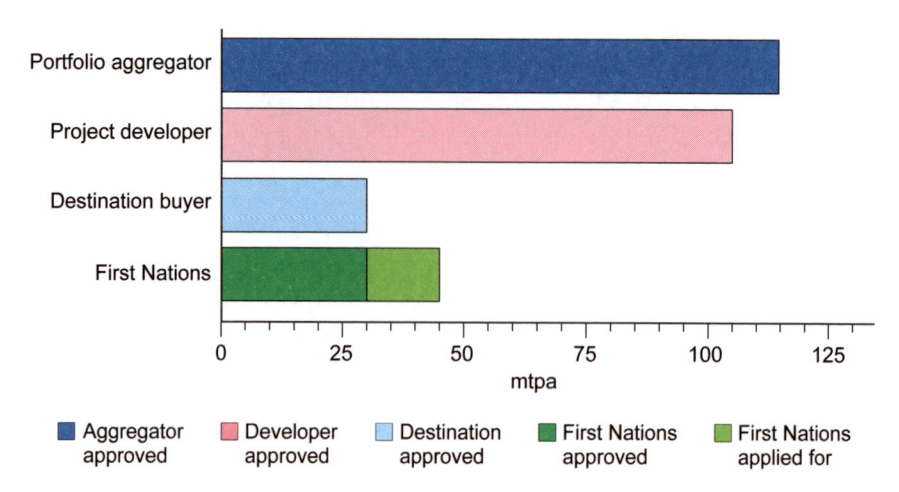

Figure 5.6: Capacity of proposed British Coumbia LNG export project by sponsor
Source: NEB, author's database.

For example, ExxonMobil's 30 mtpa WCC LNG project, sponsored by an ExxonMobil affiliate, competes against the 15.6 mtpa Golden Pass project in Texas as well as other company options. In this case Golden Pass has lower-cost supply and a brownfield cost advantage but has an independent partner, while WCC has a transportation advantage to Asia, the ability to book reserves, and an affiliate partner. ExxonMobil's decision is pending, but in the current market environment it would seem that Golden Pass's advantages are more attractive. Table 5.8 lists the projects that had received NEB approval as of December 2015.

Table 5.8: Approved British Columbia projects (as of December 2015)

Plant	Ownership	Planned capacity (mtpa)
Aurora LNG – Grassy Point	CNOOC, INPEX, JGC	12
BC LNG Cooperative – Douglas Channel FLNG	Alta Gas, Idemitsu	0.55
Canada Stewart LNG	Canada Stewart Energy	30
Discovery LNG	Quiksilver Resources	20
Grassy Point LNG	Woodside	20
Kitsault Energy	Kitsault Energy	20
KM LNG (Kitimat)	Chevron, Woodside	10
LNG Canada	Shell, KOGAS, Mitsubishi, Petrochina	24

Plant	Ownership	Planned capacity (mtpa)
New Times LNG	New Times Energy	12
Orca LNG	Orca LNG	25
Pacific NW LNG	Petronas, JAPEX, Brunei, Indian Oil, Sinopec	18
Prince Rupert LNG	BG, Spectra	21
Steelhead LNG	Steelhead LNG, Huu-ay-aht First Nation	30
Triton LNG	Alta Gas, Idemitsu	2.3
WCC LNG	ExxonMobil, Imperial	30
Westpac Midstream LNG	Westpac	3
Woodfibre LNG	Woodfibre	2.1
Total		**279.95**

Source: NEB and author's database.

The Canadian First Nations issue. For much of Canada, the government negotiated treaties with its aboriginal people – the First Nations – resolving various issues and establishing the Crown's title to the land. The Government signed 11 treaties between 1871 and 1921. But in BC, with few exceptions, such treaties were not negotiated. As a result, most of the BC First Nations retain ownership rights to land on which pipelines and some LNG plants are to be constructed.[53] Thus project developers find themselves dealing with groups that effectively control their access to sites and pipeline routes. For sites, there may be only one First Nation tribe involved, but long-distance pipelines may cross the territory of a number of different tribes, significantly complicating the negotiations.

Since many First Nations tribes control portions of the required land rights, project developers are trying to develop joint agreements with tribal groups. Petronas' Pacific Northwest LNG project has made most progress in this and thus represents a test case for what is possible.

Successes and failures have occurred in the negotiation process. The BC government successfully negotiated a revenue sharing agreement with 28 First Nations in May 2015.[54] On the other hand, Pacific Northwest LNG offered the Lax Kw'alaams First Nation a Cn$1.15 billion (US$1 billion) bonus in its negotiations over the right to a site near Prince Rupert. The

---

[53] www.theglobeandmail.com/globe-debate/if-aboriginal-issues-sink-northern-gateway. (Last visited 30 June 2015.)

[54] http://businessfinancia;post.com/news/energy/first-nations-lng-deals-with-b-c-will-help-in. (Last visited 12 July 2015.)

tribe initially turned down the offer because of its concerns over the effect that a project sited at the mouth of the river would have on spawning salmon.[55] Had the company capitalized that bonus, the increase in the cost over the life of the project would amount to one quarter of the transportation advantage that BC enjoys over the US Gulf. Subsequently, a Lax Kw'alaams' declaration calling for the protection of the site was endorsed by other First Nations tribal leaders.[56] Additionally, the Gitga'at First Nation sought a judicial review of a BC Environmental Assessment in the Pacific Northwest LNG case.[57] While these difficulties may be resolved, they threaten to slow the approval process and increase project costs.

Two First Nations groups are negotiating equity positions as their payment for land access. The Haisla First Nation is negotiating with potential developers for three projects – Cedars 1, 2 & 3. And the Huu-ay-aht have entered into a partnership with the sponsors of the Steelhead LNG project.

Supply challenges. A major issue for all of these projects is supply. BC is a part of the Western Canadian Sedimentary Basin, a gas-producing region. In 2014 it produced 43.6 bcm of marketable gas.[58] Smaller LNG projects might be willing to rely on existing BC supply, but larger projects would require very large expansions of production. For example, the 12 mtpa Pacific Northwest LNG would require a 43 per cent increase in local production. Many projects in the Prince Rupert and Kitimat area have arranged for separate pipelines to bring gas from the Horn River and Montney shales. These involve long distances (between 500 and 1,000 km) (Gomes, 2015), construction in mountainous terrain, and will thus be costly. The timing, cost, and permitting of these pipelines is also crucial for LNG projects to move ahead.

Eastern Canadian projects. The appeal of Eastern Canadian LNG plants (see Table 5.9) is their shorter distance to transatlantic markets than those in the US Gulf coast. There is a $0.33/MMBtu tanker transportation advantage[59] for Eastern Canada over the Gulf for shipments to Europe and to India.

---

[55] http://www.theglobeandmail.com/report-on-business/industry-news/energy-and-resources. (Last visited 12 December 2012.)

[56] www.alaskahiwaynews.ca/regional-news/declaration-calls -for-protection-of-lelu-i. (Last visited 26 January 2016.)

[57] www.vancouversun.com/news/First+Nation+lunches+court +action+against+Pacific. (Last visited 12 July 2015.)

[58] British Columbia Natural Gas & Oil Statistics.

[59] Author's estimate based on an LNG economics model using 170,000 cubic metre tankers.

The major disadvantage to Eastern Canadian projects is that – as of year-end 2015 – there are significant questions regarding the source of the gas supply, and its price. The resulting uncertainties surrounding project economics pose a significant challenge to developers in their attempts to find customers who will sign on to SPAs to provide volume certainty and who are willing to assume significant supply risk.

Four of the proposed plants are in the Maritime Provinces and would be served by the Maritimes and Northeast System (M&NE). Another is in Quebec and would be served by the TransCanada Pipeline system (TCPL).

Table 5.9: Eastern Canadian projects

Plant	Location	Planned capacity (mtpa)	Its attraction
Bear Head LNG	Point Tupper, NS	12	Partial infrastructure
Canaport LNG	St. John, NB	5	Existing import terminal
H Energy LNG	Melford, NS	13.5	Indian company backing
Peridae Energy	Goldboro, NS	10	5 mtpa E.On Heads of Agreement
Energie Saguenay	Saguenay, Que	11	Pipeline connection to Western Canadian Gas (650 km)
Total		**51.5**	

Source: NEB and author's database.

Since Nova Scotia's production is limited and declining, supply for the projects in the Canadian Maritime Provinces is expected to come primarily from the USA via a reversed M&NE pipeline or from Western Canada. If US-sourced gas is to be exported, the US DOE would require an export licence if the destination is a non-FTA buyer. Any necessary pipeline expansion in the USA would need a FERC Certificate.

The supply problems facing all of the projects is the substantial reorientation of Eastern North American supply and pipeline systems, and its effect on physical flows and on price relationships. The fastest growing shale basin in the USA is the Marcellus, located in the Appalachian states of New York, Pennsylvania, and West Virginia. Production from Marcellus has grown so rapidly that the region has become a major exporter, resulting in gas being cheaper in Pennsylvania than it is in Louisiana.

At the same time, growth of gas demand in New England has taxed available pipeline capacity and New England prices can experience shortage spikes in winter. Since a reversed M&NE pipeline to feed the Maritime

246   *LNG Markets in Transition*

projects would originate in New England, the distortions of traditional pricing differentials is a serious problem. There are plans for pipeline projects that would increase the takeaway capacity from the Marcellus and provide the north-east with greater access to its supply. The two pipelines which now provide supply from the south-west have competing proposals for pipeline expansions to New England. But there is substantial local resistance to pipeline expansion into New England and it is not clear how it will be resolved. Alternative ways of delivering US and Western Canadian gas through TCPL to M&NE via a Maine connection would be less direct.

The Quebec project would rely on traditional sources delivered via TCPL, but this would necessitate a 650 km pipeline to connect to TCPL. This project, like the possible use of Western Canadian supply in the Maritimes, faces an additional potential issue in that TCPL may decide to convert part of its capacity to an oil line for shipping oil sands crude oil to the east.

The competitive outlook for North American projects
Contractual commitments
To arrange non-recourse financing, a project must demonstrate that it has contractual commitments for the output, either from traditional buyers in destination markets or portfolio aggregators. Contracts signed by project developers are usually reported in the press, but the contractual commitment negotiations of portfolio aggregators are often internal to the company, making it more difficult to judge where they stand.

While Canada is still in the early stages of the SPA process, contracts from US LNG projects indicate current market conditions. As of year-end 2015, the five US projects under construction (representing 64 mtpa of capacity) had secured SPAs totalling 56.5 mtpa. This leaves 7.5 mtpa available to place in the market either as additional long-term contracts or as trading volumes. Three of the five also had expansion applications before FERC and were actively marketing another 14 mtpa. Table 5.10 shows the balance of SPAs for the five projects.

Table 5.10: Balance of SPAs in US LNG projects under construction (at end 2015)

	mtpa committed	*Percentage*
Portfolio contracts	23.28	39.9%
Destination: Northeast Asia	17.49	29.9%
Destination: Spain	7.99	13.9%
Destination: India	5.8	9.9%
Destination: other Europe	3.29	5.6%
Destination: rest of world	0.6	1.0%

Source: Author's database.

Sixty per cent of the SPAs are contracts for delivery to specific destinations, although this LNG may be re-traded depending on the markets' appetite. But almost 40 per cent are portfolio contracts which may be placed in a given market through secondary long-term contracts, or reserved for speculative short-term trading. While north-east Asia, Spain, and India appear as the largest buyers, China is absent and the rest of Europe has made only a small commitment.

The Canadian and Oregon projects all need buyers who will accept the supply risks and sign the necessary SPAs. The extent to which buyers are prepared to take the supply risks in these regions will be important in determining the success of these projects. Since the first movers have sought out the larger, more creditworthy buyers, there is a risk that later projects will have to rely on less attractive customer commitments.

How do projects' financial feasibility compare?
There are two crucial elements for the financial feasibility of LNG projects: the price they can obtain from markets and the cost of supply.

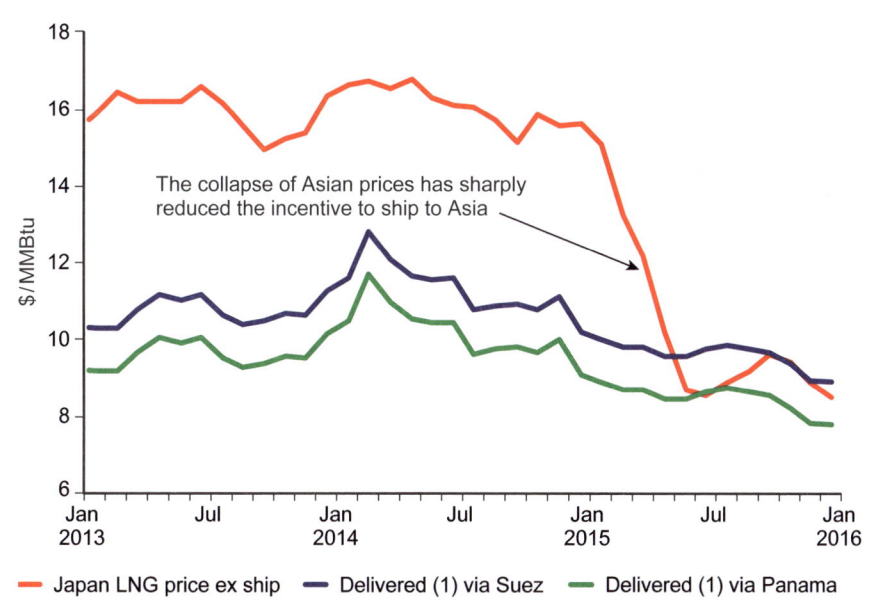

(1) Assumes three 4.5 mtpa trains, 170,000 m³ tankers, current Suez and proposed Panama Canal tolls.

Figure 5.7: Illustration of the incentive that the Asian Premium created

Note: Estimates based on the 2015 version of the author's proprietary LNG economics model.

The price environment has changed drastically with the collapse of oil prices and of Asian import prices. US LNG has now lost its price advantage at 2016 oil price levels. Figure 5.7 compares the Japanese LNG price with the estimated laid in cost of US Gulf coast supplies. The disappearance of the Asian premium has adversely affected all three types of buyers – Asian destination buyers, non-affiliated project developers, and portfolio aggregators. Nevertheless, destination buyers may still find the diversified pricing clause structure to be an advantage despite the narrowing of the price advantage.

Meanwhile, Figure 5.8 compares the recent TTF hub price with the estimated cost of delivering Gulf coast gas to the Netherlands, illustrating that TTF prices may at times not be enough to cover fully allocated delivery costs from the USA. Europe has been a difficult market for LNG, with strong variations in LNG imports (see Chapter 2). It is also not a monolithic market: a country-by-country analysis by Anouk Honoré (2014) shows that it is likely to be regionally uneven, while production from the North Sea and Groningen faces decline. Europe is also interested in diversifying its supply away from Russia. These factors will create LNG import opportunities, albeit with significant price risk.

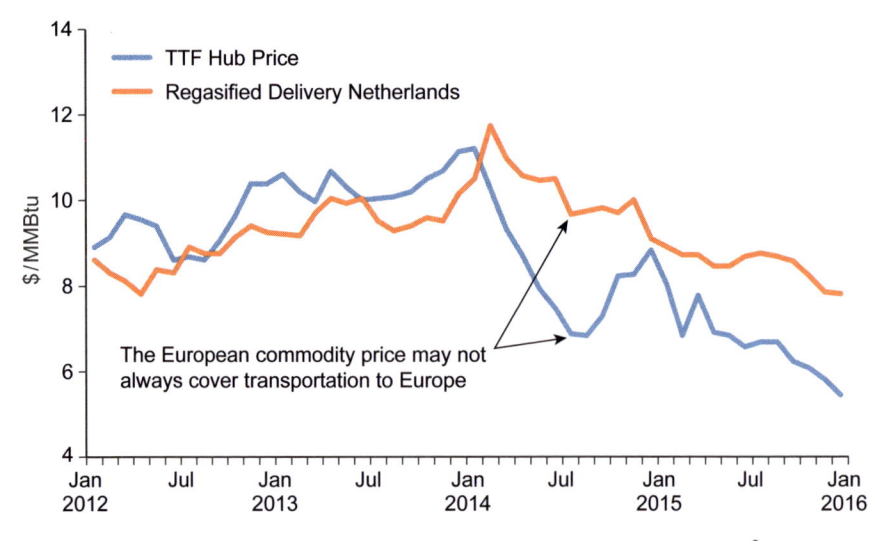

(1) Economics assume three 4.4 mtpa Greenfield trains and 170,000 m³ tankers.

Figure 5.8: Illustration of the price risk in delivering LNG to Europe from the US Gulf coast

Note: The delivered cost estimates are based on the 2015 version of the author's proprietary LNG economics model.

The potential protection that the Asian premium provided for European spot deliveries is illustrated in Figure 5.9. It shows HH prices compared to netbacks to the Gulf, from the European TTF hub, and from Japanese ex-ship LNG. From March to October 2014, when the netback from Europe was less than HH, Figure 5.9 substitutes the netback from Japan (if the Panama Canal had been available). The resulting composite netback remained above HH. With the collapse of Asian prices in early 2015, the Asian 'safety net' is no longer an option.

Consequently, all potential customers will find the price risks greater and have more difficult feasibility decisions than they did in early 2014. European buyers may find it advantageous to buy directly rather than rely on aggregators. An analysis by Kenneth Medlock argues that under equilibrium commodity pricing conditions, US exports to Europe or to Asia are losing propositions. Using Rice's proprietary world gas model,

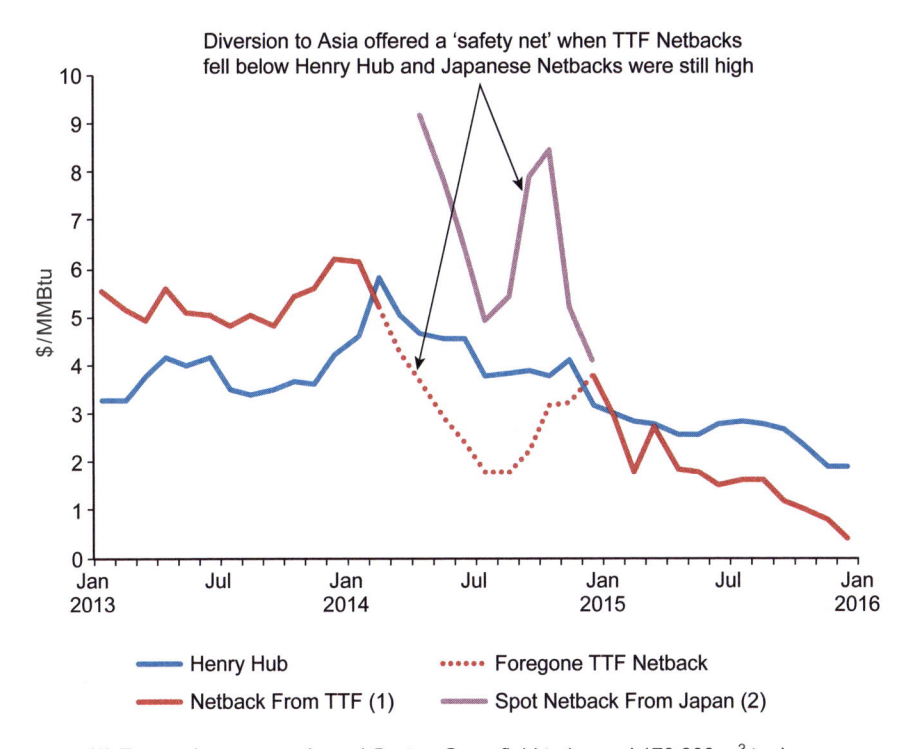

(1) Economics assume three 4.5 mtpa Greenfield trains and 170,000 m³ tankers.
(2) Netbacks from the Asian 'Safety Net' using an expanded Panama Canal.

Figure 5.9: Illustration of the Asian spot price 'safety net'

Note: Estimates based on the 2015 version of the author's proprietary LNG economics model.

he estimates a negative margin for both trades going forward.[60] The possible negative impact of equilibrium commodity pricing for existing contracts would be shared according to the risk-sharing provisions of the contract. But the financial incentive for new investments would be impaired.

The evolution of North American gas prices is another key uncertainty. Faced with opposition from consumer advocates (especially from an industrial group, America's Energy Advantage, led by Dow Chemical,[61] which campaigns to keep access to cheap US gas for the use of US businesses) the US Energy Information Administration (EIA) did an analysis and a later update of the response of prices to different levels of exports and the rate at which they might be implemented.[62] The scenarios which showed the highest price increases were those in which the EIA assumed conservative resource recovery – a low Estimated Ultimate Recovery (EUR). In their 2012 study, the highest average price increase from 2015 to 2025 over the reference case was $2.13; in the most recent analysis it was only $1.30.

To provide perspective on the potential impact on the economy, in 2012 EIA hired the economic consulting firm NERA. In its analysis, using somewhat different assumptions, NERA concluded:

> The largest price increase that would be observed after 5 or more years of potentially growing exports could range from $0.22 to $1.11 (2010$/MCF [thousand cubic feet]). The higher end of the range is reached only under conditions of ample US supplies and low domestic gas prices.

It has since updated it for Cheniere Energy with largely similar conclusions.[63]

The primary focus of the NERA analyses was the effect of domestic price increases on the economy. But NERA also ran its world gas model in both studies to see how sensitive LNG exports were to the estimated price levels.

The NERA model assumes pricing equilibrium, making it a challenge to adapt it to a world in which different pricing systems coexist. In its International Reference case in the 2012 study, it found there was no

---

[60] 'US LNG Exports: Truth and Consequences', Kenneth Medlock, James A. Baker III Institute for Public Policy, Rice University, 10 August 2012, 30.

[61] America's Energy Advantage filing, in DOE Freeport LNG proceeding – FE Docket No. 11-161-LNG, 15 November 2013.

[62] 'Effect of Increased Natural Gas Exports on Domestic Energy Markets', EIA, January 2012; 'Effect of Increased Levels of Liquefied Natural Gas Exports on U.S. Energy Markets', EIA, 29 October 2014;

[63] 'Updated Macroeconomic Impacts of LNG Exports from the USA', NERA, March 2014.

economic incentive to export LNG. In the 2014 study, its export level for the same scenario for 2028 was 1.63 Tcf (33.5 mtpa) despite the fact that 63.5 mtpa of capacity is currently under construction.

Dow sponsored a rebuttal to the first NERA study from Charles River Associates,[64] focusing on the adverse effects of exports on manufacturing. However, in October 2105 the DOE issued a study done by Oxford Economics and Rice University's Baker Institute that again confirmed positive macroeconomic effects for the US economy from LNG exports.[65]

Consulting geologist Arthur E. Berman raised opposition to LNG exports on technical grounds.[66] Fracked formations have very unusual characteristics. They are in effect highly permeable fracture zones within a highly impermeable host shale rock. They are subject to very rapid initial decline followed by a long runout 'tail'. Berman argues that it is inappropriate to use traditional hyperbolic decline curves to determine the Estimated Ultimate Recovery (EUR). He contends that fracked formations do not conform to the traditional curve and that economic recovery will end much sooner, adversely affecting the EUR.

An additional cost concern in Canada is that the country is facing a shortage of skilled labour in the oil and gas labour market and has a limited specialized LNG-skilled workforce. Project developers therefore fear that labour costs could get out of control, as happened in Australia, which could further undermine the feasibility of planned projects in the country.

Transporting LNG to markets

Given its geographic position, North American LNG can feasibly reach all global gas markets. US east coast and Canadian LNG and Gulf coast LNG have an advantage to Europe, while Oregon and BC projects are better placed to reach Asia. However, the expansion of the Panama Canal from 2016 onwards will open up opportunities for cheaper shipments from the Gulf to East Asia.

The Panama Canal uses two sets of parallel locks on the Atlantic and Pacific sides to enable vessels to transit Gatun Lake, which is 26 metres above sea level. The capacity of the canal is determined by the rate at which the locks can be cycled. By 2006, the canal had reached capacity operation to the point of overload, and the government of Panama made the decision to expand the canal. The expansion will add a third – and

---

[64] 'US Manufacturing and LNG Exports: Contributions to the US Economy', CRA, February 2013.

[65] 'The Macroeconomic Impact of Increasing U.S. LNG Imports', Oxford Economics LTI and The Center for Energy Studies, Rice University.

[66] 'U.S. Shale Gas; Less Abundance, Higher Cost', Arthur E. Berman and Lynn F. Pittinger, *The Oil Drum*, 5 August 2011.

252   *LNG Markets in Transition*

larger – set of locks parallel to the old locks. The additional capacity will permit much larger vessels to transit the canal. Less than 10 per cent of the LNG tanker fleet can use the existing canal, but the new locks will accommodate 80 per cent of the fleet.[67]

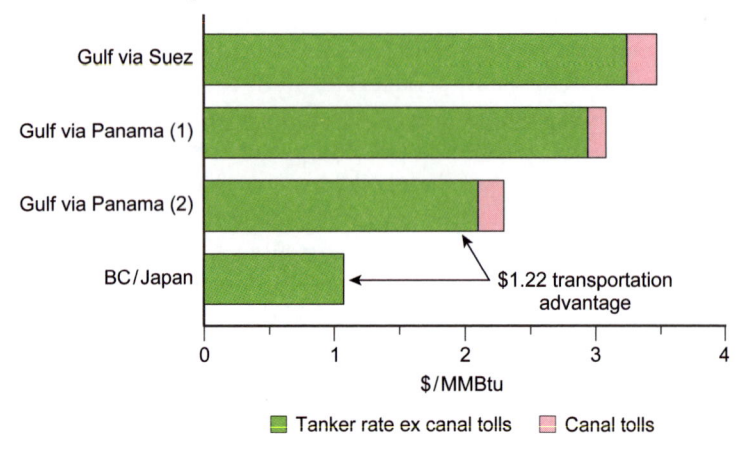

(1) Hypothetical 'Panamax' 50,000 m³ tanker, old Panama Canal tolls.
(2) 170,000 m³ tanker, new Panama Canal tolls.

Figure 5.10: Tanker rates to Japan
Note: This assumes 170,000 m³ vessels, identical gas and liquefaction costs.
Source: 2015 version of the author's proprietary LNG economics model.

BC shipments to Japan enjoy a $2.44/MMBtu rate advantage over shipments from the US Gulf to Japan via the Suez Canal.[68] This comparison assumes the use of 170,000 m³ tankers and identical plant and liquefaction costs. The expansion of the Panama Canal reduces the BC advantage to $1.22/MMBtu (see Figure 5.10).

In FY2014, the existing twin sets of locks handled 13,492 transits[69] or 18.5 transits per day for each set of locks. The expectation is that the new locks will accommodate 12 to 14 transits of the larger vessels per day.[70] A single LNG ship will require two transits for a round trip voyage. The symptoms of overload for the existing canal have been long queue lines and occasional bonuses paid for moving up in the queue. An obvious question is, 'How much LNG traffic will the expanded canal be able to handle before it, too, reaches capacity?'

---

[67] *Medium Term Oil and Gas Markets 2010*, International Energy Agency, page 264.
[68] Estimates based on the 2015 version of the author's proprietary LNG economic model.
[69] Canal de Panama, Statistics and Models Unit (MEEM).
[70] 'Panama Canal Expansion Study', U.S. Maritime Administration, November 2013, xiii.

Future LNG Supply 253

There is no easy answer to this question. When the initial studies were undertaken, the added demand was expected to come primarily from container ships that operate to a strict timetable, thus suiting the Panama Canal's transit booking system. These ships, like LNG vessels, were increasing to sizes that the canal could no longer handle. Since the decision to expand was undertaken in 2006, planning for the expansion did not reflect the later interest in LNG shipments from the US Gulf to Asia. Thus the added LNG demand will be superimposed on a planned demand growth that did not envision it. A further complication for the canal authorities is that the timing of LNG ships will be less regular than that of the container ships, creating potential logistical problems.

One way of looking at the problem is to determine what percentage of the expanded capacity is required to accommodate various levels of contract commitment. Figure 5.11 assumes that north-east Asian buyers choose to ship their contract commitments through the canal. Assuming 170,000 m^3 ships and a capacity of 12 transits per day, this would require 9.3 per cent of the expanded capacity. In addition, while it is clear that some of the portfolio commitments envision European or other destinations, if all portfolio shipments also went to East Asia through the Canal, the demand on Canal expansion capacity would increase to 24.8 per cent. These estimates are based on commitments already made and do not include any contract volumes for the many projects that are still in the planning stage. As a result, the increasing risk of canal congestion may dissuade some portfolio projects from going forward.

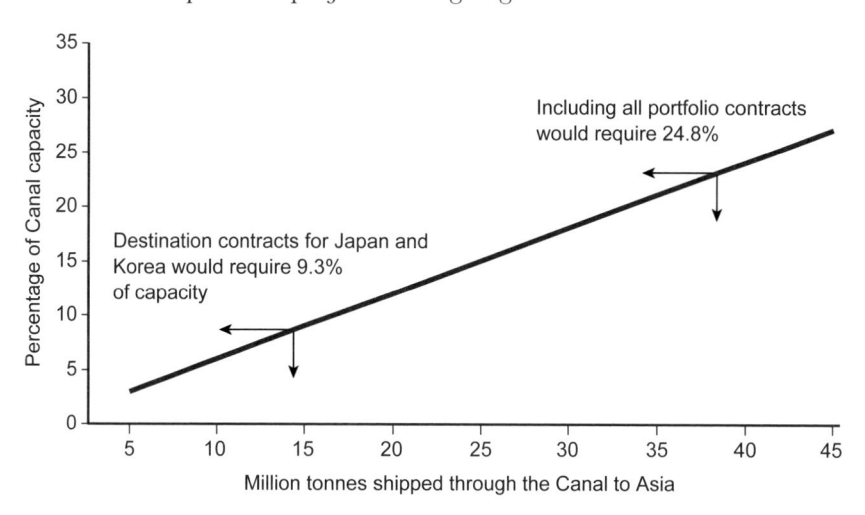

Figure 5.11: Percentage of expanded Panama Canal capacity needed to accommodate potential shipments from the US Gulf to Japan in 170,000 m^3 vessels

Source: 2015 version of author's proprietary LNG economics model.

On the other hand, the long distances involved in moving LNG from the US Gulf to Asian buyers may drive greater optimization of global LNG movements, and improve the efficiency of the LNG industry, notably by using swap agreements. In July 2015, Kansai Electric and Engie (GdF Suez) announced a new working agreement,[71] whereby Engie agreed to purchase 0.4 mtpa from Kansai's North American production, largely for its European markets. Depending on market conditions, Engie could sell an equivalent amount from its portfolio to Kansai in Japan. This swap arrangement effectively moves North American LNG to Asia by displacement from Europe, rather than by direct shipment.

The displacement option is probably most evident in the case of ExxonMobil's and Qatar Petroleum's Golden Pass facility in Texas. By converting Golden Pass to an export terminal and using it to supply their UK South Hook terminal, ExxonMobil/QP could displace the current supplies back to Qatar for export to Asia. There are other possible swap pairings involving North America, Europe, and Asia, but most of them are not as favourable as the Golden Pass/South Hook/Qatar example, and indeed destination restrictions will limit some of them.

Conclusions

In the space of a decade, North America has gone from being one of the largest potential LNG importing regions to a significant potential exporter. The capacity under construction would rank North America third in world trade. An additional 687 mtpa of export applications have been filed with the DOE and NEB, a volume equivalent to 2.8 times total world trade in 2015. Clearly most of these projects will never be built. And if the Canadian Pacific Northwest LNG – the most advanced Canadian project – were to go forward, it could add as much as 18 mtpa to the total. If this capacity were to operate at a typical 85 per cent capacity factor, North America would then provide 70 mtpa or nearly 29 per cent as much LNG as 2015 world trade.

This surge of interest in North America has been driven not only by the growth in LNG markets, but significantly by the recent disequilibrium in international gas prices. All these factors have changed with the collapse of oil prices and the effect on oil-linked LNG prices. At recent oil price levels, North American LNG is no longer cheaper for Asian buyers, although the supply diversification incentive remains. For speculative project developers, the potential for profitable investment has been sharply reduced. And for portfolio aggregators, the trading price risks are now higher. They may be

---

[71] 'Engie enters into a partnership agreement on LNG with Kansai Electric', Engie website, 21 July 2015. www.gdfsuez.com/en/journalists/press-releases/engie-agreement-kansai-electric.

less willing to speculate on competitive markets, suggesting a possible trend towards greater direct purchasing by companies in those markets.

World LNG is currently in surplus, with both weak demand and weak prices. Virtually all of the North American capacity and much of the new Australian capacity has yet to hit the market. This suggests that the surplus could easily get worse before it gets better. Given that outlook, it is difficult to see much additional North American capacity being approved during this investment cycle (say out to 2019). It is possible that even the potential 70 mtpa might not be realized if some project construction were to be delayed deliberately and some capacity operated below target levels.

But assuming the investment cycle lasts no more than four years, demand for new capacity should resume and North America is potentially a competitive source. The extent to which the USA participates will be influenced by the impact of greater exports on wellhead prices and on the extent to which political opposition to greater export levels materializes. Neither of these factors is very clear at present.

For Canada, the political issues that have slowed the process may be resolved, and the large resource base in the Montney and Horn River shales may drive increased exploration in BC, providing additional supply for LNG exports. As a result, it is highly likely that North American projects will participate in the next investment cycle, once the current glut has reduced, but at this stage the significant number of domestic and global market uncertainties make any attempt at a concrete forecast too speculative to be taken seriously.

The outlook for Russian LNG: current delays, long-term upside

Introduction

Several aspects of the Russian gas industry have delayed Russia's plans to take advantage of the spectacular growth in global LNG trade: the legacy Soviet and Russian gas business was developed as a pipeline business; Russian gas fields are located deep inland and far from export markets or marine ports; and the industry has a monopolistic structure, with a state monopoly on natural gas pipeline and, until 2013, on LNG exports. As a result, although the concept of LNG exports was considered in the Soviet era as early as the 1970s, and in Russia during the 1990s when Gazprom first took control of the Shtokman field in the Barents Sea, it was the early 2000s before the company truly expanded its horizons beyond the European gas market and towards LNG, with its potential to make it a global gas player. Sakhalin 2, Russia's first and unique LNG project, only started operating in 2009.

The Russia government now sees LNG as a path towards the achievement of a number of core objectives: expanding gas exports and accessing new markets, encouraging technological development in Russia, supporting the development of remote resources in areas such as the Yamal Peninsula and the Barents Sea, fostering the development of geopolitically important regions such as the Arctic and the Far East of Russia and, finally, expanding Russia's commercial (and therefore political) reach to new regions such as South America and north-east Asia. As such, the most recent Russian Energy Strategy (published in 2009) foresaw a rapid increase in Russian LNG output, with a plan to reach 15 per cent of the global LNG trade by 2030.[72] The Russian government provided an incentive to reach this target by reducing the export tax on LNG exports to zero (compared to the 30 per cent rate for pipeline gas exports).

The country's first LNG project, the Sakhalin 2 development, is remotely located in the Far East of Russia, but it has significant gas reserves in close proximity to the premium markets of Japan and Korea; it was originally managed by Shell and its partners Mitsubishi and Mitsui, as a result of the drive to attract foreign investments into the oil and gas sector in the 1990s. However, in 2006 Gazprom acquired a 50 per cent interest, following a series of environmental investigations which were widely perceived as the application of government pressure to secure a sale of equity to a state-owned company.[73] Despite significant delays caused both by the technical challenges of operating in icy offshore waters and the difficulty of securing rapid approvals from Russia's bureaucratic government structures – in addition to a cost overrun that saw capital expenditure double to $20 billion – Sakhalin 2 produced its first LNG in the first quarter of 2009.[74] By 2011 it had reached a peak output of 10.8 mt, exceeding its design capacity of 9.6 mt and sending cargoes to a variety markets in north-east Asia, with Japan and Korea being the main buyers.

However, apart from Sakhalin 2, the prevailing story of Russian LNG has been one of relative disappointment, as the realities of the global gas market, including the impact of the 2008 economic crisis and the emergence of numerous alternative sources of supply, have undermined the demand outlook for Russian LNG exports. In particular, the shale gas revolution in the USA has meant that the anticipated growth in US LNG demand never

---

[72] The Energy Strategy of the Russian Federation for the period up to 2030, 13 November 2009, sourced from http://minenergo.gov.ru/aboutminen/energostrategy/ on 15 July 2015.

[73] 'Shell cedes control of Sakhalin 2 to Gazprom', *The New York Times*, 21 December 2006.

[74] Sourced from 'SAKHALIN-2 – AN OVERVIEW', (on the website of Shell Global: www.shell.com/about-us/major-projects/sakhalin/sakhalin-an-overview.html, accessed on 15 April 2016).

materialized, which severely dented the prospects for the giant, but technically challenging and expensive, Shtokman field in the Barents Sea. Furthermore, disputes between Gazprom and its international partners, Total and Statoil, over the development concept and project timetable for Shtokman, combined with a lack of fiscal support from the Russian government, also undermined the project which has now effectively been postponed indefinitely.[75] Gazprom also failed to secure the future of its Baltic LNG scheme, which was first announced in 2004 as a project to liquefy gas brought by pipeline from West Siberia for onward sale into the Atlantic Basin market. PetroCanada was brought in as a core partner, and Gazprom had plans to take a stake in a Canadian regasification asset as part of a swap deal, but once again a combination of deteriorating market conditions, a shortage of funds following the economic crisis, and a perception at the time that Shtokman was Gazprom's priority LNG project led to the cancellation of Baltic LNG in 2009 (Mitrova, 2013, 15).

Despite its failure to create a robust portfolio of LNG projects, Gazprom has attempted to develop a presence on the global LNG market via its trading arm, Gazprom Marketing and Trading (GMT). As shown in Figure 5.12, GMT has sold an increasing number of spot cargoes since 2005, and it has also committed to sales contracts including a 3 mtpa deal to supply the Indian company GAIL for 25 years from 2019.[76]

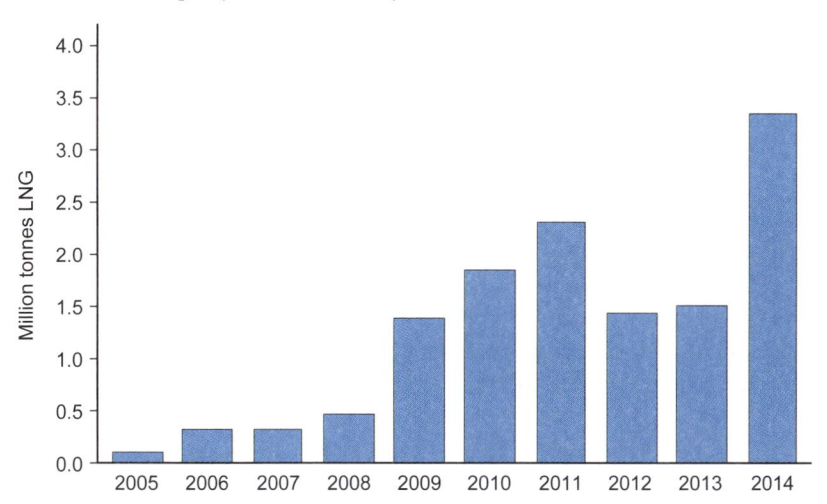

Figure 5.12: Spot LNG volumes traded by Gazprom Marketing and Trading
Source: Gazprom presentation, 'Gazprom in Global LNG Industry', 18 April 2014, slide 4, Gazprom Analyst Databook 2015.

---

[75] 'Total could quit Shtokman gas field', *The Moscow Times*, 24 September 2013.
[76] Gazprom signs 25-yr LNG contract with Indian GAIL', *Interfax*, 19 June 2014.

Nevertheless, the slow pace of development in Russia's domestic LNG industry in the 2000s prompted a radical change in the institutional structure of the industry in Russia. Historically, Gazprom has been the sole exporter of Russian gas, based on its ownership of the trunk pipeline system (the Unified Gas Supply System or UGSS),[77] and this monopoly position was extended to the LNG business *de facto*, because Gazprom was the only Russian company with any LNG plans. However, while Gazprom delayed its projects, its main competitors in the domestic market, Novatek and Rosneft, began to develop their own LNG plans.[78] Once it became clear that these could not be financed without individual export rights, both companies used their significant influence with the Russian government to lobby for change. By May 2013, Russian Prime Minister Dmitry Medvedev announced that if they could show negotiated sales contracts for their projects, then they would be granted export rights.[79] After rapid marketing tours of Europe and Asia, sufficient contracts were secured, at least in initial form. Consequently by October 2013 the Russian Ministry of Energy had approved a new law liberalizing LNG exports and by 1 December it had been passed by the Russian Duma and signed into law by President Putin.[80] The new law, however, is rather specific in its definition of allowable LNG exports, restricting them either to: licences where the right to construct an LNG plant is already included, or to offshore licences that are operated by companies which are at least 50 per cent owned by the state.[81] This currently limits the number of non-Gazprom projects to three: Novatek's Yamal LNG and Arctic LNG and Rosneft's Far East LNG. Nevertheless, it is clear that the competition which had already emerged in the Russian domestic market between Russia's three largest gas producers has now spread to the export market.

Indeed the future story of Russia's LNG industry largely depends on the relative abilities of Gazprom, Novatek, and Rosneft to establish which of them will lead the country's push into this new technological area. The Russian government is keen not only to establish a more robust presence in the global LNG market but also to create a domestic LNG design and manufacturing industry that can reduce its reliance on foreign

---

[77] Russian Federal Law on Gas Exports, No.117-F3, 18 January 2006, amended 13 November 2013.

[78] 'Gas Business Development', slide 2, Rosneft Presentation at Rosneft Investor Day, 23 April 2013,.

[79] 'Rosneft and Novatek expand their LNG exports after signing supply contracts with buyers', OilCapital.ru, 22 May 2013.

[80] 'V.Putin signed a law that ends Gazprom's monopoly' RBK, 2 December 2013.

[81] 'Russian LNG: Export Liberalisation', King and Spalding, Energy Newsletter, February 2014.

LNG technology. This is particularly important to Russia at a time when the US and EU sanctions are affecting the oil and gas industry, and when the threat of further sanctions – which could include a ban on the transfer of LNG technology – is considered as a real risk.

Russia's ambitions in the global LNG market

The number of proposed LNG projects (eight) in Russia highlights the country's ambition to become a key LNG player. Table 5.11 summarizes the country's existing and potential projects, which have a total capacity greater than 100 mtpa (larger than Qatar's current export capacity). Table 5.11 also includes an assessment of the current state of the projects as of early 2016; this shows that although one is online all the other schemes face significant issues which could delay, or which already have delayed, their implementation. As such, although Russia retains significant ambition in the LNG market, the reality is that its objective to become a major player is unlikely to be reached before the mid-2020s at the earliest.

The reasons for this are a combination of generic industry problems and specific Russian issues. In general, Russian LNG projects are facing concerns common to all current LNG projects, which include low oil and gas prices that impact revenues and financing and uncertain demand in Europe and Asia, the key markets for most developments. When this is combined with the fact that all the Russian projects bar one (Sakhalin 2 expansion) are greenfield schemes with relatively high capital expenditure requirements, and they are often in remote regions with challenging geographic conditions, it is clear that it will be difficult to generate commercial returns at current low gas prices. Furthermore, the projects also face issues specific to Russia. Notably, US sanctions have targeted certain fields and companies – including Rosneft and Novatek – making access to technology and finance difficult. Furthermore, although LNG projects in general have not been sanctioned, the threat of possible future action has also put off potential customers and partners, who are reluctant to commit to any new projects in Russia. Additionally, competition between the three major players – Gazprom, Rosneft, and Novatek – has undermined the potential for generating synergy benefits; in some cases this has meant that projects cannot proceed because of a lack of gas supply. As a result, the potential competitiveness of Russian LNG is undermined both by the difficulties of developing new projects in a remote greenfield environment and also by geopolitical and domestic regulatory and corporate issues.

Table 5.11: Assessment of current state of Russian LNG projects

	Russian operator	Partners	Volume (mtpa)	Status
Sakhalin 2 Existing	Gazprom	Shell, Mitsubishi, Mitsui	10	Producing since 2009
Sakhalin 2 Expansion	Gazprom	Shell, Mitsubishi, Mitsui	5	Possible FID in 2016
Yamal LNG	Novatek	Total, CNPC	16.5	Under construction; first output planned 2017/18
Baltic LNG	Gazprom		10	Start-up planned for 2020, but still in planning stages
Far East LNG (Sakhalin 1)	Rosneft	Exxon, Sodeco, ONGC	5–10	Initially planned for 2019, but now postponed to early 2020s
Vladivostok LNG	Gazprom		10–15	Postponed until beyond 2020
Arctic LNG	Novatek		16.5	New LNG concept based on Gydan peninsula fields. Possible start-up in mid-2020s
Pechora LNG	Rosneft	Alltech	4	Concept outlined, but no firm plans yet
Shtokman (Phase 1)	Gazprom	Total, Statoil	15	Postponed indefinitely

Source: Author's assessment based on news reports and company announcements.

Gazprom's dilemma – whether to prioritize pipeline or LNG exports

Other than its involvement in the Sakhalin 2 project, Gazprom's LNG strategy over the past five years has involved a series of apparently random moves that reflect its historical focus on being a gas pipeline company with little experience in the LNG business. In addition, the fall in the oil price has reduced both Gazprom's existing export revenues and its cash flow available for investment, while increasing competition in its traditional business areas in Europe, the FSU, and Russia. These challenges further complicated the establishment of a new core business within its broadening portfolio, which now includes oil and power generation. Furthermore, a series of commitments to build new export pipelines to Europe and Asia has left question marks over how much extra investment can be made in expensive LNG schemes, especially at a time when global gas prices are hardly encouraging the development of new projects.

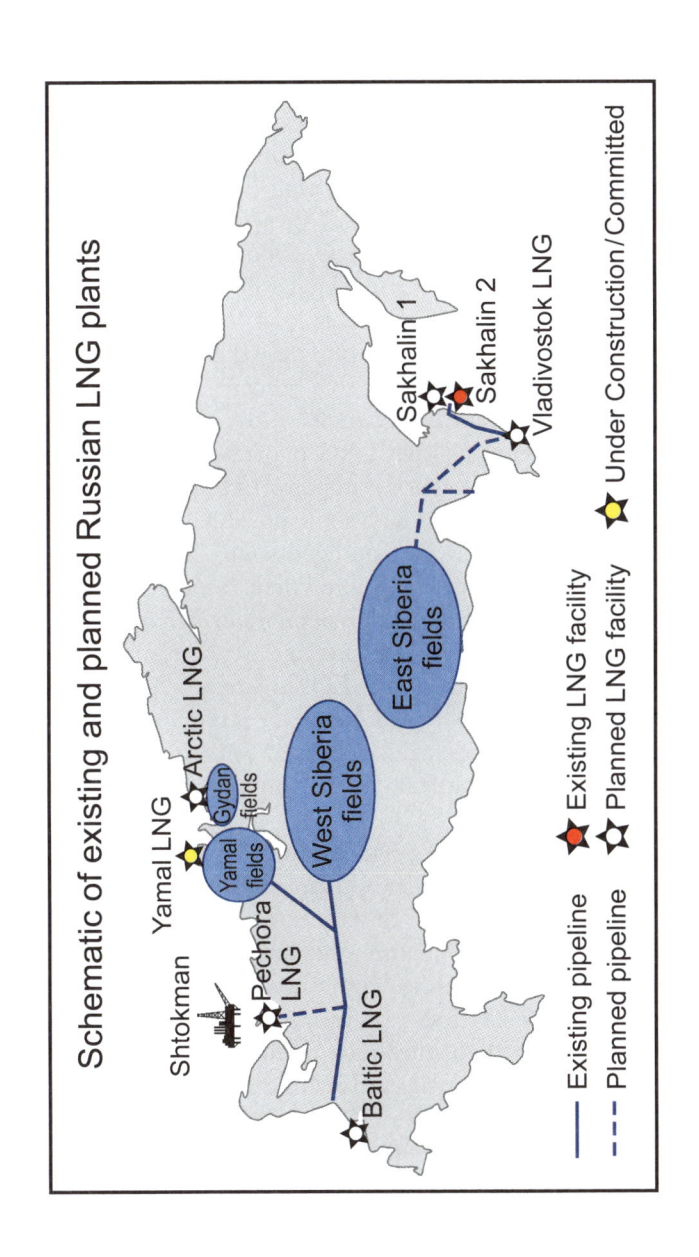

Map 5.4: Schematic of Russia's existing and potential LNG projects

Sakhalin 2 expansion

Nowhere is this confusion more evident than in the delay over Gazprom's most obvious next LNG project, the addition of a third train at the existing Sakhalin 2 site, where although space for a third train has existed since 2009 a final decision on the exact timing of an extended development has yet to be taken.[82] One of the major concerns is the source of extra gas, as the existing Sakhalin 2 fields have no extra production capacity, while other potential resources around the island bring their own specific difficulties. One obvious source is the Sakhalin 1 project, where 8 bcm of annual associated production is being reinjected into the oil reservoir and where development of gas reserves at the Chayvo field have been on hold for a number of years as the field partners look for an appropriate market. Gazprom has made several offers to purchase the gas for use at Sakhalin 2, but none have been at an acceptable price.[83] Furthermore, the main Russian partner at Sakhalin 1 is Rosneft, whose rivalry with Gazprom has encouraged it to develop its own LNG plans (see below) rather than co-operate with a fellow state-owned company.[84] However, the impact of low prices and sanctions, combined with some possible coercion by the Russian government, appears to have encouraged some dialogue concerning the possibility of the two projects combining their resources. The first signs of potential compromise were seen in September 2015, when both sides agreed that discussions might be possible, with a subsequent meeting between the Gazprom and Rosneft CEOs in January 2016 encouraging the hope that a solution might be found. However, it remains to be seen whether the Russian state companies, as well as their foreign partners, can find an outcome that is both politically and commercially acceptable to all concerned.

The potential impact of foreign partners at Sakhalin 2 is important because of the agreement signed by Gazprom with Shell at the St Petersburg Economic Forum in June 2015[85] and the subsequent sanctions imposed on the South Kirinskoye field (within the Sakhalin 3 licence) by the US authorities.[86] Initially Gazprom committed, under a new partnership agreement, to supply gas for a 5 mtpa third train at Sakhalin 2, and furthermore also agreed to introduce Shell as an equity stakeholder in Sakhalin 3 as a source of financial and technical support for the development

---

[82] See picture at 'Sakhalin II', Gazprom website, www.gazprom.com/about/production/projects/lng/sakhalin2/, accessed 17 July 2015.

[83] 'Gazprom offered to raise price for Sakhalin-1 gas', *Interfax*, 8 October 2013.

[84] 'Rosneft and Gazprom: two behemoths battle it out', *The Financial Times*, 2 July 2014.

[85] 'Gazprom set to build global strategic alliance with Shell', Royal Dutch Shell press release, 20 June 2015.

[86] 'US adds Russian oil field to sanctions list', Reuters, 7 August 2015.

of South Kirinskoye, where the 700 bcm of gas reserves have long been seen as the obvious source of extra gas for an expanded Sakhalin 2.[87] However, a decision by the US authorities in August 2015 to single out this specific field for inclusion on its sanctions list has put these plans in serious doubt, in particular because Gazprom has, to date, struggled with the challenges of the Sakhalin 3 fields. As a result, even the relatively conservative 2021 start-up date for a third train at Sakhalin 2 may not be achievable,[88] further undermining Gazprom's LNG plans.

Vladivostok LNG – a priority, a bargaining chip or a white elephant?
The sanctions imposed on South Kirinskoye could have a double impact, as its gas had also been identified as one potential source of supply to the Vladivostok LNG project, which is 100 per cent controlled by Gazprom. The company announced plans for a 10–15 mtpa plant in 2011 and took what it considered to be a final investment decision in 2013, with plans to send out a first LNG cargo in 2018.[89] Furthermore, it also announced a co-operation agreement with a consortium of Japanese companies to conduct a feasibility study on the project – prior to making final commitments on financing and implementation, and on signing gas contracts.[90]

Once again, however, uncertainty over Gazprom's priorities and its ability to provide a realistic source of gas for the new plant has caused confusion for potential partners and customers. It appeared that the original concept behind Vladivostok LNG was to provide Gazprom with some influence in its negotiations with CNPC over pipeline exports from fields in East Siberia to north-east China. Gazprom planned to use Vladivostok as a bargaining tool, arguing that it was an alternative route for East Siberian gas – in the same way that Rosneft had used the extension of the ESPO (Eastern Siberia Pacific Ocean) oil pipeline to the Pacific coast to create pricing pressure for its direct sales to China.[91] However, it soon became clear that the commercial logic was flawed because of the vast transport distances and the extra cost of building a liquefaction plant; this led Gazprom to suggest that the gas for Vladivostok LNG might instead come from a closer source in Sakhalin (South Kirinskoye), and via an existing

---

[87] 'US sanctions put Gazprom–Shell alliance plans in jeopardy', Reuters, 10 August 2015.
[88] 'Third train at Gazprom's Sakhalin 2 plant could be launched in 2021', Reuters, 30 July 2015.
[89] 'Gazprom adopts final investment decision for Vladivostok LNG', Gazprom press release, 21 February 2013.
[90] 'Gazprom and consortium of Japanese companies sign MoU on Vladivostok LNG project', Gazprom press release, 22 June 2013.
[91] 'Russia–China crude oil deals', Reuters, 19 February 2014.

pipeline.[92] The indecision over gas supply caused concern both for possible foreign partners at Vladivostok and also for potential customers, who were unclear about the long-term viability of the project and therefore the security of any contracts they might sign. US imposition of financial sanctions magnified this concern. Although the sanctions do not directly affect Gazprom, they have reduced the willingness of many Asian buyers to take on the extra risk of signing new contracts with any Russian energy companies.[93]

Gazprom's negotiations with China have further reduced the likelihood of Vladivostok LNG moving ahead on its original schedule. A first deal was signed in May 2014 to send gas from East Siberia via the Power of Siberia pipeline to north-east China,[94] but with no mention of extending the pipeline to the Pacific Coast. A subsequent deal to export gas through a second pipeline via the Russian province of Altai was then agreed in May 2015,[95] with Gazprom's CEO suggesting that this project might take precedence over the Vladivostok LNG plans.[96] Finally, Gazprom has subsequently suggested that gas from Sakhalin might be shipped to China by pipeline in the future, further undermining any LNG plans.[97] Indeed, it appears that Gazprom has reverted to its traditional role of gas pipeline exporter in the Far East, and has put its LNG plans on hold; official statements at a Gazprom Investor Day in February 2016 confirmed that the Vladivostok project had effectively been indefinitely postponed.[98]

Baltic LNG – return of Gazprom's Atlantic Basin LNG strategy
As Gazprom's Asian LNG strategy appears to be reducing in importance, so the company has somewhat opportunistically rekindled the idea of a Baltic LNG scheme. It has explained its strategy as being driven by the

---

[92] The Sakhalin–Khabarovsk–Vladivostok pipeline, constructed in 2011, which has a current capacity of 5 bcm/year but which could be expanded to 30 bcm/year with extra compression. See 'Sakhalin–Khabarovsk–Vladivostok Strategy', Gazprom website at www.gazprom.com/about/production/projects/pipelines/shvg/ for detail.

[93] Although Gazprom has now been directly affected by the sanctions on South Kirinskoye, it is not on the list of Russian energy companies which are restricted in their ability to raise long-term finance on international capital markets.

[94] 'Gazprom, CNPC sign 30-year natural gas supply contract', *Oil and Gas Journal*, 21 May 2014.

[95] 'Gazprom, CNPC sign heads of agreement on western route', *Oil and Gas Journal*, 11 May 2014.

[96] 'Gazprom considers shelving Vladivostok LNG project', *The Financial Times*, 10 October 2014.

[97] 'Gazprom finds a new way to supply gas to China', *Oil Voice*, 27 August 2015.

[98] 'Gazprom: navigating a new market environment', slide 42, Presentation at Gazprom Investor Day, February 2016.

chance to exploit an emerging LNG bunker fuel market in the Baltic Sea and to open up more distant gas markets in South America. In addition, the company is also under pressure from the Russian government to provide LNG to the Russian region of Kaliningrad, which at present can only be supplied via a pipeline through the Baltic states, now regarded as a strategic risk. As a result, Gazprom has proposed a 5–10 mtpa Baltic LNG project to be based at Ust Luga, close to St Petersburg, and has outlined a timetable which could see first output in 2021.[99]

Ostensibly the project is an attractive commercial proposition, taking cheap Russian gas (which is currently priced below $2/MMBtu in the Leningrad region) and transporting it to markets with much higher prices. The key question, though, is the cost of building the new liquefaction plant, which will determine the effective tolling fee that would need to be charged to generate an economic return. A total capital expenditure estimate of RR1 trillion (around $15.2 billion at an exchange rate of US$1=RR66) made by the head of the Ust Luga port appears very high and could undermine the commercial rationale for the project, unless Gazprom can secure government support for the 'associated infrastructure' which the estimate is said to include.[100] Furthermore, it remains unclear how large the bunker market for LNG in the Baltic will be, and if Russian LNG from a new project can really hope to compete in South America with US LNG exports from the much closer Gulf of Mexico schemes. In addition, the possible arrival of Gazprom LNG in Europe could undermine its own pipeline sales, implying that the Baltic LNG project is another scheme which could be postponed, despite the fact that Gazprom has apparently made its final investment decision.[101]

Novatek – set to become Russia's primary LNG producer?

Having established itself as the largest independent gas producer in Russia and a significant competitor to Gazprom in the domestic market, Novatek is now embarking on a strategy that could see it become the country's largest LNG exporter by the early 2020s. Its flagship Yamal LNG project, located on the north-eastern tip of the Yamal peninsula, plans to produce 16.5 mtpa of LNG from three trains, based on gas supply from the 900 bcm South Tambey field.[102] The project is located within the Arctic Circle in

---

[99] Ibid., slide 9.
[100] 'Baltic LNG plant, associated infrastructure to cost about 1trln roubles – Ust-Luga chief', *Interfax*, 16 June 2015.
[101] 'Gazprom approves Baltic LNG investment decision, signs declarations with Leningrad region', *Interfax*, 17 April 2015.
[102] 'Russia's natural gas frontiers: Harnessing the energy of the Far North', Novatek presentation, April 2013.

extremely harsh climatic conditions. Ice blocks the shipping lanes for seven months per year and the extreme cold and barren conditions will increase the cost of the large amount of new infrastructure that is required in this remote region. Indeed it is very unlikely that the project would have been commercially viable without a significant level of government support which included tax concessions, $1.5 billion of funding for the construction of port facilities (Mitrova, 2013, 29), and the provision of nuclear-powered ice breakers through state-owned company Rosatom.[103] The government provided this support to underpin the development of major infrastructure in the High North of Russia and to establish a Russian presence in the Arctic with access to the Northern Sea Route to Asia, which is likely to be politically as well as commercially important. In addition, the owners of Novatek are believed to be closely related to the Kremlin,[104] while their company can also provide a useful catalyst for action in Gazprom at a time when President Putin fears that:

> ... if we do not pursue an active policy [in LNG], we risk completely surrendering this market to competitors.[105]

Importantly, Novatek has also brought in three foreign partners who bring vital attributes to the project. Total acquired a 20 per cent interest in 2011,[106] bringing with it significant expertise in the development of LNG projects around the world,[107] while CNPC acquired a further 20 per cent in 2013, bringing access to the fastest growing gas market in the world, in China.[108] Finally, in December 2015 the sale of a 9.9 per cent stake to the Chinese Silk Road Fund was confirmed;[109] this sale brought with it a small

---

[103] 'New icebreakers open way for Russia in Arctic', *Barents Observer*, 5 May 2015.

[104] 'Novatek: The challenger takes on Gazprom in Russia', *The Wall Street Journal*, 19 June 2013.

[105] Statement from President Putin at the Hearing of the Commission for Strategic Development of the Fuel and Energy Sector and Environmental Security, Novo-Ogaryevo, 13 February 2013.

[106] 'Total buys 20 per cent stake in Yamal LNG', *LNG World News*, 6 October 2011.

[107] See 'Our priority: Put our deep offshore and LNG expertise to work for you', Total company website, (www.total.com/en/energies-expertise/oil-gas/exploration-production/strategic-sectors/lng/total-world-class-player/strategy-for-growth?%FFbw=kludge1%FF), where Total claims to be the second-largest LNG player in the world.

[108] 'CNPC buys stake in Novatek's Yamal LNG project', Bloomberg, 5 September 2013.

[109] 'Silk Road Fund and Russia's Novatek sign agrements on Yamal LNG project', *China Daily*, 17 December 2015.

direct loan[110] and, perhaps more importantly, confirmation of the Chinese government's commitment to the project, which has now resulted in key bank financing being provided by the country's banking system. This has become particularly relevant since Novatek was included on the list of companies sanctioned by the USA and prevented from accessing any debt in dollars with a duration of more than 30 days.[111] The sanctions have significantly increased the risk for western banks who might provide loans to the Yamal LNG project, and their impact can be seen in the delay that has occurred in the finalizing of project finance.[112] In addition, the importance of the relationship with China has been further underlined by the signing, in 2014, of a long-term contract with CNPC, who will purchase 3 mtpa of LNG from Yamal.[113]

Novatek and the Yamal project partners have responded to the impact of US and EU sanctions in a number of ways. Firstly, they have continued to fund the continuing capital expenditure from their own balance sheets, and had transferred almost $13 billion to the project company out of the total expected $27 billion cost as of December 2015.[114] Secondly, they have turned to the Russian government for support, requesting rouble loans from the National Well-being Fund, which has provided RR150 billion (around US$2.3 billion) in two tranches during 2015.[115] Thirdly, they have turned to two Russian banks (Sberbank and Gazprombank) who have provided €3.6 billion via a 15-year credit line.[116] Finally, after lengthy negotiations which threatened to delay the entire project, two Chinese institutions (China Development Bank and China Eximbank) have offered two further 15-year loans, one for €9.3 billion and a second for Yuan9.8 billion (€1.3 billion).[117] As a result, although a number of deadlines for the final completion of the financing deal were initially missed, the funds required have ultimately arrived, and in any case the project is so far

---

[110] 'Chinese Investment Firm signs stake and loan deal for Yamal LNG project', *Natural Gas Europe*, 17 December 2015.

[111] See US Department of the Treasury website at www.treasury.gov/resource-center/sanctions/OFAC-Enforcement/Pages/20140716.aspx.

[112] 'Sanctions bite massive gas project in Russian Arctic', *The Wall Street Journal*, 27 August 2015.

[113] 'Novatek and China's CNPC sign LNG supply deal', *The Moscow Times*, 20 May 2014.

[114] 'Russia's Novatek CEO says investments in Yamal LNG project reached $15 billion', Reuters, 18 January 2016.

[115] 'Ministry to release second NWF tranche after Yamal LNG reports on use of first', *Interfax*, 9 July 2015.

[116] 'Sberbank, Gazprombank may provide $4bln for Yamal LNG; loans to total $20bln overall', *Interfax*, 5 June 2015.

[117] 'Yamal LNG completes external financing', 29 April 2016, *Natural Gas Europe*.

advanced that it seems certain to be completed, especially as all the equipment for the first train has been delivered and will be ready to operate on schedule.[118] Indeed the signing of a number of contracts that will cover almost the entire output of the three trains indicates that Yamal LNG must ultimately come online (see Table 5.12). As a result, a conservative estimate might be that the first train will come online as planned in 2017, but that the second and third trains could be delayed for perhaps six months each given the extended time taken to negotiate the financing. However, this would still see the plant fully operational by 2020, as currently estimated by the project operator Novatek.

Table 5.12: LNG contracts signed by Yamal LNG and Novatek

Original purchasers	Volume (mt)	Duration (years)
Gas Natural	2.50	Long-term
Gazprom	2.90	20
Novatek Gas and Power	2.86	Long-term
Total Gas and Power	4.00	Long-term
CNPC	3.00	15
Total	**15.26**	
Total capacity	***16.50***	
Onward sales		
Novatek Gas and Power	2.86	
Shell	0.90	20
Engie	1.00	23
Total	**1.90**	

Source: Novatek, Yamal LNG.

However, Novatek's LNG ambitions go beyond the Yamal LNG project. The company also owns licences on the Gydan peninsula (on the other side of the Ob–Taz Bay from Yamal) which have also been granted LNG export status.[119] Two fields (Salmanovskoye and Geofizicheskoye) contain combined proved reserves of almost 400 bcm, and the company believes that further exploration and appraisal can lead to an ultimate gas resource that could support a second 16.5 mtpa LNG project, currently being referred to as 'Arctic LNG'. It is very early to say when this might come online, but Novatek has already indicated that it is selecting appropriate

---
[118] 'Yamal LNG progressing despite sanctions', *Upstream*, 27 February 2015.
[119] 'Novatek to export LNG from Gydan peninsula', Rusmininfo, 14 October 2014.

LNG technologies for the scheme and is designing a development concept,[120] with a FID possible in 2016.[121] As a result, it is conceivable that by the mid-2020s Novatek could be operating more than 30 mtpa of LNG production, with an equity share of 50 per cent or more in each of two projects.

Rosneft – LNG ambitions could be undermined by sanctions and low oil price

Prior to 2014 Rosneft was as keen as Novatek to challenge Gazprom as a gas exporter from Russia, with plans to construct the Far East LNG project on Sakhalin Island.[122] Following the announcement of its partnership in the Arctic with ExxonMobil in 2011, Rosneft also convinced the US major to invest in a 5–10 mtpa scheme that will source its gas from the Sakhalin 1 fields,[123] which have almost 500 bcm of proved gas reserves.[124] Following the lifting of Gazprom's LNG export monopoly, Rosneft CEO Igor Sechin rapidly signed three provisional contracts to cover the first 5 mt train of the project (see Table 5.13), while promising that the plant could be expanded to 10 mtpa if more gas is discovered in the company's licences around Sakhalin and in the nearby Sea of Okhotsk.[125]

Table 5.13: Contracts for LNG supply from Far East LNG

Purchasers	Volume (mt)	Duration
Sodeco	1.00	Long-term
Marubeni	1.25	Long-term
Vitol	2.75	Long-term
Total	**5.00**	

Source: Rosneft.

---

[120] 'Novatek selecting from among three technologies for future Gydan LNG plant', *Interfax*, 5 June 2015.
[121] 'Novatek to decide on building 16.5mtpa LNG plant at Salmanovskoye filed in 6-12 months', Interfax, 24 April 2015.
[122] See 'Gas Strategy', Rosneft website (http://rosneft.com/Upstream/GasStrategy/ accessed on 17 July 2015).
[123] 'Rosneft and ExxonMobil extended agreement on implementation of the Far East LNG project', Rosneft press release, 23 May 2014.
[124] 'Rosneft to develop North Chayvo together with Sakhalin-1 consortium', *Interfax*, 24 September 2014.
[125] 'Rosneft's Sakhalin LNG plant passes preliminary feasibility study – governor', *Interfax*, 6 June 2014.

However, since this positive start, numerous problems have accumulated for both Rosneft itself and the Far East LNG concept. It now appears unlikely that any production will be seen before 2020 at the earliest, with the possibility that the project may be deferred completely if an agreement can be reached with Gazprom over use of the proposed third train at Sakhalin 2 (see 'Sakhalin 2 expansion', page 262). Two main issues have emerged. The first is that Gazprom's refusal to allow Sakhalin 1 gas into its trans-Sakhalin pipeline undermined the project partners' original plan to locate the liquefaction plant in the ice-free waters to the south of Sakhalin. Rosneft challenged this decision, but it was subsequently upheld by the Russian courts.[126] The location has now been moved north to De Castri, from where Sakhalin 1 oil is exported, and although this is not a major problem, the dispute has caused some delays. The second issue has been a debate over whether the LNG project should be included within the Sakhalin 1 PSA; this would allow the partners to reclaim the $8 billion cost of the LNG plant against current oil revenues, improving the project economics. However, the Russian government does not seem happy to concede on this issue, understanding the potential loss of short-term revenue.[127] The energy minister has denied that the PSA terms will be changed, potentially undermining the LNG plans.[128]

When these two problems are combined with the financial problems that Rosneft is facing because of both the low oil price and its inclusion on the US sanctions list, it is clear that Far East LNG is likely to become a lower priority. Furthermore the head of Rosneft's gas business, Vlada Rusakova, has pointed out that the company must also consider the condition of the global gas market, where prices have fallen sharply in the company's target Asian market and demand is rising less rapidly than anticipated.[129] As a result, it appears that first LNG has been delayed by at least two years from its original 2019 launch, with a five year delay also being possible.[130] Indeed, it is possible that the project could be cancelled altogether if Rosneft and Gazprom can end their differences over use of Sakhalin 1 gas at the Sakhalin 2 project. The construction of a third train at Sakhalin 2 supplied by gas from Sakhalin 1 would be a very logical commercial solution, if all the parties can agree how to share the costs and

---

[126] 'Regulator suspends case on Rosneft access to Sakhalin-2 gas pipe', *Interfax*, 20 May 2015.
[127] 'Sakhalin-1 LNG plant to reduce state revenue under PSA – Audit Chamber', *Interfax*, 16 January 2015.
[128] 'Option of including Rosneft LNG project in Sakhalin-1 not under discussion – minister', *Interfax*, 13 April 2015.
[129] 'Launch of Far East LNG might be postponed by situation, not location change', *Interfax*, 3 June 2015.
[130] 'Rosneft's Sakhalin LNG plant delayed for at least two years', Reuters, 7 April 2015.

the revenues. To date this has not been possible, but the current state of the global gas market may ultimately encourage a common sense outcome, for the overall benefit of both parties and the Russian state.

A second possible Rosneft-related project is Pechora LNG, which was initially proposed as a private venture by Alltech Group. Rosneft is negotiating to buy a 51 per cent stake. The LNG plant would be based in the Timan Pechora region of north-west Russia and would have a capacity of 4 or 8 mtpa, based on production from two nearby gas fields,[131] with a wide range of cost estimates between $5.5 and $12 billion.[132] There is some commercial logic for a plant located on the shores of an ice-free sea and close to gas production, but Pechora LNG remains the only proposed Russian scheme which does not yet have export approval, as it does not meet the criteria outlined above.[133] As a result, a proposed start-up date of 2017 now looks impossible, and the future of the project will probably rest on the conclusion of the sale process, as the influence of Rosneft will almost certainly be needed to catalyse project development. If it can move forward, though, it could provide a third west-facing LNG project run by a third different Russian operator, creating more competition for Gazprom in the Atlantic Basin market.

Conclusion – Russia can be a major LNG player in the mid to late 2020s, but not before

Apart from the existing Sakhalin 2 project, the Russian development with the most immediate chance of completion appears to be Novatek's Yamal LNG, which is pushing ahead despite the delay in raising project finance caused by US sanctions. Investments of more than $10 billion have already been made in the project, and it therefore seems inevitable that it will be pushed to completion by the project partners, who have signed multiple sales contracts and received significant Russian government support. A delay in full completion of all three trains is certainly possible, but significant production before 2020 is very likely. Sakhalin 2 expansion appears to be the most logical short-term addition, but sanctions have now created a major barrier. Another Gazprom project, Baltic LNG, also seems logical, although the current cost estimate for the plant and its associated infrastructure could make the scheme uneconomic in the face of global competition, despite the low cost of the feed gas in the Russian market.

Indeed, by the end of the decade, Novatek could be exporting as much

---

[131] 'Alltech expands resource base of Pechora LNG', *Interfax*, 22 January 2015.

[132] 'Rosneft continuing talks on purchase of Pechora LNG, wants 100 per cent', *Interfax*, 3 June 2015.

[133] 'Allowing Pechora LNG to export gas needs further discussion – Dvorkovich', *Interfax*, 19 September 2014.

272 *LNG Markets in Transition*

LNG as Gazprom, depending on the exact timing of the development start-ups. Beyond 2020, the trend of Russian competition for Gazprom in the global gas market could be set to continue. Figure 5.13 shows two potential scenarios for Russian LNG over the next 15 years, as well as the possibility of output from the Shtokman field by 2030 (although this should be regarded as speculative given the current state of the project). In a conservative case, the only projects to proceed would be the existing Sakhalin 2 project plus a one train expansion, Yamal LNG, and Baltic LNG. This would lead to approximately 27 mtpa of output by 2020 and 42 mtpa of output by 2030, if Baltic LNG reaches its full 10 mtpa capacity. A more optimistic higher-case scenario would then include the five other projects shown in grey, namely Novatek's Arctic LNG, Rosneft's Far East LNG and Pechora LNG, and Gazprom's Vladivostok LNG plus the speculative Shtokman, which could add a combined 18 mtpa by 2025 and 39 mtpa by 2030. This is clearly a much more speculative case, as the source of gas from Vladivostok LNG is unclear and Rosneft's Far East LNG could be cancelled if Sakhalin 1 gas goes to Sakhalin 2 train 3.

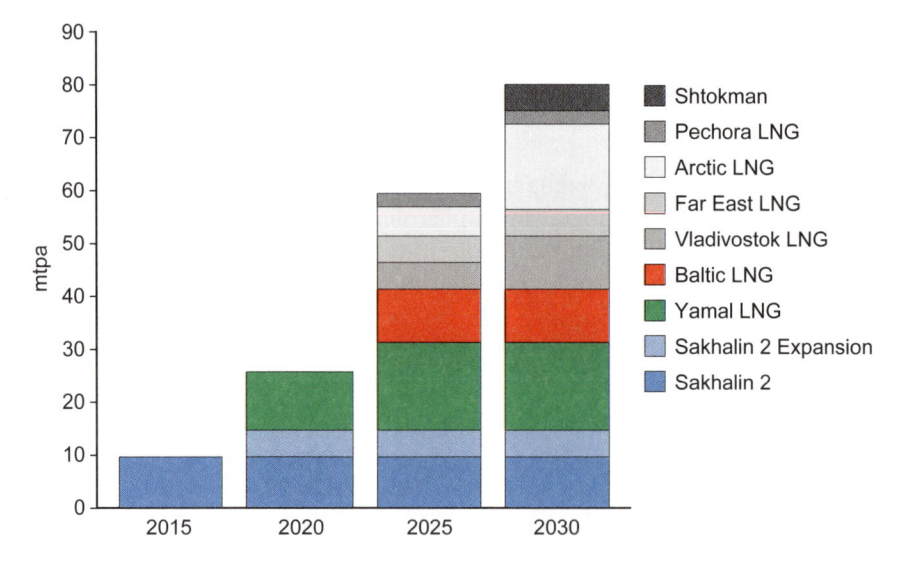

Figure 5.13: Possible outlook for Russian LNG production
Source: Author's estimate.

Nevertheless, the upside potential is obvious and the trend towards a diversification of producers is also clear, as within the outcome shown in Figure 5.13, by 2030 the split between Gazprom and non-Gazprom output could be exactly 50:50. Indeed, if Gazprom continues with its current strategy of focusing on its core pipeline business, the independent sector, and in particular Novatek, could possibly become the prime driver of Russia's LNG strategy over the next 15 years.

Eastern Africa – beyond 2020

Eastern Africa has emerged over the past five years as a serious contender on the global LNG scene. With an estimated 165 tcf (4.7 tcm) of recoverable gas resources (IHS data), the region, taken as a whole, rivals many existing and would be LNG exporters. As a comparison, offshore discoveries in Israel and Cyprus amount to 40 tcf (1.1 tcm), while Nigeria's proven gas reserves total 180 tcf (5.1 tcm) (BP, 2015).

It is crucial to set the scene for gas exports from 'Eastern Africa'. So far, there are really only two countries in that area with significant gas resources, Mozambique and Tanzania. Discoveries made so far in Kenya are much smaller.[134] The proximity and the volume of the discoveries in Mozambique and Tanzania have led some to analyse these countries together. This is a mistake – these two countries are as different as the neighbours Australia and Papua New Guinea. Among their differences are: size of gas resources, timing of potential LNG exports, regulatory, fiscal, and political frameworks, government objectives for domestic gas utilization, and project sponsors.

Table 5.14: Key indicators for Mozambique and Tanzania

	Mozambique	*Tanzania*	*Year*
GDP ($ billion)	16.4	49.1	2014
GDP growth	7.4%	7.0%	2014
Population (million)	26.47	50.7	2014
TPES (mtoe)	10.44	22.16	2012
Bioenergy in TPES	80%	85%	2012
Gas in TPES	1%	4%	2012
Oil in TPES	8%	10%	2012
Coal in TPES	0%	0%	2012
Hydro in TPES	12%	1%	2012
Electricity consumption (TWh)	11.44	4.81	2012
Electricity per capita (kWh)	414	101	2012

Sources: World Bank, IEA.

---

[134] Recoverable gas amounts to only 1 tcf (IHS).

One factor that the two countries share is the location of their resources, which are broadly located in the same region: the Rovuma basin, off the northern coast of Mozambique, and its northern extension into Tanzanian waters. Despite a few existing gas discoveries, the region had been generally overlooked, as it was considered to hold few significant source horizons and to be more gas-prone at a time when companies were looking for oil.[135] Planned investments are considerable seen against the countries' economies. Mozambique's GDP was $16.39 billion in 2014 compared with Anadarko's expected investments of $24 billion for two LNG trains.[136] Tanzania's GDP amounts to $49.1 billion, against an estimated $15–20 billion investments for two LNG trains.[137] Both countries' energy balances are heavily dominated by bioenergy, with only a small share (15–20 per cent) of modern energy. Electrification needs are immense in both countries and rank top of the governments' energy priorities. Only 24 per cent of Tanzania's households are electrified,[138] while 40 per cent of Mozambicans have access to electricity.[139] Both countries are looking to jump start their economies by developing their respective gas resources. The challenge is to keep these developments economically viable while meeting local expectations in terms of jobs, business creation, and economic growth. The resources are considered too big and costly to serve only an embryonic domestic market. And as regional markets such as South Africa are distant, investors are giving priority to LNG.

Gas resources

In February 2010, Anadarko Petroleum struck gas with its Windjammer well, 30 miles from the coast of Mozambique.[140] Anadarko has had a

---

[135] 'East Africa's potential unmarred by limited drilling', *Offshore*, 1 October 2003. www.offshore-mag.com/articles/print/volume-63/issue-10/technology/east-africas-potential-unmarred-by-limited-drilling.html.

[136] *Africa Intelligence*, September 2015.

[137] 'Exclusive: Tanzania LNG project set for step forward – sources',Reuters, 22 November, 2013 6:20pm GMT. http://uk.reuters.com/article/2013/11/22/uk-tanzania-gas-idUKBRE9AL0XK20131122; United Republic of Tanzania, IMF Country Report No. 14/121, May 2014. https://www.imf.org/external/pubs/ft/scr/2014/cr14121.pdf.

[138] The Draft National Energy Policy 2015, United Republic of Tanzania, Ministry of Energy and Minerals, Dar es Salaam, January 2015. https://mem.go.tz/wp-content/uploads/2015/02/NATIONAL-ENERGY-POLICY-2015-Feb-2015.pdf.

[139] 'Over 10 million people in Mozambique have domestic electricity', MacauHub, 15 July, 2014. www.macauhub.com.mo/en/2014/07/15/over-10-million-people-in-mozambique-have-domestic-electricity/.

[140] 'Windjammer Exploration Well, Mozambique', offshore technology.com. http://www.offshore-technology.com/projects/windjammer/windjammer2.html.

licence in Area 1 in the Rovuma basin since December 2006, but this was the first significant gas discovery. Many finds followed, not only in Area 1, but also in ENI's adjacent Area 4. In Tanzania, Ophir's first discoveries occurred in October and December 2010, while Statoil discovered gas in 2012. Gas resources in both countries are deep or ultra-deep offshore.

Despite the large amount of recoverable gas discovered so far – 132 tcf for Mozambique and 34 tcf for Tanzania – surveys suggest that Mozambique could have around 276 tcf of discovered and undiscovered gas resources (ICFI, 2012), while in 2012 USGS estimated Tanzania's mean undiscovered gas resources at 67 tcf.[141] But enough gas has already been found, at least in Mozambique, to support both significant LNG exports and domestic use.

Table 5.15: Shareholdings in licences with significant discoveries

	Gas resources recoverable	Operator	Consortium partners
Mozambique			
Area 1	75 tcf	Anadarko (26.5%)	Mitsui (20%), OVL (16%), ENH (15%), Bharat PetroResources (10%), PTTEP (8.5%), OIL (4%)
Area 4	57 tcf	ENI (50%)	CNPC (20%), ENH (10%), KOGAS (10%), Galp Energia (10%)
Tanzania			
Block 1	17.1 tcf	BG (60%)	Ophir (20%), Pavilion Energy (20%)
Block 3		Ophir (80%)	Pavilion Energy (20%)
Block 4		BG (60%)	Ophir (20%), Pavilion Energy (20%)
Block 2	16.4 tcf	Statoil (65%)	ExxonMobil (35%)

Sources: Companies' websites, IHS.

Recent gas discoveries in Mozambique are located exclusively in offshore Area 1 and Area 4, in the northernmost part of the country. Anadarko reports 75 tcf of recoverable gas in Area 1 and ENI estimates 88 tcf of gas in place in Area 4 (IHS data reports 57 tcf of recoverable gas resources). Gas resources are lean, which simplifies the development but will not bring much additional oil or condensate revenues. Four neighbouring areas have not yielded any discoveries; Statoil abandoned Areas 2 and 5 in

---

[141] 'Assessment of Undiscovered Oil and Gas Resources of Four East Africa Geologic Provinces', Fact Sheet 2012–3039, World Petroleum Resources Project, USGS, April 2012. http://pubs.usgs.gov/fs/2012/3039/contents/FS12-3039.pdf.

276 *LNG Markets in Transition*

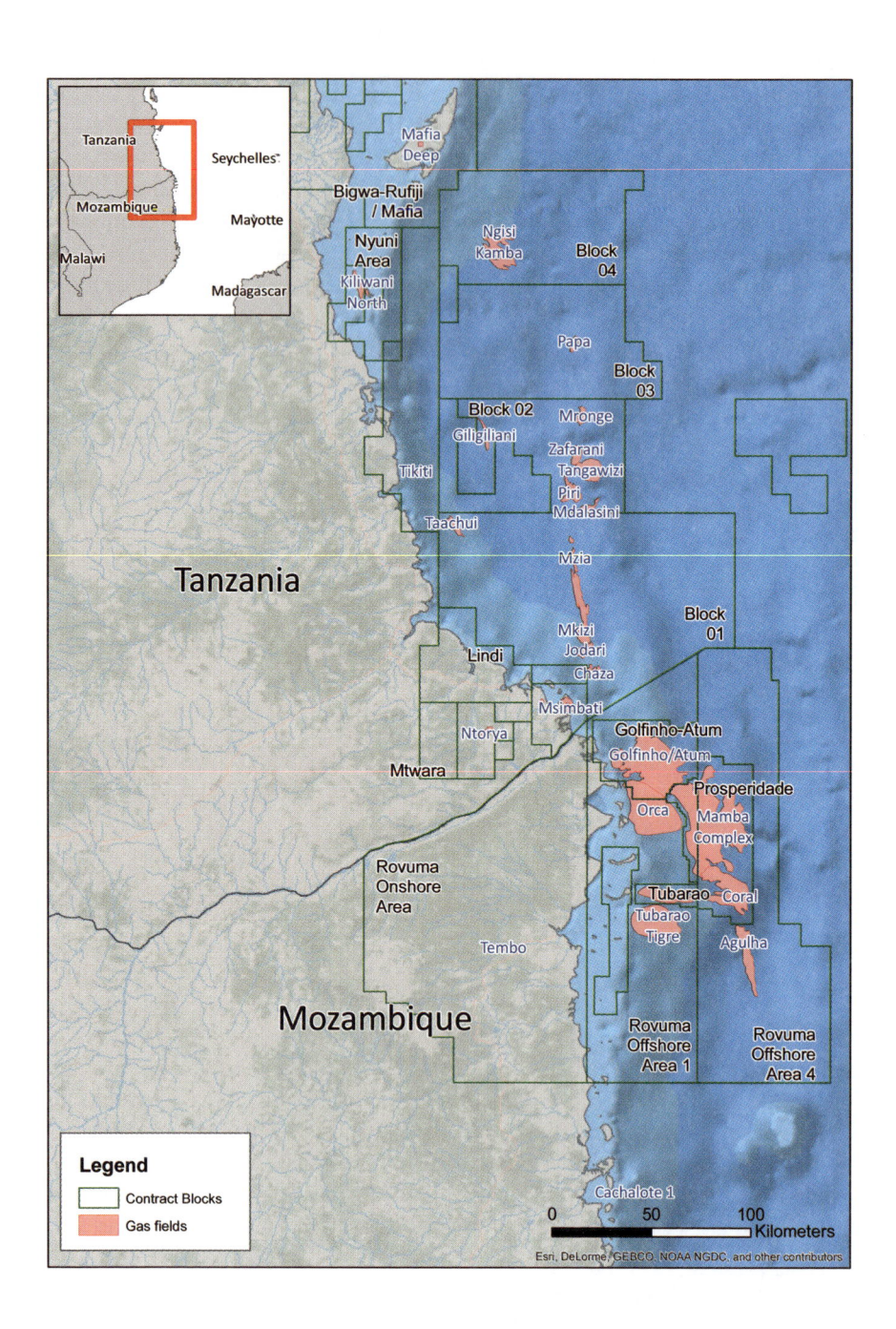

Map 5.5 Eastern Africa's gas resources

early 2015. The Pande and Temane gas fields, which have been producing since 2004, are located much further south, and only produce 4 bcm together.

In Tanzania, the offshore discoveries are smaller and scattered over four blocks. They lie in the south of the country, a few hundred kilometres away from Dar es Salaam and close to the Songo Songo and Mnazi Bay coastal fields. As a comparison, the largest Tanzanian gas find so far, Mzia, is ten times smaller than Mozambique's Prosperidade complex. In 2015 the government increased its recoverable resource estimate from 46.5 tcf to 55 tcf, while companies' data give an estimated 17 tcf of recoverable gas in Blocks 1, 3, and 4 and 16.4 tcf in Block 2.[142] Block 3 has only yielded one discovery so far, prompting BG to exit it in 2014. Independent Ophir took over its share, but decided to relinquish it in July 2015. They only retained Blocks 1 and 4, with BG as operator.[143] The proximity of Tanzania's finds to Mozambican fields has not so far prompted a joint resource development between the two countries.

LNG project development

LNG concept: will FLNG be part of the development?

Many uncertainties remain as to how much LNG will be ultimately developed, given the size of these discoveries, especially in Mozambique. Current analyses range between 10 and 89 mtpa in Mozambique and between 10 and 20 mtpa in Tanzania (see Figure 5.14). While they give an idea of the current thinking, – highlighting the uncertainty in Mozambique – they give little indication of what the future may be. Despite the low oil price environment, the IMF has substantially increased its estimates on future LNG capacity from 20 to 89 mtpa and assumes that 13 onshore LNG trains and four FLNG will be built.[144]

Companies have proposed both onshore LNG and FLNG concepts in each country. The FLNG option could offset cost uncertainties resulting from the remote location and absence of a qualified domestic workforce, but there are many uncertainties around FLNG costs depending on the concept (see Chapter 4). The higher estimates would not sit well in a $40–50/bbl environment. In addition, FLNG implies many fewer local jobs and business opportunities, and may not be compatible with the development of infrastructure to supply the domestic market.

---

[142] Statoil quotes 22 tcf in place (IHS).

[143] 'Our Assets', Tanzania, Ophir Energy company website . https://www.ophir-energy.com/our-assets/tanzania/.

[144] Republic of Mozambique, IMF Country Report, No 16/9, January 2016. www.imf.org/external/pubs/ft/scr/2016/cr1609.pdf.

278   *LNG Markets in Transition*

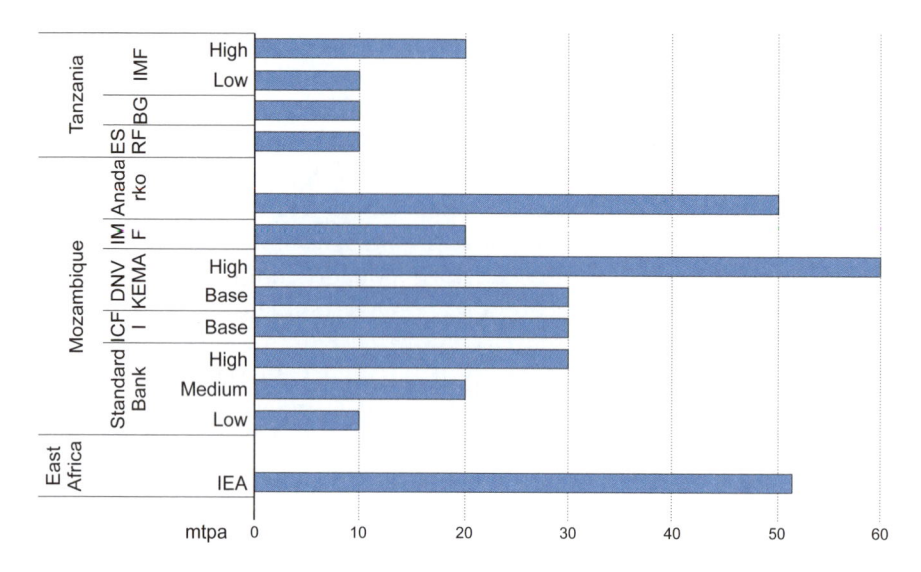

Figure 5.14: Different scenarios for LNG developments in Eastern Africa

Note: Apart from the IEA looking at 2040, other estimates relate to 2030 or have no date.

Source: IEA, Standard bank, DNV, ICFI, IMF, ESFR, BG, Anadarko.

The current state of project development gives an overwhelming advantage to Mozambique, where three different fields/complexes will support competing LNG projects:

- Area 4's Coral field for ENI's 2.5 mtpa FLNG;

- Area 1's Golfinho-Atum fields for Anadarko's 12 mtpa two-train onshore; and

- The Prosperidade/Mamba complex, straddling both areas, for the 10 mtpa Mamba project.

Both Anadarko and ENI have postponed final investment decision (FID), now expected in 2016 – Anadarko was initially stating that it would take FID in 2013 (Ledesma, 2013). Even its last schedule of taking FID on its 12 mtpa two-train onshore plant in 2015 has been postponed to 2016. The company has been facing issues which include the Exim Bank's shutdown in mid-2015, impacting project financing,[145] as well as low oil

---
[145] 'Financing issues plague Anadarko in Mozambique', *Interfax*, 31 July 2015. http://interfaxenergy.com/gasdaily/article/16953/financing-issues-plague-anadarko-in-mozambique.

and gas prices. Even though Anadarko announced 8 mtpa of HoAs as of mid-2015, it is uncertain whether this will be achieved. BP has concluded a non-binding deal with ENI on its 2.5 mtpa FLNG.[146,147] Its fields' resources would allow ENI to develop one more FLNG, based on Coral, while Anadarko could build two more trains based on Golfinho.

However, the largest discoveries are the Prosperidade/Mamba complex, which has an estimated 78 tcf of recoverable reserves (according to IHS). The complex's reserves allow for up to 50 mtpa to be developed. Anadarko and ENI had agreed in 2012 to conduct coordinated offshore development activities and build common onshore liquefaction facilities. This agreement was later abandoned, though the companies kept Afungi as the common site for the onshore infrastructure. Unitization was required under the Decree Law passed on 2 December 2014; otherwise, the government would nominate an expert to design the unitization plan. In June 2015 the companies reached an agreement, one month after the decree's deadline:[148] ENI would be the operator of the Mamba project, initially involving two onshore LNG trains, with FID planned for 2016–17 and start-up in 2022. In December 2015, the companies announced that an agreement with the Mozambique government to develop 24 tcf of resources (12 tcf for each company) had been reached.[149] This project could potentially threaten Anadarko's development if its FID is delayed to late 2016, given the bottlenecks on the government's side. The Ministry of Energy and Natural Resources, which has to confirm the Plan of Development, is also responsible for mining and electricity. Both companies lack LNG operatorship experience: ENI was involved in Nigerian and Angolan LNG projects as a minority stakeholder, while Anadarko has a wealth of experience in deep oil fields but none in LNG. This may be an opportunity for Anadarko to develop new skills and for ENI to acquire FLNG experience.

In Tanzania, the projects are much less advanced due to the presidential elections in October 2015, a regulatory framework which has not been finalized, and a handover from BG to Shell. The Tanzania Petroleum

---

[146] *Investor Book*, Andarko Petroleum, April 2015. www.anadarko.com/content/documents/apc/Operations/ANADARKO_InvestorPresentation_April.pdf.

[147] 'BP named as buyer for Eni's FLNG in Mozambique', *Interfax*, 9 October 2015. http://interfaxenergy.com/gasdaily/article/17846/bp-named-as-buyer-for-enis-flng-in-mozambique.

[148] 'Eni, Anadarko agree unitisation of straddling Mozambique gas', Interfax, 5 June 2015. http://interfaxenergy.com/gasdaily/article/16347/eni-anadarko-agree-unitisation-of-straddling-mozambique-gas.

[149] 'Development plans finalized for areas offshore Mozambique', *Oil and Gas Journal*, 3 December 2015. www.ogj.com/articles/2015/12/development-plans-finalized-for-areas-offshore-mozambique.html?cmpid=EnlDailyDecember32015&eid=311852417&bid=1248502.

Development Corporation (TPDC) only acquired the land for the onshore LNG trains in early 2016.[150] Given the current delays, compounded by a perceived LNG glut for the coming five years and low oil prices, Tanzania's project partners may only take the FID by 2020, implying first exports by 2025. A striking difference in comparison with the position in Mozambique, however, is that in Tanzania the companies are cooperating. At the request of the government, the companies have set up an integrated project team to develop a joint onshore LNG facility. BG had been designated as the lead developer during the pre-FEED stage. The initial concept is an onshore two-train 10 mtpa project. Meanwhile, Ophir is proposing an additional 3 mtpa FLNG. Importantly, the three IOCs have a good track record in terms of LNG development. Ophir has less financial strength, no LNG experience, and another more advanced FLNG project in Equatorial Guinea. The impact of Shell's acquisition of BG is not clear cut: it gives Shell an entry to the region, but brings the project into competition with others in its portfolio. Shell might also want to change Tanzania's onshore concept to FLNG to apply its experience with Australia's Prelude FLNG.

Asia challenges IOCs' dominance
One interesting angle to the story is how these discoveries have attracted the attention of oil and gas companies worldwide. Asian companies have established a strong position in Mozambique, while there is a large presence of IOCs and medium-sized companies in Tanzania, but only one Asian company (see Table 5.15).

Timing was essential. Before 2010, Japan's Mitsui trading house, India's Bharat Petroleum, and Videocon acquired shares in Area 1 while Korea's KOGAS took 10 per cent from ENI in Area 4. Acquisition prices were moderate then: Videocon paid $75 million for its 10 per cent stake.[151] However, after the first discoveries in 2010 the battle became particularly intense and the price of acquisition sky rocketed, discouraging many, even IOCs. In 2012, PTTEP outbid Shell and acquired Cove Energy's 8.5 per cent stake in Area 1 for $1.9 billion, almost 30 times more on a per unit basis than Videocon had paid.[152] Later on, OVL and OIL jointly acquired Videocon's 10 per cent share for $2.475 billion, while OVL acquired 10 per cent from Anadarko for $2.64 billion. On ENI's side, there were fewer buy-ins: in 2012, CNPC acquired a 28.57 per cent interest in ENI East Africa

---

[150] 'Lindi is ready for LNG', Africa Oil and Gas Report, 5 January 2016. http://africaoilgasreport.com/2016/01/gas-monetization/lindi-is-ready-for-lng/.

[151] 'India's Videocon, Bharat Petroleum buy 10 pct each in Mozambique block', ADVN. www.advfn.com/nyse/StockNews.asp?stocknews=APC&article=27890303.

[152] 'Cove Energy Takeover Finally Over', Rigzone, 17 August 2012. www.rigzone.com/news/oil_gas/a/120069/Cove_Energy_Takeover_Finally_Over.

(including 20 per cent in Area 4) for $4.21 billion.[153]

This reduced Anadarko's share in Area 1 from 85 per cent (including the 15 per cent holding of national company ENH) in 2006 to 26.5 per cent in 2015, but the Anadarko company still retains the operatorship. Consequently 58.5 per cent of Area 1 is now in the hands of Asian companies. Apart from the Ichthys project under construction in Australia, this is the first time in LNG history that Asian buyers have taken such an important role as shareholders outside their countries (see Figure 5.15). Meanwhile, ENI has retained a 50 per cent share in Area 4, where Asian companies control 30 per cent. With Asia seen as the growing LNG market, Asian companies' ownership and long-term contracts are advantageous in securing loans from Asian banks. JBIC announced in 2015 that it would strengthen its financial backing for specific developments in which Japanese firms were engaged, notably Anadarko's project.[154] Chinese financial support will also be crucial, either through export credit agencies or commercial banks.

Both ENI and Anadarko are rumoured to want to divest.[155] ENI's 50 per cent share gives it some margin, though the company has announced it will cut spending and sell €8 billion ($8.5 billion) of assets over the next four years, given the low oil price environment.[156] Chinese companies and ExxonMobil are reported to be interested.[157] Meanwhile, Anadarko can either sell its shares in Area 1 or be acquired as a company. ExxonMobil and Qatar Petroleum are said to be interested, but an acquisition at a relatively late stage could imperil Anadarko's initial LNG project development.

Tanzanian fields saw fewer transactions. IOCs moved quickly to acquire shares through farm-in agreements in the small time window between the Mozambican and Tanzanian discoveries – February–October 2010. This implies that IOCs had been following Eastern African gas developments even before discoveries were made and acted rapidly, conjecturing that Tanzania might also have large gas resources. Blocks 1, 3, and 4 were

---

[153] 'CNPC and ENI sign two cooperation agreements', Europétrole, 18 March 2013. www.euro-petrole.com/cnpc-and-eni-sign-two-cooperation-agreements-n-i-7311.

[154] Petroleum Argus, 12 June 2015.

[155] 'Eni talks on Mozambique sale sticking in oil slide', Reuters, 29 May 2015. www.reuters.com/article/2015/05/29/mozambique-ma-eni-idUSL5N0YI4IA20150529; 'Exclusive: Anadarko considers selling Mozambique gas assets to Exxon', Reuters, 17 April 2015. www.reuters.com/article/2015/04/17/us-anadarko-exxon-exclusive-idUSKBN0N823C20150417.

[156] 'Eni to Cut Spending, Slash Dividend and Sell Assets Amid Low Oil Price', *The Wall Street Journal*, 13 March 2015. www.wsj.com/articles/eni-to-cut-spending-slash-dividend-and-sell-assets-amid-low-oil-price-1426259098.

[157] LNG Intelligence, 24 December 2015.

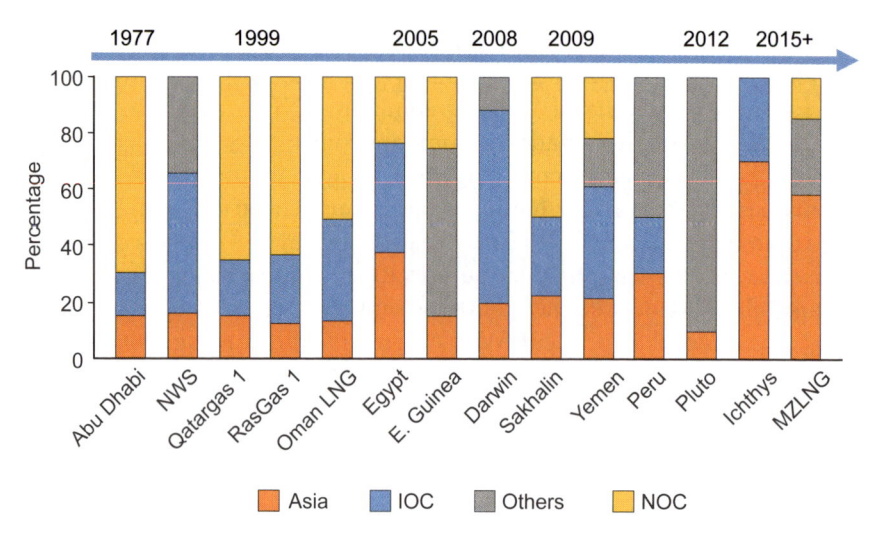

Figure 5.15: Asian companies' shareholding in relevant LNG projects
Source: GIIGNL.

originally awarded to Ophir in 2005 and 2006. Then the company farmed out a 60 per cent stake and operatorship to BG in 2010, a few months before hitting gas. Statoil concluded a farm-out agreement with ExxonMobil in 2010. In November 2013, Ophir sold a 20 per cent stake in its blocks to Pavilion Energy, a subsidiary of Singapore's investment company Temasek, for $1.288 billion, marking the first and only entry of Asian companies in Tanzania.

Can Mozambique and Tanzania compete in global markets?

Both countries present advantages when compared with their competitors in North America, Australia, and Russia. The region's location is within easy reach of all the LNG-importing markets. It offers arbitrage opportunities to companies and enables them to redirect LNG cargoes without suffering too great a transport cost differential. Compared to other LNG suppliers, neither country would tend to be the closest supplier to markets, except for India – explaining the involvement of three Indian companies in Mozambique. From the buyers' perspective, both countries provide supply diversity away from traditional LNG suppliers, even though LNG cargoes and installations could be exposed to piracy.[158]

Reported FOB breakeven costs of around $7–9/MMBtu,[159] lower than

---

[158] 'Tanzania arrests 7 pirates after attack on oil vessel', Reuters, 4 October 2011. www.reuters.com/article/2011/10/04/tanzania-pirates-idUSL5E7L43LO20111004.

[159] Deutsche Bank, Poten and Partners.

many other projects, notably Australian ones, represent a major advantage. This is attractive for LNG buyers looking for low prices in the aftermath of the shale gas boom. But this can be still considered to be high in a low oil price environment, unless project sponsors are successful in reducing costs. LNG from Eastern Africa would be competitive with US LNG if Henry Hub (HH) prices were around $3–4/MMBtu. Upstream costs in Mozambique are assumed to range around $1.74–2.1/MMBtu for the Prosperidade, Mamba, and Golfinho/Atum fields (ICFI, 2012). In Tanzania, upstream costs are estimated at $3/MMBtu, making LNG slightly more expensive. The capital costs of LNG trains would decrease if more were built. Meanwhile, transport costs to various markets would range between $0.8 and $1.6/MMBtu with oil prices at $50/bbl, and $1–1.9/MMBtu at $100/bbl (see Figure 5.16).

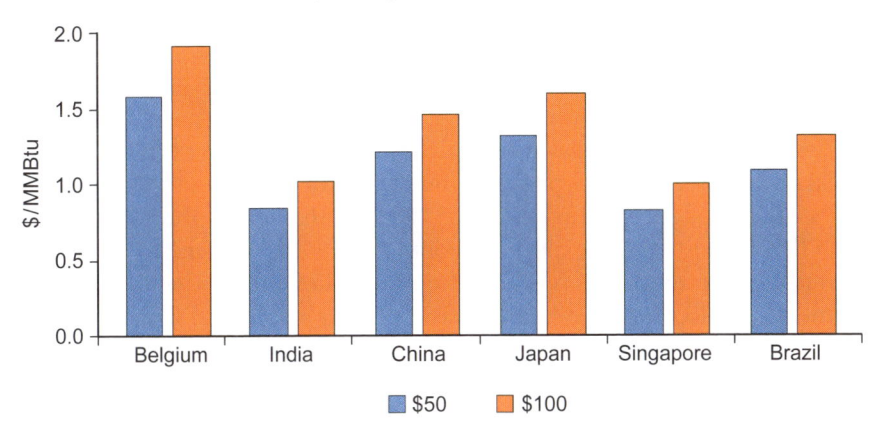

Figure 5.16: Transport costs to various markets at different oil prices from Eastern Africa
Source: Nexant World Gas Model.

The large reserves underpinning developments in Mozambique provide a sense of supply security to buyers, while the involvement of major players in the projects gives them confidence in their progress as well as access to equity LNG. Anadarko's project is expected to use a model similar to a conventional merchant model, with which buyers are comfortable. LNG is reported to be priced with oil indexation and DES (delivered ex-ship) terms, which could be slightly disappointing for Asian buyers looking for flexibility. The high involvement of Asian buyers could be a double-edged sword, however, as it makes Mozambique's LNG projects more exposed to this region's future LNG demand.

Reserves are much smaller in Tanzania, and the government wishes to give priority to the domestic market. But the IOCs' involvement would allow them to include this LNG in their portfolio and be less dependent on one specific region.

Challenges still ahead

In both countries, the challenges are essentially above-ground. Projects need regulatory, political, and fiscal stability to proceed. These challenges are even more relevant in this period of intense competition for courting potential investors. While Mozambique's 2014 presidential elections ensured continuity, with power staying within the Frelimo party, there have been some recent tensions with Renamo.[160] In Tanzania, the CMM party faced strong opposition during the 2015 presidential elections, although they won the elections. One can also expect both countries to move from overseas aid to resource dependence, and therefore increase fiscal demands on extractives industries (Frühauf, 2014).

Tackling regulatory uncertainties
In 2014 Mozambique passed essential laws to clarify the regulatory and fiscal framework for LNG players. The government took time to negotiate the terms, to avoid repeating the same mistakes that it had previously made with Sasol. Existing gas exports to South Africa have generated very little government revenue as a result of the removal of the production-sharing element, the acceptance of an 'abusive' pricing formula to determine the sale price of gas, and significant capital cost overruns (CIP, 2013).

While the Petroleum Law and Fiscal laws passed in August 2014 set the general framework governing petroleum exploration, production activities, and fiscal legislation, they needed to be completed by one decree (passed on 2 December 2014) clarifying the specific LNG development conditions for ENI and Anadarko. The decree included the possibility of renegotiating the royalty rates after 10 and 20 years, increasing it from 2 per cent to 4 per cent and 6 per cent, to increase the state's benefits in the event of successful operations. Gas sales revenues can be held offshore, and restrictions on the debt–equity ratio have been lifted (unlike the terms in the Petroleum Law). However, companies would need to be listed on the Mozambican stock exchange and the government is required to approve the terms of gas sales agreements. But decrees specifying how to apply the LNG decree are still required.[161] Meanwhile, the discovery of undisclosed loans of over $1 billion that were kept secret from the International Monetary Fund

---

[160] 'Foes from Mozambique's war spar as energy windfall looms', New Zimbabwe, 27 January 2016. www.newzimbabwe.com/news-27384-Money+Tsunami+stokes +Renamo,+Frelimo+rows/news.aspx.
[161] *Africa Intelligence*, June 2015.

(IMF) could have far-reaching implications for the attractiveness of Mozambique.

In Tanzania, the legislation necessary to develop its LNG projects has been lacking for a long time. The delays have been exacerbated by lengthy discussions in parliament, to ensure gas developments benefit the country – in contrast with those in the gold sector, which is perceived as benefiting private mining companies too greatly. Three essential laws were passed in July 2015: the Petroleum Act 2015, the Oil and Gas Revenues Management Act 2015, and the Tanzania Extractive Industries Bill 2015. President Kikwete used a certificate of urgency to ensure the laws were passed, but prompted criticism from the Tanzanian Civil Society Coalition and the opposition, due to the alleged lack of discussion. Besides setting the royalties and establishing ranges for governmental profits, the laws also set up a regulator and an advisory bureau and reinforced the role of the TPDC as the future NOC in the upstream, midstream, and downstream sectors. Amendments are needed to finalize the law. In addition, the different PSA terms vary widely, creating uncertainty over whether any one, or which, would prevail. Deloitte reports three different master PSAs (MPSAs) (2004, 2008, and 2013), with the 2004 MPSA being the basis for many of the PSAs in effect. The new 2013 MPSA appears to create a significant tightening of the fiscal terms (Deloitte, 2016).

Both countries use relatively complex PSAs and include a whole range of government take mechanisms, such as royalties, profit oil share, and income tax (see Table 5.16). There is also an Additional Profit Tax, a Petroleum Production Tax in Mozambique, and a withholding tax in both countries. A comparison of fiscal terms shows that the main terms – royalty, cost recovery limit, and ministry's share of profit gas – tend to be more favourable for the investors in Mozambique than in Tanzania, where companies have been disappointed by the high fiscal take from the government in the last MPSA. One potential issue is that there seems to be no provision for state participation to be carried during the development phase (unlike the exploration phase), which means it cannot be funded with the government's share of profit gas. However, paying such investments up-front could be a challenge for Mozambique and Tanzania.

Managing local expectations
Gas discoveries have created huge expectations among both population and government in terms of local content. However, a single standalone LNG plant creates very few employment opportunities once it is operational – a few hundred per train. The construction of Anadarko's two trains is expected to create around 10,000 jobs, but how many of those will be for local workers? Even something as apparently simple as catering is not

Table 5.16: Fiscal terms

	Mozambique		Tanzania
	Area 1	Area 4	Petroleum Law 2015
Royalty	2%, 4% after 10 years, 6% after 20 years		7.5% onshore (12.5% onshore/shelf)
Corporate tax	24% for 8 years, 32% afterwards		30%
Cost recovery limit	65%	75%	50%
Ministry share of profit gas			
R <1	10%	15%	0–149.999 mscf/d	60%
R 1–2	20%	25%	150–299.999	65%
R 2–3	30%	35%	300–449.999	70%
R 3–4	50%	45%	450–599.999	75%
R >4	60%	55%	600–749.999	80%
			750 +	85%
State's participation (optional)	15%	10%		25%

Sources: CIP, Petroleum Law.

straightforward. Farming in the two countries is mostly subsistence – farmers would need to be trained to provide fruit and vegetables on a continuous basis. Roads are undeveloped and there is not a single company in Mozambique able to provide 30,000 meals a day.

Most companies are informally run. Even responding to a tender in a limited number of weeks would be a challenge for most SMEs in these countries, not to mention complying with requirements to provide three years of audited financial statements to project developers. In Mozambique there is very little diversity in the industrial sector: it is highly concentrated around metals manufacturing (Mozal), mining, and food and beverages. Local content laws require local suppliers to be given preference. In Mozambique, locals will be chosen if their prices are only up to 10 per cent higher than those of foreign competitors; however, foreign companies coming to Mozambique usually get a 10-year tax holiday and do not pay import taxes, which can double the cost of the products. Tanzania's draft local content policy for the petroleum industry generally aims at ensuring that Tanzanians participate strategically in the oil and gas sector – a foreign entity providing goods and services must operate from Tanzania and partner with a Tanzanian-owned and registered company – and are given priority in terms of procurement, as well as ensuring capacity-building. However, the devil is in the detail.

Building infrastructure for domestic gas use
Despite limited gas and power infrastructure, both countries have ambitions to develop power plants and industries and to try to put in place domestic market obligations (DMO). However, most analysts consider that the domestic markets in Mozambique and Tanzania are too small and too spread out to be in a position to use that much gas. Stakeholders have looked at various domestic market options, including power plants, GTL, methanol, fertilizer, and small industries, but LNG remains the first choice. This assumption may have to be challenged if LNG development is delayed or does not happen at all, while the rationale of basing gas developments on key mega-projects remains.

DMO is set at 25 per cent in Mozambique, but ENI is unlikely to burden its FLNG project development with this additional infrastructure while it is still being negotiated for Anadarko. Taking Anadarko's 12 mtpa as a basis, the DMO implies around 5 bcm of gas – for a market currently consuming 0.2 bcm. In December 2015, Anadarko signed an MOU to provide 0.5 bcm per train from offshore Area 1 to the domestic market – this is lower than the DMO. However, the concessionaires are prepared to sell up to 3 bcm of additional volumes into the domestic market in future years as projects are matured and commercial terms agreed.[162] Tanzanian gas policy would prioritize the domestic market, but no specific percentage has been set for a DMO: each PSA has different terms, though Statoil has said 'up to 10 per cent of the gas produced'. Besides the DMO issue, the governments need to decide how much of the government take should be in cash or in kind.

Another key issue is the price at which gas will be marketed domestically. This is a sensitive issue for producers, as it directly impacts their profitability and it is a political issue as consumers expect gas to be cheap. A study examining the potential regional use in eight Eastern African countries suggests that, based on a cost-plus approach, gas could be delivered at the city gate for an average regional price of $5.2/MMBtu in a baseline scenario, but at $10.3/MMBtu in a high-cost scenario, with lower demand and higher investment costs (Demierre et al., 2014). The higher price would be difficult to accept, as all exporting countries with no imports keep gas

---

[162] 'Anadarko Achieves New Mozambique LNG Milestones', PRNewswire, 3 December 2015. www.prnewswire.com/news-releases/anadarko-achieves-new-mozambique-lng-milestones-300187547.html.

prices below $4/MMBtu (IGU, 2015). Meanwhile, if they do not achieve a decent return on investment, producers will feel less incentivized to develop the domestic market, while low gas prices could exacerbate demand.

Long distances represent a further challenge: Maputo is some 2,700 km away by road from Palma, which implies a significant cost for pipeline infrastructure. Meanwhile, meeting high local expectations represents another issue. In Tanzania, current production from the Songo Songo and Mnazi Bay fields is exported to Dar es Salaam; the recently built pipeline has seen riots from local people deprived of benefits from what they considered to be 'their gas resources'. The country has been plagued by recurrent power shortages due to the droughts. Tanzania had to shut down some hydro plants in late 2015. In 2014 Tanzania had 1.6 GW of capacity, 31 per cent of thermal generation, 33 per cent of gas, and 35 per cent of hydro. There are ambitions to install 10 GW by end-2025, including 4.5 GW of gas-fired generation which could serve as anchor customers (see Figure 5.17). Building up reliable power generation sources is high on the government's agenda in any discussions about the development of gas discoveries (Deloitte, 2016). This aim will be challenged if LNG drives new developments. Looking at Tanzania's geography, Block 4 is close to the producing Songo Songo field, but further away from Blocks 1 and 2, and could be potentially earmarked for domestic use if the price is satisfactory.

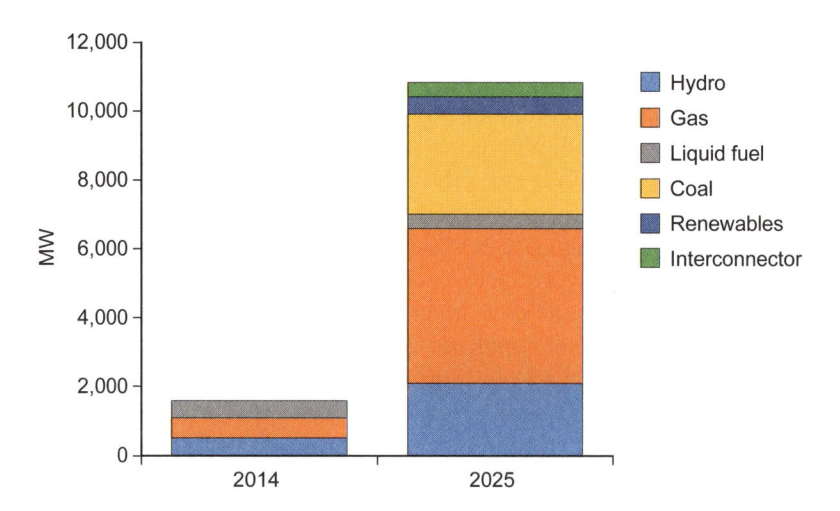

Figure 5.17: Tanzania's plans to increase power capacity
Source: Electricity Supply Industry Reform Strategy and Roadmap 2014–25.

Mozambique has a small market where gas is used by small industries and, since 2014, also by power plants. Developing power plants means facing the reality of an undeveloped country where future power developments would be export-orientated. This is why the power issues should be viewed regionally, for the whole Southern Africa region. Fertilizer production could be an interesting option in a country with much agricultural potential, but most farmers would not be able to afford expensive fertilizer products, which would then be exported. Meanwhile, the Gas Master Plan for Mozambique recommended establishing some mega-projects in Palma to promote regional economic activity.

How does LNG fit in companies' overall portfolios?
Taking a step back, another key aspect is that these LNG projects are in competition not only with other projects worldwide, but also against other projects in the investor companies' portfolios (Table 5.2). At a time when most firms are reassessing priorities in a lower cash-flow environment, any country with oil and gas assets could see its project pushed back on the basis of its competitiveness and overall costs. Majors like ExxonMobil and Shell/BG are engaged in other LNG projects at different stages of advancement, while Ophir has another FLNG project in Equatorial Guinea. For ENI, Anadarko, and Statoil, these LNG projects are key and quite unique. However, ENI's Zohr discovery in Egypt could represent serious competition for its projects in Mozambique.

Conclusion

There is no longer any expectation that Mozambique and Tanzania will enter the global gas scene by 2018 and their objectives of bringing on stream 50 mtpa and 20 mtpa, respectively, appear ambitious at this point. Mozambique and Tanzania have already missed a window of opportunity. If the FID had been taken in 2014, their projects would not have to contemplate the endless flow of competing US projects moving ahead since October 2014. There is no point criticizing the governments for being slow: most LNG projects have taken decades to move from discoveries to FIDs. If FIDs are taken over 2016–18, that would be only six to eight years after first discovery, which would already be quite remarkable.

Investors are set to take FIDs in a difficult environment. Competition between projects in different regions, but also within investors' portfolios, is intense. If the regulatory, fiscal, and cost conditions are not favourable, projects can be put on the back burner for years or indefinitely postponed. These conditions, added to a challenging global LNG market environment, mean that operators have a strong disincentive to move away from the traditional long-term contract model and there is no indication that they would wish to use hybrid indexation rather than oil indexation. At best, Tanzanian LNG could be marketed as portfolio LNG and added to the volumes of globally flexible LNG. The contribution of either country to global LNG markets thus remains uncertain in terms of timing and scale; the two countries are set to face different futures despite their proximity, as illustrated in Figure 5.18. Mozambique is clearly in the lead and is more likely to be first to export LNG, though still not before 2020 and probably even later if FID is not taken in 2016. While Mozambique's resources are too large to be ignored, and it has made significant efforts to push projects ahead, the ball is in the hands of companies which face global competition and financing issues. Due to delayed legislative and regulatory frameworks and uncompetitive fiscal terms, Tanzanian LNG may not start before 2025, and there is a possibility that LNG there may never go ahead.

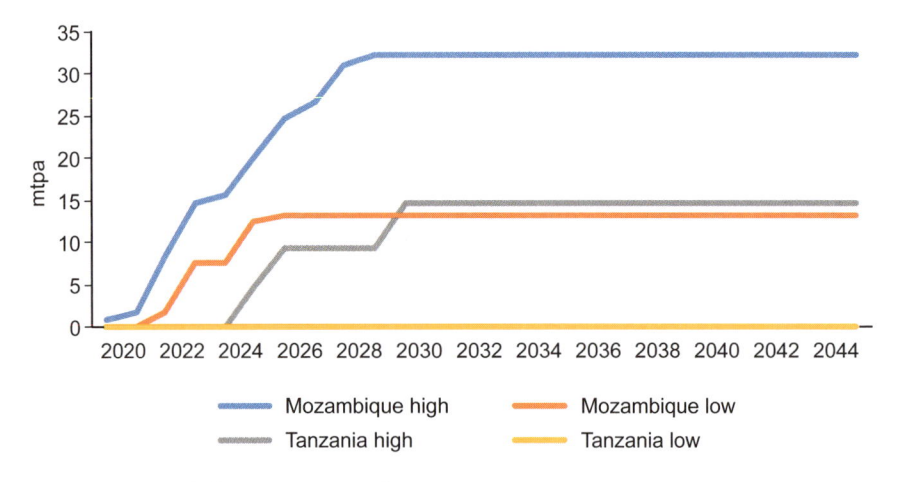

Figure 5.18: LNG exports scenarios
Source: Author's research.

Other potential LNG supplies

Beyond the large and potentially imminent developments discussed above, a number of other countries have plans to develop gas resources for export via LNG. Meanwhile existing LNG exporters will continue to play a significant role in future LNG supplies. Table 5.17 provides an overview of the existing LNG facilities across the world, which have a combined capacity of over 300 mtpa.

Table 5.17: LNG liquefaction capacity and LNG production (2015)

	No. of sites	Total trains	Total capacity (mt)	First output year	2015 sales (mt)	% change (2015/ 2014)
Atlantic Basin						
Algeria	5	17	28.5	1972	12.13	−4%
Angola (stopped)	1	1	5.2	2013		−100%
Egypt (stopped)	2	3	12.2	2005		−100%
Equatorial Guinea	1	1	3.7	2007	3.65	7%
Libya (stopped)	1	4	3.2	1970		na
Nigeria	3	6	21.8	1999	19.5	2%
Norway	1	1	4.3	2007	4.33	20%
Trinidad & Tobago	3	4	15.5	1999	11.81	−10%
Sub-Total	*17*	*37*	*94.4*		*51.42*	*−2%*
Middle East						
Abu Dhabi	1	3	5.8	1977	5.7	−7%
Oman	1	3	10.7	2000	7.56	−2%
Qatar	12	14	77	1999	78.4	3%
Yemen (stopped)	1	2	6.7	2009	1.52	−76%
Sub-Total	*15*	*22*	*100.2*		*93.18*	*−3%*
Pacific Basin						
Australia	7	10	36.6	1989	29.45	25%
Brunei	1	5	7.1	1973	6.48	6%
USA	1	1	0.4	1969	0.32	7%
Indonesia	3	11	31.9	1977	18.03	4%
Malaysia	4	9	24.2	1983	24.99	1%
PNG	1	2	6.9	2014	7.18	111%
Peru	1	1	4.5	2010	3.57	−11%
Russia	1	2	9.6	2009	10.57	0%
Sub-Total	*19*	*41*	*121.2*		*100.59*	*12%*
Total	51	100	315.8		245.19	3%

Source: GIIGNL Annual Report 2016.

Middle East production and prospects

The Middle East currently holds four LNG exporters and accounted for almost one-third of global capacity and 38 per cent of global output in 2015. Qatar is the largest LNG exporter in the world, with 14 trains with a total capacity of 77 mtpa and a very low cost of production, estimated to be below $2/MMBtu thanks to its associated liquids output (Fattouh et al.,

2015, 9–12). However, despite a strong position and the potential for further expansion, the Qatari government continues to keep in place a moratorium on production increases that was first introduced in 2005, and which limits output to the level seen in 2015. The possibility of removing the moratorium seems to be reviewed on a regular basis, but will ultimately depend on a geological review of the potential of the North field, as well as an assessment of the state of the global gas market. As of May 2016 it seems unlikely that production capacity will increase in the near future, as the country focuses more on how it plans to compete with the imminent surge in production from the USA and Australia rather than on increasing its own capacity.[163] The one exception which could cause a review of output strategy is the prospect of Iran becoming a major LNG player (see below for discussion), as Iran's South Pars field is essentially the same structure as Qatar's North field. As such, Qatar might fear losing some gas reserves if Iran increases output rapidly to support LNG projects, and might respond by increasing its own production.[164] However, given the current state of Iran's gas plans this outcome is not imminent.

The Middle East's three remaining LNG producers face different issues as they seek to maintain their output. Oman's capacity continues to be significantly underutilized due to an increase in domestic demand over the past few years. LNG production in Oman has been progressively declining since 2007. A portion of the country's liquefaction capacity could be decommissioned, but to date it seems that the government and Oman LNG, the domestic operator, are keen to try and maintain the ability to reinvigorate the industry.[165] However, the relatively high cost of new gas production in the country, combined with increasing competition both regionally and globally, may ultimately force some of the LNG plant offline. Indeed the option of importing additional gas, on top of Qatari imports, is even being considered, as this may be a cheaper option than developing the country's own resources.[166] However, two rays of hope are apparent. Firstly, BP is set to bring two phases of the Khazzan gas field online in 2017 and 2020, and with production set to peak at 15.5 bcm/year this could provide a boost to the country's LNG potential.[167] Secondly, Iran has begun

---

[163] 'No plans to lift Qatar LNG capacity', *The Australian*, 14 July 2014.

[164] 'Iran, Qatar in competition over world's biggest gas field', Natural Gas Europe, 23 December 2015.

[165] 'Oman exports more LNG in move with implications for oil', Platts, 18 August 2015.

[166] 'Oman said to consider LNG imports as domestic demand surges', Bloomberg, 30 August 2015.

[167] 'BP extends scope of Khazzan gas field development in Oman', Reuters, 14 February 2016.

discussions to use any spare LNG capacity to liquefy its gas, which could be exported via offshore pipeline. Negotiations are at an early stage, but could provide an alternative to new infrastructure offshore Iran.[168]

Yemen has also seen a decline in output, mainly driven by political issues. Yemen LNG began operations in 2005 and has sufficient reserves to supply up to 6.7 mtpa for 20 years, but output declined by 8 per cent in 2014 as civil unrest started in the country and force majeure on all contracts was declared in April 2015 as the security situation worsened.[169] The liquefaction plant is currently in preservation mode and it is unclear when it will be able to come back online.

On a more positive note the region's oldest liquefaction plant (in Abu Dhabi), which first came online in 1977, saw production increase by almost 20 per cent in 2014, and although it fell back in 2015, output remains close to full nameplate capacity. However, this result masks the fact that the UAE remains a net gas importer due to the high levels of domestic demand, with gas arriving via the Dolphin pipeline from Qatar and through an LNG terminal off the coast of Dubai.[170] As a result, no increase in exports can be expected, and indeed discussion over the construction of a new LNG regasification terminal to facilitate an increase in imports commenced in 2015.[171] Furthermore, the current LNG export contract ends in 2019, with the possibility that the plant could be closed down, which would clearly transform the country's position with regard to the LNG market.

In terms of potential growth, Iran is perhaps the most interesting prospect in the LNG sector as a whole because of its potential size. Iran holds the world's largest gas reserves,[172] but has been prevented from exploiting them for export due to US sanctions. The initiation of the process to remove sanctions in 2015 has catalysed a review of Iran's gas sector, and in particular its previous plans to export 40–70 mtpa of LNG from six production facilities.[173] The head of the National Iranian Gas Company (NIGC) has mentioned a two to three year timetable for reviving investment in LNG after the ending of sanctions is confirmed. Shell, Total,

---

[168] 'Iran begins discussions with Oman on using spare LNG facilities', Natural Gas Asia, 21 March 2016.

[169] 'UN sanctions Houthis as Yemen LNG halts production', *The Financial Times*, 14 April 2015.

[170] EIA Country Analysis (www.eia.gov/beta/international/analysis.cfm?iso=ARE, sourced on 12 Oct 2015).

[171] 'New LNG import terminal is a possibility, energy minister says', The National, 15 June 2015.

[172] BP (2015); Iran is quoted as having 34 tcm of proved reserves compared to 32.3 tcm in Russia.

[173] 'Iran eyes resuming huge LNG project with Germany', Natural Gas Europe, 7 May 2015.

and Repsol, the original companies involved in the plans, are mentioned as future partners. However, expectations for imminent development of new projects must be tempered by a number of factors including rising domestic demand, which will no doubt need to be satisfied first, as well as Iran's plans to export gas to neighbouring countries via pipeline. A 10 bcm contract has already been signed with Oman, and Iran is also targeting supply to other Persian Gulf countries. A pipeline to India via Pakistan that could link the giant South Pars field to Karachi and Delhi is under discussion.[174] As a result, although Iran clearly has the potential to become a significant LNG exporter over time, early enthusiasm will inevitably become a longer-term negotiation over contractual terms and gas market priorities, meaning that major LNG projects will not be developed until well into the 2020s at the earliest.

Political issues also surround another potential LNG scheme in the Middle East, with the possibility of Israel and Cyprus combining to develop a project based on two large discoveries in the Mediterranean. A number of discoveries have been made in the Israeli sector with the largest, Leviathan, certainly offering the potential for an LNG project. Cyprus has one major find, Aphrodite, which contains estimated reserves of 5 tcf of gas. Both countries have contemplated a joint LNG scheme that could be located either on Cyprus or on the Israeli mainland, although the option of selling gas to Egypt's currently redundant liquefaction plants has also been suggested. However, domestic politics in both countries are hindering progress. The Israeli government is insisting on domestic market priority and declaring the Leviathan project a national security issue, while in Cyprus, the Turkish government has sought to delay any gas project that does not involve both sides of the disputed island. Furthermore, the option to export gas to Egypt has apparently been undermined by ENI's recent discovery of the giant Zohr offshore field, which could contain up to 30 tcf (850 bcm) of gas reserves. Consequently, pipeline gas sales to neighbouring Middle Eastern countries such as Jordan, or sales north into Turkey, may be a better option than an LNG project. With the security situation in the region also very uncertain, any projects will likely be delayed into the 2020s, with discussions over the mix of domestic sales, pipeline exports, and LNG supply continuing for the next few years.

Africa

Supply problems in North Africa are affecting three of the continent's main LNG exporters, Egypt, Algeria, and Libya. Egypt's LNG exports halted completely in 2014, having already declined 97 per cent from their

---

[174] 'Iran–Pakistan–India pipeline is still a possibility', The Hindu Business Line, 18 March 2015.

peak during 2014. BG declared force majeure in 2014 as the Egyptian government diverted gas towards the domestic market, while Union Fenosa mothballed its Damietta plant in 2013.[175] Low domestic gas prices have encouraged a continuing increase in demand, while indigenous supply has been hit by a lack of investment due to the turbulent political situation in the country. More encouragingly, the Zohr discovery, made by ENI in 2015, has encouraged speculation that LNG exports could resume by the end of this decade.[176] However, the potential for production to start by 2017 as announced depends on the field's appraisal and on negotiations with the government, which may well insist on the majority of the gas being sold domestically. Consequently, little if any LNG is likely to leave Egypt before 2020.

Meanwhile, Algerian facilities are also operating well below capacity due to a combination of rapidly increasing demand and a poor investment climate in the upstream sector, which has resulted in declining production since 2005. Sonatrach has announced significant investment plans to 2020, but the most recent licensing round produced disappointing results, with only four of 31 blocks taken up (IEA, 2015, 86). Foreign investment is therefore set to remain low, and Sonatrach is likely to see its capital expenditure constrained by low oil prices, meaning that any further sharp increase in LNG exports is unlikely, despite the addition of a new plant in 2014. Indeed output fell by a further 4 per cent in 2015. Meanwhile Libya's LNG plant, which was damaged during the civil war in 2011, has been offline ever since and there is no imminent sign of it returning to production.[177]

Another existing producer, Nigeria, offers the possibility of additional LNG output based on its gas reserves (which are the ninth largest in the world). However, while LNG exports increased in 2014 and 2015 after a number of disappointing years, above-ground risks in the country appear to limit the prospects for further growth. Poor governance and an uncertain legislative and judicial system do not encourage foreign investment, especially in a low commodity price environment. Overall gas production is expected to be stagnant to 2020, and LNG exports will most likely remain stable or decline slightly.

The main potential for growth in Africa's LNG output is in Angola, where Chevron brought a 5 mtpa scheme online in 2013, but then shut it down for major repairs in early 2014 following serious operational issues.

---

[175] 'BG Group says natural gas operations in Egypt remain at risk', *The Financial Times*, 31 July 2014.

[176] 'Gas find promises sea change in the Med', *The Financial Times*, 6 September 2015.

[177] EIA Libya Country Review, 25 November 2014. (Sourced on 18 September 2015 at www.eia.gov/beta/international/analysis.cfm?iso=LBY.)

However, as the project does not have any long-term contracts in place, it is unclear exactly how soon output can reach design capacity of 5.2 mtpa, given low prices and increasing competition in the LNG market. Indeed in 2015 the plant remained closed, and is only expected to re-open in mid-2016, at which point Chevron will clearly be keen to start generating cash flow from the project.[178]

Output from Equatorial Guinea has been much more stable, with all the country's exports being purchased by BG under a 17-year contract that started in 2007; the government has suggested that the country's gas resources could justify construction of a second liquefaction plant.[179] This project, called Fortuna, is operated by Ophir, and is planned to be a FLNG project. Total capacity is planned to be 2.2 mtpa using a vessel built by Golar, and a FID may be take in 2016 if market conditions do not undermine the project's economic viability.[180]

Meanwhile FID was taken in 2015 for a new FLNG scheme in Cameroon, developed by Perenco and Golar to liquefy gas produced by GDF Suez and the Cameroon state oil and gas company SNH. The 1.2 mtpa plant is expected to commence operations in 2017, based on the timetable agreed by the project partners.[181] The FLNG scheme will be operated on a tolling basis, with the upstream producers supplying the gas from the offshore Kribi field, which contains approximately 500 bcf (14 bcm) of proved reserves. The relatively small size of the upstream asset means that the project is only expected to have an eight year timescale, although the liquefaction facility will have two extra trains which could increase output if additional gas reserves are discovered over the next few years. However, the difficult operating and business environment in Cameroon raises concerns about the future of the scheme. While the final tolling agreement was signed by the end of 2015, and the FLNG ship is under construction in a Singapore shipyard, the possibility of delay must remain.[182]

---

[178] 'Angola LNG company returns to production in June 2016', *Hellenic Shipping News*, 18 March 2016.

[179] 'Equatorial Guinea discoveries advance LNG expansion plans', *Petroleum Economist*, 4 January 2013.

[180] 'Fortuna LNG nears FID with new partner lined up', Natural Gas Europe, 25 January 2016.

[181] 'Golar and Perenco agree the material commercial terms for the floating liquefied natural gas export project in Cameroon', Golar LNG Press Release, 30 June 2015.

[182] 'Cameroon eyes floating LNG plant', *The Economist*, 9 October 2014.

Latin America

Trinidad and Tobago is Latin America's largest LNG exporter, but the Atlantic LNG consortium faces the problem of a continuing decline in the country's gas reserves, which has been reflected in a 10 per cent fall in LNG output in 2015. The future of Trinidad's LNG output is likely to depend upon international companies investing in upstream projects, and in turn this will rely on agreement being reached with Venezuela over the development of resources located between the two countries.[183] Active discussions are ongoing, but until this issue is resolved, it is difficult to forecast any return to historic output levels, let alone further growth in the country's gas business. Meanwhile, in Peru, the potential for increasing gas production and the planned construction of new pipeline infrastructure have encouraged discussion of a second plant in the country, either as an expansion of the existing 4.5 mtpa scheme or located at a new energy complex on the southern coast.

Interestingly, four possible new LNG projects are located in Latin America, although there is some significant doubt attached to the outlook for all of them. The most concrete plan to date had appeared to be in Colombia, where Pacific Rubiales Energy announced a plan in 2011 to monetize its stranded gas asset at La Creciente in the north of the country using a floating liquefaction scheme.[184] EXMAR was contracted to build a $180 million liquefaction, regasification and storage vessel, as well as an $80 million storage barge, for delivery in the first half of 2015, with a plan to supply small-scale LNG to buyers in the Caribbean and Central America. However, lack of demand meant that this strategy was converted into a 4 year sales agreement with Gazprom, signed in December 2014, to supply all 0.5 mtpa of the project's output to the Russian company's trading subsidiary.[185] Then in early 2015, Pacific Rubiales announced the postponement of the entire project, citing unfavourable market conditions; it now appears to be looking for alternative uses for the EXMAR facilities, as it began capacity payments for the vessel in June 2015.[186]

Venezuela and Brazil have also discussed LNG exports in the past but now seem focused on satisfying domestic demand. Although the former sits on potentially large gas reserves, it continues to import gas from Colombia.

---

[183] 'LNG breadbasket Trinidad and Tobago facing production challenges', Natural Gas Intelligence, 26 June 2015.
[184] 'Pacific Rubiales' LNG project in Colombia delayed: Partner', Platts, 30 January 2015.
[185] 'Pacific Rubiales delays Colombia FLNG export project', ICIS, 29 January 2015.
[186] 'Pacific Rubiales says impossible to predict Colombia LNG start-up', Reuters, 2 February 2015.

Any gas discoveries, such as the recently developed Perla field, will likely be directed towards the domestic market before exports are considered.[187] Meanwhile Brazil has also reined in its gas export ambitions due to a combination of growing domestic demand and the impact of US shale on the global gas market. Previously conceived FLNG plans for deepwater fields are now looking commercially unviable and politically unacceptable.[188]

Although Mexico is a significant net importer of gas, both via pipeline from the USA and also via LNG, the country is also now exploring the possibility of becoming an LNG exporter, taking advantage of both its own gas production and also the growing shale gas output in the southern states of the USA. A number of companies have been assessing the possibility of building liquefaction facilities close to existing regasification plants on the west coast of the country, in order to take advantage of the relatively short journey time to Asia. Sempra, for example, has proposed a potential 2 mtpa plant at Costa Azul in partnership with Pemex,[189] while Houston-based DKRW has suggested a 4 mtpa facility in Sonoma, a state in the north-west of Mexico connected to the US pipeline system.[190] Mexican state company Pemex is also considering a project in the south-west of the country near Salina Cruz, but this potential floating LNG scheme would use domestically produced gas transported across from the Gulf of Mexico. However, all these projects are likely to be delayed by access to gas issues, in particular because domestic demand needs to be satisfied and the pipeline network needs to be extended.[191] As a result, although the country's LNG import terminals do offer the potential to become export facilities, this is unlikely to occur before the mid-2020s despite Pemex's enthusiasm.

Asia

In Asia, Malaysia has been the region's second-largest LNG supplier (after Australia), with 25 mt of output. However, in common with a number of other gas producers in the region, Malaysia is currently experiencing high levels of gas demand growth combined with stagnant gas production, with the result that the level of future export sales is in doubt. Petronas, the state energy company, is developing new liquefaction capacity, with one FLNG plant coming online in 2016 and another scheduled for 2020, while an expansion of the existing Bintulu plant is also under way. This could expand

---

[187] 'Venezuelan LNG on hold as Perla field production begins', ICIS, 8 July 2015.
[188] 'Brazilian natural gas demand rises 12.5 per cent year-to-date', Platts, 25 September 2014.
[189] 'Sempra joins Pemex for first gas export terminal in Mexico', Bloomberg, 19 February 2015.
[190] 'Developers mull Mexican LNG export projects', ICIS, 14 July 2014.
[191] 'Mexican LNG exports will not come soon', Platts, 7 October 2014.

overall capacity by over 5 mtpa by the end of the decade, but on the same timescale the construction of new regasification terminals to increase imports could offset any possible increase in net exports.

Indonesia is encountering similar issues, with production having fallen from a high of 86 bcm in 2010 to 73 bcm in 2014 while domestic demand is increasing due to economic growth and subsidized prices. Furthermore, the domestic market is favoured over exports, with producers required to sell at least 25 per cent of their output to local consumers. Meanwhile some of the country's older liquefaction capacity is being shut down, with the Arun export plant sending out its last cargo in October 2014. Some new liquefaction plants have been built at Donggi-Senoro and Sengkang, with the first coming online in 2015, which helped to catalyse a rebound in LNG sales during the year, but nevertheless it would appear that the overall outlook for Indonesian LNG supply is one of decline.

Of the remaining Pacific Basin producers, output from Brunei is also declining in the face of rising domestic demand and changes to a number of its export contracts – in particular, reduced offtake from Japan. Although Brunei is looking for new short-term contracts, and did see a rebound in LNG sales in 2015, it seems likely that exports will continue to be constrained by domestic needs and that LNG output will continue its downward trend.

On a more positive note, production from ExxonMobil's new PNG LNG facility in Papua New Guinea began in 2014, with full output being reached in 2015 when the second train came online. Further expansion is also being discussed, with government agreement for a third train and plans for a FID set for 2017. In addition Total has now been appointed to run a new LNG scheme in the country called Elk-Antelope, which could be a separate two train project or could be tied into the existing ExxonMobil site.

Conclusions

The LNG industry is set to experience an unprecedented surge in output that was triggered by high prices and a consequent surge in FIDs for new projects in the 2010–14 period. As a result, although oil and gas prices have since fallen sharply, approximately 150 mt of new LNG capacity will come online between 2015 and 2020. The main countries involved in this growth will be Australia and the USA, which will become the first and third ranked LNG producers in the world by the end of this decade. New production will also be likely to arrive from Russia in the form of Yamal LNG, although other projects here and in another potential growth area, Eastern Africa, are likely to be deferred. Nevertheless, global LNG production will increase by 50 per cent over the next five years.

Some of this growth will be offset by declines among existing producers. Domestic demand growth in Malaysia and Indonesia will see net exports fall, while a similar theme can be seen in the Middle East, where Oman and Abu Dhabi are starting to import gas to supplement their own production. In North Africa rising gas demand, encouraged by subsidized prices, is also affecting exports from Algeria, while the volatile politics of the region is further undermining the ability of operators to maintain LNG exports, with Libya and Egypt having had to shut down their export facilities altogether. Meanwhile Yemen has had to declare force majeure on its LNG exports due to the civil war in the country, while other countries such as Trinidad & Tobago are just experiencing natural declines in output after many years of production.

Within this volatile picture, the stability of Qatar remains a constant, with the country having introduced an output moratorium of 77 mtpa in 2005 and seemingly having no plans to alter its position in the foreseeable future. The country's low cost of production, estimated at below $2/MMBtu, means that it is one of the few suppliers relatively unaffected by the low prices seen in 2015, and it is set to remain a core producer for many years to come.

However, for many of the existing and expanding producers discussed in this chapter, the fall in the oil price, and the consequent reduction in LNG prices, has had a profound impact. Even US projects, which have been the basis for the introduction of a new market-based pricing methodology linked to the Henry Hub price, have found their economic advantage undermined by a low oil price, as the total cost of LNG delivered to Europe or Asia is now above the prices being paid in the markets under existing long-term contracts or on the sport market. As a result, although five US projects with 64 mtpa of capacity have been approved and are under construction, the owners of the LNG output face the prospect of having to sell it at prices that may only cover short-run marginal costs, at least in the short term. This suggests that the pace of development in the USA, which can be judged by applications for the more expensive FERC approval, may well slow over the next few years until prices return to a level which can underpin the long-term marginal cost of US LNG (approximately $8–9/MMBtu in Europe and $10–11/MMBtu in Asia).

The high cost of new projects in Australia means that the low-price environment will also hurt project sponsors, but again the output from seven new schemes recently in production or currently under construction will inevitably arrive on the global gas market before 2020. Indeed, cargoes from two coal seam gas projects had already started by the end of 2015, while a third has commenced in the first quarter of 2016, at the same time as the first train of the offshore Gorgon project in the north-west of the country started. The consequent ramp up in production will only add to the global oversupply, while also affecting prices in the domestic market. A key question will be whether any new projects will follow, once the current surge in output has ended. The analysis in this chapter suggests that the new plateau of 86 mtpa may well be the limit of Australian output for some years, although the potential for brownfield expansion is evident in many of the projects under construction. Although it is not possible to predict which are likely to proceed, we estimate that there is upside potential for a further 20 mtpa of capacity to be approved by 2020, if the price environment improves, meaning that total Australian capacity could exceed 100 mtpa by 2025.

However, for other producers with ambition to grow, the outlook is not so positive. Over the past few years eight new projects have been discussed in Russia (including one brownfield expansion), but a combination of high costs, uncertainty over sources of supply, the impact of sanctions, and reduced availability of investment funds means that many of these have now been delayed or effectively cancelled. Indeed only one, Novatek's Yamal LNG project, is likely to be online by 2020, while in our base case scenario two others (a third train at the existing Sakhalin 2 project plus Baltic LNG), may be operational by 2025. This would take Russia's overall LNG output to just over 40 mtpa. However, it now appears that other projects, such as Shtokman and Vladivostok LNG, will be postponed until the end of the decade at least. One other notable aspect of Russia's LNG future is that Gazprom is unlikely to dominate as it does with pipeline exports, and it is conceivable that Novatek could become, and remain, the country's major participant in the LNG market, if it can finally get full financing for its Yamal project.

In Eastern Africa, where discoveries in Mozambique and Tanzania have created the potential for major LNG developments, progress has slowed not only due to market conditions but also because of the difficulties inherent in establishing the regulatory, legislative, and operational foundations for major investments in countries with a limited hydrocarbon industry. The upside potential in both countries is clear, but the need to resolve issues such as local content, domestic gas market development, and logistical support for major industrial developments, as well as the more fundamental tax and governance regimes, has meant that delays have been inevitable. We see no prospect of LNG production before 2020, but believe that the ENI and Anadarko projects in Mozambique could produce a total of 32.5 mtpa by the end of the next decade, while output in Tanzania could reach 15 mtpa on the same timescale. However, we also acknowledge that in a downside low-price environment, Tanzania could fail to develop an LNG export business altogether, while Mozambique's output could be limited to 10–15 mtpa.

Canada is another country facing the possibility of its LNG ambitions being severely limited by market conditions and domestic issues. Although theoretically 350 mtpa of new capacity has been mooted, no project has yet taken a FID, highlighting the contrast with the situation in the USA. A major stumbling block is cost, as all the Canadian projects would be new greenfield schemes, as opposed to the brownfield conversions that account for many of the US projects. In addition, the projects on the west coast of Canada will rely on gas being brought 1,500 km through the Rockies by pipeline, across territory where negotiation with the indigenous First Nations population can be lengthy and expensive. On the east coast, meanwhile, the gas supply would come mainly from the USA, implying both infrastructure issues in the north-western US states as well as regulatory hurdles to be crossed with the US authorities. Furthermore, project developers have been seeking to sign oil-linked relatively high-priced contracts with consumers who are now keener to use market-based mechanisms; this means that no projects have yet secured adequate sales contracts to move ahead. The overall conclusion is that Canada has missed the short-term LNG window and that we will not see any cargoes from projects there until well into the 2020s.

Beyond the countries discussed in detail in this chapter, a few other potentially large new sources of LNG are emerging. The ending of sanctions against Iran, which contains the world's largest gas reserves, has led to a flurry of excitement about the rekindling of LNG plans at the giant South Pars field. To date Iran's gas has been used domestically or has been reinjected to sustain oil production, but if a number of IOCs can be tempted back and encouraged to invest, then gas exports are certainly feasible. However, current interest appears to be more focused on regional markets that can be accessed via pipeline, and it may therefore be some time before LNG exports are approved. Furthermore, continued uncertainty over the future of Iran's relationship with the west may undermine IOC confidence in making billion dollar investments in new long-term gas projects when shorter-term returns may be made from refurbishing the country's oil industry.

Elsewhere, politics will also have a significant role to play in the possible development of LNG in the East Mediterranean, where discoveries offshore Israel and Cyprus could underpin the construction of a liquefaction plant. However, numerous issues remain – not the least being the impact of the conflict in Syria – but also the difficult decision of where to locate the plant, the potential for using under-utilized facilities in Egypt, the option of piping gas to Jordan or Turkey, and the need to satisfy the domestic markets in both countries. Again, both above and below ground risks have been exacerbated by the gas market conditions in 2015, meaning that rapid development of an LNG project is unlikely.

Overall, the outlook for new FIDs for LNG projects beyond the current schemes under construction looks relatively bleak and it is easy to see why the analogy of a classic commodity business 'boom–bust' cycle has become prevalent in the industry. It is difficult to see how new projects will be able to justify committing to major investments, or how they will persuade banks to back them with project financing, until the current oversupply situation has unwound. Given uncertainties over demand both in Asia and Europe it is impossible to forecast when this might occur, undermining any attempt to forecast which projects may move ahead next. However, some clues may be found in the ownership structures of proposed projects, as consumers (especially from Asia) are taking an increasing role as upstream and midstream partners. As global demand and supply for gas starts to move back into balance (perhaps by the end of this decade) it may be these projects which have a greater chance of securing customers and will thus be able to move ahead most quickly.

Another trend which is emerging, especially in the USA, is the presence of aggregators as either owners of projects or as purchasers of LNG on a tolling basis, based on gas priced on a market basis. As companies purchase gas for their LNG portfolio, rather than for a specific customer, so the marketing of LNG may become more short-term as sellers search for the best spot market options in markets across the world, rather than regional long-term contracts. Furthermore, optimization of portfolios by IOCs with projects in different regions and with different, and changing, cost bases will also influence the timing of new developments. Indeed distance to market may become less relevant to specific project economics if companies can increasingly swap cargoes between regions and re-arrange deliveries with customers and other suppliers.

In the end, though, the fundamental principles of LNG economics will ultimately be the cornerstone of the future development of the industry. Brownfield expansion is likely to be preferred over greenfield development, thanks to the lower cost brought by synergy benefits. Developments in countries with stable fiscal and regulatory regimes will be preferred over those associated with significant political and fiscal risk. Access to low-cost sources of gas will remain vital, as will the size of the reserve base, while existing industrial infrastructure with high quality local contractors will remain an advantage. All this points towards countries with existing projects being at an advantage when it comes to the next stage of LNG development post-2020. However, this does not mean that new regions cannot emerge and prosper. It does mean, though, that in order to succeed, governments will have to ensure that they offer terms that allow companies to make adequate returns in a very competitive global gas, and energy, market, and also that they put in place secure regulatory regimes that encourage multi-billion dollar long-term investment. Again, this may suggest that the prospects for politically and commercially volatile areas such as Africa, the Middle East, and Latin America have been significantly undermined by the current collapse in energy prices, meaning that brownfield expansion of existing projects in more stable areas is the most likely source of new LNG capacity once the current oversupply situation has started to dissipate.

BIBLIOGRAPHY

BP (2015). *BP Statistical Review of World Energy 2015*, London: BP.

Cassidy, N. and Kosev, M. (2015). 'Australia and the Global LNG Market', Reserve Bank of Australia Bulletin, March Quarter, 2015.

CIP (2013). 'Pande Temane gas exports to South Africa', Centro de Integridade Publica Mocambique, Edition 17/2013. www.cip.org.mz/cipdoc/274_Pande%20Temane%20Gas%20exports%20to%20South%20Africa%20by%20Sasol.pdf.

Corbeau, A.-S., Braaksma, A., Hussin, F., Yagoto, Y., and Yamamoto, T. (2014). *The Asian Quest for LNG in a Globalising Market*, IEA Partner Country Series, Paris: OECD/IEA. http://www.iea.org/publications/freepublications/publication/PartnerCountrySeriesTheAsianQuestforLNGinaGlobalisingMarket.pdf. Deloitte (2016). *Oil and gas taxation in Tanzania*, Deloitte Taxation and Investment Guide, January 2016. https://www2.deloitte.com/content/dam/Deloitte/global/Documents/Energy-and-Resources/gx-er-oil-and-gas-tax-guide-tanzania.pdf.

Demierre, J., Bazilian, M., Carbajal, J., Sherpa, S., and Modi, V. (2014). 'Potential for regional use of East Africa's natural gas', Briefing Paper, Columbia Center on Global Energy Policy. http://energypolicy.columbia.edu/sites/default/files/energy/Potential-for-Regional-Use-of-East-Africas-Natural-Gas-SEL-SDSN.pdf.

Ellis, M., Heyning, C., and Legrand, O. (2013). 'Extending the LNG Boom: Improving Australian LNG productivity and competitiveness', Oil & Gas and Capital Productivity Practices, McKinsey & Company, May.

Fattouh, B., Rogers, H., and Steward, P. (2015). 'The US shale gas revolution and its impact on Qatar's position in gas markets', Center on Global Energy Policy Working Paper, Columbia SIPA, March. http://energypolicy.columbia.edu/sites/default/files/energy/The%20US%20Shale%20Gas%20Revolution%20and%20Its%20Impact%20on%20Qatar%27s%20Position%20in%20Gas%20Markets_March%202015.pdf.

Frühauf, A. (2014). 'Mozambique's LNG revolution – A political risk outlook for the Rovuma LNG ventures', OIES Working Paper NG 86, Oxford Institute for Energy Studies, April. https://www.oxfordenergy.org/wpcms/wp-content/uploads/2014/04/NG-86.pdf.

Gomes, I. (2015). 'Natural Gas in Canada: what are the options going forward?', OIES Working Paper NG 98, Oxford Institute for Energy Studies. https://www.oxfordenergy.org/2015/05/natural-gas-in-canada-what-are-the-options-going-forward/.

Honoré, A. (2014). 'The Outlook for Natural Gas Demand in Europe', OIES Working Paper NG 87, Oxford Institute for Energy Studies, June. https://www.oxfordenergy.org/publications/the-outlook-for-natural-gas-demand-in-europe/.

ICFI (2012). 'The Future of Natural Gas in Mozambique: Towards a Gas Master Plan', Report by ICF International for The World Bank and Government of Mozambique Steering Committee, 20 December.

IEA (2015). *Medium-Term Gas Market Report: Market Analysis and Forecasts to 2020*, OECD/International Energy Agency.

IGU (2015). *Wholesale Gas Price Survey – 2015 Edition: a global review of price formation mechanisms 2005–2014*, International Gas Union. www.igu.org/sites/default/files/node-page-field_file/IGU%20Whole%20Sale%20Gas%20Price%20Survey%20Report%20%202015%20Edition.pdf.

Ledesma, D. (2013). 'East Africa Gas – Potential for Export', OIES Working Paper NG 74, Oxford Institute for Energy Studies. www.oxfordenergy.org/2013/03/east-africa-gas-the-potential-for-export/.

Ledesma, D., Henderson, J., and Palmer, N. (2014). 'The Future of Australian LNG Exports: will domestic challenges limit the development of future LNG export capacity?', OIES Working Paper NG 90, Oxford Institute for Energy Studies, September. www.oxfordenergy.org/wpcms/wp-content/uploads/2014/09/NG-90.pdf.

Mitrova, T. (2013). 'Russian LNG: The Long Road to Export', IFRI, Paris.

Songhurst, B. (2014). 'LNG Plant Coast Escalation', OIES Working Paper NG 83, Oxford Institute for Energy Studies, February. www.oxfordenergy.org/wpcms/wp-content/uploads/2014/02/NG-83.pdf.

CHAPTER 6

LNG DEMAND POTENTIAL

Anouk Honoré, Howard Rogers, Sylvie D'Apote, and Anne-Sophie Corbeau

Introduction

The year 2015 marks a turning point for LNG markets. First, after three years of being flat, LNG trade picked up again by 2.5 per cent. The main issue over 2011–14 was not a lack of demand but supply constraints: existing suppliers such as Yemen and Egypt stopped producing and others, such as Indonesia, saw a drop in their LNG exports. But LNG supply rebounded in 2015 on the back of new liquefaction plants coming online (Chapter 2 and Chapter 5). Second, 2015 marks the entry of three new LNG importers (Egypt, Jordan, and Pakistan): all three faced acute gas shortages, opted for FSRUs, and had to resort to tenders and spot markets to source the bulk of their supplies. Egypt is the first African country to import LNG, potentially starting a new trend in a region which has been, so far, an important gas exporter to Europe, but has never imported from other regions. Third, the three largest LNG markets – Japan, Korea, and China –stumbled as their LNG demand dropped.[1] While this was expected in Japan – nuclear generation was at zero and could not possibly become negative to make more room for LNG – it was more surprising for Korea and China, where a combination of lower economic growth, restart of nuclear, and strong competitiveness of coal impacted natural gas demand. These changes underline a more worrying trend that Asian LNG demand may not be as strong as expected, or that these markets might need a set of special conditions to attract more LNG. Finally, some LNG moved back to Europe. A rebound in the region's consumption, together with a further decline in production, created a higher call on imports. This left enough room for an increase in both pipeline and LNG imports, without creating a suppliers' war between Russia and LNG exporters.

Are these signs a taste of things to come? Demand for LNG is the result of a delicate balance involving not only an understanding of the primary energy mix of the various regions (including the role devoted to natural

---

[1] There is some inconsistency in respect of data on Chinese LNG demand in 2015. Some sources report an increase.

gas) but also of the way in which LNG imposes itself in the gas supply mix, both on top of domestic production and in competition with pipeline gas supplies. In many regions, pipeline gas takes a back seat and the main factor is the evolution of domestic gas production and the opportunity to develop indigenous gas resources, against importing LNG.

- Will LNG demand from mature LNG markets – Japan, Korea, and Taiwan – continue on a declining trend?

- Will an increasing number of developing countries become LNG importers? For example, LNG demand from MENA (Middle East and North Africa) countries multiplied by a factor of 2.5 in 2015, rising to 4 per cent of total LNG trade, and is set to increase further as more countries look at LNG imports to meet their growing needs. LNG demand in south-east Asia (including Pakistan) has reached similar levels in 2015. Such a trend is also present in Latin America. The main issues on the demand side are the competitiveness of gas against (domestic) fuels, notably coal and renewables, and affordability.

- And finally how will Europe and China accommodate LNG imports along with pipeline imports from incumbent suppliers.

This chapter investigates potential LNG demand in five key regions: 1) Europe, 2) the mature Asian markets, 3) new and developing Asian markets, 4) Latin America, and 5) the Middle East and North Africa.

What role for Europe in the global LNG market?

Europe[2] is acting as the swing market for LNG, and as a result the region is expected to help absorb the LNG surplus coming on to the market in the second half of the 2010s and early 2020s. But the region is facing major uncertainties. The future role of natural gas in the whole energy system is a question mark, primarily as a result of greater governmental support for renewables. Nonetheless, with declining indigenous production, the region will see its imports rise, but by when, by how much, and from which sources is still unclear. The scenarios on gas supply and demand balances for the region

---

[2] Unless otherwise stated, the term 'Europe' in this section applies to a region which encompasses 35 countries: EU28 + Albania, Bosnia and Herzegovina, Macedonia, Norway, Serbia, Switzerland, and Turkey. Due to availability of data, some statistics may apply to different groups of countries representing Europe; details will be given where appropriate.

show a very wide range of possibilities, which makes it difficult to interpret the consequences for the LNG market. This section focuses on the regional gas market fundamentals and the repercussions for LNG at the 2030 horizon.

Europe as the residual market for LNG

In 2015, the European market(s) represented 15.3 per cent of the global LNG market.[3] Eleven countries imported 51 bcm of LNG: Belgium, France, Greece, Italy, Lithuania, the Netherlands, Poland, Portugal, Spain, Turkey, and the UK.[4] Volumes imported to the region vary greatly from one year to another as seen in Figure 6.1. Imports of LNG halved between

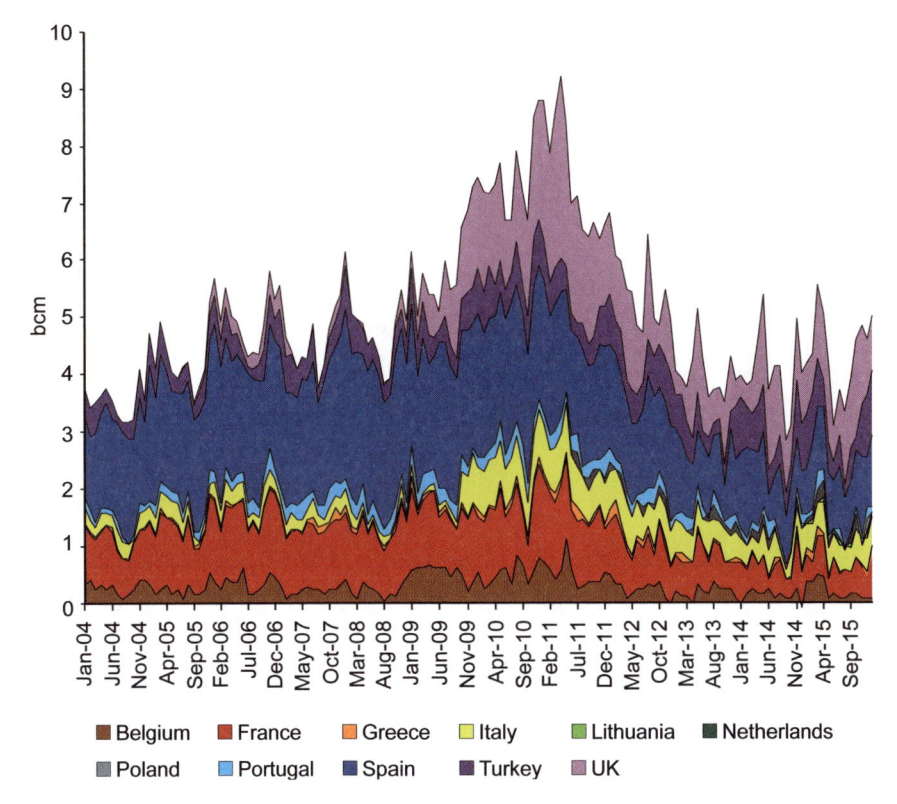

Figure 6.1: European LNG imports per month by country of destination, 2004–16 (bcm)

Source: Platts LNG database

---

[3] Down from its highest point of 29.4% in 2010. GIIGNL (2016, 20).
[4] Not including small-scale LNG. For more details on this issue, see 'Small Scale LNG Map', Gas Infrastructure Europe website (www.gie.eu/index.php/maps-data/gle-sslng-map).

310 *LNG Markets in Transition*

2011 and 2014[5] following the Fukushima disaster, making Europe a residual market for the volumes Asian countries did not need. By end-2014 cargoes had begun to return, as a consequence of lower demand in Asia and of the redirection of Qatari volumes. The level of re-export was still high, with reloading reaching 8.2 bcm in 2014 and 3.6 bcm in 2015.[6]

The total regasification capacity in these countries was 210 bcm in 2015,[7] which represented a rate of utilization of about 24 per cent on average – although important differences exist from one country to another. This means that theoretically, the region could receive about 160 bcm of additional LNG just with the existing capacity. However, about 36 per cent

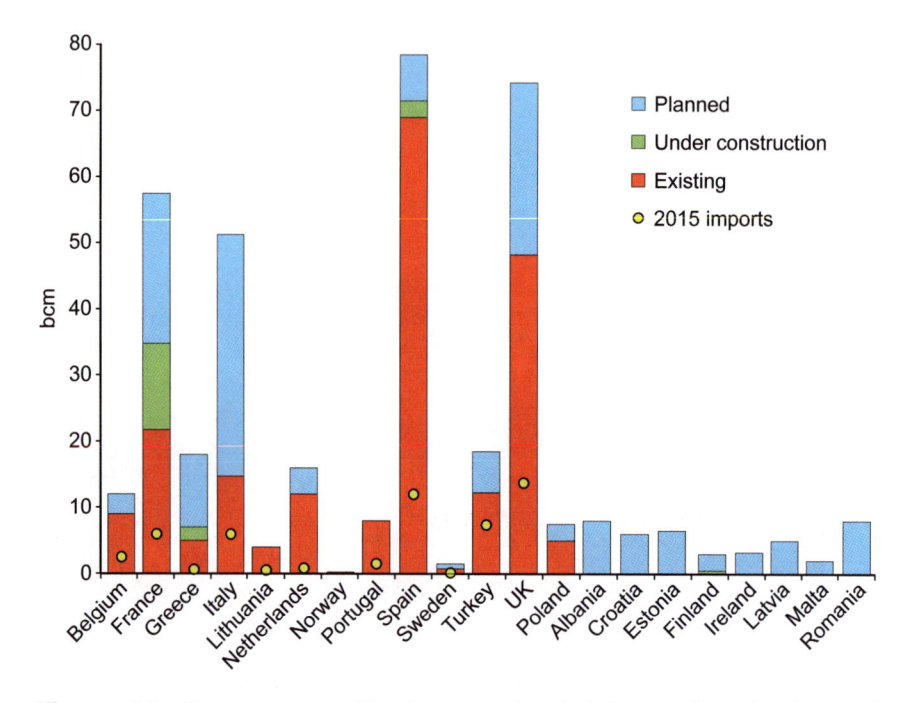

Figure 6.2: European regasification capacity (existing and projects) as of 31 December 2015 vs LNG imports in 2015 (bcm)

Note: Poland started importing in December 2015 but GIIGNL (2016) does not provide any data.

Source: GLE – Gas LNG Europe (2015), GIIGNL (2016), and author's updates.

---

[5] LNG imports to Europe declined from 87.2 bcm in 2011 to 43.6 bcm in 2014. Source: GIIGNL data.

[6] Reloads were concentrated in Spain: 5.2 bcm in 2014 and 1.2 bcm in 2015. The national gas market is over contracted and has limited pipeline interconnections with the rest of Europe. Source of data: GIIGNL (2016, 21).

[7] GIIGNL (2016, 31) and author's update (Polish terminal added).

of this unused capacity was located in Spain alone, a country with limited pipeline interconnections with the rest of Europe, and 22 per cent in the UK, also a relatively isolated market (compared with other countries in north-west Europe). Notwithstanding this low utilization rate, as of April 2016, additional terminals were under construction (18 bcm) or planned (171 bcm) across Europe as seen in Figure 6.2.[8] Despite this apparent keen interest for LNG, the fundamentals of the gas industry in the region are complicated and it is difficult to predict how much LNG will be needed in Europe at the 2030 horizon.

Unknown pace and scale of the region's production decline

Indigenous production represented 250 bcm, or just about 50 per cent of the regional gas needs in 2014 (IEA, 2015e; author's estimates for non OECD markets), but the trend is downward everywhere apart from Norway. However, even for this country, the most likely scenario shows a plateau followed by (gradual) decline post-2020 (Norway, 2015, 13). In a low energy price environment, it is difficult to envisage more optimistic scenarios. A major challenge for the region will be to foresee as accurately as possible the pace and the scale of this decline, in order to secure the adequate level of imports (and build the necessary infrastructure whether pipeline, LNG, interconnections, and/or storage).

Three countries accounted for 86 per cent of the total: Norway, the Netherlands, and the UK. The first two export part of their output while the UK is a net importer with a production that declines slowly in the late 2010s before a sharper deterioration post 2020 (DECC, 2016). The major unknown comes from the Netherlands. Following fears of earth tremors in the Groningen province, total production from the field was capped in 2014 and 2015, with the latest revision setting the maximum production at 30 bcm for 2015[9] (and even 27 bcm for the gas year 2015/16[10]), a sharp drop compared to the output of nearly 54 bcm in 2013.[11] Uncertainties prevail as to future limits. With smaller fields also in decline, the question is how quickly the production will drop. This more rapid rate of decline will have a major impact, not only on the country itself but also on north-west Europe as a whole, with repercussions on import needs that have already started to be felt. As of 2015, the author expects total European (conventional)

---

[8] See Map 2.1 European LNG terminals, page 50.
[9] Platts 'International Gas Report' Journal, 29 June 2015, 'Dutch cut Groningen to 30 bcm'.
[10] Argus News and Analysis, 18 December 2015, 'Groningen cap kept at 27bn m³ for 2015/16 gas year'.
[11] 'Natural gas production reduced and funds earmarked for Groningen', Government of Netherlands, 17 January 2014.

production to decline by 25 bcm in 2020 (compared with 2015) and 89–117 bcm (about 41 per cent) by 2030.[12] In addition to total volumes, Europe is also going to lose the sources of flexibility which had been provided by some of the UKCS and Dutch fields.

There is major interest in the development of unconventional gas reserves, but no serious research sees any output of magnitude in Europe in our timeframe. The only country which has drilled enough wells to make some kind of judgement is Poland,[13] and the results have been disappointing with most of the majors leaving the country one after the other.[14] In the other countries, progress is even slower and most activity is at a very preliminary stage. Some countries have even imposed outright bans (or moratoria) on drilling and fracking.[15] In the European Union, unconventional gas production is expected to remain well below 20 bcm by 2035 (IEA, 2013, 118), which will have little impact on the major decline in conventional gas production (by 2030).

Green gas production is encouraged in many countries, and Europe already produces the equivalent of about 18 bcm of biogas – mostly in Germany.[16] Biogas production could increase to 28–40 bcm in 2020 (about 7 per cent of demand) according to national renewable energy plans[17] and maybe close to 50 bcm by 2030 (about 9 per cent of demand) (EurObserv'ER, 2015, 49). There are several problems around green gas, including the costs of production, but biogas is expected to be much more important for European gas supply than unconventional gas – and also to attract much less opposition.

Limited options for additional pipeline gas, apart from Russia

With indigenous gas production declining, Europe anticipates an increase of imports, but by how much, and from which sources, is unclear (and will depend on the level of demand). In 2015, most of the gas imported arrived

---

[12] The range of indigenous production in Europe is expected to be 213–239 bcm in 2020 and 133–161 bcm in 2030. Sources: National statistics and author's assumptions.

[13] About 70 wells had been drilled by mid-2015. Source: 'Polish shale gas exploration: the way forward', Shale Gas Information Platform, July 2015.

[14] Conoco Philips was the latest major to leave the country, after ExxonMobil, Chevron, Total, Talisman, and Marathon. Even the state controlled companies appear to have scaled back their activities. Source: 'Eastern European shale exploration on ice as boom turns to bust', *Financial Times*, 28 October 2015.

[15] Countries such as France, the Netherlands, Luxembourg, the Czech Republic, and Bulgaria. Source: IEA (2014, 82).

[16] Data for 2014, Source: EurObserv'ER (2015, 43–4).

[17] 'National Action Plans', European Commission. http://ec.europa.eu/energy/en/topics/renewable-energy/national-action-plans.

in the form of pipeline gas (87.7 per cent of total demand) while LNG represented only 12.3 per cent (for data on OECD Europe: IEA, 2015e).

The main exporter was Russia with 158 bcm of natural gas (physically) exported to Europe,[18] which represented 33 per cent of total demand. Following the various crises with Ukraine in 2006, 2009, and again – albeit for different reasons – in 2014[19] the European Union has been keen to look for ways to reduce its reliance on Russian gas. However, the possibilities of a rapid reduction are limited. Up to the mid-2020s, European companies are contractually obliged to import at least 115 bcm of Russian gas, a figure which reduces to around 80 bcm by 2030.[20]

Pipeline gas imports from other sources are not expected to increase substantially in the period considered:

- The long-standing European gas suppliers from North Africa (Algeria, Egypt, and Libya) have faced several problems post-2011 and their gas exports have shrunk from 56 bcm in 2011 to 46 bcm in 2014 (IEA, 2015b, 62–77). Despite large reserves in the three countries, difficulties in attracting investment in upstream, and meeting fast rising national gas demand, make gas export potential very uncertain. By 2020, no increase in exports from the region is envisaged, and the outlook for 2030 is also unpromising unless the 2015 gas discovery off the coast of Egypt is bigger than advertised and, even more importantly (and perhaps also more uncertain), is developed fast enough to feed both the national and the international markets.[21]

- In the East Mediterranean region, several gas discoveries made in 2009 offshore Israel and Cyprus have also sparked high expectations, but the development of the fields is complicated. A pipeline to Turkey would be politically difficult and expensive (albeit maybe possible by 2030) and a pipeline to Greece would be too long and technically complicated. Some exports of Israeli gas are possible (about 10 bcm) in the 2020s, probably via an FLNG option.[22]

---

[18] Gazprom data for 2015, Source: 'Delivery Statistics, Gas Supplies to Europe', Gazprom Export. www.gazpromexport.ru/en/statistics/.

[19] For more details on these crisis, see Stern (2006), Stern, Pirani, and Yafimava (2009), and Stern et al. (2014).

[20] For additional details on Russia's exports, see Stern et al. (2014), and Henderson and Mitrova (2015).

[21] The Zohr field was discovered by ENI in 2015. For additional details, see Chapter 5.

[22] Exports are critical to develop the Leviathan field as Israel's market is too small to make the project viable on its own, but this would require (regional) political stability and the timely development of the reserves. For additional details, see Chapter 5.

- Major gas pipeline projects, such as the Southern Gas Corridor, are also expected to play a big role in the diversification of European gas supplies, at least on paper, but the reality is complicated. Azerbaijan is most likely the only country to possibly increase pipeline exports to Europe before 2030, thanks to the development of Shah Deniz 1 & 2 and some other fields. It could offer a maximum of 24.4 bcm by 2020 (which would be split between Turkey and the rest of Europe), with a possible increase to 27 bcm post-2023. However, the 2015 restart of imports from Gazprom to fulfil its national demand (which includes oil field reinjection), suggests major problems of supply from old fields and cast doubt on potential export volumes to Europe.[23] The other potential sources of gas are also facing major challenges: Turkmenistan has large reserves but has important commitments towards China and it lacks a direct export route to reach Europe; Uzbekistan and Kazakhstan also have agreements with China; Iran, with its world-class reserves, is not expected to become a major gas exporter to Europe anytime soon (except from already existing exports to Turkey[24]) and nor is Iraqi Kurdistan (albeit maybe possible by 2030).

All in all, aside from Azerbaijan, some additional pipeline gas could be sourced from Central Asia and the Middle East, but the volumes are highly uncertain and probably post-2025, at best.

As a consequence, if Europe wants to reduce its imports of Russian gas, it appears that alternative sources for pipeline gas (both indigenous production and imports) are limited. This result means that LNG could play a greater role in the future, but exactly how much is difficult to grasp. This is because it is not only a question related to LNG itself, but to the future of natural gas demand in general, which is becoming more and more uncertain.

Security of gas demand in question ... and will it recover?

Natural gas is a significant contributor to the European energy supply, with a 22.4 per cent share of the total primary energy supply (TPES) in 2014.[25] After a fast and fairly continuous increase from the early 1970s, gas consumption remained relatively flat between 2005 and 2010 and, contrary

---

[23] 'Report: Gazprom starts gas supply to Azerbaijan', *Natural Gas Europe*, 1 October 2015.

[24] There may be LNG exports towards the end of the period. For more information on the Iranian market, see Hassanzadeh (2015).

[25] Data for OECD Europe in 2014, Source: IEA (2015b, IV.35).

to earlier scenarios,[26] gas demand fell in the early 2010s (between 2010 and 2014) to levels not seen since the late 1990s.[27] Most of the sectors have been hit by the combined effects of slow economic growth, improvements in efficiency measures, relatively high gas prices, and the development of renewable energy. However, the most impressive evolution happened in the power sector, which represented just 26 per cent of total gas consumed in 2014 as seen in Figure 6.3.[28] Total gas demand picked up again in 2015, mainly thanks to colder temperatures, and reached 494 bcm (IEA, 2015e; author's estimates for non OECD markets).

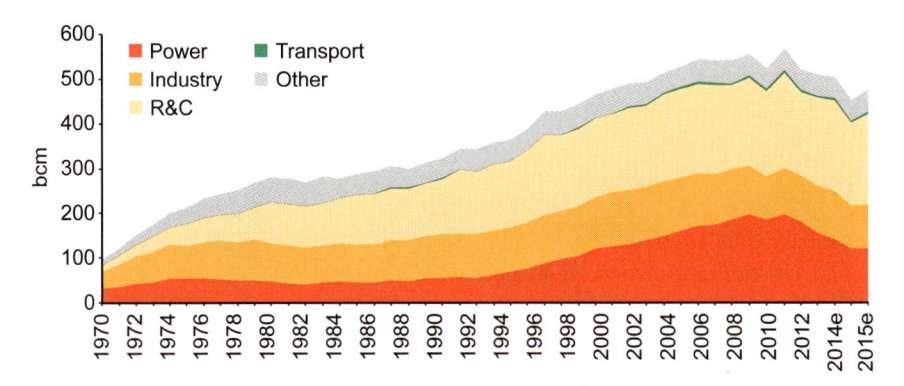

Figure 6.3: Natural gas demand in OECD Europe, by sectors, 1970–2015 (bcm)
Source: IEA (2015b) and previous annual reports.

In 1990s and the 2000s, natural gas was the fuel of choice for new power generation capacity in a liberalized market and was seen as the key driver for additional demand in the next two to three decades at least ... albeit with growing uncertainty in the 2000s and downward revisions of expectations as time passed by. In the first half of the 2010s, not only has gas demand for power generation declined faster than total gas consumption[29] but gas has also lost market share to other fuels. A combination of factors explain this:

---

[26] See IEA, annual series of the *World Energy Outlook*, for an example.
[27] For more details, see Honoré (2014).
[28] The power sector represented 26% of total gas demand in 2014 (35% in 2010), industry: 21% (18%), R&C: 41% (38%), transport: <1% (0.5%), others: 11% (9%). These are data for OECD Europe, sources: IEA (2015b) for 2010 data and author's estimate for 2014 data.
[29] Natural gas demand for power has declined faster than total consumption since 2010. In 2015, gas demand for the power sector was almost 40% below 2010 – equalling levels not seen since the late 1990s – while total demand declined by 16% over the same period. These are data for OECD Europe, sources: IEA (2015b) for 2010 data and author's estimate for 2015 data.

the economic slowdown has restricted power demand growth which, combined with the fast increase of renewable energy,[30] left little room for other fuels in the generation mix. A sharp drop of coal prices since 2011 made coal more competitive than gas,[31] a situation reinforced by the parallel decline of the price of carbon in the EU ETS.[32] From early 2012, spark spreads have been negative, or at least well below dark/clean dark spreads, in most European countries. Between 2010 and 2015, the share of natural gas in total generation dropped from 24 per cent to 16 per cent – not far from its share in 2000 (15.7 per cent) – while other shares remained relatively flat, with the exception of renewables whose share increased sharply (5 per cent to 13 per cent).[33]

With energy policies supporting renewables in the mix, will gas for power demand ever recover? This will depend on several – sometimes conflicting – factors.

- First of all, the continued policies aimed at improving energy efficiency mean that even with some GDP growth,[34] the effects on energy and power demand are likely to be flattened by these measures.[35]

- Second, renewable energy is expected to continue to rise (albeit at a slower pace than seen since the early 2000s due to the downward revision of support schemes across Europe), at least for new capacity. However, upgrades and better interconnections between countries will contribute to sustaining the role of renewables, in order to meet the EU 2020 and 2030 targets.

---

[30] Thanks to the support schemes put in place to reach the EU 2020 targets, more than 50% of the new generation capacity since 2000 has been in some form of renewable energy; this has near zero marginal costs, priority dispatch, and guaranteed access to the grid. Data Source: EWEA (2016, 7).

[31] In early January 2011, coal prices (CIF ARA) were $131/mt. In early January 2016, coal prices were $44.5/t. Source: Platts Power in Europe 10 January 2011 and 18 January 2016. For more information on coal, EU ETS, and gas prices in the early 2010s, see Honoré (2014).

[32] European Union Emissions Trading Scheme. The carbon price in the EU ETS has declined from above €25/t in 2008 to €5–8/t since 2013 (time of writing: March 2016).

[33] These are data for OECD Europe, sources: IEA (2015a) for 2010 data and author's estimate for 2015 data.

[34] GDP growth is not expected to be impressive in the period considered in this book, and forecasts in the early 2010s have been revised downwards several times. See International Monetary Fund, bi-annual World Economic Outlook reports for an example, https://www.imf.org/external/pubs/ft/weo/2016/update/01/.

[35] The EU energy savings expected thanks to the (non binding) 2020 targets will probably reach 17% (maybe as high as 18–19%) by 2020, mostly thanks to the impacts of the financial crisis –and will miss the 20% target by 1–2%. In 2014, the EU countries agreed on a new energy efficiency target post-2020 of 27% (or greater) by 2030.

- Third, the competitiveness of gas prices against coal prices is not expected to change dramatically over the period. This is because coal prices are expected to remain low, and the pricing of carbon within the EU ETS is unlikely to climb high enough to make a difference in the dispatch order, despite a series of measures envisaged by the European Commission.[36] The low(er) LNG prices expected in the second half of the 2010s and early 2020s (see Chapter 8) will create some demand in the power sector, but gas prices will need to drop to very low levels to start making a real difference in the regional mix. It is impossible to give a 'magic price' (of gas, coal, or EU ETS) at which coal-to-gas switching would start to happen in the whole region, due to the wide heterogeneity of the market.[37] As an illustration, in a market with spare capacity to be used and highly efficient gas and coal plants, at a gas price of $4/MMBtu and a coal price of 50 $/t, switching may happen at a carbon price of about 20 €/tCO$_2$ as seen in Figure 6.4.[38] Some coal-to-gas switching started to happen in winter 2015/16 in the UK. At that time, the UK carbon price floor (a national measure which comes on top of the EU ETS price and which reached £18 in April 2015[39]) finally had some impact on the relativity of the spark and clean dark spread in the country, with more gas being used in the system, and gas plants becoming more profitable than coal plants. The special characteristics of the market have also contributed to this change.[40] More limited switching also happened in other markets, such as France and Belgium (at peak times). There is a different story to tell for each country, but gas

---

[36] For more information on the EU ETS, see 'The EU Emissions Trading System (EU ETS)', Climate Action, European Commission. http://ec.europa.eu/clima/policies/ets/index_en.htm.

[37] This would depend on various factors including plant efficiencies, the type of plants in the market (combined cycles, combined heat and power, heat plants), the national mix, the available capacity and interconnections with other markets, and any measures affecting the relationship between these prices – such as the carbon price floor in the UK for instance. For more information on the gas/ coal/EU ETS price relationship and additional details at the national level in Europe, see Honoré (2014).

[38] With highly efficient gas plants and less efficient coal plants, switching may happen at a much lower carbon price (about €/5t CO$_2$). Source: author.

[39] For more information on the UK carbon price floor, see 'Carbon price floor: reform', Business tax – policy paper, UK Government. https://www.gov.uk/government/publications/carbon-price-floor-reform.

[40] These characteristics include the type of gas plants in the market (mostly CCGTs belonging to utilities which are more reactive to price changes), the closure of several GWs of coal capacity due to the LCPD, the still relatively low level of renewables (including hydro), and maybe even more importantly, the limited interconnections with the rest of the European system. Source: author.

prices would probably need to drop below $3.5/MMBtu in 2016 in western Europe before switching starts to happen (for baseload generation).

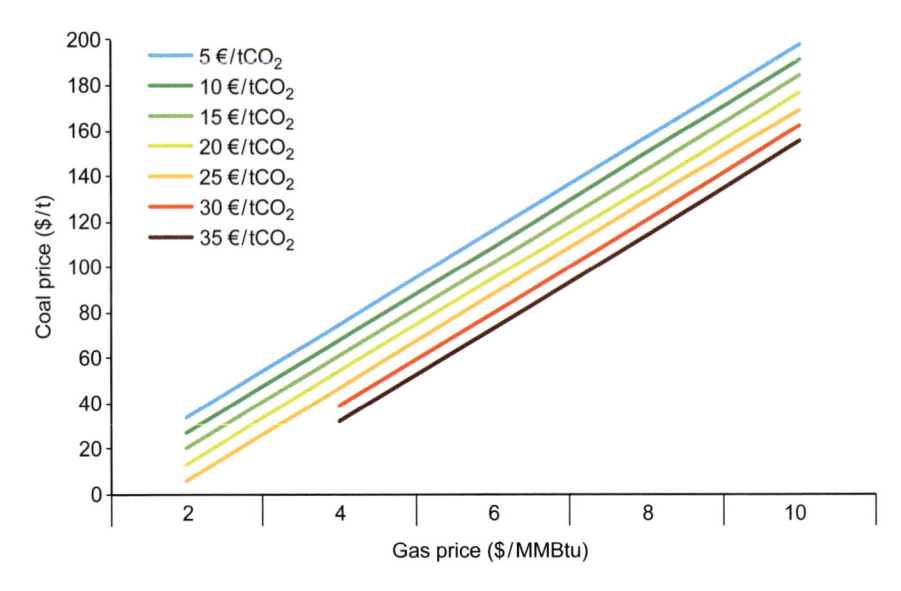

Figure 6.4: Relationship between gas prices ($/MMBtu), coal prices ($/mt), and EU ETS prices (€/tCO$_2$) in Europe in 2015
Source: Author.

The power sector lost about 75 bcm between 2010 and 2015, but even a theoretical scenario for 2016, such as a return to the level of competitiveness between coal and gas seen in 2010, would probably translate into 30–40 bcm of additional gas demand (10 bcm in the UK alone) due to the rise in renewable generation in the mix (because renewable generation is dispatched first, reducing the need for other types of generation), all other factors being equal.[41]

The factors mentioned above will not act in favour of more gas being used for power generation in Europe. However, one must also remember that 'all things will not remain equal' and some existing capacity will close down in the timeframe, due to old age and inefficiency.[42] Some plants have been pushed out of the system already, as a result of the Large Combustion

---

[41] This is for OECD Europe, Source: author's estimates.

[42] About 320 GW are older than 30 years, 60% of which are fossil fuelled (mostly coal and oil), but there are (in the UK for instance) also some old nuclear plants that may shut down. Source: author's assumption.

Plant Directive, or LCPD (around 55–60 GW by the end of 2015),[43] and some additional ones will also opt out of the Industrial Emissions Directive (IED) and will close down by the first half of the 2020s. Although it was too soon to tell at the time of writing, as many generators decided to include their plants in the National Transition Plans which gives them time to decide to invest or not to comply with the directive,[44] the IED will probably lead to the closure of between 50 and 100 GW. Finally, some nuclear capacity will shut down due to political decisions to either phase out nuclear or to decrease the role of nuclear in the mix.[45] The removal of this (large amount of firm) capacity will create a gap between the need for power generation and the capacity in place. Much will depend on how the gap is filled (and how big the gap is). The main unknown is whether gas will be able to play its role when the time comes. About 50 GW of gas-fired plants were closed down or mothballed in the first half of the 2010s[46] and very few new non-renewable plants have taken FID since the 2008/9 crisis – apart from Turkey.[47] If capacity mechanisms are put in place in an efficient and timely manner, then gas used for power starts to recover slowly post 2020, when much nuclear capacity gets retired and coal starts – hopefully – to decline in the mix.[48]

As for non-power sectors, the industry sector was also particularly hit by the 2008/9 economic crisis and the subsequent recession. This triggered some relocation in other regions, structural changes (a shift to less gas-intensive sectors), and technological improvements (less gas used in production process) as well as efficiency measures. Gas demand peaked in 2000 and fell by 15 per cent between 2000 and 2013,[49] while output rose by 2 per cent, a clear sign of energy savings improvements. There are few expectations of much additional gas consumption in this sector even with

---

[43] Data Source: author's estimates. For more details on the LCPD, see http://ec.europa.eu/environment/archives/industry/stationary/lcp/implementation.htm.

[44] For more details on the IED, see 'The Industrial Emissions Directive', Environment, European Commission. http://ec.europa.eu/environment/industry/stationary/ied/legislation.htm.

[45] A phase-out has been decided in Germany (2022), Belgium (2025), Spain (2028). The role of nuclear is expected to decrease from about 75% to 50% in France (2025).

[46] This is difficult to estimate as some plants formerly declared mothballed were only shut down for the summer months; others only mothballed part of their total capacity, and some mothballed plants will re-open (such as the SSE Keadby gas-fired power station in the UK for instance). Data Source: author's estimates.

[47] Uncertainty on future load factors and revenues means investment decisions are more difficult; there will be no new conventional thermal plant while there is a merchant risk and zero long-term price visibility.

[48] See Honoré (2014) for details on assumptions and country-by-country scenarios.

[49] And even by 17% without Turkey. The data is for OECD Europe. Source: IEA (2015b).

lower gas prices, except maybe for a small growth in Germany, Turkey, and in eastern Europe. The same remark can be made for the residential and commercial sector, despite some switching to gas from oil and coal in the heating sector, although the seasonal variations will remain. An interesting new market is the use of LNG as a marine fuel, which could offer some demand in the late 2010s and beyond, especially following the introduction of new emissions regulations for the sector from 1 January 2015,[50] but this would probably equate to rather small volumes.[51]

In this scenario, no substantial additional gas consumption is envisaged, but total natural gas demand in the 35 countries of the European market may still rise to about 508 bcm by 2020 and 562 bcm by 2030,[52] still well below the record level of 594 bcm (IEA, 2015b) in 2010. This scenario would leave a gap unfilled by indigenous production of about 235–261 bcm in 2020 and 336–364 bcm in 2030, as seen in Figure 6.5.

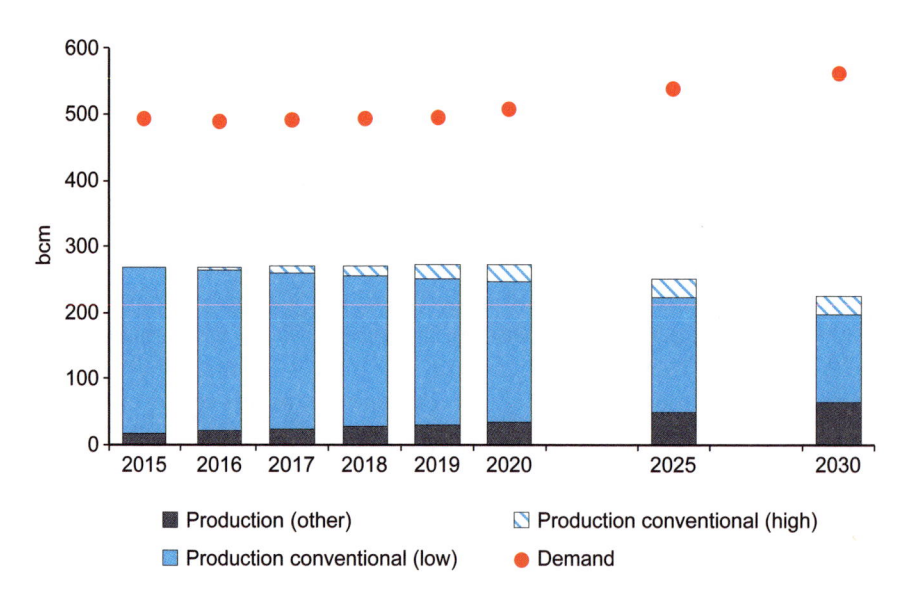

Figure 6.5: Scenarios for natural gas demand and indigenous production in Europe, 2015–30 (bcm)

Source: Author.

---

[50] For more details, see 'Sulphur limits in emission control areas from 1 January 2015', International Maritime Organization. www.imo.org/en/MediaCentre/HotTopics/GHG/Documents/sulphur%20limits%20FAQ.pdf.

[51] See Le Fevre (2014) for additional details on the transport sector, and Chapter 7.

[52] Source: author's estimates. For detailed assumptions on general trends by countries, see previous scenarios in Honoré (2014).

LNG Demand Potential 321

This gap will be fulfilled by both pipeline gas and LNG imports. A first logical step would be to look at pipeline gas. This gas may or may not be delivered, but it cannot be redirected to other regions as easily as LNG, due to the infrastructure in place. Figure 6.6 shows scenarios for natural gas demand compared to scenarios for supply from indigenous production and pipeline gas imports. For each year, it presents a case of low production and a case of high production (as already seen in Figure 6.5). The volumes of Russian gas included in long-term contracts are shown at three different levels: ToP (take-or-pay) of 70 per cent and 85 per cent, and ACQ (Annual Contract Quantity). Non-Russian pipeline gas is included in 'other pipeline gas' and details are provided in Table 6.1. Even at ACQ levels of Russian gas, a small gap remains to fulfil total demand up to 2020, but the gap grows quickly post 2020 when Russian long-term contracts reach the end of their lifetimes.

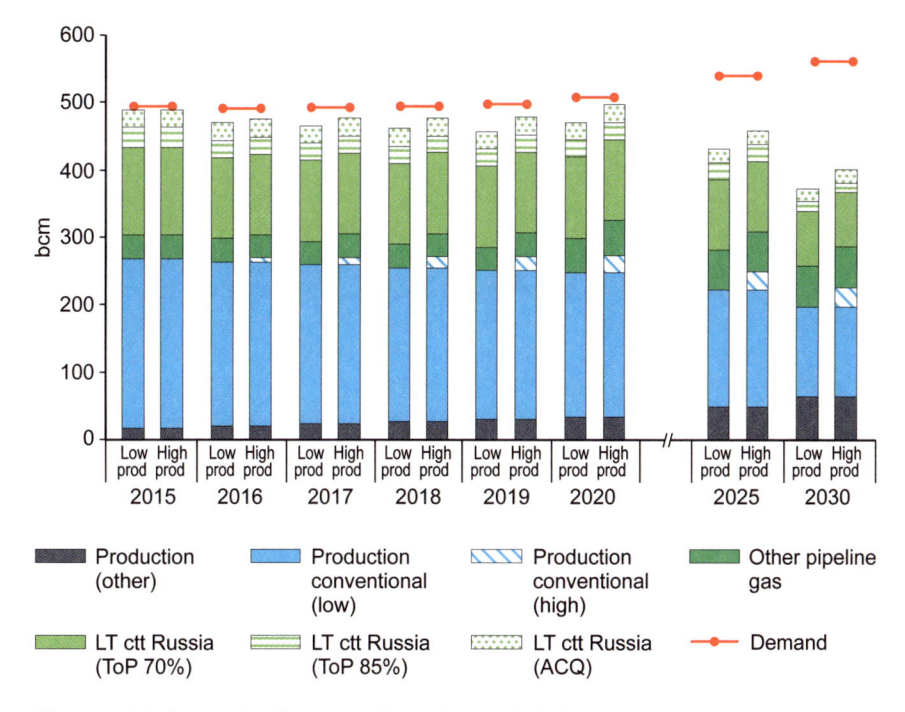

Figure 6.6: Scenarios for natural gas demand, indigenous production (high and low), and pipeline imports, in Europe, 2015–30 (bcm)

Note: Russian gas in long-term contracts at 70 per cent TOP, 85 per cent TOP, and ACQ.

Source: Author.

In a scenario of high production and high Russian gas (in other words, Russian long-term gas contracts at ACQ), the gap is limited to 11 bcm in 2020. In a scenario of low production and low Russian gas (namely Russian long-term gas contract at 70 per cent TOP), the gap is much more important at 88 bcm in 2020. Similarly, the potential gap oscillates between 161 and 223 bcm in 2030 (see Table 6.1). As a result, Europe will need to secure additional gas to meet its demand.

Gas supply challenges: what role for LNG?

Despite low demand growth, declining indigenous production means that Europe will have to increase its gas imports. Due to limited supply options in our timeframe, the competition is likely to be concentrated between Russian gas and LNG.

With global LNG production on the verge of significant increases, the interest in unused capacity at European regasification facilities is growing. In a surplus global LNG market in 2015–20, the region could be the recipient of substantial LNG supplies at prices competitive with pipeline gas. However, for as long as existing long-term contracts remain in place, Russian gas sales to Europe will meet a price challenge from surplus LNG. The region will remain Gazprom's main market at least for the next decade (2025), as other options for its gas are questionable.[53] The company will likely look to keep its share of the market[54] and with a surplus of about 100 bcm of relatively low-cost gas, it will be in a position to compete not only with all other pipeline gas but also with LNG (including US LNG) supplies throughout the period to 2030. Gazprom could keep gas prices at $4–6/MMBtu (or Henry Hub + $2/MMBtu) for quite a long time even if it would prefer to avoid this.[55] It is unlikely that offtakers[56] of US LNG would send large volumes of loss-making LNG to Europe, as their concerns may also include further depressing the hub prices if a large quantity of LNG is shipped, as this would result in higher losses for further LNG deliveries.[57] If there is a price war, Gazprom is likely to win. If the company maintains its market share

---

[53] See Henderson and Mitrova (2015) for additional details.

[54] 'Gazprom to defend market share', Argus Analysis, 3 February 2016.

[55] OIES data suggest that the most expensive Russian gas (from the Yamal Peninsula) can be delivered to Europe for €19–25/MWh ($6–8/MMBtu). Assumptions: $8 at an exchange rate of $1 = 30RR; $4/MMBtu at $1 = 60RR but exchange rate advantage unwinds by 2018. Source: Henderson and Mitrova (2015).

[56] Offtakers include Shell, the UK's BG, Spain's Gas Natural Fenosa, France's Total, and the UK's Centrica.

[57] A spread of at least $2/MMBtu between the US and European gas hubs is needed to promote LNG exports to Europe. Source:'Half of Cheniere's LNG bound for Europe', Argus, 18 November 2015. See also Rogers (2015) for additional details.

between 27 per cent and 33 per cent, as indicated by deputy chief executive Alexander Medvedev in early 2016,[58] then the gap remaining to be filled in 2020 oscillates between 15 bcm (high production and Russian gas at 33 per cent of the market) and 71 bcm (low production and Russian gas at 27 per cent of the market), as seen in Figure 6.7. This gap is likely to be filled by LNG due to the lack of options other than Russian gas. In 2030, this gap oscillates between 90 bcm and 151 bcm. However, after that date, Gazprom will need to send volumes not covered by long-term contracts to keep its market share within the bracket.[59] In addition, some further pipeline gas may have become available to Europe by this date, especially from Azerbaijan and Iraqi Kurdistan. If this happens, then the need for LNG would oscillate between 68 and 129 bcm, depending on the level of indigenous production (especially Norwegian supplies) and the market share of Russian gas.

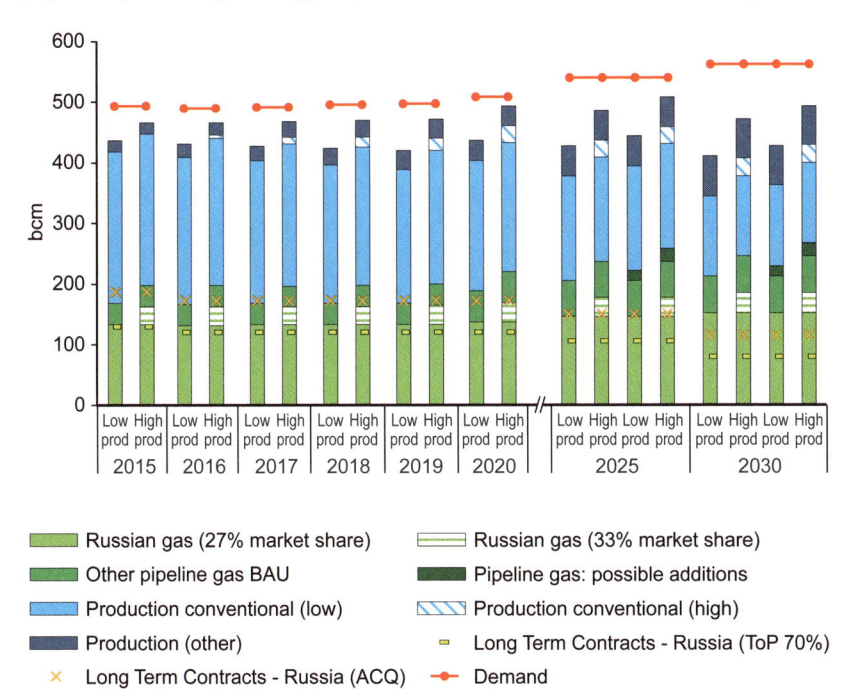

Figure 6.7: Scenarios for natural gas demand, indigenous production (high and low) and pipeline imports in Europe, 2015–30 (bcm)

Note: With Russian gas at 27 per cent and 33 per cent of the market.
Source: Author.

---

[58] 'Gazprom to defend market share', Argus Analysis, 3 February 2016.
[59] ACQ levels in long-term Russian gas contracts cover around 33% of the market in 2020, and just about 27% in 2025. For a discussion about transit capacity for Russian gas to the European market, see Pirani and Yafimava (2016).

Even if the LNG price advantage is challenged, LNG is still an attractive option for Europe for two main reasons: security of supply and flexibility.

- Gas is an energy security issue in Europe; the EU wants to diversify its supply of gas and make it more resilient to supply disruptions.[60] LNG is seen as a strong asset in terms of security of supply, as it offers not only the potential for additional volumes, but also the access to diversified sources in the global market. Increased LNG deliveries would help in covering the region's needs and free up pipeline gas for other parts of Europe with no access to LNG. In February 2016, the European Commission unveiled the EU LNG Strategy, which calls for the construction of necessary infrastructure to complete the internal market and changes to gas market rules.[61] While the European network has not been designed to flow gas from LNG terminals along the 35 countries (the system was primarily designed to accommodate historical predominant flows from North to South and East to West), the development of reverse-flow capacities substantially increased in the early 2010s, and significant investments are planned to enable a major LNG 'counterflow' to central and eastern Europe.[62] Nonetheless, new regasification units in the Baltic and in central and south-east Europe are planned for which the investment will be mainly driven by security of supply issues. Lithuania opened its terminal in 2014, and the Polish terminal in mid 2016. These terminals may not be fully used, but they give the countries the ability to decrease their dependence on Russian gas – or at least, to put Gazprom in a competitive position simply by creating an opportunity for market players to import gas from the global market. On the other side of Europe, the Croatian project is also a strategic one. With interconnections in place, these three terminals not only offer alternatives to the importing countries, but also to neighbouring markets to diversify their own imports.

---

[60] For additional details see 'Gas and Oil Supply Routes', Energy, European Commission. https://ec.europa.eu/energy/en/topics/imports-and-secure-supplies/gas-and-oil-supply-routes.

[61] For more information, see 'Consultation on an EU strategy for liquefied natural gas and gas storage', Energy, European Commission. https://ec.europa.eu/energy/en/consultations/consultation-eu-strategy-liquefied-natural-gas-and-gas-storage.

[62] To help create an integrated EU energy market, the European Commission has drawn up a list of 248 projects of common interest (PCIs). These projects may benefit from accelerated licensing procedures, improved regulatory conditions, and access to financial support. For more details, see 'Projects of common interest', Energy, European Commission. https://ec.europa.eu/energy/en/topics/infrastructure/projects-common-interest.

- LNG offers diversification, but on the other hand Europe is not alone on the global LNG market; in period of tighter supply, the LNG flow could be driven away from Europe to the higher-paying markets in, for instance, Asia and Latin America unless the European countries are prepared to pay higher prices for their gas. With access to pipeline gas and LNG, some European countries will also benefit from the opportunity to arbitrage and re-export LNG.

- Another important component of LNG is its flexibility. Seasonality – an important feature of gas demand in Europe – has been covered by a mix of storage, additional production, and imports.[63] With rising renewables on the demand side and declining flexible indigenous production from the UKCS and Groningen on the supply side,[64] Europe will need to develop new forms of flexibility. Better interconnections within the region and the development of liquidity at hubs will play a role, but LNG could also be a key component. In other words, at times of surplus, or with a low demand for LNG in China, LNG could almost eliminate the need for flexible pipeline gas in Europe.

Conclusions

The future of natural gas demand in Europe remains a concern, especially in relation to the outlook for the gas-fired power generation sector. It is unclear how much gas the region will need, with scenarios mostly depicting slow growth, although in some cases a decline is possible by 2030 – and the scenarios on gas balances are even more complicated and diversified at the national level. Over the same period, the region will face a decline of its indigenous production, which will increase the need for imports. Additional pipeline gas is expected to come from the Southern corridor post-2020, albeit with some uncertainties on available volumes, but the major potential comes from Russia, which will be the main competitor to LNG in Europe. Russia has a surplus capacity and could send additional gas to Europe at prices competitive to LNG, in order to keep its market share between 27 and 33 per cent, even if it would prefer to avoid low prices. What happens on the other side of the globe, in Asia, will determine how keen the LNG suppliers are to send LNG to Europe, at the risk of depressing hub prices

---

[63] The difference between a cold and a warm winter represents about 50 bcm. Source: author.

[64] In addition to meeting the majority of the Netherlands' domestic gas requirements, the giant Groningen onshore gas field has also played a key role in providing annual base supply, as well as winter 'swing' flexibility to neighbouring NWE markets. The UKCS also used to provide important flexibility, but this feature has been declining alongside the total production volumes.

even more. If Gazprom competes for its market share, the room left for LNG will be somewhere between 15 and 71 bcm in 2020, depending on the level of indigenous production and the share kept by Russian gas. In 2030, some additional pipeline gas could also be envisaged, essentially from the Southern Corridor (Azerbaijan and Iraqi Kurdistan being the two likely sources). If this happens, the room left for LNG would be between 68 and 129 bcm in 2030 as seen in Table 6.1, which shows the assumptions used in this section. LNG has two main advantages over long-distance pipeline gas from Russia (and elsewhere): the security of supply it offers by giving access to world suppliers, and its flexibility. These two features are actively being encouraged by the European institutions (European Commission, 2016), and could ultimately contribute to supporting additional LNG to Europe at the 2030 horizon.

Table 6.1: Assumptions used in this section for natural gas demand and supply balances in Europe, 2015–30 (bcm)

	2015	2016	2017	2018	2019	2020	2025	2030
DEMAND Europe 35	494	489	492	494	496	508	540	562
Production (conventional low)	250	243	235	228	220	213	173	133
Production (conventional high)	250	248	246	243	241	239	200	161
Production (other)	18	21	24	28	31	34	50	65
GAP demand: low production	*226*	*226*	*232*	*239*	*245*	*261*	*317*	*364*
GAP demand: high production	*226*	*220*	*222*	*223*	*224*	*235*	*290*	*336*
PIPELINE LT ctt Russia (ToP 70%)	130	120	120	120	120	120	105	80
PIPELINE LT ctt Russia (ToP 85%)	160	145	145	145	145	145	130	95
PIPELINE LT ctt Russia (ACQ)	186	171	171	171	171	171	150	114
PIPELINE North Africa (BAU)	20	20	20	20	20	20	24	24
PIPELINE Azerbaijan and Caspian (BAU)	7	7	7	7	7	24	27	27
PIPELINE Iran (BAU)	8	8	8	8	8	8	8	10
GAP demand: low prod., pipeline gas BAU with 70% ToP Russian gas	*60*	*70*	*77*	*84*	*90*	*88*	*153*	*223*
GAP demand: low prod., pipeline gas BAU with 85% ToP Russian gas	*30*	*45*	*52*	*59*	*65*	*63*	*128*	*208*
GAP demand: low prod., pipeline gas BAU with ACQ Russian gas	*5*	*19*	*25*	*32*	*39*	*37*	*108*	*189*
GAP demand: high prod., pipeline gas BAU with 70% ToP Russian gas	*60*	*65*	*66*	*68*	*69*	*62*	*126*	*195*
GAP demand: high prod., pipeline gas BAU with 85% ToP Russian gas	*30*	*40*	*41*	*43*	*44*	*37*	*101*	*180*

	2015	2016	2017	2018	2019	2020	2025	2030
GAP demand: high prod., pipeline gas BAU with ACQ Russian gas	5	14	15	17	18	11	81	161
PIPELINE share of Russian gas at 27%	133	132	133	133	134	137	146	152
PIPELINE share of Russian gas at 33%	163	162	162	163	164	168	178	185
PIPELINE North Africa (BAU)	20	20	20	20	20	20	24	24
PIPELINE Azerbaijan and Caspian (BAU)	7	7	7	7	7	24	27	27
PIPELINE Iran (BAU)	8	8	8	8	8	8	8	10
PIPELINE possible additions (4th corridor)	0	0	0	0	0	0	17	22
Demand for LNG: low prod., pipeline gas BAU with 27% Russian gas	57	58	64	70	76	71	112	151
Demand for LNG: low prod., pipeline gas BAU with 33% Russian gas	27	29	35	41	46	41	80	118
Demand for LNG: high prod., pipeline gas BAU with 27% Russian gas	57	53	54	54	55	45	85	123
Demand for LNG: high prod., pipeline gas BAU with 33% Russian gas	27	24	24	25	25	15	53	90
Demand for LNG: low prod., pipeline gas with 27% Russian gas – possible additions	57	58	64	70	76	71	95	129
Demand for LNG: low prod., pipeline gas with 33% Russian gas – possible additions	27	29	35	41	46	41	63	96
Demand for LNG: high prod., pipeline gas with 27% Russian gas – possible additions	57	53	54	54	55	45	68	101
Demand for LNG: high prod., pipeline gas with 33% Russian gas – possible additions	27	24	24	25	25	15	36	68

Source: Author.

Mature Asian markets: limited growth potential

Introduction

This section describes the markets generally viewed as the 'mature' Asian LNG importers (namely Japan, South Korea, and Taiwan), addresses the factors which have influenced their LNG consumption trends to date, and derives views of possible future demand paths. These three markets commenced LNG imports in 1969, 1986, and 1990 respectively. As a group they accounted for in excess of 60 per cent of global LNG imports from 1980 to 2006.

These countries have minimal domestic gas resources and depend on natural gas to differing degrees in their power and non-power sectors. All three markets have enjoyed economic growth based on export-oriented manufacturing and technology goods production, however, with the slowdown in Chinese economic growth and the limits to growth inherent in this economic model, there are questions regarding their future economic performance. Japan, in particular, is struggling to stimulate domestic demand in the face of high personal and corporate savings levels and ongoing deflationary tendencies. Declining population trends are also a relatively new challenge for these countries, threatening domestic consumption growth and workforce renewal.

The largest uncertainty impacting future gas (LNG) consumption trends, however, is uncertainty in future energy consumption growth and energy mix. With the challenge of GHG emission reduction, especially post COP21, strategies incorporating energy efficiency and renewables have been proposed, with nuclear aspirations constrained either by public opinion or (in the case of Japan) restart logistics and approval processes. While an indicative share for gas in the energy mix is often included in policy documents, competition with (cheaper) coal in the power sector is an open issue which requires a more robust policy framework than generally exists at present. Typically, the continued presence of coal in the energy mix is offset by assumed future energy efficiency gains and aggressive renewable capacity growth. The reality of such aspirations will presumably become clear once National Determined Contributions (agreed at COP21) are tracked by the Monitoring, Reporting, and Verification process, albeit from 2020 at the earliest (IIGC, 2015, 4–5).

The following sections describe the individual markets with the objective of addressing the drivers of future LNG demand. With this as the primary focus, it is inappropriate to dwell on the details of individual LNG contracts and import infrastructure. For such information the reader is directed to GIIGNL, which provides an annual update on these and other aspects of the LNG market at a country level.

Japan

Energy mix

Japan is the world's third-largest economy with a population of 126.2 million in 2014,[65] though this is viewed as being in long-term decline. Decades of low economic growth and heavy government spending to support the economy have left Japan with the world's highest public debt at almost 250 per cent of GDP. The Abe government in 2012 commenced a three-part plan of stimulus spending, monetary easing, and structural reforms. In mid-2015 commentators appeared cautiously optimistic that

---

[65] 'Japan's population slide set to accelerate', *Financial Times*, 2 July 2015. www.ft.com/cms/s/0/41aace5e-208f-11e5-aa5a-398b2169cf79. html?siteedition=uk#axzz3fr7DgV1U.

Japan's growth of 3.9 per cent (annualized) in the first quarter of 2015[66] heralded a sustained recovery after 2014's zero GDP growth. However, GDP data in September 2015 indicated a figure of just 1 per cent annualized growth, consumer spending and investment remained sluggish, and exports were dampened by decelerating growth in China.[67] Japan's GDP comprises: agriculture 1.1 per cent, industry 25.6 per cent, and services 73.2 per cent (CIA, 2015b; Index Mundi, 2015). Japan's manufacturing sector has a significant element of high energy intensive industries such as metals, chemicals, and machinery manufacture.

Total Japanese primary energy consumption reached a plateau in the mid-2000s with gas and coal gaining share from oil and nuclear. The post financial crisis year of 2009 reduced energy consumption from all sources, but 2010 showed a significant recovery. On 11 March 2011 the Great East Japan Earthquake and its Tsunami resulted in a nuclear accident at the Fukushima Daiichi Nuclear Power Station. This led to the policy-induced shutdown of all Japan's nuclear generation plant.[68] The loss of nuclear generation was partially compensated for by an increase in gas, coal, and oil-fired generation. The total energy consumption for 2014 was below the level of 2009.

Gas consumption
Japanese gas demand has a space heating seasonal peak in winter (peak month generally February) and a less pronounced peak in summer, due to additional power generation usage for air conditioning.[69] Japan manages seasonal demand fluctuations by varying the stock of LNG held in storage tanks at regas terminals, and by increasing the frequency of cargo deliveries during high-demand periods.

City gas consumption became increasingly dominated by the industrial sector through the 2000s, with the residential and commercial sectors having remained stagnant from 2000. The average annual growth rate in industrial sector gas consumption was 10 per cent from 2000 to 2007, slowing to 2.6 per cent from 2008 to 2013.

In FY 2013[70] gas accounted for only 11.6 per cent of industrial sector energy, having grown from a much lower base in the early 2000s. Industrial

---

[66] 'Japan economy grows 3.9% in first quarter', *Financial Times*, 8 June 2015. www.ft.com/cms/s/0/6a1ae4a0-0d89-11e5-b850-00144feabdc0.html#axzz3frCyYjrF.
[67] '2016's economic outlook' *The Japan Times*, 11 January, 2016. www.japantimes.co.jp/opinion/2016/01/11/editorials/2016s-economic-outlook/#.VpYtThWLSCo.
[68] For a comprehensive review of the impact of Fukushima see Miyamoto et al. (2012).
[69] Figure 4.1 in Miyamoto (2008, 127).
[70] Note: The Japanese fiscal year runs from April to March of the following year. Fiscal Year 2013 ends in March 2014.

330 *LNG Markets in Transition*

energy consumption has reduced considerably since FY 2007. In general, gas has gained share from oil products but coal consumption has grown.

The scope for further future growth of gas in the industrial sector was addressed in a 2012 OIES paper (Miyamoto et al., 2012) where the importance of access to gas (infrastructure), together with price competitiveness relative to other fuels, were viewed as key determinants of future consumption growth. The authors concluded that industrial demand would continue to grow at 2.85 per cent per year to 2020, but that residential demand would reduce by 0.57 per cent per year, while the commercial sector would grow at 0.42 per cent per year; with an aggregate city gas sector growth of 1.6 per cent per year. In 2013, city gas comprised 30 per cent of total gas demand and the power sector 70 per cent.

Gas consumption in the power sector remained reasonably constant in the period 2000 to 2006, grew modestly to 2010, and then expanded dramatically by some 20 bcm/year after Fukushima.

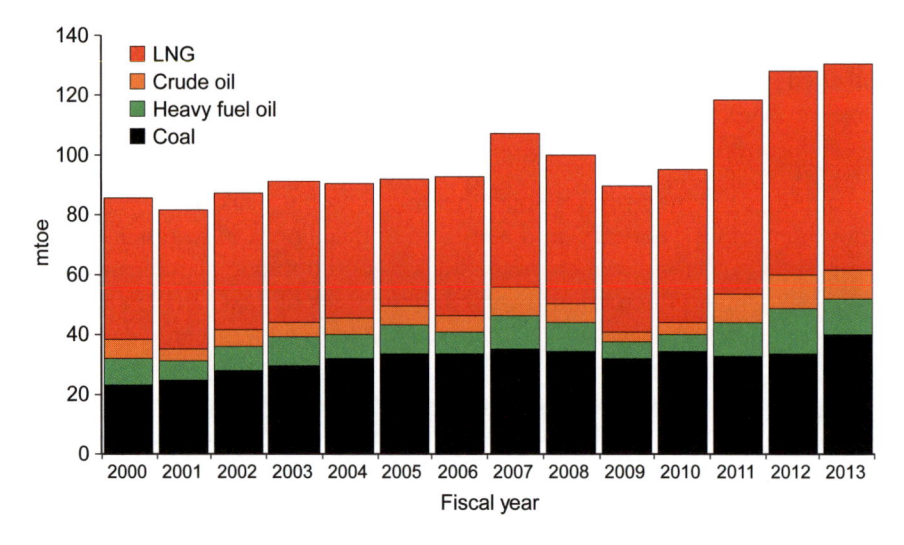

Figure 6.8: Fuel consumption for electricity generation (general electric utilities)
Source: IEEJ/EDMC (2015, 210).

Figure 6.8 shows the consumption of fuels in thermal generation. The graph also enables us to deduce that the loss of nuclear generation post Fukushima was compensated for by broadly comparable increases in crude and heavy fuel oil on the one hand, and natural gas on the other.

In July 2011, immediately following the Fukushima disaster, the Energy & Environment Council (Enecan) was established to make recommendations on Japan's future energy strategy; proposing a phase-out of nuclear power by 2040. Operable reactors would be allowed to restart once they had gained permission from the Nuclear Regulation Authority (NRA), but a 40 year operating limit would be imposed. Enecan proposed a 'green energy policy framework' focused on LNG, coal, and an expanded use of renewables. This provoked a strong response from industry, with a consensus that a 20 to 25 per cent share of nuclear was necessary to avoid severe economic penalties. The succeeding government (Liberal Democratic Party) abolished Enecan, placing the responsibility for energy policy matters in the hands of METI (the Ministry of Economy, Trade and Industry).

In June 2015 the government's draft plan for electricity generation to 2030 was approved; this has nuclear at 20–22 per cent, renewables at 22–24 per cent, LNG at 27 per cent, and coal at 26 per cent, with an aim to reduce CO_2 emissions by 21.9 per cent by 2030 from the 2013 level, and to improve energy self sufficiency measures to 24.3 per cent from 6.3 per cent in 2012.[71] The plan aims to achieve ambitious energy efficiency savings. By 2030, economic growth would normally be assumed to increase energy demand to 411.3 billion litres (oil equivalent) from the 2013 figure of 361 billion litres (oil equivalent). Efficiency measures are assumed to be capable of reducing this figure to 326 billion litres (oil equivalent) by 2030.[72]

Achieving these goals will be challenging, however. Early difficulties with renewables expansion surfaced in October 2014, when at least seven of the then major utilities limited the access of renewable energy to their grids due to potential overloads.[73] Solar capacity tripled in the fiscal year ending in March 2014 due to the high feed-in tariff introduced in 2012. Even so, renewables (excluding hydro), only accounted for 2.2 per cent of Japan's electricity output in fiscal year 2013.[74] Of perhaps greater concern, the energy efficiency goals in the 2015 draft plan assume a similar path to that which was achieved in the period 1970–90.[75] Achieving this will likely be difficult, Japan being already regarded as the sixth most energy efficient nation in a global survey.[76]

The process for restarting nuclear plant comprises a safety assessment by the NRA and the briefing of local governments by the operators. The NRA process includes the review of detailed design, site inspection,

---

[71] 'Nuclear Power in Japan', April 2015, World Nuclear Association. www.world-nuclear.org/info/Country-Profiles/Countries-G-N/Japan/.
[72] Slide 8 in IEEJ (2015).
[73] Slide 8 in IEEJ (2015).
[74] 'Outlook cloudy for Japan's renewable energy drive', *Financial Times*, 20 April, 2015. www.ft.com/cms/s/0/dae47c8c-d927-11e4-b907-00144feab7de.html#axzz3g2zV8Sl6.
[75] Slide 13 in IEEJ (2015).
[76] 'The International Energy Efficiency Scorecard', American Council for and Energy Efficient Economy. http://aceee.org/portal/national-policy/international-scorecard.

and an assessment of operating management systems. Local government consent is required before restart can occur. Kyushu Electric Power Co.'s Sendai 1 began full commercial operations on 10 September 2015, and Sendai 2 on 17 November.[77] These are both 890 MW reactors. By end-November 2015 both plants had reached full capacity. Kansai Electric Power Co. received local approval for the restart of its Takahama 3 and 4 reactors, but start-up was delayed until late January and late February 2016 pending preparations for final on-site checks by Japan's Nuclear Regulation Authority. The court decision to start up the plant was opposed by public opinion. The Ikata 3 reactor gained approval for restart from the Ehime Prefecture on 29 October 2015. The 846 MW reactor was expected to start in early 2016.

There are still uncertainties as to the pace and extent of the nuclear restart process. Of the 42 operable reactors, in October 2015 Reuters reported (based on NRA inspection data, court rulings, and interviews with local authorities, utilities, and energy exports), that seven rectors are likely to restart over the next few years (down from 14 in a similar 2014 survey). The fate of the remaining potentially operable reactors appears uncertain.[78]

Under a high case scenario developed by Itochu, about 10 reactors could be restarted every year, with a total of 35 units back online within five years.[79] Delays observed to the process to date seem likely to continue going forward, however.

Assuming (for the purpose of this analysis) that Japan's renewables growth, and its coal and oil power sector constraint ambitions are achieved, the outlook for LNG in the power sector depends primarily on the achievement of energy efficiency goals and the pace of nuclear restarts.

To explore the sensitivities, the following scenarios for nuclear restarts were considered:

- Fast restart – where Japan achieves 35.45 GW of operational capacity by 2020 which operates at an assumed historic average of 70 per cent send-out (with modest assumed additional efficiency growth to 2030).

- Slow restart – where a similar level of nuclear capacity is achieved more gradually – in other words, by 2030.

---

[77] Japan Nuclear Update, Nuclear Energy Institute, 21 April 2016. www.nei.org/News-Media/News/Japan-Nuclear-Update.

[78] 'Japan Nuclear Power Outlook Bleak Despite First Reactor Restart', Reuters, 1 September 2015. www.reuters.com/article/us-japan-nuclear-restarts-analysis-idUSKCN0R022Q20150901.

[79] 'Reactor restarts in Japan', 30 January 2015, Nuclear Monitor. www.wiseinternational.org/nuclear-monitor/797/reactor-restarts-japan ..

- Partial restart – where only 50 per cent of the previous scenario's capacity is achieved.

The trends in nuclear generation for these scenarios are shown in Figure 6.9.

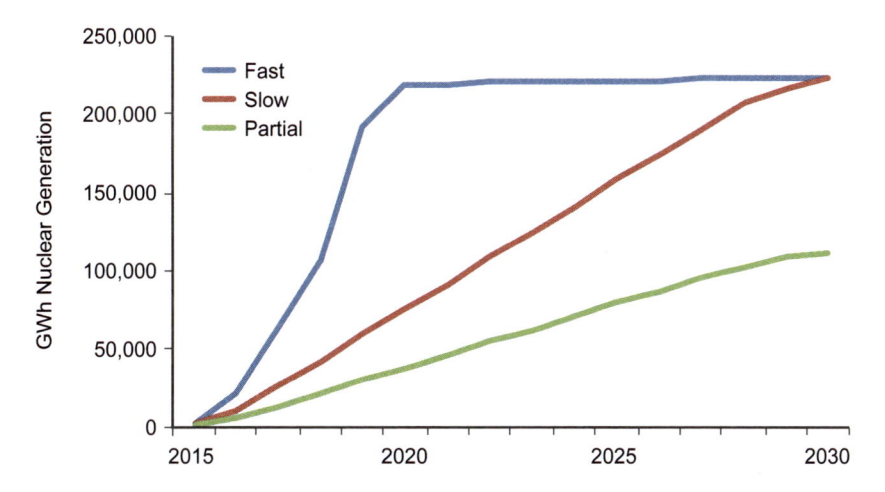

Figure 6.9: Japanese nuclear restart scenarios
Source: Author's assumptions.

Six scenarios were constructed by combining the three nuclear restart cases with two power generation energy efficiency cases:

- No efficiency saving case: 1,278 GWh power generation in 2030 with 21 per cent nuclear on the 'fast restart assumption', 23 per cent renewables, 26 per cent coal, 3 per cent oil, and 27 per cent LNG.[80]
- Target efficiency saving case: with the three nuclear start-up assumptions.

The considerable variation in the consumption of gas in power generation for these cases is shown in Figure 6.10 (overleaf).

The future gas demand outlook for Japan in aggregate is shown in Figure 6.11. In these cases 'High Demand' relates to 'No Efficiency Saving', and 'Low Demand' relates to 'Target Efficiency Saving'. Note that the 2030 figure of 62 mtpa (84 bcm/year) of LNG imports in 2030 (consistent in the Japanese Target-energy efficiency scenario described above) is met only by two of the cases in Figure 6.11. Despite the potential for some

---

[80] Slide 9 in IEEJ (2015).

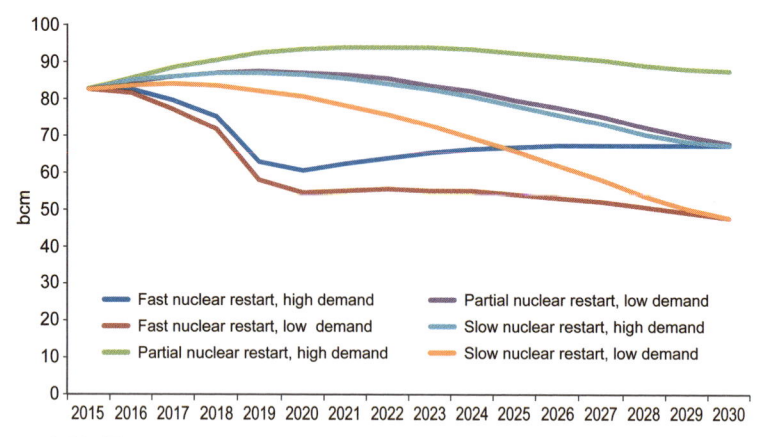

Figure 6.10: Future power generation gas consumption for six cases
Source: Author's calculations.

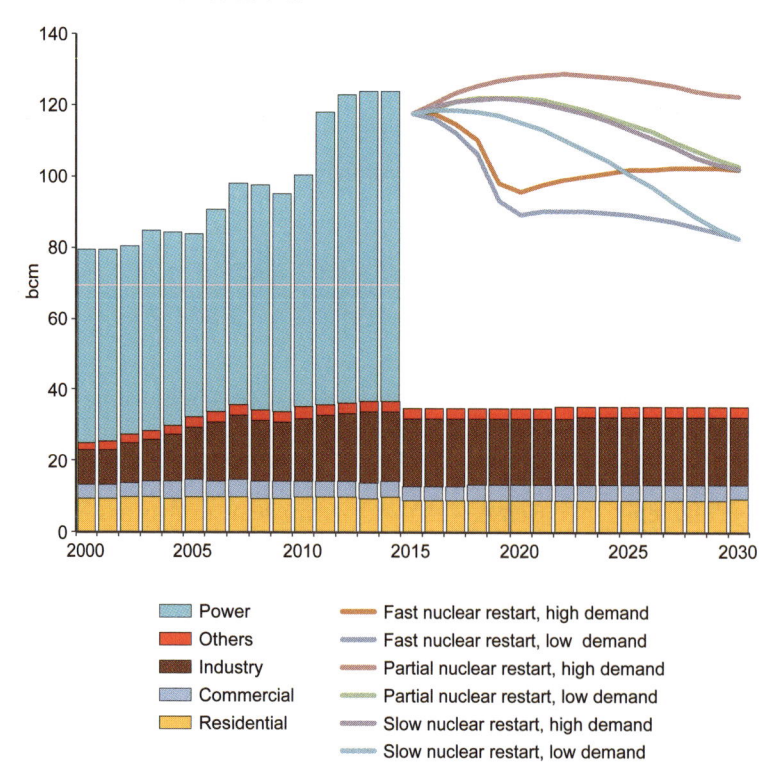

Figure 6.11: Historical and future Japanese gas demand
Source: Produced from Balance derived from IEEJ/EDMC (2015, 178, 180, and 184) and author's analysis.

demand growth by 2020 (due to a slow or partial nuclear restart pace) the overall outlook is one of limited scope for significant gas demand upside, at least based on the assumptions presented here. It should also be noted that higher than average temperatures in the fourth quarter of 2015 suppressed space heating demand, which contributed to a decline in 2015 consumption compared to 2014.[81]

Gas supply
Japan has some 3.2 bcm/year of associated and non-associated domestic gas production from numerous small fields. Gas production peaked at 3.73 bcm/year in FY 2007 and is in slow decline. Japan also produces minor volumes of synthetic gas (1.4 bcm/year in FY 2012) from petroleum and (until 2008) from coal (IEEJ/EDMC, 2015, 180). Overwhelmingly, however, Japan relies on imported LNG. It has 33 regas terminals with an aggregate capacity of 267 bcm/year (GIIGNL, 2014), however, limits on the number of vessels entering Tokyo Bay (under an agreement with the fishing industry), a ban on night-time navigation, and (possibly) transmission system constraints appear to limit annual imports to around half of the nameplate capacity stated here.[82] Regas capacity is driven by peak rather than average demand, Japan having minimal geological gas storage capacity. Japan's most significant LNG suppliers, in volume terms, are Qatar, Australia, Malaysia, and Russia; however the portfolio is diversified.

Given the uncertainty over future demand, particularly in the power sector given the variable rate and extent of future nuclear restarts, it is instructive to look at Japan's LNG supply position (Figure 6.12) superimposed on the demand scenarios developed above. For 2010 to 2014 the yellow bars represent historic volumes purchased on spot or other short-term arrangements. These volumes increased significantly post Fukushima. The green bars represent disclosed short-term contracts (term equal to or less than four years), some of which proceed beyond 2014. Dark blue represents historic supplies purchased under medium- and long-term contracts. Light blue represents the future volumes committed to under medium- and long-term contracts (ACQs) in force from non-US sources, and red from US LNG export facilities.

---

[81] 'Japan's imports of liquefied natural gas reached 85.05 million mt in 2015, a drop of 3.9 percent as compared to the year before', *LNG World News*, 25 January 2016, https://www.lngworldnews.com/japans-annual-lng-imports-drop-for-first-time-in-six-years/.

[82] For example see 'Energy in Japan', 26 April 2012, Credit Suisse, https://doc.research-and-analytics.csfb.com/docView?sourceid=em&document_id=x446745&serialid=vPH7BrABSVBiMmvPreIYc4%2F6gyIbeVxKu8MBtpsV5G4%3D.

336 · *LNG Markets in Transition*

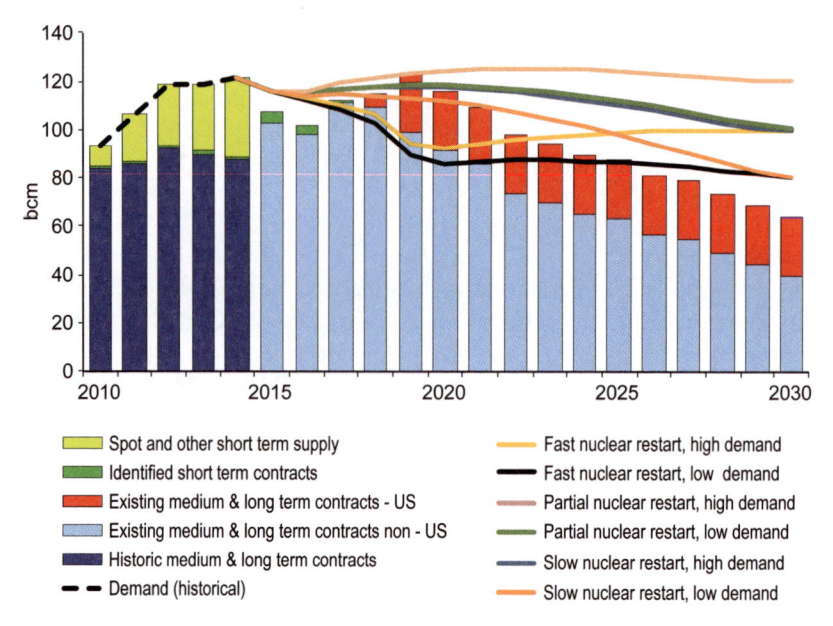

Figure 6.12: Japan's LNG supply outlook and demand uncertainty, 2010–30
Source: Author's analysis.

Figure 6.12 suggests that Japan's future contracted LNG position is manageable, at least to the early to mid-2020s, over the range of the future demand cases derived above. In the fast nuclear restart cases, Japan has limited exposure to non-US long-term contract commitments above its demand requirements. This could be managed by exercising downward tolerance in its LNG contracts in the 2018 to 2020 period. Its US LNG contract commitments are, by their nature, destination flexible; however, in the fast nuclear restart cases, Japan would need to develop a strategy to 'trade-on' these volumes in what may be a low-priced market (in terms of European hub and spot LNG prices). In the slow and partial nuclear restart scenarios, Japan could continue to balance its LNG import requirements using spot LNG cargoes to the early 2020s, before possibly needing to sign up new medium- or long-term contracts.

Conclusions: Japan
Japan is the world's largest LNG importer, with gas in 2014 representing some 22 per cent of its primary energy mix. It is an industrialized economy which has suffered from low growth since the early 1990s. Its economic prospects began to tentatively improve in 2015 following intense government policy aimed at economic stimulus; however, prospects for sustained recovery are still in doubt. Longer term, however, its low birth rate and

population decline emphasize the need for exports rather than domestic consumption, to provide a key element of economic growth.

Since 2011, Japan's energy policy has been overshadowed by the aftermath of the Fukushima disaster, which required increased imports of LNG, crude, and oil products to offset the loss of nuclear generation at a time of historically high oil and LNG contract and spot prices. LNG provided some 50 per cent of the additional power generation necessary to offset the loss of nuclear. Future LNG demand will be directly influenced by the pace and extent of the nuclear restart programme – which seems at present subject to uncertain delays.

A related and important issue is Japan's Kyoto commitment and its need to reduce its CO_2 emissions by 2020. Nuclear restart will be driven by considerations of safety assurance, together with political and public approval issues at the prefecture level. A slow or partial restart will require Japan to focus on renewables growth (whose scale potential may be questionable on the grounds of cost, land availability, and infrastructure issues) and the need to reduce the share of coal and oil in industry and power sector consumption. This would provide additional scope for LNG demand growth, but this is difficult to define at present.

A low and a high LNG import requirement case are shown in Table 6.2.

Table 6.2: Japanese low and high LNG import cases

	2010	2011	2012	2013	2014	2015	2016	2017	2018	2019	2020
bcm/year											
Low case	93.5	107.0	118.8	119.0	122.0	115.7	112.3	108.3	102.9	89.6	86.0
High case	93.5	107.0	118.8	119.0	122.0	115.7	116.3	119.4	121.8	123.5	124.6
mtpa											
Low case	68.7	78.6	87.4	87.5	89.7	85.1	82.6	79.6	75.7	65.9	63.3
High case	68.7	78.6	87.4	87.5	89.7	85.1	85.6	87.8	89.5	90.8	91.7

	2021	2022	2023	2024	2025	2026	2027	2028	2029	2030
bcm/year										
Low case	86.9	87.3	87.3	87.0	86.5	85.7	84.7	83.5	82.2	80.6
High case	125.4	125.7	125.6	125.3	124.7	123.9	122.8	121.7	120.8	120.3
mtpa										
Low case	63.9	64.2	64.2	64.0	63.6	63.0	62.3	61.4	60.4	59.3
High case	92.2	92.4	92.4	92.1	91.7	91.1	90.3	89.5	88.8	88.4

Note: The low case corresponds to the fast nuclear restart, low power demand; the high case corresponds to the partial nuclear restart, high power demand.

Source: GIIGNL and author's analysis.

South Korea

South Korea in the 1960s had a GDP per capita comparable with the poorer countries of Africa and Asia. Since then, it has generally enjoyed strong economic growth and increasing global integration and has become a high technology industrial power; it is currently the world's twelfth largest economy. South Korea's export-oriented economy was hit by the 2008 global economic crisis but rebounded swiftly, with GDP growth in 2010 reaching 6.3 per cent. Since 2010, growth has been muted due to economic and export market slowdowns in the USA, China, and the Eurozone, requiring a refocus away from exports towards domestic-oriented industry and services. Longer-term challenges include an ageing population, inflexible labour market, and the dominance of large conglomerates/incumbents.[83]

The relative contribution of agriculture, industry, and services to South Korea's economy is 2.6 per cent, 39.2 per cent, and 58.2 per cent (2013) (CIA, 2015b; Index Mundi, 2015). Industries include textiles, steel, shipbuilding, car manufacturing, and electronics. South Korea has pursued a strategy of being a 'fast follower', with the government taking on foreign loans and allocating capital to strategic industries, which led to a massive influx of foreign capital goods and turnkey plants. In the 1990s, the focus switched from imitating and assimilating mature foreign technologies to in house R&D, drawing upon emerging new technologies. However, slower growth, reduced job prospects, and the deteriorating performance of South Korean companies all indicate that its past strategy is perhaps no longer effective. The government has responded with a new vision labelled the 'creative economy'; generating growth by facilitating cross-fertilization of IT and other areas.[84]

In 2014 gas accounted for 15.7 per cent of the primary energy mix and was 9 per cent below consumption levels of 2013. Total energy consumption has been essentially flat from 2011, despite the 7 per cent rebound in 2010 after the post crisis year low in 2009. This is in marked contrast to the period 1999 to 2008, during which energy consumption grew by 3 per cent per year on average. While nuclear contributed 13 per cent to the energy mix, it was dominated by coal (31 per cent) and oil (39.5 per cent) in 2014.

Gas consumption

Gas consumption in the non-power sectors declined in 2014, partly due to a warm winter. However, growth was significant from 2010 to 2012, both

---

[83] 'South Korea', Forbes, December 2015, www.forbes.com/places/south-korea/.

[84] 'Lessons to be learned from South Korea's stellar rise', Sung Chulchung, *Europe's World*, 23 February 2015. http://europesworld.org/2015/02/23/lessons-learned-south-koreas-stellar-rise/#.VakacPlVhBc.

in the industrial and district heating sectors. This said, the proportion of natural gas in terms of total industrial energy consumption is low (6.9 per cent in 2014).

Gas in industrial use appears to have plateaued at a level of 7 to 8 per cent post 2011, with industrial energy consumption dominated by oil products and coal; the latter having grown significantly since 2009.

South Korea's power sector is less significant relative to other gas consumption sectors, accounting for 43 per cent of total gas consumption in 2014. Figure 6.13 illustrates the minor role played by gas in power generation. Gas has a 20 per cent share in a sector dominated by coal and nuclear.

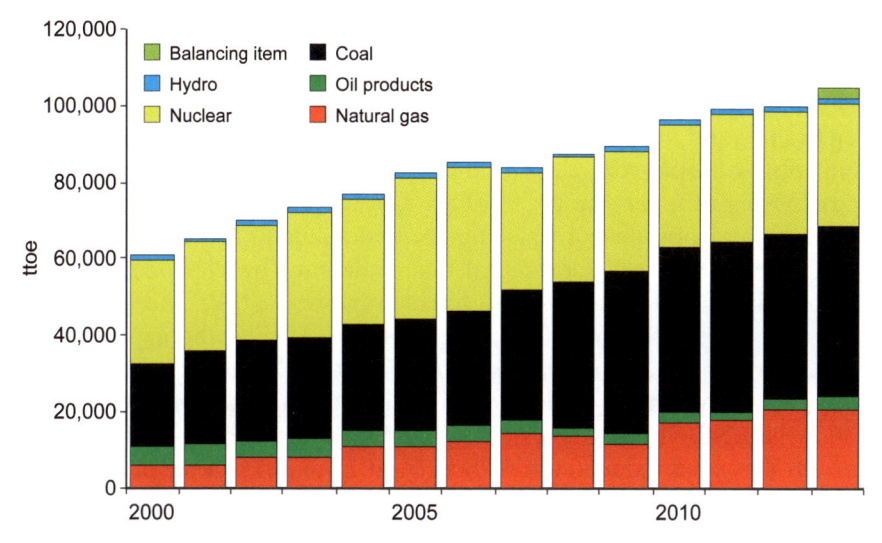

Figure 6.13: South Korea fuel consumption for power generation, 2000–14
Source: KESIS.

The growing role played by coal in South Korea's energy mix in the past two decades is reflected in the country's CO_2 emissions which, although having plateaued since 2010, were in 2014, three times those of 1990. The government's current goal is to achieve a 37 per cent decrease in 'business as usual' GHG emissions by 2030.[85]

Gas supply
South Korea's gas supply is overwhelmingly from LNG imports. Domestic production peaked at 0.6 bcm in 2010 and has since declined. After strong growth post 2010, LNG imports declined in 2014 and 2015. In terms of

---
[85] 'South Korean energy plan sees two more reactors', *World Nuclear News*, 22 July 2015. www.world-nuclear-news.org/NP-South-Korean-energy-plan-sees-two-more-reactors-2207154.html.

the sources of LNG imports, Qatar has grown, since 2011, to become the dominant source, followed by Indonesia, Malaysia, Oman, and Nigeria.

Energy policy and future gas demand drivers
President Park Geun-hye's government took power in February 2013. The most recent power sector plan (June 2015) coincided with the cancellation of four new coal-fired plants (total capacity 3.74 GW), with modest future growth in nuclear and gas envisaged. Targets for power generation shares in 2029 are: nuclear 28.5 per cent, coal 32.2 per cent, gas 24.7 per cent, renewables 4.6 per cent, CHP 5.8 per cent, and oil and pumped storage 4.2 per cent.[86] The envisaged share for gas in 2029 is unchanged from the latest comparable figure (for 2013) from the Korean Energy Economics Institute. The 2015 plan assumes a minor decrease in coal's share of 2029 power generation relative to 2013's levels, with compensating increases in renewables and nuclear. The government expects power demand to grow annually by 2.2 per cent, the World Nuclear Association expects this figure to be 2.5 per cent per year to 2020.[87] However, this appears to conflict with South Korea's objective of reducing power demand in 2035 by 15 per cent relative to current levels (and overall energy demand by 13 per cent), which was stated in its 2014 Energy Master Plan (Korea, 2014). The June 2015 plan was superseded in December 2015 by MOTIE[88] who expressed an expectation that demand for gas would drop to 34.65 mtpa in 2029. The use of gas in power generation would fall to 9.48 mtpa while domestic and industrial LNG consumption would rise to 25.17 mtpa.[89] LNG import data for 2015 shows a reduction to 45 bcm/year from 2014's level of 50 bcm/year, due to higher coal consumption and the restart of nuclear power plant temporarily shut down due to safety considerations.

Any outlook of South Korean gas demand must take account of:

- The slowdown in overall energy consumption since 2010, apparently as a result of reduced consumption in South Korea's manufactured goods export markets, and the extent to which this situation changes in the future. This will impact power generation and industrial consumption sectors.

---

[86] 'UPDATE 1-S.Korea axes four coal plants, plans two new nuclear units', Reuters, 8 June 2015. http://uk.reuters.com/article/2015/06/08/energy-southkorea-nuclear-idUKL3N0YU0AJ20150608.

[87] 'Nuclear Power in South Korea', World Nuclear Association, April 2016. www.world-nuclear.org/info/Country-Profiles/Countries-O-S/South-Korea/.

[88] MOTIE – Ministry of Trade, Industry and Energy, South Korea.

[89] 'South Korea's gas demand to drop 5 percent by 2029', *LNG World News*, 28 December 2015. www.lngworldnews.com/south-koreas-gas-demand-to-drop-5-percent-by-2029/.

- Consumption trends within the domestic non-power sector, given the outlook for low or negative population growth.

- The assumed rate of power generation growth and the share of gas within it. Government messages on this have been conflicting in recent years.

An illustrative outlook, based on MOTIE's December 2015 view is shown in Figure 6.14.

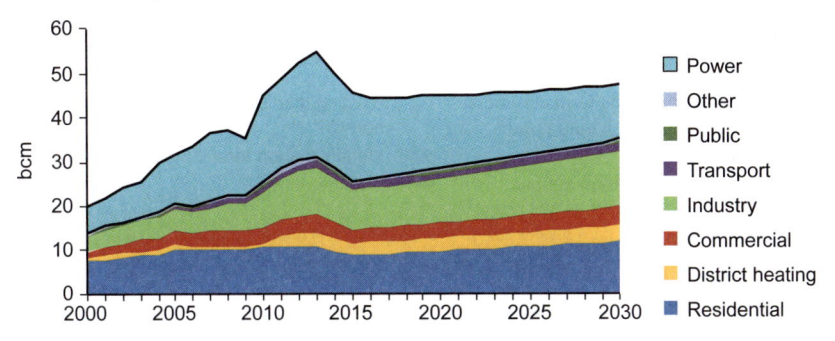

Figure 6.14: Historic and illustrative future South Korean gas demand
Source: KEEI (2015), author's assumptions.

Future annual growth assumptions for specific sectors, as shown in Figure 6.14 are:
Residential, District Heating, Commercial: 2 per cent;
Transport: 2.1 per cent;
Industry: 2.5 per cent;
Power: −2.7 per cent.
(Note that 2014 and 2015 sectoral divisions are notional in order to achieve aggregate consumption levels).

Total demand in 2030 amounts to 47.5 bcm compared with 44 bcm in 2015.

Figure 6.15 superimposes the illustrative demand outlook (Figure 6.14) on South Korea's LNG contractual supply position.

Existing JCC and US offtake contracts should be sufficient to cover South Korea's LNG requirements until the mid-2020s, although re-sale of short-term contract volumes was required to manage the situation in 2015 and 2016. Post 2025, South Korea will likely seek new supply contracts to offset the sharp decline in its existing portfolio. This will provide an opportunity to change the price formation balance of its supply away from oil indexation if so desired.

342 *LNG Markets in Transition*

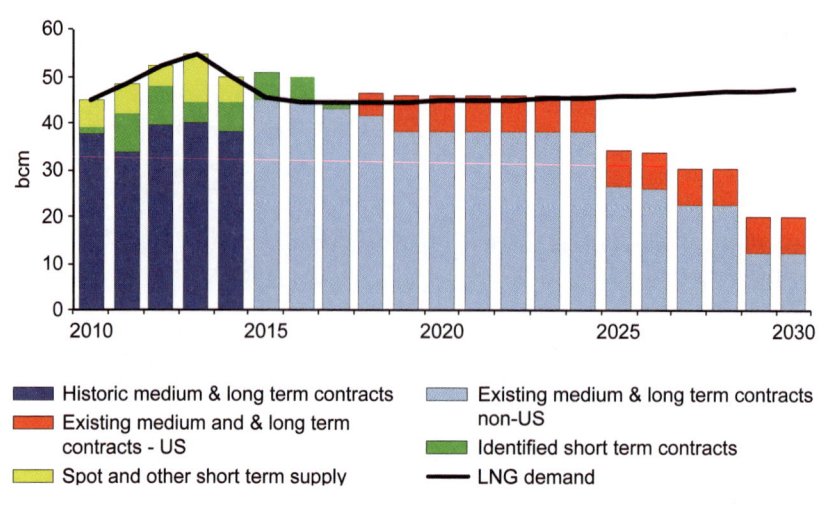

Figure 6.15: South Korea's LNG supply outlook and demand uncertainty, 2010–30
Source: GIIGNL (2014), author's analysis.

Conclusions: South Korea
South Korea is Asia's second-largest LNG importer, but with gas in 2014 representing only 15.7 per cent of its primary energy mix. Despite past periods of strong economic growth, the slowdown in the USA, China, and the Eurozone has required a refocus away from export industry to domestic-oriented industry and services. Longer-term challenges include an ageing population, inflexible labour market, and the dominance of large conglomerates/incumbents. This is relevant to LNG – which in South Korea is dominated by KOGAS, the world's largest corporate LNG purchaser. With negligible domestic production, South Korea's gas market development is directly reflected in its LNG import requirements.

South Korea's future LNG demand will be determined by:

- The extent to which it can regenerate economic growth and the balance between energy intensive manufacturing and domestically focused service industries.

- The need to reduce the role of coal and oil in its energy mix in order to reduce GHG emissions. The extent to which gas plays a role in achieving this is at present uncertain.

- The extent to which the government is able to achieve its future target for nuclear power generation, given a degree of popular opposition to it. In a GHG emission-constrained world this could increase LNG demand.

Despite the rather muted demand outlook, at least in comparison to historic LNG consumption growth trends, the need for new contracted supplies in the 2020s, as existing long-term contracts expire, places South Korea (and by definition KOGAS) in the front line of buyer-initiated moves away from JCC-linked contract pricing.

Table 6.3 shows a high case for South Korean imports based on the June 2015 power sector plan discussed above, and a low case consistent with MOTIE's revised view of December 2015.

Table 6.3: South Korea LNG imports – low and high cases

	2010	2011	2012	2013	2014	2015	2016	2017	2018	2019	2020
bcm/year											
Low case	45.0	48.4	52.3	54.8	49.8	45.5	44.4	44.5	44.6	44.7	44.8
High case	45.0	48.4	52.3	54.8	49.8	45.5	44.9	45.4	45.9	46.4	46.9
mtpa											
Low case	33.1	35.6	38.5	40.3	36.6	33.4	32.7	32.7	32.8	32.8	32.9
High case	33.1	35.6	38.5	40.3	36.6	33.4	33.0	33.4	33.7	34.1	34.5

	2021	2022	2023	2024	2025	2026	2027	2028	2029	2030
bcm/year										
Low case	44.9	45.1	45.3	45.6	45.8	46.1	46.4	46.7	47.1	47.5
High case	47.4	48.0	48.5	49.1	49.6	50.2	50.8	51.4	52.0	52.7
mtpa										
Low case	33.0	33.2	33.3	33.5	33.7	33.9	34.1	34.4	34.6	34.9
High case	34.9	35.3	35.7	36.1	36.5	36.9	37.4	37.8	38.3	38.7

Source: GIIGNL and author's analysis.

Taiwan

Introduction

Over the past 50 years the Taiwanese government and private sector have co-operated to continuously enhance industrial competitiveness and achieve steady economic growth. Taiwan has become the global centre for semiconductors, flat panel displays, and many other high-tech products. Exports led by electronics, machinery, and petrochemicals have provided the impetus for economic development but this heavy export dependency has exposed the economy to fluctuations in world demand. Free trade agreements have proliferated in east Asia in recent years with the Economic Cooperation Framework Agreement, signed with China in June 2010, being a notable landmark. Since 2009, Taiwan has gradually loosened its rules governing Chinese investment on the island, and has also secured greater market access for its investors in the mainland. Taiwan's diplomatic isolation, low birth rate, and rapidly ageing population are other major long-term challenges (CIA, 2015a).

Taiwan's energy mix is heavily dominated by oil and coal (76 per cent combined, in 2014 with gas constituting 13.8 per cent). After rapid growth from 1995 to 2007 (4.5 per cent per year), energy consumption growth has been muted following the 2008 financial crisis.

Gas consumption
In the non-power sector, residential consumption has increased by 2 per cent per year since 2010 but, more remarkably, industrial and services consumption has risen by 4.8 per cent per year in the same period. Taiwan's use of gas is dominated by the power generation sector, with city gas accounting for only 21.5 per cent in 2014. Power sector gas consumption surged post 2009, with annual growth from 2010 to 2014 at 5.1 per cent per year. The growth of gas-fired generation post 2010 has been at the expense of oil and, to a lesser degree, coal. The growth of coal in the power generation sector and in the energy mix more generally has directly contributed to Taiwan's CO_2 emission profile. Although having plateaued post 2007, Taiwan's 2014 CO_2 emissions are 2.45 times their 1990 level (BP, 2015).

Gas supply
Taiwan currently has some 0.4 bcm/year of domestic production from nine onshore fields on the western side of the island, and three offshore platforms on the CBK 1–3 gas fields.[90] The overwhelming source of gas supply is from LNG imports.

Historically, Taiwan's main LNG suppliers have been Indonesia and Malaysia. By 2010 the supply portfolio had become diversified, with the addition of Qatar, Nigeria, Oman, Australia, and others; however, by 2014 Qatar had grown to represent 45 per cent of LNG imports.

Energy policy and future gas demand drivers
Despite Taiwan's economic success, it faces challenges on the energy policy front. Its ambiguous relationship with mainland China and consequently limited international diplomatic relationships, together with minimal

---

[90] 'Energy Profile of Taiwan', Encyclopedia of Earth, October 2007. www.eoearth.org/view/article/152534/.

domestic energy endowment, have engendered concerns over security of energy supply. Its goals for CO_2 abatement (set in 2008) are to reduce CO_2 emissions to 2008 levels by 2020, and to 2000 levels by 2025 (Huang and Ko, 2009). Taiwan's energy policy focuses on energy efficiency, the deployment of renewables (wind and solar) to reach 16.1 per cent of generation capacity by 2030, a phase out of nuclear, and the 'reasonable use of natural gas for security of energy supply'. No mention is made of specifically cutting coal consumption (Taiwan, 2015a).

Two major barriers to progress are:

a) the low domestic price of electricity and gas, which has led to a huge cumulative debt on the part of CPC Corp. and Taipower (Liao and Jhou, 2013), and which does not allow decarbonization investment costs to be passed on to consumers;

b) anti-nuclear public opinion, catalysed by the Fukushima disaster, which has led to the mothballing and suspension of two reactors under construction at the Lungmen nuclear power plant.[91] The six existing reactors are planned to be phased out between 2018 and 2025.

The outlook for future gas demand in Taiwan critically depends on the future growth of power demand, the relative shares of gas and coal in power generation (in the context of the intent to phase out nuclear power), and whether policies will emerge to favour gas over coal.

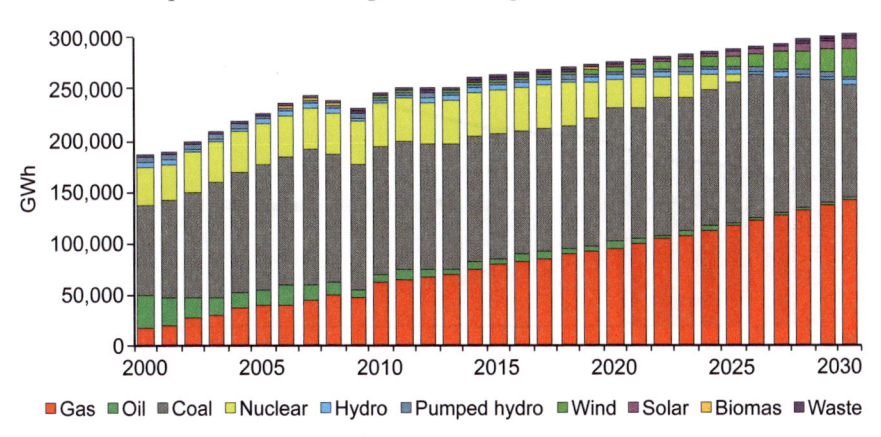

Figure 6.16: A possible future generation outlook to 2030 for Taiwan
Source: Taiwan (2015b, 87), author's assumptions and analysis.

---

[91] 'Political Discord Places Lungmen on hold', *World Nuclear News*, 28 April 2014, www.world-nuclear-news.org/NN-Political-discord-places-Lungmen-on-hold-2804144.html.

346   *LNG Markets in Transition*

For an assumed future power demand growth of 1 per cent per year, Figure 6.16 shows a scenario where nuclear is phased out as currently anticipated, wind and solar generation grow at an assumed 20 per cent per annum, oil continues to be squeezed, gas grows at an assumed 4 per cent per annum, and coal supplies the balance. Gas-fired generation continues on its 2000 to 2014 trend, coal increases as nuclear plants are shut down, but due to an assumed continued growth of renewables and gas, by 2030 coal consumption in power is 10 per cent lower than in 2014.

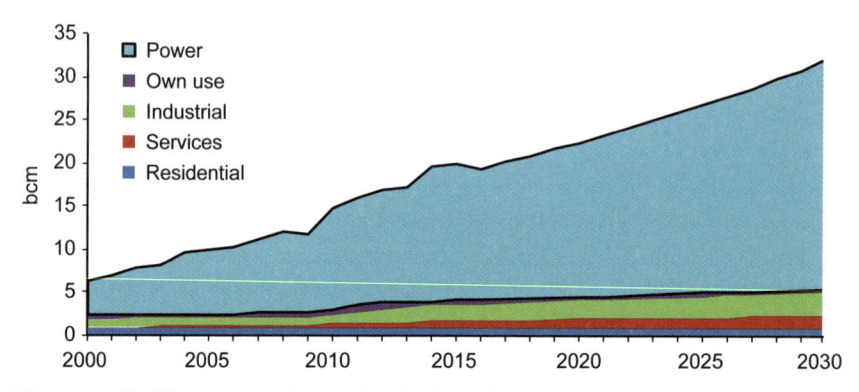

Figure 6.17: Taiwan gas demand outlook to 2030
Source: Taiwan (2015b), author's assumptions and analysis.

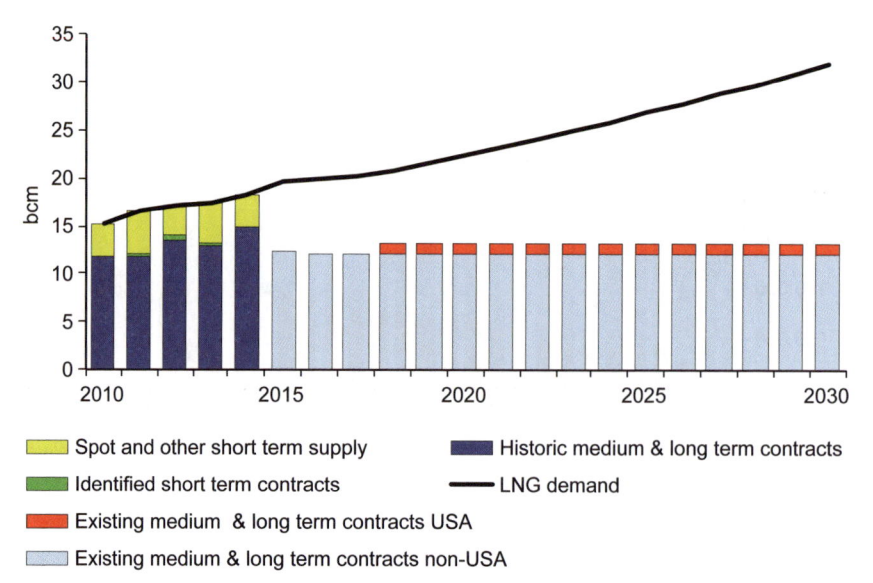

Figure 6.18: Taiwan future LNG demand and contractual position
Source: GIIGNL (2014), author's assumptions and analysis.

The resulting total gas demand outlook is shown in Figure 6.17, with gas demand by 2030 reaching 32.1 bcm compared to a 2015 figure of 19 bcm.

The combination of this LNG demand outlook with Taiwan's contractual position is shown in Figure 6.18. Taiwan has a stable long-term contract portfolio of some 13.1 bcm/year; all but 1.1 bcm/year (US-sourced LNG under a contract with GDF-Suez) of this being predominantly JCC price-linked. Taiwan, in the face of significant uncertainty over its future energy mix (as opposed to its policy intentions), will need to consider entering into additional medium- or long-term LNG contracts towards the end of this decade if it wishes to avoid increasing dependence on the spot LNG market to fulfil its import requirements.

Conclusions: Taiwan

Taiwan has developed a successful high technology-focused export-led economy which has in recent decades enjoyed high (if at times volatile) economic growth. It has based this on a high carbon intensity energy mix in which coal and oil are dominant. While gas represented only 13.8 per cent of primary energy consumption in 2014, its use has been growing at 5 per cent per year on average since 2010. Taiwan's gas consumption is dominated by the power sector. Taiwan's quest to reduce its CO_2 emissions and energy import dependency are challenged by: a popular revolt against nuclear power; and, low regulated domestic prices for gas and electricity.

Even assuming high growth rates of future wind and solar investment (20 per cent per year) the challenge for Taiwan is one of containing coal consumption. It is feasible therefore that the growth of gas demand (and LNG imports) could continue to follow its 2010–14 trend of 4 per cent per year. This would add an additional import requirement by 2030 of 14 bcm/year over 2014's level.

Table 6.4 shows the 'high case' discussed above and a 'low case' in which power demand growth for gas is only 1 per cent per year.

Table 6.4: Taiwan LNG import outlook – low and high cases

	2010	2011	2012	2013	2014	2015	2016	2017	2018	2019	2020
bcm/year											
Low case	14.8	16.1	16.8	17.2	18.1	19.7	19.2	19.5	19.7	20.0	20.3
High case	14.8	16.1	16.8	17.2	18.1	19.7	19.9	20.1	20.9	21.6	22.4
mtpa											
Low case	10.9	11.9	12.4	12.7	13.3	14.5	14.1	14.3	14.5	14.7	14.9
High case	10.9	11.9	12.4	12.7	13.3	14.5	14.3	14.8	15.4	15.9	16.5

Table 6.4 *continued*

	2021	2022	2023	2024	2025	2026	2027	2028	2029	2030
bcm/year										
Low case	20.5	20.8	21.0	21.3	21.6	21.8	22.1	22.4	22.6	22.9
High case	23.3	24.1	25.0	25.9	26.8	27.8	28.8	29.8	30.9	32.1
mtpa										
Low case	15.1	15.3	15.5	15.7	15.9	16.1	16.2	16.4	16.6	16.8
High case	17.1	17.7	18.4	19.0	19.7	20.4	21.2	21.9	22.7	23.6

Source: GIIGNL and author's analysis.

Conclusions: mature Asian LNG markets

Japan, South Korea, and Taiwan have together accounted for around 60 per cent of world LNG demand since 1980. Despite their differences, the three countries face some common issues which will impact their future LNG demand:

- The future of nuclear power. Following the Fukushima disaster, Japan's future LNG requirements are expected to be the most directly influenced by the pace and extent of the programme for restarting its nuclear power plant. South Korea has restarted nuclear plant that had been temporarily shut down due to safety considerations, and government policy sees a continuing role for nuclear which might in future be contested. In Taiwan, government policy sees a phase-out of nuclear plant by 2025.

- Coal is the most price-competitive power generation fuel in all three countries. How the obvious clash between this and GHG obligations made at COP21 will be resolved remains to be seen. For now, these counties are relying on (challenging) assumptions of energy efficiency and rapid renewable capacity growth to meet such targets.

- All three counties face the issues of low birth rates, ageing populations, and hence long-term population decline. In terms of their economic model, this emphasizes the need for export-orientated activity rather than domestic consumption to provide economic growth. Taiwan's diplomatic isolation and South Korea's inflexible labour market and the dominance of large conglomerates/incumbents, are other long-term challenges.

- Future economic growth is a key factor affecting power and industrial demand. Japan is an industrialized economy which has suffered low growth since the early 1990s. South Korea's previous strong economic growth has been muted since 2010 due to economic slowdown in the

USA, Asia, and the Eurozone. Whether these economies can maintain growth by stimulating domestic demand is an open question at present. Taiwan has also relied on export markets for its high-tech products; however, it remains to be seen whether its trade agreements signed in recent years, including with China, will extend its existing business model.

Overall the LNG demand outlook for these three countries is somewhat less optimistic than historic trends might suggest.

More recent and emerging Asian LNG markets

Introduction

This section covers a range of markets, from China and India where LNG, as an already established channel of gas supply, could grow to levels of major global importance, to more recently emerged (and also potential new) importers, where future LNG requirements are uncertain (such countries as Singapore, Thailand, Indonesia, Malaysia, Pakistan, Bangladesh, and Vietnam).

Each country has specific needs in terms of LNG imports, based on its gas demand expectations and its domestic production and pipeline gas import outlook. This section reviews each in detail, with common strands brought together in the concluding summary.

China

With a population of 1.37 billion[92] and the world's second-largest economy in 2014, China has experienced exceptional economic growth since 1995: an annual average of 9.6 per cent. In 2015 attention focused on the slowdown

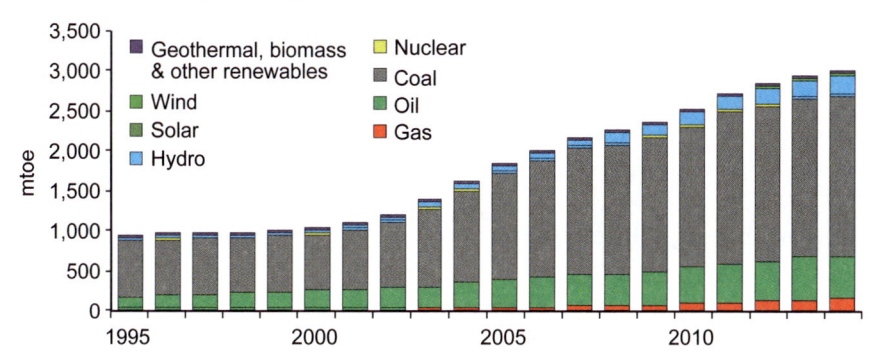

Figure 6.19: Primary energy mix of China, 1995–2014
Source: BP (2015).

---

[92] Countrymeters – website of key country statistics – (China): http://countrymeters.info/en/China.

in China's economic growth, which was officially around 7 per cent in terms of GDP year on year, but in terms of observed commodities imports and manufacturing output may have been lower than this. Figure 6.19 shows China's primary energy mix from 1995 to 2014, demonstrating that its economic growth, in energy terms, has been driven overwhelmingly by coal.

In 2014, the share of gas in China's energy mix stood at 5.6 per cent, with coal at 65.7 per cent, oil at 17.9 per cent, and hydro at 8 per cent. Despite its minor contribution, gas consumption has grown at an average rate of 13.2 per cent per year from 2010 to 2014 (compared with total energy consumption growth of 4.7 per cent). Energy consumption growth slowed in 2014, however, achieving only a 2.5 per cent increase over 2013 (the corresponding increase for gas being 8.4 per cent). Of particular note is that coal consumption in 2014 was virtually unchanged on the 2013 level.[93]

Gas consumption

Residential and commercial demand has increased by 20 per cent on an annual average basis between 2005 and 2012, manufacturing by 13.3 per cent, and power by 42.5 per cent. The main industrial growth areas for gas demand are Chemicals, Fuel Processing, Metal and Metal Products, and Machinery and Transport Products. Although these sectors saw a dip in demand during the post-crisis year of 2009, strong growth had been re-established by 2011. In all these sectors however, gas plays 'second or third fiddle' to coal and oil.

In the power sector, gas continues to play a very minor role compared to coal and hydro. In 2012 gas provided only some 2 per cent of power generation compared with coal (76 per cent) and hydro (18 per cent); this despite gas-fired generation having grown by an estimated 24 per cent per year on average between 2009 and 2012.

Monthly data for China's gas consumption is not available in a comprehensive form. While Kong, Dong, and Xhou noted limited seasonality on the basis of import patterns to end 2012 (Kong et al., 2015), the need for gas storage facilities in addition to the mid-2015 total of 7.3 bcm appears to be growing, to deal with peak demand periods.[94]

---

[93] Note that other sources suggest that 2014 saw coal consumption decline by 2.9% from 2013's level. 'Official data confirms Chinese coal use fell in 2014', Carbon Brief, 26th February 2015, www.carbonbrief.org/official-data-confirms-chinese-coal-use-fell-in-2014.

[94] China Natural Gas Map, www.chinagasmap.com/theprojects/gasstorage.htm.

Chinese natural gas supply and demand (historical)

From 2006 onwards gas demand outstripped growing domestic production, with the balance initially being supplied by LNG imports. Pipeline imports from Turkmenistan and Central Asia commenced in 2010 and from Myanmar in 2014. Domestic production is overwhelmingly from conventional sources, with coal bed methane and shale gas contributing only 3.6 and 1.3 bcm in 2014 respectively.[95] The revised (downward) target for shale gas in 2020 is 30 bcm.[96] China has commenced a programme of producing natural gas from coal (synthetic natural gas). While this may alleviate the particulate pollution deriving from coal combustion in power generation and other uses, the process (without CCS) produces higher net CO_2 emissions and is a heavy consumer of water. The original intention was to produce 50 bcm/year of 'synthetic' natural gas by 2020; however, it is likely that this will be scaled back to 15 bcm/year.[97] The sources of China's LNG imports between 2006 and 2014 were initially dominated by Malaysia, Indonesia, and Australian, but Qatar became the largest supplier from 2012. In 2015 China's largest three gas producers limited gas production in the face of demand slowdown, but nevertheless China had to resell some long-term contracted LNG volumes.

Chinese energy policy

In June 2014, President Xi Jinping called for an energy policy shift based on five key areas: consumption, energy mix, technology, the energy system, and international co-operation. The government aims to cut coal consumption by 160 million tonnes by 2020. China intends to increase the share of gas in its energy mix to 10 per cent, in addition to achieving 100 GW of wind capacity by 2015, and further growth of solar PV from 21 GW in 2015 (Ma, 2015). China's energy policy gained greater international prominence through the joint announcement of national climate targets by President Barack Obama and President Xi Jinping in November 2014, ahead of the December 2015 Climate Summit. China intends that its CO_2 emissions will peak around 2030 and will use

---

[95] 'China's unconventional output up', Platts International Gas Report, Issue 766, 26 January 2015.

[96] 'Yin and Yang of Chinese shale gas', Audrey Raj, *Asian Oil & Gas*, 27 May 2015. www.aogdigital.com/component/k2/item/4912-yin-and-yang-of-chinese-shale-gas.

[97] 'In China, a tug of war over coal gas: Cleaner air but worse for the climate', Simon Denyer, *The Washington Post*, 5 May 2015, https://www.washingtonpost.com/world/in-china-a-tug-of-war-over-coal-gas--cleaner-air-worse-for-the-climate/2015/04/27/b10992cc-e380-11e4-ae0f-f8c46aa8c3a4_story.html.

352   *LNG Markets in Transition*

its best efforts to bring that date forward.[98]

From 2011, Chinese policy makers have undertaken a reform of Chinese natural gas pricing in the domestic market, progressively linking city gate prices to a formula including competing fuels, notably fuel oil and LPG, albeit with delayed re-calculation.[99] This was an attempt to rationalize the internal pricing system in terms of the price competitiveness of gas with competing fuels; and to ensure an economic logic to the matrix of Chinese supply sources (imports and domestic production) in terms of wellhead cost of supply, contractual price formulae, and transport costs. This reform process has run into headwinds. The calculation of prices under the Chinese competing fuel price formula has resulted in domestic gas prices above those in international (LNG spot) markets, and an oversupply in the domestic market. With oil and oil product prices low (since the oil price slump of late 2014), gas faces challenges in achieving government energy mix targets in China unless prices are further liberalized. Wood Mackenzie estimate that China faces an oversupply of 18 bcm/year of contracted gas between 2015 and 2017 due to lower than expected demand growth.[100] It has been suggested that the government take advantage of the oversupply to push natural gas market reform and boost its share in transportation fuels.[101]

Future Chinese natural gas demand

In early 2014 the Chinese National Development and Reform Commission (NDRC) indicated that by 2020 it would raise its total natural gas supply capacity to between 400 bcm/year and 420 bcm/year.[102] As China's economy began to slow during 2014 CNPC, in December 2015, provided a more modest demand outlook of 300 bcm/year by 2020 on a 'Business as Usual Scenario' (CNPC, 2015). The IEA, in its 2015 World Energy Outlook, showed a gas demand figure for China of 315 bcm/year for 2020 in a 'New Policies Scenario' (IEA, 2015a, 196). These demand outlooks to

---

[98] 'China Energy Outlook 2015', Alexandra Cheung, Imperial College London, 1 April 2015, http://wwwf.imperial.ac.uk/blog/climate-at-imperial/2015/04/01/china-energy-outlook-2015/.

[99] For a comprehensive description see Chen (2014).

[100] 'High prices threaten Beijing's target of natural gas accounting for 10pc of energy use', Eric Ng, *South China Morning Post*, 21 June 2015, www.scmp.com/business/china-business/article/1824591/high-prices-threaten-beijings-target-natural-gas-accounting.

[101] 'China seen holding off LND deliveries amid glut and high-cost domestic output', *South China Morning Post*, 29 November 2015, www.scmp.com/business/markets/article/1884381/china-seen-holding-lng-deliveries-amid-glut-and-high-cost-domestic.

[102] 'China to raise natural gas supply to 400–420 billion cubic metres by 2020: NDRC', *The Economic Times*, 24 April 2014. http://articles.economictimes.indiatimes.com/2014-04-24/news/49378338_1_ndrc-natural-gas-supply-national-bureau.

2030 are shown in Figure 6.20. Due to a combination of high regulated gas prices and a slowdown in economic activity, China's gas consumption for 2015 appeared (in October 2015) to be only 2.6 per cent higher than 2014.[103] This serves to cast doubt on some of the more aggressive demand trends in Figure 6.20. For the purpose of this analysis, Figure 6.20 includes a High Demand Case Assumption (dashed orange line) which converges on the IEA New Policies case by 2020; and a Low Demand Case Assumption (dashed blue line) which by 2020 and beyond is the average of the CNPC 2015 Business as Usual and Low cases. It should be stressed that these two cases are illustrative and not based on quantitative analysis. CNPC (2015), however, presents a useful benchmark for the scope for potential coal-to-gas switching, driven by government policy with the aim of reducing CO_2 and particulate emissions: 40 bcm/year in power generation, 55 bcm/year in industry, and 20 bcm/year in space heating. The proposed timescale for this total 115 bcm/year of coal-to-gas substitution is five years.[104]

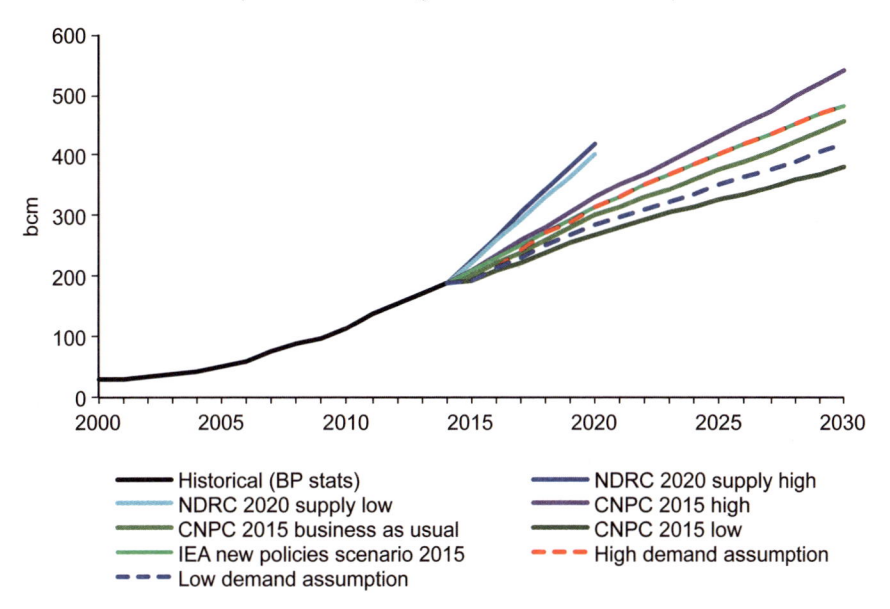

Figure 6.20: Chinese historical and future natural gas demand from various sources

Sources: BP (2015), 'China to raise natural gas supply to 400-420 billion cubic metres by 2020: NDRC', *The Economic Times*, 24 April 2014 (http://articles.economictimes.indiatimes.com/2014-04-24/news/49378338_1_ndrc-natural-gas-supply-national-bureau), CNPC (2015, 196).

---

[103] 'China's weak natural gas demand cuts into LNG imports', ICIS, 7 October 2015. www.icis.com/resources/news/2015/10/07/9930658/china-s-weak-natural-gas-demand-cuts-into-lng-imports/.
[104] Slide 19 in CNPC (2015).

China's future natural gas supply mix

It is fair to say, in early 2016, that all elements of Chinese natural gas supply are prone to considerable future uncertainty. In the face of weak demand for natural gas in 2015, Chinese upstream companies were reported to have reduced conventional gas output while striving to meet targets for shale gas production.[105]

Chinese domestic supply includes conventional gas, shale gas, coal bed methane, and synthetic gas (gas from coal). There are few sources which provide a comprehensive outlook for each. The IEA in its 2015 World Energy Outlook (New Policies Scenario) provides a total Chinese domestic gas production total. CNPC (CNPC, 2014) provides a useful breakdown based on analysis presented in November 2014. The outlooks from both the IEA and CNPC are shown in Figure 6.21. (Note that the CNPC estimates of domestic production from various sources are only available for the period 2015 to 2020).

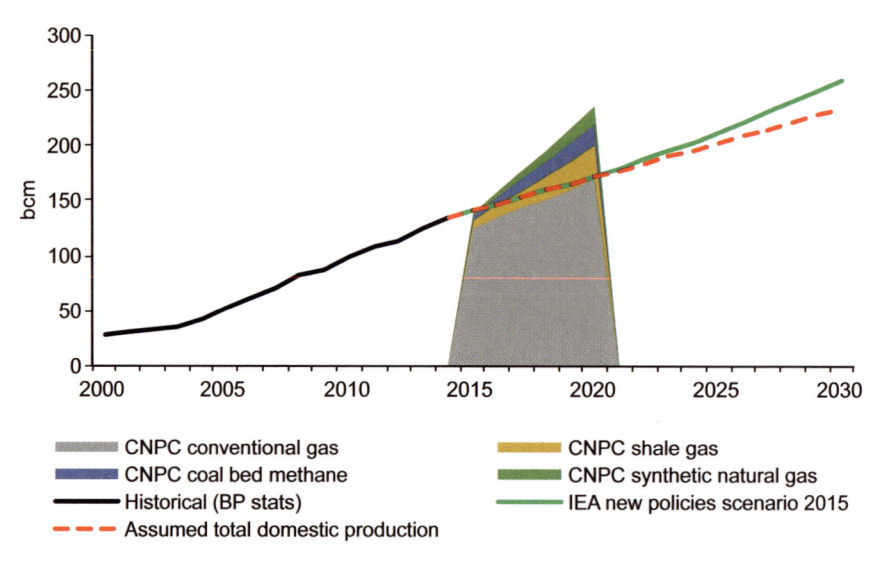

Figure 6.21: Historical and future Chinese domestic natural gas production
Source: BP (2015), IEA (2015c), CNPC (2014).

Clearly CNPC sees greater potential for domestic production, with anticipated growth from shale gas, coal bed methane, and synthetic natural gas than is implied in the IEA New Policies Outlook. The analysis in the remainder of this section will be based on the assumption that Chinese

---

[105] 'China curbs conventional gas output, keeps shale target', Reuters, 10 September 2015. www.reuters.com/article/china-gas-idUSL3N10N44X20150910.

domestic production follows the dashed orange line in Figure 6.21; this tracks the IEA's 2015 New Policies Scenario assumption between 2015 and 2020 but then continues on a lower linear trend (in other words, it diverges from the IEA case, which assumes an acceleration in domestic production in the 2020s). The author is inclined to take this conservative view given the lack of positive news on the progress of unconventional gas development in China.

To varying degrees, CNPC has invested both in upstream field development and in pipeline infrastructure to bring gas from Turkmenistan, Kazakhstan, and Uzbekistan (entering at China's north-west border) to key demand centres. In 2014 total imports via this route amounted to 28.3 bcm, although existing and future pipeline capacity could raise this figure to 65 bcm/year. In 2014 China imported 3 bcm/year from Myanmar with the potential to increase this to 10–12 bcm/year in the future.[106] China's two pending pipeline import deals with Russia were prominent in the media in 2014 and 2015; namely a 38 bcm/year contract to supply gas from East Siberian fields (the 'Power of Siberia' project) entering China at its north-east border; and a 30 bcm/year contract to supply West Siberian gas at China's north-west border, the 'Altai Pipeline'. These supplies were expected to come on stream around 2020. However, in mid-2015, media reports cast doubt on whether these arrangements would progress. The border price required by Gazprom in 2015 appeared high in comparison with contract and spot LNG import prices, while weakening Chinese gas demand growth has eased the pressure on China to fully consummate these two contracts.

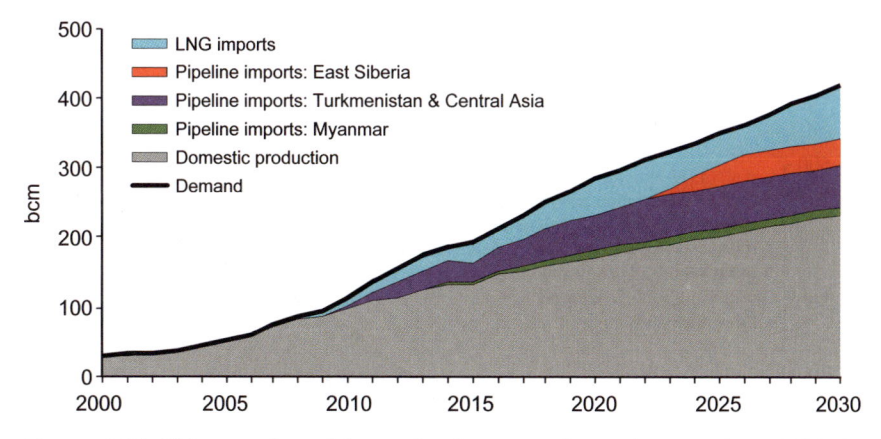

Figure 6.22: China supply and demand on base-case demand assumptions, 2000–30
Source: BP (2015), IEA (2015c), GIIGNL(2014), author's assumptions.

---

[106] 'Natural Gas Imports into China – Prospects for Growth', King & Spalding Energy Newsletter, September 2014. www.kslaw.com/library/newsletters/EnergyNewsletter/2014/September/article1.html.

Taking the 'Low Demand Case Assumption' view of Chinese gas demand shown in Figure 6.20, a possible disposition of Chinese supply is shown in Figure 6.22, from conventional and unconventional sources and based on assumptions of future pipeline import levels.

In Figure 6.22, Myanmar pipeline imports are assumed to grow by 1 bcm per year to reach 11 bcm/year by 2022, imports from Turkmenistan and Central Asian grow from 2015 to reach 60 bcm/year by 2022, and the Russian East Siberian project is assumed to proceed with imports commencing in 2023 and growing to 38 bcm/year by 2026. LNG is assumed to make up the balance, reaching some 56 bcm/year in the early 2020s and 75 bcm/year by 2030. Table 6.5 summarizes the balance at five-yearly intervals.

Table 6.5: China supply and demand on base case demand assumptions (bcm/year)

	2015	2020	2025	2030
Demand	192	285	350	418
Domestic production	133	172	203	234
Pipeline imports: Myanmar	4	9	11	11
Pipeline imports: Turkmenistan & Central Asia	28	50	60	60
Pipeline imports: East Siberia	0	0	30	38
Pipeline imports: West Siberia	0	0	0	0
LNG imports	27	54	46	75
Total supply	192	285	350	418

Source: BP (2015), IEA (2015c), GIGNL (2014), author's assumptions.

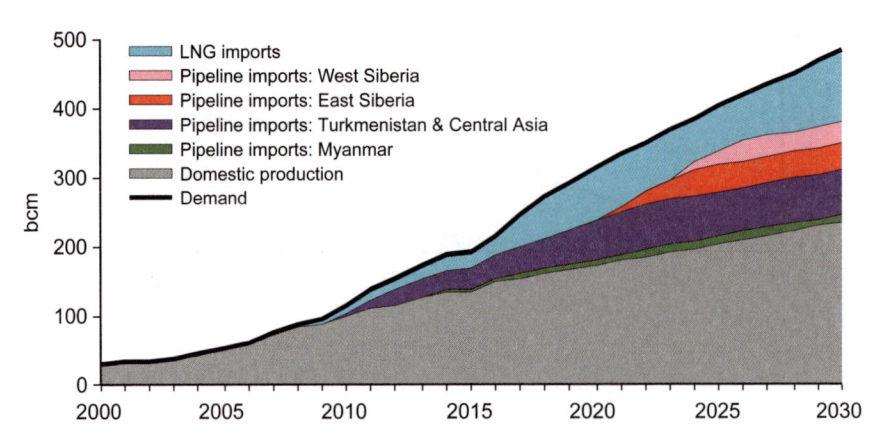

Figure 6.23: China supply and demand – high demand assumption, 2000–30
Source: BP (2015), IEA (2015c), GIIGNL(2014), author's assumptions.

LNG Demand Potential 357

A 'High Demand Case Assumption' could yield the balance shown in Figure 6.23. Here, imports from Turkmenistan and Central Asian grow to 65 bcm/year by 2022; the Russian East Siberian project is assumed to commence in 2021 and grow to 38 bcm/year by 2024; and the West Siberian project (Altai line) is assumed to start in 2024 and reach 30 bcm/year by 2026. LNG is assumed to make up the balance, reaching some 105 bcm/year by 2030. Table 6.6 summarizes the balance at five yearly intervals

Table 6.6: China supply and demand on high case demand assumptions (bcm/year)

	2015	2020	2025	2030
Demand	**192**	**315**	**403**	**483**
Domestic production	133	172	203	234
Pipeline imports: Myanmar	4	9	11	11
Pipeline imports: Turkmenistan & Central Asia	28	55	65	65
Pipeline imports: East Siberia	0	0	38	38
Pipeline imports: West Siberia	0	0	20	30
LNG imports	27	79	66	105
Total supply	**192**	**315**	**403**	**483**

Source: BP (2015), IEA (2015c), GIGNL (2014), author's assumptions.

Figure 6.24 shows future LNG import requirements related to these two demand cases, and compares them with China's current portfolio of future long, medium, and short-term contracts. Historic data on China's LNG imports (long, medium, and short-term contract deliveries, and spot transactions) is also shown.

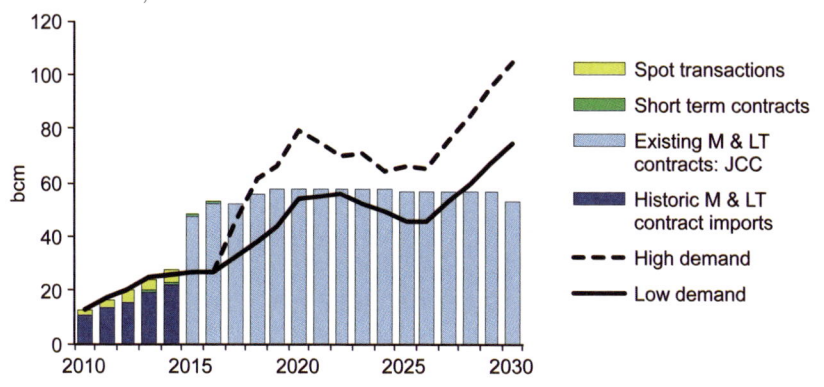

Figure 6.24: China's LNG import requirements on base and high future demand cases and contractual commitments

Sources: GIIGNL(2014), author's calculations.

358   *LNG Markets in Transition*

In 2015 and 2016, China was already in an 'over-contracted' position in terms of LNG contracts it had entered into, relative to its ability to absorb such volumes. In the Low Demand Case defined above, China would continue to be over-contracted to varying degrees until the mid-2020s. Postponement of the second Russian pipeline project and/or reducing take-up of Turkmen/Central Asian volumes would mitigate this position. Failing this, China would be required to sell-on contracted LNG volumes (as it did in 2015) potentially incurring a loss relative to contract price.

China conclusions
Over the past 10 years or so, China has been the source of demand for a range of imported commodities including oil and natural gas. China's situation has changed, however, as from 2014 it appeared to enter a phase of lower growth, re-focusing away from energy intensive state-directed infrastructure and manufacturing activity, towards domestic consumption and services. Any move to a lower carbon intensive economy on the part of China needs to address its overwhelming reliance on coal. Growth in nuclear, hydro, wind, and solar PV will help in this regard, but the timescales required to achieve targets through such investment programmes are often underestimated. Gas has an obvious role to play, but China is rightly concerned to ensure firstly, that it maximizes its domestic production capabilities and secondly, that prices for contracted imported supplies are acceptable and such arrangements do not preclude future evolutions to more liberalized energy market pricing constructs. The challenge for China is to manage all of the above in the context of uncertain future energy requirements and fuel mix.

Table 6.7 summarizes China's LNG import requirements for the cases discussed above.

Table 6.7: China LNG import cases

	2010	2011	2012	2013	2014	2015	2016	2017	2018	2019	2020
bcm/year											
Low case	13.1	17.8	19.9	25.3	25.8	27.2	27.0	32.5	38.0	43.5	54.0
High case	13.1	17.8	19.9	25.3	25.8	27.2	26.8	45.6	61.4	66.2	79.0
mtpa											
Low case	9.6	13.1	14.7	18.6	19.0	20.0	19.9	23.9	27.9	32.0	39.7
High case	9.6	13.1	14.7	18.6	19.0	20.0	19.7	33.5	45.1	48.7	58.1

Table 6.7 *continued*

	2021	2022	2023	2024	2025	2026	2027	2028	2029	2030
bcm/year										
Low case	54.8	55.6	52.4	49.2	46.0	45.4	52.8	60.2	67.6	75.0
High case	74.4	69.8	71.2	64.6	66.0	65.8	75.6	85.4	95.2	105.0
mtpa										
Low case	40.3	40.9	38.5	36.2	33.8	33.4	38.8	44.3	49.7	55.1
High case	54.7	51.3	52.4	47.5	48.5	48.4	55.6	62.8	70.0	77.2

Source: GIIGNL, author's analysis.

India

India has a population of 1.2 billion and its GDP growth has exceeded the world average in every year since 2001. Its economy, in 2014, in terms of GDP comprises agriculture (18 per cent), industry (31 per cent) and services (51 per cent);[107] it is thus more highly dependent on agriculture than other major Asian LNG importers. After low economic growth in 2013, the incoming Prime Minister Narendra Modi has promised to implement economic reform to attract private sector investment. India's economy, however, continues to operate far below its potential with corruption, poor infrastructure, and fiscal deficits all being major obstacles to economic growth (IEF, 2016a).

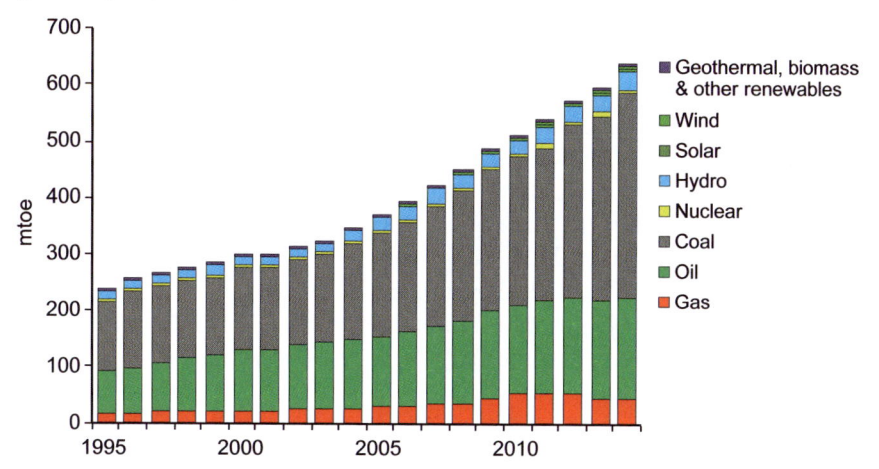

Figure 6.25: Primary energy mix of India, 1995–2014
Source: BP (2015).

---

[107] 'Sector-wise contribution of GDP of India', *Statistics Times*, 8 July 2015. http://statisticstimes.com/economy/sectorwise-gdp-contribution-of-india.php.

India's primary energy consumption trends are shown in Figure 6.25. The energy mix is dominated by coal (56.5 per cent in 2014) and oil (28.3 per cent in 2014), with gas coming a poor third, at 7.1 per cent. The decline in gas use since 2011 is a consequence of a reduction in domestic production (see below). Total energy consumption has grown by 5.8 per cent per year on average between 2010 and 2014, while coal consumption in the same period saw a corresponding growth of 8.5 per cent per year.

The key dynamic of India's gas supply/demand position in recent years has been the decline in overall demand post 2011; the result of abruptly falling domestic production which was not compensated for by an increase in LNG imports. Trends post 2005 show a stable level of industrial consumption, higher consumption as a domestic fuel post 2009/10 (but with limited growth thereafter), a growing consumption in fertilizer production to 2009/10 (again stagnant in recent years), and a power sector demand which grew rapidly to 2010/11 but which has reduced after this peak.

For a description of the Indian domestic gas market, the reader is directed to a paper ('Gas Pricing Reform in India: Implications for the Indian gas landscape') by Anupama Sen (Sen, 2015). The following summarizes key points from this paper.

Gas consumption in India is governed by the 'Gas Utilisation Policy' which supports the rationing of domestically produced gas to Tier 1 'priority sectors' with the resulting balance released for sale to the wider Indian market. The major 'priority sector' customers are: city gas for households and transportation, fertilizers, LPG extraction plants, and grid-connected power plants. Industrial users, which include steel, refineries and petrochemicals plant, commercial users, and merchant power plants, are regarded as Tier 2, or lower priority users in this allocation system.

Prices received by producers of domestic gas are determined by state regulation and vary depending on the original licensing terms. The majority of domestic gas prior to the price reform implemented in April 2015 received $4.20/MMBtu. While observers expected the price reform to result in a near doubling of this price, in the event (by selecting a basket dominated by relatively low international reference prices: US Henry Hub, Canadian hub prices, and Russian domestic price as prime examples) the post reform price rose modestly to $4.66/MMBtu.

LNG is imported at prices determined by contractual terms (historically an oil price linkage) or spot prices. Some LNG may be directed to Tier 1 consumers (with the state or state-owned entities funding any subsidies involved). Tier 2 consumers will pay the import price of LNG consumed, plus any additional transportation and other costs.

India consumes some 30 million tonnes/year of fertilizer, second only to China. Of the urea manufactured in India, 81 per cent derives from gas feedstock. Farmers receive a subsidy amounting to 50 per cent of the cost of urea. While a growing population and economic wealth will support increased underlying demand for fertilizer, the ability of farmers to pay the 'real' price of urea (or the government's ability to fund the current subsidy arrangement) may act to dampen its availability.

In the power sector, gas-fired generation accounts for just under 10 per cent of total installed capacity. Power demand is limited by the geographical extent and capacity of distribution grids. Gas-fired power suffers due to its higher cost relative to domestic or imported coal.

City gas consumption shows continued growth potential both in terms of domestic and commercial consumption and in transportation. Again actual demand growth may be supressed by infrastructure constraints and by supply availability. This sector is generally able to pay prices based on LNG imports. The outlook for industrial demand is less clear.

Onshore gas production has been stable at around 8.5 bcm/year during this period. Offshore production rose dramatically in 2008/9 and 2009/10 with the development of the KG-D6 eastern offshore gas field. Production from this field has declined, apparently due to poor well performance and higher than anticipated water influx from the reservoir.[108]

In Sen (2015), the outlook for increased domestic production is not an optimistic one. Significant additional resource potential could be accessed by exploration and development, but only at wholesale or 'beach' prices above $8/MMBtu. As policymakers seem unwilling or unable to either set the regulated price at a level which would incentivize further domestic supply development, or allow wholesale prices to be determined by the forces of supply and demand, any future growth in Indian gas demand will need to be met by (and be able to pay for) LNG imports. The IEA, in its World Energy Outlook 2015 New Policies Scenario anticipates Indian production reaching 55 bcm/year by 2030, presumably assuming a change in pricing policy prior to the 2020s (Figure 6.26). On the demand side, Figure 6.26 shows two rather optimistic outlooks (Vision 2030 cases) which were derived with the intention of making a case for policy reform to stimulate the domestic gas industry. The IEA 2015 New Policies Scenario case, by contrast, shows a more measured growth to 2020 followed by an acceleration to reach 121 bcm/year by 2030. The IEA Current Policies Scenario by 2030 is little changed from the New Policies case (4 per cent lower); the '450 Scenario' however has modestly higher gas demand growth in the 2020s (achieving 134 bcm/year by 2030).

---

[108] 'RIL, BP offer $5 billion to hike KG D6 gas output', 1 May 2013, *Oil and Gas Journal*. www.ogj.com/articles/print/volume-111/issue-4/exploration---development/ril-bp-offer-5-billion-to-hike.html.

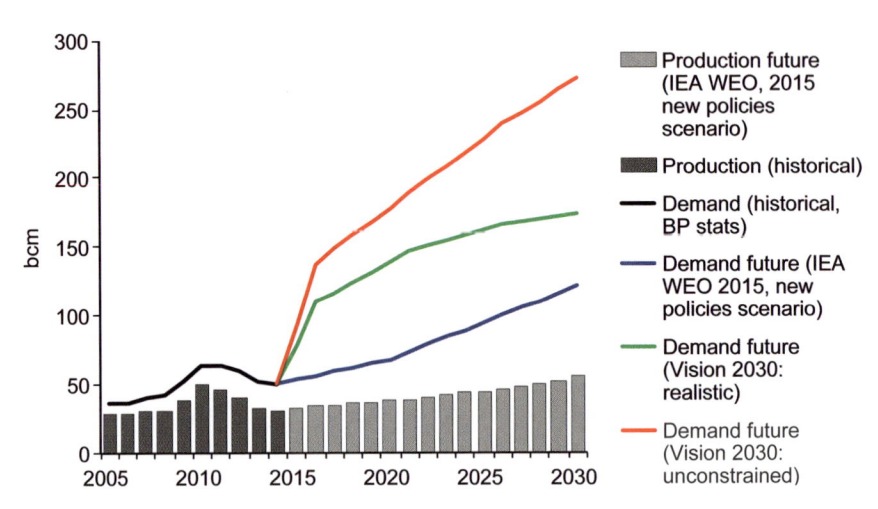

Figure 6.26: Indian demand outlooks and domestic gas production, 2005–2030
Sources: IEA (2015c), India (2013), BP (2015).

India began LNG imports in 2004. To end 2014, Qatar has supplied 80 per cent of India's LNG with Nigeria and, prior to 2014, Egypt as the main secondary suppliers. In December 2015, India's Petronet negotiated a 50 per cent reduction in price under a contract signed with Qatar in 1999 and was not required to pay for volumes not imported in 2015 under the take-or-pay clause. While India's potential future market size was certainly an issue to consider, the wisdom of signing the initial deal on what is alleged to have been a fixed price of $12 to $13/MMBtu is certainly questionable.[109]

India's energy policy and future gas demand

India's energy policy continues to appear somewhat unfocused, notably the expedient handling of the issue of gas price reform and the 'wishful thinking' support of solar and wind (given the realistically achievable scale of such capacity build). There appears to be an acceptance that coal will provide for the main growth of power generation, and no specific policy for natural gas. The future growth of gas will be hindered by a number of factors. On the supply side, domestic production will not materially increase until wholesale/beach prices are either liberalized or at least linked to a credible international index. Additional supply will be in the form of LNG imports, with the low probability of completing pipeline import projects due to demand uncertainties, linking infrastructure build requirements,

---

[109] 'Petronet strikes deal with Qatar's RasGas to get LNG at half-price', *The Hindu Business Line*, 31 December 2015. www.thehindubusinessline.com/news/qatar-agrees-to-lower-price-in-gas-deal-with-india/article8049876.ece.

and pricing issues. The process of gas allocation in the domestic market and attendant subsidies is a further barrier to establishing a market price based on supply/demand dynamics, especially with no obvious plan to extend pipeline infrastructure.

Estimating future demand trends for natural gas in India is therefore problematic at this juncture. In the absence of any rational alternative scenario, the LNG import requirement derived from the IEA WEO 2015 New Policies Scenario is used as a 'default base case', albeit that its assumptions regarding future domestic production growth appear optimistic.

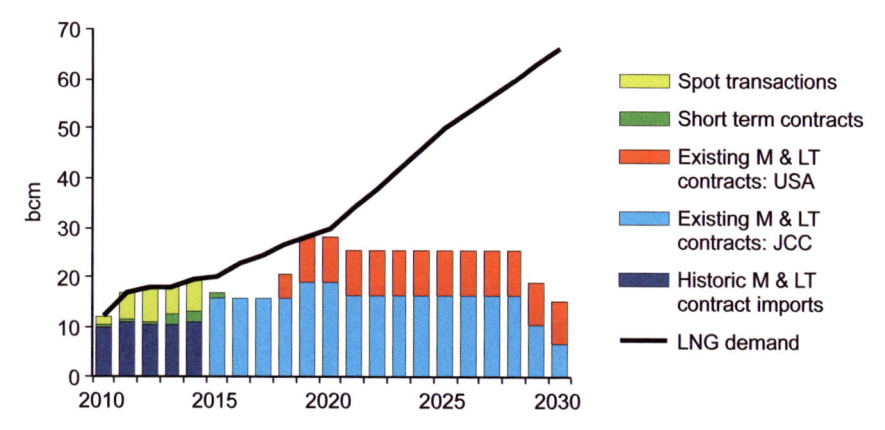

Figure 6.27: India's future LNG import requirements and contractual commitments
Source: IEA (2015c), GIIGNL(2014), author's analysis.

Figure 6.27 overlays the LNG import requirement derived from the IEA's 2015 view of India's future gas demand and domestic production, with its historic LNG imports and future contractual positions. With continued purchase of spot and short-term LNG and its commitment to purchase US LNG export volumes, India's LNG import needs are covered on this outlook until the early 2020s.

Table 6.8 shows India's tentative LNG import requirements. The outlook described above is labelled the 'low' case and a notional future additional growth of 20 per cent constitutes the 'high' case. In the context of the uncertainty surrounding India's future energy mix, this upside could occur in response to rising air quality problems due to the reliance on coal and domestically burned biomass, or alternatively as a consequence of domestic production growth failing to emerge.

364   *LNG Markets in Transition*

Table 6.8: India LNG import requirements

	2010	2011	2012	2013	2014	2015	2016	2017	2018	2019	2020
bcm/year											
Low case	12.2	16.8	18.1	17.8	19.8	19.9	22.6	24.5	26.3	28.2	30.0
High case	12.2	16.8	18.1	17.8	19.8	19.9	27.2	29.4	31.6	33.8	36.0
mtpa											
Low case	9.0	12.3	13.3	13.1	14.5	14.6	16.6	18.0	19.3	20.7	22.1
High case	9.0	12.3	13.3	13.1	14.5	14.6	20.0	21.6	23.2	24.8	26.5

	2021	2022	2023	2024	2025	2026	2027	2028	2029	2030
bcm/year										
Low case	34.0	38.0	42.0	46.0	50.0	53.2	56.4	59.6	62.8	66.0
High case	40.8	45.6	50.4	55.2	60.0	63.8	67.7	71.5	75.4	79.2
mtpa										
Low case	25.0	27.9	30.9	33.8	36.8	39.1	41.5	43.8	46.2	48.5
High case	30.0	33.5	37.1	40.6	44.1	46.9	49.8	52.6	55.4	58.2

Source: GIIGNL, author's analysis.

India has four existing LNG terminals with an aggregate capacity of 20.7 mtpa (GIIGNL, 2014, 29) or 28.2 bcm/year. While prospective terminals are planned, the need to secure demand centres and to access infrastructure for future projects will likely constrain both low and high cases from the mid to late 2010s, unless these projects proceed in a timely manner.

Singapore

Singapore has a developed a successful free market economy relying heavily on exports in consumer electronics, information technology products, pharmaceuticals, and a growing financial services sector. Singapore has experienced comparatively high rates of GDP growth; in the period 2004 to 2007 these were in the range 7.5 per cent to 9.5 per cent per year (World Bank, 2015). Singapore's energy mix comprises: oil products (87 per cent in 2014), natural gas 12.8 per cent, and renewables 0.2 per cent. The average annual increase in primary energy consumption between 2010 and 2014 was 2.4 per cent (BP, 2015).

Gas consumption and supply
In 2014 Singapore consumed 10.7 bcm[110] of natural gas, overwhelmingly in the power generation sector, with industry a distant second. The rapid

---
[110] The comparable figure in the *BP Statistical Review of World Energy, 2015* is 10.8 bcm/year.

growth in gas demand for power has been mainly driven by a displacement of oil products; in 2010 gas accounted for 80.6 per cent of the generation fuel mix, by 2014 it was 95.4 per cent (EMA, 2015a). Annual electricity demand growth in Singapore has been 2.1 per cent on average between 2010 and 2013 (EMA, 2015b).

Having no domestic production, Singapore has imported gas by pipeline from Malaysia (from 1992) and Indonesia (from 2001), and since 2013, LNG from a number of suppliers. Indonesian pipeline volumes were reduced in favour of LNG in 2014 and Singapore has a policy of discouraging new pipeline supply as it pursues its goal of becoming a regional LNG trading centre. The Indonesian pipeline contracts are expected to end between 2015 and 2025 (Fadillah, 2012). It is assumed that the Malaysian pipeline contracts also end in 2025.

The outlook for Singapore's LNG requirements is shown in Figure 6.28. On the demand side a future 1.5 per cent annual growth in gas consumption in the power and industrial sectors is assumed, and 0.5 per cent in other sectors. With the fall off in pipeline imports discussed above, this results in an LNG requirement in 2020 and 2030 of 6.6 and 13.8 bcm/year respectively.

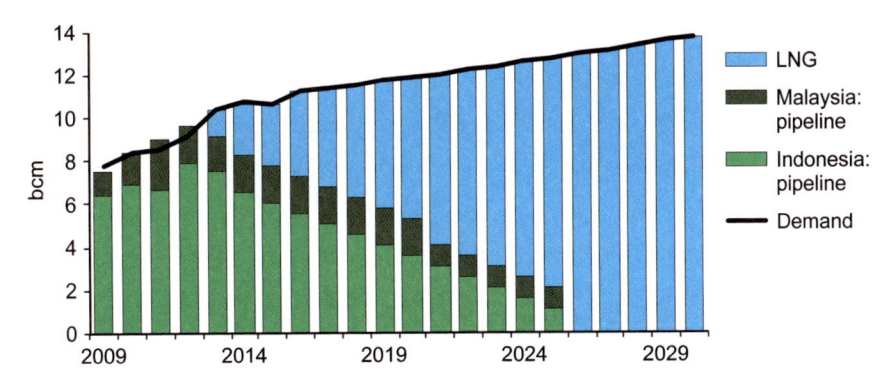

Figure 6.28: Outlook for Singapore gas demand and supply
Source: BP (2015), EMA (2015b), GIIGNL (2014), author's assumptions.

Singapore has an LNG contract with BG for 3 mtpa (4.1 bcm/year), in force from 2013 to 2033 (GIIGNL, 2014, 10). In addition to existing arrangements, the Singapore Energy Market Authority is pursuing a second tender to attract LNG importers whose role would be to act as importers and re-sellers both to domestic buyers in Singapore and also to LNG bunker fuel consumers and buyers from other importing markets.[111]

---

[111] 'Appointment of New Liquefied Natural Gas Importers for Singapore', 29 May 2015, Energy Market Authority. https://www.ema.gov.sg/cmsmedia/Gas/Post-3%20Mtpa%20RFP%20Document%20Stage%20Two%2029May2015.pdf.

Table 6.9 shows the outlook for LNG imports (low case) based on Figure 6.28. A high case was constructed based on a 2 per cent per year growth of gas use in power and industry and 1 per cent in other sectors.

Table 6.9: Singapore LNG import outlook

	2013	2014	2015	2016	2017	2018	2019	2020	2021
bcm/year									
Low case	1.2	2.3	2.8	3.9	4.6	5.2	5.9	6.6	8.0
High case	1.2	2.3	2.8	4.0	4.7	5.5	6.2	6.9	8.4
mtpa									
Low case	0.9	1.7	2.1	2.9	3.4	3.8	4.3	4.8	5.8
High case	0.9	1.7	2.1	2.9	3.5	4.0	4.6	5.1	6.2

	2022	2023	2024	2025	2026	2027	2028	2029	2030
bcm/year									
Low case	8.6	9.3	10.0	10.7	13.0	13.2	13.4	13.6	13.8
High case	9.1	9.9	10.6	11.4	13.8	14.0	14.3	14.6	14.9
mtpa									
Low case	6.3	6.8	7.4	7.9	9.5	9.7	9.8	10.0	10.1
High case	6.7	7.3	7.8	8.4	10.1	10.3	10.5	10.7	10.9

Source: GIIGNL, author's analysis.

Thailand

Since 2000 Thailand's annual GDP growth has averaged 3.9 per cent (World Bank, 2015), although it has been somewhat volatile. Notwithstanding political uncertainty since the 1970s, Thailand has moved from a low to an upper income country in less than a generation. The global economic recession cut exports, and in late 2011 Thailand's recovery was interrupted by severe flooding in the industrial areas of Bangkok and surrounding provinces. In 2013, agriculture comprised 12.1 per cent of GDP, with industry and services 43.6 per cent and 44.2 per cent respectively (CIA, 2015b; Index Mundi, 2015). Leaders in place since a military coup in May 2014 have come under criticism by the international business community for micro-management and lacking an economic strategy.[112] No timetable is in place at the time of writing

---

[112] 'Thailand's Generals Don't Have an Economic Plan', *Bloomberg View*, 4 August 4 2015. www.bloombergview.com/articles/2015-08-04/thailand-s-generals-don-t-have-an-economic-plan.

for the election of a new government and the prospect of economic stagnation must be considered in the absence of positive political and economic management developments. The share of gas in Thailand's primary energy mix is substantial (39 per cent in 2014), second only to oil.

Gas consumption and supply

Thai gas consumption has steadily increased from 2000. Although the power sector dominates (where gas consumption has been stagnant for 2012–14), industry and use as fuel in its large gas separation plant (producing ethane, propane, and other NGLs from domestic wet gas production) are also significant.

On supply, Thailand's domestic production appears to have reached a plateau. Thailand imports gas from fields located offshore in the Myanmar sector of the Gulf of Thailand. Established infrastructure configurations could serve to safeguard this gas for Thailand, despite a need for more gas in Myanmar.

Thailand commenced LNG imports in 2011 through its Map Ta Phut regas terminal (capacity 7.3 bcm/year) (GIIGNL, 2014, 30). If the IEA's expectation of rapid future declines in Thailand's domestic production are borne out (IEA, 2015d, 42), Thailand will need to expedite plans for further LNG import capacity to maintain, let alone grow, gas demand.

In its 2015 Power Development Plan (Thailand, 2015), Thailand assumes a growth in power demand of 3.9 per cent per year. Through expanding the role of renewables and hydro, it seeks to limit the growth in gas and coal-fired generation. The plan also assumes nuclear power commencing in 2029.

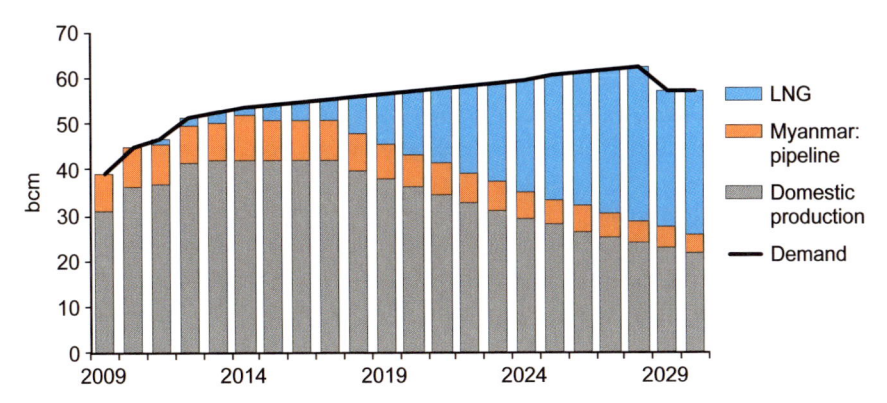

Figure 6.29: Thailand gas supply and demand outlook, 2009–30

Note: Reduction in demand in 2029 and 2030 is due to the government's assumed start of nuclear power.

Source: EPPO (2015), GIIGNL(2014), author's assumptions.

This forms the basis of a reasoned, if somewhat speculative, outlook for Thailand's future LNG requirements. On the demand side, power sector consumption is based on the plan referred to above, industry growth is assumed at 1.5 per cent per year. Together with a 1 per cent per year growth in NGVs and 'other/unaccountable' this would take Thailand's gas consumption from 53.7 bcm in 2014 to 57.1 bcm in 2030. If we assume that Thailand's domestic production, and the offshore Myanmar fields exporting gas to Thailand, begin their production decline in 2017, at 5 per cent per year, Figure 6.29 paints a picture of a growing and substantial market for LNG. LNG imports, on these assumptions, would in 2020 and 2030 be 13.9 and 31.2 bcm/year respectively.

Table 6.10 shows the outlook for LNG imports (high case) based on Figure 6.29. A low case was constructed based on an assumption that domestic production in future declines at 2.5 per cent per year (rather than 5 per cent), as a consequence of further exploration success and field development.

Table 6.10: Thailand LNG import outlook

	2010	2011	2012	2013	2014	2015	2016	2017	2018	2019	2020
bcm/year											
Low case	0.0	1.1	1.4	2.0	1.9	3.7	3.9	4.9	7.0	9.0	11.0
High case	0.0	1.1	1.4	2.0	1.9	3.7	3.9	4.9	8.0	11.0	13.9
mtpa											
Low case	0.0	0.8	1.0	1.5	1.4	2.7	2.8	3.6	5.1	6.6	8.1
High case	0.0	0.8	1.0	1.5	1.4	2.7	2.8	3.6	5.9	8.1	10.2

	2021	2022	2023	2024	2025	2026	2027	2028	2029	2030
bcm/year										
Low case	13.0	14.9	16.7	18.6	20.4	22.1	23.8	25.5	21.3	22.5
High case	16.7	19.4	21.9	24.4	26.8	29.1	31.3	33.4	29.6	31.2
mtpa										
Low case	9.5	10.9	12.3	13.6	15.0	16.3	17.5	18.8	15.6	16.5
High case	12.3	14.2	16.1	17.9	19.7	21.4	23.0	24.6	21.7	22.9

Source: GIIGNL, author's analysis.

Indonesia

Comprising an archipelago of which the major islands are Sumatra, Java, Sulawesi, the southern part of Borneo, and the western section of New Guinea (Irian Jaya), Indonesia is a populous country (256 million) whose

GDP (2014 data) comprises agriculture 14.2 per cent, industry 45.5 per cent, and services 40.3 per cent. Energy intensive industries include oil and gas, mining, chemicals, textiles, products derived from processing agricultural inputs, and tourism (CIA, 2015a). Indonesia has enjoyed consistently high GDP growth (average of 5.3 per cent, 2000–14) (World Bank, 2015), with positive growth having been maintained through the 2008/9 financial crisis period. Indonesia was (in 2014) the world's third-largest coal producer (after China and the USA) (BP, 2015) and one of the world's largest coal exporters. Its first oil discovery was in 1885, with Shell taking a leading role from 1890. Indonesia became an LNG exporter in 1977 with Japan as its first market (see Chapter 1) (Cedigaz, 2004).

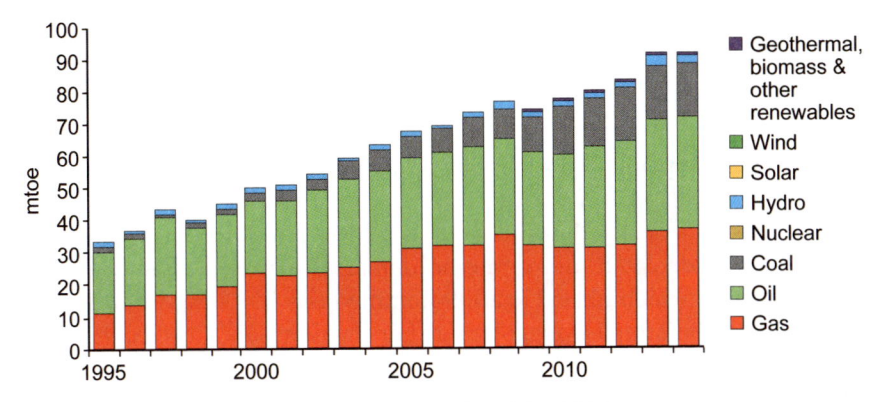

Figure 6.30: Indonesia primary energy mix, 1995–2014
Source: BP (2015).

As Figure 6.30 shows, gas consumption has been generally stagnant since the early 2000s while overall energy consumption has grown by (on average) 4.1 per cent per year. Coal has been the main beneficiary. Industry and power generation are the key gas consumption sectors, having grown at 2.8 per cent and 4 per cent respectively per year on average between 2010 and 2013. Note that in addition to the above consumption categories, some Indonesian production is flared, consumed as 'own use' or as 'gas lift and reinjection'.

Recent government policy moves to increase gas consumption, in order to displace oil products, are described in Seah (2014). Achieving consistent future gas consumption growth will require the provision of gas supply and distribution infrastructure across the archipelago, and this is progressing.

Figure 6.31 shows Indonesia's total production and use of gas. Considerable volumes are used to maintain oil field production ('own use' and 'gas lift and reinjection') and flaring continues. The category 'LNG plant fuel consumption' appears high but probably includes significant statistical errors. The scale of LNG and pipeline exports is evident.

370   *LNG Markets in Transition*

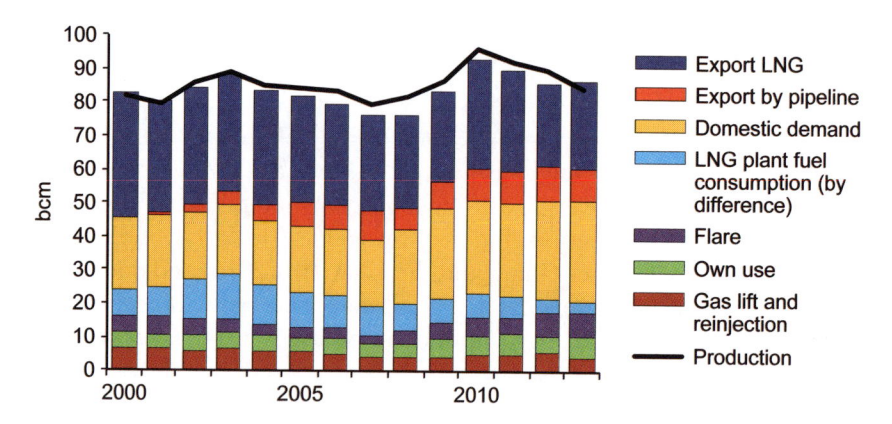

Figure 6.31: Indonesia production and consumption of natural gas, 2000–13
Source: Indonesia (2014, 82–3).

Indonesia's pipeline exports to Singapore began in 2001 and to Malaysia in 2009. LNG exports from the early Bontang (Kalimantan) and Arun (Sumatra) plants declined in the early to mid-2000s as feed gas supplying fields became depleted and domestic demand increased. The Tangguh (Papua) project which started in 2009 stemmed this LNG export decline to some extent. The 2 mtpa Donggi-Senoro liquefaction plant started operations in 2015 and the 0.5 mtpa Sengkang liquefaction plant is expected to start in 2016/17. In addition, the Arun export facility on Sumatra is being converted to an import terminal.[113] Indonesia's LNG story is thus evolving into one of intra-archipelago trade as well as one of net exports of LNG.

The decline in output from Bontang and Arun from the mid to late 2000s was reflected in lower exports to Japan and Taiwan. The start-up of Tangguh underpinned the increase in exports to South Korea and the start of exports to China, as well as more opportunistic cargoes to Mexico, India, Thailand, and Singapore. Of note is the start of trade flows within the Indonesian archipelago from 2012.

The IEA (IEA, 2015b, 41) anticipates strong natural gas demand growth in Indonesia, especially in the industrial sector; growth between 2015 and 2020 of 4.1 per cent is noted. Figure 6.32 shows Indonesia's balance with a post 2014 domestic demand growth assumption of just 2.3 per cent and pipeline exports to Singapore declining, as noted previously. Assuming a future production decline (net of flaring, reinjection, and own use) of 5 per cent per year (but with Tangguh expansion – 5.2 bcm/year – starting in 2019), Indonesia would become an LNG net importer by 2023 in the

---

[113] 'Indonesia's share of global LNG supply declines due to global and domestic demand growth', EIA, 10 March 2014. www.eia.gov/todayinenergy/detail.cfm?id=15331.

absence of significant new gas discoveries. On these assumptions, its LNG net import requirement by 2025 would be some 5 bcm/year and by 2030 21 bcm/year. The domestic demand within the archipelago for LNG is assumed to grow at 2.5 per cent per year. Until now this has been provided for by Indonesian-sourced LNG, which inevitably reduces net exportable LNG volumes.

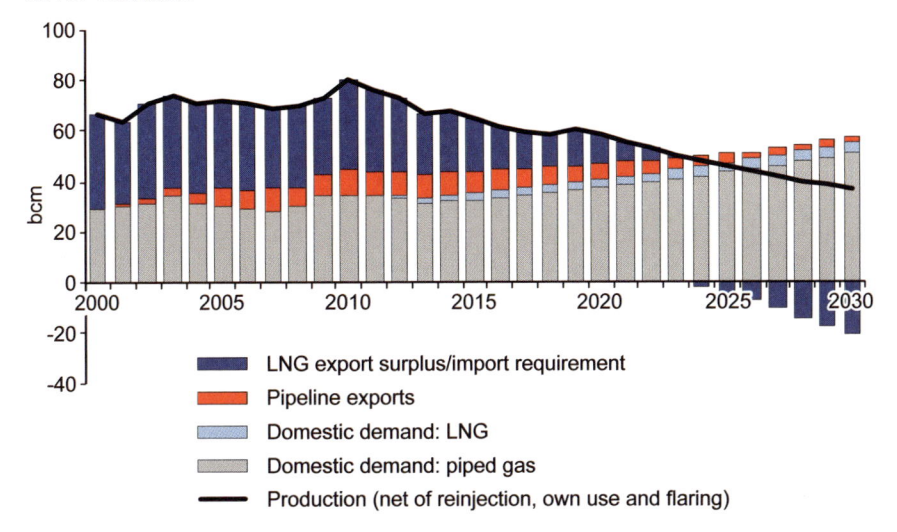

Figure 6.32: Natural gas balance, 2000–30
Source: Indonesia (2014, 82–3), BP (2015), author's assumptions.

Table 6.11 shows the outlook for LNG imports (high case) based on Figure 6.32. A low case was constructed based on an assumption that domestic production in future declines at 2.5 per cent per year (rather than 5 per cent), as a consequence of further exploration success and field development. In the low case Indonesia would still be a net exporter of LNG in 2025.

Table 6.11: Indonesia net LNG import outlook

	2010	2011	2012	2013	2014	2015	2016	2017	2018	2019	2020
bcm/year											
Low case	0.0	0.0	0.0	0.0	0.0	0.0	0.0	0.0	0.0	0.0	0.0
High case	0.0	0.0	0.0	0.0	0.0	0.0	0.0	0.0	0.0	0.0	0.0
mpta											
Low case	0.0	0.0	0.0	0.0	0.0	0.0	0.0	0.0	0.0	0.0	0.0
High case	0.0	0.0	0.0	0.0	0.0	0.0	0.0	0.0	0.0	0.0	0.0

Table 6.11 *continued*

	2021	2022	2023	2024	2025	2026	2027	2028	2029	2030
bcm/year										
Low case	0.0	0.0	0.0	0.0	0.0	0.0	1.1	3.8	6.5	9.3
High case	0.0	0.0	0.0	1.9	4.9	7.3	10.7	14.1	17.5	20.8
mtpa										
Low case	0.0	0.0	0.0	0.0	0.0	0.0	0.8	2.8	4.8	6.9
High case	0.0	0.0	0.0	1.4	3.6	5.4	7.9	10.4	12.9	15.3

Source: GIIGNL, author's analysis.

Malaysia

Malaysia's land mass is separated by the South China Sea into two similarly sized regions: Peninsula Malaysia (north of Singapore) and East Malaysia (the northern part of the island of Borneo – excluding Brunei). Although Malaysia saw GDP falling 1.9 per cent in 2009, its average annual GDP growth from 2000 to 2014 was 5.1 per cent (World Bank, 2015). Malaysia is an open upper/middle-income economy. Formerly (in the 1970s) a producer of raw materials such as tin and rubber, Malaysia now has a diversified economy and has become a leading exporter of electrical appliances, electronic parts and components, palm oil, and natural gas.

Malaysia's energy mix is shown in Figure 6.33. Its annual average energy consumption has grown by 4.3 per cent between 2000 and 2014 and its gas consumption has grown by 4.4 per cent on average between 2010 and 2014. Since 2000, coal consumption has increased significantly, but it still amounts to only 17 per cent of the total energy mix.

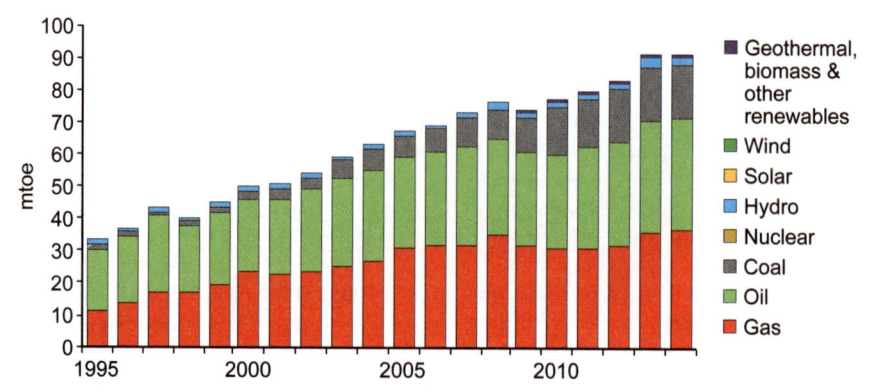

Figure 6.33: Malaysia energy balance, 1995–2014
Source: BP (2015).

LNG Demand Potential 373

Malaysia's oil and gas industry commenced with Shell drilling an oil well in Miri, Sarawak in 1910. The offshore discovery of large natural gas reserves in the 1960s resulted in the Bintulu liquefaction plant.[114] Gas resources are chiefly offshore to the north-west of Peninsula Malaysia and north of the Sarawak region. More than 80 per cent of domestic gas consumption is in Peninsula Malaysia. LNG exports commenced in 1983 and pipeline gas exports to Singapore in 1992. Malaysia imports pipeline gas from Indonesia, the Malaysia/Thailand Joint Development Area, and the Malaysia/Vietnam Commercial Arrangement Area (CAA) (Malaysia, 2014a, 35). Malaysia also began importing LNG in 2013.

Gas consumption by sector in Malaysia in 2012 comprised: power generation 56 per cent, non-energy 23 per cent, industry 20 per cent, transportation 1 per cent, and residential and commercial 0.1 per cent (Malaysia, 2014a, 22). Of the industrial demand: 55 per cent was consumed in rubber, food, beverages, and tobacco; 20 per cent in metal and non-metallic mineral products; 8 per cent in chemicals; and 17 per cent in 'others' (Malaysia, 2014a, 23). This suggests that, in the absence of a high-growth technology-based industrial sector, Malaysia's future demand is primarily driven by the power sector, although recent trends (see (Malaysia, 2014b, 33) suggest that coal will supply incremental power demand growth in the future.

Malaysian LNG imports in 2013 and 2014 were between 2 and 2.3 bcm from a range of countries including: Algeria, Brunei, Nigeria, and Yemen, primarily on the basis of spot or short-term contracts.

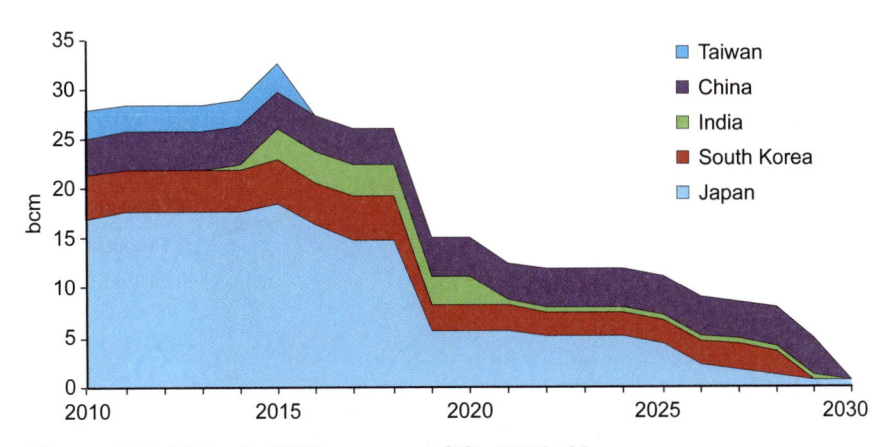

Figure 6.34: Malaysia LNG contract ACQs, 2010–30
Source: GIIGNL (2014).

---

[114] 'The History of Shell in Malaysia', Shell website. www.shell.com.my/aboutshell/who-we-are/history/malaysia.html.

LNG exports have grown slowly since 2006 to around 35 bcm/year and are primarily to Japan, South Korea, and Taiwan. Chinese deliveries have grown since 2009 and other minor spot trades make up the difference. Future LNG contractual commitments fall significantly towards the end of the 2010s as shown in Figure 6.34.

Outlook for Malaysian gas
The outlook for natural gas in Malaysia is coloured by its maturity as a gas producing province (new resources are generally in deeper water) and the low regulated price in the Malaysian domestic market. Coal has already established itself as the fuel to supply incremental power generation. Whilst higher regulated gas prices would stimulate more domestic production, this would enhance the competitiveness of coal in the power sector, in the absence of a more specific carbon abatement policy. Malaysia's 2014 CO_2 emissions for reference were 4.3 times higher than in 1990 (BP, 2015). Malaysia has embarked upon the use of LNG imports to supply the Malacca region on the Malaysian Peninsula and has plans for further import terminals: one in the Sabah region (Island of Borneo) and another at Johor on the Malaysian Peninsula (EIA, 2014, 13).

In addition to its existing land-based liquefaction facilities (Satu, Dua, and Tiga in Bintulu), Malaysia is progressing two or more small floating LNG production facilities offshore Sarawak and Sabah (EIA, 2014, 13).

An illustrative supply outlook for Malaysia is shown in Figure 6.35. This assumes a decline in domestic production from 2018 of 2.5 per cent per year from 2018, a gradual reduction in pipeline imports, but a notional growth of 0.25 bcm/year per year in LNG imports.

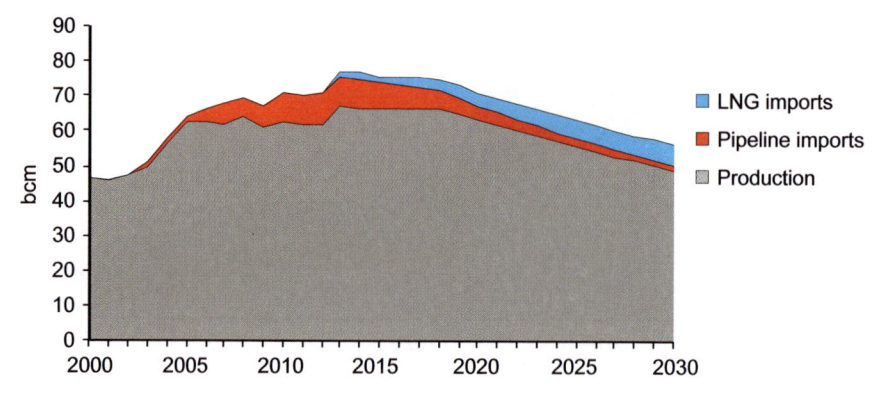

Figure 6.35: Malaysian supply outlook to 2030
Source: BP (2015), GIIGNL (2014), Malaysia (2014b, 23), author's assumptions.

LNG Demand Potential 375

On the demand side, Figure 6.36 shows an assumed domestic demand growth of 1 per cent per year, a tapering in pipeline exports and LNG exports as a balancing item. LNG exports in all years to 2030 are in excess of the aggregate ACQs of existing contracts.

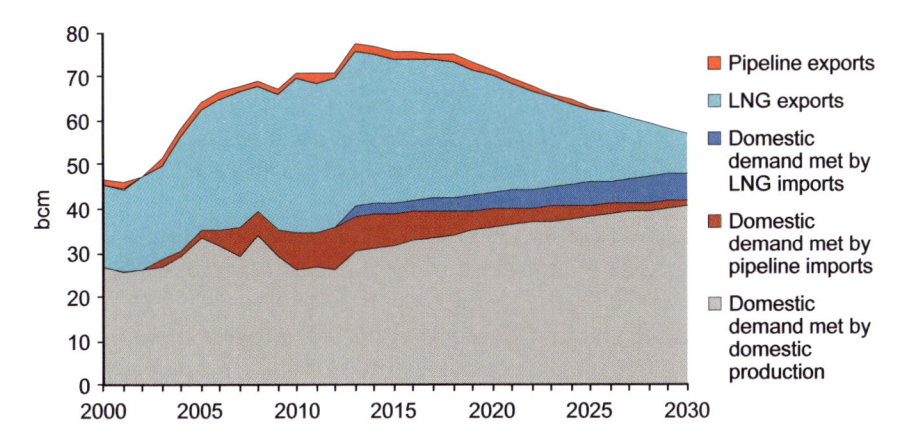

Figure 6.36: Malaysian demand and export outlook to 2030
Source: BP (2015), GIIGNL, Malaysia (2014b, 23), author's assumptions.

The outlook for Malaysia is therefore one of a significant participant in LNG trade into the 2020s, but one whose LNG export surplus is progressively declining due to the maturity of its gas resource.

For the cases considered, Malaysian LNG import volumes are as shown in Table 6.12. To 2025 there is no difference in LNG imports. The high LNG import case assumes a 5 per cent decline in future domestic production (as opposed to 2.5 per cent in the low case represented in Figure 6.36) with, post 2025, a requirement for higher LNG imports to meet overall domestic demand while meeting LNG export contract ACQs.

Table 6.12: Malaysia LNG import outlook

	2010	*2011*	*2012*	*2013*	*2014*	*2015*	*2016*	*2017*	*2018*	*2019*	*2020*
bcm/year											
Low case	0.0	0.0	0.0	2.0	2.2	2.1	2.7	3.0	3.2	3.5	3.7
High case	0.0	0.0	0.0	2.0	2.2	2.1	2.7	3.0	3.2	3.5	3.7
mtpa											
Low case	0.0	0.0	0.0	1.5	1.7	0.5	2.0	2.2	2.4	2.6	2.8
High case	0.0	0.0	0.0	1.5	1.7	1.5	2.0	2.2	2.4	2.6	2.8

Table 6.12 *continued*

	2021	2022	2023	2024	2025	2026	2027	2028	2029	2030
bcm/year										
Low case	4.0	4.2	4.5	4.7	5.0	5.2	5.5	5.7	6.0	6.2
High case	4.0	4.2	4.5	4.7	5.0	5.2	5.5	5.7	8.2	10.7
mtpa										
Low case	2.9	3.1	3.3	3.5	3.7	3.9	4.0	4.2	4.4	4.6
High case	2.9	3.1	3.3	3.5	3.7	3.9	4.0	4.2	6.0	7.9

Source: GIIGNL, author's analysis.

Pakistan

While Pakistan's GDP growth from 2000 to 2014 averaged 4.2 per cent per year (World Bank, 2015) the country saw a degree of stagnation post 2008. Pakistan's problems have been described in these terms: 'corruption, lack of accountability, and lack of transparency continue to pervade all levels of government, politics, and the military' (Gomes, 2013; IEF, 2016b). Agriculture, industry, and services in 2013 contributed 25.3 per cent, 21.6 per cent, and 53.1 per cent to GDP respectively (CIA, 2015b; Index Mundi, 2015).

Pakistan's total energy consumption has plateaued since 2008. Gas has consistently formed 50 to 55 per cent of the energy mix, with coal between 5 and 8 per cent; the gas industry beginning in earnest with the discovery of 10 tcf in Balochistan province in 1952. In addition to state-controlled companies, several international companies are currently present in the Pakistan upstream sector. ENI is currently the largest international player with production operations and participation in several offshore exploration blocks. In 2014, Pakistan had no export or import trade flows in gas; its production and consumption grew rapidly between 2000 and 2005 but growth has since been meagre.

Pakistan has latent demand potential which is constrained by available supply. Gomes (2013) cites un-met demand in 2012 of between 18 and 26 bcm/year comprising: potential for fuel oil switching in power generation and industry and unutilized capacity. The scope for additional demand above available domestic production is estimated at 13–26 bcm/year in 2015, rising to 41–49 bcm/year in 2020.

In the early 2010s an assessment of yet-to-find reserves on an unrisked basis suggested 3.6 billion barrels of oil and 66.3 tcf of gas. However, over the last few years there has actually been a decline in the country's gas reserves. The situation is not helped by the low domestic price of gas – in

2012 some $5/MMBtu (Gomes, 2013, 15 and 25).

The Iran Pipeline Project was first discussed in the early 1990s. Plans to include India as a secondary market foundered in the 2000s. Although it is alleged that Iran has completed 900 of the 1150 km of this pipeline on its own territory, Pakistan's section has yet to be built. While some of the agreement suite appears to have been concluded, pricing has been revisited several times (Gomes, 2013, 30). This said, the 2015/16 rapprochement on Iranian nuclear issues and potential for lifting of sanctions might in time allow the project to achieve completion.[115] Initial gas volumes are planned to be 7.8 bcm/year. The Turkmenistan–Afghanistan–Pakistan–India (TAPI) pipeline project was initiated in 2004. The project was designed as an alternative to the Iran Pipeline Project and while it has US State Department support, in practical terms the security situation in Afghanistan renders its implementation 'on hold' for the foreseeable future.

In March 2015 Pakistan began importing LNG from Qatar and, from July 2015, Nigeria. Using a floating storage and regasification unit and ship-to-ship transfer, the gas is injected into the grid in the vicinity of Karachi. In 2015, some 1.5 bcm was imported. Full regas capacity of this system/configuration is 4 bcm/year.[116] Pakistan has signed a 15 year contract with Qatar for between 2 and 4 bcm/year at prices of around $7/MMBtu at mid-2015 oil prices.[117] Plans to build a second terminal of around 4 bcm/year capacity are at an advanced state, to be operational in 2016/17.

Pakistan outlook

Figure 6.37 shows an illustrative outlook for Pakistan's gas supply and demand position to 2030. The notional 'Potential Demand' is guided by research in Gomes (2013). Future domestic production assumes a decline of 5 per cent per year from 2016. Actual consumption (as has been the case for the past few years) will be a function of gas supply availability (and the ability of consumers to pay a cost reflective/market price). This is predicated upon the successful conclusion of current and future LNG import projects and of the Iran Pipeline Project ('IPP' in Figure 6.37).

---

[115] 'Will the Iran Deal Help the Iran–Pakistan Pipeline Project?', *The Diplomat*, 28 July 2015. http://thediplomat.com/2015/07/will-the-iran-deal-help-the-iran-pakistan-pipeline-project/.

[116] 'Pakistan to join LNG Importers club soon', 10 March 2015, *LNG World News*. https://www.lngworldnews.com/pakistan-to-join-lng-importers-club-soon/.

[117] http://arynews.tv/en/pakistan-to-sign-15-year-deal-to-import-gas-from-qatar-official/.

378   *LNG Markets in Transition*

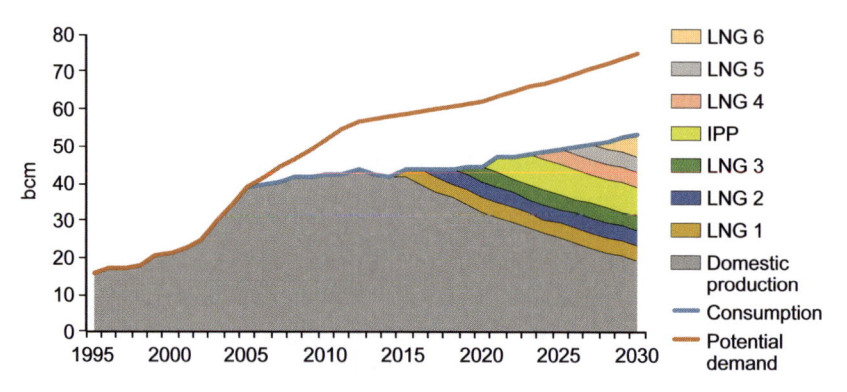

Figure 6.37: Pakistan gas supply and demand outlook, 1995–2030
Sources: Gomes (2013, 11), BP (2015), author's assumptions.

While highly speculative, this view indicates an LNG import requirement for 2020 and 2030 of 12 and 26 bcm/year respectively, albeit below the potential country demand. This 'lagged response' will be due to a lack of focused policy and detractions from powerful lobbies, project execution delays (including finance concerns), and end-user payment collection issues.

Pakistan LNG import volumes are as shown in Table 6.13. The high case corresponds to the discussion above. A low case assumes a domestic production decline of 2.5 per cent per year.

Table 6.13: Pakistan LNG import outlook

	2010	2011	2012	2013	2014	2015	2016	2017	2018	2019	2020
bcm/year											
Low case	0.0	0.0	0.0	0.0	0.0	1.4	4.0	4.0	6.0	8.0	10.0
High case	0.0	0.0	0.0	0.0	0.0	1.4	4.0	6.0	8.0	10.0	12.0
mtpa											
Low case	0.0	0.0	0.0	0.0	0.0	1.1	2.9	2.9	4.4	5.9	7.4
High case	0.0	0.0	0.0	0.0	0.0	1.1	2.9	4.4	5.9	7.4	8.8

	2021	2022	2023	2024	2025	2026	2027	2028	2029	2030
bcm/year										
Low case	12.0	12.0	12.0	12.0	14.0	14.0	14.0	14.0	14.0	14.0
High case	12.0	12.0	12.0	14.0	16.0	18.0	20.0	22.0	24.0	26.0
mtpa										
Low case	8.8	8.8	8.8	8.8	10.3	10.3	10.3	10.3	10.3	10.3
High case	8.8	8.8	8.8	10.3	11.8	13.2	14.7	16.2	17.6	19.1

Source: GIIGNL, author's analysis.

Bangladesh

Bangladesh is one of the world's most densely populated countries; poverty is deep and widespread, however in recent years it has reduced population growth and improved health and education. The major employer is agriculture. The country is trying to diversify its economy, with industrial development a priority. Bangladesh spent 15 years under military rule and, although democracy was restored in 1990, the political scene remains volatile. Bangladesh's GDP growth has averaged 5.7 per cent from 2000 to 2014, with no years of negative growth (World Bank, 2015). Pakistan Petroleum Limited discovered gas at Sylhet in 1955; commercial production commenced in 1960 with the supply of 4 million cubic feet a day to a cement factory (Gomes, 2013, 42). Natural gas is the predominant primary energy source with coal playing a minor, if growing, role.

While most categories of demand have stabilized since 2009/10, power generation is still on a generally rising trend. Potential gas demand in 2015 is some 10 bcm above available supply (Gomes, 2013, 47). However, with limited future prospectivity and low domestic prices, the outlook for increased domestic production is not encouraging.

In 1997, Bangladesh expressed interest in a project to import pipeline gas from Myanmar; this, however, was not progressed and given Myanmar's future gas pipeline export obligations it is unlikely to proceed in the future.

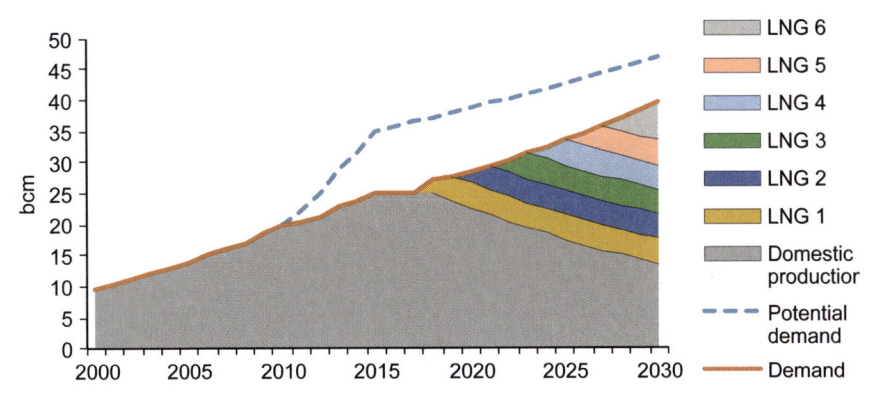

Figure 6.38: Bangladesh potential gas supply and demand to 2030
Sources: BP (2015), Gomes (2013), author's assumptions.

Bangladesh in 2010 announced its intention to build an LNG import terminal for 5 bcm/year; this did not materialize due to issues of buyer creditworthiness, poor infrastructure connectivity, and the lack of a strong project sponsor/financing (Gomes, 2013, 60–1). In 2015 however, Reliance Power signed an MOU to develop a floating regas unit and associated power plant.[118] In the absence of sufficient gas to meet latent demand, Bangladesh is turning to coal and fuel oil in power generation.

Figure 6.38 shows a potential outlook for Bangladesh's supply and demand to 2030. Assuming domestic production declines at 5 per cent per year from 2018, LNG imports could maintain the recent trend of gas consumption growth, although probably leaving substantial 'unmet' demand potential. Bangladesh's LNG import volumes are as shown in Table 6.14. The high case corresponds to the discussion above. A low case assumes a domestic production decline of 2.5 per cent per year.

Table 6.14: Bangladesh LNG import outlook

	2010	2011	2012	2013	2014	2015	2016	2017	2018	2019	2020
bcm/year											
Low case	0.0	0.0	0.0	0.0	0.0	0.0	0.0	0.0	0.0	2.0	4.0
High case	0.0	0.0	0.0	0.0	0.0	0.0	0.0	0.0	2.0	4.0	6.0
mtpa											
Low case	0.0	0.0	0.0	0.0	0.0	0.0	0.0	0.0	0.0	1.5	2.9
High case	0.0	0.0	0.0	0.0	0.0	0.0	0.0	0.0	1.5	2.9	4.4

	2021	2022	2023	2024	2025	2026	2027	2028	2029	2030
bcm/year										
Low case	4.0	4.0	6.0	8.0	8.0	10.0	12.0	14.0	16.0	18.0
High case	8.0	10.0	12.0	14.0	16.0	18.0	20.0	22.0	24.0	26.0
mtpa										
Low case	2.9	2.9	4.4	5.9	5.9	7.4	8.8	10.3	11.8	13.2
High case	5.9	7.4	8.8	10.3	11.8	13.2	14.7	16.2	17.6	19.1

Source: GIIGNL, author's analysis.

Vietnam

Vietnam has seen consistent high GDP growth with an annual average of 6.4 per cent in the period 2000 to 2014 (World Bank, 2015). The country has been transitioning from a centrally planned economy since 1986. Agriculture's share of economic output has shrunk from about 25 per cent in 2000 to 18 per cent in 2014, while industry's share increased from 36 per cent to 38 per cent in the same period. State-owned enterprises now account for about 40 per cent of GDP. Vietnam joined the WTO in 2007, which has

---

[118] 'Reliance Power to develop LNG Power Project', LNG Industry, 8 June 2015, www.lngindustry.com/liquid-natural-gas/08062015/Bangladesh-LNG-power-project-moving-forward-909/.

promoted more competitive, export-driven industries. Vietnam's economy continues to face challenges from an undercapitalized banking sector, and non-performing loans weigh heavily on banks and businesses (CIA, 2015a).

The country's modern natural gas industry began in 1995 when associated gas from the Bach Ho oil field (less than 3 million cubic metres per day) was sent to the Ba Ria Power Plant. In 2008, Vietnam used about 90 per cent of its natural gas production for power generation, with the remainder supplying the industrial and fertilizer sectors. Gas made up about 50 per cent of the power sector's generation requirements in 2010. Gas markets will be able to expand in the central and northern areas of Vietnam once pipeline infrastructure develops (EIA, 2012). Vietnam's National Gas Master Plan projected that gas consumption in the country would increase to over 13 bcm/year by 2015. In 2013, the IEA was reported as expecting that Vietnam's gas production would rise to 13 bcm/year (2014 production 10.2 bcm/year (BP, 2015)) and then remain at 12 bcm/year until 2035. PetroVietnam predicts there will be a gas supply gap of 13 bcm/year by 2025 as demand outstrips supply in the country.

Vietnam has been expected to become an LNG importer for some time; however, its two planned regas terminal projects have been subject to rolling delays. The country had been expected to receive its first cargo in 2018 or 2019, based on expectations that a PetroVietnam subsidiary had hoped to award its first LNG contract in 2015.[119] The LNG is intended to be sold to industrial users and fertilizer plants that buy gas at a price linked to alternative fuels such as oil (close to the world market price for LNG). The reality of Vietnamese LNG imports appears, however, to be subject to rolling delays at the time of writing.

A low and a high case for LNG imports is shown in Table 6.15, assuming a 4 per cent per year future demand increase, and a 2.5 per cent and 5 per cent decline respectively in domestic production post 2020.

Table 6.15: Vietnam LNG import outlook

	2010	2011	2012	2013	2014	2015	2016	2017	2018	2019	2020
bcm/year											
Low Case	0.0	0.0	0.0	0.0	0.0	0.0	0.0	0.0	0.0	0.0	0.0
High Case	0.0	0.0	0.0	0.0	0.0	0.0	0.0	0.0	0.0	0.0	0.0
mtpa											
Low Case	0.0	0.0	0.0	0.0	0.0	0.0	0.0	0.0	0.0	0.0	0.0
High Case	0.0	0.0	0.0	0.0	0.0	0.0	0.0	0.0	0.0	0.0	0.0

[119] 'Vietnam will need imports, but again delays its first LNG', Alaska Natural Gas Transportation Projects, 8 December 2014. www.arcticgas.gov/2014/vietnam-will-need-imports-but-again-delays-its-first-lng.

Table 6.15 *continued*

	2021	2022	2023	2024	2025	2026	2027	2028	2029	2030
bcm/year										
Low case	1.0	1.7	2.6	3.5	4.4	5.3	6.2	7.1	8.1	9.1
High case	1.2	2.3	3.5	4.6	5.7	6.9	8.0	9.1	10.3	11.4
mtpa										
Low case	0.7	1.3	1.9	2.6	3.2	3.9	4.6	5.2	6.0	6.7
High case	0.9	1.7	2.6	3.4	4.2	5.1	5.9	6.7	7.6	8.4

Source: GIIGNL, author's analysis.

Conclusions: more recent and emerging Asian LNG markets

Whilst it is difficult to draw common conclusions for such a diverse group of countries, it is perhaps worth grouping these in terms of three drivers which will determine their future LNG import requirements.

The first is the likely/impending decline in existing domestic production or pipeline gas supplies. This is especially relevant where such supplies of natural gas historically have given rise to the situation where gas has become a major share of the energy mix and where this would be difficult to markedly reduce in the space of five to 10 years. Countries where a **decline in domestic production or pipeline gas supplies** will likely lead to increased LNG imports to 2025 are: Singapore (pipeline supply), Indonesia, Pakistan, Bangladesh, Thailand, Malaysia, and Vietnam.

The second driver is **uncertainty around the future exergy mix** and government policy. Thus Taiwan and China have the potential for increased LNG imports depending on their choice of coal dependency levels (and GHG emission targets). This category also includes Thailand, India, Malaysia, Pakistan, and Bangladesh, insofar as they may be unable to achieve acceptable (to other COP21 parties and domestic populations) energy mixes without significantly increasing LNG imports to displace coal, especially if renewables targets and energy efficiency goals are not met.

The third driver relates to **investment frameworks and regulated domestic gas price levels**. If these are deficient, they may slow the development of domestic gas resources and give rise to increased LNG imports (albeit these may cost more in the short to medium term). Examples here are: Bangladesh, Pakistan, Vietnam, Malaysia, India, and Thailand.

Note that some recent and emerging LNG importing countries appear in more than one of the above categories.

Conclusions: Asian LNG markets

The preceding sections of this chapter have reviewed the range of LNG import requirements for the Asian markets, whether they are existing or prospective importers. A 'low' and 'high' case has been derived for each country. The low case is shown in Figure 6.39 and the high case in Figure 6.40.

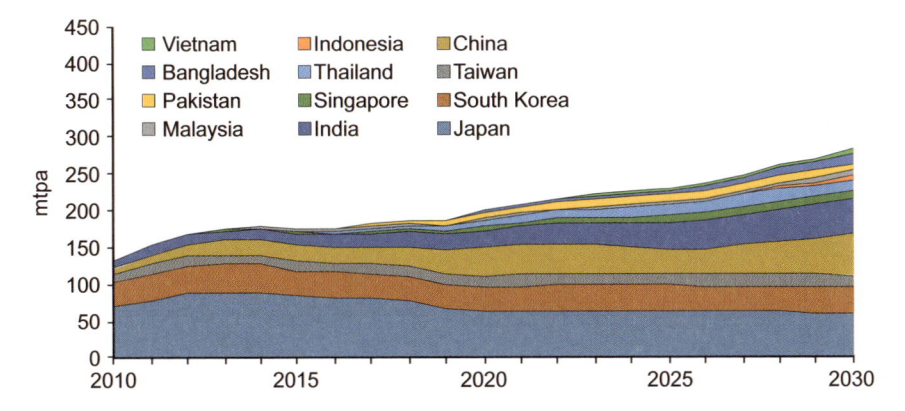

Figure 6.39: Asian LNG imports, 2010–30: low case
Source: Author's analysis.

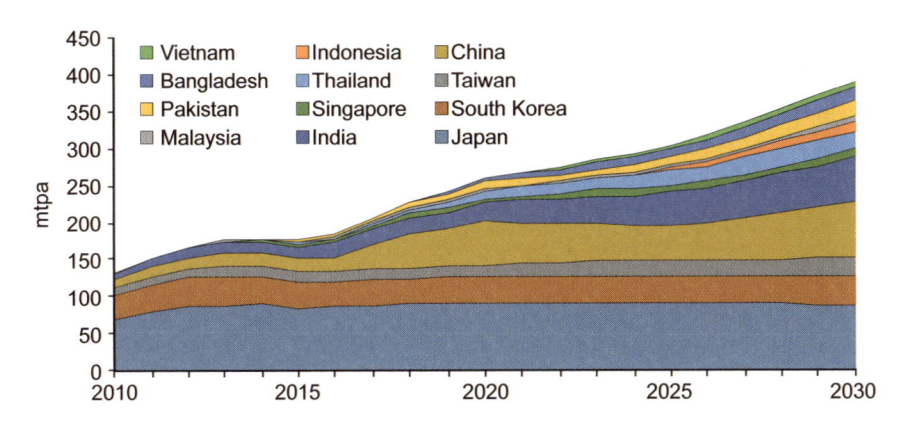

Figure 6.40: Asian LNG imports, 2010–30: high case
Source: Author's analysis.

In both the low and high cases the dominant markets, in terms of absolute volumes, are Japan, South Korea, China, and India. By 2030, the total LNG import volumes from all countries considered here ranges from 283 to 390 mtpa, compared with the 2015 total of 175 mtpa. In the low and high cases, the annual average aggregate growth in LNG demand growth is 3.2 per cent and 5.2 per cent respectively. It is instructive to look at the country-level variances between low and high cases – shown in Figure 6.41, as this highlights the key uncertainties for the period.

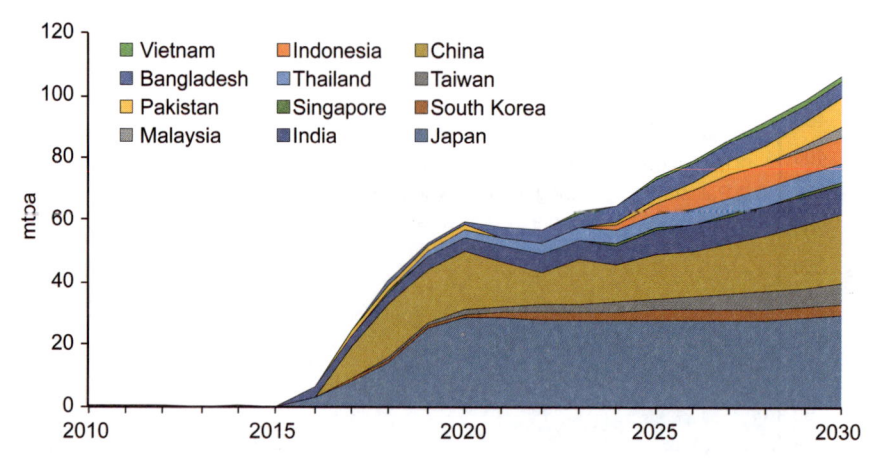

Figure 6.41: Asian LNG imports, 2010–30: differences between low and high cases
Source: Author's analysis.

China and Japan dominate the picture between 2015 and the early 2020s. In the case of China the uncertainties relate to gas demand growth in the economic 'new normal', where government policy will be crucial in establishing a more material role for gas in the power sector (for CO_2 and particulate pollution abatement reasons) and in providing access infrastructure to enable growth in the residential and industrial sectors. The future LNG requirement is also, however, subject to uncertainties in the gas supply mix; these include conventional and unconventional domestic gas production, the scale and timing of future pipeline imports from Turkmenistan and Central Asian, as well as the scale and timing of Russian pipeline gas imports from East and West Siberia. With Japan, the main uncertainty is the pace and extent of the start-up of nuclear power plant, reducing the requirement for LNG imports, and achieving long-term energy efficiency goals.

In the case of Taiwan and South Korea, the scale of future LNG imports depends on uncertain economic growth prospects and energy mix policy. With Thailand, Indonesia, Malaysia, and Vietnam a major uncertainty is the future decline of domestic production, as exploration prospectivity declines due to province maturity, often exacerbated by low regulated domestic pricing policies. While the future scope of LNG imports is difficult to ascertain, this is likely to be an increasingly widespread dynamic and an important source of new global LNG demand in markets where natural gas already has a strong presence. The same issue applies to Pakistan and Bangladesh, but with the added complication of delays to building import infrastructure due to poor investment frameworks, governance, or end user credit worthiness. This highlights an opportunity for future LNG supply projects, but it requires a markedly more proactive marketing stance and greater capability in credit-risk management than has traditionally been the case in the LNG business. The use of floating LNG regas units, however, is an added incentive towards ensuring that LNG supplied is paid for.

The high and low LNG import cases to 2025 are shown in Table 6.16.

Table 6.16: Low and high LNG import cases to 2030 (mtpa)

	\multicolumn{5}{c}{Low case}	\multicolumn{5}{c}{High case}
	2010	2015	2020	2025	2030	2010	2015	2020	2025	2030
Japan	68.7	85.1	63.3	63.6	59.3	68.7	85.1	91.7	91.7	88.4
South Korea	33.1	33.4	32.9	33.7	34.9	33.1	33.4	34.5	36.5	38.7
Taiwan	10.9	14.5	14.9	15.9	16.8	10.9	14.5	16.5	19.7	23.6
China	9.6	20.0	39.7	33.8	55.1	9.6	20.0	58.1	48.5	77.2
India	9.0	14.6	22.1	36.8	48.5	9.0	14.6	26.5	44.1	58.2
Singapore	–	2.1	4.8	7.9	10.1	–	2.1	5.1	8.4	10.9
Thailand	–	2.7	8.1	15.0	16.5	–	2.7	10.2	19.7	22.9
Indonesia	–	0.0	–	–	6.9	–	0.0	–	3.6	15.3
Malaysia	–	1.5	2.8	3.7	4.6	–	1.5	2.8	3.7	7.9
Pakistan	–	1.1	7.4	10.3	10.3	–	1.1	8.8	11.8	19.1
Bangladesh	–	0.0	2.9	5.9	13.2	–	0.0	4.4	11.8	19.1
Vietnam	–	0.0	–	3.2	6.7	–	0.0	–	4.2	8.4
Total	**131.2**	**175.0**	**198.8**	**229.6**	**283.0**	**131.2**	**175.0**	**258.5**	**303.6**	**389.8**

Source: GIIGNL, author's analysis.

LNG demand perspectives in Latin America and the Caribbean

Introduction

Latin America and the Caribbean is a vast region encompassing more than 40 countries across two continents (North and South America) and stretching more than 10,000 km from Northern Mexico to the southern tip of Argentina and Chile. This region is neither uniform, nor is it integrated in terms of either economics or energy. There are four sub-regions which are loosely interconnected through trade exchanges and in some cases through energy trade. These are the **Southern Cone**;[120] the **Andean Region**; the so-called **Greater Caribbean** (including the Caribbean

---

[120] Geographically, Bolivia should be included in the Andean Region, but because of its natural gas interconnections with Brazil and Argentina, it will be treated as being part of the Southern Cone.

islands and countries, Central America, and three countries on the north coast of South America[121]; and **Mexico** (see Map 6.1).

Table 6.17 presents some comparative socio-economic and energy data for the region's 23 largest countries.

Table 6.17: Comparative demographic, economic, and energy indicators

Country	Land area (thousand km²)	Population (million)	GDP per capita (US$)	Primary energy consumption (Mtoe)	Power generation (TWh)	Primary energy consumption per capita (toe)	Power generation per capita (MWh)	Share of natural gas in primary energy consumption
South America								
Argentina	2,737	43	12,569	81	139	1.9	3.2	52%
Bolivia	1,083	11	3,236	8	8	0.8	0.8	38%
Brazil	8,358	206	11,385	294	570	1.4	2.8	11%
Chile	744	18	14,528	39	73	2.2	4.1	10%
Colombia	1,110	48	7,904	32	65	0.7	1.4	27%
Ecuador	248	16	6,322	15	23	1.0	1.5	4%
Paraguay	397	7	4,729	5	60	0.8	9.2	–
Peru	1,280	31	6,551	22	43	0.7	1.4	27%
Uruguay	175	3	16,807	5	12	1.3	3.4	1%
Venezuela	882	31	16,615	69	123	2.2	4.0	31%
Central America								
Costa Rica	51	5	10,415	5	10	1.0	2.2	–
El Salvador	21	6	4,129	4	6	0.7	1.0	–
Guatemala	107	16	3,667	12	10	0.8	0.6	–
Honduras	112	8	2,435	5	8	0.7	1.0	–
Nicaragua	120	6	1,963	4	4	0.6	0.7	–
Panama	74	4	11,949	4	9	1.0	2.3	–
Caribbean								
Cuba	106	11	-	12	19	1.0	1.7	7%
Dominican Republic	48	10	6,147	8	18	0.7	1.7	11%
Haiti	28	11	824	4	1	0.4	0.1	–
Jamaica	11	3	n.a.	3	4	1.1	1.5	–
Puerto Rico	9	4	n.a.	n.a.	21	n.a.	n.a.	n.a.
Trinidad & Tobago	5	1	n.a.	20	10	14.5	7.0	92%
Mexico	1,944	125	10,230	191	297	1.5	2.4	32%
Latin America	20,042	626		839	1,534	1.3	2.4	23%

Sources: World Bank data (2015, data are for 2014); IEA statistics (2015, data are for 2013).

---

[121] Three countries/territories (French Guiana, Guyana, and Suriname) which, while being geographically located on the Caribbean coast of South America, are part of neither the Southern Cone nor of the Andean region; they are often included in the Caribbean area of influence.

Map 6.1: Latin America's four sub-regions
Source: Author's analysis.

Latin America is a region well-endowed with energy resources; these include oil, gas, hydropower, wind, solar, biomass-based fuels, coal, and geothermal. It has a well-developed hydropower capacity and is a world leader in the use of biomass to produce commercial fuels and biomass-fired electricity.

The region holds 4 per cent of global proved gas reserves. Figures for the size of these reserves have been growing in the last decade; this trend is expected to continue in the next decade, due in particular to the large resources found off the coast in Brazil (Presalt) and the initial development of unconventional resources in Argentina and Colombia.

The gas reserves are unevenly distributed: Venezuela by itself holds 70 per cent of Latin America's total proven reserves. Figure 6.42 summarizes current natural gas proven reserves, production, and consumption for the main gas producing countries in Latin America.

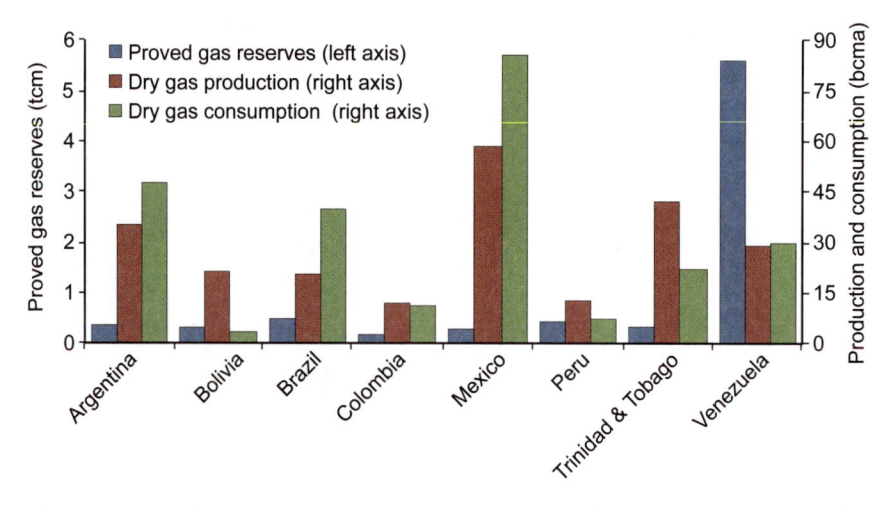

Figure 6.42: Natural gas reserves, dry gas production, and consumption by country, 2014

Source: BP (2015).

Natural gas has a relatively recent history in Latin America (IEA, 2003): with the exception of Argentina and Mexico, most countries only started to develop their markets in the 2000s. In 2013, the share of gas in the region's primary energy demand mix was 23 per cent. There are large variations among countries, as can be seen in Figure 6.43, but overall the power sector has been the driving force for gas demand growth in most countries. It accounted for 40 per cent of the region's natural gas demand in 2013, up from 22 per cent in 1990. Industry is the second largest user (28 per cent) while the residential sector accounts for only 6 per cent, given that the region is largely tropical.

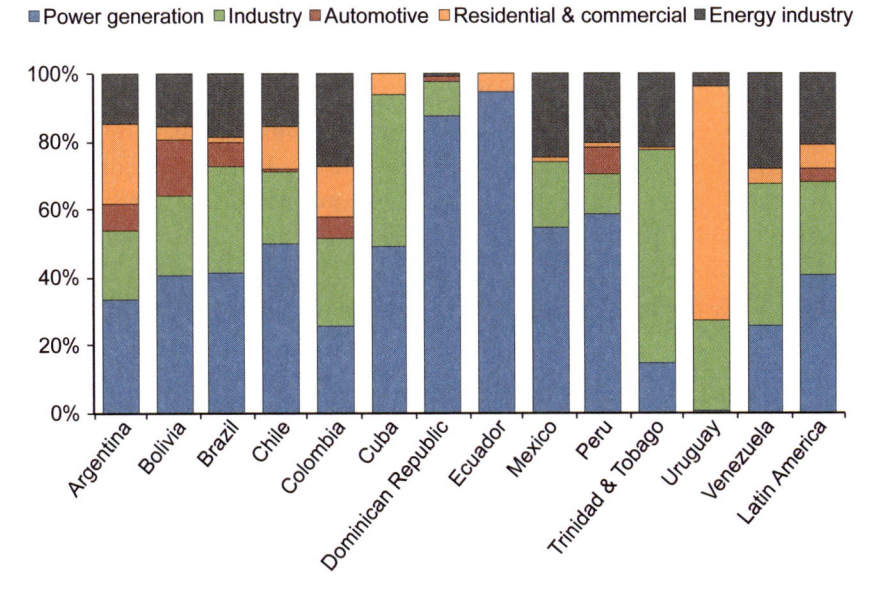

■ Power generation ■ Industry ■ Automotive ■ Residential & commercial ■ Energy industry

Figure 6.43: Natural gas demand by sector of use in Latin America, 2013
Source: IEA (2015), data are for 2013.

Gas market development in Latin America required the construction of a number of very long gas pipelines in the 1990s and early 2000s: from Bolivia to Argentina and Brazil, from Argentina to Chile, Uruguay, and Brazil, Bolivia to Brazil, from Colombia to Venezuela. But this infrastructure has remained limited to a few binational pipelines and has never amounted to a real regional integrated network.

Natural gas integration by pipelines in Latin America is made difficult by the large distances in a vast and relatively under-populated continent, as well as by formidable geographical features such as the Andean *cordillera*, the Amazon forest, and the insularity in the Caribbean. Meanwhile, essential conditions for solid regional integration, such as common policy objectives, harmonized regulation, and common pricing were, and still are, lacking. In 2014, cross-border pipeline gas trade in South America was 17.8 bcm, about 10 per cent of total gas consumption. Mexico, on the other hand, imported 20.5 bcm from the USA, 24 per cent of its consumption (BP, 2015).

These conditions have led six Latin American countries to look at LNG for new or additional gas supply. Puerto Rico and the Dominican Republic in the Caribbean were the first to build LNG regasification terminals in the early 2000s, followed by Mexico (two terminals in 2006 and 2008). The

Southern Cone followed with Argentina (2008 and 2011), Chile (2009 and 2010), and Brazil (2008, 2009, and 2013). There are currently 12 regasification terminals (including five FSRUs) with a total importing capacity of 60 bcm/year (Table 6.18). Two additional regasification terminals are currently under construction in Uruguay and Colombia with a capacity of 3.7 and 4.1 bcm/year respectively. In addition, there are some 10–15 proposed regasification terminals at various stages of planning and development (Table 6.19).

Table 6.18: Latin America's existing regasification terminals and those under construction

Country	Plant	Type	Status	Capacity (bcm/year)	Capacity (mtpa)	Start-up year
Argentina	Bahía Blanca GasPort	FSRU	Operational	5.1	3.7	2008
Argentina	GNL Escobar	FSRU	Operational	5.1	3.7	2011
Brazil	Pecém	FSRU	Operational	2.5	1.8	2009
Brazil	Guanabara Bay	FSRU	Operational	7.2	5.3	2009
Brazil	Bahia LNG	FSRU	Operational	5.0	3.7	2013
Chile	Quintero	Onshore	Operational	3.7*	2.7*	2009
Chile	Mejillones GNL	Onshore**	Operational	2.0	1.5	2010
Colombia	LNG Cartagena	FSRU	Under construction	4.1	3.0	2017
Dominican Rep.	AES Andrés LNG	Onshore	Operational	2.3	1.7	2003
Dominican Rep.	AES Andrés LNG exp.***	Onshore	Under construction	-	-	2016
Jamaica	Montego Bay	FSRU	Under construction	n.a.	n.a.	2016
Jamaica	Old Harbour	Onshore	Under construction	0.3	0.2	2018
Mexico	Altamira	Onshore	Operational	7.8	5.7	2006
Mexico	Costa Azul	Onshore	Operational	10.3	7.6	2008
Mexico	Manzanillo	Onshore	Operational	5.2	3.8	2012
Puerto Rico	Peñuelas	Onshore	Operational	3.8	2.8	2000
Uruguay	GNL del Plata	FSRU	Under construction	3.7	2.7	2019

* Regasification capacity is being expanded to 5.5 bcm/year.
** Terminal with onshore regasification and floating storage.

*** The expansion of the AES Andrés terminal involves a second LNG storage tank, but no increase in regasification capacity.

Source: GIIGNL; author's research.

Table 6.19: Latin America's proposed regasification terminals

Country	Plant	Type	Status	Capacity (bcma)	Capacity (mtpa)	Start-up year
Chile	GasAtacama LNG	FSRU	Proposed	2.0	1.5	?
Chile	Penco Lirquén	FSRU	Proposed	4.0	3.0	2019
Chile	San Vicente Bay	FSRU	Proposed	2.7	2.0	?
Brazil	Rio Grande Tergas	FSRU	Proposed	5.1	3.7	2019/20
Brazil	Suape	FSRU	Proposed	5.1	3.7	2019/20
Brazil	Porto de Sergipe	FSRU	Proposed	2.6	1.9	2020/21
Dominican Republic	San Pedro de Macorís	Onshore	Proposed	1.3	1.0	?
El Salvador	Energía del Pacífico	FSRU	Proposed	0.6	0.4	2018
Panama	Costa Norte LNG	FSRU	Proposed	0.5	0.4	2018
Puerto Rico	Aguirre Gasport	FSRU	Proposed	5.1	3.7	2017

Source: GIIGNL; author's research.

The reasons behind the decision to import LNG vary across countries, ranging from insufficient production development to match growing demand in Argentina, Mexico, and Colombia to the lack of alternatives for Puerto Rico and the Dominican Republic. Another reason is supply security: Chile and Uruguay depended on imported gas from Argentina, but found their supply curtailed when Argentina started to lack gas for its own market. Finally, Brazil imports LNG to complement domestic production and pipeline imports from Bolivia – in particular as a source of flexible supply to meet peak demand from the power sector.

As shown in Figure 6.44, LNG imports in Latin America have grown rapidly since 2000 and reached 28.5 bcm in 2015 (21 mtpa). In 2015, LNG imports decreased by 3.3 bcm from the 2014 figure, because of reduced demand in Brazil, Argentina, and Mexico. In Brazil, LNG imports were down in 2015 because of higher hydropower production, in Argentina because of a warmer winter and slightly higher domestic production, and in Mexico because of increased pipeline imports from the USA.

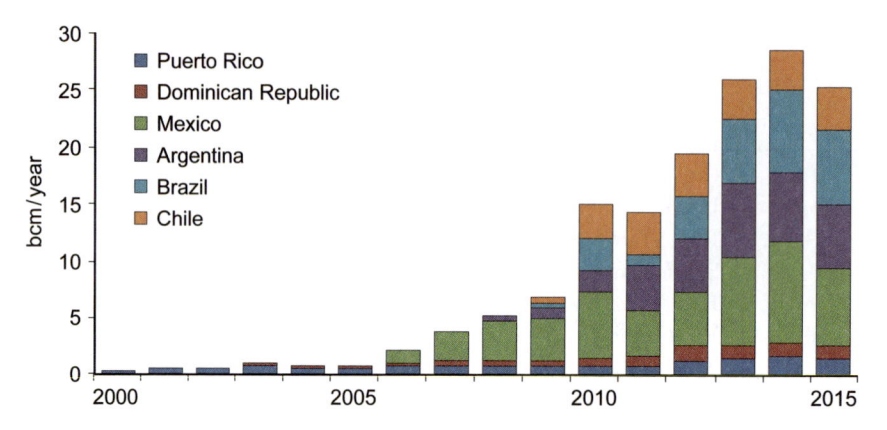

Figure 6.44: Historical growth of LNG imports in Latin America by country of destination
Source: GIIGNL (2016).

Interestingly, the region also has two LNG exporters: Trinidad and Tobago and Peru. Nevertheless, for a number of commercial and political reasons, there has been limited intra-regional LNG trade. Peru exports LNG to Mexico under a long-term contract, and Trinidad and Tobago exports short-term volumes and spot cargoes to Argentina, Brazil, Chile, the Dominican Republic, Mexico, and Puerto Rico. All in all, intra-regional LNG trade in Latin America amounted to just 9.7 bcm in 2015 (without considering LNG received as re-exports).

The Southern Cone

The Southern Cone has long been self-sufficient in natural gas, with Argentina supplying its own large and diversified market, as well as exporting to Chile, Uruguay, and Brazil, while Bolivia[122] emerged as an important exporter to Brazil (IEA, 2003). The plans to build regional gas infrastructure collapsed after Argentina faced gas shortages and cut export contracts in the 2000s. Meanwhile nationalization in Bolivia generated

---

[122] Geographically, Bolivia should be included in the Andean sub-region, but because of its natural interconnections with Brazil and Argentina, it will be treated as being in the Southern Cone.

Map 6.2: South America's main pipelines, existing and proposed LNG terminals
Source: Author's research.

doubts on its future ability to supply its domestic and export markets. This resulted in new interconnection projects grinding to a halt. Governments reacted by reinvigorating the concept of natural gas as a 'strategic resource' and focused on supply security and energy diversification (D'Apote and Castaño, 2012). Producing countries gave priority to their domestic market, while importing countries started looking for alternative supplies, notably LNG. Even liquid fuels recovered their importance in the power generation and industrial segments.

The LNG demand outlook in the Southern Cone will depend upon:

- The development of domestic gas production in Argentina and Brazil, which depends among other things on oil price recovery;

- The evolution of Bolivian gas exports. Increasing exports to Brazil and Argentina, coupled with increasing domestic demand, led to a rapid depletion of reserves, which were not replenished by new exploration and discoveries. Following the gas resource nationalization in 2006 and increase of the government take from 18 per cent to 82 per cent, operators have been reluctant to make new exploratory investment. Although reserves have not been certified in Bolivia since 2005, they are now estimated to be lower than 300 bcm. However, the Bolivian government has launched a series of incentives aimed at promoting private investment in exploration. It is still too early to say whether these new measures will be sufficient to reverse the trend that is expected to see exports gradually shrink over the next decade;

- Natural gas demand growth. In Argentina, gas demand has been constrained for several years by lack of supply, but new growth is likely to be restrained by low economic growth and price increases. In Brazil, natural gas demand growth depends crucially on the new gas-fired power projects and on the dispatch of thermal power plants, which in turn depends on hydrology.

Argentina
Argentina has a mature gas industry and a gas-intensive economy. Gas accounts for 52 per cent of total primary energy demand, and it is well distributed across all sectors. The power sector accounts for 35 per cent of gas demand, while gas is responsible for 50 to 55 per cent of power generation depending on the year (and on hydrology).

Argentina has a temperate climate, similar to that of Europe, and as result, the residential sector accounts for 24 per cent of total demand, as an annual average figure; however, in the coldest winter month residential demand can be five to seven times higher than in the summer, reaching

40–50 per cent of total demand. Total demand, however, is only about 20 per cent higher in the coldest month than in the warmest month because in winter, power plants and industrial consumers reduce their gas consumption to give priority to residential demand (Figure 6.45).

The development of the Argentine natural gas industry within a context of regional market integration was interrupted by the Argentine economic and financial crisis of 2001/2. In the aftermath of the crisis, the government implemented gas (and power) price controls that kept prices at artificially low levels, which stimulated demand growth, while discouraging investment in exploration and production. As gas production eventually started to decrease, Argentina's gas exports progressively dropped. This led Argentina to cut exports and to resume gas imports from Bolivia, signing a 20-year contract which started at 1.8 bcm/year in 2007 and will increase gradually to 10 bcm/year by 2021.

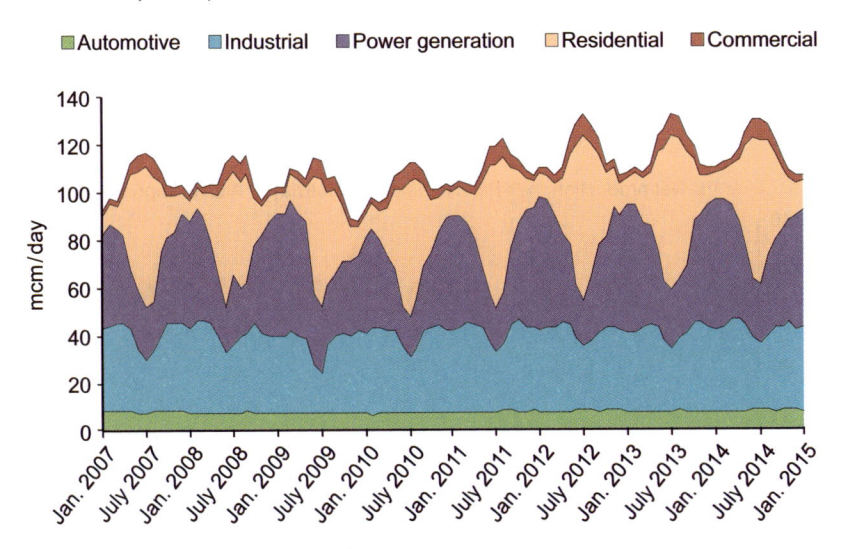

Figure 6.45: Argentina's natural gas consumption
Note: Excludes losses, system use, and statistical differences.
Source: ENARGAS (2016).

In June 2008, Argentina became the first South American country to import LNG, with the commissioning of the 3.7 bcm/year Bahía Blanca regasification terminal. The terminal's capacity was later expanded to 5.1 bcm. Another 5.1 bcm/year terminal was inaugurated in Escobar in 2011. Both are FSRUs permanently moored at the new port facilities. LNG was initially imported only during the winter,[123] when residential demand

---
[123] Southern Hemisphere winter is June to August.

soars due to space heating. However, LNG imports rapidly increased from 0.5 bcm in 2008 to 5.5 bcm in 2015 (with a peak of 6.4 bcm in 2013) and LNG is now imported the whole year round. Since 2008, Argentina has been a net gas importer, and its import dependence has grown steadily as can be seen in Figure 6.46.

Estimating future LNG demand in Argentina is not easy, as there are great uncertainties with respect to the pace of development of the country's large unconventional gas resources, given that almost all conventional fields are mature, with several in the declining stage. According to the 2013 EIA shale study (EIA, 2013), Argentina has the second largest shale gas resources and the fourth largest shale oil resources outside North America, estimated at 22.7 tcm of natural gas and 27 million barrels of oil. Vaca Muerta in the Neuquén Basin is the main formation for both oil and gas. Oil and gas production from unconventional resources has been increasing gradually. In August 2015, it reached 26,000 bpd of oil and 7 bcm of natural gas. These figures include production from both tight sands reservoirs and shale formations – 90 per cent of the oil comes from shale and 80 per cent of the natural gas comes from tight sands (Código Energético, 2015).

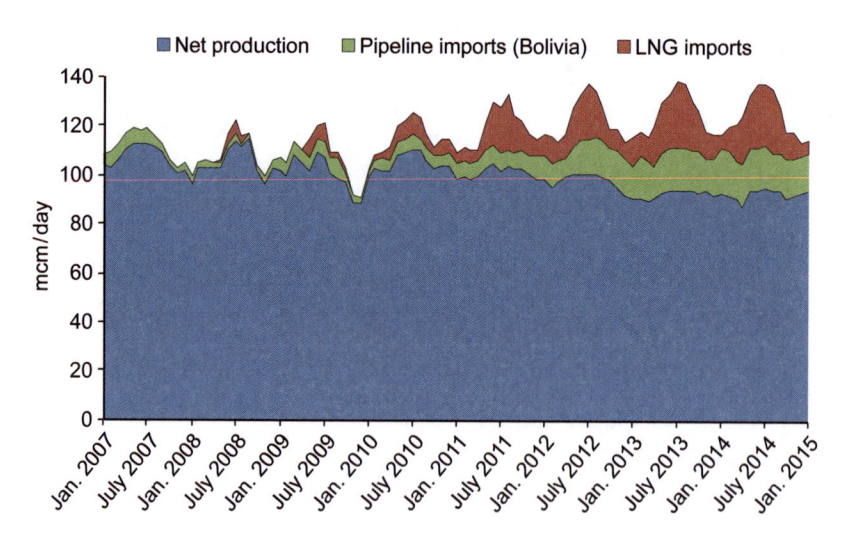

Figure 6.46: Argentina's domestic natural gas production and imports
Source: ENARGAS (2016), AliceWeb, Instituto Argentino de la Energía 'General Mosconi'.

Argentina's shale gas resources are located in regions that are already traditional natural gas and oil producers and therefore have significant infrastructure already in place – with increasing availability given the decline of conventional production. But their economic exploitation implies huge investments, the development of infrastructure, as well as a reliable institutional and regulatory context, and all of these will take time to materialize. The state-owned energy company YPF has been making a large effort to develop partnerships with major oil companies for tight gas and shale exploration. The pumping capacity for hydraulic fracturing available in Argentina is now the largest in Latin America. But some important challenges remain: Argentina's macroeconomic instability which has led to foreign exchange and capital controls, penalizing external investments and imports of goods and services; government-controlled gas pricing; lack of transparency and predictability of policy and regulation; and the country's labour market, which has traditionally been affected by excess regulation and strikes, especially in an environment of high and rising inflation (Almeida, D'Apote, and Fritsch, 2015).

Artificial prices for oil and gas[124] protect existing operators from low international prices, but the new liberal government that came into power following elections in October 2015 is not likely to keep these artificial prices for long. [125] Currency controls and limitations on repatriation of dividends, among other rules, have been strong barriers that made foreign investors cautious, despite the country's large resources. A 2015 Hydrocarbons Law tried to simplify and improve the attractiveness of the regulatory framework for private investment: among other changes, it unified the rate of royalties across the country and allowed operators to export 20 per cent of production without paying export tax (limited to those operators with investments above $1 billion in a five year period). These changes are welcome, but still provide insufficient incentives. It is yet to be seen if the new liberal government will be able to implement the major changes in regulation (and in the economy in general) that would be needed to attract the very high investment required to develop Argentina's unconventional resources at a sustained pace.

The global oil price will also be a key driver of the pace of development: with the barrel at $50, only a few sweet spots in Vaca Muerta are viable,[126] slowing the development of the whole play. Higher oil prices would gradually increase the quantity of viable fields, attracting more investments,

---

[124] A price floor of $77/bbl of oil (Medanito quality) and $7.5/MMBtu of natural gas (specifically for new and unconventional gas production) was put in place by the previous administration.

[125] When President Macri took office, expectations were that he would remove all price interventions. However, as of May 2016, the new government had yet to make any significant move in that direction, as a result of the aligned pressure of provincial authorities, unions, and existing producers. Only a 12% downward adjustment to the oil price floor, and none to the gas price floor, had been implemented at the time of writing (May 2016).

[126] Author's private communications.

accelerating the learning curve and decreasing costs, thus fostering production growth of both oil and natural gas.

Another uncertainty relating to gas supply is linked to the level of imports from Bolivia; these are supposed to gradually increase to 10 bcm in 2021 and continue at that level until 2026. In the absence of substantial investment in new exploration, Bolivia's production is expected to start declining shortly after 2020, while internal demand is rising. Although Argentina will have priority over Brazil after the Bolivia–Brazil contract expires in 2019, there are still uncertainties as to how much longer into the next decade Bolivia will be able to sustain exports to Argentina.

While there are also uncertainties about future increases in natural gas demand, these are less pronounced than those related to natural gas supply, because Argentina is a mature gas market. By 2016, it is expected that the natural gas coverage of the country will be close to 100 per cent, so there will be limited gas demand growth due to network expansion. A moderate increase in gas demand is expected, with demand growth in the residential sector dampened by the likely increase of gas prices from the current very low subsidized levels, while demand growth in the industrial sector will be limited by weak economic growth.

Combining our High and Low Scenarios for (a) domestic production, (b) Bolivian imports, and (c) demand, we obtain a wide range of projections for LNG imports. Table 6.20 shows our Higher and Lower LNG Demand Scenarios for Argentina.

Table 6.20: Argentina's LNG import outlook range (bcm/year)

Scenarios	2013*	2014*	2015*	2016	2017	2018	2019	2020	2025	2030
High	6.4	6.0	5.6	6.9	7.8	9.3	10.8	11.3	16.1	20.1
Low	6.4	6.0	5.6	5.5	4.4	3.4	2.4	1.1	-	-

*Actual imports (GIIGNL, 2016)
Source: Author's estimates.

Clearly, the demand for LNG imports is highest (and growing) in the scenarios with lower domestic production growth[127] and higher demand growth.[128] Conversely, in the scenarios with high domestic production

---

[127] The Low Domestic Production Scenario assumes a moderate increase of unconventional production (12% p.a. in 2015–30) and a 3% annual decline in conventional production. The High Production Scenario assumes a higher growth of unconventional production (17%) and the same decline in conventional production.

[128] The High Demand Scenario assumes a 3% p.a. growth (in line with historical growth), while the Low Demand Scenario assumes a 2% p.a. growth.

growth, we can expect a gradual substitution of LNG imports (and Bolivian imports) with domestic production from unconventional sources. LNG imports decrease and eventually disappear between 2020 and 2026, depending on the demand scenario and on the Bolivian imports assumption.

However, even in the scenarios where domestic production is sufficient to supply demand, there could still be seasonal imports to cover the winter peaks. In the absence of any storage capacity, seasonal LNG imports could be a more economical solution to meet peak demand than having to scale up the entire production and transportation infrastructure to meet the winter peak. Of course, Argentina may build storage capacity in the future, thereby reducing the need for seasonal LNG imports.

Since Argentina's current total LNG import capacity at its two terminals is 10.2 bcm/year, there will be a need for additional import capacity from 2024 in the highest LNG demand scenario; this could come either from a new regasification plant in Argentina or (more likely in our view) from a plant which is being planned in neighbouring Uruguay.[129] A 26 km pipeline between Argentina and Uruguay already exists, and this could be expanded and reversed.

For winter peak demand,[130] LNG imports via Chile may also be an option, using idle LNG regasification capacity in Chile (and idle cross border pipelines). The Argentine and Chilean governments announced, in February 2016,[131] an agreement by which Argentina will import 5.5 mcm/day from Chile from May through September 2016.

Brazil

Brazil is the largest energy market in Latin America, accounting for about 35 per cent of the region's total energy demand. Gas, however, still accounts for a relatively small proportion of Brazil's primary energy mix and of its power generation mix, respectively 12 and 14 per cent in 2014 (Brazil, 2015a). In 2015, Brazil's gas consumption was 36 bcm, half of which was imported (11.7 bcm from Bolivia and 6.5 bcm of LNG) (Brazil, 2016). A large, but very volatile proportion of gas demand is used for power generation (Figure 6.47). Brazil has a large hydropower capacity, but hydropower generation depends on river levels and ultimately on rain, even though hydropower plants have significant reservoir capacity. The last

---

[129] In 2013, ANCAP (Uruguay) and YPF (Argentina) signed an MOU establishing that Uruguay will export to Argentina part of the natural gas it will produce in the regasification plant expected to be built close to Montevideo. (https://www.presidencia.gub.uy/comunicacion/comunicacionnoticias/acuerdo-ancap-ipf)

[130] Winter in Argentina starts 21 June and ends 21 September.

[131] 'Chile to export gas, electricity to Argentina', Andrew Baker, 1 February 2016. www.bnamericas.com/en/news/oilandgas/chile-to-export-gas-electricity-to-argentina.

three years (2013 to 2015) have been unusually dry, requiring a much higher level of dispatch of the gas-fired plants, and hence a much higher LNG demand.

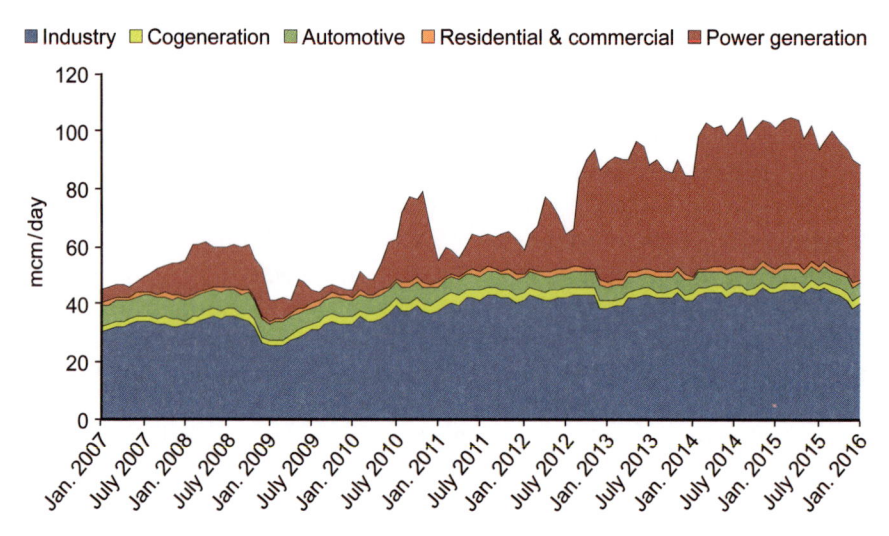

Figure 6.47: Brazil's natural gas consumption
Source: ABEGÁS (2016), Brazil (2016).

Although the upstream sector was opened to private companies in the mid-1990s, Petrobras is still the dominant company in oil and gas production. Natural gas reserves in Brazil are largely associated with oil and offshore, which explains why historically a large proportion of the gross production of gas was reinjected, flared, or used as a fuel on the platforms. Even today, only 65–70 per cent of gross gas production is sent to market.

Since there is no storage capacity in Brazil, and most gas production is associated with oil, there is very little flexibility in the Brazilian gas supply system. The flexibility in the import contract with Bolivia[132] became insufficient when gas-fired power plant capacity started to grow.

Thus, in 2006, Petrobras made a decision to build two regasification terminals as a way of procuring flexible gas and as an insurance against cuts from Bolivia (Almeida and Trebat, 2007). The two regasification terminals, located in Baia de Guanabara (Rio de Janeiro) in the south-east and in Pecém (Ceará) in the north-east are moored FSRUs. Both were commissioned in 2009 with an initial capacity of 2.5 and 5 bcm/year

---

[132] The contract has a take-or pay clause that allows Brazil to reduce monthly demand to 80% of maximum contracted volume (within the limit of 90% of annual contracted volume).

respectively. Later on, in 2014, a third FSRU of 2.5 bcm/year was added, in Salvador de Bahia, while the capacity of the Baia de Guanabara terminal was increased to 7.2 bcm/year. Brazil currently has a regasification capacity of nearly 15 bcm/year. Petrobras is the operator and, so far, the sole user of these terminals.[133]

Because power plant dispatch is very variable and highly unpredictable, Petrobras has opted to acquire LNG in the spot market and has signed 83 Master Sales Agreements (MSAs) with numerous companies, including NOCs, majors, international utilities, and trading companies. This allows Petrobras to quickly acquire a spot cargo when needed. In 2014 Petrobras bought 116 LNG cargoes, of these 101 were received in Brazil and 15 were resold.

The demand for LNG in the last three years (2013 to 2015) has been exceptionally high compared to that in previous years, due to the high level of dispatch of the country's gas-fired plants (Figure 6.48).

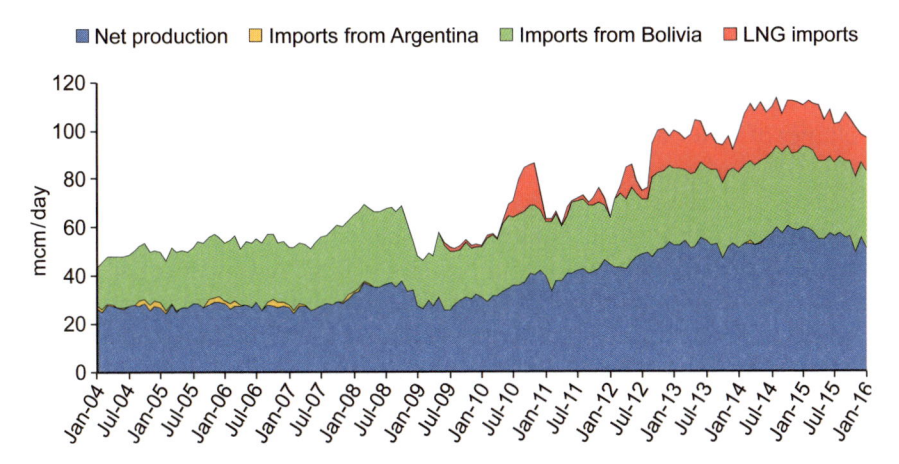

Figure 6.48: Brazil's domestic natural gas production and imports
Source: ANP (2016); Brazil (2016).

Petrobras is currently the only company importing and selling LNG in Brazil. However, with the current low LNG prices, there has been a wave of interest from other companies, in particular from power developers and large industrial users, in building new LNG regasification terminals. Three regasification projects stand out because they are integrated LNG/power projects and the power developers have successfully obtained a 25 year

---

[133] In Brazil there is no regulatory requirement for third-party access for regasification terminals, but Petrobras has announced that it would be willing to offer some capacity to other users.

power purchase agreement (PPA) in the 2013 and 2014 nationwide power auctions, which means the projects will have to be ready to generate by 2019 and 2020.[134]

Two of the integrated LNG/power projects are being developed by local conglomerate Grupo Bolognesi. They both involve gas-fired power plants of 1.238 GW capacity fuelled by LNG supplied through purpose-built FSRUs, one to be located in the port of Suape (Pernambuco State, north-east of Brazil) and the other in the port of Rio Grande (Rio Grande do Sul, Brazil's southernmost state). However, other locations are said to be under consideration. The capacity of the terminals has not yet been defined, but Bolognesi has announced that it plans to build the terminals with a capacity of 5.1 bcm/year, so it will also be able to sell LNG to local industries, on top of supplying the power plants.

Genpower, which won a 25 year PPA in 2015 for a 1.5 GW power plant, to be located in Santo Amaro das Brotas in the state of Sergipe, is developing the other integrated LNG/power project, due to start operating in 2020. In order to supply the plant at full capacity, a regasification capacity of at least 2.6 bcm/year will be required.

Looking ahead, the consensus is that Brazil will import increasing volumes of LNG, at least for the next decade or so, albeit with large month-to-month and year-to-year variations, due to gas demand from power plants, which in turns depends on hydrology.

Although there is no doubt that Brazil will be able to substantially increase its natural gas production, given the large resources of associated gas in the Presalt and some substantial onshore associated and non-associated resources (both conventional and unconventional), there is great uncertainty about the pace of these developments. This will depend on four main factors: (a) the oil price, (b) the ability of Petrobras to recover from its current financial crisis, (c) the willingness of the government to change current legislation to allow for a wider participation of private companies in the Presalt and (d) the improvement of policies and regulations to support onshore exploration and production.

There is also uncertainty about the future level of imports from Bolivia, as the current 20 year supply contract (11 bcm/year) will expire in 2019. In the absence of substantial investment in new exploration in Bolivia, Bolivia will soon be unable to supply both its export markets (Brazil and Argentina) and its own rising internal demand. Once the Bolivia–Brazil export contract expires in 2019, Argentina will have priority over Brazil.

---

[134] In order to participate in the power auction, power developers need to demonstrate that they have secured a gas supply agreement enabling the power plant to run at 100% capacity for a 25 year period. It does not have to be a final supply contract, which can be signed after the auction, but a draft agreement or a letter of intent.

Uncertainties in the demand outlook stem from the evolution of industrial gas demand (which in turn depends on the country's economic performance), and from the pace of construction of new gas-fired power plants and their utilization rate. The latter depends critically on assumptions regarding the reservoir capacity of existing hydropower plants, delays in the commissioning of large new hydropower projects under construction, and the performance of existing and new wind farms. Furthermore, the daily operation of the thermal power generation capacity (which is largely based on natural gas) depends on the level of available hydropower generation, which in turns depends on river levels and reservoirs capacity.[135] The end result is that the dispatch of gas-fired plant is highly variable and mostly unpredictable, and increasingly so. However, there is a consensus that thermal power plant dispatch will increase on average, because the latest large hydropower plants built, or under construction, have increasingly smaller reservoirs and are basically run-of-river plants (with production sometimes varying in a range from 1 to 10, between dry and rainy periods).[136] Gas demand from power plants today can vary from 3.6 bcm/year (minimum dispatch) to 19.6 bcm/year (100 per cent dispatch). In 2030, we expect power plant gas demand to vary between 10 bcm/year and 43 bcm/year. Minimum dispatch is not zero because some power plants have contractual levels of minimum dispatch.

Official projections (Brazil, 2015b) for the period 2015–24 show that if imports from Bolivia continue at current levels and domestic production increases at about 5 per cent per year, the capacity of the existing regasification plants plus the three new LNG regasification projects will be sufficient to supply additional demand, even considering peak demand for power plants. Apart from the assumptions on domestic production and imports from Bolivia, the Government's projections critically depend on the assumption that all the projected hydropower plants will be commissioned according to schedule and that wind farms will perform as

---

[135] In Brazil, the decision to dispatch thermal power plants depends on a complex stochastic calculation; this calculation takes into account not only how much water there is in the hydropower reservoirs at any given moment, but also the probability that there will be sufficient water in the reservoir to cover power demand in the next 24 months, given power demand projections and a very large number of historical series of monthly regional rain patterns, with an acceptable risk of undersupply of no more than 5%. This calculation is done weekly by the national Power System National Operator on a rolling 24 month basis, with the first 12 months having greater importance. Apart from these stochastic calculations, dispatch occasionally takes place out of the merit order (for various technical and non-technical reasons).

[136] There are increasing issues of social acceptance regarding hydropower projects with large reservoirs, as they involve inundation of very large areas (often in sensitive areas like the Amazon forest) and displacement of communities.

projected, which are unrealistic assumptions in this author's opinion.

In order to explore the sensitivity of LNG demand in Brazil (and the need for additional LNG import capacity), this author has built detailed supply and demand scenarios with high and low assumptions for gas demand, domestic production, and imports from Bolivia. As can be expected, the Higher LNG Demand Scenario implies lower domestic production and lower imports from Bolivia, while the Lower LNG Demand Scenario implies higher domestic production and higher imports from Bolivia, although there is little difference in the high and low scenario up to 2020. The largest uncertainty, however, relates to gas demand, which will vary significantly depending on whether we assume a 'year of average hydrology' with average thermal power plant dispatch, or a 'very dry year' with 100 per cent thermal power plant dispatch during most of the year.

The results are summarized in Figures 6.49 and 6.50, and in Table 6.21. It appears that in most scenarios, LNG demand will continue to grow in Brazil, reaching between 30 and 40 bcm/year in 2030, under a 'maximum dispatch' assumption or a 'very dry year' situation. Clearly this is not likely to happen every year. Most years will have 'average hydrology' and therefore 'average power plant dispatch'. Although it may seem that until 2022–4, LNG may not be needed in a year with average hydrology, in reality even in an 'average year' there will be days or weeks with peak LNG demand. Thus in any given year (even in an average year), LNG imports will typically vary between 0 and a maximum corresponding to 100 per cent power plant dispatch. Hence, the system (including infrastructure and import contracts) must be able to cope with peak LNG demand at any time, although in most years the LNG infrastructure is unlikely to be fully utilized during the whole year.

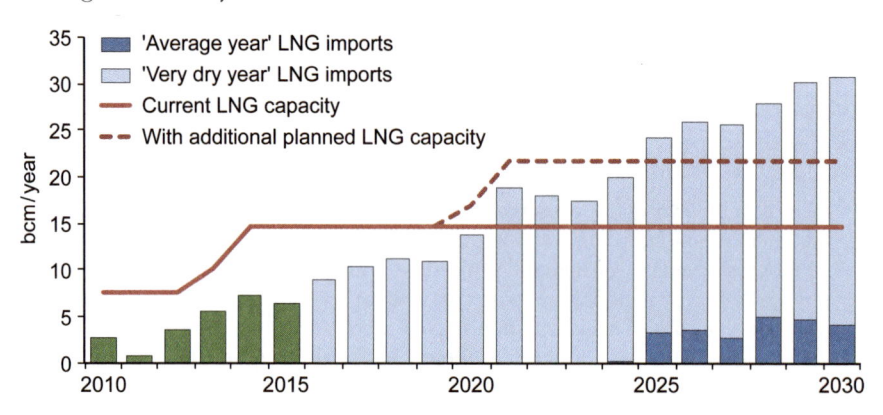

Figure 6.49: Brazil's LNG import scenarios (bcm/year): Lower LNG Demand Scenario

Source: Author's estimates.

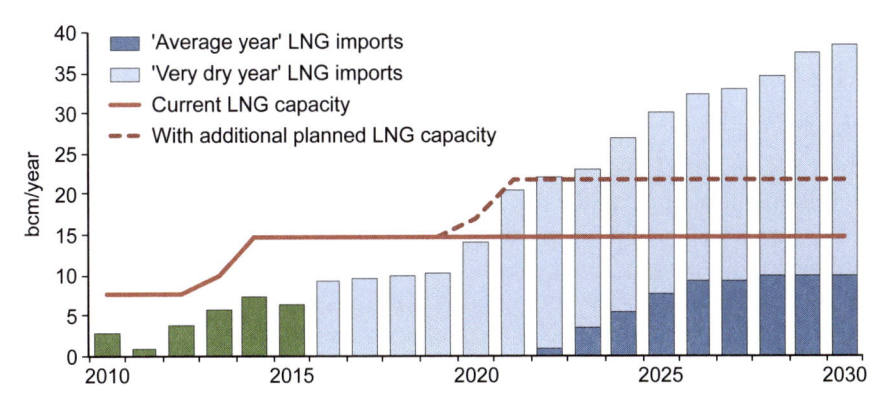

Figure 6.50: Brazil's LNG import scenarios (bcm/year): Higher LNG Demand Scenario

Source: Author's estimates.

Table 6.21: Brazil's LNG import outlook range (bcm/year)

Scenarios	2015*	2016	2017	2018	2019	2020	2025	2030
Lower LNG Demand Scenario								
With average power plant dispatch	6.5	–	–	–	–	–	3.2	4.2
With highest power plant dispatch**	6.5	9.1	10.5	11.2	11.1	13.7	24.1	30.7
Higher LNG Demand Scenario								
With average power plant dispatch	6.5	–	–	–	–	–	7.7	9.8
With highest power plant dispatch**	6.5	9.2	9.6	10.0	10.2	14.0	30.0	38.3

* Actual LNG imports (GIIGNL, 2016)

** The values in this second line represent both peak demand in any year, and maximum annual demand in a very dry year.

Source: Author's estimates.

Given that Brazil's regasification capacity is currently 15 bcm/year, new regasification capacity will be needed in both the high and low scenarios from 2021. Several terminals are being planned or discussed, of which three terminals are linked to power projects totalling 7 bcm/year or more. As of June 2016, none of the three planned terminals is yet committed.

Chile

Both Chile and Uruguay are poor in hydrocarbon resources and the development of their natural gas markets has been based on imported gas from Argentina, which at the time had abundant production available at relatively low prices. These imports soared until 2004, when Argentina started to restrict gas exports. When imports gradually dried up, both Chile and Uruguay turned to LNG to secure a stable and reliable source of natural gas supply.

Chile has a small production in the far south of the country, which is not connected to the other parts of the country. Gas in Chile is mainly used for power generation, with new high efficiency gas-fired plants gradually replacing old and polluting oil-fired and coal-fired plants, but use in the industrial, commercial, and residential sectors is also rising. In 2004, Chile was importing 5.2 bcm from Argentina, which were gradually curtailed to 0.6 bcm in 2008. Chile reacted very quickly, building two onshore regasification terminals. The first terminal in Quintero near Santiago (3.7 bcm/year) was commissioned in 2009 and the second in Mejillones (2 bcm/year), in the north of the country, started up in 2010 and supplies mostly power generation for the mining industry. LNG imports amounted to 3.5 bcm in 2014.

Chile's LNG demand is expected to continue to expand as a result of demand from new gas-fired power plants as well as increased use in the residential, commercial, and industrial sectors (Table 6.22). This increase will be supported by the proposed expansion of the existing LNG terminals, as well as by two or three new proposed LNG regasification terminals.

Table 6.22: Chile's LNG import outlook range (bcm/year)

Scenarios	2013*	2014*	2015*	2016	2017	2018	2019	2020	2025	2030
High	3.6	3.5	3.7	4.3	4.9	5.4	5.9	6.5	8.9	11.3
Low	3.6	3.5	3.7	4.0	4.3	4.7	5.0	5.4	7.1	8.8

* Actual LNG imports.

Source: Author's estimates.

Two projects are competing to supply the centre–south region of Chile, which is not interconnected with the centre and currently receives CNG by truck from the Quintero LNG terminal. The Penco Lirquén project, formerly known as the Octopus LNG project, will be located in Concepcion Bay, in Chile's Biobio region, and will supply a 640 MW CCGT. Cheniere is both a 50 per cent partner in this terminal (together with local power generator Biobiogenera) and the LNG supplier, expected to deliver approximately 0.6 mtpa of LNG for 20 years beginning in 2019 from its Corpus Christi Liquefaction Project currently under construction in Texas.[137] The Penco Lirquén partners reportedly contracted Norway's Höegh LNG for the 20 year chartering of a FSRU with a capacity of 4 bcm/year.[138] In order to reach a final investment decision and start construction, the power plant and the terminal must receive regulatory and environmental approvals and obtain financing. The other terminal for the centre–south region is being proposed by ENAP in Baia de San Vicente, where ENAP is seeking to develop a gas-fired power plant which would also supply its Aconcagua oil refinery.

Another FSRU project was being planned by GasAtacama, a Chilean energy company. This terminal would be located in Mejillones in the north of Chile and would potentially compete with the existing Mejillones terminal. This terminal is aimed at fuelling one or more power plants to supply the local mining companies' expansion plans. But lower copper prices, higher costs, and local opposition have delayed the companies' expansion plans in the Atacama Desert, postponing the power and LNG projects.

Uruguay

Uruguay does not currently produce hydrocarbons, although it is exploring both offshore and onshore. So far all domestic gas demand is met by imported gas from Argentina. Argentina did not cut exports to Uruguay, as it did with Brazil and Chile, but has been keeping them at a minimum volume to supply Uruguay's residential and commercial demand, which in 2015 amounted to around 55 mcm.

Uruguay has long been seeking a solution to the problem of increasing its gas supply and of diversifying its sources of supply. The country aims at converting several oil-fired power plants and building a new 530 MW CCGT. For this reason, the Uruguayan government, through Gas Sayago (a joint venture between Uruguay's state oil company Ancap and the state power company Ute), is actively supporting the construction of an LNG regasification terminal in Punta Sayago, close to Montevideo.

---

[137] 'Cheniere Marketing and Central El Campesino Sign 20-Year LNG Sale and Purchase Agreement', PR Newswire, 30 July 2015. www.prnewswire.com/news-releases/cheniere-marketing-and-central-el-campesino-sign-20-year-lng-sale-and-purchase-agreement-300121610.html.

[138] 'Höegh LNG signed 20-year FSRU Contract with Chilean Octopus LNG SpA', Vessel Finder, 28 May 2015. https://www.vesselfinder.com/news/3480-Hegh-LNG-signed-20-year-FSRU-Contract-with-Chilean-Octopus-LNG-SpA.

The terminal was to be developed by a consortium led by France's Engie (GNLS) under a 15 year Build-Own-Operate-Transfer contract, and the FSRU – which is being constructed by Mitsui OSK Lines (MOL) – was initially due to arrive at Punta Sayago in Uruguay in mid-2017. However, following a series of difficulties with the terminal contractors (AOS) and doubts whether the project would be economically sound, Engie and its partner Marubeni walked away from the project in September 2015. Nevertheless, the Uruguayan government is going ahead with the project and has reached a basic agreement with MOL, who will now build, own and operate the FSRU.[139] The whole project is now likely to suffer delays, although sources from the Uruguayan government have confirmed that it will not be cancelled.[140] The construction of the CCGT is going ahead and the plant may have to be initially fuelled with diesel.

The Punta Sayago FSRU is the world's largest FSRU booked so far, with a storage capacity of 263,000 cubic metres and a regasification capacity of 3.65 bcm/year, expandable to 5.5 bcm/year. And this is part of the problem because Uruguay, with a population of 3 million, a large hydropower capacity, and growing renewable resources, does not need all that LNG and had been planning to sell both gas and gas-based power to Argentina during the winter months. However, at the time of writing, Argentina had not committed firmly to the project. Power exports to Brazil and/or LNG re-exports in smaller cargoes to potential regasification terminals in southern Brazil, are also a possibility.

Based on the above, we expect that Uruguay will start importing LNG in 2019 or 2020 (Table 6.23). Our outlook for Uruguay's LNG imports only includes the expected volumes that would be consumed in Uruguay, because the possible exports to Argentina and Brazil have already been considered in those two countries' outlooks; in other words, we have considered that Argentina could either import LNG at one of its own terminals or could indirectly import LNG through Uruguay.

Table 6.23: Uruguay's LNG import outlook range (bcm/year)

Scenarios	2015	2016	2017	2018	2019	2020	2025	2030
High	–	–	–	–	0.5	0.9	1.2	1.4
Low	–	–	–	–	0.2	0.4	0.5	0.6

Source: Author's estimates.

[139] 'Mitsui OSK and Gas Sayago agree to continue Uruguay FSRU project', *LNG World Shipping*, 5 October 2015. www.lngworldshipping.com/news/view,mitsui-osk-and-gas-sayago-agree-to-continue-uruguay-fsru-project_39374.htm.
[140] Author's private communication.

The Andean Region

The Andean countries include one LNG exporting country, Peru, and the largest reserve holder of the whole region, Venezuela. In spite of the Venezuelan government's announcement in 2009 of a 'Socialist Gas Revolution' to double the natural gas production and to begin exporting natural gas by 2015, Venezuelan natural gas continues to be a great unfulfilled promise. Political instability remains the main challenge to making gas projects attractive. Domestic natural gas pricing remains a crucial risk factor for private investors, while LNG export projects require a very high level of investment, which is difficult to justify given the country's political instability. Meanwhile, Peru's LNG exports are expected to remain stable, but are unlikely to be expanded in the next decade due to the growth of domestic demand (see Chapter 5 on LNG Supply).

Colombia

The Colombian natural gas market has experienced significant expansion since the mid-1990s, when Colombia launched an ambitious and highly successful Natural Gas Expansion Programme. In 2014, natural gas production was 11.8 bcm, almost twice that in 2000 (6 bcm). Of this, 10.8 bcm was consumed domestically and 1 bcm was exported to Venezuela. Gas is mostly used by the energy industry itself (27 per cent in 2013), followed by power generation (26 per cent) and the industrial sector (25 per cent). Colombia has significant hydropower capacity, but hydropower generation varies significantly from year to year depending on hydrology: in 2013 hydro accounted for 69 per cent of the total generation, with natural gas providing 18 per cent, while in 2007 and 2008, hydropower accounted for 80 and 83 per cent and gas for 12 and 10 per cent (IEA, 2015f).

Colombia began exporting gas to neighbouring Venezuela in 2008, through the 224 km 5 bcm/year Antonio Ricaurte pipeline. The flow on this pipeline was supposed to be reversed in 2012, when gas production in Venezuela was expected to increase, but this plan has been delayed several times and it is uncertain when (if ever) Venezuela will finally begin exporting to Colombia. In mid-2015, Venezuela announced that the start of production in its giant offshore gas field (Perla) would allow exports of gas to Colombia to start in January 2016, but that plan was indefinitely postponed in December 2015 due to the severe drought conditions caused by El Niño which mean that Venezuela needs the gas to generate electricity itself. Colombia invoked the same reason in April 2014, to temporarily suspend gas exports to Venezuela because of drought conditions.

Oil and gas reserve growth has lagged behind the rise in production, and the country's resource base is a concern. To stimulate gas exploration and production, the government has, in recent years, introduced fiscal incentives for natural gas: onshore and shallow-water gas fields and deep offshore gas pay only 80 and 60 per cent of the level of royalties paid by oil fields, respectively. In addition, the government has introduced new regulation and incentives, in order to attract investment for unconventional gas. Colombia has important yet to be tapped coal bed methane resources, and also some shale gas resources.

According to Unidad de Planeación Minero Energética (UPME), the government's energy planning institution, gas demand is expected to grow at an annual average rate of between 1.4 and 3.3 per cent in the next 15 years (2014–29) depending on the GDP scenario (Colombia, 2015); during the previous 15 years it had grown at 4.8 per cent per year. Given that domestic production is declining, Colombia will have to start importing gas or LNG by 2017 or 2018 depending on the demand scenario (see Figure 6.51). Even assuming that Venezuela will indeed start exporting to Colombia, this would only delay the need for other sources of supply (LNG) by one or two years.

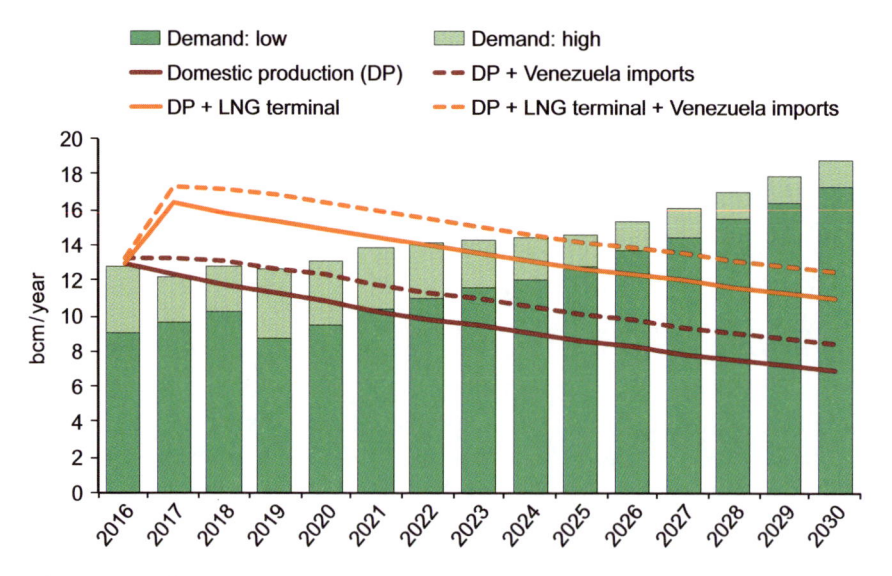

Figure 6.51: Projected supply–demand balance in Colombia, 2016–30
Source: Author's estimates based on Colombia's UPME scenarios (2015).

Concerned with the lack of new gas discoveries, Colombia has been considering importing LNG for some time. The country's first LNG terminal, located close to Cartagena on the Atlantic coast, is currently under construction and is expected to be commissioned in late 2016 or

LNG Demand Potential 411

early 2017. The terminal is being developed by a consortium of three Colombian power generators (TEBSA, Celsia, and Termocandelaria). The consortium has already signed a 20 year charter deal with Höegh LNG for a 4.1 bcm/year FSRU, and has started negotiations for contractual volumes.

Even with the Cartagena regasification terminal, supply will come short of demand between 2022 and 2026, depending on the demand scenario and on whether Venezuela honours its export commitments (Table 6.24). Thus, Colombia will need additional regasification capacity. Options include: an expansion of the Cartagena terminal (or adding another terminal on the Atlantic coast) or building a new terminal on the Pacific coast. UPME has analysed the overall costs of the two options and concluded that a terminal on the Pacific coast would be cheaper in terms of pipeline network expansion needs, and would also increase supply security by diversifying the LNG supply sources.

Table 6.24: Colombia's LNG import outlook range (bcm/year)

Scenarios	2016	2017	2018	2019	2020	2025	2030
High	–	–	1.1	1.4	2.4	5.9	11.9
Low	–	–	–	–	–	2.7	8.9

Source: Author's estimates.

Surprisingly, there was also a small liquefaction project in Colombia, Pacific Rubiales' Caribbean FLNG project, which monetizes the gas reserves found in the La Creciente onshore field. However, Pacific Rubiales announced in February 2015 that the project has been suspended because of low oil prices and changes in the LNG market.

The Greater Caribbean

The Greater Caribbean is defined here as the region around the Caribbean Sea which includes: the Caribbean islands, the six countries of Central America, and three countries on the north coast of South America (French Guiana, Guyana, and Suriname).

The Caribbean islands are characterized by a scarcity of energy resources such as hydrocarbons and large-scale renewable energy. Therefore, most islands are highly dependent on liquid fuel imports to meet their energy needs. In particular, power generation is mainly based on diesel and fuel oil. The only exceptions are Trinidad and Tobago, which is a major natural gas producer and LNG exporter, and Cuba, which has some limited oil and gas production but relies on liquid fuels imports

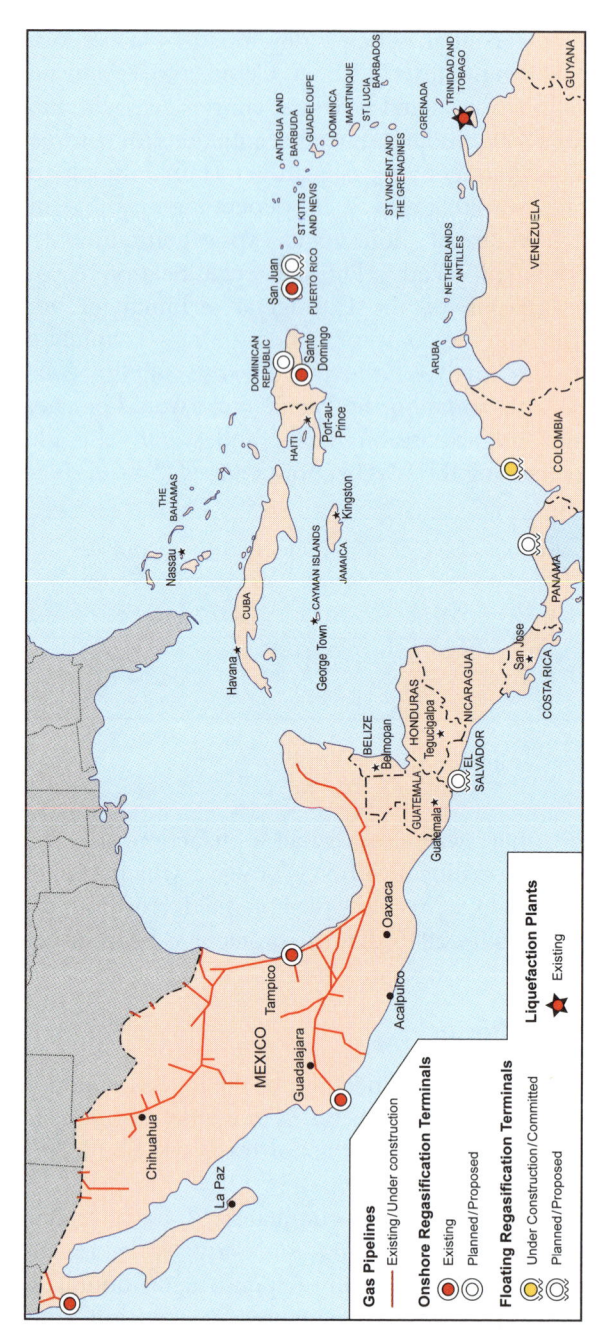

Map 6.3: Main pipelines, existing and proposed LNG terminals in Mexico, Central America, and the Caribbean

Source: Author's research.

LNG Demand Potential 413

for 60 per cent of its primary energy supply.

Central America has no natural gas production or consumption. The energy matrix is more diversified than in the Caribbean, with a larger use of renewable resources, especially hydropower. However, like in the Caribbean, most countries are dependent on imported oil products for a large share of their power generation.

This energy mix (Figure 6.52) has resulted in high and volatile electricity prices for the countries of this region and significant environmental impacts (Bailey, 2013; Castalia, 2014). The predictable ending of the PetroCaribe trade programme[141] will further increase energy costs for the Caribbean countries which were part of this programme.

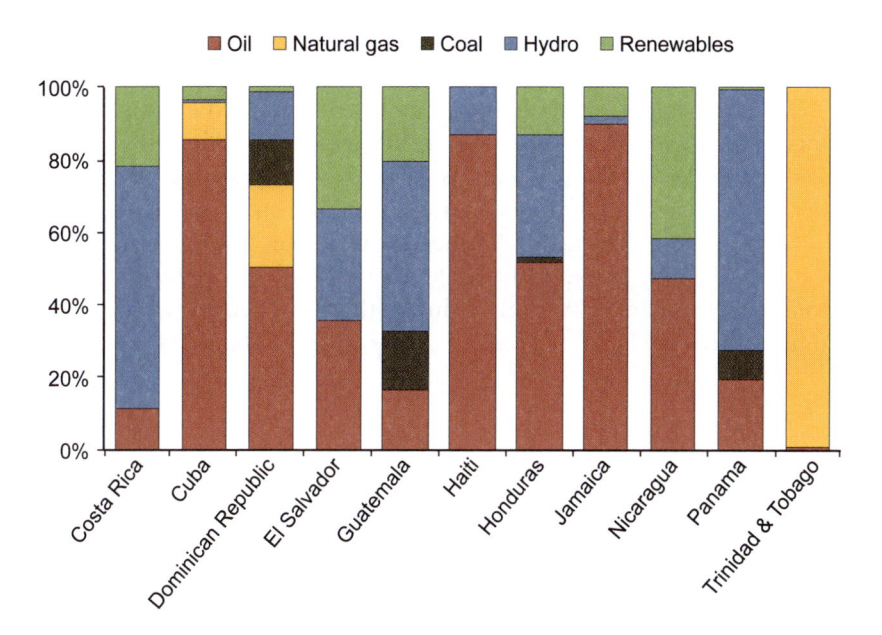

Figure 6.52: Power generation mix in selected Caribbean and Central American countries, 2013
Source: (IEA 2015f).

Many governments in this region are looking at options to diversify both their energy matrix and their suppliers, aiming at a cleaner and cheaper

---

[141] The region has been favoured since 2005 by the PetroCaribe trade programme, in which Venezuela sells subsidized oil and diesel to many Caribbean countries and territories. But the reduced global oil price scenario and the decline of Venezuela's oil production are putting pressure on the viability of this programme. PDVSA's oil production has declined from 3.5 million bpd in 1998 to 2.7 million bpd in 2014.

energy mix. Many countries are launching programmes to increase the use of renewable energy, such as wind and solar. Several countries are also exploring the possibility of importing LNG and converting existing power plants to natural gas, partly because of the proximity of regional suppliers, such as Trinidad and Tobago and the USA.

Puerto Rico and the Dominican Republic have been importing LNG since 2000 and 2003 respectively. However, there were significant special features in these two early projects that are hard to replicate nowadays. Haug and Cumberland (2013) discusses the success factors of the two projects, and identifies the challenges faced by new small emerging markets; they have small energy markets, often requiring sub-optimal logistics and they lack: large established LNG customers with a good credit history; receiving facilities or a reliable market; and clear regulations and pricing mechanisms.

The technologies and business models in the LNG industry have changed considerably in the last decade, bringing new options to new small emerging markets. One important issue used to be the scale of the projects, since the countries' small power markets were not sufficient to anchor the development of a world-scale regasification terminal (Institute of Americas, 2013). FSRUs now allow smaller-scale solutions at a much lower cost than an onshore terminal. For a more in-depth discussion on smaller LNG terminals and smaller LNG carriers, please refer to Chapter 4.

Puerto Rico

Puerto Rico was the first country in the region to build a regasification plant (in 2000). LNG imports remained around 0.7 bcm until 2010 and then grew rapidly to 1.7 bcm in 2014.

Puerto Rico's first regasification plant is an onshore integrated facility with a 3.7 bcm/year regasification terminal and a 540 MW power plant, operated by the company Ecoeléctrica; it is owned by Gas Natural Fenosa (47.5 per cent), Edison (50 per cent), and General Electric (2.5 per cent). Gas Natural Fenosa holds exclusive import rights for Puerto Rico. The Ecoeléctrica gas-fired power plant accounts for 9 per cent of Puerto Rico's installed capacity and 15 per cent of its power generation. The LNG terminal still has substantial spare capacity and gas consumption could be expanded.

Because of the high dependency of Puerto Rico's power sector on imported oil, power prices in Puerto Rico are about two to three times the US average. To reduce fuel costs, PREPA, the local public electric utility which owns Puerto Rico's five oil-fired power plants (totalling about 4.1 GW and responsible for two-third of total power generation) has announced plans to convert all its oil-fired plants to dual-firing with natural gas. A first conversion, at the Costa Sur 990 MW power station, was completed in 2013, but the other four conversions depend on the construction of new LNG import terminal and natural gas distribution infrastructure.

A second regasification terminal is being planned: the Aguirre Offshore Gasport terminal will be a FSRU located off the southern coast of Puerto Rico, chartered with Excelerate Energy. The terminal will be located close to PREPA's large Aguirre power complex in Salinas (1.6 GW). The project has already received FERC authorization and is scheduled to start construction in 2016 and operation in 2017. The FSRU will have a capacity to regasify 5.1 bcm/year, but will initially deliver 2.5 bcm/year to the PREPA plants to be converted to natural gas.

Later on, when distribution lines are installed, the terminal could also supply PREPA's two other power plants, San Juan and Palo Seco, which total 1.4 GW.

Dominican Republic

The Dominican Republic has imported LNG since 2003, when the Andrés regasification plant started operation in Punta Caucedo. Natural gas represents 11 per cent of the total primary energy demand, and 23 per cent of the power generation mix.

The Andrés terminal, operated by AES Dominicana, has a 2.3 bcm/year regasification capacity and was initially aimed just at supplying two local gas-fired power plants, with a combined capacity of 555 MW. However, since 2005, it has been supplying LNG to other final consumers through seven distribution companies, transporting natural gas to final consumers by CNG or LNG trucks. In 2014, LNG imports reached 1.1 bcm and sales were made to more than 80 final consumers.

AES expects that total natural gas demand in the Dominican Republic will more than double by 2018, mostly driven by increasing demand from power generation. To meet this demand, AES is planning to expand the Andrés terminal by building a second LNG storage tank, apparently without increasing the regasification capacity. AES is also redesigning the Andrés terminal to adapt it for re-load operations onto vessels between 10,000–60,000 cubic metres. The objective is to provide natural gas to smaller markets in the region, with the LNG received in the AES Andrés terminal. This new business model could help spread the use of natural gas in other Caribbean countries that have too small a demand to build an independent standard-size LNG terminal. The terminal will be ready for re-load operations in the third quarter of 2016.

In 2014, the Dominican government announced the construction of a second regasification terminal, to be located in the coastal city of San

Pedro de Macorís. The terminal, which is being developed by Antillean Gas Ltd. (a consortium of six domestic and foreign firms) will be able to receive about 1.3 bcm/year and will supply approximately 300 MW of existing power plants which are barely used at present because they are too expensive to operate using other fuels. The status of the project is not clear from available information.

Other Caribbean countries
Several other Caribbean countries are attracted by the possibility of substituting liquid fuels with a cleaner and cheaper fuel. Low US gas prices and the prospect of US LNG exports at HH-linked prices have spurred a new wave of LNG regasification projects; however none has yet come to fruition.

Jamaica has long wanted to become an importer of LNG to substitute oil imports in its power generation plants. After several failed tenders, Jamaica is expected to start importing LNG in 2016. Jamaica Public Service (JPS) has contracted US-based New Fortress Energy (NFE) to supply LNG to its 120 MW power plant at Bogue in Montego Bay in western Jamaica and, later, to a new 190 MW gas-fired power plant to be constructed at Old Harbour on the southern coast of Jamaica. NFE will initially supply LNG in Montego Bay through an FSU vessel chartered on a two year contract from Golar, until it completes the construction of an onshore terminal in Old Harbour. First LNG delivery at Montego Bay has been announced for August 2016. Engineering work has already started on the Old Harbour onshore LNG terminal. Both the terminal, expected to regasify 0.2 mtpa, and the power plant are expected to be operational by mid-2018.

The *Haiti* government, concerned about the need to dramatically increase power supply while reducing dependence on expensive liquid fuels, called for developers to come forward with an adequate LNG plan for Haiti. The developers (a joint venture of four international companies) are proposing a 'mini' regasification terminal located 14 km north of Port-au-Prince, with an initial storage capacity of 15,000 m^3 rising in a second phase to 30,000 m^3. The terminal will supply a 40 MW gas-fired power plant. In a second stage of the project, a pipeline will be constructed to supply the industrial area of Port-au-Prince. In order to secure supplies on a small scale, the companies will procure gas from intermediary LNG storage facilities elsewhere in the Caribbean. Construction began in August 2013, but suffered delays and interruptions in 2014.

Central America
Importing natural gas has long been a common objective in the region. The first attempts started in the 1990s through proposed regional pipelines bringing imported gas either from the north (Mexico) or from the south

(Colombia and Venezuela), but these proposals failed. Early LNG projects were considered in *El Salvador* and in *Honduras*, but did not go ahead. More recently, there has been a wave of LNG regasification projects involving the construction of one terminal supplying power plants in two or more countries, to achieve minimum economies of scale, but none so far have come to fruition.

Currently, there are two ongoing projects to import LNG in Central America. In *El Salvador*, Quantum Energy is developing a LNG regasification terminal integrated with a 380 MW power plant in the port of Acajutla, planned to start in 2018. The power plant would require gas supplies of around 500–600 mcm/y.

Panama is devising a similar integrated project. The LNG Group Panama is planning to construct a 350 MW gas-fired CCGT with a regasification terminal located on Telfers Island in Colon, at the Caribbean Sea entrance of the Panama Canal. Terminal construction is planned to begin in early 2016, with commercial operations planned for 2018. The particularity of this project is that its jetty will be able to accommodate multiple sizes of LNG carriers ranging from Q-Flex to barges, and small and mid-size LNG carriers, with capacities as low as 5,000 m^3 or less. This will enable Panama to function as a regional LNG hub, with the capability to offtake LNG from full-scale vessels and re-export it in smaller carriers towards regional markets. The terminal will also have facilities to ship LNG by truck and could be a bunker supply port.

Range of future LNG imports in the Greater Caribbean
There is no doubt that there is a large gas demand potential in the region, as power demand is still growing strongly and natural gas seems to be the fuel of choice for new thermal power plants, and to complement renewables. It is more difficult, however, to make a projection of LNG imports into the region because there are many LNG regasification projects, but past records indicate that only a few of them will actually come to fruition.

We feel reasonably certain that both Puerto Rico and the Dominican Republic will gradually increase their LNG demand and will, at some point, build a second terminal or expand the existing ones. We also feel that there are good chances that one terminal will be built in Central America during this decade, and perhaps another two in the next decade.

Using both a bottom up approach (analysing power demand growth, gas substitution for other fuels, and the need for new generating capacity (Castalia, 2014) and a top–down approach (assessing the regasification capacity that might be built or expanded), we converged to a range of between 15 and 20 bcm/year of LNG imports in the region in 2030 (Table 6.25).

Table 6.25: LNG import outlook range for the Caribbean and Central America (bcm/year)

Scenarios	2014*	2020	2025	2030
High	2.8	9.5	15.5	20.3
Low	2.8	7.5	11.8	14.8

* Actual imports.
Source: Author's estimates.

Mexico

Since the country is interconnected with the USA through 16 gas pipelines, the dynamics of the Mexican gas market are linked more with North America, than with Central and South America.

In the last 10 years natural gas demand in the country has increased rapidly, fuelled by the power sector. Mexico's gas demand increased from 53 bcm in 2004 to 75 bcm in 2014. In 2014, the power sector accounted for 49 per cent of gas demand, followed by the oil sector (32 per cent) and the industrial sector (18 per cent) (Mexico, 2015). Gas share in power generation has increased rapidly from 20 per cent in 2000 to 56 per cent in 2013 (IEA, 2015f).

On the other hand, between 2006 and 2014, Mexico's natural gas production stagnated at around 45–50 bcm.[142] More than two-thirds of gas production was from associated oil fields. At 348 bcm, Mexico's natural gas proven reserves are modest, only equivalent to six years of current production. Nevertheless, Mexico has one of the world's largest shale gas resource bases, estimated at 15 tcm of technically recoverable shale gas – the sixth largest in the world according to the EIA (2013). In order to develop its gas potential, both conventional and unconventional, Mexico needs to attract private investment. Historically, Pemex's exclusive rights over the upstream have been an important obstacle to increasing gas exploration in the country. But in 2013 a much awaited Constitutional Reform opened the way to private investment. However, the implementation of an adequate regulatory framework, sufficiently attractive and transparent to compete with investments in the USA and Canada, will take time.

In this context, natural gas imports increased from 12 bcm in 2004 to 30 bcm in 2014. Three regasification terminals were built between 2006 and 2012: one on the Atlantic coast (in 2006 at Altamira, 7.8 bcm), and two

---

[142] Mexico (2015). In the same period Mexico's oil production actually fell by 25%.

on the Pacific coast (in 2008 at Costa Azul, 10.3 bcm and in 2012 at Manzanillo, 5.2 bcm), adding 23.3 bcm/year of regasification capacity. The Costa Azul terminal in Baja California was intended to supply LNG to the US west coast, while the other two were targeting the Mexican market. However, the US shale gas boom has fostered a new market dynamics in both the USA and Mexico, and the three terminals have remained largely underutilized. US gas pipeline imports became a cheaper gas supply option than LNG, and now represent an important threat to LNG demand in Mexico. The utilization of the three terminals has remained low (peaking at 39 per cent in 2014) as LNG cargoes procured under long-term contracts are diverted to other destinations (mainly to Asia, with significant arbitrage gains). LNG imports into Mexico gradually grew to 9 bcm in 2014 and fell to 7 bcm in 2015.

The gas boom in the USA is fostering a wave of pipeline projects to export cheap US gas to Mexico. Currently, Mexico imports 30 bcm through 16 gas pipelines interconnections with the USA and an additional 10,000 km of new gas pipelines is under construction in Mexico, which will increase significantly Mexico's capacity to import US natural gas.

The construction of these new import pipelines and increased internal gas transportation capacity is fostering a large increase in demand, driven in particular by the higher demand in the power sector, due to the large number of new gas-fired power stations being built. The industrial sector is also expected to absorb a large part of the imported gas. The Mexican Secretaría de Energía (SENER) expects that natural gas demand will increase from 75 bcm in 2014 to 107 bcm in 2029. During the same period, domestic production (including both conventional and, eventually, unconventional gas) is expected to grow from 45 bcm in 2014 to 67 bcm in 2029 in the high production growth scenario. In the low production growth scenario, it will grow more slowly up to 2025 and then start to decline, to 39 bcm in 2029 (Mexico, 2015). The results for net imports are shown in a Figure 6.53. In the low production scenario, net imports will more than double from 30 bcm in 2014 to 70 bcm in 2029 (in the high production scenario, imports jump to 52 bcm in 2016 and then decline back to 30 bcm in 2025, going back to 42 bcm in 2029). However, LNG imports will not take a share in this import bonanza. The Mexican Secretaría de Energía sees LNG imports decreasing substantially and disappearing altogether 'in the next few years'.

As to the use of Mexico's three regasification terminals, there have been suggestions that one or two of them be converted into liquefaction plants, on the model of US regasification plants. However, that would require significant investment and Mexico would have to apply to the US Department of Energy for authorization to export to non-FTA countries.

420   *LNG Markets in Transition*

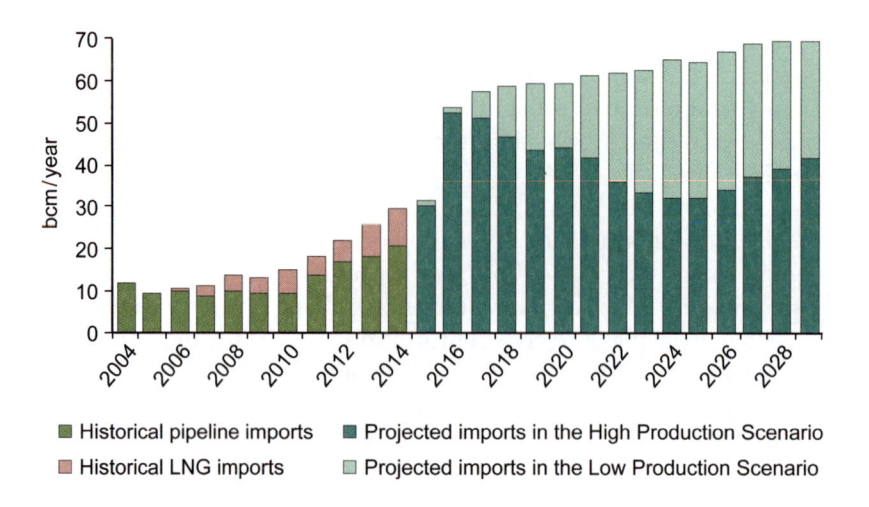

Figure 6.53: Pipeline and LNG imports in Mexico (bcm/year)

Note: In SENER's outlook, natural gas imports are projected as the difference between expected demand and expected production. The large jump in imports in 2016 is due to a significant increase in demand, mainly in the electricity sector (+17 per cent), in the industrial demand (+13 per cent), and in the oil sector (Pemex) (+54 per cent). The first two are easily explained: many new import pipelines (and a few internal trunk pipelines) are coming on stream in 2016; this increasing supply will fuel new gas-fired power plants and will encourage the conversion of existing oil-fired power plants and industrial complexes to natural gas. The reason for the large increase in Pemex's gas use is not clear.

Source: Mexico's Secretaria de Energia (2015).

Conclusion: Latin America

The natural gas markets in Latin America have evolved considerably over the last decade, and LNG is an important factor in this wave of change. While LNG was initially introduced as an emergency measure in face of supply shortages in countries that traditionally depended on their domestic production or on the supply of pipeline imports from neighbouring countries, LNG is now here to stay. Abundant and flexible supply, as well as attractive prices, are helping LNG to achieve a more permanent role in the region's energy mix.

A few new features of the global LNG industry have facilitated LNG projects in Latin America (as in other non-traditional markets). In particular, there are three important ingredients of the success story:

a) Availability of new technologies (FSRU) shortening the implementation time and lowering capital costs;

b) A diversity of players along the gas chain, with different portfolios and different risk perceptions;

c) A wider variety of contractual and pricing arrangements.

The region now has the largest number of FSRUs in the world, and the two largest regional importers (Argentina and Brazil) rely on the spot and short-term contract markets to procure their LNG cargoes.

The first 12 terminals now in operation involved the support or participation of state companies or large (often international) industrial conglomerates with good credit ratings. But the next wave of projects is being sponsored by smaller – often local – companies which face more difficulties in accessing credit. Many projects are facing challenges in aligning all the stakeholders of a LNG regasification project (often linked to a power project), and in securing financing for the project.

Despite these difficulties, we believe that there is substantial potential for additional LNG imports in the region. This is because energy demand (and in particular power demand) is still growing at income elasticities above 1, and because the development of local gas resources is taking more time than expected. Given that most countries in the region have substantial hydropower generation capacity, and/or substantial potential for other intermittent renewable sources (like wind and solar), natural gas has a role to play as a cleaner and efficient complementary source of firm energy, but flexibility of supply is an important element.

All in all the region is expected to require between 37 bcm and 103 bcm of LNG in 2030 (Table 6.26). The large difference between the lower and higher outlooks reflects, on the one hand, uncertainties about the pace of development of the local gas resources, and on the other the great variability of LNG demand in Brazil, which substantially depends on the availability of hydropower energy and ultimately on the amount of rain during the year.

Table 6.26: Latin America LNG import outlook range (bcm/year)

	2015*	Low 2020	Low 2025	Low 2030	High 2020	High 2025	High 2030
Argentina	5.6	1.1	–	–	11.3	16.1	20.1
Brazil	6.5						
Average		–	3.2	4.2	–	7.7	9.8
Max.**		13.7	24.1	30.7	14.0	30.0	38.3
Chile	3.7	5.4	7.1	8.8	6.5	8.9	11.3
Uruguay	–	0.4	0.5	0.6	0.9	1.2	1.4
Colombia	–	–	2.7	8.9	2.4	5.9	11.9
Caribbean & C. America	2.7	7.5	11.8	14.8	9.5	15.5	20.3
Mexico	6.7	–	–	–	–	–	–
Total	25.3						
With Brazil average		14.4	25.3	37.3	30.6	55.3	74.9
With Brazil max.		28.1	46.1	63.8	44.6	77.5	103.4

* Actual imports (GIIGNL 2016).

** The values in this second line represent both peak demand in any year, and maximum annual demand in a very dry year.

Source: Author's estimates.

The Middle East and Africa region

Introduction

The Middle East and Africa region is a paradox. It has ample gas resources, but many countries are facing gas shortages, forcing them to turn to LNG imports. The Middle East holds 79.8 tcm (43 per cent of the world's proven reserves), while Africa holds 14.2 tcm (BP, 2015). However, these reserves are not homogenously spread: Iran and Qatar hold three-quarters of the Middle East's proven reserves, while Algeria and Nigeria hold two-thirds of Africa's.

The Middle East is highly dependent on gas, which represents 51 per cent of its primary energy mix (as of 2013). In contrast, it accounts for only 13 per cent of Africa's primary energy demand, far behind bioenergy.

The combination of rapid population growth and economic and industrial development in the Middle East and North Africa (MENA) have spurred a rapid increase in energy, and therefore in gas, demand. In contrast, gas demand developments are limited in sub-Saharan Africa (apart from Nigeria). In 1990, the Middle East's gas demand was only 97 bcm (or 5 per cent of the world's demand), but rose to 465 bcm in 2014 (14 per cent of global demand). Africa's gas demand tripled from 40 bcm to 120 bcm over the same period.

While most Middle Eastern countries consume gas, Algeria and Egypt represent two-thirds of Africa's demand. Algeria's gas consumption grew from 20 bcm to 38 bcm over 1990–2014, which has reduced the quantities it has been able to export. Egypt's consumption has been curtailed by shortages for a few years despite a halt in exports (see Chapter 2): from 8 bcm in 1990, demand peaked in 2012 at 53 bcm, but it dropped to 48 bcm in 2014. In contrast, demand from the rest of Africa accounts for around 40 bcm; this is concentrated in Nigeria, Tunisia, and Libya, while most other countries consume very limited amounts of gas due to lack of resources, or infrastructure.

In the Middle East and Africa, natural gas is mostly consumed in the power generation, water desalination, and industrial (petrochemical) sectors; only Iran, Egypt, and Algeria use gas in the residential and commercial sector, while Iran has a large number of natural gas vehicles.

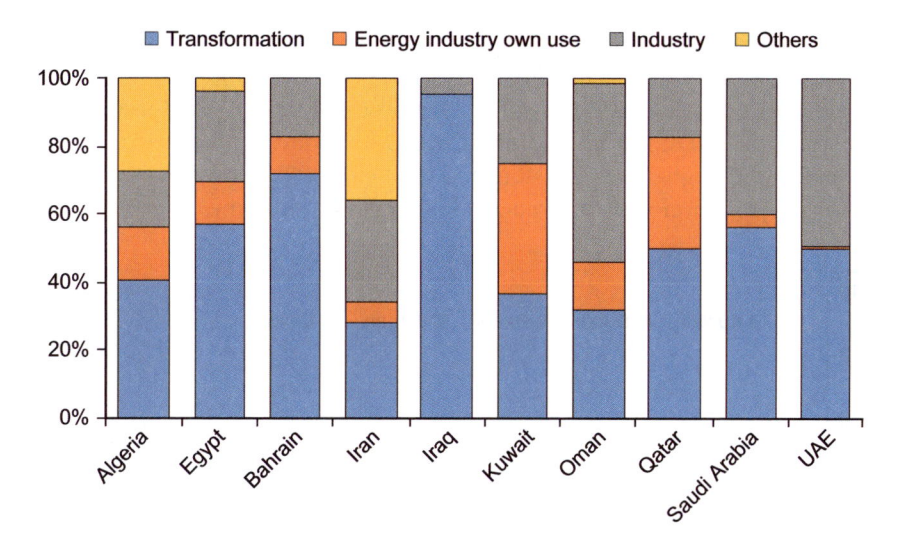

Figure 6.54: Sectoral gas use in selected MENA countries (2013)

Note: 'Industry' includes non-energy use; 'Others' includes transport, residential/commercial, and losses.

Source: IEA.

Historically, the region has been an important source of LNG (and pipeline) exports. Algeria was the first LNG exporting country in 1964. It was joined by Libya in 1970 and Abu Dhabi in 1977 (Chapter 1). While the region's role in global LNG supply declined over 1980–95 as other producers appeared, it regained significance when new countries started exporting LNG: Qatar started in end-1996, followed by Nigeria in 1999, Oman in 2000, Egypt in 2005, Equatorial Guinea in 2007, and Yemen in 2009. The decisive factor was the substantial expansion of Qatar's LNG capacity over 2009–11; this enabled the region's LNG exports to represent in excess of 50 per cent of global LNG trade.

However, LNG exports are often challenged by developments in domestic demand. Exports from Libya, Yemen, and Egypt have stopped and exports from Oman and Abu Dhabi could also stop when contracts expire. The interesting development since 2009 has been that five countries have turned to LNG imports to meet their increasing demand (see Chapter 2). Imports of LNG have more than doubled, to 9.8 mtpa, from 2014 to 2015 and will expand further as demand for natural gas grows. More facilities are at the planning stage, and one of the key features of these LNG import schemes is that all the facilities built so far have been floating storage and regasification units (FSRUs), enabling rapid construction. Such units also make it possible to meet seasonal demand only, if required (most of the power demand occurs during summer due to air conditioning needs). While domestic demand has grown, gas production has failed to grow at the same pace. Due to low domestic gas prices, development of the new generation of 'tight' or non-associated gas fields often makes no economic sense; project developers thus need a higher price and some cross subsidies.

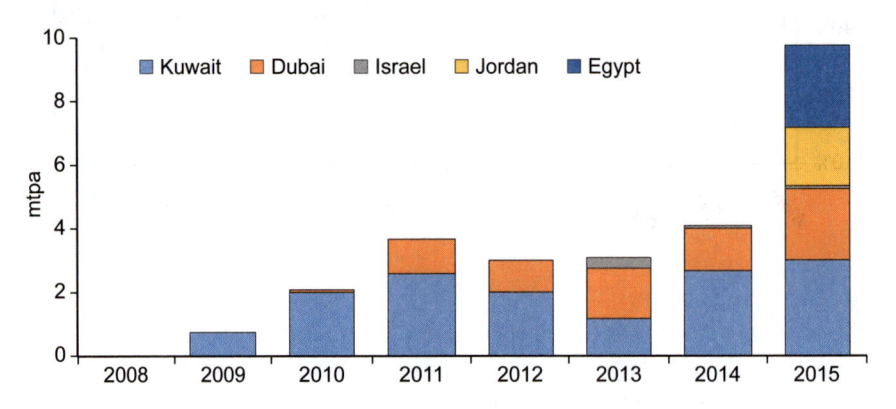

Figure 6.55: LNG imports from MENA countries
Source: GIIGNL

Both the Middle East and Africa remain net gas exporting regions: theoretically Qatar, Iran, Nigeria, Egypt, and Algeria could be the logical pipeline suppliers to their neighbours, but unlike the situation in Europe, intraregional trade has never developed in a significant way. Qatar exports about 20 bcm per year to the UAE and Oman, but does not plan to export more due to the moratorium and the low price of these exports. Iran does not export to any GCC country, while Egypt stopped exporting after a few years, and Nigeria has never exported pipeline gas in a significant manner. Algeria exports pipeline gas to Tunisia and Morocco, mostly as a payment for transit.

Wholesale gas prices in the region are often regulated below cost and struggle to cover the upstream development costs (notably for non-associated gas). But this is changing as prices are progressively increased in the MENA region (Corbeau et al., 2016).

There is a range of key features that will drive LNG imports in the Middle East and Africa:

- The region's gas consumption is expected to increase substantially over the coming decades. BP estimates that the Middle East's demand will gain 20 per cent by 2035 (BP, 2016), while Nexant's world gas model foresees a 50 per cent increase for the Middle East. The IEA foresees a 90 per cent increase of Africa's gas demand by 2035, compared to the 85 per cent suggested by BP. However, the impact of price increases on future demand developments is still unknown.

- While domestic production will grow, most of the gains will be in Iran, Qatar, Iraq, and Saudi Arabia, which will mostly feed either their domestic market or their exports of LNG. Similarly in Africa, production gains are likely to be in Eastern Africa, Algeria, Nigeria, and Egypt.

- Intra-regional pipeline trade developments are expected to remain limited (with the exception of the planned Iran–Oman pipeline or pipeline exports from Mozambique to South Africa) so that gas-short countries will have to resort to LNG imports to meet their growing gas demand. This also implies that an analysis of the region's future LNG demand requires a country-by-country study. Due to the political complexity of developing pipelines between countries, it can take decades to get them built. Exporters are also reluctant to export more gas at low prices (such as Qatar to the UAE or Mozambique to South Africa). Many West African countries currently looking at LNG imports are too remote for pipelines to be developed, while the existing West African Gas Pipeline from Nigeria to its neighbours has failed to meet expectations.

- While some countries are considering land-based LNG import facilities, both the Middle East and Africa can be expected to prefer FSRUs.

- Due to the low oil and gas price environment and the LNG oversupply situation, new buyers in the Middle East and Africa have expressed interest in LNG imports. They are currently in a good position to negotiate prices and contractual terms, although the low-price environment and the oversupply may not last. These buyers seem, nevertheless, to be reluctant to commit to 20-year long-term contracts, and have used tenders or short-term contracts to source LNG supplies.

The Middle East

Four countries import LNG in this region: Kuwait, the United Arab Emirates (Dubai), Israel, and Jordan. Altogether they imported 7.2 mtpa in 2015. All countries besides Israel can be expected to see their LNG imports increase over the long term. Bahrain is advanced in developing its LNG terminal while Oman has been rumoured to be considering LNG imports.

As highlighted in Chapter 2, the region's first LNG importer was Kuwait in 2009, when an FSRU built by Excelerate Energy went into operation, enabling imports of 0.6 bcf/d during the summer months. This helped to increase gas consumption from 12.4 bcm in 2009 to 20.1 bcm in 2014, driven by demand from the power generation sector (BP, 2015). In 2014, a larger FSRU, the Golar Igloo, was installed, enabling imports to gain 17 per cent, to 3 mtpa in 2015. Looking forward, Kuwait has significant associated gas resources, whose output is limited by OPEC quotas, while the development of Jurassic gas fields has proved challenging so far. However, Kuwait Oil Company (KOC) tendered three contracts worth $5.7 billion for the development of these reserves in late 2015, and this could bring as much as 10 bcm of additional production by 2022 and impact LNG imports needs. Kuwait could be burning fuel oil or diesel as an alternative, but this is inefficient, more expensive, and less environmentally friendly than using gas, and increasing domestic oil demand could impact the country's exports – and therefore revenues – in the long term. The lease for the new FSRU expires in 2019, but it could potentially be extended. Additionally, Kuwait is planning to build a new 11 mtpa land-based terminal at Al-Zour that would be starting at end-2020 to meet increasing demand from power generators. KPC signed a six-year LNG supply deal with Shell and a five-year supply deal with BP for the existing FSRU, but has not signed any long-term LNG contract for the new plant.

Dubai, in the United Arab Emirates (UAE), started importing LNG in 2010 due to a significant gas deficit. The FSRU Golar *Freeze* was chartered by Dubai Supply Authority (Dusup) from Golar LNG. In 2015, a newer and higher capacity FSRU replaced the original FSRU, and will be able to receive twice the number of cargoes than the original design. Dubai imported 2.2 mtpa in 2015. Looking forward, the UAE's gas demand has doubled since 2000 to 69 bcm in 2014 and it is expected to increase further, but growth will be dampened due to the development of nuclear generation (four reactors under construction are planned to start between 2017 and 2020) and renewables; this will reduce the dependency of the power generation sector on gas. Most of the demand growth looking forward is expected to come from industry. Gas in non-associated fields is sour and the development of the Bab field was postponed in the current low oil price environment. The UAE plans to build a larger LNG import facility (9 mtpa) at Fujairah. The project is sponsored by EmiratesLNG, a joint-venture of two government-owned companies – Mubadala Petroleum and International Petroleum Investment. However, the company announced in May 2016 that it was looking at other options including storing gas at the site, reloading it on ships for resale, and supplying LNG as a marine fuel. Another factor which could have a negative impact on LNG imports would be if Abu Dhabi were to stop exporting LNG when the contracts expire in 2019, and redirect the gas resources to its domestic market.

Israel started importing LNG in 2013 after Egypt stopped delivering gas through the Arab Gas Pipeline after the Arab Spring. Before this point, Israel used to get around 2 bcm from Egypt. The Israel Electric Corporation (IEC) concluded an LNG supply deal with BP for the delivery of two cargoes per month from December 2012 until May 2013. However, Israel is still importing LNG (0.12 mtpa in 2015) and in 2015 the Public Utilities Authority approved the continued use by IEC of the FSRU to import LNG until 2019 (Cohen, 2015). However, Israel's LNG import needs are likely to be limited, given the development of the Tamar field, and it could even become an LNG exporter with the development of the Leviathan field. Consequently, Israel is not expected to be importing LNG after 2019.

In contrast, due to its limited domestic production, Jordan was particularly affected by the cuts in Egypt's pipeline exports – imports from Egypt used to be at a rate of around 3 bcm. Jordan's FSRU started operating in May 2015, enabling the country to import 1.9 mtpa in 2015. Such import levels are still below the volumes that Jordan used to import from Egypt, so there is a margin for them to expand back to historical levels of consumption and beyond, as LNG will displace oil products in power generation (which has caused financial difficulties for power companies). The project's economics have benefited from the existence of pipeline infrastructure and CCGTs.

Bahrain stands to be the next LNG importer in the Middle East region, with first LNG imports planned for 2018. Bahrain's gas demand has almost doubled in recent years, from 9 bcm in 2000 to 17 bcm in 2014, driven by the power and industry sectors. Bahrain plans to add 1.5 GW of gas-fired plant by 2017 at the Al Dur power and desalination plant, while the aluminium producer Alba plans to build a 1.35 GW plant by 2016. While the country aims to expand its associated gas production by around 3.5 bcm from the oil field Tatweer, it is also looking at LNG imports (MEES, 2015b). Bahrain is planning to develop a floating storage unit (FSU); located in the Hidd Industrial area, this will have a capacity of around 8 bcm/year and will be owned and operated under a 20-year agreement starting in July 2018 (MEES, 2015b). It will help the country meet increasing demand from industry. The Oil and Gas Holding Company (Nogaholding) awarded the project to a consortium comprising Teekay LNG, Samsung, and the Gulf Investment Corporation (GIC). The project will be owned and operated by a joint venture, Bahrain LNG, comprising: Nogaholding (30 per cent), Teekay LNG (30 per cent), Samsung (20 per cent), and GIC (20 per cent). This represents the first public–private partnership of this kind in the region and Teekay LNG will supply the vessel through a 20-year time charter.

Finally, in 2015 Oman had been rumoured to be considering LNG imports to meet its growing demand, but there is no concrete plan so far. LNG imports could be avoided if Oman stops exporting LNG when contracts expire in the mid-2020s, or if it builds a pipeline from Iran. Meanwhile, in 2012 Lebanon expressed some interest in building a 3.5 mtpa FSRU in the Port of Beirut to service the Deir Amar power plant. However, the project has been postponed due to regional instability. Saudi Arabia is planning to increase the share of gas in its energy mix from 50 per cent to 70 per cent; this could include importing gas if it is at competitive costs. Besides pipeline gas from Qatar, which has not yet lifted its moratorium on exports, this leaves LNG as the main alternative.

Africa

Egypt turned from being an exporter of pipeline and LNG (18 bcm in 2009) into an LNG importer in 2015. This switch was due to domestic production having plummeted from 61 bcm in 2012 to 49 bcm in 2014, while Egypt's gas needs kept rising. Despite a complete halt of all pipeline and LNG exports in 2014, the country still needed more gas to face demand in its power sector (see Chapter 2). In November 2014 EGAS concluded a contract with Höegh for an FSRU which started operating in April 2015. A second FSRU was contracted from BW Shipping and started operations in October 2015. Both are located in Ain Sokhna and represent an importing capacity of 13 bcm/year. Egypt imported 2.6 mtpa in 2015. It is likely that LNG imports will continue to increase in the short term to meet additional demand. The long-term horizon is more complex as it depends on the evolution of domestic production and on the way in which demand rebounds. The Zohr field, discovered in 2015, is expected to start in 2017 and add around 12 bcm by 2019, while other fields would add another 12 bcm. These developments would bring production back to levels largely above peak production (63 bcm in 2007) even though existing fields are likely to decline. But gas consumption has been constrained both in the power and industry sectors and could rebound strongly when supply becomes available. Depending on the size of future demand growth, timeliness of production, and affordability of LNG beyond 2020, LNG imports could either stop or continue beyond 2020.

Ghana plans to start importing LNG in early 2017. Ghana National Petroleum Corporation and Quantum Power signed heads of terms to build a 3.4 mtpa FSRU (see Chapter 2). The Tema LNG project will be implemented on a build-own-operate-transfer basis, with the assets transferring to GNPC after 20 years. The project is seen as being necessary to complement measures to provide security of gas supplies in Ghana, while the output from the Jubilee and other fields is expected to increase (ACEP, 2016). Another planned terminal is the integrated gas-to-power solution from Endeavour Energy and GE at Takoradi; this would feed a 1,000 MW plant.

Morocco has been considering building an LNG terminal for some time. Unlike other countries where LNG supplements domestic production, LNG imports would replace Algerian pipeline imports after 2021, when the Algerian transit contract expires. Supplies to Morocco's gas-fired plants (Tahaddart and Ain Beni Mathar) had been covered by payment in kind for gas transit until 2011. But in 2011, a 10-year supply contract was agreed to supply the plants. The LNG terminal is planned in the port of Jorf Lasfar, 100 km south of Casablanca. It will be connected to the existing pipeline system transiting Algerian gas to Spain. Several companies – including Engie, Shell, Gazprom, and Taqa – have expressed interest in the $4.6 billion project. Morocco plans to import 2 mtpa starting in 2020, to be increased to 3.5 to 4 mtpa by 2025. This is part of a wider plan to build up power capacity by increasing renewables (Morocco plans to add 2 GW of wind, 2 GW of solar, and 2 GW of hydro capacity), and also by adding 2.4 GW of gas-fired capacity. Another 6.3 GW of gas-fired capacity could be installed in the longer term (MEES, 2015a).

South Africa also has plans to import LNG, due to growing shortages in the power sector. Earlier work from the government has highlighted the need for 3,126 MW of gas-fired capacity to contribute towards energy security. Another 3 GW could be added by 2025 and again by 2030 (IPP Gas, 2016). Another issue for the country is that Eskom, the South African power company, has been increasingly using diesel to generate electricity, and this is more expensive than electricity from coal-fired plants when oil prices are high. The government has determined that Eskom must switch from diesel to gas, which would be achieved between 2017 and 2018. However, the country has limited gas reserves, in spite of some shale gas potential which could be developed in the long term. Pipeline imports from Mozambique look challenging due to the distance between the resources and South Africa, together with existing history on the current pipeline imports. This leaves LNG imports (or possibly CNG) as the main solution to the problem of supporting the development of power generation capacity. In May 2015, the South African Department of Energy released the Gas to Power Request for Information. The department is considering two options: either a bundled project including everything from the gas supplier, the import facility, and the power plant, or an unbundled project with the elements separated. This comes on top of the development of a 'Gas Utilisation Master Plan' for South Africa. One of its key objectives is to enable the development of indigenous gas resources and to create the opportunity to stimulate the introduction of a portfolio of gas supply options, while providing long-term gas demand centres. Several locations are envisaged for the terminal(s) including Saldanha Bay, Richards Bay, and Coega.

Other West African countries, including Senegal, Côte d'Ivoire, and Benin have expressed interest in LNG supply to support LNG-to-power projects. As many as five FSRUs are planned including the two in Ghana. Besides meeting growing power demand, the projects would also limit the countries' reliance on refined products. In Senegal, the state-owned utility Senelec has signed a deal with Mitsui and Nebras Power to build an FSRU and couple it with a 400 MW gas-fired plant. In Côte D'Ivoire, Endeavor Energy is planning another gas-to-power project: the 375 MW Songon IPP, near Abidjan. Finally, in Benin, Gasol is planning an FSRU that would be located in Cotonou harbour. The LNG would be distributed to Benin, Togo, and Ghana via the existing West African Gas Pipeline, which has substantial spare capacity. Gasol has signed a long-term cross-border agreement to supply Ghana's Volta River Authority in 2014, and another offtake agreement with the Benin Electricity Community. Some of these projects have been on the cards for many years and have not moved forward, but as LNG suppliers are looking for markets, there is an opportunity for these countries to move the projects ahead. A critical element will be the financial viability of the projects and the creditworthiness of the counterparties.

Conclusions: the Middle East and Africa

Historically, the Middle East and Africa region was considered as an LNG exporter rather than a potential LNG demand centre. However, rapidly increasing demand set against production, limited intraregional pipeline trade, and in some cases the wish to replace oil or refined products in the power sector mean that LNG imports have become a reality. As much as 10 mtpa was imported in 2015, and imports could increase further. However, a growing trajectory should not be taken for granted. Table 6.27 provides our low and high LNG demand cases for the Middle East and Africa, highlighting the uncertainty in terms of future LNG demand. Many importing countries have plans to develop domestic production, even though some developments are technically challenging. Some limited intraregional trade could change LNG dynamics, while countries such as Oman and Abu Dhabi could stop exporting and redirect domestic gas supplies to the market. Finally, there is a lot of uncertainty regarding the developments of LNG imports in Africa. The region has largely been overlooked, but projects exist and some are relatively advanced. LNG would create an opportunity for Africa to provide power supply to the millions who have no access to it.

Table 6.27: Middle East and Africa LNG demand (mtpa)

	2015	*2020*	*2025*	*2030*
Africa: high case	3	8	14	21
Africa: low case	3	1	4	6
Middle East: high case	7	16	20	29
Middle East: low case	7	12	14	15
Total: high case	**10**	**24**	**34**	**50**
Total: low case	**10**	**13**	**18**	**20**

Conclusions

The small cosy club is fully over, as the map of LNG demand is slowly redrawn with the appearance of new players across Asia, Latin America, and MENA. Many buyers are not as creditworthy as those of the past (or as sellers would like them to be), have different requirements in terms of seasonality and flexibility, and they can be quite price sensitive. But as we stand in 2016, sellers are investigating these buyers' needs in the hope of reducing the oversupply. The current low oil (and gas) price environment is actually seen as an advantage in building up demand in developing markets and in helping to develop infrastructure to secure long-term demand. FSRUs are seen as the best tool to attract new potential LNG importers. Finally, sellers do not neglect existing LNG importers – either the mature ones or those which started importing over the past 10 years.

Our analysis shows that demand paths could vary significantly depending on the different assumptions taken. It may be misleading to add up the highest LNG demand numbers for each region. Even within a region, factors determining the low and high cases are not always associated – a lower production in Bangladesh or India has nothing to do with Japanese nuclear policy. Consequently, one Asian country could follow one scenario and its neighbour another one. Similarly, Argentina and Mexico could face different fates when it comes to developing unconventional gas production. Also a high demand scenario in one region could imply less LNG being available for other regions, as has been the case with LNG being diverted away from Europe over 2011–14. Still, it remains interesting to add up those numbers to estimate the lowest and highest LNG demand potential.

With no surprise, given that it represented 72 per cent of LNG demand in 2015, Asia shows the largest variation between low and high demand estimates by 2030, with a gap of 107 mtpa. However, some distinction must be made between the mature markets (Japan/Korea/Taiwan), China/India, and other Asian markets. The LNG demand uncertainty by 2030 for the three groups of Asian countries is actually quite similar, ranging from 32 mtpa (China/India) to 40 mtpa (J/K/T). Albeit remaining significant, the share of the historical players will decline. The low and high scenarios feature either a declining or an increasing demand for LNG for these markets, whereas LNG demand increases in China/India and the other Asian markets in both scenarios. In both cases, LNG demand in China/India is almost catching up with the mature markets by 2030. At the country level, the largest uncertainty comes from Japan: decisions on the future of nuclear energy will be crucial in determining LNG demand. Still, Japan remains the largest world's LNG importer in all scenarios.

Europe presents a relatively high uncertainty in terms of LNG demand by 2030, owing to the role of pipeline gas in its gas supply. Even though current market conditions seem to point to a return of LNG toward Europe, a combination of high production and pipeline gas imports could keep LNG at bay for an extended period – in this scenario, by 2030 LNG imports would be barely higher than in 2015. A higher share of LNG imports is clearly favoured from a political point of view, but it remains to be seen how this will fit with market realities. But a different environment could also lead to a continuous increase in LNG imports. In any case, these ranges are an indication of the low and high points, from a European perspective. As demonstrated over the previous years, Europe is often serving as the balancing market for global LNG.

Latin American, the Middle East, and Africa are three regions where regional LNG demand is deemed to increase. Latin America is particularly interesting as some countries, such as Mexico and Argentina, could stop importing altogether. At the country level, the largest uncertainty in this region comes from Argentina and its success in developing its unconventional gas resources, while the largest incremental LNG demand could potentially originate from a relatively new and underdeveloped market – the Caribbean and Central America. A very important feature of Latin America is the variability of LNG demand depending on the hydro conditions in Brazil. A dry year could see Brazil LNG demand soar and significantly impact the global LNG balance.

The Middle East and Africa have not been studied in depth in this book.[143] They represent a small but rapidly growing share of LNG demand – around 10 mtpa in 2015. By 2020, the United Arab Emirates, Bahrain, Kuwait, and Jordan are all likely to be importing (in some cases through expanded LNG terminals), while Lebanon could join them later. In Africa, only Egypt is importing as of 2016, but Ghana, Morocco, and South Africa are seriously looking at LNG imports. The question of access to electricity is crucial in Africa (aside from North Africa and South Africa) and the case of Ghana could set a precedent for LNG to power development in the region.

Obviously LNG demand cannot be considered separately from supply (Chapter 5). The major question is whether there will be a supply gap after 2020 or whether supply growth will resume immediately after the current wave of LNG supply is finished. A pause in LNG supply development would inevitably impact future LNG demand, as it did over 2011–14. Meanwhile, for future LNG supply to be sanctioned in a period of low oil and gas prices, there must be some certainty about future demand growth.

---

[143] For more information on the Middle East and North African markets see *Natural Gas Markets in the Middle East and North Africa*, Fattouh, B., and Stern, J.P. (eds.), Oxford: OUP/OIES, 2011.

BIBLIOGRAPHY

ABEGÁS (2016). Monthly statistics available at: www.abegas.org.br/Site/.

ACEP (2016). 'Ghana To Reposition Petroleum Sector To Boost Economy', 27 April 2016. www.acepghana.com/news/171/.

AliceWeb (2016). Monthly trade statistics for Brazil, available online at: http://aliceweb.desenvolvimento.gov.br/.

Almeida, E. (2005). 'The Brazilian Natural Gas Sector', in Blanco, P. and Benavides, J. (ed.). *Gas Market Integration in the Southern Cone*, Washington DC: Inter-American Development Bank.

Almeida, E. and Trebat, N. (2007). 'A crise na Bolívia e seus impactos para a indústria de gás', in Bicalho, R. (ed.), Ensaios sobre Política Energética, Rio de Janeiro: Interciência.ANP (2016). Monthly statistics available at: http://www.anp.gov.br/.

Almeida, E., D'Apote, S., and Fritsch, W. (2015). 'Natural Gas', in Fresco, F. and Pereira, E. (ed.) *Latin American Upstream Oil and Gas: A Practical Guide to the Law and Regulation*, London: Globe Law and Business.

Bailey, J. (2013). 'Pre-feasibility study of the potential market for natural gas as a fuel for power generation in the Caribbean', Technical Note 600, Inter-American Development Bank, https://publications.iadb.org/handle/11319/6015?locale-attribute=en.

BP (2015). *BP Statistical Review of World Energy June 2015*. Data obtained from workbook at: www.bp.com/en/global/corporate/energy-economics/statistical-review-of-world-energy/downloads.html.

BP (2016). 'Outlook to 2035 – energy use to rise by a third', BP Energy Outlook. www.bp.com/en/global/corporate/energy-economics/energy-outlook-2035/energy-outlook-to-2035.html.

Brazil (2015a). 'Balanço Energético Nacional – 2015', Ministry of Energy and Mines, Brasília: MME/EPE.

Brazil (2015b). 'Plano Decenal de Expansão de Energia 2024', Ministry of Mines and Energy. Brasília: MME/EPE.

Brazil (2016). Ministry of Energy and Mines. 'Boletim Mensal de Acompanhamento da Indústria de Gás Natural'. Monthly bulletin available at: www.mme.gov.br/web/guest/secretarias/petroleo-gas-natural-e-combustiveis-renovaveis/publicacoes/boletim-mensal-de-acompanhamento-da-industria-de-gas-natural?_20_displayStyle=descriptive&p_p_id=20.

Castalia (2014). 'Natural Gas in the Caribbean – Feasibility studies', Report to the Inter-American Development Bank, Castalia, August 2014.

Cedigaz (2004). 'LNG Trade and Infrastructures', CEDIGAZ, February 2004.

Chen, M. (2014). 'The Development of Chinese Gas Pricing: Drivers, Challenges and Implications for Demand', OIES Working Paper NG89, Oxford Institute for Energy Studies. http://www.oxfordenergy.org/2014/07/the-development-of-chinese-gas-pricing-drivers-challenges-and-implications-for-demand/.

CIA (2015). *CIA World Factbook*, https://www.cia.gov/Library/publications/the-world-factbook/geos/print/country/countrypdf_pk.pdf, and other countries covered by service.

CNPC (2014). 'Challenges for Imported LNG in China', Dai Jiaquan, Director of Oil Market Department, CNPC Economic & Technology Research Institute, LNG Producer–Consumer Conference, Tokyo, Japan, 6 November 2014. http://aperc.ieej.or.jp/file/2014/11/20/s2_d5_cnpc.pdf.

CNPC (2015). 'Prospects of Gas Market in China', Shan Weiguo, CNPC, Presentation at IEF, 9th December 2015. www.globallnghub.com/custom/domain_4/extra_files/attach_139.pdf.

Código Energético (2015). 'Hidrocarburos no convencionales', October 2015 Report, Argentina.

Cohen, H. (2015). 'IEC extends LNG floating tanker contract', Globes, 3 November 2015. www.globes.co.il/en/article-iec-extends-lng-ship-contract-1001078472.

Colombia (2015). 'Balance de Gas Natural en Colombia 2015-2024 – Agosto 2015'. Unidad de Planeación Minero Energética (UPME/MINMINAS). http://www1.upme.gov.co/sites/default/files/BALANCE_GAS%20NATURAL_Agosto_2015.pdf.

Corbeau, A., Shabaneh, R., and Six, S. (2016). *The Impact of Low Oil and Gas Prices on Gas Markets: A Retrospective Look at 2014–15*, KS-1634-DP028, KAPSARC, May 2016.

D'Apote, S. and Castaño, A. (2012). 'Geopolitics and Natural Gas in South America', in International Gas Union (IGU), International Gas, April–September 2012.

DECC (2016). *UKCS Oil and Gas Production Projections*, Department of Energy & Climate Change, UK Government, February 2016. https://www.gov.uk/government/uploads/system/uploads/attachment_data/file/503852/OGA_production_projections_-_February_2016.pdf.

EIA (2012). 'Vietnam', Country Analysis Briefs, Energy Information Administration, 9 May 2012. www.iberglobal.com/files/vietnam_eia.pdf.

EIA (2013). 'Technically Recoverable Shale Oil and Shale Gas Resources: An Assessment of 137 Shale Formations in 41 Countries Outside the United States', June 2013, Washington DC.

EIA (2014). 'Malaysia', International Energy Data and Analysis, Energy Information Administration. www.eia.gov/beta/international/analysis.cfm?iso=MYS.

EMA (2015a). 'Singapore Energy Statistics 2015', Singapore Energy Market Authority. www.ema.gov.sg/cmsmedia/Publications_and_Statistics/Publications/SES2015_Final_website_2mb.pdf.

EMA (2015b). 'Statistics', Singapore Energy Market Authority. www.ema.gov.sg/Statistics.aspx.

ENARGAS (2016). Monthly statistics available at: www.enargas.gov.ar.

EPPO (2015). 'Energy Statistics', Energy Policy and Planning Office, Ministry of Energy, Thailand. www.eppo.go.th/info/index-statistics.html.

EurObserv'ER (2015). *The State of Renewable Energies in Europe*, Edition 2015, www.eurobserv-er.org/15th-annual-overview-barometer/.

European Commission (2016). 'Liquefied Natural Gas and gas storage will boost EU's energy security', Press Release, European Commission, 16 February 2016. http://europa.eu/rapid/press-release_MEMO-16-310_en.htm.

EWEA (2016). 'Wind in Power, 2015 European Statistics', European Wind Energy Association, February. www.ewea.org/fileadmin/files/library/publications/statistics/EWEA-Annual-Statistics-2015.pdf.

Fadillah, R. D. (2012). 'Singapore LNG policy won't affect RI exports: BPMigas', *The Jakarta Post*, 6 March. http://imo2.thejakartapost.com/news/2012/03/06/singapore-lng-policy-won-t-affect-ri-exports-bpmigas.html.

Financial Times (2015). *The New Bolivia*, October 2015.

GIE (2015). 'GIE LNG Map Dataset in Excel-format', Gas Infrastructure Europe, www.gie.eu/index.php/maps-data/lng-map.

GIIGNL (2014). *The LNG Industry in 2014*, International Group of Liquefied Natural Gas Importers, GIIGNL (Groupe International des Importateurs de Gaz Naturel Liquéfié) Annual Report). www.giignl.org/sites/default/files/PUBLIC_AREA/Publications/giignl_2015_annual_report.pdf.

GIIGNL (2016). *The LNG Industry in 2015*, International Group of Liquefied Natural Gas Importers, GIIGNL (Groupe International des Importateurs de Gaz Naturel Liquéfié) Annual Report 2016. www.giignl.org/publications.

Gomes, I. (2013). 'Natural gas in Pakistan and Bangladesh: current issues and trends', OIES Working Paper NG77, Oxford Institute for Energy Studies. www.oxfordenergy.org/2013/06/natural-gas-in-pakistan-and-bangladesh-current-issues-and-trends/.

Gomes, I. (forthcoming). 'Shale Gas in Argentina: Will it become a real game changer?', OIES Paper, Oxford Institute for Energy Studies.

Hassanzadeh E. (2015). *Iran's Natural Gas Industry in the Post-Revolutionary Period: Optimism, Scepticism, and Potential*, Oxford: OUP/OIES.

Haug, D. and Cumberland, S. (2013).'LNG for power in small emerging markets', Arctas Capital Group, www.gastechnology.org/Training/Documents/LNG17-proceedings/3-7-David_Haug.pdf.

Henderson J. and Mitrova T. (2015). 'The Political and Commercial Dynamics of Russia's Gas Export Strategy', OIES Working Paper NG 102, Oxford Institute for Energy Studies, September. https://www.oxfordenergy.org/publications/the-political-and-commercial-dynamics-of-russias-gas-export-strategy/.

Honoré, A. (2014). 'The Outlook for Natural Gas Demand in Europe', OIES Working Paper NG 87, Oxford Institute for Energy Studies, June. https://www.oxfordenergy.org/publications/the-outlook-for-natural-gas-demand-in-europe/.

Honoré, A. (forthcoming). 'South American Gas Markets and the Role of LNG', OIES Paper, Oxford Institute for Energy Studies.

Huang, C. and Ko, F. (2009). 'Nuclear Power Generation and CO_2 Abatement Scenarios in Taiwan', World Academy of Science, Engineering and Technology 30 2009. http://db.foresight.kr/sub03/research/filedown/id/719/field/file_saved_name/rfile/182daf033c260eb8b8ee02898a8340f4.

IEA (2003). *South American Gas – Daring to Tap the Bounty*, Paris: OECD/International Energy Agency.

IEA (2013). *World Energy Outlook 2013*, Paris: OECD/International Energy Agency, November.

IEA (2014). *Medium Term Gas Outlook 2014*, Paris: OECD/International Energy Agency.

IEA (2015a). *Electricity Information 2015*, Paris: OECD/International Energy Agency.

IEA (2015b). *Natural Gas Information 2015*, Paris: OECD/International Energy Agency.

IEA (2015c). *World Energy Outlook 2015*, Paris: OECD/International Energy Agency.

IEA (2015d). *Medium-Term Gas Market Report: Market Analysis and Forecasts to 2020*, OECD/International Energy Agency, June.

IEA (2015e). 'Monthly gas statistics', Provisional data for OECD countries for 2015. www.iea.org/statistics/monthlystatistics/monthlygasstatistics/.

IEA (2015f). Country energy statistics (up to 2013) available online at: www.iea.org/statistics.

IEEJ (2015). 'The Best Energy Mix for Japan', Masakazu Toyoda, Presentation, The Institute for Energy Economics, Japan, 4 June. https://eneken.ieej.or.jp/data/6119.pdf.

IEEJ/EDMC (2015). 'EDMC Handbook of Japan's & World Energy & Economic Statistics 2015'.

IEF (2016a). 'India', 2016 Index of Economic Freedom, The Heritage Foundation/Wall Street Journal. www.heritage.org/index/country/india.

IEF (2016b). 'Pakistan', 2016 Index of Economic Freedom, The Heritage Foundation/*Wall Street Journal*. www.heritage.org/index/country/pakistan.

IIGC (2015). 'COP21 in Paris – a guide for investors', Institutional Investors Group on Climate Change, October 2015. www.iigcc.org/files/publication-files/IIGCC_2015_Paris_COP_Guide_for_Investors.pdf.

Index Mundi (2015). 'Japan GDP: Composition by sector', Index Mundi. www.indexmundi.com/japan/gdp_composition_by_sector.html.

India (2013). *"Vision 2030" Natural Gas Infrastructure in India*, Report by Industry Group for Petroleum & Natural Gas Regulatory Board. www.pngrb.gov.in/Hindi-Website/pdf/vision-NGPV-2030-06092013.pdf.

Indonesia (2014). 'Handbook of Energy & Economic Statistics of Indonesia', Ministry of Energy and Mineral Resources, Republic of Indonesia. http://prokum.esdm.go.id/Publikasi/Handbook%20of%20Energy%20&%20Economic%20Statistics%20of%20Indonesia%20/HEESI%202014.pdf.

Institute of Americas (2013). 'Natural Gas in Central America: Seizing the benefits and overcoming challenges', San José, Costa Rica: 2nd Annual Forum on Prospects for LNG and Natural Gas in Central America, October 2013.

IPP Gas (2016). 'Gas to power programme', accessed in May 2016. https://www.ipp-gas.co.za/

KEEI (2015). 'Monthly Energy Statistics', Volume 31-06, 2015.6, Korea Energy Economics Institute. www.keei.re.kr/keei/download/MES1506.pdf.

KESIS. 'Fuel Consumption in Generation', Korea Energy Statistics Information System. www.kesis.net/flexapp/KesisFlexApp.jsp?menuId=Q0109&reportId= &chk=Y.

Kong, Z., Dong, X., and Zhou, Z. (2015). 'Seasonal Imbalances in Natural Gas Imports in Major Northeast Asian Countries: Variations, Reasons, Outlooks and Countermeasures', *Sustainability*, 7(2), 1690–1711. www.mdpi.com/2071-1050/7/2/1690.

Korea (2014). 'Korea Energy Master Plan Outlooks and Policies to 2035', Ministry of Trade, Industry and Energy (MOTIE), January 2014.

LeFevre C. (2014). 'The Prospects for Natural Gas as a Transportation Fuel in Europe', OIES Working Paper NG 84, Oxford Institute for Energy Studies, March. https://www.oxfordenergy.org/wpcms/wp-content/uploads/2014/03/NG-84.pdf.

Liao, H. and Jhou, S. (2013). 'Taiwan's Severe Energy Security Challenges', Taiwan–U.S. Quarterly Analysis, No. 12 of 20, Brookings Institution, September. www.brookings.edu/research/opinions/2013/09/12-taiwan-energy-security-liao.

Ma, D (2015). 'Rebalancing China's Energy Strategy', Paulson Papers on energy and Environment, January 2015. www.paulsoninstitute.org/wp-content/uploads/2015/04/PPEE_Rebalancing-Chinas-Energy-Strategy_Ma_English.pdf.

Malaysia (2014a). Page 35 of 'Malaysia: Natural Gas Industry Annual Review – 2014 Edition', Malaysian Gas Association. www.malaysiangas.com/portal/document/publication/1419816334_Malaysia%20G.pdf.

Malaysia (2014b). 'Malaysia Energy Statistics Handbook 2014', Suruhanjaya Tenaga (Energy Commission). http://meih.st.gov.my/documents/10620/adcd3a01-1643-4c72-bbd7-9bb649b206ee.

Matthews, S. (2009). 'Powering Kuwait', Arabian Oil and Gas, 15 March 2009. www.arabianoilandgas.com/article-5127-powering-kuwait/1/print/.

MEES (2015a). 'Morocco's $4.6bn LNG Scheme Continues To Drum Up Interest', MEES, Volume: 58 Issue: 20, 15 May 2015.

MEES (2015b). 'Bahrain LNG plans', MEES, Volume: 58 Issue: 50, 11 December 2015.

Mexico (2015). 'Prospectiva de Gas Natural y Gas L.P. 2015-2029', Secretaría de Energía (SENER), https://www.gob.mx/cms/uploads/attachment/file/44326/Prospectiva_Gas_Natural_y_Gas_LP.pdf.

Miyamoto, A. (2008). 'Natural Gas in Asia', 2nd edition in Stern, J., OIES: 2008. www.oxfordenergy.org/shop/natural-gas-in-asia-the-challenges-of-growth-in-china-india-japan-and-korea-2nd-edition/.

Miyamoto, A., Ishiguro, C., and Nakamura, M. (2012). A Realistic Perspective on Japan's LNG Demand after Fukushima, OIES Working Paper NG62, Oxford Institute for Energy Studies NG 62, June. https://www.oxfordenergy.org/wpcms/wp-content/uploads/2012/07/NG-62.pdf.

Norway (2015). *Norwegian Gas Update*, Presentation at Flame conference in Amsterdam by Erik Johnsen, Norwegian Ministry of Petroleum and Energy, 15 April 2015.

Pirani, S. and Yafimava, K. (2016). 'Russian Gas Transit across Ukraine Post-2019: pipeline scenarios, gas flow consequences, and regulatory constraints', OIES Working Paper NG 105, Oxford Institute for Energy Studies, February. https://www.oxfordenergy.org/wpcms/wp-content/uploads/2016/02/Russian-Gas-Transit-Across-Ukraine-Post-2019-NG-105.pdf.

Rogers H.V. (2015). 'The Impact of Lower Gas and Oil Prices on Global Gas and LNG Markets', OIES Working Paper NG 99, Oxford Institute for Energy Studies, July. https://www.oxfordenergy.org/publications/the-impact-of-lower-gas-and-oil-prices-on-global-gas-and-lng-markets-2/.

Seah, S. (2014). 'Can Indonesia's policy of reconfiguring its energy mix by increasing natural gas usage support its initiatives to reform subsidies?', OIES Working Paper NG 93, Oxford Institute for Energy Studies, November. www.oxfordenergy.org/2014/11/can-indonesias-policy-reconfiguring-energy-mix-increasing-natural-gas-usage-support-initiatives-reform-subsidies/.

Sen, A. (2015). 'Gas Pricing Reform in India: Implications for the Indian gas landscape', OIES Working Paper NG 96, Oxford Institute for Energy Studies, April. https://www.oxfordenergy.org/wpcms/wp-content/uploads/2015/04/NG-96.pdf.

Stern J., Pirani S., and Yafimava K. (2009). 'The Russo-Ukrainian gas dispute of January 2009: a comprehensive assessment', OIES Working Paper NG 27, Oxford Institute for Energy Studies, February. https://www.oxfordenergy.org/publications/the-russo-ukrainian-gas-dispute-of-january-2009-a-comprehensive-assessment/.

Stern, J. (2006). 'The Russian-Ukrainian gas crisis of January 2006', OIES Working Paper, Oxford Institute for Energy Studies, January. https://www.oxfordenergy.org/publications/the-russian-ukrainian-gas-crisis-of-january-2006/.

Stern, J., Yafimava, K., Rogers, H., Pirani, S., El-Katiri, L., Honoré, A., Henderson, J., Hassanzadeh, E., and Dickel R. (2014). 'Reducing European Dependence on Russian Gas – distinguishing natural gas security from geopolitics', OIES Working Paper NG92, Oxford Institute for Energy Studies, October. https://www.oxfordenergy.org/publications/reducing-european-dependence-on-russian-gas-distinguishing-natural-gas-security-from-geopolitics/.

Taiwan (2015a). 'New Energy Policy of Taiwan', Bureau of Energy, Ministry of Economic Affairs (MOEA). http://web3.moeaboe.gov.tw/ECW/english/content/Content.aspx?menu_id=969.

Taiwan (2015b). 'Energy Statistical Hand Book', Taiwan Bureau of Energy, Ministry of Economic Affairs (MOEA), May 2015. https://web3.moeaboe.gov.tw/ECW/english/content/SubMenu.aspx?menu_id=1537.

Thailand (2015). 'Thailand's Power Development Plan 2015', Mr. Chavalit Pichalai, Director General, Energy Policy and Planning Office, Ministry of Energy. www.renewableenergy-asia.com/Portals/0/seminar/Presentation/02-Overview%20of%20Power%20Development%20Plan%20(PDP%202015).pdf.

United Nations (2012). 'Jamaica: Rapid Assessment and Gap Analysis', Sustainable Energy for All Initiative. www.se4all.org/wp-content/uploads/2015/05/Jamaica_RAGA.pdf.

Vidal, M. (2015). 'GNL Mejillones: acceso abierto al GNL y mucho más', Santiago: XIV Encuentro Energético ElecGas 2015.

Viscidi, L. et al. (2015). 'Natural Gas Market Outlook – How Latin America and the Caribbean Can Benefit from the US Shale Boom', Energy Working Paper, September 2015, The Dialogue. www.thedialogue.org/wp-content/uploads/2015/09/Natural-Gas-Market-Outlook.pdf.

World Bank (2015). World Bank indicators. http://data.worldbank.org/indicator/NY.GDP.MKTP.KD.ZG.

Yépez-Garcia, R. A. and Dana, J. (2012). 'Mitigating Vulnerability to High and Volatile Oil Prices: Power Sector Experience in Latin America and the Caribbean', Washington, DC: World Bank.

CHAPTER 7

LNG AS A TRANSPORT FUEL

Chris Le Fevre

Introduction

Natural gas has a number of environmental and financial advantages over oil-based fuels in most markets, and it has been used as transport fuel in vehicles for many years, primarily in the form of compressed natural gas (CNG). However, it has always struggled to gain market share against the more efficient and established fuels.

The emergence of LNG, which brings some additional cost and technical advantages over CNG as a fuel, is more recent. In particular, LNG provides two and a half times the energy of an equivalent volume of CNG, thereby increasing range and efficiency (IGU, 2012). This makes LNG a practical fuel for heavy road vehicles and ships and, where existing LNG infrastructure is available, the fuel is beginning to make inroads.[1] Furthermore legislative changes mean that LNG is becoming established in North American marine shipping and in northern Europe.

LNG is already used as a fuel in many LNG tankers but its use more widely as a transport fuel is a new application. It is very difficult to determine the present size of the market for LNG as a transport fuel, though total marine usage in 2013 has been estimated at 1.5 mt (DNV-GL, 2015).

The market for LNG as a transport fuel brings together two major existing industries and a large number of potential players with a multiplicity of backgrounds, skills, and experience. These will include oil and gas majors with well-established petroleum retailing businesses, global shipping and logistics companies, as well as new entrants who could bring innovation as well as over-commitment.

There is a wide range of uncertainties regarding levels of future growth of LNG used in transportation as the market is still relatively new. It is likely that growth will be slow initially, though the potential size, in LNG terms, could be significant. Not all of the demand for LNG will necessarily be for

---

[1] LNG is not a suitable fuel for passenger cars, primarily due to the lower utilization levels creating major problems with boil-off though refuelling; the weight of storage tanks is also an issue.

'primary LNG', some will be sourced from market-based liquefaction of natural gas or biomethane. Analysis is complicated by the immature nature of the market, which means that there is a lack of consistent information/definitions in different countries. Furthermore the regulatory environment has yet to emerge fully.

This chapter looks at the market for LNG as a transport fuel in two dimensions – the types of customer and the main geographic markets – before considering growth forecasts.

The main customers for LNG as a transport fuel

Overview

This section provides a broad overview of the market for LNG as a transport fuel. It can be characterized by both demand pull and supply push characteristics; these are described in broad terms and then discussed in greater detail in the specific markets.

From a demand perspective, the attractions of LNG are primarily dependent on the level of financial and environmental advantage enjoyed in comparison to other fuels. In road transport, the financial case for LNG is normally set against that for diesel, and the price paid for both fuels can be materially impacted by national taxation levels. In marine markets, the competing fuel is primarily heavy fuel oil (HFO), though diesel (referred to marine gasoil or MGO) is also important in some markets. Marine fuel prices are generally untaxed, so the price comparison is usually on a commodity basis.

The second key advantage of natural gas relates to emissions. The main areas of concern in transportation are emissions of carbon dioxide (CO_2), nitrogen oxides (NO_x), and particulate matter (PM), as well as sulphur oxides (SO_x) in maritime transport. Carbon dioxide and nitrous oxide (N_2O) are greenhouse gases and their global warming potential (GWP) is typically measured on a CO_2-equivalence basis. PM, SO_x, and NO_x can cause health problems[2] and sulphur dioxide (SO_2) is also responsible for acid rain.

The combustion of natural gas generates lower levels of CO_2 emissions and virtually no NO_x, SO_x, or PM emissions, in comparison with the combustion of diesel or fuel oil. On the other hand, methane is an important greenhouse gas (GHG), so any emissions that might be associated with the

---

[2] PM emissions are caused by the incomplete combustion of fuel; they are easily inhaled into the lower respiratory tract and have been found to contain potentially carcinogenic organic compounds. See the UK Health and Safety Executive Circular OC 292/2, 'Diesel engine exhaust emissions', www.hse.gov.uk/foi/internalops/ocs/200-299/oc292_2.htm.

production, transportation, dispensing, or incomplete combustion[3] of natural gas should also be captured. The International Panel on Climate Change (IPCC) has updated its assessment of the GWP of GHGs and these are shown in Table 7.1.

Table 7.1: One-hundred-year GWP for the main GHGs (Fifth assessment from IPCC)

Greenhouse gas	CO_2 equivalent (CO_2 eq)	
	Without feedback	*With feedback*
CO_2	1	1
Fossil methane (CH_4)	30	34
Nitrous oxide (N_2O)	265	298

Note: 'With feedback' includes the indirect effects of the gas on global warming.
Source: Trottier (2015).

The environmental driver prevails where legislation requiring action on environmental protection is in force – such as the International Maritime Organization (IMO) rules (referred to as **MARPOL VI**) banning fuel oil whose sulphur content is above a certain level, in some regions. There is also increasing evidence that governments and companies are seeking to promote LNG as a fuel for environmental reasons.

On the supply side the attractiveness of LNG as a fuel has been partly driven by the increased availability of LNG and LNG terminals – many of which have spare capacity. In some markets, factors such as an existing off-grid sector supplied by LNG and declining demand from traditional consumers could also be important. This has led to the development of a so-called 'virtual pipeline' for LNG in some countries (such as Norway); in other words a cryogenic supply chain that moves LNG to end-users through a variety of stages. These can include:

- road tankers,
- bunker vessels and barges,
- rail wagons, and
- intermediate and end-user storage facilities.

---

[3] Incomplete combustion with methane venting to the atmosphere is referred to as 'methane slip'.

LNG as a Transport Fuel 445

The volumes consumed by different vessels or vehicles can vary quite significantly, as illustrated in Table 7.2. The significantly higher levels of LNG required to serve marine usage indicates that this area can achieve scale more quickly than road-based applications.

Table 7.2: Comparison of natural gas consumption for different types of vessels and vehicles

Vessel/vehicle	Annual LNG/CNG consumption of a single vessel/vehicle		Approximate number of vessels/vehicles with the same consumption
	MWh	*m³*	
Ferry	395,000	37,335,000	1
Port vessel (tug)	5,900	557,700	65
Fishing boat	3,000	283,600	130
Bus	290	27,400	1,300
Taxi	40	3,800	10,800

Source: Lage and Pilskog (2014).

The supply and demand factors have to be assessed in the context of the perspective of the various key stakeholders. Le Fevre (2014) suggests that in broad terms there are four groups of stakeholders:

- Vehicle or vessel owners/operators.
- Manufacturers (OEMs) and distributors of vehicles and vessels.
- Fuel suppliers and refuelling infrastructure providers.
- Government and other policy makers.

In addition to the actions of stakeholders, the pace and scale of roll-out will be determined by a number of global/regional factors that may be only tangentially linked to the issue of LNG in transportation, but which could nevertheless be crucial determinants. These include:

- global energy prices and interfuel competition,
- technological developments,
- levels of economic activity, and
- demand for transport.

Finally the there are a number of barriers that can hinder the uptake of LNG in the various market sectors. The most important obstacles are:

- availability of appropriate vehicles and refuelling infrastructure,
- certainty over pricing issues, and
- regulatory treatment.

There are two major market user categories[4] – road and marine. These markets and the issues involved are covered in the following sections.

Marine bunkers

In the marine sector, global shipping is almost wholly reliant on oil. The IEA (2014) estimates global marine bunker fuel consumption to be in the region of 4 million barrels of oil equivalent per day (mboe/d), which equates to 4.4 per cent of total oil product consumption. Approximately 80 per cent of this figure is in the form of low-price, low-quality fuel oil, with much of the remainder being diesel (often termed marine gasoil or MGO). Cargo ships account for some 90 per cent of global consumption. Other vessels such as passenger ships, fishing vessels, tugs, and naval craft consume the rest.

LNG is a feasible marine fuel; it has been used as the prime source of propulsion in LNG tankers for many years and is becoming established in other ships in parts of Europe.[5] The prime driver for this change is emission control legislation, known as MARPOL VI, though there are also some potential price advantages. The other important factor is the relative scale involved in marine usage, in comparison with road-based usage (see Table 7.2); this makes it an attractive new sector for fuel marketers and bunkerage ports (Danish Maritime Authority, 2011). While ships can be converted to LNG use, LNG is more likely to be chosen for newbuild vessels.[6] Refuelling can be achieved from onshore bunkers, LNG barges, or LNG trucks.

As explained above, stakeholder positions are key to assessing the overall market potential. Table 7.3 shows the main stakeholders.

---

[4] Rail and inland waterways may also be of interest in some parts of the world, though relative volumes are small.

[5] DNV-GL (2015) reports that there were 63 LNG-fuelled vessels (excluding LNG carriers) in operation as at May 2015, with a further 76 on order. Ninety-two per cent of the existing vessels are in Europe and the vast majority are in Norway.

[6] Some new vessels are being built to be adaptable to LNG in the future. See DNV-GL (2015).

Table 7.3: Main stakeholders in marine transport

Stakeholder	Typical players	Active companies
Vessel owners/ operators	Container lines Ferries Cruise ship operators	Tote Shipping, Crowley Fjord Lines, EMS Carnival Cruise lines
Manufacturers	Ship builders Engine makers	Wärtsilä Rolls Royce
Fuel/infrastructure providers	Integrated oil companies Port operators LNG terminals	GasNor (Shell) Port of Antwerp GATE LNG
Government/ policy makers	National governments The EU The IMO Standards setting bodies Lobbying groups	DNV-GL Lloyds Register Society for Gas as a Marine Fuel

Source: Author's analysis.

The key stakeholder is the International Maritime Organization (IMO), a specialized agency of the UN, whose responsibilities include the prevention of marine pollution. Annex VI of the MARPOL convention[7] established emissions standards for oceangoing ships for SO_x, NO_x, and PM, both globally and in defined emission control areas. The standards include a global limit (established in August 2012) of 3.5 per cent sulphur in fuel and from January 2015, in emission control areas, a 0.1 per cent limit. In addition a global 0.5 per cent limit is planned to apply by January 2020, though this may be deferred to 2025 depending on the outcome of a fuel availability study that is due to report in 2018. The NO_x limits are based on engine size and date of installation.

The emission control areas are shown in Figure 7.1:

- **North America**[8] – the area 200 nautical miles from the coasts of US, Canadian, and French territories.

- **US Caribbean** – waters off the coasts of Puerto Rico and US Virgin Islands.

---

[7] The IMO has no powers of enforcement and is reliant on national governments to establish the necessary legislation. Nearly 95% of the world's shipping tonnage are parties to Annex VI. Full details are on the IMO website: www.imo.org/en/MediaCentre/PressBriefings/Pages/44-ECA-sulphur.aspx#.VpO5NpOLRBx.

[8] Includes PM and NO_x.

- **Europe** – the Baltic, North Sea, and English Channel.

In addition Hong Kong created an emission control area for vessels berthing in the port from July 2015.[9]

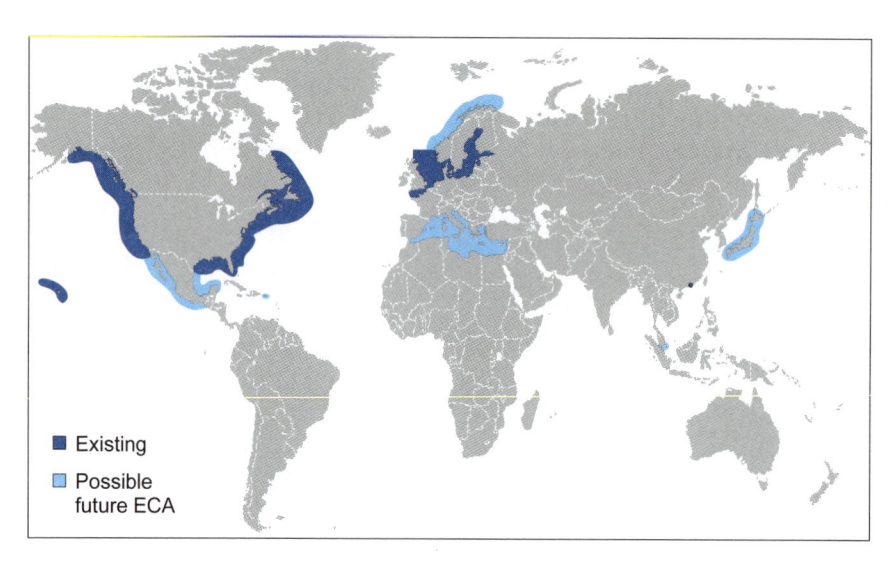

Figure 7.1: Existing and possible new emission control areas (ECAs)
Source: IMO (2012)/American Nautical Services.

LNG is particularly attractive compared to fuel oil, as it has no sulphur emissions and virtually zero PM, it also emits 20–25 per cent less CO_2 and 90 per cent less NO_x. Some comparisons are shown in Table 7.4.

Table 7.4: Comparison of emissions by fuel type

Marine fuel type	Sulphur emissions (ppm)	NO_x (g/kWh)	PM (g/kWh)	CO_2 (g/kWh)
Residual fuel oil	35,000–45,000	9–12	1.5	580–630
Marine distillate	15,000–20,000	8–11	0.25–0.5	580–630
Marine gasoil (low sulphur)	1,000	8–11	0.15–0.5	580–630
Ultra-low sulphur diesel	15	8–11	0.15–0.25	580–630
LNG	1	2	0	430–480

Source: Deal (2013).

[9] 'Hong Kong Sets Emissions Enforcement Date', *The Maritime Executive*, 12 March 2015, http://maritime-executive.com/article/hong-kong-sets-emissions-enforcement-date.

The comparisons in Table 7.4 do not take account of different types of vessel, or of the usage patterns of the full 'well to propeller' impact of LNG compared to other fuels.[10] Thomson et al. (2015) demonstrate that for a range of simulations LNG has a materially improved performance for both GHGs and other emissions.

The other important stakeholders are the vessel owners and operators who must decide how to meet the MARPOL requirements. LNG is not the only option available, and some may decide to install emission-scrubbing technology or purchase more expensive MGO – particularly if their vessels are only operating in emission control areas for part of the time. However, these solutions do not deal with NO_x or PM; Aagesen (2013) suggests that for the longer term, a significant proportion of vessel owners (particularly container line and cruise ship operators) are considering LNG.

The other critical issue for operators is the cost of fuel, which can range between 58 per cent and 78 per cent of a vessel's operating expenses (DNV, 2012). The commodity price of natural gas has been below that of gasoil in most markets, though the gap has decreased since 2013. This is illustrated in Figure 7.2, which shows selected prices for natural gas and the two main competing fuels.

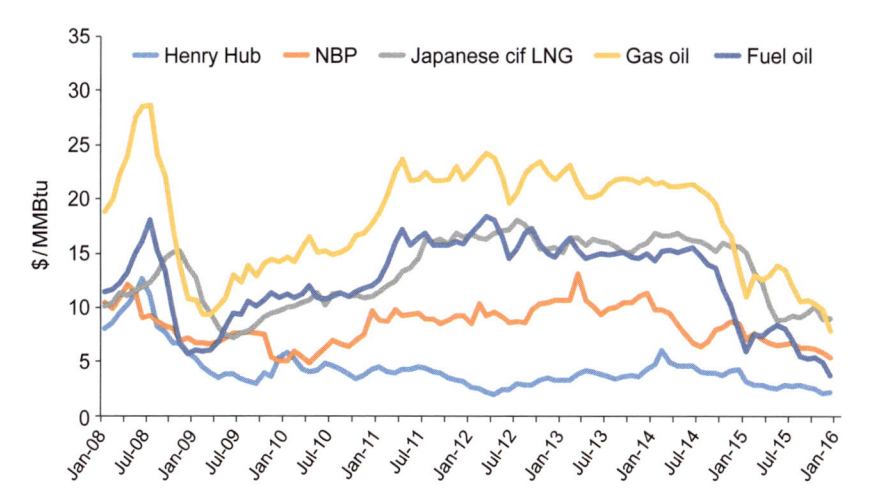

Figure 7.2: Marine fuel price comparisons with regional gas prices
Source: Argus. (Gas oil and Fuel oil prices are those quoted for NW Europe.)

The comparison in terms of differentials is shown in Figure 7.3. It could be argued that in the emission control areas of North America and Europe,

---

[10] This is often referred to as 'total fuel cycle analysis', and it includes the emissions associated with the extraction, transportation, and processing of LNG.

the important differential is between the local gas price and gasoil, as fuel oil is no longer appropriate. This is shown as the Henry Hub (HH) or NBP price minus the local gasoil price.[11] In Asian markets, fuel oil is likely to prevail at least until 2020, so the average price of LNG imported into Japan minus the price of Singapore shipping fuel (180 CST) is the basis for calculating differentials. Figure 7.3 shows that natural gas has generally been cheaper than gasoil in Europe and the USA, although the differential has narrowed as a result of the recent fall in oil prices. Differentials between LNG and fuel oil in Japan are generally narrower, which is to be expected given that the price of most Japanese LNG is still linked to oil prices.

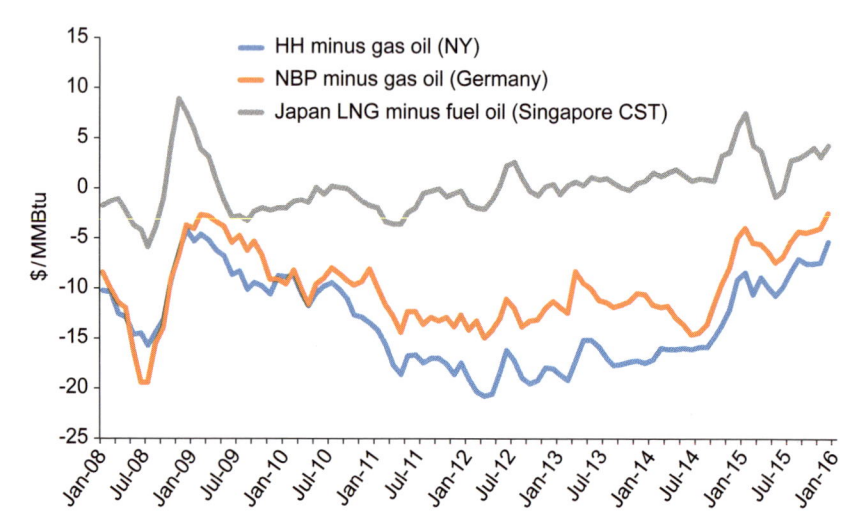

Figure 7.3: Marine fuel price differentials with regional gas prices (negative differential means gas is cheaper)

Source: Argus.

In practice the actual price paid by LNG marine fuel users will depend on factors such as point of delivery and other contractual terms. Various pricing arrangements are beginning to emerge. These include:

- 'hub plus' pricing – this is where the LNG price is linked to a gas trading hub such as HH or NBP and a predetermined mark-up is added,

- 'oil product minus' pricing – where there is a guaranteed margin against a competing fuel such as FO or MGO.

---

[11] New York No. 2 and German heating oil quoted by Argus.

Some of the hub prices may display marked seasonality – particularly in Europe – which is not so apparent in oil indexation; there are also varying levels of hub liquidity around the world. Regional oil product prices are also better understood and more widely available than gas prices in some markets. For these reasons, buyers may prefer an 'oil minus' arrangement rather than a 'gas hub plus' approach. There is also the possibility of a new LNG bunkering index once liquidity has reached a satisfactory point, though this would be strongly influenced by overall LNG pricing dynamics which could be a drawback for some buyers.

The benefits of LNG in terms of reduced fuel costs have to be considered against the higher capital charges for a new or converted LNG-fuelled vessel. These relate primarily to the higher costs of an LNG-fuelled engine and of the storage and delivery system. Mc Gill et al. (2013) estimate that newbuild LNG vessels cost around 25 per cent more than conventional ones, whilst the cost of retrofit ranges from €5.8 million for a tug boat to €19 million for an inshore bulk carrier.

Semolinos et al. (2013) have analysed the economics of newbuild LNG shipping versus the two alternatives (HFO plus scrubbers and burning MGO):

- For LNG to be more attractive than HFO plus scrubbers, a discount at or below $2/MMBtu is required for most vessel types (tankers, container ships, ferries, and most cargo vessels). Very large bulk carriers with high fuel economy require a discount of nearly $5/MMBtu.

- For LNG to be more attractive than the MGO option, a discount of between 2 and $4/MMBtu is required for most vessel types, while very large bulk carriers require a discount of around $6/MMBtu.

This analysis suggests that LNG would typically be the preferred option on financial grounds in the European and North American markets for all vessels, whilst the situation in Asia is less clear cut.

A further important driver in the marine market will be the readiness or otherwise of ports to develop LNG bunkering facilities. Table 7.5 shows the largest existing FO bunker locations in terms of throughput and the location of nearby LNG terminals. These 10 ports account for approximately 35 to 40 per cent of global marine fuel demand and the table suggests that a comparatively small number of major bunkering ports could provide LNG bunkering facilities to a significant proportion of the global large ship fleet. It should, however, be noted that many of these ports are also locations for major oil refineries, and the increasing availability of very low value fuel oil may drive re-configuration. This could have a consequent impact on the cost effectiveness of LNG versus gasoil.

A survey by Lloyds Register (2014b) of 22 ports showed that nearly 60 per cent had specific plans for LNG bunkering. In the short term, ports were expected to use barges and road tankers to provide LNG, though most were expecting to install shore-based tanks in the longer term. The survey indicated that most progress was being made in European ports, where 76 per cent expected to have LNG available by 2020.

Table 7.5: Top ten bunkering ports and LNG terminal locations

Port/Region	Bunker throughput (mt)	Market share (%)	Nearest LNG terminal
Singapore	39.0	17	Singapore (Regas)
Rotterdam	13.0	6	GATE Rotterdam (Regas)
Fujairah (UAE)	9.5	4	Abu Dhabi and Oman (Liquefaction) Fujairah (Regas) – Planned
Antwerp	6.1	3	GATE Rotterdam, Zeebrugge (Regas)
Hong Kong	5.4	2	Dapeng Bay (Regas)
Gibraltar	5.0	2	Huelva (Regas)
Korea (Busan)	4.6	2	Tongyeong (Regas)
West Africa	4.1	2	Bonny Island, Nigeria (Liquefaction)
Tokyo Bay	3.5	2	Tokyo Bay (Regas)
Iran	3.1	1	Ras Laffan, Qatar (Liquefaction)

Source: Lloyds Register (2014a), Le Fevre et al. (2014).

There is still a great deal of uncertainty over the eventual level of take-up of LNG as a fuel in the maritime market. The main barriers to growth are: uncertainty over the timing of future MARPOL restrictions on FO, concerns over the competitiveness of LNG versus competing fuels, the different regulatory and procedural requirements around the world, and doubts over the availability of cost effective bunkering facilities.

Road vehicles

LNG in road transport is of most interest to operators of large trucks – often referred to as heavy goods vehicles (HGV). The category most suitable for LNG usage is normally above 15 tonnes gross laden weight (GLW), with a power rating of between 250 and 800 horsepower (HP). However, whilst the definition of HGVs can vary between countries, they are generally defined as those with a GLW in excess of 3 to 4 tonnes; in addition, road vehicles are limited to 330 horsepower (HP) in Europe and 450 HP in the USA and China. Table 7.6 shows estimates of the global HGV population as a proportion of the total number of commercial vehicles.

Table 7.6: Estimated commercial vehicle populations (thousands) and 2013 sales

Region/ Country	Total commercial vehicles stock	of which HGVs (>15t GLW)	Commercial vehicle production (annual)	HGV production (>16t GLW)
Europe	38,203	3,779	1,559	129
USA	118,456	2,702	6,699	252
China	21,844	6,500	3,858	700
Other	131,385	9,519	16,105	659
World	309,888	22,500	21,523	1,740

Source: Le Fevre et al. (2014).

LNG as a fuel is proven technically and there are a number LNG-fuelled trucks in operation – most notably in China – though efficiencies and power range are still less than those of diesel vehicles.

As explained above, stakeholder positions are key to assessing the overall market potential. Table 7.7 shows the main stakeholders and the key drivers behind a potential decision.

Table 7.7: Main stakeholders in road freight transport

Stakeholder	Typical players	Active Companies
Buyers/users	Large fleet operators Major retailers	UPS, Ryder, Tesco, Walmart
Manufacturers	Truck makers Engine makers	Volvo, Scania Westport, Cummins
Fuel/infrastructure providers	Integrated oil companies Fuel distributors Petroleum retailers	Shell, Engie Linde/BOC Chive Fuels (SHV/Calor), ENN
Government/ policy makers	National governments The EU Pan-national organizations Standards setting bodies Lobbying groups	NGVA Blue Corridors Project

Source: Author's analysis.

The key decision maker in this sector is the vehicle owner/operator, which in many countries means the operators of large fleets. These can be haulage providers, parcel distributors, or large retail organizations with extensive distribution chains.[12] The decision to opt for LNG-fuelled vehicles is typically taken at the time of vehicle renewal and the financial case is crucial, although environmental considerations are becoming increasingly important.

The financial case is a trade off between the discounted price of LNG versus the higher capital cost for an LNG-fuelled vehicle. Though the premium paid for LNG trucks is falling, they still cost between €20,000 and €40,000 more than an equivalent vehicle in Europe (Kantor 2014) and $50,000 more in the USA (WSJ, 2014). The commodity price of LNG, whilst it varies around the world, is usually well below the price of diesel, though the actual differential will often depend heavily on taxation at the point of sale. In most EU countries, taxation accounts for around two-thirds of the retail price (European Commission, 2015), while in the USA the equivalent taxation figure is only around 13 per cent (Morse et al., 2013). Retail LNG prices are not generally available, though a proxy can be used in the form of published CNG prices. Table 7.8 illustrates the differential with diesel in some key markets.

Table 7.8: Retail and wholesale natural gas prices and retail diesel, in $/MMBtu for Q4 2015

Product	Market		
	USA	*UK*	*China*
Diesel	20.1	49.0	51.3
CNG	18.3*	33.6	22.0
Wholesale natural gas	2.3 (Henry Hub)	5.4 (NBP)	8.0 (LNG import price)

*LNG is quoted at $16.7/MMBtu

Source: US EIA and Dept. of Energy, Argus, CNG Europe, Automobile Association.

The fuel price advantage of LNG has been eroded in some markets by falling oil prices – particularly in the USA where taxation has a lower impact. Nevertheless, there are still substantial potential fuel cost savings in Europe and China. These saving must be weighed against lower efficiencies,

---

[12] Large retailers may outsource distribution but require their contractors to use clean fuels.

the increased vehicle cost, and slightly higher operating costs. The payback period will depend crucially on distances travelled; for vehicles operating distances of around 100,000 km per year, the payback period would be between three and four years in Europe (Le Fevre, 2014).

Refuelling infrastructure and vehicle availability are also important concerns for operators. Whilst a wider range of trucks is becoming available, there is nothing like the extensive maintenance and repair network that is available for diesel vehicles. Outside a small number of countries, the LNG-refuelling network is non-existent and only large-scale operators are in a position to invest in their own facilities. Until vehicles can establish a significant track record with regard to reliability, and there is reasonable coverage for refuelling, many operators will be reluctant to change from the well tried and tested diesel option – particularly if there is little pressure from their customers or government.

Truck and engine manufacturers, as well as infrastructure providers, are likely to reflect this reluctance and resist over-committing to new investments until their customers' needs are clearer. This so-called chicken and egg syndrome will act as a brake on rapid roll-out in this sector in most countries.

For government stakeholders, the key issue relates to environmental performance. Measuring the environmental advantages of natural gas in comparison to other road transport fuels is complicated and the most commonly accepted approach for passenger vehicles is to measure well to wheel (WTW)[13] emissions; this figure incorporates the entire life cycle of the fuel from production to combustion including extraction, separation and treatment, transportation, refining, and distribution to the tank of the relevant vehicle. Though the calculation of WTW emissions may be relatively straightforward for passenger vehicle emissions (which are calculated per unit of either energy consumed or distance travelled by a vehicle, see Edwards et al., 2011 and 2013), establishing an effective comparative environmental metric for freight vehicles is more difficult. Measures such as emissions per ton-mile will vary for different sizes of vehicle and usage pattern (for example, long-distance haulage versus urban delivery with frequent stops) and this can distort comparisons. The focus has therefore tended to be on engine rather than vehicle performance (Ricardo-AEA, 2012), though as events relating to VW in September 2015 have demonstrated, actual performance can differ from that claimed by manufacturers.[14]

Evidence of environmental benefits relating to LNG use in road

---

[13] This combines the well to tank (WTT) and tank to wheel (TTW) measures. See European Commission (2007) and Huss et al. (2013).

[14] See 'Volkswagen: The scandal explained', BBC News, 10 December 2015. (www.bbc.co.uk/news/business-34324772) for a summary of the issues.

transport to date is inconclusive. Some trials have been undertaken in various countries and these suggest WTW CO_2 savings of 8 per cent and reduced NO_x and PM emissions of 85.6 per cent and 97.1 per cent respectively (PWC, 2013). However, the efficiency of engines, together with the extent to which unburnt LNG is contained in the exhaust (this is referred to as methane slip), can be crucial. A 2014 German study (Wurster et al., 2014) suggests that when these factors are taken into account, the WTW performance of LNG was worse than that of diesel in 2013. (The study did not consider the impact of NO_x or PM and also concluded that LNG will be better than diesel by 2030 as efficiencies improve.)

One challenge for government is to deal with regulatory uncertainty. Issues that need to be addressed include: standardized pricing formats so that users can easily compare fuel costs, regulations pertaining to the construction and operation of refuelling stations, and ensuring that LNG filling stations are treated as end-users rather than licensed gas suppliers.

The main regional markets for LNG as a transport fuel

Global overview

Table 7.9 provides an estimate of global fuel consumption in the marine and truck (primarily HGV) sectors by major region.

Table 7.9: Global oil demand in transportation, in million b/d

Region	Total transport demand (2012)	Marine demand (2010)	Truck demand (2012)
OECD America	13.1	0.6	2.2*
OECD Europe	5.9	0.9	n.a.
OECD Asia Oceania	2.7	0.3	n.a.
OECD Total	21.7	1.8	n.a.
Non-OECD Asia	8.2	1.1	n.a.
Other	15.5	1.1	n.a.
World	**45.5**	**4.0**	**9.0**

* USA only in 2011 (see Davis et al., 2013).

Source: IEA (2014), OPEC 2014, author's estimates.

The main regional markets considered in this section are North America (mainly the USA), Europe, and China.

North America

The size of the long-haul road freight sector in North America and the extensive use of coastal shipping suggest that this market may have potential for the use of LNG in transport. This potential is enhanced by a number of factors.

- The widespread availability of indigenous gas production – some of which is presently flared – makes natural gas significantly cheaper than diesel and marine fuel oil in many locations.
- The USA already has an extensive LNG infrastructure in the form of peak shaving units and satellite storage facilities,[15] coastal import terminals, and some export facilities under construction. In addition, there is a significant level of exports of truck-borne LNG to Mexico (EIA 2014), while LNG bunkering facilities are being developed in Gulf Coast locations such as Louisiana and Florida.
- The North American Emission Control Area extends 200 miles from the coast and so environmental legislation driven by MARPOL VI is encouraging the use of LNG in shipping.
- A number of companies have invested in LNG production and refuelling networks. These include Clean Energy Fuels, which has two LNG production plants, 60 LNG delivery tankers, and a 'Natural Gas Highway' of 150 LNG refuelling stations across the country.[16]
- There is a vibrant vehicle and engine sector with a number of players keen to innovate. Canadian engine manufacturer Westport has been at the forefront of NG engine design, and truck manufacturers are now providing vehicles based on the Cummins Westport ISX 12G engine.[17]

The main barriers to market development include the taxation of LNG and gaps in the refuelling network. Under Federal rules, LNG is taxed on a volume basis rather than on energy content. This results in LNG attracting taxation that is 1.7 times higher than diesel. Individual states have moved to rectify this, but it creates challenges for interstate operators and shipments of LNG. In July 2015 the Senate Finance Committee approved a bipartisan

---

[15] See US Department of Transportation for details.
[16] Graphic of US Nationwide Network, Clean Energy Website.
https://www.cleanenergyfuels.com/why-clean-energy/#Robust-Nationwide-Network/.
[17] For details of the ISX 12G engine see the Cummins Westport website:
www.cumminswestport.com/models/isx12-g.

bill to put LNG on an equal footing with diesel for the highway excise tax[18] and plans are underway to extend this arrangement to inland waterways.

An LNG storage and refuelling network is being developed, though rollout is not taking place as rapidly as some forecasts had initially suggested. For example, Shell has cancelled plans to build its own network of small-scale LNG plants and will source the fuel from other suppliers.

Nevertheless, a number of major operators have begun to switch to natural gas (though some of this may be in the form of CNG rather LNG). These include Lowe's, Procter & Gamble, and UPS. In October 2013 Lowe's announced a new LNG truck fleet to begin operating out of Texas, 20 per cent of P&G's trucks are being converted to run on natural gas, and UPS was operating more than 1,000 LNG trucks by mid-2015.[19] In Canada, the proximity of mining, drilling, and large-scale timber operations are creating synergies that can facilitate the development of an LNG fuelling hub. An example of the type of project that is emerging is the deal Shell has signed with Caterpillar to test a new engine using LNG, for use in the trucks and equipment used in oil sands mining in northern Alberta.

The USA and Canada also have potential for LNG to be used as a fuel in the rail sector and LNG demand could be as high as 4.6 mtpa by 2030 (EIA, 2014). (Unlike most regions with extensive rail networks and high levels of long-haul freight, there is a relatively low level of electric-powered traction.) There are, however, some major operational challenges in switching to LNG, such as dual fuelling and inter-operability between systems. Operators would also have to underwrite the investment in new fuelling facilities.

Europe

In terms of road haulage distances and use of coastal shipping, Europe has many similar features to North America. The main drivers for LNG in transportation include:

- Lower fuel costs for the road haulage sector in comparison to diesel, though taxation is major driver.

- MARPOL VI ban on fuel oil in the Baltic and North Sea emission control areas.

- EU initiatives aimed at encouraging the use of LNG as fuel.

---

[18] 'U.S. Legislation Lowers Tax on LNG', NGV Global News, 31 July 2015. www.ngvglobal.com/blog/u-s-legislation-lowers-tax-on-lng-0731.

[19] 'Agility Facilitates 1,600 NGVs for UPS', Fleets and Fuels.com, 1 April 2015. www.fleetsandfuels.com/fuels/cng/2015/04/agility-facilitates-1600-ngvs-for-ups/.

- A large number of LNG import terminals, many with spare capacity, together with a cryogenic distribution network in some countries – notably Spain.

The main source of policy support for LNG is via the European Commission's Alternative Fuel Infrastructure Directive (European Commission, 2014) which sets out timelines for the development of marine and road-based refuelling facilities. This requires common technical standards by 2016, and LNG refuelling stations every 400 km on the core

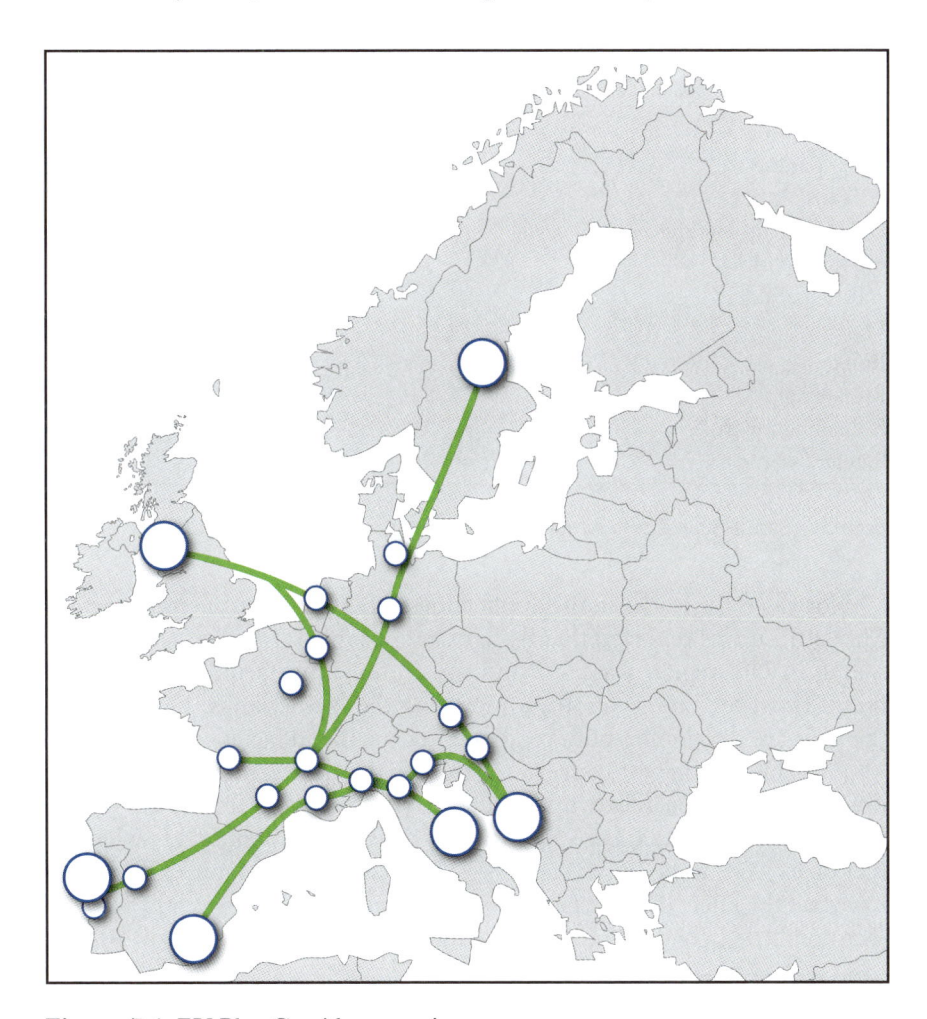

Figure 7.4: EU Blue Corridors – main routes
Source: 'LNG Blue Corridors', Seventh Framework Programme, http://lngbc.eu/.

TEN-T network and at 'sufficient' seaports by 2025. The LNG Blue Corridors project has been established to meet these arrangements. The project reported that at the end of 2014 there were around 1,300 LNG-fuelled trucks in Europe, of which nearly half were in the UK with the Netherlands and Spain accounting for most of the rest (Pilskog, 2015).

Figure 7.4 shows the main areas to be covered by the Blue Corridors project and Table 7.10 summarizes the situation regarding infrastructure within the EU as provided by Gas Infrastructure Europe.[20]

Table 7.10: LNG infrastructure in Europe

	Operational	*Under construction*	*Planned*
LNG terminals			
Re-loading	15	2	12
Transhipment	3	2	4
Bunker ship loading	9	7	11
Truck loading	19	8	5
Rail loading	–	–	4
Liquefaction	22	n.a.	2
Bunkering for ships	26	5	22
Bunker ships	5	4	6
Refuelling for trucks	70	14	19
Satellite storage	>1000	n.a.	n.a.

Source: Small-Scale LNG Map, Gas Infrastructure Europe, May 2015.

Norway is the leader in the application of LNG for marine transport. In May 2015 it was reported that 81 per cent of all LNG-fuelled vessels were sailing in Norwegian waters,[21] and most bunkering facilities are located there. However, other countries (including the Netherlands, Finland, and the UK) are developing both road and marine based facilities.

Probably the biggest concern for users is the degree to which fuel price differentials can be relied upon. Their concerns were illustrated by the proposed Energy Tax Directive (European Commission, 2011) whereby fuel taxes were to be based on energy and CO_2 components. This would have had the effect of increasing the tax on natural gas by over 300 per cent (Kantor, 2014). The proposal was withdrawn at the beginning of 2015,[22]

---

[20] LNG map, Gas Infrastructure Europe, www.gie.eu/index.php/maps-data/lng-map.
[21] DNV-GL (2015) – excludes LNG tankers.
[22] The Legal Helpdesk, Energy Taxation in the EU, www.keepontrack.eu/contents/virtualhelpdeskdocuments/energy-taxation_1718.pdf.

though it remains a concern for those looking to invest.

China

China is a major LNG importer and also has significant and growing onshore LNG production capability. This was originally built to serve remote networks and off-grid customers (in part due to the difficulty in accessing monopoly gas networks) and had a capacity of around 64 mmcm/d by the end of 2014.[23] The country has the world's largest inland goods transport market with over 9,000 bn tonne-km shipped in 2012, of which nearly 6,000 bn was road transport (OECD, 2015). Growing concern over air quality has resulted in Government support for gas-fuelled vehicles. In 2013, the Government indicated that it required the volume of LNG used in inland transportation vessels to be above 10 per cent of total fuel consumption by 2020.

Whilst most gas-fuelled vehicles in China use CNG, at the end of 2013 there were an estimated 100,000 LNG vehicles, making it by far the largest LNG-fuelled fleet in the world. Growth is expected to continue, with numbers reaching as much as 220,000 by the end of 2015. Most of the vehicles (over 80 per cent) are buses and coaches, with heavy duty trucks only accounting for 10 per cent of the fleet, though this share is likely to increase. This growth in fleet size is matched by a rapid increase in LNG refuelling stations; the figure for these stood at 1,100 by the end of 2013, and it is forecast to reach 3,000 by 2015 (Le Fevre et al., 2014).

Growth projections for LNG as a transport fuel

The increasing interest shown in the use of natural gas in transportation has stimulated a number of forecasts of future demand. There are, however, some difficulties:

a) The market is still very small and so minor differences in growth assumptions can result in a wide range of outcomes over a 20 year horizon.

b) Many forecasts fail to distinguish between LNG and CNG, or whether LNG is imported or liquefied locally (some of it could be from biomethane).

c) Some estimates are global, but many just relate to one or two regions, such as Europe or North America.

---

[23] 'China's LNG truck transportation faces oversupply, low crude', Sun Xuelian, ICIS News. 10 April 2015. www.icis.com/resources/news/2015/04/10/9873410/china-s-lng-truck-transportation-faces-oversupply-low-crude/'

LNG Markets in Transition

Nevertheless most forecasts agree that the pace of MARPOL roll-out and the future level of gas versus oil price differentials are the key drivers in the marine sector. In the case of MARPOL, the main uncertainties relate to whether additional emission control areas are declared and the timing for extending the 0.1 per cent limit on sulphur emissions to all shipping. The expected price differential between LNG and alternative fuels will be the key driver in determining both the extent to which operators opt for LNG over other options, and the timescales over which these decisions are implemented. The availability of LNG bunkering outside North America and Europe will also be a factor.

In road vehicles, the pricing issue is the most important determinant, although this requires a view to be taken on future levels of taxation, as well as on commodity price differentials. A further important element is the extent to which government support might be available to assist with the capital cost of refuelling facilities or of new vehicle purchase.

In the light of the foregoing, it is not surprising that forecasts generated to date cover a wide range of possible outcomes. Most global forecasts have focused on the marine sector; however, as shown in Table 7.11, the global road sector could also be significant.

Table 7.11: Selected forecast for global LNG consumption in transport (mtpa)

Source	Sector	2025	2030	2035
BCG (base case)	Marine	72	141	–
Lloyds		0.7–69.6	–	–
Cedigaz		20.2–55.5	26.3–89.6	47.1–120.4
Shell		15–25	25–40	45–65
Gazprom		28.0–86.4	50–154.1	107–223.7
Cedigaz	Road	9–132	15–193	21–227
Shell		13–22	–	–

Source: 'Forecasting the Future of Marine Fuel', BCG Perspectives 17 March 2015. https://www.bcgperspectives.com/content/articles/transportation_travel_tourism_energy_environment_forecasting_future_marine_fuel/, Aagesen (2013), Le Fevre et al. (2014).

It is clear that there is a wide range of possible outcomes, even on a ten-year horizon. LNG could become a significant source of demand by 2030, though it would appear that some of the higher-range forecasts are unlikely to materialize at present rates of build up.

Conclusions

The concept of LNG as a transport fuel adds another dimension to the dramatic changes occurring in the LNG industry. The combination of demand for cheaper, more environmentally friendly fuels is coinciding with a period of LNG over-supply and increased contractual flexibility. There is therefore a strong likelihood that LNG will feature as a transportation fuel in the next 20 years. It is not yet clear whether LNG will break out from its current, relatively minor niche role in some regional markets to become a significant global fuel. The key determinant is likely to be whether LNG prices remain competitive, both with existing fuels and new alternatives.

Developments in the maritime sector are likely to be key, as this will provide a platform of significant scale to allow road-based usage to develop in a relatively risk-free environment. The greatest challenge is likely to be from competing technology – such as electric traction and possibly CNG.

The early stage nature of the market means that there are likely to be periods of stop–start investments in infrastructure. During periods of under-investment users will be reluctant to commit, whilst periods of over-investment will lead to under-utilization and failure to make promised returns. Timescales will be extended by the fact that most decisions to switch to LNG will take place at the point of vehicle/vessel renewal.

This underlines the fact that it is still too early to form a definitive conclusion on overall prospects, but if conditions remain favourable the acceleration in take-up could become quite rapid.

BIBLIOGRAPHY

Aagesen J. (2013). 'LNG-fuelled Deep Sea Shipping – The outlook for LNG bunker and LNG-fuelled newbuild demand up to 2025', Lloyds Register Group PowerPoint. www.skibsteknikselskab.dk/public/dokumenter/Skibsteknisk/Foraar%202013/25.02.2013/IDA%20Feb%202013%20LR%20Bunkering%20Study.pdf.

Danish Maritime Authority (2011). Reference Documents, The LNG Infrastructure Project, May 2012. www.dma.dk/themes/LNGinfrastructureproject/Sider/ReferenceDocuments.aspx.

Davis, S.C., Diegel, S.W., and Boundy, R.G. (2013). Transportation Energy Data book, Edition 32, Oakridge National Laboratory, July 2013, http://info.ornl.gov/sites/publications/Files/Pub44660.pdf.

Deal A.L. (2013). 'Liquefied Natural Gas as a Marine Fuel – A Closer Look at TOTE's Containership Projects', NEPI Working Paper, May 2013, www.glmri.org/downloads/lngMisc/NEPI%20LNG%20as%20a%20Marine%20Fuel%205-7-13.pdf.

DNV (2012). Shipping 2020, a report on technology uptake for the maritime shipping industry for DNV Maritime Oil and Gas. www.dnv.nl/binaries/shipping%202020%20-%20final%20report_tcm141-530559.pdf.

DNV-GL (2015). In Focus – LNG as Ship Fuel, LNG Report No. 01 2015, DNV-GL. http://production.presstogo.com/fileroot7/gallery/dnvgl/files/original/124feddb807045969b3071a55f73c80b/124feddb807045969b3071a55f73c80b_low.pdf.

Edwards R., Larivé, J.-F., and Beziat, J.-C. (2011). 'Well-to-wheels Analysis of Future Automotive Fuels and Powertrains in the European Context', Appendix 2 (WTW GHG-Emissions of Externally Chargeable Electric Vehicles), JRC Scientific and Technical Reports, JEC Joint Research Centre-EUCAR-CONCAWE collaboration, European Commission Joint Research Centre Institute for Energy and Transport, EUR 24952 EN-2011. http://iet.jrc.ec.europa.eu/about-jec/sites/iet.jrc.ec.europa.eu.about-jec/files/documents/wtw3_wtw_appendix2_eurformat.pdf.

Edwards, R., Larivé, J.-F., Rickeard, D., and Weindorf, W. (2013). 'Well to Tank report Version 4.0, JEC Well-To-Wheels Analysis, Well-To-Wheels Analysis of Future Automotive Fuels and Powertrains in the European Context', JRC Technical Report, JEC Joint Research Centre-EUCAR-CONCAWE collaboration, EUR 26028 EN-2013.

EIA (2014). *Annual Energy Outlook 2014 with projections to 2040*, US Energy Information Administration, DOE/EIA-0383(2014). http://www.eia.gov/forecasts/aeo/pdf/0383(2014).pdf.

European Commission (2007). 'Well-To-Wheels Analysis of Future Automotive Fuels and Powertrains in the European Context', Version 2c, EUCAR, CONCAWE, and JRC (the Joint Research Centre of the EU Commission), March 2007. http://iet.jrc.ec.europa.eu/sites/about-jec/files/documents/WTW_Report_010307.pdf.

European Commission (2011). COUNCIL DIRECTIVE amending Directive 2003/96/EC restructuring the Community framework for the taxation of energy products and electricity COM(2011)169.

European Commission (2014). DIRECTIVE 2014/94/EU OF THE EUROPEAN PARLIAMENT AND OF THE COUNCIL of 22 October 2014 on the deployment of alternative fuels infrastructure, Brussels, October 2014. http://eur-lex.europa.eu/legal-content/EN/TXT/?uri=CELEX:32014L0094.

European Commission (2015). Excise Duty Tables, Part II – Energy Products and Electricity, Ref 1038 Rev 1, July 2013. http://ec.europa.eu/taxation_customs/resources/documents/taxation/excise_duties/energy_products/rates/excise_duties-part_ii_energy_products_en.pdf.

Huss, A., Maas, H., and Hass, H. (2013). 'Tank-to-Wheels Report Version 4.0, JEC Well-to Wheels Analysis, Well-To-Wheels Analysis of Future Automotive Fuels and Powertrains in the European Context', JRC Technical Reports, JEC Joint Research Centre-EUCAR-CONCAWE collaboration, Report EUR 26027 EN-2013.

IEA (2013). *Medium-Term Gas Market Report 2013, Market Trends and Projections to 2018*, International Energy Agency.

IEA (2014). *World Energy Outlook 2014*, Paris: OECD/International Energy Agency, November.

IGU (2012). *Natural Gas for Vehicles (NGV)*, IGU and UN Economic Commission for Europe Joint report, June 2012.

IMO (2012). *International Shipping Facts and Figures – Information Resources on Trade, Safety, Security, Environment*, International Maritime Organization, 6 March 2012, (available from Knowledge Centre, IMO).

Kantor (2014). 'Regulatory implications of New developments in the gas supply chain', Report by Kantor Management Consultants for Agency for the Cooperation of European Regulators (ACER), October 2014.

Lage, M. and Pilskog, L. (2014). 'European Market for Natural Gas (methane) as a vehicle fuel', Presentation by GASNAM/NGVA, 27 April 2014. http://gasnam.es/wp-content/uploads/2014/07/Presentation_NGVA_ _GASNAM_-_European_market_for_NG_as_vehicle_fuel.pdf.

Le Fevre C. (2014). 'The Prospects for Natural Gas as a Transportation Fuel in Europe', OIES Working Paper NG 84, Oxford Institute for Energy Studies, March. www.oxfordenergy.org/2014/03/the-prospects-for-natural-gas-as-a-transportation-fuel-in-europe/.

Le Fevre C., Madden M., and White N. (2014). *LNG in Transportation*, a report for Cedigaz, September 2014.

Lloyds Register, (2014a). *Global Marine Fuel Trends 2030*, Report by Lloyds Register Marine and University College London for Lloyds Register, www.lr.org/en/_images/213-34172_Global_Marine_Fuel_Trends_2030.pdf.

Lloyds Register, (2014b). *LNG Bunkering Infrastructure Survey 2014 – The outlook of Ports on provision of LNG bunkering facilities*, Lloyds Register Marine, www.lr.org/en/_images/213-35940_lloyd_s_register_lng_bunkering_ infrastructure_survey_2014.pdf

Mc Gill, R., Remley, W., and Winther, K. (2013). *Alternative Fuels for Marine Applications*, A Report from the IEA Advanced Motor Fuels Implementing Agreement, IEA-AMF, Energy Technology Network, May 2013.

Morse, E. L., Yuen, A., Kleinman, S. M., Wetherbee, C., Thein, T., Michaeli I., Cunningham, G., and Smith, R. P. (2013). 'ENERGY 2020: TRUCKS, TRAINS & AUTOMOBILES: Start Your Natural Gas Engines!', Report Series, Citi Global Perspectives & Solutions, June 2013, https://www.citivelocity.com/citigps/ReportSeries.action?recordId=19.

OPEC (2014). *2014 World Oil Outlook*, Organization of Petroleum Exporting Countries, OPEC Secretariat, 2014. https://www.opec.org/opec_web/static_files_project/media/downloads/ publications/WOO_2014.pdf.

OECD (2015). *ITF Transport Outlook 2015*, International Transport Forum and OECD, OECD Publishing. www.oecd-ilibrary.org/transport/itf-transport-outlook-2015_9789282107782-en.

Pilskog, L. (2015). 'Potential for Natural Gas and BioMethane in Transports', Geneva 2015, www.unece.org/fileadmin/DAM/energy/se/pp/geg/geg2_ jan2015/ai9_2_Pilskog.pdf.

PWC (2013). 'LNG-as-a-fuel – why it's the next big thing for the transport sector', www.icisconference.com/uploads/assets/2013_PwC_LNG_FOR_THE_ TRANSPORT_SECTOR_v1.pdf.

Ricardo-AEA (2012) *Opportunities to overcome the barriers to uptake of low emission technologies for each commercial vehicle duty cycle*, A report for the Low Carbon Vehicle Partnership, November 2012, www.lowcvp.org.uk/assets/reports/Opportunities%20for%20low%20emission%20HGVs%20-%20final%20report%202012.pdf.

Semolinos P., Olsen, G., and Giacosa, A. (2013). 'LNG as Marine fuel – Challenges to be overcome', Presentation at 17th International Conference & Exhibition on liquefied natural gas (LNG 17), Houston 17 April 2013.

Thomson, H., Corbett, J., and Winebrake, J. (2015). 'Natural gas as a marine fuel', *Energy Policy*, 87(2015), 153–67.

Trottier, S. (2015). *Understanding the Changes to Global Warming Potential (GWP) Values*, Ecometrica, February 2015. http://ecometrica.com/assets/Understanding-the-Changes-to-GWPs.pdf.

WSJ (2014). 'Slow Going for Natural-Gas Powered Trucks', *Wall Street Journal*, 25 August 2014. www.wsj.com/articles/natural-gas-trucks-struggle-to-gain-traction-1408995745.

Wurster, R., Weindorf, W., Zittel, W., Schmidt, P., Heidt, C., Lambrecht, U., Lischke, A., and Müller, S. (2014). *LNG as an alternative fuel for the operation of ships and heavy-duty vehicles*, Study for Federal Ministry of Transport and Digital Infrastructure (BMVI), Munich/Ottobrunn, Heidelberg, Berlin, 6 March 2014.

CHAPTER 8

LNG PRICING: CHALLENGES IN THE LATE 2010s

Jonathan Stern

Introduction

Chapter 1 briefly reviewed the pricing problems encountered in early LNG projects and explained their origins, contrasting these with the expectations of the pioneering exporters, particularly those in Algeria. That chapter also set out the basic elements of gas pricing in the USA, Europe, and Asia up to 2000, highlighting the differences between how gas and LNG was priced in these three regions. In this chapter we show how these pricing developments have evolved since 2000 and examine the emerging price dynamics and challenges. The major question posed in this chapter is whether LNG pricing in Asia (where three-quarters of global LNG was traded in the first half of the 2010s) is likely to move in the same direction as gas pricing in North America and Europe – away from oil-linked pricing and towards market (spot/hub) pricing – and if so how and by when this is likely to be achieved.

Gas price formation and change in the USA and Europe: the impact on LNG import contracts

Since the mid-2000s, there has been a trend away from oil-linked pricing and towards market pricing in international gas trade. 'Market pricing' is taken to mean prices which are based on gas supply/demand dynamics in the country or region where it is sold; such prices are most often quoted at market hubs or on financial exchanges.[1] In 2005 more than 60 per cent of global gas imports were priced in relation to oil, with 20 per cent being

---

[1] Market pricing is also known as 'gas-to-gas competition', 'spot' or 'hub' pricing (although there are differences between these terms). The International Gas Union classification (on which its annual global price survey is based) defines gas-to-gas competition pricing as 'determined by the interplay of supply and demand ... traded over a variety of different periods ... Trading takes place at physical hubs ... or notional hubs ... If there are longer term contracts these will use gas price indices to determine the price.' IGU (2015, 7).

market-priced; by 2015 the figures were 49 per cent and 45 per cent respectively. But the change was almost entirely in pipeline import pricing where, by 2015, 52 per cent of imports were market priced compared with 38 per cent being oil-linked. The share of market-priced LNG increased but only from 25 to 31 per cent between 2007 and 2015.[2]

Market pricing began in North America in the mid-1980s (much earlier than in the rest of the world) when regulated prices were progressively abolished and a deregulated market moved first to pricing gas at hubs (with Henry Hub as the principal national reference) and then to the gas futures contract quoted on the New York Mercantile Exchange (NYMEX) from 1990.[3] In the UK (where gas prices were never linked to oil to the same extent as those in continental Europe), a virtual hub was created at the National Balancing Point (NBP) as the market liberalized in the 1990s; this became the price discovery point and benchmark for all gas sold in one of Europe's two largest gas markets.[4]

In continental Europe, gas prices were traditionally set according to the netback market value principle (also known as the Groningen principle) and this remained the dominant price formation mechanism until the early 2010s. The 'netback market value' principle is, essentially, that the price paid for gas at the border of a country is based on the weighted average price of the fuels with which gas competes in the energy market of the importing country, adjusted to allow for transportation and storage costs from the border plus any taxes on gas. In the majority of continental European countries, the principal fuels which competed with gas were gasoil and fuel oil, and therefore the prices of gas in long-term import contracts were linked closely to the prices of these products.[5]

This picture began to change after 2008 when a number of factors came into play:

- recession (which caused a sharp drop in energy and gas demand);

- liberalization of gas markets (a long-term process resulting from EU and national regulation);

- a surplus of gas (particularly LNG) supplies (these had been developed for the US market but were not needed due to the shale gas revolution); and

- a massive increase in oil prices above $100/bbl.

---

[2] Figures 3.3, 3.5, and 3.8 in IGU (2016, 9–12).

[3] As noted in Chapter 1, this was the major reason for the demise of US LNG imports in the 1980s. A detailed account of the evolution of hub pricing in the USA (and also Canada) can be found in Foss (2012).

[4] For details of the evolution of NBP and gas trading in the UK see Heather (2010).

[5] For a detailed account of the principle see Stern (2012), especially 54–9.

These factors combined to place utilities that imported gas in huge financial difficulty.[6] The emergence of gas hubs in many European countries has seen a progressive move away from oil-linked prices, towards market prices in the majority of large gas markets (Heather 2015). By 2015, 64 per cent of gas sold on wholesale markets was priced in relation to hub levels. However, this figure is a European average: in north-west Europe (which accounts for roughly 50 per cent of total European demand) 92 per cent of gas was market priced; in central Europe (10 per cent of demand) the figure was 56 per cent; in Mediterranean Europe (30 per cent of demand) it was 32 per cent (overwhelmingly concentrated in Italy); and in south-east Europe it was around 5 per cent; while in Scandinavia and the Baltic countries (with a very small share of total demand) it increased to around 15 per cent in 2015, largely due to the introduction of LNG (IGU 2016, 39–42).

These regional differences are important because in 2015, market pricing had not yet reached Spain, a country where LNG had become the dominant gas supply source during the 2000s, and this had reinforced the dominance of oil-linked prices.[7] Aside from its link to Portugal, Spain's only other connection with the rest of continental Europe is one pipeline, of very limited capacity, to France. For this reason, and because of the dominant influence of LNG imports in Spain (which, as noted above, have remained largely priced in relation to oil), by 2015 the Spanish market had not adopted the market-based pricing which had evolved in all other significant European gas markets with major exposure to international trade, despite the existence of the Spanish AOC market hub.[8]

Regional price dynamics and price levels

The relative dominance of domestically produced and imported pipeline gas in the majority of North American and European markets provides a sharp contrast to the dependence of Asian markets on imported LNG, and hence explains the willingness of the latter to pay much higher prices if this is necessary to ensure delivery of the required volumes. This has meant that, for long periods of time post-2000, Atlantic Basin LNG imports have been affected by the relative prices in regional gas markets – increasing as

---

[6] The evolution from oil-linked to market prices in continental Europe is described in detail in Stern and Rogers (2014) especially 8–39.

[7] Figure 32 in Honoré (2011, 54). Spain, with a regas capacity of nearly 50 mt had net LNG imports of only 8.8 mt of LNG in 2015, but re-exported a significant volume of LNG, which meant that in terms of the actual volumes consumed that year, pipeline imports exceeded those of LNG. (Communal data.)

[8] For an assessment of the development of the Spanish AOC hub see Heather (2015, 35–8).

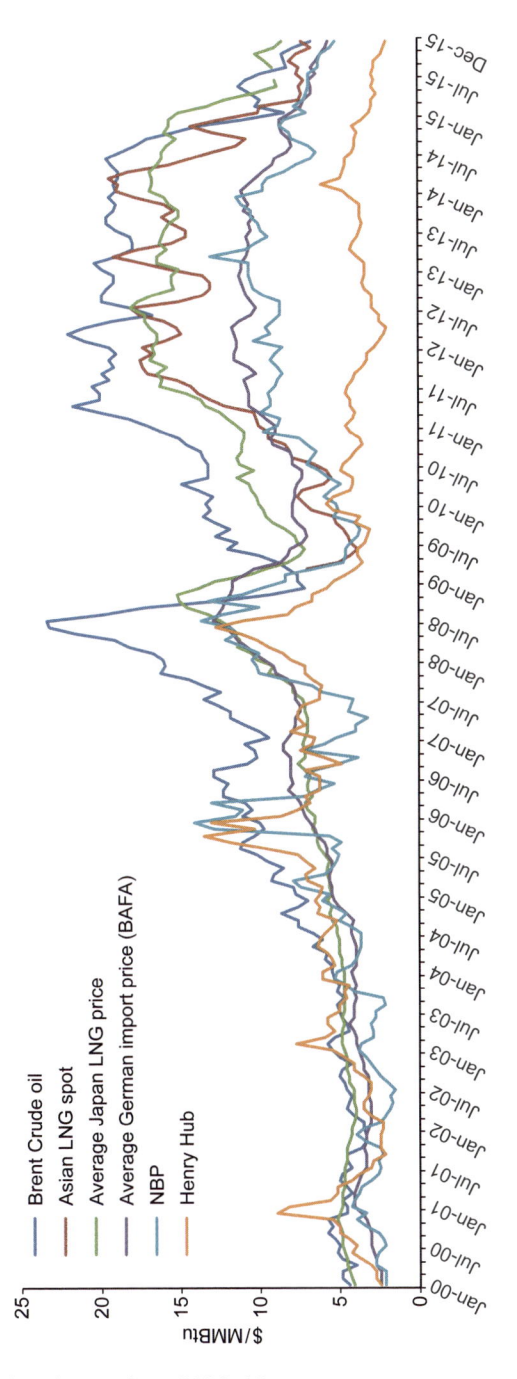

Figure 8.1: Regional gas prices, 2008–15
Source: Figure 6 in Stern and Rogers (2014); Figure 1 in Rogers (2015).

European and North American prices approached those of Asia, and falling as Asian prices rose well above those of the Atlantic Basin. Figure 8.1 shows these price fluctuations, which have become more pronounced since 2005, in the different regional markets.

The increase in Henry Hub prices in the mid-2000s, with peaks of up to $14/MMBtu in 2005 and 2008, gave rise to a frenzy of regasification terminal construction in the USA. These terminals began to come on stream in the late 2000s and early 2010s, just as the shale gas revolution was driving down prices below $5/MMBtu, much too low for any imported LNG to be commercially viable.[9] This price cycle caused US LNG imports to increase from very low levels to 3–5 mtpa in the early 2000s, and to 10–15 mtpa in the period 2003–7, rapidly subsiding thereafter to marginal levels by 2013, by which time Mexico and even Puerto Rico had become, and have remained, larger importers (see Chapter 2).[10]

In Europe the picture was more complicated, partly because of the progressive decoupling of gas and oil prices in many countries, noted above, but also because of the concentration of European regasification capacity in a small number of countries (in particular Spain, France, and the UK since 2008). For the period 2000–8, the steady rise in continental European long-term contract gas prices (represented in Figure 8.1 by BAFA, the average German import price) reflects the increase in oil prices; this contrasts with the variations in the NBP hub price – set mainly by the forces of gas supply and demand rather than by oil. Starting in 2009, discounts to the traditional oil-linked formula were introduced, and as long-term contract gas prices were progressively renegotiated towards hub prices, the BAFA price converged with NBP.[11]

As oil prices climbed increasingly rapidly towards, and then above, $100/bbl post-2010, the gap between European hub prices and traditional oil-linked contract gas prices widened substantially. The appearance of low-cost shale gas production meant that LNG imports were not competitive in the USA at a time when substantial new LNG supply was coming on stream,[12] and European countries were able to access these cargoes at attractive prices relative to pipeline gas, where contracts were still being adjusted to emerging hub prices. European LNG imports rose sharply

---

[9] With the exception of the New England region (Foss, 2012).

[10] Communal data.

[11] In fact, continental European hub prices tend to be based on or linked to TTF (in the Netherlands) rather than NBP, but the differences for most of the year are minimal. Hub price differentials in Europe since 2007 are discussed in Petrovich (2013) and (2014).

[12] LNG trade increased by 40 per cent (around 69 mtpa) from 2008 to 2011.

from around 40 mt in 2007/8 to a peak of 65 mt in 2011.[13] However, the Fukushima disaster in Japan, followed by the closure of that country's nuclear power stations, completely changed the market situation: long-term contract LNG prices had been driven up by the oil price, and spot LNG prices rose to equivalent levels (partly) due to much higher demand in Japan. At those levels, LNG had great difficulty remaining competitive in European markets, where hubs were progressively setting the price level, and by 2015, despite the addition of three importing countries, European imports were still 40 per cent below their 2011 peak (see Chapter 2).[14]

Asia: LNG pricing in the 2000s

In Chapter 1, the origins and rationale of the Japan Customs Cleared Crude Oil Price Mechanism (or JCC, established in the 1980s), were explained, including the importance of the slope, S-curve, and the applicable range mechanisms, in long-term LNG contracts. The first strains on the JCC mechanism became evident during the 2000s, because of the increase in oil prices to levels far above those which had been contemplated in these contracts.

The impact of these problems was different for different countries. In Japanese contracts between 2004 and 2010, many prices were outside the applicable range which had been agreed, and were therefore on a provisional basis until agreement was reached.[15] At the end of the decade, the 'average' price of $10–$11/MMBtu for Japanese LNG imports concealed a range of prices of $5–$13/MMBtu in contracts which had been signed at different times – and therefore at very different oil prices and with different slopes.[16] In Korea, the lack of S-curves and of an applicable range in most contracts resulted in significantly higher prices for LNG purchased from many of the same producers (Figure 8.2). Taiwanese contracts also did not have an applicable range and therefore were also higher than those of Japan for most of this period. The lowest LNG prices in Asia during this period were for Chinese and Indian imports. Chinese buyers had signed contracts with Australian, Indonesian, and Malaysian sellers at oil prices in the $20–$40/bbl range, with slopes of 5.25–7 per cent. Contracts signed later in the decade with Qatar, Total, Australia, and Papua New Guinea were at much higher oil price levels, with slopes of 14–16 per cent. India's first LNG contract with Qatar started deliveries in 2004 at a delivered price of $2.80/MMBtu fixed for five years, subsequently

---

[13] Communal data.

[14] But this was also due to recession, and therefore lower gas demand, in countries strongly impacted by recession, such as Spain and the UK (see Chapter 6).

[15] This paragraph is substantially based on Flower and Liao (2012), especially 345–52.

[16] Figure 11.5 in Flower and Liao (2012, 347).

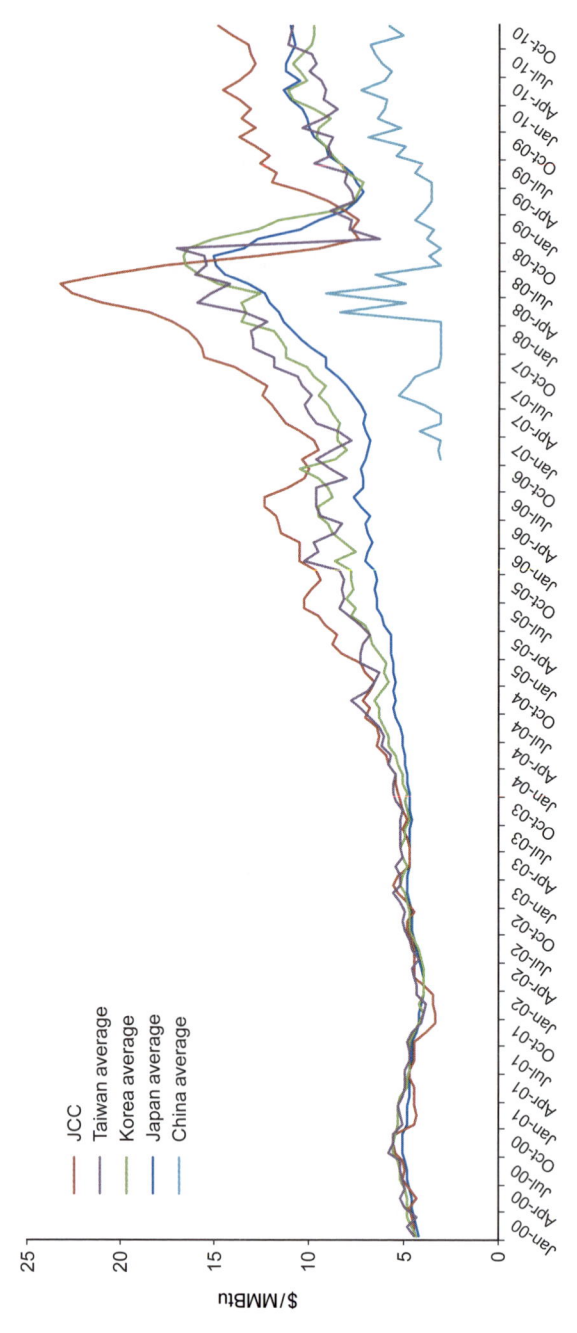

Figure 8.2: Average monthly LNG import prices in Japan, China, Korea, Taiwan and China, 2000–10 ($/MMBtu)

Source: Figures 11.4–11.8 in Flower and Liao (2012, 346–51).

rising to 100 per cent oil linkage with a slope of 12.65 per cent over the subsequent five years.

By the end of the 2000s evidence of the problems created by the rigidity of long-term contracts in the context of fluctuating – but generally increasing – oil prices was mounting. Miyamoto and Ishiguro developed a 'netback market value' (NMV) methodology for LNG pricing in the five major Asian importing markets.[17] They examined the weighted average cost of fuels competing with gas in the relevant importing country and compared this NMV price with JCC import prices at various oil price levels. In the 1970s and 1980s, crude oil and oil products were clearly the main competing fuels for LNG in Japan (the major importer) and hence the formulaic linkage of the LNG contract price to the JCC crude price had some validity. But notwithstanding the introduction of 'S-curves' (to dampen both volatility and the impact of wide fluctuations in oil price on LNG prices) the applicability of JCC prices to market conditions had become increasingly questionable.

Miyamoto and Ishiguro's survey of the energy products competing with gas in the five main Asian LNG importing countries in the period 1979–2006 found that by the end of the period, coal and oil were comparable competitors in Japan and Korea, and coal was extremely important in the other countries. The research compared the NMV with the average price of imported LNG up to a $90/bbl crude oil price. Above $40/bbl, the JCC price exceeded the average Asian NMV for LNG, and at $90/bbl the difference was very substantial for most countries. Only for Korea did NMV exceed the JCC price up to a $90/bbl crude oil price; in all other countries (with the exception of India where there are special circumstances) NMV was significantly below JCC, with the gap between the two values growing wider at oil prices above $60/bbl.[18]

By 2010 it had therefore become clear that although market fundamentals differed between the Asian LNG importing countries, even in countries such as Korea, India, and China where oil products remained important competitors to gas, 100 per cent linkage to crude oil (let alone to Japanese crude oil imports) had ceased to be a logical way to price LNG. Pressure for a change in price formation, away from JCC, was to increase substantially in the 2010s.

---

[17] Table 4 in Miyamoto and Ishiguro (2009, 26).

[18] The data set used by Miyamoto and Ishiguro covered the period 2000–7, but the authors projected their results to 2014; this showed there had been very little change in the relationship between gas and competing fuels since they completed the original research. Stern and Rogers (2014, 20–1).

Post 2010 LNG pricing in Asia: developing alternatives to JCC

The 2010–16 period: peak followed by collapse

As already noted, in 2011 two major events occurred in Asian LNG markets: oil prices rose above $100/bbl and the Fukushima nuclear accident created significant additional demand for LNG which had not been foreseen. The result was that LNG imports rose substantially, mainly in Japan but also in China and south-east Asian markets. But also (and discussed in Chapter 9) companies started to rely more on spot/flexible/short-term contracts to 'top up' their supply requirements.

Figure 8.3 shows that for the 2011–14 high oil price period, LNG import prices averaged $14–$18/MMBtu for Japan, Korea, and Taiwan; and $9–$14/MMBtu for China and India. By early 2016, prices for all importers were in the range of $6–$8/MMBtu and had moved much closer together. The collapse in oil prices, which started in mid-2014, resulted in prices in the $35–$60/bbl range in 2015, with corresponding JCC-linked LNG contract prices falling to $6–$10/MMBtu and spot prices at similar levels; by early 2016 spot prices were in the $4–5/MMBtu range. At the time of writing, it is too early to be clear about the longer-term supply and demand impact of the oil price collapse on Asian LNG markets, and the likely duration of this lower price range. However, the collapse of Asian spot gas prices at the beginning of 2014 (well ahead of long-term contract prices), together with a very substantial volume of supply from new projects starting up during 2016–18 (see Chapter 5), and lower than expected demand, especially in Asia (see Chapter 6), suggests that a lower LNG price environment could last for some years.

The period of oil prices in excess of $100/bbl resulted in significant financial burdens being placed on Asian buyers. China benefitted from advantageous, often 'fixed price', contracts with Australia and Indonesia from the early 2000s. By 2013, however, these had been subsumed in a portfolio of higher-priced JCC deals – resulting in average LNG import prices generally reaching levels of above $11/MMBtu.[19] In Japan, average spot and contract prices in this period were in the range $15–$17/MMBtu. With limited ability to pass these costs through to end-users, Japanese utilities began to make multi-billion dollar annual losses.[20] Calls for lower-priced LNG imports grew, because much lower prices in North America

---

[19] Also in 2014, the Tangguh contract price was revised upwards from $3.4 to $8.00/MMBtu which was (at that date) still at a discount to JCC-based prices. Corbeau et al. (2014, 31).

[20] Figure 7 in Rogers and Stern (2014, 16–17) shows that in fiscal years 2011 and 2012 losses for major utilities – excluding Tokyo Electric where Fukushima clean-up costs were immense – exceeded $10 bn per year.

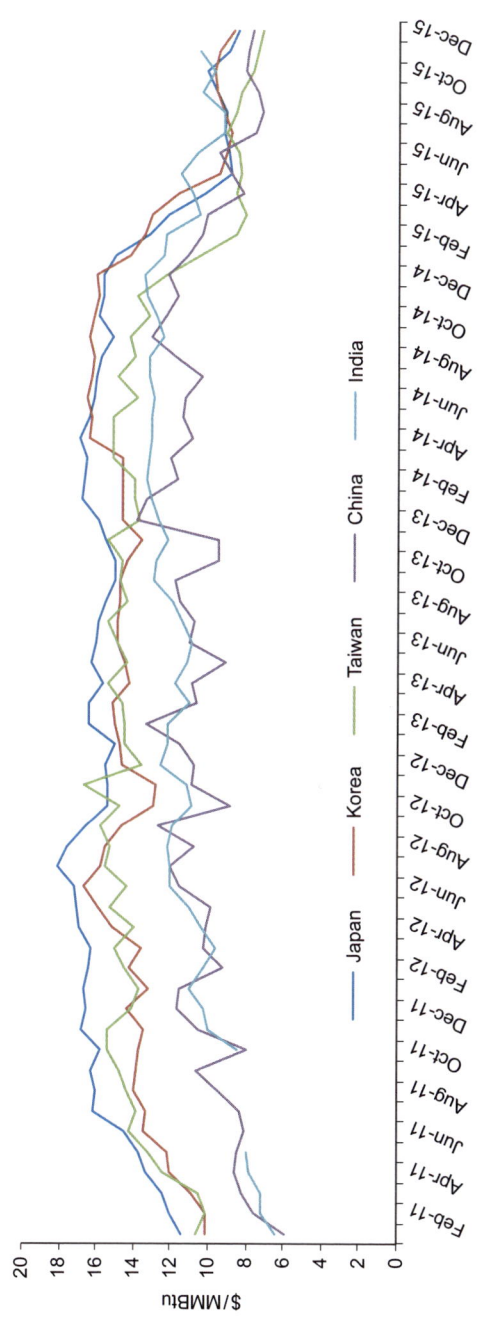

Figure 8.3: Average monthly Asian LNG import prices in Japan, Korea, Taiwan China, and India, 2010–15

Source: Argus Global LNG for respective years

478   *LNG Markets in Transition*

and Europe imposed a significant competitive disadvantage on Japanese industry, and triggered a search for alternatives to JCC pricing in Asia.

The oil price collapse had a profound effect on Asian LNG prices. Within a period of a year, the 'Asian premium' was greatly reduced – or entirely eliminated.[21] This lifted much of the financial pressure on Asian buyers, some of whom had seen their demand falter in the mid-2010s for a number of reasons, which probably included the effects of the high price levels in 2011–14. Partly as a result of this, there is some evidence that buyers may be over contracted in the late 2010s (see Chapter 6) and therefore have less reason to purchase short-term LNG cargoes, unless they are attractively priced (IEA 2015, 108–11). Problems could arise for long-term contracts if lower levels of demand persist and short-term LNG cargoes are available at prices significantly below those in long-term contracts for an extended period. This could result in buyers taking less than their long-term contract obligations, placing serious pressure on JCC pricing (we return to this below).[22] As a result, despite the reduction in urgency (due to lower price levels), the search for alternatives to JCC pricing has remained high on the agenda of buyers, and is confirmed by market developments.

US LNG export contract structures and the introduction of Henry Hub-based prices

The US LNG export projects – the first of which, at Sabine Pass in Louisiana, was commissioned in early 2016 – are based on a business model and a price formation mechanism which are radically different from those employed by traditional LNG projects. The US company Cheniere developed a business model to sell LNG to buyers on an FOB basis using the following price formula:

P(LNG) = 1.15 * HH + B

Where:

HH is the Henry Hub futures price on the New York Mercantile Exchange (NYMEX) for the month of lifting; 1.15 represents a 15 per cent premium over the Henry Hub price to cover the cost of acquisition, the fuel to run the LNG plant, and a margin;[23]

B is a constant agreed between Cheniere and each buyer.

---

[21] For an estimate of the Asian premium see note 50 below; JCC prices in late 2015 were similar to those in Europe and the USA, allowing for liquefaction and transportation costs.

[22] This is what happened in Europe post-2008 and was a catalyst for the move to hub prices. Stern and Rogers (2014, 11–20).

[23] There is anecdotal evidence that in other contracts this factor can be as high as 1.25.

Starting in 2011, Cheniere Energy signed 20 year contracts with six buyers (two of whom are in Asia) for LNG from the five trains of the Sabine Pass terminal, for a total of 20 mtpa. The constant B in the price formula increased from $2.25/MMBtu in the first contract with BG Group (now part of Shell), to $2.49/MMBtu for the second contract with the Spanish company Gas Natural Fenosa, and to $3/MMBtu for all other buyers and subsequent contracts. This translates into an annual fee which varies from $274 million to $723 million per year depending on the volume purchased; in each case a portion (11.5–15 per cent) of the fee is subject to inflation.[24] The fee provides Cheniere with the revenues to cover the capital and operating cost of the liquefaction plant. Cheniere's Corpus Christi terminal has the same commercial structure but with B set at $3.50/MMBtu for all buyers.[25] It is worth noting that there is no price review clause for the constant (tolling fee) in these contracts.

This arrangement (where Cheniere sources the gas and delivers it at the outlet of the liquefaction plant) is a 'modified tolling' model, in contrast to other US LNG projects, such as Sempra's Cameron terminal, which are 'pure tolling' models, where the buyers source their own gas and toll it through the plant (see Chapter 3). If offtakers choose not to take LNG they still incur the fixed fee.[26] US LNG offtake agreements can therefore be viewed as a 'call option' with the cost being the liquefaction tolling fee. If it takes delivery of LNG the offtaker will also incur the shipping and regas costs at the destination market. In many cases the offtaker is an aggregator/portfolio player who intends to sell cargoes on a flexible basis to markets offering the highest netback.

Some of the prospective US LNG export volumes have, however, been 're-sold' on medium to long-term contracts to (typically) Asian buyers on a pricing basis of acquisition plus shipping cost plus a premium – a fully built-up long-run marginal cost basis. The key price uncertainties to which such Asian buyers will be exposed are the variations in future Henry Hub and oil price levels.[27] Figure 8.4 provides an illustrative comparison of LNG prices in Asia indexed to JCC and Henry Hub.[28]

---

[24] Personal communication with Cheniere Energy.

[25] No commercial terms of other US LNG export projects are available but it is believed that the tolling fee for most projects is around $3.50/MMBtu.

[26] And will also need to give Cheniere notice that they do not need gas to be purchased, to avoid incurring a cancellation fee.

[27] In addition to price uncertainties there are also demand uncertainties. However, the FOB purchase contract allows buyers to have complete destination flexibility so that if they do not need the LNG they can sell it elsewhere.

[28] The comparison can only be illustrative because it will depend on: the slope and the constant in the specific JCC contract; the fixed fee in the Henry Hub contract; and the shipping cost from the USA to Asia which will depend on the Panama Canal tariff, the fuel cost, and the charter rate (here assumed to be $70–$80,000/day).

480 *LNG Markets in Transition*

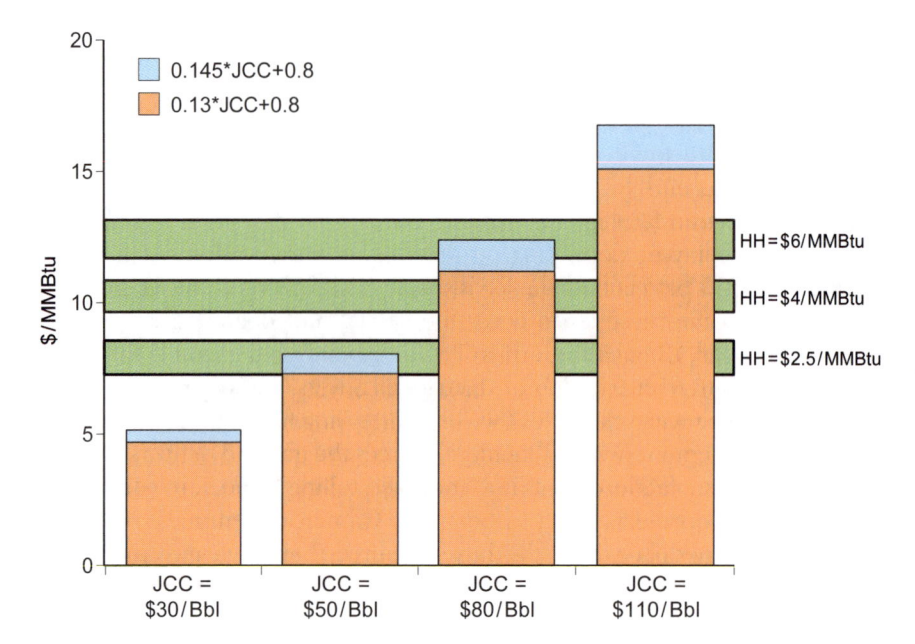

Figure 8.4: Illustrative prices of LNG in Asia indexed to JCC and Henry Hub at different price levels

Note: The figure shows JCC prices at two different slopes (13 per cent and 14.5 per cent) and a constant of $0.8/MMBtu. In the Henry Hub contract: the premium is assumed to be $1.15–$1.25, the fixed fees are assumed to be $2.50–$3.50/MMBtu, and the shipping cost from the USA to Asia $2.00–$2.50/MMBtu.

Source: Andy Flower.

Some very broad conclusions from Figure 8.4 are that:

- at any crude oil price below $50/bbl, JCC-based pricing (with a slope of 13 per cent or below) results in a lower delivered price than a formula based on a Henry Hub price below $2.50/MMBtu with full cost recovery;
- if the Henry Hub price rises to $4.00/MMBtu then oil prices will need to be around $80/bbl for US LNG to be competitive;
- at a crude oil price of $110/bbl, US LNG exports will be competitive even at a Henry Hub price of $6.00/MMBtu.

The 'full cost recovery' assumption is important as US buyers may be forced to regard the tolling/liquefaction (and perhaps also part of the shipping) fee as sunk costs; they will in any case be contractually required to take LNG even if they are not covering their full costs. However, by early 2016 when the first US cargoes were shipped from the Gulf coast, prices in both Asia and Europe were at levels which made it impossible for deliveries to those markets to recover full costs (but they could still make a positive margin over operating costs). Nevertheless, prolonged inability of offtakers to recover full costs plus a profit margin will have an important influence on whether contracts for additional US exports will be signed and on what terms. The idea has been advanced of an LNG Index base – separate from the Henry Hub price – that would provide a reference price for LNG shipped on an FOB basis from the Gulf of Mexico, based on the large new US LNG export volumes coming from that region starting in 2016 with rapid expansion up to 2020. Volumes would represent around 50 mtpa of supply volumes on an annual basis, contracted by a variety of market players. The coal industry developed a similar index with the globalCoal NEWC Index.

This illustrates a potential dilemma for Asian buyers: whether Henry Hub-related pricing (or in the future a Gulf of Mexico index) provides a lower-risk option than JCC-related contracts with inflexible linkage to crude oil prices. Evidence that Asian buyers refused to contract for North American LNG at JCC-related prices suggests that, at a minimum, contracts related to North American prices provide a way of diversifying price risk and, for the first time in many decades, an alternative to JCC (ICIS Heren, 2014, 12).

This rapid change in oil and gas prices illustrates the importance of differentiating between price *formation* and price *level*, which is a common failure in Asian price discussions. When the first US contracts were signed in 2011/12, Henry Hub prices were in the $2.75–$4.00/MMBtu range and oil prices were around $100/bbl. Figure 8.4 shows that at these Henry Hub prices, US LNG would be delivered to Asia at $8–$11/MMBtu, compared with JCC at $15–$16/MMBtu. Although the 2015 Henry Hub price was below (and in the latter part of the year substantially below) $3.00/MMBtu, the fall in oil prices had eroded the advantage of US LNG over long-term JCC-linked imports. Should oil prices remain in the $30–$50/bbl range for a prolonged period of time, this will cause problems for all offtakers of US LNG who have 20-year contracts to pay for LNG and capacity; and should Henry Hub prices rise, these problems will increase substantially. This illustrates the risks of purchasing long-term contract LNG at prices which are based on the fundamentals of the market where the gas is being produced, rather than on those of the market in which it is being sold.

482   *LNG Markets in Transition*

Asian spot-indexed prices

When short-term trading expanded significantly in Asia in the second half of the 2000s (see Chapter 9 and Figure 9.3), Asian buyers needed to offer prices that were higher than either Henry Hub or NBP (to attract cargoes away from the Atlantic Basin), and generally at a premium to all Japanese LNG imports (Flower and Liao, 2012, 353–6). As spot trade increased, a number of different Asian spot price indices started to be published, of which the four best known are:

- JKM (or Japan/Korea Marker) from Platts,
- EAX (East Asia Index) from ICIS,
- ANEA (North East Asia) from Argus and
- RIM, from RIM Intelligence.

Figure 8.5 shows JKM prices from the start of the series in 2009 to the end of 2015, with the UK NBP price for comparison.[29] Figure 8.5 also includes the Japanese Ministry of Economy, Trade and Industry's (METI) spot JOE prices, which have been reported since April 2014.[30] Each month METI reports a 'contract-based' price and an 'arrival-based' (or spot) price, but in some months (May and July 2015) fewer than two cargoes were received and therefore no data was published.[31] At the end of 2015, no contracts had been reported as having used the JOE price as a marker or index.

A related METI 2012 initiative to set up a gas futures market seemed doomed to fail without an underlying physical market.[32] In order to address this problem, in June 2014 a joint venture between the Tokyo Commodity Exchange (TOCOM) and Ginga Energy launched an OTC LNG platform for forward trading which they somewhat confusingly named JOE, with the intention that this should become a futures market (Seki, 2014, 8–9). This platform traded its first contract only in August 2015 and its level of activity since then is not known.[33]

---

[29] For a brief history of JKM since it started in 2009 see Box 2 in ten Kate et al. (2013, 67).
[30] JOE prices are reported every month on the METI website: www.meti.go.jp/english/statistics/sho/slng/.
[31] METI publishes the JOE spot price ' ... only in the cases where there are two or more reporters that imported spot LNG. If there is only one reporter or none at all, we will not publish a price'.
[32] Box 12 in Corbeau et al. (2014, 95).
[33] *International Gas Report*, 10 August 2015, 20.

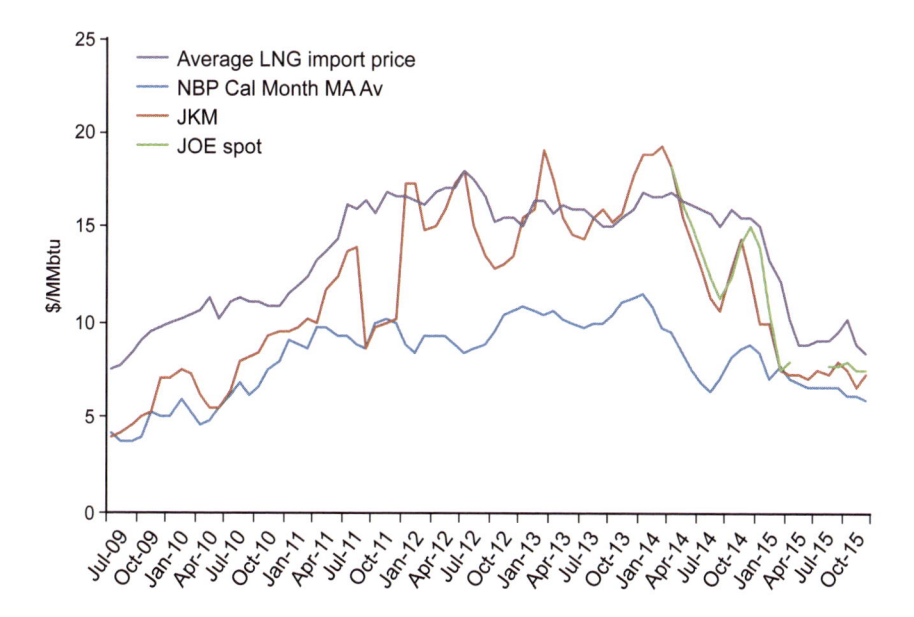

Figure 8.5: JKM, NBP, and JOE Prices, July 2009–December 2015

Notes: NBP is the calendar month-ahead average price. The JOE spot price 'refers to LNG that is traded on a cargo to cargo basis, and does not mean term contracts of LNG (so-called long, medium, short-term contracts). In addition, spot LNG for which the price is linked to a particular price index (for example Henry Hub or JKM) is excluded from these statistics. These statistics are for cargoes where the price is determined at the time of the contract (so-called 'fixed price').

Source: Platts for JKM and NBP, METI for JOE, Argus for average Japan LNG imports.

The Asian spot indices are based on a subset of the volumes in Figure 9.3 (see Figure 9.4 for the different streams of short-term trade) and liquidity has also been constrained by the physical size of LNG cargoes – in other words, on the 'lumpiness' of this market. Total spot trade in Asia in 2015 was 46.77 mt (or 6.15 bcf/d), and given that an average LNG cargo is 2.8 bcf of natural gas, even if all spot trades were reported, the deal frequency would be around two cargoes per day plus any re-trades (Rogers, 2015, 34). Moreover, Figure 8.5 shows significant seasonal price volatility during 2011–13. Sellers would, with some justification, claim that such spot indices lack depth, exhibit too much volatility, and could be influenced by individual players. But even though they have yet to become part of the pricing or indexation process in long-term LNG contracts, there is anecdotal evidence that these indices (especially JKM and RIM) have already become part of an index for some medium and shorter-term contracts, and also for tenders. With greater liquidity in short-term LNG markets, the importance of these spot indices could increase, particularly if the surge of new LNG supplies expected in the late 2010s and early 2020s results in substantially increased traded volumes.

Pricing at an Asian gas hub (or hubs) and market liberalization

From 2011 to 2014, the gap between Asian LNG prices and the hub-based gas prices in North America and Europe – the so-called 'Asian premium' – created active discussion around the idea of creating an Asian gas hub or hubs.[34] There are several major differences between the current position of Asian markets and the experiences of North America and Europe in relation to hub development. The most important is that both the latter were mature pipeline gas markets with (aside from particular regions such as New England and individual countries such as Spain) the ability to access large volumes of domestic and imported pipeline gas. By contrast, some large Asian gas markets (such as China and India) have relatively short histories, while most lack national pipeline networks. Moreover, due to a combination of geography and politics, it has proved very difficult for Asian gas markets to achieve substantial cross-border pipeline interconnections and this situation is likely to continue.[35] This means that key Asian markets – in particular Japan, Korea and Taiwan – are almost completely dependent on LNG imports.

Secondly, both North America and Europe created hubs as part of deregulation (in North America) and liberalization (in Europe) reforms which required several years (and decades in continental Europe) to develop. Three elements in this process proved crucial: first liberalization of the market allowed the entry of players other than the established utility companies. Second, pipeline transportation was separated from gas supply, allowing new entrants access to networks on the same terms as incumbents. And third, the practice whereby utilities could pass through gas purchase costs to their customers was abolished. The result was the emergence of gas-to-gas competition, and spot and futures pricing at market hubs. Similar reforms have been slow to develop in Asia, but over the next decade, this situation may change.

In the transition to hub prices, a major lesson to be learned from the North American and European gas markets is that the financial distress of

---

[34] Flower and Liao (2012, 366–7); ten Kate et al. (2013); Corbeau et al. (2014, 117–9); Stern and Rogers (2014, 38–41).

[35] With the exception of China and some south-east Asian countries, none of the major Asian LNG markets have pipeline connections with any other country.

major utilities is transformative. The multi-billion dollar losses incurred by Japanese utilities in the early 2010s (referred to above) indicated that pricing and contractual mechanisms would have to change. Japan has a tradition of commodities futures trading extending over 300 years and it remains by far the largest LNG importer in Asia (and the world). What has been lacking in enabling the formation of a liberalized and traded gas market, is a hands-off government approach, and effective unbundling of transportation from supply. Onshore gas infrastructure is regionally segmented (although there are some connections) and this is not counterbalanced by flexible LNG, as there is no workable third-party access (TPA) to LNG import terminals and pipeline infrastructure.

However, in 2015, legislation to liberalize the Japanese wholesale gas market, reinforcing access rights to LNG terminals and pipelines (which had existed but in a largely unworkable form) passed through the Diet. This means that complete liberalization of the retail market and access to LNG terminals for third parties will become law towards the end of 2017; separation of pipeline operations from supply is scheduled for April 2022 but only for the three major gas companies.[36] While much will depend on the detail of the regulatory framework which will be needed to enforce these measures, this should facilitate short-term trade which would provide the basis for a physical spot market on which a futures market could eventually be based. But only in 2016 did serious and detailed discussion begin to surface in Japan about the creation of a hub (Walker, 2015, 1–2).[37] A major milestone was the publication by the Japanese Ministry of Economy, Trade and Industry (METI) of an LNG Strategy at the G7 Ministerial Meeting that year setting out a roadmap to create an LNG hub in the early 2020s (METI, 2016).

As the largest Asian gas market, China has domestic production, pipeline imports from both Central Asia (mainly Turkmenistan) and Myanmar, deliveries from Russia which are contracted to begin by 2021, and a variety of LNG suppliers (Chen, 2012). The gas industry is dominated by three national oil companies and there has been no regulated access to pipeline or LNG infrastructure. But in 2015, plans were announced to create a new national company which would own the pipeline transportation and storage infrastructure (but not the LNG assets) of the three major companies (WGI, 2015, 4–5; Li, 2016, 7). The major price reform which started at the end of 2011 introduced the 'Shanghai hub', but in a gas context this was more akin to a city gate benchmark than a hub price

---

[36] Tokyo Gas, Osaka Gas, and Toho gas.
[37] For example from METI and JERA (the Tokyo Electric/Chubu Electric joint venture set up to purchase LNG.

(Chen, 2012 and 2015).[38] Shanghai could evolve into a physical gas hub, although there is a potential problem with this; the Shanghai Petroleum Exchange – on which gas and LNG is traded and prices are quoted – is majority owned by gas industry participants, which compromises its independence.

In its early stages, the Chinese reform looked more like a (traditional continental European) netback price based on alternative fuels than a traded market. Nevertheless, small quantities of LNG are being traded in Shanghai, and the first steps have been taken towards setting a price which reflects market fundamentals. A key step will be for each province to develop prices based on differential costs of supply, provided that rules and tariffs for third-party access and storage are developed and regulated effectively. If that happens, China might gradually move to hub-based pricing (at least for a portion of its supplies and facilitated by regional exchanges) in order to allow gas to flow to regions that have the highest demand and the greatest ability to pay (Chen, 2015).

Despite the many obstacles in China, the country is far ahead of India, where reforms have yet to resolve the fundamental issue of raising prices to levels which could create incentives to develop domestic gas and ensure that imported LNG is profitable to sell (Sen, 2015). Until the Indian government is willing to allow domestic prices to reflect a balance of domestic development costs and import prices, the prospect of any kind of genuine gas market, and therefore of hub development, will remain remote.

Korea's KOGAS is the world's largest LNG importer, and given the country's winter demand needs and lack of underground gas storage, it has been a substantial purchaser of short-term LNG and proactive in securing US LNG export volumes. However, the market is dominated by KOGAS, and although legal rights to access the company's three LNG terminals exist, no requests have been received and little progress has been made towards liberalizing the market (Corbeau et al., 2014, 95–6). Wholesale gas prices are regulated on an import cost pass-through basis, limiting incentives for spot trade and the creation of a hub.

Singapore was the first country in Asia to develop a competitive natural gas market and a trading hub (Ledesma, 2012, 276–8). It has pipeline connections with Malaysia and Indonesia, and is home to Asia's first open-access LNG terminal (SLNG), which started operations in 2013. With unbundling of gas transport activities, deregulation of the wholesale

---

[38] A citygate benchmark is a price derived from averaging prices of domestic and imported gas, and prices of fuels which compete with gas (in this case oil products and LPG), delivered at the citygate. This price is then periodically revised (taking into account changes in gas and alternative fuel prices) usually every 3–6 months. A hub price changes on a daily (and possibly within daily) basis depending on market conditions.

market, and trading teams from many of the major global LNG players already in place, it was the majority view that Singapore was the strongest candidate for Asia's first gas hub (Corbeau et al., 2014, 102).

In 2015, the Singapore SGX LNG Index Group launched the so called 'SLInG' (pronounced 'sling') price.[39] However, in 2014, Singapore gas demand was only 11 bcm, with LNG accounting for less than a quarter of that volume and, although there are plans to expand LNG receiving terminal capacity to more than 10 mt by 2020, this is a relatively small figure in relation to Asian trade.[40] Nevertheless, Singapore has first-mover advantage and by 2016 the first derivative contract based on the SLInG price had been reported.[41] Although it is difficult to see how the SLInG marker can develop sufficient liquidity to become a reference price across Asia, it could certainly become a south-east Asian regional price reference for small-scale LNG. With LNG trade in Malaysia, Indonesia, Thailand, and Vietnam set to increase significantly (see Chapter 6), SLInG could become established as a south-east Asian hub price, particularly given the calculation method published by the Singapore Exchange and the Energy Market Company which notes:

> By Singapore FOB, we mean a cargo in the vicinity of Singapore or any other Asian port … the price is intended to be an Asian proxy without specific consideration for the conditions in SLNG or any other terminal. (Singapore Exchange, 2015)

This suggests that Singapore FOB is intended to become a virtual LNG hub for south-east Asia.

Individual Asian markets will have different conceptions of how a national hub could be formed: a Japanese hub would be for LNG (one comprising LNG cargoes), whereas Shanghai will be a gas hub (for pipeline gas and LNG). The question then arises as to whether the hub should be physical like Henry Hub, or virtual like the NBP. Shanghai looks like developing a physical hub. In Japan, a physical hub may be easier to start with, but this could over time (and with greater national pipeline interconnection) become virtual. Singapore has already suggested that its SLInG price could represent the whole of south-east Asia which is, thus far, the only suggestion that a regional hub is under development, as opposed to under discussion.

---

[39] The initiative dates from 2014 but the price appears to have only become active in June 2015.

[40] Communal data; BP (2015, 23 and 28); Scott (2015).

[41] Reuters (2016). The importance of this contract is that it was for a very small volume (10,000 MMBtu), demonstrating the ability of the exchange to trade a small share of a standard physical LNG cargo.

Hybrid pricing

With great uncertainty surrounding the future of oil prices and the impact on LNG spot prices of very large volumes from new projects being delivered to markets, combined with uncertain demand, negotiations for some new contracts have been based on 'hybrid' pricing. The IEA has used this term to denote a mixture of Henry Hub and JCC for new projects in Mozambique and Canada, and also for contracts between portfolio sellers (Total and BG Group) with buyers in Singapore and China.[42] However, there seems to be no reason why hybrid pricing could not encompass different combinations of JCC, Henry Hub, NBP, and Asian spot – and (eventually) hub prices (Koyama, 2015). There are also suggestions that hybrid long-term contract pricing could encompass a mixture of these international prices and domestic indicators (such as electricity and coal prices), as well as possibly a fixed price element. The advantage of such hybrid pricing is that it spreads risk in the event that one element of the formula rises steeply due to the supply/demand dynamics of a particular fuel or market. The disadvantage is that it moves Asian LNG trade further away from what should be the ultimate aim: a price that reflects gas supply/demand conditions in the market into which the LNG is being sold. Thus hybrid pricing can be regarded as a transitional process – allowing the hedging of exposure until existing long-term contracts expire and the entire price formula can be revisited. Arguably, the way of dealing with price uncertainty is not to use an average of a large number of international and domestic gas (and other fuel) prices with the aim of hedging risk in an unfocused way, but to insert review clauses into contracts which can then periodically adjust prices to changing market conditions.

Anecdotal evidence suggests that buyers are also using average prices of LNG imported into Japan – so-called 'JLC prices' – for short-term contracts. Figure 8.5 shows average import prices compared with JKM and JOE spot prices over the period 2009–15. Although an average import price may provide a better hedge against oil-related prices than a hybrid price composed of several indicators, given the dominance of JCC in long-term contracts, for most of the 2009–15 period, it resulted in higher values than spot prices.

Price review

In contrast to the situation in continental Europe, where long-term gas contracts always included regular price reviews, such review clauses were not included in most long-term LNG contracts in Asia until the 1990s.[43]

---

[42] Table 4 in Corbeau et al. (2014, 44), ibid., 116.
[43] For an overview of price review see Levy (2014).

In European contracts, the most usual price review period is three years, but in Japanese contracts it has been typically every five years – and in some cases every 10 years – since the early 1990s. The use of an applicable range, under which the parties agreed 'to meet and discuss in good faith' the pricing formula when JCC prices moved out of an agreed oil price range, resulted in many price renegotiations being triggered after 2003. Experience in the other established markets – Korea and Taiwan – has been different, with relatively few price reviews taking place and only limited modifications to prices being implemented.[44]

Negotiations with Japanese buyers have often been protracted, for example the pricing provisions for Abu Dhabi's ADGAS project took over six years to resolve (Dargin and Flower, 2011, 460). However, the delivery and receipt of LNG has not been interrupted, even when the parties have been far apart in their negotiations. Furthermore, despite the existence of arbitration clauses in many long-term contracts, there is no public record of a price dispute in an Asian LNG contract having been referred to arbitration.[45] This contrasts with the situation in the Atlantic Basin where, post-2008, price review arbitrations have become relatively common events in relation to both pipeline and LNG contracts. In particular, the case of Atlantic LNG (sales of gas from Trinidad and Tobago to the USA and Spain) where, as a result of the price being referred to arbitration, the tribunal fundamentally changed the price formula in the long-term contract (Griffin, 2014, 143–4). However, the Atlantic LNG contract was precedent-setting in that it combined sales to a gas-to-gas competitive market in the USA with an oil-linked contract market in Spain.[46]

Although contracts finalized in recent years with Asian buyers have generally included price reviews that are triggered after a set number of years from the start of deliveries, and at regular intervals thereafter, they typically say very little about the factors that will be taken into account in any resulting renegotiation. Most review clauses include rather general language along the following lines:[47]

---

[44] Much of this paragraph is taken from Flower and Liao (2012, 352–3).

[45] In 2015, South Korea and Taiwan were not listed among the states which had ratified the 1958 New York Convention on the Recognition and Enforcement of Arbitral Awards. (Website of New York Arbitration Convention: www.newyorkconvention.org/contracting-states/list-of-contracting-states.)

[46] As a result, the pricing clause is unusual and a tribunal would have been compelled to create a different formula even if Atlantic LNG had won its case. Shepherd and Ball (2006).

[47] These phrases are taken from Griffin (2014a) which has a substantial legal discussion of good faith, reasonable endeavours, and other issues in LNG contracts written under English law.

> If either party considers that the Contract Price no longer represents a price appropriate for long term sale and purchase of LNG ... then [the parties should] meet together to hold discussions in good faith with an objective of agreeing appropriate amendments ... in order to take account of such changed circumstances and ... use all reasonable endeavours to agree appropriate amendments ... which are fair and justified ...

These generalities would make it very difficult for an arbitral tribunal to make a ruling on how prices should be revised. The outcome of price revision negotiations has generally been retention of the oil price linkage with changes to the constant and, less frequently, to the slope, rather than a move to a fundamentally different approach, such as the introduction of a full or partial linkage to alternative indices.

There are a number of different options which Asian buyers could consider in relation to price reviews; these could include clauses which would prevent them having to pay prices higher than those being charged to other regional buyers (or other customers of the same buyer), or the ability to redirect cargoes for which they have no immediate market requirement (Corbeau et al., 2014, 112–3). An indication of this was seen at the end of 2015 when India's Petronet was able to negotiate a price reduction of around 50 per cent, by changing the indexation of its LNG price from a 60 month average of the JCC price to a three month average.[48] Greater flexibility of offtake and, specifically, the abolition of destination clauses (which prevent buyers from selling contracted LNG elsewhere), is also something for which Asian buyers have long campaigned.[49]

However, a different order of difficulty would be involved in writing – and getting suppliers to accept – a price review clause which would allow for a complete change of price formation in the event of a market hub being created in either the buyer's country or the region. Given that, over the life of a new 25-year contract, large-scale spot trading and market hubs are likely to emerge in Asia, it will be increasingly important for contracts to include specific price review provisions which allow for such circumstances, although this is likely to be resisted by sellers embarking on

---

[48] A very important indicator from this episode is the increasing difficulty experienced by sellers in insisting that long-term contract price terms should be honoured if cheaper spot cargos are available. Petronet also persuaded Qatargas to set aside a $1 bn take-or-pay penalty which it had incurred by purchasing cheaper spot cargoes of LNG, rather than its contractual quantities, although the importer will be required to take these quantities in future years. Katakey and Chakraborty (2015); Financial Express (2015).

[49] For a statement calling for the removal of destination clauses in Asia see IEEJ (2015). For an account of the process by which they were removed in Europe see Chapter 4 of Talus (2011).

new baseload export projects with uncertain cost profiles.

Interestingly, US LNG contracts do not seem to include any wording that relates to price renegotiation; this would be useful in the case that companies, having contracted US LNG, find themselves in financial difficulty because they are selling LNG on the basis of variable costs and have to consider the liquefaction fee as a sunk cost. The length of time for which some companies could continue with such a financial burden may be questionable.

Pricing and 'security'

Before concluding this chapter, it is important to make the connection which exists, particularly in the culture of Asian LNG buyers and their governments, between pricing and security of supply. Because of the near-total dependence of Japan, Korea, and Taiwan on imported LNG, a culture of security of supply has emerged in which their governments became very much involved (see Chapter 1); this is somewhat different from the position in other countries. This is a major reason why Asian buyers have been willing to pay a premium for LNG (and it was also a major reason for the inclusion of destination clauses in long-term contracts). This strategy has been very successful over the past several decades in ensuring secure gas supplies for countries (and companies) with physically isolated gas markets lacking easily available alternatives to LNG, but it came at a cost.[50]

Fundamental changes in long-term gas contracts and price formation are interpreted by many in Asia as a threat to security of supply. While this is not necessarily correct – since those offering the highest price/netback to the seller should always be able to attract as many LNG cargoes as they need – a change from the traditional long-term contract/JCC/destination clause model creates uncertainty. Shorter-term contracts with much more rapid price adjustments introduce unpredictability and increase the possibilities of short-term price volatility. They may also fail to provide a sufficient financial basis for investments in new (particularly greenfield) LNG projects with the risk that, by the time market prices begin to rise (as the supply/demand balance tightens), long construction lead times will then create shortage and high prices, leading to the familiar 'boom and bust' commodity cycle.[51] These are important reasons why there has been

---

[50] Corbeau et al. (2014, 20–5) suggests that the premium to European prices paid by Japan was around 20 per cent in the early 2000s, but it widened substantially post 2010.

[51] With around five years being needed to build an onshore greenfield liquefaction facility, unless demand can be foreseen and investments can be taken ahead of actual requirements, it will be difficult to avoid the traditional commodity cycle.

resistance to a move away from traditional contract and pricing models. During a period of lower oil prices, surplus supplies, and greater competitive pressures on utilities, this position may change as demand for flexibility increases (see Chapter 9). But reluctance to change, and aversion to taking any significant risk in relation to supply security remain much greater issues in Asia than in the rest of the gas world, and these factors should not be underestimated as obstacles to market evolution.

Summary and conclusions

Market (hub)-based gas prices have been dominant in North America for the past quarter century. The UK has had a similar mechanism for nearly 20 years and, since 2008, major continental European gas markets have made a transition away from oil-linked to market prices. But in all of the major gas markets of these regions, prices were related to (domestic or imported) pipeline gas, with LNG as a marginal source of supply. The exception is Spain where – due to the influence of LNG and lack of pipeline links to the rest of Europe – oil-related gas prices remained dominant, largely due to Asian LNG prices remaining tied to the traditional JCC crude oil-related formula which was created in the 1980s and has changed relatively little since then.

By the late 2000s, the price levels created by these different formation mechanisms had begun to create a consensus that a 'global gas market' was developing, and with it a global gas price. This seemed persuasive for a period of about six months up to the middle of 2008 when Henry Hub, European (contract and spot), and Japanese LNG import prices came together. But in the early 2010s, the spread increased to the point where Asian LNG prices were six to seven times higher than Henry Hub (Figure 8.1). This did not necessarily mean that no price connection between regions existed, only that the dynamics of regional gas supply and demand, industry structure, and commercial contractual arrangements, remained fundamentally different.

Post 2010: a coincidence of 'Black Swan' events

The coming together of regional prices in 2008 can be seen as a coincidence, and a further coincidence of events then drove prices apart during 2010–14. None of these events could have been foreseen:

- shale (oil and) gas development in North America drove gas prices down and held them down below $5/MMBtu (and, for long periods, below $3/MMBtu);

- oil prices rose above $100/bbl, remaining at and above that level until mid-2014;

- high oil prices, combined with the impact of recession and liberalization, forced European gas markets to move rapidly away from oil-linked and towards market pricing;

- the Fukushima nuclear disaster of March 2011 and the subsequent closure of Japanese nuclear plants (plus some problems in the Korean nuclear sector and rapid economic growth in China) created far higher demand for LNG in Asia than had been anticipated.

Not only did these events result in very high prices for Asian LNG buyers, they created a mindset among sellers that these buyers would always be willing to pay $15–$18/MMBtu for LNG, and would have no other option but to do so. This in turn created unrealistic producer expectations, particularly in relation to new projects for which costs had risen sharply in the late 2000s and early 2010s (see Chapter 4). Moreover, the regional gas price spread created by these events would ultimately prove unsustainable.

Viewing the 2010–14 period from a perspective of less than two years – as this book is being completed – not only could these events not have been predicted, but the conditions they created are unlikely to be repeated. Starting in mid-2014, the decline in oil prices and a commensurate decline in Pacific Basin LNG prices, meant that by the end of 2015 regional prices had substantially converged to the point where, taking transportation costs into account, they could be said to be reasonably (although certainly not perfectly) aligned. Post-2014 – with an apparent slowdown in the Chinese economy and the expectation that some Japanese nuclear stations would restart (see Chapter 6) – doubt had also been cast on projections of continued high Asian LNG demand growth rates.

Over the period 2008–15, global LNG trade grew by more than 40 per cent and projects currently under construction mean that it will expand by a similar percentage by 2020. This huge increase in global trade (and the potential for a similar expansion of short-term trade) means that it is difficult to imagine similar extreme and enduring conditions which could lead to a repeat of the regional price differentials seen during 2010–14. However, this might happen if JCC-indexed gas prices were to diverge substantially from spot and short-term LNG prices (due to some future combination of an oil price increase or spot price collapse), at which point Asian buyers would once again be exposed due to their JCC-based long-term contracts. To avoid this risk, Asian buyers would need to move their long-term contracts to reflect market (supply/demand) prices which, following experience elsewhere in the world, would require short-term trading at national hubs or a regional hub. Another potential scenario explained in Chapter 9 is that only part of the volumes in contracts reaching expiry would be extended, increasing the availability of spot cargoes. When added to uncommitted LNG volumes, and flexible US LNG, this would increase the volumes of spot and short-term LNG, providing further encouragement for the creation of national price references (and perhaps eventually a regional reference) in Asia.

Challenges to market pricing of LNG in Asia

The fall in oil and LNG prices post-2014 eliminated the 'Asian premium' and gave buyers some breathing space to consider their options. As a result of the 2010–14 experience, Asian buyers had already been forced to consider a number of different options – including spot indexation and pricing at different hubs – one or more of which could be utilized in Asia. During that period, a number of tolling (and modified tolling) contracts were signed for imports of US LNG which would result in Asian buyers paying a Henry Hub price plus costs of liquefaction and transportation. Early negotiations on new long-term contracts for East African and Canadian LNG were reported to have included a 'hybrid' JCC/Henry Hub price, but this may no longer be the case. While Henry Hub prices looked very attractive in comparison with JCC when oil prices were at $100/bbl, the benefit is very much reduced, and may be reversed, at oil prices below $50/bbl; this highlights the importance for Asian buyers of focusing on price formation as opposed to price level, and on supply/demand fundamentals in their national markets as opposed to the fundamentals in US (Henry Hub) and European (NBP/TTF) markets.

In 2015/16, lower oil price levels, combined with anticipation of a global LNG surplus in the late 2010s, reduced the urgency to change traditional JCC pricing. But to protect against future divergence of long-term contract and spot prices, buyers will need to develop other price formation options. While it can be very difficult to agree to change a price in an existing contract, particularly if a price review clause is either absent or couched in very general terms, the expiry of existing (or the negotiation of new) contracts provides an opportunity to rethink the price formation mechanism. Japanese and Korean buyers have long-term contracts involving significant volumes of LNG which will expire in the early to mid-2020s (see Chapter 9); whether (and when) they will need to sign new long-term contracts will depend on demand developments as well as on their appetite for flexibility (see Chapter 6).

Given the anticipated surplus of global supply development in the late 2010s, the most immediate outcome is likely to be a much more active short-term traded market with cargoes potentially available at prices significantly below JCC levels. Short-term contracts have already been signed which include Asian spot indices as part of the price formula. A deep and liquid short-term market would provide the physical basis for creating a hub reference price for LNG in Asia. But at the time of writing, the prospect of any of the major Asian LNG import markets liberalizing and establishing a hub with sufficient liquidity to become a credible price reference for Asian LNG trade only seems likely in a five to ten year time frame. Singapore has been a front runner in this process, and although its SLInG price seems unlikely to become a reference for long-term contracts across the entire Pacific region, it could become a credible regional pricing reference for the growing traded volumes in south-east Asia.

Of the other candidates for an Asian hub, China is the furthest advanced, with reforms well on the way towards establishing a credible city gate supply/demand gas price in Shanghai. In time, this will become a reference for all long-term gas contracts with Chinese buyers and – given the growing importance of the Chinese gas market in Asia – will have an influence on regional pricing. Liberalization of access to pipelines, with the expectation that a national pipeline company (independent of the major supply companies) could be created in 2016, will be an important step in this direction; although neither mandatory access to pipelines or LNG terminals is yet part of an enforceable regulatory framework. In Japan, the passage of legislation to liberalize the market will create the conditions for hub pricing, but probably not until the early 2020s, and the government's May 2016 LNG strategy confirmed this had become official policy. Korea is much less well advanced in this respect.

Therefore the answer to the question posed at the start of this chapter – as to whether Asian LNG contracts will undergo a transition similar to that seen in North America and Europe (from oil-linked to market pricing) – is that this is highly probable, but it is likely to take up to a decade to achieve in most countries. Aside from the inertia created by the longevity of the current commercial long-term contract framework, the difficulty of converting existing JCC-based contracts to any other price formation mechanism will be a major barrier to change. Events could be accelerated by a change in market conditions (if spot prices were to fall significantly below long-term contract prices for a protracted period of time); this was illustrated, at the end of 2015, by the conversion of the price in an Indian long-term contract from a 60 month, to a three month, average of JCC prices.

The emergence of a much larger and more liquid short-term traded market would be a catalyst for a more radical change in long-term contract LNG prices – to the use of spot indices and, eventually, to hub creation.

This interim five to ten year period is likely to see the evolution of hybrid pricing with short – and perhaps also longer – term contracts based on a mixture of hub (Henry Hub, NBP/TTF), spot (JKM, Argus, RIM, ICIS), and traditional JCC prices. A potentially better alternative are prices based on an average price of all LNG (under long-term and spot contracts) imported into the relevant market, such as JLC for Japan and KLC for Korea. However, all of these can be regarded as unsatisfactory transitional measures from which a price mechanism will eventually evolve which will reflect supply/demand conditions on a flexible basis, and will be accepted by the majority of Asian LNG players.

This in turn raises the question of whether such a transition can be achieved without the contractual discontinuities and litigation which have been seen in Europe and North America. Liberalization of access to LNG terminals and pipelines could allow new players to import cargoes at prices which would significantly undercut those of established utilities under long-term JCC-linked contracts. With demand not increasing as fast as expected, and perhaps falling in Japan and Korea, the established utilities could find themselves losing market share to new entrants and struggling to meet their take-or-pay commitments.

At that point, established utilities would be forced to offer lower prices to prevent their customers switching to new entrants, while being contractually required to continue to take-or-pay for minimum volumes at JCC-linked prices. A consequence of such developments could be severe financial hardship, and possibly litigation launched by buyers. This would be revolutionary in a region with no culture or tradition of long-term gas contract litigation, but in North American and European markets it has been a catalyst for (painful) change. Buyers must hope that by the time they face the possibility of exposure to such risks, sufficient long-term contracts will have expired for them to be able to renegotiate (or terminate) the volume and price terms of their contracts, in order to ensure a 'smooth transition' to a new contractual status quo. The alternative would be a 'contractual train wreck' of litigation with uncertain outcomes.[52]

---

[52] Rogers and Stern (2014, 48–9), advanced the following scenarios for Asian long-term gas contracts: 'Smooth Contractual Transition: new contracts start to be signed with a mix of oil, hub and spot prices (perhaps from various regions of the world), with price review clauses which mandate renegotiation of prices after a number of years, anticipating the creation of an Asian hub or hubs. There are challenges to existing contract prices, but renegotiations result in adjustments which are tolerable for both buyers and sellers with no fundamental changes or litigation ... Contractual Train Wreck: [where buyers'] losses from existing contracts become financially untenable and [they] demand price renegotiations; these are resisted by suppliers ... Litigation ensues with unpredictable results.'

During this transitional period, it will become increasingly obvious (if it is not already) that traditional JCC pricing has reached the end of its useful life and will be progressively replaced by mechanisms that are more market related. A transition away from JCC, and towards market, pricing in Asia will promote regional price convergence and hence a reasonable approximation of a 'global LNG price' (taking transportation costs into account). Signals in this direction will come from: progress in liberalization of national gas markets, the price terms agreed in new (and extensions of existing) contracts, and whether short-term trade can expand to the point where it becomes sufficiently liquid to constitute a credible price reference for long-term contracts, prior to national hubs being created in Asia.

BIBLIOGRAPHY

BP (2015). *BP Statistical Review of World Energy 2015*, London: BP.

Chen, M. (2015). 'China's Pricing Reform: how far and how fast?', *Oxford Energy Forum* No. 101, 17–19.

Chen, M.X. (2012). 'Gas Pricing in China', Chapter 10 in Stern, J.P. (ed.), *The Pricing of Internationally Traded Gas*, Oxford: OUP/OIES.

Corbeau, A.-S., Braaksma, A., Hussin, F., Yagoto, Y., and Yamamoto, T. (2014). *The Asian Quest for LNG in a Globalising Market*, IEA Partner Country Series, Paris: OECD/IEA. www.iea.org/publications/freepublications/publication/PartnerCountrySeriesTheAsianQuestforLNGinaGlobalisingMarket.pdf.

Dargin, J. and Flower, A. (2011). 'The UAE Gas Sector', Chapter 13 in Fattouh, B. and Stern, J.P. (eds.), *Natural Gas Markets in the Middle East and North Africa*, Oxford: OUP/OIES.

Financial Express (2015). 'Qatar's RasGas to waive $1 bn penalty on Petronet LNG Ltd for lower gas offtake', *The Financial Express*, 23 November. www.financialexpress.com/article/economy/qatars-rasgas-to-waive-1-bn-penalty-on-petronet-lng-ltd-for-lower-gas-offtake/169431/.

Flower, A. and Liao, J. (2012). 'LNG pricing in Asia', Chapter 11 in Stern, J.P. (ed.), *The Pricing of Internationally Traded Gas*, Oxford: OUP/OIES.

Foss, M.M. (2012). 'North American Gas Pricing', Chapter 3 in Stern, J.P. (ed.), *The Pricing of Internationally Traded Gas*, Oxford: OUP/ OIES.

Griffin, P. (2014a), 'A New Approach to LNG Price Reopeners in Asian Markets?', Allen & Overy LLP, 2014.

Griffin, P. (2014). 'The Future for Price Reviews', in Levy, M. (ed.), *Gas Price Arbitrations: a practical handbook*, Globe Business Publishing.

Griffin, P. ed. (2012). *Liquefied Natural Gas: the law and business of LNG* (2nd Edition), Globe Business Publishing.

Heather, P. (2010). 'The Evolution and Functioning of the Traded Gas Market in Great Britain', OIES Working Paper NG 44, Oxford Institute for Energy Studies, August. www.oxfordenergy.org/2010/08/the-evolution-and-functioning-of-the-traded-gas-market-in-britain/.

Heather, P. (2015). 'The Evolution of European Traded Gas Hubs', OIES Working Paper NG 104, Oxford Institute for Energy Studies, December. www.oxfordenergy.org/2015/12/the-evolution-of-european-traded-gas-hubs/.

Honoré, A. (2011). 'The Spanish Gas Market: demand trends post-recession and consequences for the industry', OIES Working Paper NG 55, Oxford Institute for Energy Studies, July. www.oxfordenergy.org/wpcms/wp-content/uploads/2011/08/NG_552.pdf.

ICIS Heren (2014). 'North America: US developers line up for project sanction', in *Focus: The LNG Outlook for 2014*, ICIS Heren Global LNG Markets 2 January, 2014. www.icis.com/resources/news/2014/01/02/9739206/focus-the-lng-outlook-for-2014/.

IEA (1996). *Asia Gas Study*, Paris: OECD/International Energy Agency.

IEA (2008). *Natural Gas Market Review 2008*, Paris: OECD/International Energy Agency.

IEA (2015). *Medium-Term Gas Market Report: Market Analysis and Forecasts to 2020*, OECD/International Energy Agency.

IEEJ (2015). 'What need to be done in the changing LNG market? – Recommendations for a better functioning LNG market in Asia', LNG Producer–Consumer Conference 2015, 16 September, 2015, Tokyo, Japan, http://aperc.ieej.or.jp/file/2015/9/18/S3-6+Mr.+Masakazu+Toyoda_IEEJ.pdf.

IGU (2015). *Wholesale Gas Price Survey – 2016 Edition: a global review of price formation mechanisms 2005–2015*, International Gas Union. www.igu.org/sites/default/files/node-page-field_file/IGU%20Whole%20Sale%20Gas%20Price%20Survey%20Report%20%202015%20Edition.pdf.

Katakey, R. and Chakraborty, D. (2015). 'Petronet LNG breaks Qatar contract to gain from low spot prices', Live mint, 30 September. www.livemint.com/Companies/Lk2NOm5DvuqeqxTCcKD19J/Petronet-LNG-breaks-Qatar-contract-to-gain-from-low-spot-pri.html.

Koyama, K. (2015). 'Japanese LNG import prices – are alternatives to JCC evolving', *Oxford Energy Forum* No. 101, 19–22.

Ledesma, D. (2012). 'Pricing of Pipeline Gas and LNG in South East Asia', Chapter 8 in Stern, J.P. (ed.), *The Pricing of Internationally Traded Gas*, Oxford: OUP/OIES.

Ledesma, D., Henderson, J., and Palmer, N. (2014). 'The Future of Australian LNG Exports: will domestic challenges limit the development of future LNG export capacity?', OIES Working Paper NG 90, Oxford Institute for Energy Studies, September.

Levy, M. (2014). 'Drafting an effective price review clause', in Levy, M. (ed.), *Gas Price Arbitrations: a practical handbook*, Globe Business Publishing, 9–20.

Li, X. (2016). 'China's NOCs stall on third party terminal access', *Interfax Natural Gas Daily*, 26 January 2016.

METI 'Spot LNG price statistics', Ministry of Economy, Trade and Industry, Japan. www.meti.go.jp/english/statistics/sho/slng/.

METI (2016). *Strategy for LNG Market Development: creating flexible LNG market and developing an LNG trading hub in Japan*, METI, 2 May 2016. http://www.meti.go.jp/english/press/2016/pdf/0502_01b.pdf.

Miyamoto, A. and Ishiguro, C. (2009). 'A New Paradigm for Natural Gas Pricing in Asia: a perspective on market value', OIES Working Paper NG28, Oxford Institute for Energy Studies, February. www.oxfordenergy.org/2009/02/a-new-paradigm-for-natural-gas-pricing-in-asia-a-perspective-on-market-value/.

Petrovich, B. (2013). 'European Gas Hubs – How Strong is Price Correlation?', OIES Working Paper NG79, OIES, October. https://www.oxfordenergy.org/wpcms/wp-content/uploads/2013/10/NG-79.pdf.

Petrovich, B. (2014). 'European Gas Hubs Price Correlation: Barriers to Convergence?', OIES Working Paper NG91, Oxford Institute for Energy Studies, September. www.oxfordenergy.org/2014/09/european-gas-hubs-price-correlation-barriers-to-convergence/.

Relihan, T. (2015). 'Study says a new pipeline is not necessary, lays out alternatives', *The Recorder*, 20 August 2015.

Reuters (2016). 'Trafigura trades first Singapore derivatives contract', 25 January 2016. www.reuters.com/article/singapore-sgx-lng-idUSL3N15939T.

Rogers, H.V. (2012). 'The Interaction of LNG and Pipeline Gas Pricing: does greater connectivity equal globalisation?', Chapter 12 in Stern, J.P. (ed.), *The Pricing of Internationally Traded Gas*, Oxford: OUP/OIES.

Rogers, H.V. (2015). 'The Impact of Lower Gas and Oil Prices on Global Gas and LNG Markets', OIES Working Paper NG 99, Oxford Institute for Energy Studies, July. https://www.oxfordenergy.org/wpcms/wp-content/uploads/2015/07/NG-99.pdf.

Rogers, H.V. and Stern, J. (2014). 'Challenges to JCC Pricing in Asian LNG Markets', OIES Working Paper NG 81, OIES, Oxford Institute for Energy Studies, February. https://www.oxfordenergy.org/wpcms/wp-content/uploads/2014/02/NG-81.pdf.

Scott, C. (2015). 'Singapore – moving towards being a gas hub?', *Interfax Global Gas Analytics*, October 2015, 27–8.

Seki, R, (2014). *TOCOM Commodity Market Seminar*, https://www.tocom.or.jp/news/2014/documents/20140716_TOCOMPresentation.pdf.

Sen, A. (2015). 'Gas Pricing Reform in India: will it transform the gas landscape?', *Oxford Energy Forum* No. 101, 15–17.

Shepherd, R. and Ball, J. (2006). 'Liquefied natural gas from Trinidad & Tobago: the Atlantic LNG project', Chapter 9 in Victor, D.G., Jaffe, A.M., and Hayes, M.H., (eds.), *Natural Gas and Geopolitics: From 1970 to 2040*, Cambridge: CUP.

Singapore Exchange (2015). *Calculation Method for the FOB Singapore LNG Index Group ('SLInG')*. https://www.emcsg.com/f1415,99779/Calculation_Methodology_for_SLInG_FOB_Singapore.pdf.

Stern, J (2012). 'The Pricing of Gas in International Trade: an historical survey', Chapter 2 in Stern, J.P. (ed.), *The Pricing of Internationally Traded Gas*, Oxford: OUP/OIES.

Stern, J. and Rogers, H.V. (2014). 'The Dynamics of a Liberalised European Gas Market: key determinants of hub prices, and roles and risks of major players', OIES Working Paper NG 94, OIES, December. www.oxfordenergy.org/wpcms/wp-content/uploads/2014/12/NG-94.pdf.

Talus, K. (2011). *Vertical Natural Gas Transportation Capacity, Upstream Commodity Contracts and EU Competition Law*, Netherlands: Kluwer Law International.

ten Kate, W., Varró, L., and Corbeau, A.-S. (2013). *Developing a Natural Gas Trading Hub in Asia: obstacles and opportunities*, IEA Partner Country Series, Paris: OECD/IEA.

Walker, A. (2015). `Liberalised Asian Markets Seek Gas Indexing', *Interfax Natural Gas Daily*, 15 March 2016.

WGI (2015). 'China Pushes Competitive Gas Market', *World Gas Intelligence*, 19 August 2015.

CHAPTER 9

LNG CONTRACTS AND FLEXIBILITY

Anne-Sophie Corbeau

Introduction

Long-term contracts have long played a significant part in the financing of large capital projects (such as large pipeline projects worth billions of dollars); they have also been at the heart of the LNG industry since its inception, underpinning large financial investments along the LNG value chain. However, questions are now being asked about their future:

Would buyers accept the need to source larger quantities of their LNG supplies directly from the market?

In the wake of the rapid changes on global LNG markets, could long-term contracts disappear?

Issues such as: the growth of spot trading, the emergence of greater flexibility in the LNG value chain since 2000, and pressure on oil indexation have prompted such lines of inquiry. Many elements of the initial LNG business model (a single liquefaction plant linked to a few regasification plants through a long-term, inflexible, and oil-indexed contract) have evolved over time. While the industry — both buyers and sellers — has accepted a greater degree of flexibility, LNG suppliers are only grudgingly adjusting to the idea that gas could be priced on its own merit and not by means of indexation to another commodity (see Chapter 8).

Nonetheless, one stronghold remains: the long-term contract is still quite inseparable from the financing of the key (and most expensive) part of the LNG value chain, the liquefaction plant (Chapter 3). Despite alterations to the initial business model, long-term contracts have almost always covered a significant part of a gas liquefaction plant. To date, only one project has gone ahead without any long-term contract explicitly attached to it: the Gassi Touil LNG project in Algeria. Some projects, such as Oman LNG, have also moved ahead before all the LNG volumes were fully contracted. Meanwhile, a more recent trend has been for LNG liquefaction project sponsors to resell LNG to one of their affiliated trading arms, which will then market it to places where they have regasification capacity, at a time that they wish, or where trading hubs and third-party access (TPA) make it easy for them to sell the LNG at a spot-indexed price. Although this practice does not formally link a seller to an 'end-user', it is still a form of long-term contract. This approach, as well as a growing role for aggregators in US LNG, may precipitate changes in the overall market, by increasing quantities of spot LNG.

First, it is crucial to understand why the LNG industry maintains that long-term contracts must continue, while in the oil sector very large projects can proceed without them. A series of changes over the last 15 years in global gas markets have challenged the model's inflexibility and its oil-indexed prices, but have not yet pushed the LNG industry to a tipping point. The next five years will bring even more changes that individually would not be disruptive, but taken together with, and building upon, the challenges already established, may lead to a great reconfiguration of the LNG industry.

To aid a better appreciation of these changes, we analyse how LNG trade has evolved over the past 15 years with respect to flexibility, understanding the changes both on the supplier and buyer sides. Based on this analysis, we consider how spot and short-term LNG trade could evolve in the future and what the implications may be for the future of long-term contracts.

What makes LNG different from oil and coal?

The narrative of the LNG industry is that high costs (and high debt), coupled with long payback periods, require high payment security and secure finance. Initially, the LNG industry was in the hands of a few companies with deep pockets (Iniss, 2004). Long-term contracts – or sales and purchase agreements (SPA) – linked buyers and sellers to ensure adequate cash flows for the project. To proceed, an LNG liquefaction project needed sufficient gas resources (10 tcf for an 8 mtpa plant – see Chapter 3) and a firm market, or several markets. The development of US liquefaction capacity based on the region's gas resources, not on a specific field, is likely to be an exception rather than the rule.

Another fundamental trait of the LNG business is the sharing of risk between buyer and seller: take-or-pay commitments mean that the seller takes the price risk and the buyer takes the volume risk. In the early years of the LNG industry, such take-or-pay requirements represented between 90 and 100 per cent of contract volume, but these portions were reduced in the late 1990s, notably after Asian buyers faced a significant demand reduction in the wake of their economic crisis. Despite some concessions, there was no dramatic shift away from the long-term contract model. Contracts generally also feature a ramp-up period and a plateau volume, to take market growth into account (Jensen, 2004).

Long-term contracts are said to be inseparable from LNG projects, but is this really true? A few LNG producers have built liquefaction plants without having the full capacity booked under long-term contracts. This happened first in the early 2000s, when falling costs (the capital costs of liquefaction plants decreased from 1995 onward and the cost of LNG tanker construction decreased by half between 2000 and 2003) played a role in market players' view of LNG. The LNG industry in the early 2000s was thus experiencing a sharp decrease in costs, so that the cost of a typical two 3.3 mtpa train in West Africa would be around $5 billion – covering field development, liquefaction, tankers, and regasification (Jensen, 2004). (Upstream and liquefaction represented $2.9 billion of this total.) Such costs allowed market participants to take more risks and allow some LNG to go to the spot market (notably the US market) at a time when the European and Japanese markets were liberalizing,[1] and at these lower costs, project financing could be based on long-term contracts which covered only part of the plant's total capacity. For example:

- Oman LNG moved ahead in November 1996 with only 4.1 mtpa contracted by KOGAS (out of a capacity of 7.4 mtpa) (Ledesma, 2011). The balance buyers could only be sourced after the project had taken FID. Subsequent contracts were signed only in 1998. One of them, with Enron, never delivered LNG as the company shut the Dabhol power plant in India following a payment dispute with its sole customer, Maharashtra State Electricity Board (MSEB).

- Malaysia LNG Tiga was reported under construction in 2001. One SPA was signed for 0.9 mtpa with Tohoku Electric Power in April 2001, followed in February 2002 by another one with the Japanese Gas Consortium (comprising Tokyo Gas, Osaka Gas, and Toho Gas), and a third one in April 2002 with JAPEX. The first cargo was exported to JAPEX in March 2003.

- Nigeria train 1 was contracted at around 80 per cent when it started in 1999 (based on contracts data in GIIGNL, 2000).

---

[1] Liberalization of the Japanese gas sector began in 1995, when users with an annual contracted volume of 2 million m^3 could choose their gas supplier.

- Equatorial Guinea had a 3.4 mtpa contract with BG covering just 90 per cent of its capacity (3.7 mtpa).

- Later, Skikda and Gassi Touil in Algeria were (re)built without any long-term contract attached to them. This was largely due to the belief of Algeria's Oil Minister Chekib Kahlil that long-term contracts were much less profitable than spot sales to Asia.

Subsequent firm and binding sales were often concluded after the FID was taken, so that the main buyer did not have to wait for the seller to line up other buyers before the projects got underway.

However, even though some LNG industry players considered moving ahead without long-term contracts, no fundamental change in the industry's business model took place. The substantial increase in capital costs since 2010 changed the picture again (see Chapter 4). In this context, investors are even more wary of trying different approaches, given the scale of financing required. Projects with contracted offtake can generally take on more debt than projects that sell their product on a short-term basis for a fluctuating price. While the price could change, a long-term contract provides demand certainty for a number of years (as long as the contract is honoured).

The sheer scale of capital required is often described as being the key distinction between LNG projects and oil and coal projects. The development of LNG projects costs billions of dollars, which requires them to be more attractive than other prospects in the portfolios of large energy companies (Yergin and Stoppard, 2003). Oil projects tend now to move ahead without long-term contracts attached, while coal projects (mine and infrastructure) generally need a mix of long and short-term contracts, with the remaining output sold on spot markets.

LNG costs are higher in comparison to those of oil and coal on an energy basis. In energy terms, a 5 mtpa LNG plant produces the equivalent of a 120,000 bbl/d oil project or a 10.8 million ton coal project.[2] In today's environment, the associated costs of upstream and liquefaction would be around $4.3 billion – $8.1 billion,[3] while the equivalent cost on an energy basis for oil would be around $2 billion – $3.5 billion and $1 billion – $3 billion for coal (including the mine plus infrastructure).[4]

---

[2] Based on 6000 kcal/kg coal.

[3] See Chapter 3. The cost of upstream and liquefaction for a 8 mtpa plant ranges between $7 and $13 billion.

[4] 'Riskiest Oil Projects Are in Canada', Matthew Philips, Bloomberg Business, 15 August 2014. www.bloomberg.com/bw/articles/2014-08-15/the-biggest-oil-projects-need-high-prices-to-make-sense.

Obviously, oil still needs to be processed, while LNG needs to be regasified.

The capital cost differential for ships is also important: an LNG ship of 160,000 m^3 would cost around $200 million,[5] while a VLCC transporting 2 million barrels of oil, or around 3.4 times more than an LNG tanker on an energy basis, would cost $100 million.[6] Additionally, unlike oil, oil products, and coal, an LNG tanker loses LNG with every mile travelled due to the boil-off. Another important parameter is the cost of shipping compared to the total sales price: for oil, shipping represents a very small share, typically just a few dollars against a price that is at least 10 or even 20 times higher.[7] For coal, freight costs are often a larger percentage of the price. For example, freight costs from South Africa to Europe have varied between $4–$10/ton over 2010–14, against prices hovering between $55–$120/ton. For natural gas, shipping costs can be important. They vary depending on the distance, fuel consumed, boil-off, and port fees as well as potential transit fees through the Suez Canal (and soon the Panama Canal). For example, for a delivered price of Algerian LNG to Japan of $8.4/MMBtu in November 2015, Platts LNG Daily calculated a freight route cost for LNG of $1.48/MMBtu.[8] In its initial presentations, Cheniere was assuming a transport cost for US LNG to Asia of $3/MMBtu against a delivered price of LNG of $11.1/MMBtu in Asia.[9]

Oil has become a globally traded commodity, unlike natural gas. In its early history, oil was controlled by multinational oil companies. These companies were vertically integrated from the upstream to a part of the downstream, and most oil trading was an internal company affair; this meant that the spot market was underdeveloped. The host governments did not participate in oil production or in setting the price of oil. The oil pricing system was based on a posted price, which was used to calculate the stream of revenues accruing to host governments, but it did not reflect supply/demand dynamics. Later, over the period 1973–88, oil prices were administered by the OPEC countries, while at the same time, these got access to a share of the oil produced (Fattouh, 2011).

---

[5] 'LNG & LPG Shipping Fundamentals', Jefferies LLC, June 2013. https://www.marinemoney.com/sites/all/themes/marinemoney/forums/MMWeek13/presentations/Wednesday/4_00%20PM%20Doug%20Mavrinac-LPG.pdf.

[6] 'VLCC or Very Large Crude Carriers and ULCC or Ultra Large Crude Carriers', definitions: Maritime Connector website. http://maritime-connector.com/wiki/vlcc/.

[7] The price of transporting oil between the Middle East and Japan has typically been between $1 and $2.5/bbl in recent years (Bloomberg data).

[8] 'Freight Route Costs: Nov 4 ($/MMBtu)', Platts LNG Daily, Issue 213, Vol. 12, 4 November 2015.

[9] 'Corporate Presentation – November 2014', 5 November 2014, 6. Available on Cheniere website: http://phx.corporate-ir.net/phoenix.zhtml?c=101667&p=irol-presentations.

One of the cracks in the system in the late 1970s was caused by the appearance of many new players such as: non-concessionaire customers, independent oil companies, and trading houses. Meanwhile, existing long-term contracts forced producers to sell oil to the majors at the marker price, while those oil companies would resell it at a much higher spot price. Producers started to abandon their long-term oil contracts in order to capture higher prices on the nascent spot market. Consequently, the majors lost access to the large volumes of crude oil available under these long-term contracts, prompting them to go to the market to acquire oil based on short-term contracts, or even to the spot market. The decline in oil demand in the mid-1980s, combined with the growth in non-OPEC supply, started to challenge OPEC's administered pricing system as new producers were undercutting OPEC on the spot market. Internal disagreements between OPEC countries precipitated the end of the pricing system (Fattouh, 2011).

The development of exchange-based pricing between 1986 and 1988 enabled oil to become a global commodity. This was a very timely change as previous events had established the basis of arm's-length deals and exchange outside the vertically integrated multinational companies. The arrival of many non-OPEC suppliers, and of additional buyers, further reinforced the move towards exchange-based pricing.

Long-term contracts for oil are different from those in the LNG business. For oil, buyers and sellers typically negotiate one to two-year bilateral deals (compared to 20 years for LNG), with the price of a cargo linked to a spot price. These 'long-term' contracts are complemented by cargo transactions under which one or several cargoes are sold (Fattouh, 2011).

Coal can be sold under long-term contracts (whose length usually ranges from one to 20 years), or under spot contracts (single shipments). However, there has been a move away from export contracts to more index-priced and shorter-term deals (Eberhard, 2011). With the exception of minemouth power stations, long-term contracts for coal are less common in the Atlantic market. In the USA, there has been a shift away from long-term contracts to short-term deals (IEA CCC, 2015). Relatively higher prices in 2008, as well as the emergence of coal price indices, such as API 2, API 4, and Newcastle, drove this change. Companies such as globalCOAL and McCloskey have been instrumental in establishing assessments of spot physical prices (DES or FOB depending on the indices). Such index prices are now used as the basis of derivative contracts. The paper market has been growing steadily and, by 2007, paper volumes reached ten times physical sales in the Atlantic market. This was also helped by the creation of the SCOTA (standard coal trading agreement) in 2002.

508   *LNG Markets in Transition*

The increasing flexibility of LNG trade

Understanding the evolution of spot and short-term LNG trade

The split between spot (single cargo) and short-term LNG trade (defined by GIIGNL as contracts whose duration is less than four years) enables a better understanding of how spot and short-term trade has developed, and gives some pointers to future developments. Since 2000, the International Group of LNG Importers (GIIGNL) has become a well-known and comprehensive source of publicly available data on the LNG trade. A database that includes all data from GIIGNL's annual reports since 2000 has been created for this analysis.

This type of trade is not a novelty of the new century (Figure 9.1), but spot and short-term LNG (then defined as contracts of less than one year) represented only 1 per cent of total trade in 1992, slightly less than 1 mtpa. GIIGNL reported a spot and short-term volume (contracts of less than four years) of 5.6 mtpa in its 2000 annual report. Since 2000, the percentage of such contracts in total LNG trade has increased dramatically, from 5.4 per cent in 2000 to 28 per cent in 2015. As total LNG trade has also expanded, this means that spot and short-term volumes have grown more than tenfold since 2000 – from 5.6 mtpa to 68 mtpa. In 2000 these contracts were spread equally among all importing regions: Europe (nine contracts), the USA (eight contracts), and Asia (10 contracts) (GIIGNL, 2000). In 2014 the overwhelming majority went to Asia (74 per cent) and the Americas (18 per cent), especially Latin America. In 2015 the share of Asia dropped to 68 per cent, against 17 per cent for the Americas and 9 per cent for the MENA region.

The rise in spot and short-term trade is often attributed to Qatar's capacity increase over 2009–11. Qatar has been an active participant in spot and short-term trades since its first exports in the late 1990s. Qatar was thrust into the spot market in a more significant way when the plans to send LNG to the USA fell apart and the diversion rights present in the contracts were activated. Spot and short-term trade doubled between 2009 and 2014, with Qatar representing half of the addition and Nigeria, Indonesia, Algeria, and Yemen together contributing 45 per cent. But spot and short-term trade dropped by 1.2 mtpa in 2015, while Qatar's contribution fell from 25 mtpa in 2014 to 20 mtpa in 2015. South-east Asian LNG exporters were involved to a significant extent in short-term and spot trade before 2000, but as their short-term contracts expired around 2000, their role diminished while other countries took over. All 20 LNG exporting countries have contributed, or are still contributing, somehow to spot and short-term LNG trade.[10]

---

[10] As of mid-2016, three LNG exporting countries (Libya, Yemen, and Egypt) are not exporting. Angola restarted in June 2016.

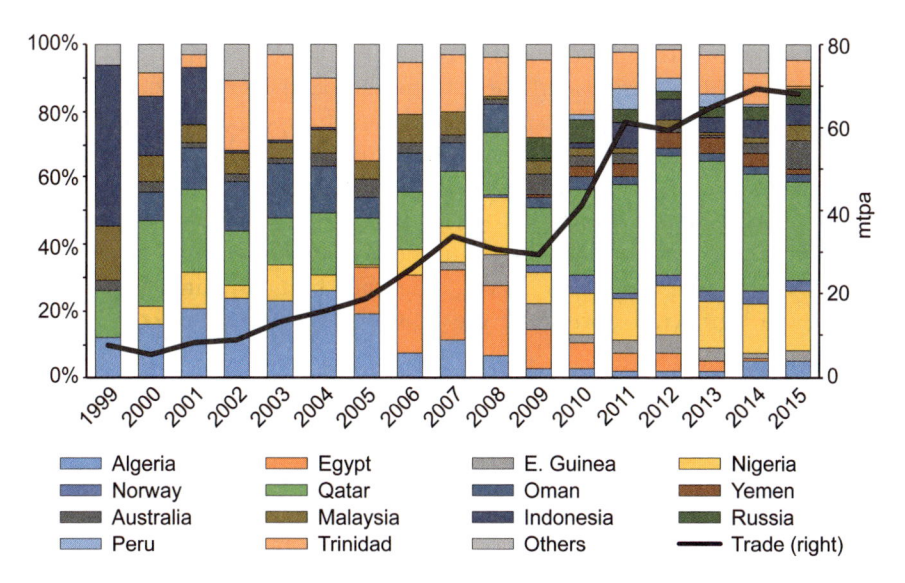

Figure 9.1: Spot and short-term LNG exports, 1996–2015
Source: GIIGNL.

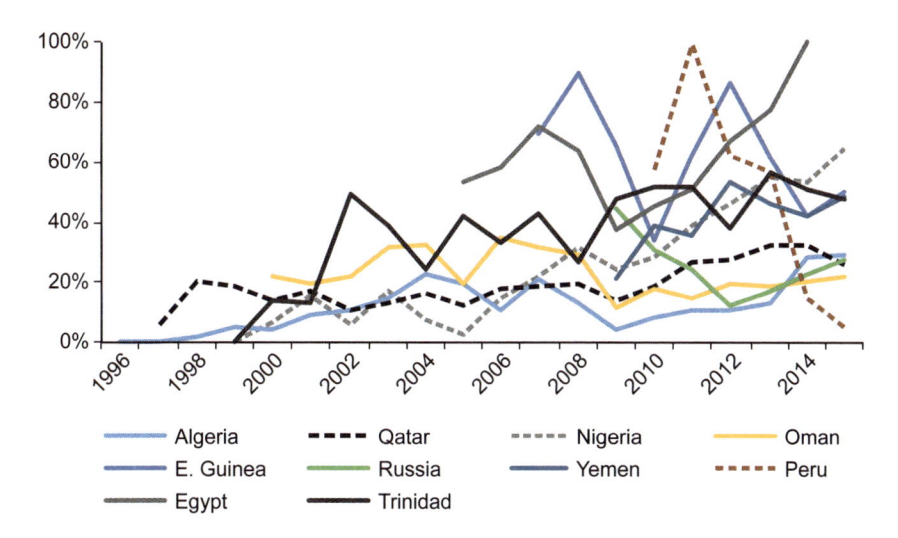

Figure 9.2: Spot and short-term trade against countries' LNG exports
Source: GIIGNL.

Another interesting aspect is the contribution of spot and short-term trade to countries' individual LNG exports; this is represented in Figure 9.2. The proportion of LNG traded short term is particularly high

– above 50 per cent – for Egypt, Nigeria, Equatorial Guinea, and Peru (except in 2014 for Peru and in 2015 for Egypt). The share of Qatar's LNG exports that are traded short term has been increasing over time, but 'only' reached 32 per cent in 2014 and dropped to 26 per cent in 2015. Plummeting LNG exports have accentuated Egypt's high share of short-term trade over the past few years. Remarkably, Trinidad has almost always had a higher share than Qatar, partly due to exports to a liquid market – the USA – and partly due to the need to divert LNG away from that market after 2009. In Egypt, Nigeria, Trinidad, and Equatorial Guinea, a significant portion of the LNG supply was contracted by the aggregators.

Jim Jensen noted in 2003 that:

> ... no country, no matter how aggressive in the short-term market, has placed as much as 30 per cent of its exports in any one year in short term trading. (Jensen, 2004)

That was certainly true then, but the evolution of the trade since 2005 shows diminishing risk aversion to significant spot market reliance among operating LNG projects, once they have started. It is important, though, to reiterate that these projects did not move ahead without the support of long-term contracts.

Contracts of less than four years duration represent a small but increasing share of total trade, reaching 7.5 per cent in 2015 (18 mtpa). They tend to be agreed upon shortly before their start, usually months (and up to two years) before, and thus they represent a small amount looking forward (Figure 9.3). The currently targeted markets are Korea, Malaysia, India, the UK, Argentina, Jordan, and Egypt whereas the USA used to be a key market. However, only two LNG suppliers have been regularly engaged in short-term contracts: Qatar since 2003 and Australia since 2009. As of 2015, 'portfolio' sales represented more than half of the short-term volumes, making it difficult to track these ships' origin.[11] Uncertainties over demand, combined with security of supply imperatives, make limited-duration contracts quite attractive, as highlighted by those signed recently by Lithuania, Egypt, and Jordan.[12] Most of the short-term contracts signed in 2015 were portfolio sales and half of them (six) targeted Egypt.

---

[11] Portfolio LNG is LNG supply often owned by an aggregator and not tied to a specific destination. The aggregator can then either sign secondary sales contracts from its portfolio without specifying the origin of the LNG, or keep it to use in spot market interventions.

[12] These contracts have a 5-year duration which means they would be considered, strictly speaking, as long-term contracts. In the case of Lithuania the contract was extended (in January 2016) from five to 10 years.

From the suppliers' point of view, such contracts are useful to test a future relationship with new buyers and the potential to extend into a more long-term relationship.

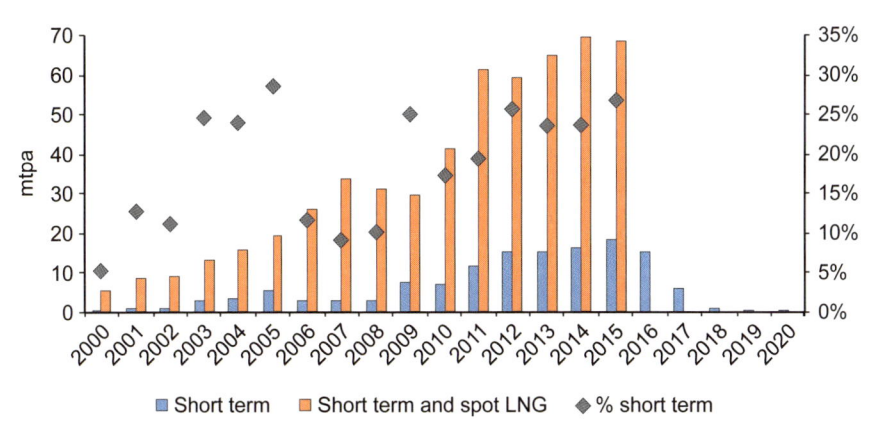

Figure 9.3: Short-term against spot trade, 2000–15
Source: GIIGNL.

Spot trading makes up the majority of short-term trade – totalling around 50 mtpa in 2015, or 20 per cent of total LNG trade. Analysing the drivers on both sides (suppliers and buyers) helps in understanding its development.

Flexibility: the suppliers' side

The 'flexibility' that spot and short-term LNG trade provides is, in part, the achievement of LNG suppliers. Spot cargoes can consist of:

1. uncommitted (or 'spare') LNG liquefaction capacity;
2. ramp-up volumes at the beginning of a liquefaction project when the market is not entirely ready to absorb volumes;
3. volumes initially committed to markets but then released and redirected (Kim, 2006); or
4. portfolio LNG: volumes (equity or not) earmarked for the aggregators, contracted by their trading arms with no specific destination attached.

Uncommitted volumes
The first source of flexibility, uncommitted liquefaction capacity, has tended to be thin. The amount of LNG spare capacity was assumed to be

around 9–14 mtpa over 2000–2, originating mostly from Africa and the Middle East (Kim, 2006). The analysis of LNG trade in 2015 indicates high spare capacity in a few countries (see Table 9.1). However, some countries among those with the highest spare capacity (notably Algeria, Indonesia, and Nigeria) are clearly not using it, or using it only partially due to gas shortages. Over the past few decades, some early long-term contracts have expired, leaving suppliers with spare capacity. Without the need to finance large investments, such suppliers may opt to keep quantities for spot trading. For example, Algeria did not extend about 9 mtpa of its long-term contracts over the period 2004–9.[13]

In analyses of spare capacity, Qatar poses a problem. The sum of all its contracts reported active in 2015 (94 mtpa) is clearly above its stated export capacity of 77 mtpa. Capacities initially contracted by companies such as ConocoPhillips have also apparently been included under other contracts, creating a double-counting effect, notably for Qatargas 2 and RasGas 3.

Table 9.1: The origins of spot cargoes: analysis of contracts, 2015

	Free capacity (mtpa)	Exports: contracts (mtpa)	Redirecting from initial market	Aggregators with contracts
Algeria	17.83	0	USA (3.2 mtpa)	ENI, Engie, Iberdrola
Angola	n.a.	0	USA (5.2 mtpa)	Chevron
Egypt	n.a.	0	USA (4.3–5.1 mtpa)	BG, BP, Engie, Shell, Gas Natural
E. Guinea	0.3	0.25	USA (3.4 mtpa)	BG
Nigeria	2.5	0.2	USA (4–8.3mtpa)	ENI, Engie, Iberdrola, Shell, Total, Gas Natural
Norway	0	0.15	USA (1.75 mtpa)	Engie, Iberdrola, Statoil, Total
Abu Dhabi	1.1	1.4		
Qatar	n.a.	n.a.	USA (>15 mtpa)	ConocoPhillips, ENI, ExxonMobil, Shell, Total
Oman	2	0		Union Fenosa
Yemen	n.a.	0	USA (4.55 mtpa)	Engie, Total
Australia	3.61	3.76		

---

[13] The 3.6 mtpa contract with Distrigaz in 2006, the 3.2 mtpa contract with Duke Energy in 2009, and the 2.9 mtpa contract with Gas Natural in 2004.

	Free capacity (mtpa)	Exports: contracts (mtpa)	Redirecting from initial market	Aggregators with contracts
Brunei	1.9	1.28		Shell
Malaysia	0.8	1.31		
Indonesia	12.59	1.1	Mexico (3.7 mtpa)	
Russia	0.5	1.47	Mexico (1.6 mtpa)	Gazprom, Shell
Peru	0.5	0	Mexico (3.95 mtpa)	Shell
Trinidad	0	0	USA (9 mtpa)	BG, BP, Engie, Shell, Gas Natural
USA	0.4	0.3		ConocoPhillips
PNG	0.4	0.68		ExxonMobil

Notes: Spare capacity is calculated as the difference between nominal capacity of the LNG plants and long-term contracts in force in 2015.

For exports, contracts are based on 2015 data.

Negative values have been set to 0.

Quantities redirected from the initial market refer to contracted quantities reported in 2008 (before the US shale gas revolution).

Source: GIIGNL, author's research.

Looking at the difference between LNG exports and long-term LNG contracts, a total of around 12 mtpa was exported in 2015 (mostly from Abu Dhabi, Australia, Brunei, Papua New Guinea, Malaysia, Indonesia, and Russia) was not attached to long-term contracts. Russia's exports are around 1 mtpa above its nominal capacity, allowing cargoes to be sold as spot. Meanwhile, around 60 mtpa originally earmarked for North America (as of 2008) have been redirected or already re-contracted, to countries such as Japan.

Ramp-up volumes

These are usually a short-term phenomenon that can occasionally boost the spot market. For example, a large share of PNG's new production served the spot market in 2014. Significant spot volumes were available because PNG had started ahead of schedule and ramped up very rapidly – the plant was operating at full capacity only two months after its start.[14] New projects tend to not contract fully in the early months (and sometimes years) as they are not sure how the new liquefaction facilities will perform. In 2015, many commissioning cargoes were sold from the new

---

[14] 'Global trade summary for 2014', BG, www.bg-group.com/assets/files/cms/BG_LNG_Outlook_2014_15.pdf.

Australian projects. QCLNG sold an estimated 1.5 mtpa during its commissioning phase.[15]

Re-direction of LNG cargoes
This third source of spot LNG was initially even thinner, as cargo re-direction was strictly prohibited under the majority of long-term contracts, with the exception of a few that sought arbitrage between destinations, such as those from Trinidad and Tobago (between Spain and the USA). As explained in the next section (Market-side developments, page 517) the increase in regasification capacity, the end of final destination clauses in Europe, and the experience of supply and demand shocks have all boosted LNG flexibility. In particular, flexibility drove the increase in re-exports, especially from Europe, which peaked at around 6 mtpa in 2014 and fell to 4 mtpa in 2015. An important amount of re-exports came from Spain, where buyers were forced to take much more contract LNG than they could use.

In 2015, some Asian buyers found themselves over contracted and were trying to dispose of their surplus LNG cargoes. If Asian demand does not pick up over the coming years (see low demand scenario in Chapter 6), more of these unwanted cargoes may find themselves on the spot market.

Portfolio LNG[16]
Volumes from aggregators[17] have grown rapidly as their role has increased. Aggregators use arbitrage strategies in such a way that they will plan to have different LNG regasification terminals available, so they can send LNG supplies to the most favourable destination, whichever it might be. They sign contracts that enable them to divert LNG to higher-value markets as the opportunity arises. This happened simultaneously with vertical integration and strategic partnerships, such as those of ExxonMobil and Qatar Petroleum, which have LNG assets ranging from Qatar to the UK (Ruester, 2009). In the same way, shipping capacity and regasification capacity at the US Lake Charles and UK Dragon terminal support BG's trading activity.

Quantities contracted by aggregators have grown almost tenfold in the new century, rising from 13 mtpa in 2000 to over 125 mtpa in 2015.

---

[15] 'A Flood Of LNG "Commissioning" Gas Starting To Create Havoc In The Short-Term LNG Market', Tim Treadgold, Forbes, 16 November 2015. www.forbes.com/sites/timtreadgold/2015/11/16/a-flood-of-lng-commissioning-gas-starting-to-create-havoc-in-the-short-term-lng-market/#4280a1533e31.

[16] In this section, we are using GIIGNL's definition of portfolio LNG. When a contract relates to portfolio LNG, the importing country is reported as 'the name of the company Portfolio' rather than the name of a country.

[17] In this chapter, the following companies are considered as aggregators: BP, BG, ENI, Enel/Endesa, Engie, ExxonMobil, Gas Natural, Gazprom, Iberdrola, Pavilion, Shell, and Total.

Meanwhile, 'portfolio LNG' quantities increased to 54 mtpa by 2015. As much as 90 per cent of portfolio LNG is in the hands of aggregators. However, this portfolio LNG is sometimes resold through secondary agreements making it, in principle, no longer available for spot trading. Interestingly, new players are now selling portfolio LNG: they are mostly Japanese buyers such as Mitsubishi, Osaka Gas, Chubu Electric, TEPCO, and Tokyo Gas. This highlights how they are trying to manage a potential contractual surplus and are interested in engaging more into LNG trade, even though most of the resales are to other Japanese companies. However, when these companies contract LNG, it is not designated as portfolio but usually earmarked for Japan.

Comparing the evolution of 'portfolio LNG' alone on Figure 9.4 (orange line) with spot and short-term LNG trade (blue line) could be misleading due to several factors: secondary sales to end-users, delayed starts of LNG plants, the beginning of many LNG contracts during the course of the year, and the role of Qatar. The grey line includes the effects of secondary sales (those with 'portfolio' as country of origin) and of delays and shortages, notably in Egypt, Nigeria, Australia, and Indonesia. Quantities of portfolio LNG may also be higher, as this does not take into account the quantities that aggregators had initially contracted for their main market(s), but that they have to resell on global markets when these markets are over-contracted (notably in Europe). The role of Qatar will be analysed later, as it presents little portfolio LNG, despite a high share of spot and short-term trading (20 mtpa in 2015).

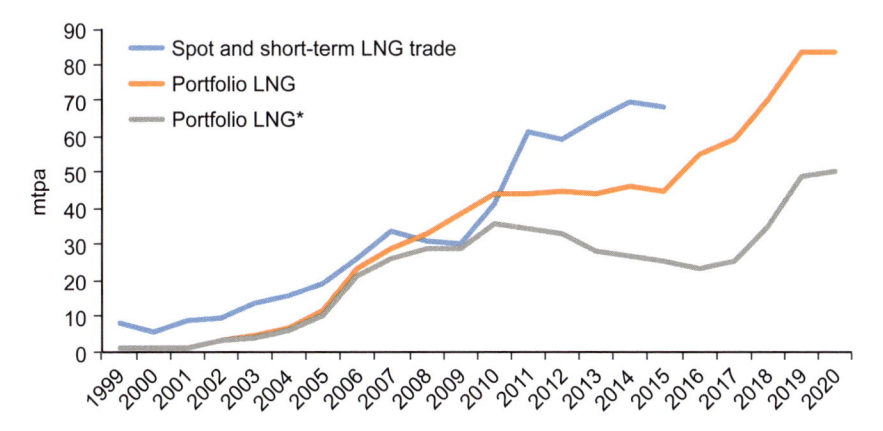

Figure 9.4: Portfolio LNG as a source of spot LNG

Note: From 2015 onwards, the grey line reflects no portfolio trade from Yemen and Egypt.

* Includes the effects of secondary sales, delays, and shortages.

Source: GIIGNL, author's analysis.

The rise of aggregators and the corresponding increase in portfolio LNG has been accompanied by challenges from new players to the traditional business models and norms of the LNG sector. While companies like Enron promoted different business models in the late 1990s, banks appeared in LNG trading during the 2000s. Those that survived the economic crisis contributed to developing the liquidity of the paper market, notably in Asia. Finally, traders such as Trafigura, Gunvor, Glencore, and Vitol are increasingly involved in LNG trade and supply. They supply existing LNG markets, with some recent major success in Mexico, Egypt, and Argentina, and are even engaged in some term deals with established buyers.

- In articles relating to **Trafigura**, it is reported that the company:

  > ... expect[s] the LNG markets to reach a tipping point during this decade that:
  > In the past, ... industry players [had] to commit to long-term contracts. Now, as infrastructure is put in place, the spot market is becoming more active and freely traded volumes are growing' (Trafigura, 2016).
  > and also that:
  > ... the majority of global LNG supplies will be traded on a short-term [basis] rather than through long-term contracts. (Shiryaevskaya, 2015)

  The amount of LNG handled by Trafigura in the financial year ending 30 September 2015 more than doubled to 4.2 mtpa, from 1.7 mtpa the year before. In order to provide confidence about security of supply to customers, and to gain a trading advantage over its competitors, Trafigura is using Petronet's underutilized Kochi import terminal in India for storage and has secured access to shipping by using cargoes without long-term commitments.

- **Gunvor Group** is reportedly set to expand into short-term buying and selling of LNG in 2014. The trading house won a tender to supply 60 LNG cargoes over 2016–20 in late 2015;[18]

- **Glencore** plans to double its global LNG trading team and trade as many as 50 cargoes over 2016 despite difficulties in late 2015; and

---

[18] 'Shell, Gunvor to supply 120 LNG cargoes to Pakistan – sources', *Hellenic Shipping News*, 17 December 2015. www.hellenicshippingnews.com/shell-gunvor-to-supply-120-lng-cargoes-to-pakistan-sources/.

- With over 2 mtpa traded in 2015, **Vitol** is using its three dedicated LNG vessels on time charters to supply LNG based on spot, short-term, and long-term contracts. In 2012, it signed a 10-year supply deal with Komipo.

Market-side developments supported the rise in flexible LNG trade
Supply and demand shocks

Developments on the supplier side would be nothing without similar developments on the market side, and these have also contributed to the increase in spot and short-term trading (Figure 9.5). LNG spot trade has been used initially to meet demand surges, or imbalances between supply and demand. For example, weather trends exacerbated US gas prices in the early 2000s and this attracted a certain number of spot cargoes (Kim, 2006). TEPCO also used spot trading to compensate for the loss of production from the Kashiwazaki–Kariwa nuclear power plant after an earthquake in 2007, and then later to source LNG for the gas-fired plants that replaced nuclear generation after the Fukushima accident.[19] In January 2009, Greece and Turkey imported spot cargoes to replace missing Russian pipeline gas supplies. Another demand shock was the disappearance of the USA as an importer and US buyers then starting to re-export cargoes from their own LNG storage tanks over the period 2008–12. However, US re-exports were short-lived as the original LNG suppliers found alternative

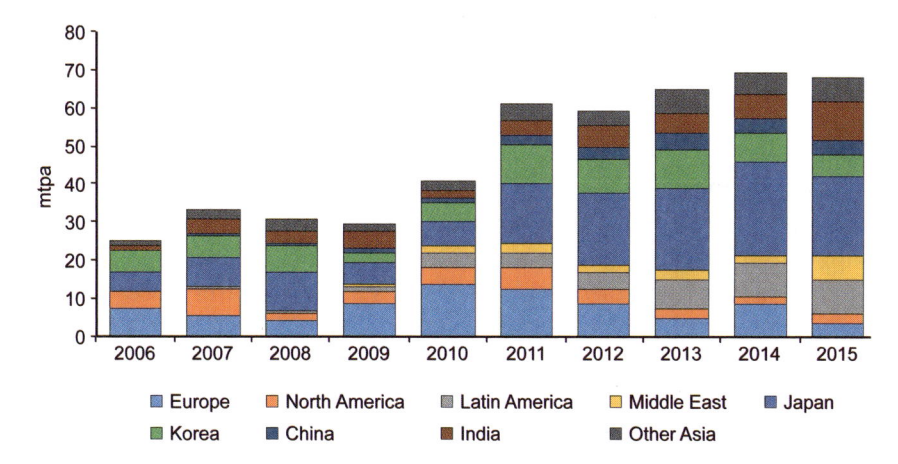

Figure 9.5: Spot LNG imports, 2006–15
Source: GIIGNL.

---

[19] 'Japan's TEPCO plans to buy spot LNG this winter', Roman Kazmin, ICIS, 13 September 2011. www.icis.com/resources/news/2011/09/13/9491808/japan-s-tepco-plans-to-buy-spot-lng-this-winter/.

markets. The shift to Asia from 2010 onwards, notably after the Fukushima accident, resulted in a switch of spot and short-term volumes from Qatar to Japan, while Europe started to take advantage of the price differential with Asia and Latin America to re-export surplus LNG.

Spot and short-term trade has increased in reaction to the markets' demand shortcomings, prompting buyers to ask for lower take-or-pay volumes. Demand shortcomings in the late 1990s contributed to increased flexibility in the terms, notably in Japan due to the changing role of LNG from a baseload source to a mid-merit or peak load source of power. As the economic crisis of 1997 reduced Asian customers' LNG demand (Morita, 2003), power and gas utilities started requiring a reduced take-or-pay coverage (down to 70–80 per cent of the contract volume). This freed up volumes as the total contract amount taken reduced, and sellers ended up with more spot LNG to sell.[20] In the case of Malaysian LNG Tiga, three Japanese customers were allowed to have 40 per cent volume flexibility, instead of the 5–10 per cent in a conventional contract. When the 20-year contract between Malaysia's Petronas and Japan's TEPCO and Tokyo Gas expired in 2002, it was extended, but with a shorter duration – 15 years. Part of the supply was put into a short-term four-year contract (TEPCO: 0.7 mtpa and Tokyo Gas: 0.5 mtpa). In addition, delivery terms changed from DES to FOB.

LNG tenders

Short-term trade was, to some extent, driven by the emergence of LNG tenders in the mid-1990s (Griffin, 2012). Their first use on a larger scale was in the period of market surplus from 2001 to 2004, where 10 producers and potential producers were offering supply. Buyers took advantage of these market conditions to invite potential suppliers to submit competitive tenders: CNOOC, for supply to the Guangdong terminal in China; CPC, for supply for the Tatan power plant in Taiwan; POSCO and K-Power for supply to the Gwangyang terminal in Korea; KOGAS for supply in 2003 and late-2004. In all these cases the buyers achieved lower prices than in the Japanese and Korean 'legacy' contracts, and in some cases the terms included oil price ceilings of around $25–$38/bbl.[21]

By the mid-2000s, tenders had become a common means of sale and purchase for suppliers and buyers. A range of buyers and also sellers (such as Nigeria and Australia's North West Shelf) were using tenders to solicit available supplies and markets. Tenders can be 'closed' (when limited to a

---

[20] If the TOP on the contract amount reduces from 90 per cent to 85 per cent, it frees up volume (5 per cent) that would otherwise have been sold term.

[21] 'Focus on pricing Gorgon gas', David Maitland, ICIS, 3 November 2005. www.icis.com/resources/news/2005/11/03/9280307/focus-on-pricing-gorgon-gas/.

number of pre-agreed companies) or open. The terms of tenders can vary: some just ask for a fixed price, others for a base price and a slope (percentage). In 2015, Nigeria LNG offered a series of cargoes asking for 10.5 per cent Brent plus Alpha, with the Alpha being the bidding number (Kazmin, 2015).

Factors influencing the development of spot LNG trade on the buyers' side
Developments in infrastructure on the demand side have enabled growth in short-term LNG trade. LNG regasification capacity has expanded much faster than liquefaction, enabling LNG suppliers to have more choice in terms of final markets (Figure 9.6). While the decoupling originally appeared in the mid-1980s, it became particularly visible after 2007, as regasification capacity gained an average of 40 mtpa per year. As of 2016, regasification capacity is more than twice as large as liquefaction capacity and almost three times the size of the LNG trade. Another key infrastructure component is shipping, since cargoes need to be easily available to transport LNG. The increase in shipping capacity and availability of second-hand cargoes also contributed to the rise of spot trading (see Chapter 4).

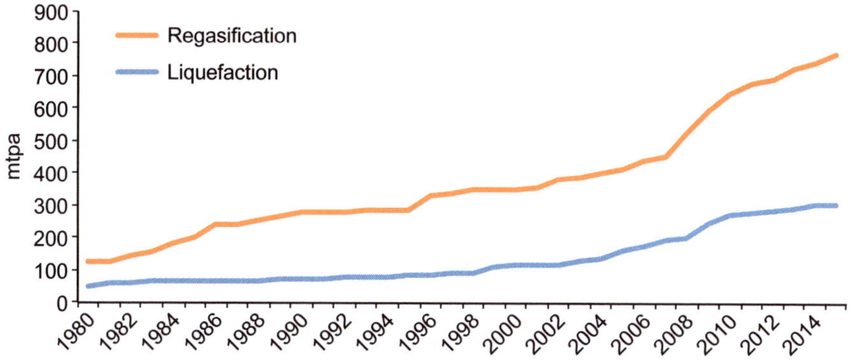

Figure 9.6: Surplus regasification capacity rises
Source: GIIGNL, author's analysis.

Literature suggests that the **gas market liberalization** processes in Europe acted as catalysts for the development of spot trading. However, this reflects only one side of the situation. The market-opening processes which took place in the United Kingdom in the 1990s, and then in Europe in the 2000s, increased the number of liquid markets with hub-indexed prices that could absorb spot cargoes based on a spot price. But more than that – they dramatically changed the buyers themselves. Originally, most buyers were government monopolies or utility companies in OECD countries, which meant that their creditworthiness was guaranteed by their governments. These buyers could pass on the costs to the final end-users. Liberalization increased the number and variety of market players, leading to the inclusion of smaller players, independent power producers, and traders seeking to profit from arbitrage opportunities between markets. Even established incumbents had to change their business models, as their market share was no longer guaranteed. In addition, many gas companies ceased to be pure gas companies and acquired power assets, often by merging with power companies. Consequently they also faced interfuel competition, one effect of which has been to considerably reduce natural gas demand in the power sector in Europe. Overall, these market players can rarely pass higher LNG costs on to their end-users. Small players are usually less able to take volume risks, their creditworthiness is weaker, and they are unlikely to obtain favourable financial terms when it comes to building LNG infrastructure if it is needed, making them natural participants in the spot market.

The existence of **trading hubs** in Europe enables the use of prices such as the UK's NBP or Dutch TTF as benchmarks. NBP and TTF have been used as references in long-term contracts, such as Qatar's sales to the UK though South Hook, its LNG sales to Centrica, or Cheniere's sales to EDF, proving that suppliers have gained some confidence in using spot prices.

Although liquid markets make the selling and pricing of spot LNG easier, those markets that have attracted spot cargoes have not always been liquid markets. For example, the USA, Spain, and Korea initially attracted the largest amount of spot and short-term trade during 1992–2003 (Kazmin, 2015). Among these, only the US market could qualify as being liberalized. Ironically, as North America ceased to be an LNG buyer and Europe lost its competitiveness against the Asian market from 2011 onwards, these liberalized markets have stopped attracting spot and short-term trading. As of 2015, Asia imported 46.8 mtpa of spot and short-term LNG trade against 3.9 mtpa for Europe (net of re-exports). However, liberalization did help in boosting spot trading: volumes earmarked for the European and North American markets could be diverted to Asian or Latin American markets at short notice and be replaced by domestic production, pipeline gas, or storage withdrawals (Thompson, 2009).

The end of **final destination clauses** in Europe was also important for the development of spot trading. These clauses forbid buyers from re-selling gas to parties in a different country, allowing a monopolist to earn more revenue through price discrimination. In a competitive market, price differentials between locations are limited to the cost of arbitraging between those locations (Hartley, 2013). The European Commission (EC) found that destination clauses did not comply with competition law.[22] Since 2001, these clauses have been progressively eliminated from existing and new contracts. In turn, this allowed a greater flow of Atlantic-based spot cargoes into Asia.

Over the past few years Asian buyers have been vocal about getting rid of the destination clauses that continue to exist in a number of Asian LNG contracts.[23] They want more flexibility in terms of destination, stressing the need to introduce FOB terms into existing contracts. Despite the possibility for them to use their downward tolerance, they feel they may also need more flexibility in a future low demand period to avoid being in the same situation as Spain, which was forced to re-export LNG due to insufficient demand.

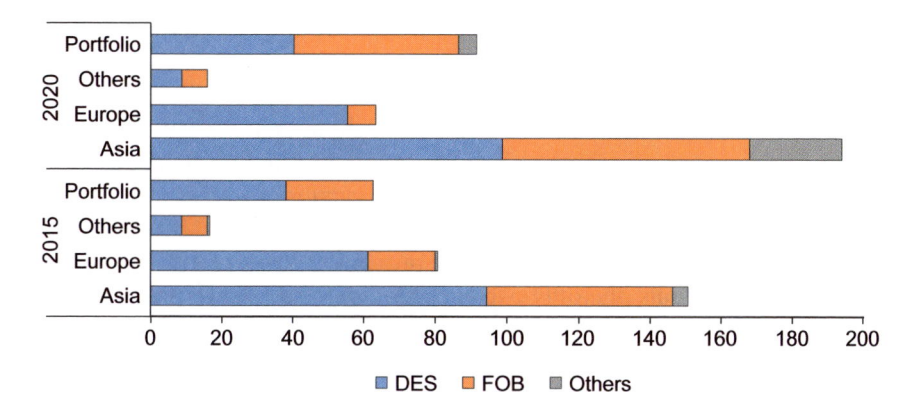

Figure 9.7: Destination flexibility in long-term contracts as of 2015

Note: 'Others' represents a category for which no information about the contract is available.

Source: GIIGNL, author's analysis.

Around two-thirds of existing long-term LNG contracts are on DES terms, aimed mostly at Asia (49 per cent), but also at Europe and other

---

[22] 'Energy Liberalisation and EC Competition Law', Michael Albers, Fordham 28th Annual Conference of Antitrust Law and Policy, 26 October 2001. http://ec.europa.eu/competition/speeches/text/sp2001_028_en.pdf. Issues in Europe regarding final destination clauses only concern DES contracts. Final destination clauses in FOB contracts are legal.

[23] 'Destination clauses on LNG will soon fade away: gas union president', Aaron Sheldrick, Reuters, 25 February 2015. www.reuters.com/article/2015/02/25/us-asia-lng-contracts-idUSKBN0LT0YY20150225; 'Buyers Market for LNG Turns Tables on Producers Amid Supply Glut', Stephen Stapczynski, Tsuyoshi Inajima, and Emi Urabe, Bloomberg Business, 5 October 2015. www.bloomberg.com/news/articles/2015-10-05/buyers-market-for-lng-turns-tables-on-producers-amid-supply-glut.

522   *LNG Markets in Transition*

markets (Figure 9.7). A significant share of these DES contracts (19 per cent) is actually portfolio LNG. A forecast for 2020 shows a higher volume of FOB contracts, but a relatively constant volume of DES contracts, pointing towards a slightly higher flexibility in terms of destination, but not a fundamental market change. Meanwhile, there is a non-negligible share of contracts for which no information regarding the destination terms is available. This is particularly true for some Chinese contracts.

Third-party access for LNG regasification terminals is another important part of the liberalization process. TPA can enable small players and new entrants without LNG infrastructure to import spot cargoes. As of end-2015, around 315 mtpa of LNG regasification terminals globally offered TPA, while another 120 mtpa provided either negotiated TPA or TPA subject to some conditions. This leaves around 340 mtpa with no TPA, as shown in Figure 9.8. However, the devil is in the detail and not all the capacity having theoretical TPA is easily accessible. Some TPA capacity, such as the 60 mtpa of US LNG capacity, is no longer relevant. TPA has not been used to date in Japan, despite around 190 mtpa of capacity with TPA or negotiated TPA. In China the government is pushing the NOCs to give better access to new entrants, such as ENN Holdings and JOVO, which have successfully concluded spot LNG purchases using CNPC's Rudong and Dalian terminals (the only two accessible as of 2015). In practice, this means that capacity with effective TPA is mostly found in Europe. According to reports from the Council of European Energy Regulators, there are no signs of capacity hoarding, while the secondary capacity market is deemed to be active in all European countries (CEER, 2014). Even though the rates of contracted capacity used have decreased since 2011, as LNG was diverted to Asia, regulatory measures have prompted unused capacity to be released to the market.

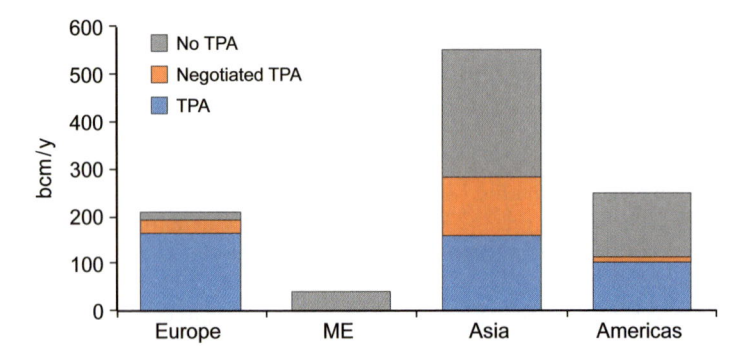

Figure 9.8: Third-party access (TPA) to LNG terminals in different regions, 2015
Source: GIIGNL, author's analysis.

Challenges to the growth of spot and short-term LNG trade

A number of constraints limiting further growth of spot trading have been identified, these include (Kim, 2006):

1. LNG quality issues;
2. Ship compatibility issues;
3. Contractual constraints;
4. Traders' creditworthiness and volatility; and
5. Need for security.

Quality specifications in different markets have been an issue due to different qualities of LNG. In the early 2000s, the emerging North American and UK LNG markets required lean LNG, imposing new constraints on the quality of gas. The emergence of the USA as an LNG exporter now poses the opposite problem. The majority of Japan's city gas has a standard heating value of 45–46MJ/m^3, against 37.3–40.1 MJ/m^3 for gas distribution in the USA (Horiike et al. 2015). This will require either specific terminals for lean LNG, or the ability to mix it with richer LNG. Alternative solutions include widening the allowed heat content of some markets, but that could in turn require some adjustments to end-user appliances.

Access for LNG cargo ships can also limit spot trade. Ships in the largest class of LNG tankers (Q-Max, with capacity of 261,000–267,000 m^3) can only access one-third of the existing terminals (Figure 9.9), but more than half of existing LNG import terminals and those under construction as of 2014 will be able to receive ships in the Q-Flex class (capacity of 210,000–217,000 m^3). Some ports have been adapted to accept larger ships and others are planning to do so. However, even though Qatar has smaller ships (allowing it to supply all importing countries) in practice cargo size remains a limitation to spot sales, as the industry has established 170,000–180,000 m^3 as the capacity of the largest mid-size trading vessels (Chapter 4).

Contractual constraints remain a challenge to spot sales in many areas. Final destination clauses remain in force in Asia, despite the push from Asian buyers to break this stranglehold given high demand uncertainties there. Availability of cargo ships occasionally represents a bottleneck, as this part of the value chain tends to be contractually locked in the hands of either suppliers or buyers. However, some shipping capacity is not linked to long-term contracts, allowing both buyers and sellers to use

524   *LNG Markets in Transition*

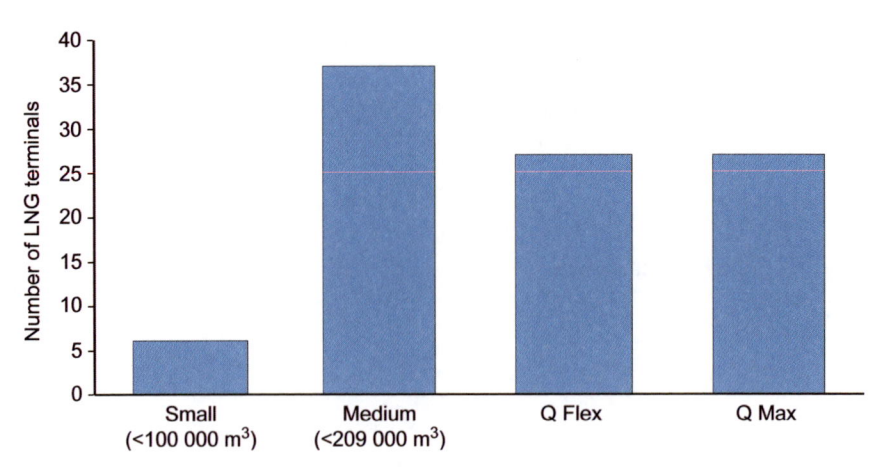

Figure 9.9: Number of LNG terminals by size of maximum cargo allowed
Source: GIIGNL (2014b).

the ships (Chapter 4). Meanwhile, the LNG industry has been trying to facilitate the use of spot contracts by coming up with a new model for an LNG master sales agreement (Ashurst, 2012), although established market participants generally want to use their own house contracts that suit their own commercial and contract preferences. There has been a convergence in the terms since the late 1990s, when spot contracts were a rare occurrence. Different MSAs have been released by industry bodies AIPN, GIIGNL, and EFET, but it remains to be seen whether one will prevail. There are also some doubts about whether market players would adopt a single set of general terms and conditions, given a widely different set of specific needs.

The emergence of new and less **creditworthy buyers** will continue (Chapter 2). They will pose a challenge not only for the support and development of LNG export projects, but also as long-term buyers of LNG. While some traditional players are more reluctant to deal with them directly, trading houses are keen to develop their role by taking and pricing in that risk.

Concerns relating to **security of demand** remain an impediment to spot sales for both sellers and buyers. The U-turn in North America reinforced the fact that sellers must be able to face strong demand variations. **Security of supply** is the other side of the coin – an argument for long-term contracts from the buyers' side. LNG is usually seen in the context of diversity of supply and often in opposition to pipeline gas, notably Russian pipeline gas. It remains to be seen whether countries entirely dependent on LNG, such as Japan and Korea, would accept a strong dependency on spot LNG without a reliable price benchmark. The Japanese government has been developing a well-balanced combination of spot, short-term, and flexible long-term contracts to import LNG. Spot and short-term contracts are growing in importance in Japan, representing 24 per cent of its LNG imports in 2015, against 10 per cent in 2010 (Vivoda, 2014).

Looking forward: the roots of the change

The LNG industry faces a daunting question: how will the evolution of spot and short-term LNG influence industry practices? To explore this question, we have created scenarios for spot trade in the future, building on the analysis done in the early part of this chapter. Our forward-looking supply analysis includes: uncontracted capacity, contracts not being extended, portfolio LNG, and the potential evolution of spot trade from Qatar and the USA. Apart from supply side considerations, there is an overarching worry on the demand side, where the appetite for additional LNG from the different players, and the need for flexible LNG, will also play a critical role.

Market demand uncertainty

All gas industry players forecast a growing role for natural gas, portraying it as the fuel of choice, whether as a destination in itself or as a bridge fuel to a lower carbon future. And yet in most parts of the world this 'inevitable' rise of natural gas is colliding with reality: gas is a high-cost energy resource trapped between cheap coal and policy-supported renewables (KAPSARC, 2015); this is leading to uncertainty, illustrated by various changes in the gas market over the last few years:

- Collapsing demand in Europe, added to increased needs from Japan following Fukushima, precipitated a 50 per cent reduction in European LNG imports over the period 2010–14.

- In 2015 the gas industry became increasingly worried that Asia may have missed its Golden Age of Gas. Chinese LNG imports dropped by 1 per cent, compared with a 10 per cent rise in 2014.[24] Japanese and Korean LNG imports were also down.

- Lower Asian LNG imports in 2015 have prompted LNG suppliers to redirect LNG to Europe, which has turned from being the market of last resort (receiving only leftovers from Asia), to the market absorbing all surplus LNG.

---

[24] 'China's LNG Demand Falls For First Time Since 2006: EIA', Christine Forster, Platts, 8 February 2016. www.platts.com/latest-news/natural-gas/sydney/chinas-lng-demand-falls-for-first-time-since-26361976.

The affordability of gas supplies will be a key factor in whether 'gas demand blues' continue, or demand rebounds.

Traditional buyers, mainly those in Asia, feel awash with more contracted gas supplies than they can absorb. Since early 2015, Asian buyers have been using a range of options as they face surplus contracted LNG: delaying deliveries, swapping LNG cargoes, or selling them on the spot market. For example in mid-2015, CNOOC sold cargoes from Australia's Queensland Curtis LNG, and Sinopec no longer seems keen to take its 7.6 mtpa of contracted LNG from Australia's APLNG.[25] This growing pain is likely to result in buyers fully using their downward quantity tolerance (DQT), putting even more volumes on the spot market unless they can organize time swaps. There will also be increased pressure to remove final destination clauses, as a means of managing lower market demand. But should they need further reductions beyond what the contracts allow, contract sanctity could be threatened.[26] Even Japan has turned from being a buyer to a seller, as it sells surplus LNG.[27] The total size of additional cargoes which may come to the market is very difficult to estimate, as it depends on how individual companies' portfolios relate to their needs.

Japan, Korea, and China – currently the three largest LNG importers – are key countries to watch. Japan is expected to remain the largest LNG buyer for the next 10 years and Korea and China will remain significant LNG importers. The liberalization of these markets, combined with an end to final destination clauses, would encourage their increased participation in spot trading. Meanwhile, effective TPA implemented in the region would enable players to move LNG more easily from one market to another.

The evolution of Japan's future LNG demand and its liberalization processes will impact companies' appetite for extensions of existing contracts. Views on future Japanese demand differ widely: while the IEA assumes a constant demand of around 100 bcm/year (74 mtpa) until 2040, Japan's Ministry of Economy, Trade and Industry (METI) announced in

---

[25] 'Origin Energy's APLNG project faces headache as Sinopec said unable to take gas', Angela Macdonald-Smith, Business Day, *Sydney Morning Herald*, 23 June 2015. www.smh.com.au/business/energy/origin-energys-aplng-project-faces-headache-as-sinopec-said-unable-to-take-gas-20150622-ghuy5i.html.

[26] 'Japan Resales Would Deal Market Body Blow', *World Gas Intelligence*, 30 September 2015.

[27] 'Japanese LNG buyers turning sellers as gas glut bites', Sarah McFarlane and Oleg Vukmanovic, Reuters, 28 January 2016.
http://af.reuters.com/article/commoditiesNews/idAFL8N15C39B.

2015 that LNG imports were expected to drop to 62 mtpa by 2030.[28] According to our analysis (Chapter 6), LNG demand in Japan could vary between 59 and 88 mtpa by 2030. Contracted LNG supply will peak by 2017 at 90 mtpa and decline progressively to 58 mtpa by 2025 and 43 mtpa by 2030 (Figure 9.10). Based on previous forecasts, Japanese LNG demand would be covered at least until 2020 and potentially for longer if Japanese companies became comfortable relying on the spot market. There are also signs that the mindset of Japanese buyers is moving away from the idea that long-term contracts bring security of supply, towards a mixed approach that enables more reactivity to market changes. In 2015 JERA, the new joint venture between TEPCO and Chubu, announced a diversification of its procurement portfolio, using long-term, mid-term, short-term, and spot transactions.[29] JERA's business plan, released in February 2016, shows that long-term contracts currently represent 35 mtpa out of a portfolio of 40 mtpa; the rest being spot/short-term LNG volumes. By 2030, these long-term contracts would account for only 15 mtpa, while the rest of its portfolio could consist of a mix of long-term and short-term/spot supplies.[30]

Adding to the gloomy demand picture, Japanese buyers – both gas and power companies – will feel increased pressure, as the residential market was liberalized in April 2016, and the citygas sector will be in 2017. Retail electricity and gas tariff regulation will be abolished, meaning that passing on fuel costs to retail rates will no longer be possible.[31] Liberalization of the gas market in Japan also includes a TPA scheme, even though some market players openly question the usefulness of this. Even if third parties had greater access to Japanese LNG terminals, the option to resell the gas would still be limited, due to the fragmented nature of the Japanese market which has no integrated transmission network covering the whole country. New entrants would therefore be forced to resell LNG to the local gas utilities that own the regional pipeline infrastructure, reducing the competitive element of the liberalization process considerably. However,

---

[28] 'Japan LNG imports to drop to 62mtpa by 2030 – METI', Ben Lefebvre, ICIS, 16 September 2015. www.icis.com/resources/news/2015/09/16/9924240/japan-lng-imports-to-drop-to-62mtpa-by-2030-meti/.

[29] 'JERA's Initiatives to Foster Evolution in the Asian LNG Market', Yuji Kakimi, President, JERA Co., Inc. 16 September 2015. http://aperc.ieej.or.jp/file/2015/9/18/S3_Mr_+Yuji+Kakimi_JERA+ver2.pdf .

[30] Total portfolio by 2030: 30–40 mtpa. JERA Business Plan, 10 February 2016. www.jera.co.jp/english/information/pdf/20160210_01.pdf.

[31] 'Developments of the LNG Futures Market', Takayuki Sumita, Director-General For Commerce, Distribution and Industrial Safety Policy, METI, LNG Producer-Consumer Conference 2015, 16 September, 2015. http://aperc.ieej.or.jp/file/2015/9/18/S3-7+Mr_+Takayuki+Sumita_METI.pdf.

gas companies in Tokyo, Nagoya, and Osaka are required to unbundle their pipeline network in April 2022.[32]

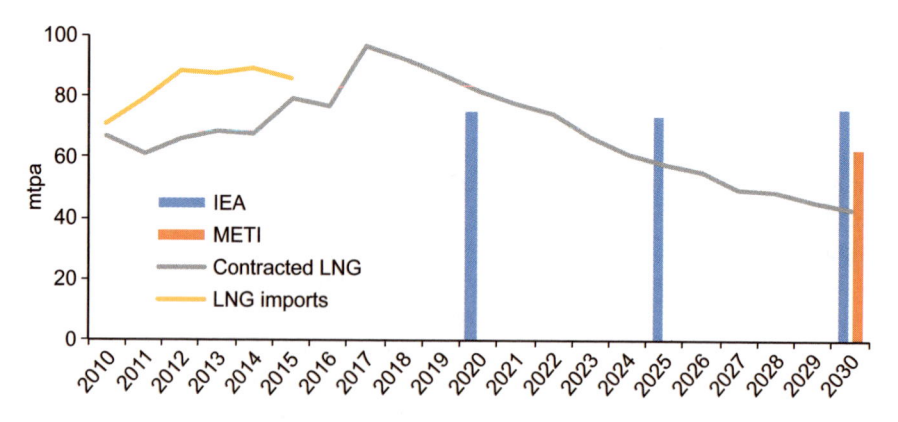

Figure 9.10: Japan's contracted LNG quantities against import needs
Source: author's research, GIIGNL, IEA, METI.

Korea offers a very different profile, as contracted LNG supply is relatively flat at around 32–35 mtpa until 2024, when it is expected to drop abruptly. Korea may be happy to keep that diminished level of contracted supply in the wake of recently declining gas demand (down 10 per cent in 2015). In late 2015, LNG demand forecasts for 2029 were downgraded to 34.65 mtpa.[33] In addition, large seasonal variations require the country to resort to spot cargoes to cover winter demand, which has already made Korea an important player on LNG spot markets. Failures to liberalize the Korean gas market have effectively left KOGAS in charge. However, the government seems uncomfortable with the KOGAS monopoly, making it difficult for KOGAS to commit to additional long-term contracts (the government did not approve the Australian contracts).

China's LNG demand is particularly uncertain, due to different scenarios in terms of demand, domestic production, and pipeline imports (Chapter 6). China is said to envisage spinning off its pipeline and storage infrastructure – but not its LNG import terminals – with the aim of providing access to the market for new entrants. The NOCs, notably

---

[32] 'Electricity and gas deregulation', Commentary, *The Japan Times*, 7 March 2015. www.japantimes.co.jp/opinion/2015/03/07/commentary/japan-commentary/electricity-gas-deregulation/#.VoPRZvl94sN.

[33] 'UPDATE 1-S.Korea sees gas demand falling 5 percent by 2029', Meeyoung Cho, Reuters, 28 December 2015. http://uk.reuters.com/article/southkorea-gas-idUKL3N14H14720151228.

CNOOC (the largest holder of regasification capacity), are currently resisting giving access to new entrants.

Apart from these big players, a number of small LNG importers have appeared, as highlighted in Chapter 2. Some, like Egypt, may have import needs of a limited but uncertain duration, as other domestic supply options arise. Most will have creditworthiness issues, forcing new buyers such as Egypt or Jordan to buy LNG by issuing tenders for a specific number of cargoes, thus relying on the spot market.

Uncommitted LNG supply

Some recent LNG export projects took FID without 100 per cent offtake commitments by buyers. This is notably the case for Australian and US LNG projects that, taken together, represent more than 12 mtpa of uncommitted capacity. Gorgon LNG and Wheatstone LNG have more uncontracted LNG than usual as two HoAs of 1.5 mtpa each with KOGAS were cancelled in 2011. Angola also has no contract attached to capacity (originally earmarked for the US market) and is likely to play a role in spot markets once the plant comes back online in 2016. South-east Asian LNG projects also have some uncontracted capacity; LNG from the two new Malaysian FLNG plants and a ninth train at Malaysia LNG have no long-term contracts attached, strictly speaking, and will be added to Petronas' portfolio.

This new uncommitted capacity builds on the existing uncommitted capacity that we have earlier assessed as having been around 10 mtpa in 2014 and 12 mtpa in 2015; the position is expected to remain relatively constant, except for potential changes in a few areas:

- Abu Dhabi, where demand for natural gas is rising and development of domestic production is hampered by low domestic gas prices.

- Nigeria, which might be able to utilize more of its LNG capacity and produce some LNG for spot trading, but this is uncertain.

All together, we estimate that between 8 and 10 mtpa of existing uncommitted LNG will be available for spot trading.

In total, uncommitted capacity is expected to almost triple by 2020 and then remain stable (Figure 9.11). However, the picture is not set in stone. It is entirely plausible that some of this LNG will eventually be contracted. Meanwhile, buyers have become extremely cautious about committing for 20–25 years and wary about sudden demand changes in their own markets. The increase in uncommitted capacity will put them in a stronger position to negotiate terms, including non-pricing terms.

530   *LNG Markets in Transition*

Finally, debottlenecking of existing plants could add spare capacity that would also be uncommitted. This is not included in the total above. For example, Qatar could add another 12 mtpa by debottlenecking its existing capacity, should the moratorium on additional exports be lifted.

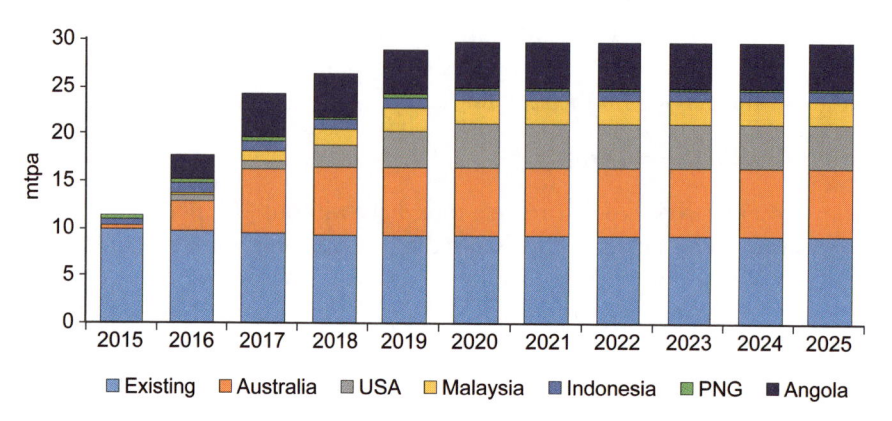

Figure 9.11: Estimated uncommitted LNG supply, 2015–25
Source: Author's research.

Contract extensions and renegotiations

Significant contracted volumes of LNG will expire over the next 10-year period, creating a renegotiation time window, particularly for key Asian players (Figure 9.12). A total of 135 mtpa of existing contract volume will expire in 2015–25 (including 54 mtpa in 2015–20), around 64 mtpa of which (originating mainly in Malaysia, Australia, and Qatar) is targeting Japan and Korea (only 1 mtpa relates to China). Another third of the 135 mtpa figure aims at supplying Europe. A third of these expiring contracts are in the hands of aggregators on the buyers' side (this includes those contracts designed as 'portfolio', Figure 9.13). Meanwhile, over 120 mtpa of new supply contracts will start from 2015, including around 35 mtpa targeting Japan, which could be replacement volumes for expiring contracts.

In the past, suppliers have sometimes let contracts expire and have then extended them with lower quantities. Unlike the position facing new liquefaction plants, at the end of a 20-year contract investments are usually already amortized. Further operation requires less financing, which may encourage suppliers to retain more output for spot market trades. But the environment today is unlike anything we have seen before. Many contracts cannot be extended, not because suppliers want to keep some LNG for spot trading, but because buyers do not wish to extend them. As explained earlier, demand uncertainty from once predictable buyers, together with issues regarding pricing mechanisms, are combining to put pressure on suppliers. Asian buyers are likely to resist extending their existing long-term contracts, either because they want more flexible deliveries or because they no longer wish to pay a JCC-indexed price. It is noteworthy that among the long-term contracts signed in 2015, half have a duration of 10 years or less.

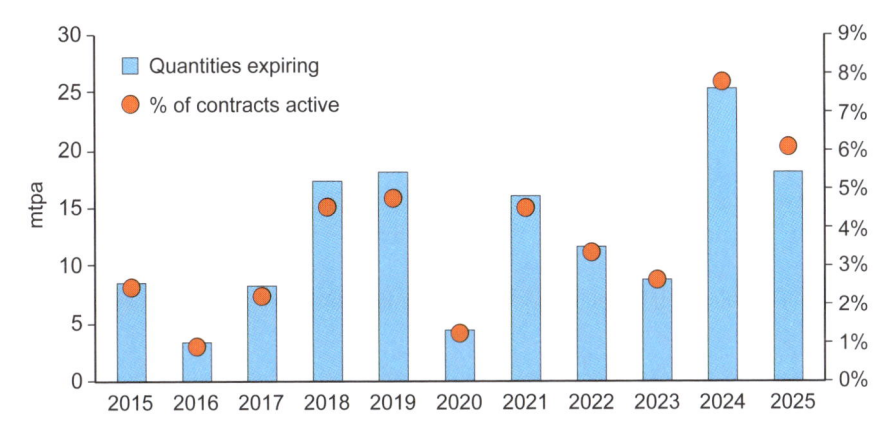

Figure 9.12: LNG contract expiry dates
Source: GIIGNL.

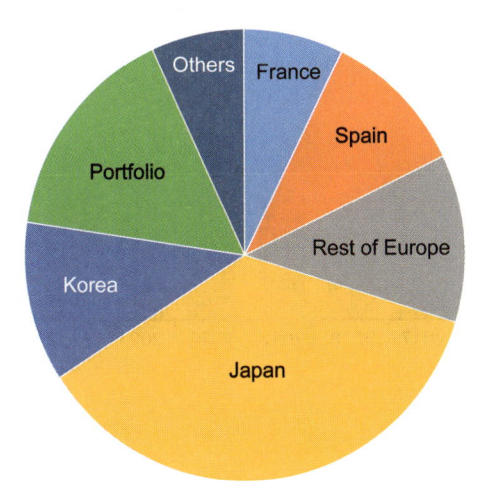

Figure 9.13: Destinations of contracts expiring over 2015–25
Source: GIIGNL.

Forthcoming changes on the suppliers' side are another aspect of the contract renegotiations. In many instances, partners in LNG projects have marketed their LNG as a group rather than as individual companies. This characteristic has been challenged in a few projects. For example, Australia's North West Shelf (NWS) partners changed their structure in 2015, to market uncommitted LNG volumes individually. This change will also affect Pluto LNG. Portfolio suppliers in NWS sought this change in order to optimize their positions. It means that uncontracted and excess LNG would be returned to individual equity partners, who would then be able to sell volumes bilaterally, either through spot trades or tenders. While this change will not affect existing long-term contracts, some contracts will expire by 2017. Woodside, which has been building an LNG trading business, could build on these volumes, along with those contracted from Wheatstone in Australia and from Corpus Christi in the USA.[34] However, smaller partners in the joint venture may see their negotiating position weakened.

Looking at each long-term contract individually, we have come up with potential ranges for the LNG supply which would not be extended. In some cases, LNG exports could stop altogether, or more LNG would be diverted to the domestic market. Portfolio LNG, which has been analysed earlier (see page 514), has been excluded to avoid double counting. Quantities potentially available to the spot market would increase regularly to around 36 mtpa, possibly reaching as much as 47 mtpa by 2025 (Figure 9.14).

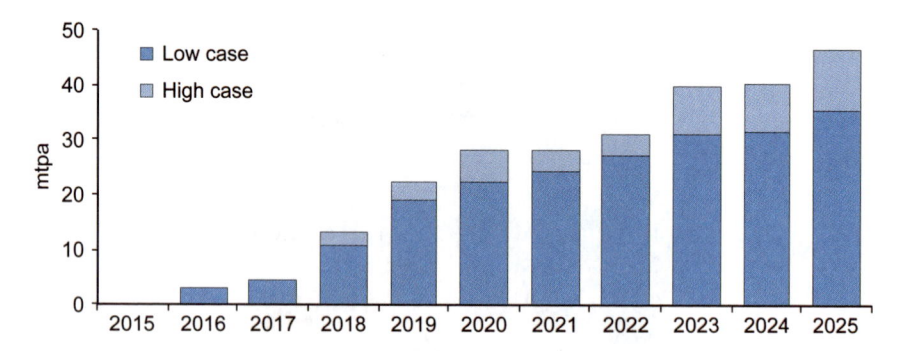

Figure 9.14: Quantities potentially available if selected contracts are not extended (excludes Qatar)

Source: author's research.

---

[34] 'Australia's North West Shelf LNG changes marketing structure from June', Lee Xieli, ICIS, 4 June 2015. www.icis.com/press-releases/aus-nws-lng-changes-marketing-structure/.

The role of Qatar

Qatar is currently the uncontested leader of the LNG market, representing one-third of total LNG trade. Due to its large LNG capacity and central position between Europe and Asia, Qatar plays the important role of 'swing producer' for the global LNG market (Al-Tamimi, 2015). Qatar's spot and short-term exports quadrupled from 2009 to 2011, from 5 mtpa to 20 mtpa, while its total LNG exports doubled over the same period. Spot and short-term exports further increased to 20.3 mtpa in 2015.

Qatar probably never intended to play such a role in the spot market. Its initial strategy was to sell LNG based on long-term contracts to Europe, Asia, and North America, but that strategy faced shortcomings when the North American LNG market disappeared, due to the rise of shale gas production. It subsequently moved to adapt to a sharply different market from that it had planned for. While these unwanted LNG volumes could have had a more long-term impact on LNG markets in 2009–10, Qatar benefited from a recovery of European gas demand in 2010. Europe then became the main recipient of spot trade from Qatar, with the UK market being linked to Qatar by the Qatar-sponsored South Hook terminal, as well as by the long-term contract between RasGas and Distrigas.

The situation changed again in 2011 due to Japan's additional needs after the Fukushima accident. From 2011 onwards, Japan and other Asian countries attracted more LNG spot cargoes, as the price gap between Europe and Asia widened. (Japan itself attracted around 27 per cent of Qatar's flexible LNG in 2015.) Consequently, increasing quantities of LNG have been redirected away from Europe towards Asia, and also towards Latin America where prices also skyrocketed. In 2014, around 17 mtpa of contracted Qatari LNG was taken away from Europe, another 3 mtpa from Canada, and 1 mtpa from China (Figure 9.15). These volumes fed LNG spot trade, while another 4 mtpa came from short-term deals. The picture changed in 2015: spot and short-term Qatari LNG volumes dropped, Asia attracted less flexible Qatari LNG, Europe took more under long-term contracts, while the MENA countries increased their imports of spot and short-term LNG. Qatar exports to most LNG importers and has therefore gained geopolitical benefits from this large LNG export portfolio. Qatar enjoys a strategic advantage by being a swing supplier and is regarded as a supply competitor to Russian pipeline gas in both Europe and Asia (Jaffe et al., 2013).

534   *LNG Markets in Transition*

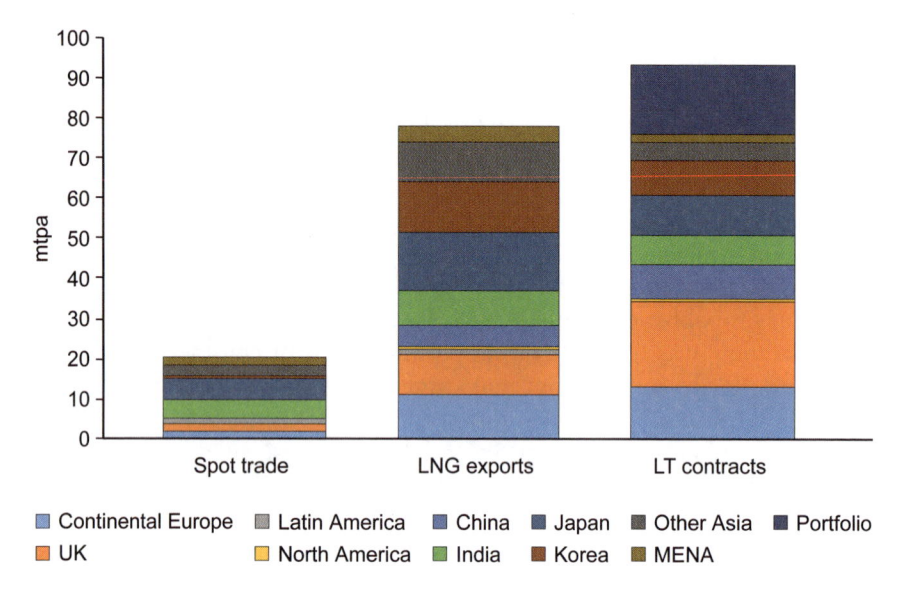

Figure 9.15: Qatar's LNG in 2015: spot trade, LNG exports, and long-term contracts

Note: Three long-term contracts have been excluded as the total contracted capacity exceeded the capacity of the LNG trains.

Source: GIIGNL.

Over the coming years, the supply scene will become quite crowded. Importantly, Qatar will lose its position as the largest supplier to Australia unless some debottlenecking takes place. The USA will challenge Qatar's position as swing producer, and will compete against Qatari exports in the European, Latin American, and Asian markets. US LNG exports are not destination-restricted, allowing them to be flexibly traded (Fattouh et al., 2015). As mentioned in the previous section, long-term contract renegotiations will be difficult for all producers, but this could be especially the case for a supplier whose rhetoric is that:

> ... Qatar has always supported the view that long term contracts based on oil indexation are a more predictable and reliable mechanism for all concerned in the industry. (Critchlow, 2014)

Still, Qatar has been adapting to these new challenges. Back in 2009 it aimed to send 15–20 mtpa to the USA and suddenly had to find new outlets for these LNG supplies. A few recent events highlight the growing pressure that buyers are applying in all regions, and give indications as to how Qatar may adapt to its changing environment.

In Europe, Qatar has already been signing shorter-duration contracts with buyers, even if its preference is still towards long-term contracts. These shorter-duration contracts are excluded from our definition of short-term contracts, as they relate to a period longer than four years, but they still represent a break away from the 20-year contracts. In 2013, Centrica extended an existing 2.4 mtpa SPA with Qatargas (signed in 2011 for 3 mtpa of LNG) for four and a half years. This DES contract is based on NBP prices. In 2014, Qatargas signed another 1.14 mtpa five-year SPA with Petronas for deliveries to its Dragon LNG terminal in the UK, and a five-year flexible SPA for 1.5 mtpa with E.ON, to be delivered at the Dutch GATE terminal and priced on a continental hub basis (Corbeau et al., 2014). These contracts will expire over 2018–19. Assuming that they could be further extended by using the same format but a slightly shorter duration, we have included these volumes in short-term LNG trade. Other contracts signed in early 2014 were more traditional 15-year contracts, with Japanese buyers. Finally, Qatar has been amending a long-term contract with Polish PGNiG for the year 2015, whereby Qatargas will place the LNG expected to be supplied to PGNiG in 2015 on other markets. This change was mostly driven by the delays of the Świnoujście LNG terminal, which only started operating in late 2015. It remains to be seen whether this amendment will be revisited over the following years if the contract price remains above the European hub gas price levels.

Qatar also provided commissioning cargoes for all new LNG importers in 2015 – Jordan, Egypt, and Pakistan – that are comfortable with a mix of short-term contracts and spot cargoes. Qatar has supplied additional LNG to them with the help of trading houses, using tenders to sell spot cargoes. Qatar also deals directly with new players, such as independent Chinese LNG importer JOVO. Qatargas CEO Khalid Bin Khalifa Al-Thani spoke of a cargo delivery to JOVO on a FOB basis as highlighting:

> ... Qatargas' ... ability to work successfully with small-scale buyers and cater to their specific needs. (Qatargas, 2014)

Meanwhile, the pressure on long-term LNG contracts from Asian buyers is rising. In mid-2015, PetroChina required Qatargas to skew deliveries under its 3 mtpa long-term contract towards the peak demand winter period.[35] Although this does not change the nature of the long-term contract, it is a major concession in terms of flexibility and shows that Qatar is ready to adapt to market requirements to keep its market share in Asia. Meanwhile, RasGas had to renegotiate its long-term contract with Petronet LNG, as the price of around $13/MMBtu (as of 2015) was much

---

[35] 'Qatar and PetroChina alter LNG supply deal, winter spot price fallout', Reuters, 26 August 2015. http://in.reuters.com/article/2015/08/26/china-qatar-lng-renegotiation-idINL5N10Y0MC20150826.

higher than Asian spot prices of $7–$8/MMBtu. India has also sought to reduce its contracted LNG imports from Qatar, taking only 70 per cent of the contract volume and potentially facing a fine as the specified DQT is only around 10 per cent. The price formula was amended, take-or-pay penalties waived, but contracted quantities increased by 1 mtpa. Qatar has also concluded a 15-year contract with Pakistan on oil-indexed terms.

Despite these growing pressures, Qatar's unique position allows it to take a potentially higher share of the spot market. It has in the past used market power and profit maximization approaches between Europe and Asia (Ritz, 2014). It already has an established infrastructure and its production costs are low compared to competitors. Qatar is well positioned to reach all markets and has a fleet of 69 vessels (42 for Qatargas and 27 for RasGas).[36] In his report on Qatar's response to the global gas boom, Naser Al-Tamimi estimated that Qatar's spot and short-term volumes could increase to almost 42.2 bcm (31 mtpa) if some contracts are not extended. Indeed, five contracts with Japan expire over 2017/18 and in 2021. Meanwhile, Qatar's European contracts may be extended in the form of shorter-duration deals, as mentioned earlier. Together, these total 13.8 mtpa by 2021.

The key question in estimating Qatar's ability to contribute to the spot market is: how much of its LNG can be diverted and to what extent is it willing or forced to divert? The country currently has 23 mtpa contracted to Japan, Korea, and Taiwan, 16 mtpa to China and India, with 34 mtpa to Europe, 3 mtpa to other destinations, with the balance being portfolio

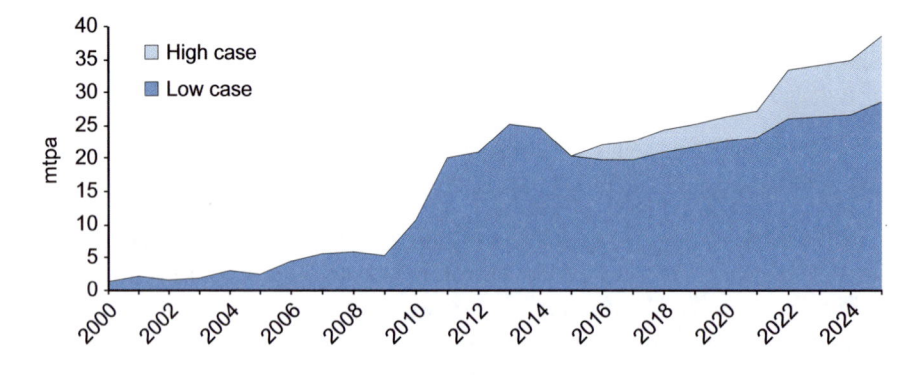

Figure 9.16: Qatar's potential spot and short-term LNG trade
Source: Author's research.

---

[36] 'Safe and Reliable Transportation', (Shipping page of RasGas website). www.rasgas.com/Operations/Shipping.html; 'Future Fleet' (Q-Flex and Q-Max page of Qatargas website). https://www.qatargas.com/English/AboutUs/Pages/FutureFleet.aspx.

LNG. Considering all the contracted LNG to Europe and other destinations as flexible and all that contracted to Asia as inflexible is too simplistic. Trade in 2014 has shown that despite a large price premium, Qatar did not send all its LNG to Asia. We can consider that the 17.6 mtpa reaching Europe in 2014 is probably the minimum volume Qatar would send, but this already included 4.6 mtpa of spot and short-term LNG. Finally, the volumes to North America or 'portfolio' supplies are considered flexible.

Meanwhile, some LNG previously diverted to Asia came back to Europe in 2015. Looking forward, Asian players will test their flexibility options. Taking into account existing contracts, as well as the appetite for flexibility from different players, we estimate that Qatar's spot and short-term trading is likely to decline or plateau over the coming years as LNG switches back to Europe under the framework of existing long-term contracts, and as increasing volumes to India and Pakistan are accounted for. However, expiring long-term contracts and the need for more flexibility from different buyers means that these quantities could range between 23 and 26 mtpa by 2020 (close to what was observed in 2014) and increase to between 29 and 39 mtpa by 2025 (Figure 9.16).

US LNG

LNG of US origin is more flexible as it is sold to offtakers at the liquefaction plant and has no destination restriction. Many Asian companies, including KOGAS, GAIL, Osaka Gas, Chubu Electric, Pertamina, Mitsui, and Mitsubishi, have contracted US LNG. It should not be assumed that these companies are end-users of this LNG. A few European companies that do not fall in our category of aggregators, such as EDF, EDP, and Centrica, have also contracted US LNG. Even though the contracted volumes could serve these companies' markets, most can also be diverted, either by those with trading experience (to capture better opportunities), or because LNG is not needed in the target market, or it is too expensive. For example, GAIL is said to have sold around 0.5 mtpa of its contracted US LNG to Shell.[37] 'Contracted' US LNG, excluding the volumes taken by aggregators and previously included in portfolio LNG, could therefore provide a significant addition to spot trade.

Against this background, the role of Cheniere is particularly interesting. Even though Cheniere is not considered here as an aggregator, the contract it signed in August 2015 with EDF for the delivery of LNG cargoes on a DES basis to the Dunkirk LNG terminal in France, followed by a further two contracts with EDF and Engie, were unusual for the company. These

---

[37] 'GAIL sells some of its U.S. LNG to Shell', Nidhi Verma and Oleg Vukmanovic, Reuters, 27 May 2015. http://in.reuters.com/article/2015/05/27/gail-lng-idINKBN0OC1UT20150527.

538 *LNG Markets in Transition*

are short-term contracts for the delivery of up to 74 cargoes in total (approximately 4.5 mtpa) through 2018; these contracts, unlike all previous ones signed by Cheniere, will be sourced from its own supply portfolio (the uncontracted capacity in Sabine Pass). This contract also breaks away from the Henry Hub cost plus approach by linking to a European spot price (TTF). On a combined basis, Cheniere Marketing's LNG portfolio is expected to have approximately 9 mtpa of LNG available from its nine liquefaction trains at Sabine Pass and Corpus Christi coming online between 2016 and 2020.

Towards an inflexion point?

Adding up all the elements analysed in the previous section (uncommitted LNG, portfolio LNG, LNG freed by the non extension of some LNG contracts, and the role of Qatar and the USA), we arrive at a range for the potential evolution of spot and short-term LNG trading (Figure 9.17). In the higher case, we included fully flexible US LNG. The higher case shows a significant rise to around 160 mtpa by 2020, increasing to 190 mtpa by 2025, while in the low case, these quantities would increase to 120 mtpa by 2020 and to 140 mtpa by 2025.

There is one caveat to this analysis: the LNG supply picture to 2020, and thus the share of spot and short-term LNG trade, can be given with some confidence, but the situation post-2020 is plagued with uncertainty. In addition, our numbers do not include any potential upside arising from future developments, such as future LNG plants that would take FID between now and 2020 and come on line before 2025. These could provide additional uncommitted or 'portfolio LNG' contracts with no resales attached and contribute to a further increase of spot LNG, or diminish the quantities going to the spot markets.

In the higher case, spot and short-term LNG trade could climb to account for 43 per cent of total LNG trade by 2020, based on existing capacity as well as capacity already under construction as of June 2016 (Figure 9.17). How the percentage of spot and short-term trade will evolve beyond 2020 depends on the structure of projects going forward and how LNG supply evolves post 2020. There is one further caveat in this analysis: some volumes will be traded under long-term contracts based on hub pricing, such as the Qatari contracts that go to the UK, Belgium, and the Netherlands that are based on NBP or TTF prices.

LNG Contracts and Flexibility 539

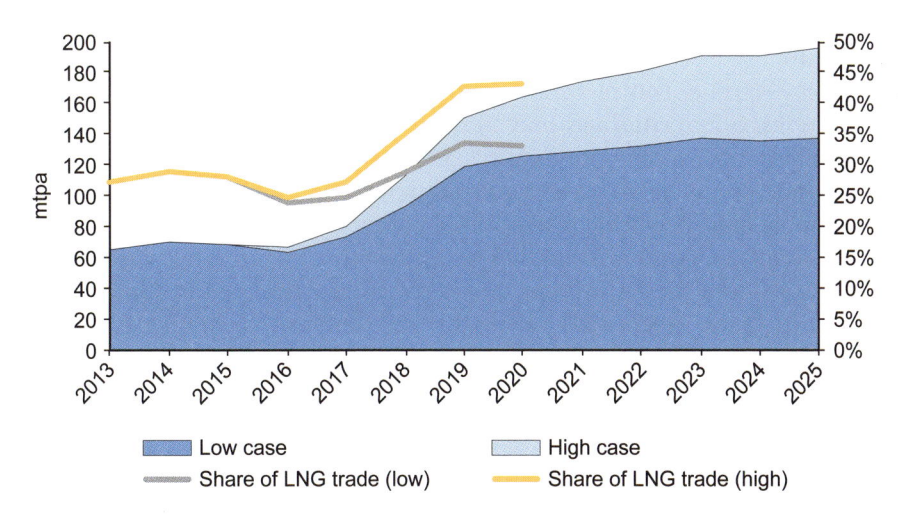

Figure 9.17: Future spot and short-term LNG trade
Source: Author's research.

Will these trends bring the LNG market to an inflexion point by 2020, ready to rely more significantly on the spot markets as the oil market did before? In 2005 the IEA identified three prerequisites for an efficient spot market (IEA, 2002):

- Large number of players, without any leading player that could manipulate prices;
- A fluid market with few or no bottlenecks. Transport of the commodity should not hinder its availability, in place or time;
- At least one place where the goods can be delivered to fulfil open deals.

The first criterion is likely to be fulfilled with Australia, Qatar, and the USA as the largest LNG suppliers. The other two criteria may still require some work.

This growth in spot market volume has two implications for long-term contracts:

Firstly, for existing long-term contracts, we believe that the current state of oversupply, combined with weakness and uncertainties regarding future demand evolution in Asia and the start of liberalization of the power and gas markets in Japan during 2016/17, will create a resistance to the extension of many long-term contracts. This is especially true if sellers are not willing to provide more flexibility in DQT and/or the pricing conditions required by buyers, or if buyers find themselves being locked into higher quantities of LNG than they need. This could be also exacerbated by a discontinuity between term and spot prices. The renegotiation of the RasGas/Petronet contract shows that buyers are determined to get better conditions. Some contracts may also be extended as short-term deals, so that buyers have more options to react to unexpected demand changes. As spot trade continues to grow, and trading houses play an increasing role, traditional players will likely trust the spot market more.

Secondly, might this mean that new projects taking FID from now until 2020 will move ahead without long-term contracts? Shell in Oman and Mobil in Qatar considered relying on spot volumes to build new LNG trains in the late 1990s, but rejected the idea as too risky (Jensen, 2004). Despite the fundamental changes coming on the LNG market and the growth in spot and short-term trading, we think that this is still a bridge too far at this stage. Current market conditions make it extremely challenging for new LNG projects to proceed without the support of long-term contracts, even though some are likely to move ahead without full coverage. There is nevertheless a push towards contracts of shorter duration, for example 10 years. Cameroon FLNG took FID supported by an eight-year contract with Gazprom Marketing and Trading. As David Ledesma states in Chapter 3, liquefaction represents roughly 75 per cent of the whole LNG chain investment for an 8 mtpa project ($6–$10 billion). Given the many uncertainties and the low oil and gas price environment as of mid-2016, the risk of FID without long-term contracts is probably too great for the moment, as LNG sponsors need visibility on revenues to secure financing. Some special circumstances might make this risk acceptable, such as a small (1–2 mtpa) project (potentially a leased FLNG) that benefits from a strategic location to reach diverse markets and the support of a player with a robust balance sheet and limited financing needs.

Meanwhile, could buyers start buying mostly or exclusively from the market? We are approaching that moment, and every percentage point increase in spot trading will bring us closer. Misalignment of existing supply conditions with buyers' needs and expectations, while alternative options exist, will provide the circumstances for a shift to occur. This shift happened in the US gas markets in the early 1980s; the first change that freed buyers from buying gas from producers under take-or-pay contracts at fixed gas supply prices came about when FERC Order 380 removed minimum bill obligations from all long-term contracts in 1984. Banning these obligations became necessary due to the mismatch of contract prices and lower market prices (Corbeau et al., 2012). US gas market liberalization culminated in Order 636 that unbundled the sale and transportation of natural gas, enabling suppliers to compete on an equal footing and fostering competition among suppliers.

Transitions rarely happen smoothly, and markets could witness a very rapid transition as changes accumulate. The drivers that could precipitate such changes are:

- A further increase in spot and short-term LNG trade, along with an expected increase in liquidity, so that market players get used to relying on spot or short-term LNG as a way of accessing LNG supplies. The analysis in this chapter suggests that this is likely to happen. As in the oil industry, the number of short-term contracts (less than four years) will increase to enable both suppliers and buyers to adapt to a rapidly changing supply and demand environment.

- Trading houses providing liquidity in the spot LNG market as they continue to build positions with both new and established players. Poten has estimated that total LNG volume delivered by traders in 2015 reached around 7 mtpa.[38] Traders can increase buyers' security of supply by providing LNG from different sources, while offering suppliers indirect access to buyers that they would not have otherwise approached. These trading houses must have access to physical shipping and, potentially, to regasification capacity (to store LNG).

- A sharp cost reduction that reduces risks for project developers. A cost reduction in the early 2000s enabled some projects to move ahead with SPAs that did not cover the entire output. But costs are now much higher than they were at that time. As noted in Chapter 3, the supply chain of an 8 mtpa plant generally costs $8.6 to 15.5 billion. The 20 mtpa Gorgon project in Australia cost $54 billion, not including tankers and regasification. LNG must become more affordable for developed and developing countries alike. This appears challenging based on the analysis presented in Chapter 4.

- Transparent price benchmarks that the LNG industry can use for trade. The industry needs a reliable price index, notably for Asia. However, an index is difficult to develop for a thinly traded market. Much less LNG is traded today than oil, and even less spot LNG is traded. Total spot and short-term LNG trade is equivalent to around two 165,000 m^3 cargoes per day. However, the spectacular growth of LNG trade, combined with an increased share of spot trading, will potentially triple these volumes over the coming five years. To that end, the example of the coal industry could be useful. Meanwhile, large LNG buyers, notably Japan, are pushing for the relaxation or elimination of the destination

---

[38] 'Traders Take More LNG Market Share in 2015', Poten LNG Opinion, Poten & Partners, June 2015.

clause present in most long-term contracts. This, along with the development of price indices reflecting LNG supply and demand, is part of Japan's strategy aimed at boosting liquidity and transparency in global LNG markets. GlobalCOAL developed an FOB index for Newcastle (the NEWC Index) by combining data on bids and offers posted on its platform as well as transactions executed on the platform. The NEWC Index has now established itself as the benchmark for the Asia–Pacific thermal coal market, underpinning significant volumes of index-linked physical coal transactions and supporting the swap market. But rather than having a daily price, it is a weekly index.[39] A weekly index smooths volatility and increases the relevance of the benchmark. Additionally, this is an FOB index; the LNG industry could potentially develop something similar in the Gulf of Mexico.

- One international project leading the way by changing business practices. As Cheniere demonstrated in the USA, one bold move by a market player is sometimes enough to trigger a complete change in practice. Only companies with great knowledge and previous experience in the spot market would consider moving with a lower contract coverage.

- Banks and lenders such as export credit agencies changing their requirements for financing LNG projects. The previous elements will be necessary for this to happen. Convincing banks and other financial institutions will nevertheless be difficult if market conditions do not improve. They have always played an important role in LNG project financing. While lending money, they have also protected themselves by requiring regular debt service payments out of the LNG project's cash flow.

Optimizing shipping

Another aspect of the great reconfiguration could affect shipping. Looking at a map representing LNG flows, shipping distances are clearly not optimized. LNG is shipped from Nigeria, Egypt, or Algeria to Asia, while the much closer European markets get Middle Eastern LNG. Despite the rise in spot trading, the majority of LNG is still linked to long-term contracts that do not always optimize shipping. When suppliers sell spot cargoes, they look at maximizing profits by optimizing operations along the entire LNG value chain, not just within transportation. Longer shipping distances may still result in increased profits, as long as the incremental shipping costs are more than offset by the overall gain (see Chapter 4) (Shcherbakova et al., 2014). An extreme example of that behaviour is the LNG re-exported from

---

[39] 'globalCOAL NEWC Index Methodology v.1h', globalCOAL website. https://www.globalcoal.com/Brochureware/NEWCIndex/Methodology/.

Europe to Asia, with the aim of capturing the price premium between the two markets.

But market conditions are changing and the advent of the USA as a major supplier is expected to further increase shipping distances globally; also, shipping US LNG to Asia, while Middle Eastern LNG goes to Europe, does not make sense in terms of shipping distances, fuel costs, and CO_2 emissions. It may still happen, though, as individual companies maximize profits, but in the current low oil and gas price environment, US LNG may be more likely to end up in Europe. Swapping cargoes would make even more sense in the case of Yamal's LNG supplies to Asia during the winter season.

Provisions for sending an LNG vessel to an alternative destination existed in the original long-term contracts, but as a solution to technical issues, such as operational constraints, and force majeure. For DES deliveries, any right for the buyer or the seller to change the destination would be a diversion right, while for FOB deliveries any right to change the destination would be called destination flexibility. Cargo swaps have been happening for almost a decade, even though they do not represent a significant part of the market. Swaps occur for two reasons:

- Shortening delivery routes when both sellers and buyers are able to receive at two different locations. In the past, that would have typically involved the USA and European markets with Africa/Europe and Trinidad as suppliers. These swaps cut transportation costs and freed up shipping capacity. A swap between Statoil and BG in 2009 with a cargo from Snøhvit ending in the UK's Isle of Grain, and one of BG's Trinidad LNG ending in the US Cove Point terminal, was reported to have saved each player $350,000 in fuel costs, without considering the reduced boil-off losses (Thompson, 2009).

- Different demand pattern between purchasers that leads to over-commitment on one side and shortage on the other. These swaps lead to increased market flexibility.

Optimizing shipping certainly refers to the first item.

Buyers and sellers are now increasingly keen to use flexibility tools for arbitrage or commercial diversion. The aim here is cost minimization and profit maximization, not optimization of the LNG fleet. As we are in a period of excess supply and very low prices, with NBP and Asian spot prices close to $4/MMBtu (as of mid-2016), margins are squeezed encouraging optimization.

Profit optimization already gives an indication of the contractual issues and technical bottlenecks that would arise if shipping were optimized. The optimization of LNG flows raises issues that include: the compatibility of the vessel with different LNG terminals, heterogeneous LNG fleets, limited berth availability at terminals, different seasonal demand patterns in LNG importing countries, impact on vessel schedules, and compatibility of the producing country and receiving country's laws.[40] Additionally, parties would want a minimum impact on their operations: the seller would want to minimize the impact of the redirected cargo on its existing customer base and to avoid any impact on normal operations in the liquefaction and shipping sectors.[41] The buyer would want any additional costs incurred in replacing the LNG to be covered. Sharing any profit arising from the diversion is a further key issue.

The rise of aggregators with 'portfolio' LNG has already been a step towards optimization, as these companies want to minimize their overall LNG fleet costs while optimizing profits. This has been BG's business model as they:

> ... manage contractual terms such as delivery schedules, optimise logistics, in particular making [their] fleet of LNG ships run as efficiently as possible, and if the opportunity presents, purchase spot cargoes. (BG Group, 2016)

When Shell acquired Repsol's LNG assets in 2013, the company mentioned that it:

> ... expects to add value to this portfolio by optimizing the new LNG flows in our world-wide customer base. (Shell, 2013)

Shell's equity LNG will increase to around 45 mtpa by 2018 once the recent merger with BG is completed.

The idea of optimizing shipping to reduce costs is certainly in the mind of buyers too. GAIL, seeking to reduce its transport cost, initiated a tender for an LNG cargo swap for up to one-third of its US LNG supplies (5.8 mtpa). Qatari deliveries to Italy provide another example, with the potential to swap with US deliveries so that US LNG reaches Italy and Qatari LNG is delivered to India.

Many studies have been conducted on optimizing LNG shipping. These often centre on the point of view of a single producer and are addressed as special cases of maritime inventory routing problems (Goel et al., 2012). A

---

[40] 'Optimising the Value of LNG Sale Agreements by Formulating Strategic Cargo Diversion and Destination Flexibility Clauses', James Atkin and Raina Lal, Bloomberg Law Reports. www.pseudology.org/gazprom/APLR_LNGArticleNovember2009.pdf.

[41] Operating an LNG liquefaction plant involves having a delivery schedule for each customer, on an annual basis (Annual Delivery Program), which tries to accommodate the expected needs of each party in a given year.

more general search for equilibrium faces the challenge that all LNG producers will seek to maximize profits and therefore target the end-user that is offering the highest price.

A study from the University of Texas looked at how parameters such as: high demand, larger capacity vessels, sailing speed, the impact of spot market trades, shipping costs, and the structure of the shipper (vertically integrated or not) influence LNG cargo movements. Taking Qatar as the equilibrium point, it concludes that LNG tankers are more likely to cross Qatar's longitude when demand and charter rates are high and when carrying a spot cargo. These are all signals that markets are tightening. Meanwhile, tankers are less likely to cross Qatar's longitude when spot shipping costs are higher and when they are operated by partly vertically integrated companies. Older vessels are less likely to embark on less efficient voyages, but vessel speed and ship size do not have a clear impact (Shcherbakova et al., 2014). Massol and Tchung-Ming (2010) looked at optimization in the framework of GECF suppliers and conclude that in the absence of a redistribution strategy, a cooperative strategy would not be implemented because it would not be a rational move for some individual exporters, despite being collectively profitable.

Using the Nexant World Gas Model, we tried to optimize shipping. If all long-term contracts are ended, the model shows a drop in total LNG trade, as some costly LNG is replaced by either domestic gas production or pipeline supplies, while natural gas demand drops due to demand-side reduction. A second modelling run designated all the LNG contracts as 'portfolio' by deleting the destination but keeping gas demand the same. In that case, LNG liquefaction plants would still have an obligation to send out LNG, while the model optimizes shipping. One downside is that this removes some LNG which is uncompetitive against either domestic gas production or against pipeline. Consequently, total LNG trade is slightly lower in the optimization case than in the base case scenario up to 2025 (by around 7 mtpa in 2020); in particular, LNG imports are lower in North America (Mexico), Europe, and Asia (China). After this point, LNG trade is roughly at the same level as in the base case.

By multiplying the LNG flows for each route by the cost of shipping, we calculate the total cost of shipping in both cases. The costs are adjusted due to the lower volumes of the optimization case. The savings that optimizing shipping would create would range from $2.0 to $2.7 billion per year over the whole period 2020–30. This means a saving of around $0.1/MMBtu, which may look small compared to the total price of delivered LNG, but is actually quite high at a time of squeezed margins.

The optimization of LNG flows would give the following results by 2020 (Figure 9.18):

- A larger share of North American LNG would go to Europe, while LNG flows to Asia would totally stop and LNG flows to Asia–Pacific (Japan and Korea) would be reduced. The flows to Latin America would remain the same.

- LNG supply from Asia–Pacific (Australia) would remain mostly within the region (Japan and Korea), while less would go to Asia and flows to Mexico would stop. But the most visible change is that inter-regional LNG flows are totally displaced.

- African LNG to Europe and Asia–Pacific are lower, while those to the Middle East stop. African LNG volumes to Latin America increase.

- Increased volumes of Middle Eastern LNG would go exclusively to Asia, Asia–Pacific, and the Middle East, but none would serve European and Latin American markets.

- Latin American LNG flows become more intra-regional; LNG flows to North America stop.

- Finally, FSU LNG exports target exclusively Asia–Pacific and Europe.

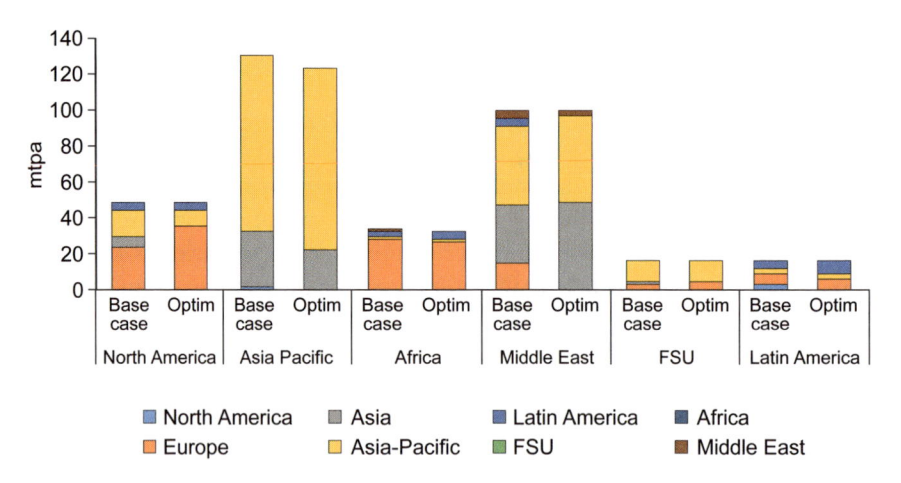

Figure 9.18: Interregional LNG flows by 2020
Source: Nexant world gas model.

The LNG industry is not quite yet at a stage where it can achieve perfect optimization of shipping. Contractual and technical constraints would make that difficult to achieve. However, it is likely that aggregators will attempt to achieve maximum optimization of their portfolios in order to preserve margins. Obviously the new Shell/BG will be a key company to observe, as well as companies such as Petronas, QatarGas, and Rasgas. Next in line would be Total, ExxonMobil, BP, and Chevron.

Conclusion

Looking at the next five years, many factors point to a change in LNG market configuration. Individually, these factors would not trigger massive changes, but together, they could create a great reconfiguration of the LNG business.

- LNG has become global and genuinely brings together buyers and sellers from all regions. This state of affairs will only increase over the coming years as additional smaller buyers appear, while demand from incumbents is more uncertain, as highlighted in Chapters 2 and 6. The advent of North America's non destination-bound LNG supply (see Chapter 5) will create a major new source of LNG, challenging traditional suppliers from the Middle East and Africa in Europe, and from Qatar and Australia in Asia. However, forthcoming US LNG sales shift both price and volume risks onto the buyers. This contrasts with the previous position where the buyer took the volume risk and the supplier the price risk. Other large future potential suppliers, such as Russia, Canada, and Eastern Africa are, for now, sticking to the traditional model of long-term contracts and oil indexation.

- The LNG market is walking into a state of oversupply, with 150 mtpa coming on line over 2015–20; this is likely to result in a boom (2015–20) then a bust. In an oversupply situation, the LNG market shifts in favour of buyers, who have been keen to obtain better contractual conditions, notably more destination flexibility and different price indexations. Any discontinuity between term and spot prices, or between buyers' LNG contracts and actual needs, could precipitate buyers (or sellers) towards increased spot trade. The renegotiation of the RasGas contract shows that contracts can be renegotiated.

- While the industry likes long-term contracts to finance its projects, it has also become accustomed to spot and short-term LNG trade to capture arbitrage opportunities. LNG flows shift in response to price fluctuations and market players' strategies, defying the inflexibility of long-term contracts.

- Volumes of spot and short-term LNG trade will increase, supported by uncontracted (spare LNG), portfolio LNG, and flexible US LNG, and also by the non-extension of some existing LNG contracts. In some cases, portfolio LNG has been re-contracted through secondary sales and is no longer available for spot trading. More often, such LNG does not have a clear target or is resold to aggregators. This structure gives suppliers the option to choose the market, but in an oversupplied market where buyers have the advantage, many suppliers are likely to end up fighting for the same buyers.

- Many LNG contracts will expire over the period 2015–25, providing an opportunity to buyers either to achieve better deals or to not re-enter long-term contracts; they may instead contract for shorter durations or rely on the spot market. In many regions, the gas industry's narrative of rapidly growing gas demand faces the reality of sluggish or declining gas consumption. For example, Japan, which restarted some nuclear power plants in August 2015, is likely to absorb less LNG in the future, while a huge question mark exists about China's thirst for LNG.

- Market players on the supply side have changed and now include IOCs, NOCs, end-users such as gas and power companies, as well as banks and trading houses. This diversity offers a possibility for change, due to the different approaches taken vis-à-vis LNG trade. In particular, trading houses will be crucial in driving these changes, as they have already taken positions in LNG trade and are proponents of spot trading. Some traders, like Trafigura, openly support:

  > ... the use of a transparent, recognisable spot LNG assessment and the increase in the liquidity of the swap market for LNG spot. (Trafigura, 2016)

- Buyers are also changing with the advent of smaller, less creditworthy buyers in developing countries. New buyers tend to issue tenders and buy smaller quantities on the spot market. Meanwhile, traditional buyers facing demand uncertainties may no longer be confident that there will be enough demand in their home market, due to lack of competitiveness of gas against coal and renewables, or due to forthcoming market liberalization processes. Consequently they will either ask for more flexibility regarding annual contract quantity (ACQ) or destination (FOB instead of DES), so they can redirect unwanted LNG. Or they may stop extending long-term contracts that are expiring, and turn to the spot market, if they feel that enough uncontracted LNG could be available at affordable prices.

- Improved third party access (TPA) and the end of final destination clauses in Europe were crucial to making Europe a more flexible market, while the development of liquid hubs enabled LNG to be delivered at spot prices. Asian buyers are becoming more vocal about the end of final destination clauses, while TPA could become more efficient in Japan and potentially in China.

- Uncommitted cargoes and surplus shipping capacity are indispensable to a more flexible LNG trade. Departing from the original business model of ships linked to specific contracts, an increasing number of ships have been built without the support of long-term contracts, in order to seize spot trading opportunities. Optimizing shipping through more widespread use of swaps may also create more free shipping capacity, but it may also break some links within the LNG value chain that would ultimately affect long-term contracts.

Over the coming 10 years, the LNG industry is expected to experience a reconfiguration, prompted by an impressive growth of spot LNG. This change will allow buyers to source their LNG supplies from the market rather than forcing them to rely on long-term contracts. The forthcoming wave of LNG supply will shift the balance of power into the hands of buyers who seek increased flexibility, and it is applying additional pressure on suppliers to adapt to their changing needs. With the emergence of smaller and less creditworthy buyers in developing markets, and rising demand uncertainties and liberalization in Asia, buyers are now increasingly exposed to market risks in deregulated markets and are careful about committing to long-term volumes.

This reconfiguration will make existing long-term contracts bend but not break over the short term, though it will also pave the way for potential further changes. In a low oil and gas price environment, cargo optimization could flourish. While it will remain difficult for new greenfield LNG projects to move ahead without the support of long-term contracts (given the high capital costs and the need to finance the project), long-term contracts covering existing projects already amortized could be at risk. In the current environment, with uncertainty around both oil and gas prices and future regional and country-specific LNG demand, project sponsors will still be reluctant to trust financial derivatives to hedge project risk on LNG projects. Taking this road without certainty on future demand may make these companies the targets of M&A activity by other players. Shell's acquisition of BG reminds everyone that big players can be absorbed as well. However, should LNG players rely increasingly on the spot market over the coming years, this could pave the way for some LNG projects to move ahead with a reduced share of long-term contracts or long-term contracts of shorter duration (a maximum of 10 years).

BIBLIOGRAPHY

Al-Tamimi, N. (2015). 'Navigating uncertainty: Qatar's response to the global gas boom', Brookings Doha Center Analysis Paper, Number 15, Brookings Doha Center, June 2015. www.brookings.edu/~/media/Research/Files/Papers/2015/06/25-tamimi-gas-boom/English-PDF.pdf?la=en.

Ashurst (2012). 'AIPN releases new 2012 version of its model LNG master sales agreement', July. https://www.ashurst.com/doc.aspx?id_Content=8088.

BG Group (2016).'Capitalising on the growth of LNG', 'About us', BG Group Website. www.bg-group.com/29/about-us/lng/.

CEER (2014). 'CEER Status Review on monitoring access to EU LNG terminals in 2009–2013', Council of European Energy Regulators, Ref. C14-GWG-111-03, 22 October.

Corbeau, A.-S., Braaksma, A., Hussin, F., Yagoto, Y., and Yamamoto, T. (2014). *The Asian Quest for LNG in a Globalising Market*, IEA Partner Country Series, Paris: OECD/IEA. www.iea.org/publications/freepublications/publication/PartnerCountrySeriesTheAsianQuestforLNGinaGlobalisingMarket.pdf.

Corbeau, A.-S., Volk, D., Sinton, J., Jiang, J., Jiang, P., Teng, T., Li, B., and Yue, F. (2012). *Gas Pricing and Regulation: China's Challenges and IEA Experience*, IEA Partner Country Series, Paris: OECD/International Energy Agency.

Critchlow, A. (2014). 'US shale no "game changer" for LNG, say Qatar energy minister', *The Telegraph*, 2 February 2014. www.telegraph.co.uk/finance/newsbysector/energy/oilandgas/10611960/US-shale-no-game-changer-for-LNG-say-Qatar-energy-minister.html.

Eberhard, A. (2011). 'The future of South African coal: market, investment and policy challenges', PESD Working Paper 100, Program on Energy and Sustainable Development Stanford, January. http://iis-db.stanford.edu/pubs/23082/WP_100_Eberhard_Future_of_South_African_Coal.pdf.

Fattouh, B. (2011). 'An anatomy of the crude oil pricing system', OIES Working Paper WPM40, Oxford Institute for Energy Studies. www.oxfordenergy.org/wpcms/wp-content/uploads/2011/03/WPM40-AnAnatomyoftheCrudeOilPricingSystem-BassamFattouh-2011.pdf.

Fattouh, B., Rogers, H., and Steward, P. (2015). 'The US shale gas revolution and its impact on Qatar's position in gas markets', Center on Global Energy Policy Working Paper, Columbia SIPA, March. http://energypolicy.columbia.edu/sites/default/files/energy/The%20US%20Shale%20Gas%20Revolution%20and%20Its%20Impact%20on%20Qatar%27s%20Position%20in%20Gas%20Markets_March%202015.pdf.

GIIGNL (2000; 2001; ... ; 2014; 2015). Annual reports from 2000 to 2014, International group of Liquefied Natural Gas Importers.

GIIGNL (2014b). 'Regas Terminal overview: Qflex/max acceptability', February 2014. www.giignl.org/system/files/q-flexq-max_acceptability_database_-_march_.pdf.

Goel, V., Furman K. C., Song J-H., and El-Bakry A. S. (2012). 'Large Neighborhood Search for LNG Inventory Routing', *Journal of Heuristics*, Volume 18, Issue 6, 821–48, December. www.optimization-online.org/DB_FILE/2012/02/3342.pdf.

Griffin, P. (ed.) (2012). *Liquefied Natural Gas: the law and business of LNG* (2nd Edition), Globe Business Publishing.

Hartley P. R. (2013). 'The Future of Long-term LNG Contracts', RISE Working Paper 14-022, Rice Initiative for the Study of Economics.

Horiike, S., Hashimoto, H., and Fukuoka, S. (2015). 'Issues surrounding planned and proposed LNG procurement from the United States', The Institute of Energy Economics, Japan (IEEJ), March. http://eneken.ieej.or.jp/data/5988.pdf.

IEA (2002). *Flexibility in Natural Gas Supply and Demand*, Paris: OECD/International Energy Agency, December.

IEA CCC (2015). 'Coal contracts and long-term supplies', International Energy Agency Clean Coal Centre. www.iea-coal.org.uk/documents/83772/9505/Coal-contracts-and-long-term-supplies,-CCC/258. (Executive Summary of: *Coal contracts and long-term supplies*, CCC/258, Paul Baruya, ISBN 978-92-9029-581-5, October 2015.)

Iniss, H. (2004). 'Operational, vertical integration in the gas industry, with emphasis on LNG: is it necessary to ensure viability?', Centre for Energy, Petroleum and Mineral Law and Policy, University of Dundee.

Jaffe, A., Elass, J., and Miller, K. (2013). 'The Gulf Cooperation Council Natural Gas Conundrum: Geopolitics Drive Shortages Amid Plenty', Harvard University's Belfer Center and Rice University's Baker Institute Center for Energy Studies, 23 October. http://belfercenter.hks.harvard.edu/files/MO-CES-pub-GeoGasGCC-102513.pdf.

Jensen, J. (2004). 'The Development of a Global LNG Markets: Is it likely? If so by when?', OIES Working Paper NG 5, Oxford Institute for Energy Studies.

KAPSARC (2015). 'Natural Gas: Entering the New Dark Age?', King Abdullah Petroleum Studies and Research Center, August.

Kazmin, R. (2015). 'Portugal's Galp shortlists five companies in LNG tender', ICIS, 31 July. www.icis.com/resources/news/2015/07/31/9908668/portugal-s-galp-shortlists-five-companies-in-lng-tender/.

Kim, B. (2006). 'The future of the LNG spot market', International Gas Union, 23 World Gas Conference, Report of Study Group D3, Amsterdam, 5–9 June.

Ledesma, D. (2011). 'Natural Gas in Oman', Chapter 12 in Fattouh, B. and Stern, J.P. (eds.), *Natural Gas Markets in the Middle East and North Africa*, Oxford: OUP/OIES.

Massol, O. and Tchung-Ming, S. (2010). 'Cooperation among liquefied natural gas suppliers: Is rationalization the sole objective?', Sixth Conference on The Economics of Energy Markets, Toulouse, France, 28–9 January.

Morita, K. (2003). 'LNG: Falling Price and Increasing Flexibility of Supply – Risk Redistribution Creates Contract Diversity', The Institute of Energy Economics, Japan (IEEJ). http://eneken.ieej.or.jp/en/data/pdf/185.pdf.

Qatargas (2014). 'Qatargas sells its first cargo of LNG to JOVO, an independent LNG importer from the People's Republic of China', Qatargas press release, 26 October 2014. https://www.qatargas.com/English/MediaCenter/PressReleases/2014/Pages/First-cargo-to-JOVO.aspx.

Ritz, R.A. (2014). 'Price discrimination and limits to arbitrage: An analysis of global LNG markets', (Revised version: June 2014), *Energy Economics*, September. www.econ.cam.ac.uk/people/research/rar36/pubs/RobertRitz_LNG_July2014.pdf.

Ruester, S. (2009). 'Changing Contract Structures in the International Liquefied Natural Gas Markets – A First Empirical Analysis', *Revue d'Economie Industrielle*, 127(3): 89–112.

Shcherbakova, A., Kleit, A.N., and Dhanurendra. B. (2014). 'Exploring shipping inefficiencies in global LNG trade patterns', Presentation at 37th IAEE International Conference, New York City, June. www.usaee.org/usaee2014/submissions/Presentations/IAEE%20presentation%20Shcherbakova.pdf.

Shell (2013). 'Shell Continues To Expand Its LNG Leadership With The Purchase Of New Positions From Repsol S.A.', Media Release, Shell, 26 February. www.shell.com/global/aboutshell/media/news-and-media-releases/2013/shell-repsol-260213.html.

Shiryaevskaya, A. (2015). 'Trafigura LNG Trading More Than Doubles on New Buyer Demand', Anna Shiryaevskaya, Bloomberg Business, 14 December 2015. www.bloomberg.com/news/articles/2015-12-14/trafigura-lng-trading-more-than-doubles-as-nations-start-imports.

Thompson S. (2009). 'The new LNG trading model, short term markets developments and prospects', Poten & Partners, Inc., paper presented to the International Gas Union 24th World Gas Conference, Argentina.

Trafigura (2016). The 'LNG' page on the Trafigura website: www.trafigura.com/our-services/oil-petroleum-products/lng/.

Vivoda, V. (2014). *Energy Security in Japan: Challenges After Fukushima*, Routledge.

Yergin D. and Stoppard M. (2003). 'The Next Prize', *Foreign Affairs*, Nov/Dec.

CHAPTER 10

CONCLUSION: LNG MARKETS – THE GREAT RECONFIGURATION

Anne-Sophie Corbeau[1]

The LNG world has been turned upside down and profoundly changed in just two years. In mid-2014 the mood had been cheerily optimistic, but it then plummeted to an air of 'doom and gloom' in early 2016 when oil prices touched $30/bbl and spot gas prices in Europe and Asia hit $4–5/MMBtu. Coal has been displacing gas in both these markets, and global LNG markets are currently oversupplied. Three factors lie behind the change in outlook:

- The LNG supply capacity coming to the markets over the period 2015–20 has proved to be much greater than required.

- LNG demand in Asia (the premium market targeted by most LNG exporters) is weaker than expected, having declined by 2 per cent in 2015 compared with 2014 (GIIGNL, 2016).

- Oil and spot gas prices have fallen to levels unseen for a decade, threatening the economics of the newest projects coming on line and placing a question mark over future LNG expansion.

The large number of projects which had previously planned to take final investment decisions (FIDs) in 2014–15 suggests that few in the industry had seen this 'triple whammy' coming.

When we began considering a book on LNG in mid-2014, our idea then was that the coming surge in LNG export capacity would have significant implications for global LNG markets and that the rise of spot-based US LNG might challenge the industry's traditional pricing and contractual practices. Around 100 mtpa of capacity had already been sanctioned in Australia, Russia, Malaysia, and Indonesia, though only one

---

[1] This chapter draws on the other chapters of this book. However, the opinions given here are solely those of the author and may differ from those of the authors of the other chapters.

US export project had received FID. A few months later three US projects – Freeport LNG, Cameron LNG, and Cove Point – were sanctioned. In 2015 one further US LNG project, Corpus Christi, as well as Cameroon LNG, also moved forward. This brought total LNG export capacity coming online over 2015–20 to around 150 mtpa – twice the export capacity of Qatar, the largest LNG exporter as of 2016. Meanwhile Asia was still considered the premium market and thought to be capable of absorbing any LNG available at any price. The 'new normal' in China – with lower economic (and hence energy and gas demand) growth – was not yet fully recognized. The last nail in the coffin of an 'optimistic LNG story' came with the abrupt decline in oil and gas prices: hub and spot gas/LNG prices declined in early 2014, to be followed by oil and oil-indexed gas/LNG prices from late 2014 onwards, bringing the gradual expectation of 'lower for longer' prices. Views on the precise definition of 'longer', and about what level of rebound may be expected, differ greatly within the industry and among analysts. Consequently this new LNG supply is arriving at a time of great uncertainty for the natural gas industry. Concerns also exist about the period post 2020, when lack of investment decisions between 2016 and 2018 could lead to a time of tight LNG supply. If demand does rise, the supply/demand cycle could turn very quickly.

Over the course of 2015 and up to May 2016, we changed our perspectives on LNG to encompass the altered situation for the gas and energy markets. The United Nations Climate Change Conference (COP21) in December 2015 failed to fully recognize the key role of natural gas in the reduction of CO_2 emissions and in the transition to a carbon-constrained world. The gas industry maintains that natural gas is the best fuel over the medium to long term, but it struggles to convince politicians and the general public of this, and has had difficulty in prompting a full consideration of coal's externalities (in terms of CO_2 emissions and particulate pollution) and their detrimental impact on health. Indeed, despite the decline in key gas price benchmarks, coal remains extremely competitive in most regions (except the USA), in the absence of an effective carbon price and policies aiming at closing coal-fired plants, and this commercial argument is currently outweighing environmental concerns

As we look forward, the LNG industry seems ripe for change or, as we see it, 'a great reconfiguration'. Over its 52-year lifetime, the LNG industry has evolved in many ways, constantly adapting itself to various supply and demand events. While the current oversupply and low-price situation is likely to have a profound impact on LNG's future supply/demand balance, the coming reconfiguration also concerns the industry's basic business model. In this model, massive investment in infrastructure, often costing tens of billions of dollars, is underpinned by long-term, oil-price linked – and often inflexible

– gas contracts. Given the present and future market uncertainties, existing buyers are no longer prepared to accept such contractual terms, while many new buyers are less creditworthy than sellers might like, and would prefer to operate and structure contractual arrangements differently from the ways adopted to date. The challenge for the industry in the future will be to find the correct balance between buyers' concerns about competitiveness and flexibility and sellers' need to secure financing and to make positive returns, in order to build a bright future for LNG.

False starts and U-turns: the non-linear path of LNG supply/demand

The evolution of the global LNG supply and demand balance has been anything but linear, and actual developments have often confounded expectations. LNG has in fact proved to be surprisingly resilient to multiple shocks. Expectations have been challenged right from its infancy. While Atlantic Basin LNG trade had been expected to expand substantially in the 1970s, with Europe as a foundation buyer and the USA likely to become a major importer, the reality proved to be entirely different. Europe was the first region to import LNG in 1964 and remained the largest importing region until 1977. Europe developed alternative supply options ranging from domestic gas to pipeline supply (notably from Russia), while pricing demands made Algerian and Libyan LNG less competitive than these alternatives. Apart from the expansion of LNG capacity in Algeria, no other large-scale supply to the Atlantic Basin came on stream until Nigeria and Trinidad and Tobago in 1999. LNG demand was therefore subdued until 2000, when domestic production started to decline and diversification of supplies was needed. The liberalization of the US gas industry after the Natural Gas Policy Act of 1978 brought a halt to US imports of LNG (Chapter 1).

Many unanticipated supply/demand shocks took place over the period 2000–16 (Chapter 2). The decline in UK domestic production from 2000 prompted the construction of major regas infrastructure in this important market with pipeline connections to north-west Europe (instrumental in catalysing hub trading in the early 2010s). The USA was transformed from a major future LNG importer into an exporter with the prospect of having the third-largest export capacity by 2020 following the boom in shale gas. The opposite situation is reflected by Egypt, which started importing LNG in 2015, only 10 years after its first LNG exports, while Libya and Yemen ceased exporting in 2011 and 2015, respectively. The abrupt halt to Angolan LNG exports in 2014 marked the first time a facility had become non-operational within a year of its commissioning; there have also been long delays in the giant Australian Gorgon project that closed for several months immediately after loading its first cargo. In contrast, the Fukushima nuclear accident in 2011 resulted in a surge in Japanese LNG imports. Combined with the growth of LNG demand in other Asian countries over 2010–14, this contributed to diverting LNG away from Europe, where LNG imports halved over that period. Meanwhile Spain, having been Europe's largest LNG importer in 2008, saw its LNG demand cut to one-third of its former level in 2014, due to poor economic growth and competition from coal and renewables. Finally, re-exports of surplus LNG highlight the differences between previous demand expectations, contracted gas supplies, and market realities.

Market developments since late 2014 point to a 'reverse demand shock' as Asian LNG demand has fallen, notably in Japan, Korea, and China. The question is whether this is a taste of things to come or just a hiccup. Asia is crucial, not only because of its historical dominance, but mostly because it is seen as the largest future LNG demand centre with limited alternative gas supply sources – an assumption already being challenged by the start-up of new gas pipeline supply from Russia to China in 2020. Should this assumption prove to be flawed, it would have tremendous implications for the LNG industry.

A bumpy ride is in sight for the next four years. The supply side transformation ahead of us is exceptional, as export capacity will rise by 150 mtpa (or 50 per cent) over 2015–20 (Chapter 5). The previous LNG supply wave, led by Qatar, from 2009 to 2011, saw only half of that volume (77 mtpa). These additions will reshuffle the rankings of LNG exporters, with Australia dethroning Qatar, both followed by the USA – in 2015, the smallest exporter. But this rapid expansion may have unintended consequences, sending the LNG industry into a major supply boom-and-bust cycle. As of May 2016, we have seen only the very early stages of this boom, as additional LNG volumes from the earliest-commissioned new projects have only come to the markets slowly. But the consequences are already apparent, with LNG spot prices collapsing to around $4/MMBtu in Asia and Europe ahead of the biggest increase in LNG supplies, which will take place over 2017–18. The compounded effects of low prices and the surge in capacity are setting the stage for a potential dearth of FIDs, and already many project FIDs originally intended for 2015 have been postponed indefinitely. The magnitude of the bust will be determined by two factors – how long this pause in FIDs lasts and when global markets are expected to rebalance. If markets rebalance faster than expected, there is a danger that supply will be inadequate when demand picks up, striking a damaging blow to the gas industry.

From a cosy club to a multi company global business

For a long time the LNG community has been a small cosy club (Chapter 1). In 1971, six countries imported LNG from three exporting countries. As of early 2000, there were still only nine importing countries, and they were facing 11 exporters. This created a 'relationship culture', especially in Asia, which from 1977 onwards became undisputedly the largest LNG importing region. Japan, Korea, and Taiwan dominated global LNG trade from then on, always accounting for more than 50 per cent (and up to 79 per cent) of global imports. They also chose to become involved in the LNG value chain: Japanese and Korean companies built liquefaction plants and invested in upstream/liquefaction and shipping. This move was prompted by security of supply concerns as these three countries depend almost entirely on LNG, with no credible alternative in sight. For them, gas is LNG. Their LNG demand was also supported by regional LNG exporters: Brunei, Indonesia, and Malaysia. Apart from Abu Dhabi, the Middle East played no part in LNG supply until late 1996, when Qatar started exporting. After 2000, Asia's import dominance was reinforced as China, India and, in the 2010s, other south-east Asian countries and Pakistan, started importing LNG.

But as time went on, the LNG industry started to diversify and develop new ideas and new technologies (Chapter 2, 3, and 4). The expansion of LNG trade after 2000 was nothing short of remarkable in terms of growth and of the regions connected. LNG trade jumped from 102 mtpa in 2000 to 245 mtpa in 2015. In 2000, no LNG was imported into Latin America, the Middle East, China, India, south-east Asia or Africa, while as of early 2016, 35 LNG countries from all regions (except the Former Soviet Union) imported LNG, while 20 countries export, or have exported, it. Qatar supplied only 7 per cent of global LNG trade in 1999, as against 32 per cent in 2015. As of May 2016, due to gas shortages and war, Egypt, Libya, and Yemen are no longer exporters, while Angola is set to restart LNG exports in 2016 – as we finalize this book. Advances in floating regasification have played a major role in enabling developing countries to access LNG. The LNG import facilities in Latin America, the Middle East, Africa, and parts of south-east Asia are largely based on floating storage and regasification units (FSRUs) (Chapter 4).

This expansion of LNG trade has triggered a substantial increase in the number and diversity of LNG players. On the liquefaction side, LNG project structures have proved to be adaptable and able to meet the changing needs of the industry (Chapter 3). Meanwhile, among Asian LNG buyers, Inpex became an LNG operator (Ichthys), while new entrant Perenco sanctioned its Cameroon floating liquefaction (FLNG) project. The first FLNG export plant is expected to start in mid 2016, enabling development of stranded gas fields. FLNG has attracted not only conventional players (Shell and Petronas), but also companies (EXMAR and Golar LNG) eager to capitalize on their experience in FSRUs (Chapter 4).

Even though new players are emerging, some consolidation is taking place in LNG supply. This has already been seen in the merger of Shell and BG. Portfolio players, using their contracted LNG supply to optimize trade depending on price differentials, are taking a central position.[2] Significantly, around half the long-term contracts and the majority of short-term contracts signed in 2015 involve portfolio players. Other key players to watch are ExxonMobil, Total, and Eni which are pursuing various projects in all parts of the world and could be potentially seeking to grow further through acquisitions during a period of low oil prices

Originally, shipping was in the hands of either exporters or importers (when LNG was bought FOB). The increase in trade, as well as the rise in spot trade, has opened the door to independent ship owners (Golar and Höegh) over the past decade, followed by players with expertise in the shipping business (EXMAR and BW Gas). In the mid-2000s, they were joined by Teekay and Greek companies (GasLog, Dynagas, and Maran Gas). Some 52 years of technical improvements have made LNG ships bigger and safer, allowing LNG to be transported at an economic cost and enabling LNG to be competitive with pipeline supply alternatives. The largest LNG carriers (Q-max) are 10 times larger than the very first LNG ship, but the need to adapt import terminals, together with constraints on transiting the Panama Canal, mean that the industry is unlikely to build bigger ships. However, Arctic ice-breaking tankers are under construction for Russia's Yamal LNG project (Chapter 4).

On the market side, new companies have appeared: smaller LNG players supporting their own country's entry into the LNG business, (former) LNG exporters, power companies, LNG traders, and new entrants challenging the dominance of incumbents. Even in Asia, there are substantial differences between countries along the gas value chain: Japan will have a multiplicity of power and gas companies while Korea and Taiwan have a single national champion – though companies such as K-Power, Posco, and more recently Hyundai, seek to further develop their LNG imports. Likewise, China has three national oil companies, which are being challenged by new entrants such as ENN and Huadian.

---

[2] Portfolio LNG is LNG supply (often) owned by an aggregator and not tied to a specific destination. The aggregator can then either sign secondary sales contracts from its portfolio without specifying the origin of the LNG, or keep it to use in spot market interventions.

A further new trend is that of cooperation among buyers. In 2015 TEPCO and Chubu Electric created JERA, a market-based aggregator in charge of upstream energy and fuel procurement. JERA is the largest global LNG buyer, with around 40 mpta contracted as of 2016. In early 2016, JERA, CNOOC, and KOGAS discussed plans to cooperate on management of their contracted oversupply. Their LNG contracts together represent around one-third of world LNG trade (80 mtpa). Tokyo Gas and Kansai Electric have also announced cooperation on LNG purchases, while Kansai also has a partnership with Engie. Buyers in other countries are also announcing trading cooperation deals to optimize their LNG supply portfolios and potentially reduce shipping costs. It remains to be seen whether buyers from different countries can cooperate, given their different demand profiles and supply portfolios. Finally, traders such as Trafigura and Vitol are taking a growing role in LNG trading, aiming at increasing flexibility and spot trading (Chapter 9).

The development of small-scale LNG (cargo lots of 6,000–10,000 mt) is still in its infancy, though the market is developing in a number of directions. These include the use of LNG as a fuel for ships (bunker fuel) and road transport, and to supply remote gas networks and medium to large gas users who are not connected to gas pipelines. Chapter 7 examines the way that this new market is growing, with LNG displacing oil products for economic as well as environmental reasons. The narrowing of the oil/gas price spread since 2015 has reduced growth expectations for LNG in transport, but the combination of legislation reducing the amount of sulphur in marine fuels and growing concerns over the impact of particulate emissions from diesel in urban areas means that demand growth in the sector is expected to be positive. Ship owners in Europe and North America are increasingly specifying 'LNG ready' vessels for new build, while a number of ferries and other ships are running on LNG, particularly in the Baltic. Also in the Baltic, LNG is supplying off-pipeline industrial users, whilst Indonesia plans considerable growth of small-scale LNG cargoes around the archipelago to supply remote power stations and industrial users. The use of LNG in road haulage in China is already significant and is expected to grow as environmental pressures mount. Even though individual buyer demand is small, cumulatively, the volumes could grow to between 25 and 50 mtpa by 2030. Probably the most important driver will be the rate of adoption of LNG as a marine fuel.

The final step may be towards a world where the distinction between buyers and sellers is no longer clear cut. Buyers will increasingly invest into the upstream to secure strategic stakes in LNG projects, while portfolio sellers will increasingly become involved in marketing the gas.

Where is LNG demand heading?

ExxonMobil envisages a tripling of LNG demand by 2040 to around 760 mtpa, from today's levels (ExxonMobil, 2015). But how we get there – if we do – remains unclear. The assumptions that prevailed until 2014 (Asian LNG demand is infinite, on the back of strong Chinese and India LNG demand, and these buyers will pay a premium for LNG) are certainly worth revisiting.

The future of LNG demand is intrinsically linked to that for natural gas (Chapter 6). But the opposite is also true: LNG is fundamental to the gas business. The 'blue fuel' faces a public image problem: despite being a low-emitting fuel it is, nevertheless, a fossil fuel. The 2011–14 period of high oil and spot gas prices have labelled gas an expensive commodity. Natural gas still struggles to compete with coal in most regions despite the decline in gas prices, since coal prices have declined as well. In addition, the low oil price environment has boosted the competitiveness of oil in the industrial and transport sectors. If the gas industry fails to convince politicians and public opinion that natural gas is a 'triple A' – affordable, abundant, and environmentally acceptable – product, the next wave of LNG demand may be much weaker than expected. But the current low oil and gas price environment provides a unique opportunity for natural gas to enter new markets in Asia (Bangladesh, Vietnam, and Myanmar), the Middle East (Bahrain, Lebanon), Africa (Ghana, South Africa, and Morocco), and Latin America (the Caribbean). These markets are the ones currently in the spotlight, but more markets could potentially be unlocked in Africa if the conditions are right. Sellers may need to be innovative to secure additional demand by providing LNG-to-power solutions, while bearing in mind that some new players may only need 1–2 mtpa. And above all, LNG needs to be affordable.

LNG demand is particularly hard to estimate, as it results from a delicate balance involving gas demand, domestic production, and pipeline imports. Counter-intuitively, it may grow in markets (such as Europe) where gas demand is stagnating, because rising global LNG supply leads to increased import requirements, and countries opt for LNG instead of pipeline gas for political, supply diversification, and flexibility reasons. LNG demand may also decline while gas demand grows, in places where rapidly growing domestic production covers demand (Argentina and Mexico); alternatively, it may proceed in 'hiccups' reflecting LNG's interaction with pipeline supplies (China).

Our analysis of the different regions in Chapter 6 underlines a wide range of potential future LNG demand paths. The main factors are:

- The evolution of economic growth and population;
- The competitiveness of gas against renewables, coal, and oil (notably whether lower gas prices will generate a demand rebound);
- Whether governments will promote natural gas as a solution to improving air quality and reducing CO_2 emissions;
- The evolution of import gaps in countries or regions, and how LNG fits in against alternative pipeline options – this is particularly relevant for Europe, China, and India;
- The political will to diversify away from existing pipeline suppliers, as is the case in Europe with Russia.

Table 10.1: LNG demand ranges (mtpa)

	2015	*2020*	*2025*	*2030*
High case				
Japan/Korea/Taiwan	133	143	148	151
China/India	35	85	93	135
Other Asia	10	31	63	104
Latin America	19	23	41	55
USA/Canada	2	0	0	0
ME-Africa	10	24	34	50
Europe (high)	*38*	*52*	*82*	*111*
Europe (low)	*38*	*11*	*26*	*50*
Case 1 (high)	*245*	*357*	*461*	*606*
Case 2 (low)	*245*	*316*	*405*	*545*
Low case				
Japan/Korea/Taiwan	133	111	113	111
China/India	35	62	71	104
Other Asia	10	26	46	68
Latin America	19	11	19	27
USA/Canada	2	0	0	0
ME-Africa	10	13	18	20
Europe (high)	*38*	*52*	*82*	*111*
Europe (low)	*38*	*11*	*26*	*50*
Case 3 (high)	*245*	*275*	*349*	*441*
Case 4 (low)	*245*	*234*	*293*	*380*

Note: LNG demand numbers have been rounded (see Chapter 6).

Source: Author research.

Table 10.1 summarizes high and low regional demand outlooks. (As highlighted in Chapter 6, these outlooks have been analysed separately, taking into account the regional market dynamics, and they are not meant to be added up.) Europe plays a balancing role, so that high LNG demand in other regions is likely to be coupled with low European LNG imports, unless the region as a whole decides to limit Russian pipeline gas for political reasons. Meanwhile, in the case of low demand in other regions, Europe will absorb additional volumes of LNG. Consequently we have four cases for LNG demand. It is important to note that LNG demand from transport – maritime and road – has not been added to this table, even though it provides an additional outlet for LNG (Chapter 7). There is a strong likelihood that LNG will feature as a transportation fuel in the coming 20 years, although it is as yet uncertain whether it will play only a minor role in transport or become a significant global fuel. The competitiveness of LNG against other fuels and new alternatives – such as ultra-low sulphur marine fuels – will be key.

The High Demand cases (Cases 1 and 2) picture a bright future for LNG, with LNG demand more than doubling by 2030, despite a slow start-up for Case 2. However, the Low Demand cases (Cases 3 and 4) paint a totally different picture. They include a fall in demand in some key markets – JKT as well as Latin America – requiring Europe to act as the balancing market (Case 3), but even that would not be sufficient to absorb all the volumes currently coming to the markets. It is very unlikely that Case 4, combining low LNG demand in all regions, could ever happen, but if it ever did, it would severely damage the global LNG industry.

It is important to underline that specific factors, such as weather conditions, can reduce or exacerbate LNG demand. In Brazil, the dispatch of thermal power plants depends on hydrology and is therefore unpredictable. The range of LNG demand on a daily or weekly basis will thus vary between minimum dispatch and 100 per cent dispatch, given that neither domestic production nor pipeline imports provide much flexibility.

The evolution of LNG demand will impact directly on the utilization of regasification capacity across the world, which already shows some significant disparities (Chapter 4). Utilization in Asia has tended to be high, while that in Europe dropped to historical lows post 2010 when LNG supplies had been diverted away. In aggregate, Europe does not need new regasification capacity, but there is a large volume in Spain which has limited interconnections with the rest of Europe. New regasification capacity may be required in eastern and south-eastern Europe to diversify away from Russia. But Europe is an exception, as it has a well-developed pipeline network allowing movement of gas across the region. This is not the case for other regions, apart from North America which will not need

LNG. In Middle Eastern, African, Latin American, and south-east Asian countries, additional LNG import capacity – mostly FSRUs – will be developed to feed individual needs. Our analysis underlines that in the High Demand case scenario, a further build-up of LNG import capacity in some Asian countries will be necessary during the next five years.

When will the market rebalance?

Demand for LNG could follow widely different paths over the coming decade, as highlighted above. Meanwhile, the existing LNG supply picture is not set in stone since some LNG suppliers, such as Abu Dhabi, may disappear by the early 2020s. Others, such as Indonesia, Trinidad and Tobago, Oman, or Brunei, may face a further decline from their current LNG export levels due to gas shortages or redirection of gas supplies towards the domestic market. The current consensus about the timing of rebalancing the markets is 'some time between 2020 and 2025'.

Whether LNG markets rebalance by 2020 or later will be a major driver behind new FIDs. Looking at LNG supply up to 2020 on the basis of projects existing and under construction – assuming that no FIDs are taken in 2016 – the figure could vary between 353 and 380 mtpa (Figure 10.1). Markets will rebalance as soon as 2020 in Demand Case 1 if LNG supply follows the low, or 'cautious' LNG supply path, and by 2022 in the high, or 'optimistic' LNG supply case. A rapid market rebalancing will require FIDs to be taken over 2016–17 (despite a low oil and gas price environment) to avoid a tightening in global LNG markets by 2021. Rebalancing would happen some two years later in Demand Case 2, which would give project sponsors more time to proceed with new projects, taking their FIDs only from 2017 onward.

The two other demand scenarios pose a different question as LNG demand would be depressed for a lengthy period of time. In Case 4, something would have to change, considering the large volumes of LNG available at distressed prices on global markets over the period 2015–20 and beyond. That would call for: a demand rebound in markets where LNG capacity is sufficient for additional LNG imports, the arrival of new markets based on FSRUs, more demand in the transport sector, or for some producers to shut in production or not lift cargoes because they can no longer cover their plants' variable costs. If this were to be combined with a low-price environment, it would cause a lasting dearth of FIDs across the world. That would be something of a nightmare scenario for the global LNG industry.

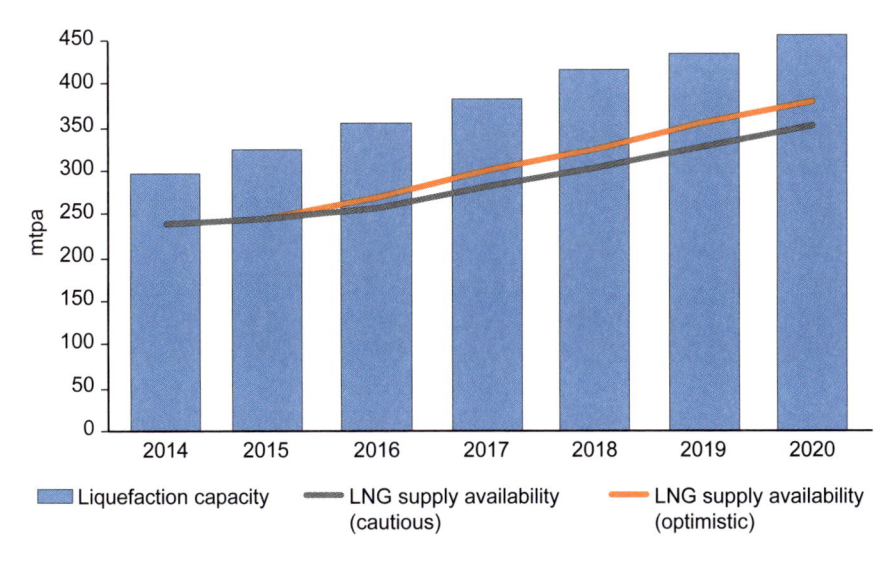

[Chart showing Supply scenarios 2014-2020 with Liquefaction capacity bars, LNG supply availability (cautious) and LNG supply availability (optimistic) lines]

Figure 10.1: Supply scenarios, 2014–20
Source: KAPSARC research.

Investing in a low oil and gas price environment

Over the period 2005–20, LNG supply came on stream in chunks rather than continuously, creating two LNG waves (2009–11 and 2015–20). Should the High Demand LNG cases come to pass, the industry would need to continue investing to make sure there will be enough LNG beyond 2020. LNG projects need six to seven years, including contract negotiations, to get production underway (around five years for construction only). With oil prices at around $40–50/bbl, the outlook for new developments, beyond the LNG export capacity currently under construction, looks relatively bleak. Very few, if any, projects would be sanctioned in an environment with a $40–50/bbl oil price and a $4–5/MMBtu gas price in Europe and Asia, unless costs are drastically cut or project sponsors take an optimistic long-term view regarding future LNG demand prospects and work actively to develop new markets. But the paradox is that if markets tighten by 2020, we will need several projects to take their FID in the current challenging price environment, while dealing with the issue of costs.

Two crucial but widely differing issues emerge:

- Project financing. Even if project sponsors are confident that oil prices (for those selling at oil-indexed prices) and gas prices in importing countries will recover and LNG demand rebounds, many will still need third-party finance. It is likely to be difficult to convince lending institutions that a price recovery is in sight while the new norm is believed to be 'lower for longer'. This would point to aggregators with robust balance sheets and plans to market the LNG themselves, as being those most likely to support FIDs in the current conditions.

- Design, engineering and construction. US projects under construction are far more in line with typical cost escalation figures in the oil and gas industry than Australian projects have been. However, costs are likely to be higher for LNG export projects subject to issues of remoteness and lack of infrastructure. Cost-reduction strategies for onshore plants could include: the use of multiple smaller plants designed on a more functional and standardized design basis rather than project-specific designs; or the choice of FLNG if an onshore development involved the construction of long offshore pipelines. Both standardization of design, and a move towards companies working together collaboratively in the supply chain, will help to cut costs. Given recent experience in terms of cost overruns, the industry must learn from its past in order to guarantee its future and find innovative ways to reduce costs (Chapter 4).

In a nutshell, the success of future LNG supply developments depends on the three 'Cs': competitiveness, collaboration, and creative thinking.

When oil and gas prices recover to levels sufficient to enable projects to be sanctioned, and investors and lenders have confidence that gas markets will rebalance within four or five years, projects will move ahead. The level of oil and gas prices that investors are comfortable with will depend on the type of indexation chosen: oil-indexed or based on spot prices in the importing market. The most competitive projects will need at least $60/bbl or $9/MMBtu. Their success will depend as much on their own technical characteristics as on their location. Countries with a stable fiscal and regulatory framework, reasonable local content requirements, and political stability will be the front runners. Predictability regarding future domestic demand – to avoid repeating the Egyptian case of halting LNG exports in order to feed the domestic market – will be an advantage. So will the availability of industrial infrastructure and a qualified workforce, unless the option of FLNG is chosen. Given the long list of proposed projects, only those governments which allow projects to make adequate returns will succeed, while those with regulations which could potentially inflate the cost of billion dollar projects, or delay them, will lag behind. Some LNG projects, such as those in Iran, may still move ahead due to pure political backing once certain concerns (such as meeting domestic requirements –

particularly for pressure maintenance injection in oil fields – and the development of progressive upstream investment frameworks) have been met, in addition to the required relaxation of sanctions. Such projects can be structured in a way that manages the necessary risks (Chapter 3), with different and new companies investing and owning assets, while others provide support through committing to capacity over the long term.

The characteristics of the projects will play an important role, especially in a low-price environment (Chapter 5).

- Brownfield expansions where resources are sufficient stand the best chances. They will benefit from the experience gained by the operator during the previous construction and operation phases, as well as significant cost reduction compared with a greenfield project.

- Among brownfield expansions, Qatar stands out as the world's lowest-cost supplier and benefits from a key geographical position. Debottlenecking of the existing capacity can be easily achieved within a couple of years. The decision to build additional liquefaction capacity beyond the planned debottlenecking will depend on the perceptions of Qatar Petroleum and its partners about market rebalancing, and of course on Qatar's willingness to relax its self-imposed 'moratorium' on further development of the North Field, which to date it shows no sign of doing.

- Another type of brownfield project is the utilization of existing plants by other countries. Such partnerships could take place with Venezuela/Trinidad and Tobago, Israel/Egypt, and Iran/Oman, whereby the first country would use the underutilized plants of the second. In all cases, geopolitics will play a central role, but clearly projects can only proceed if sufficient gas reserves are in place and committed to the project.

- FLNG – as highlighted in Chapter 4 – can in some cases be less expensive than onshore project options, especially those based on solution providers such as Golar.

- Liquids-rich projects – either brownfield or greenfield – usually stand a better chance than others since liquids provide an additional source of revenue, at least when oil prices are robust. Liquids-rich projects have been hit by lower oil, and hence liquids, prices. Lowering upstream costs through liquids revenues can offset higher liquefaction costs.

- Similarly, 'strategic' LNG projects, where buyers own a stake and bring cash from their balance sheets, and from the financial institutions of their own countries, also stand a better chance. This will be the case

568 *LNG Markets in Transition*

specifically for countries which place emphasis on security of supply. Project ownership structures will reflect the interest of consumers, mostly Asian, who will play an increasing role as upstream and midstream partners. This could be one way to avoid a supply crunch.

Around 1,000 mtpa of LNG projects are proposed as of 2016 (Chapter 5). The capacity is concentrated in four main regions: around 90 mtpa is in Australia, 666 mtpa in North America (315 mtpa in the USA, including Alaska, and 352 mtpa in Canada), 70 mtpa in Eastern Africa, and 75 mtpa in Russia. This does not mean that projects could not move ahead in other countries, depending on specific conditions. Each of our four regions faces specific issues which may delay or lessen the extent to which they will form part of any further build-up in supply (Figure 10.2).

Governments' priorities differ profoundly from those of companies. Many companies have different projects in a few countries and can therefore advance those which are the most competitive. ExxonMobil has the highest

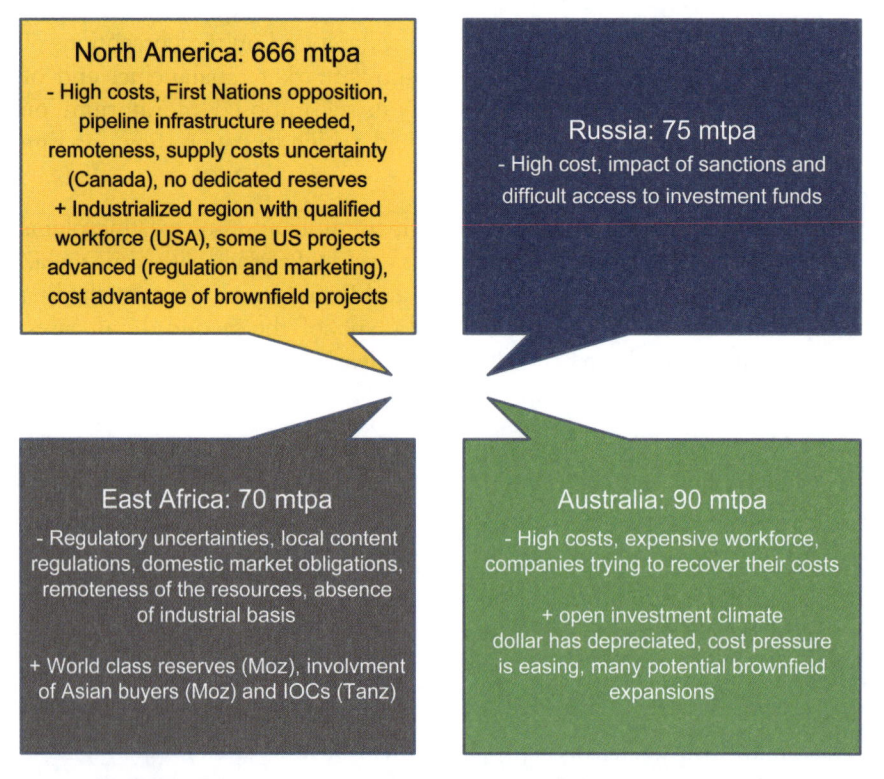

North America: 666 mtpa
- High costs, First Nations opposition, pipeline infrastructure needed, remoteness, supply costs uncertainty (Canada), no dedicated reserves
+ Industrialized region with qualified workforce (USA), some US projects advanced (regulation and marketing), cost advantage of brownfield projects

Russia: 75 mtpa
- High cost, impact of sanctions and difficult access to investment funds

East Africa: 70 mtpa
- Regulatory uncertainties, local content regulations, domestic market obligations, remoteness of the resources, absence of industrial basis
+ World class reserves (Moz), involvment of Asian buyers (Moz) and IOCs (Tanz)

Australia: 90 mtpa
- High costs, expensive workforce, companies trying to recover their costs
+ open investment climate dollar has depreciated, cost pressure is easing, many potential brownfield expansions

Figure 10.2: Key suppliers' strengths and weaknesses
Source: Author, based on Chapter 5.

number of prospective projects, strategically placed in various countries. If countries are too demanding in terms of fiscal take, or develop a regulatory environment which is either unstable or too complex, they may deter projects. The lengthy fiscal discussions in Canada have certainly resulted in the Western projects missing a key window of opportunity. This may leave some gas resources undeveloped despite their high potential.

Testing the limits of US LNG supplies

With five projects moving ahead, the USA currently occupies a special place in the LNG supply environment. It is set to become the third-largest holder of LNG export capacity by 2020. More importantly, the business model of US LNG – a tolling model in which the offtaker pays a fixed fee of around $3–3.5/MMBtu for liquefaction – means that offtakers have the option not to take their contracted LNG if market conditions are not appropriate, resulting in US capacity being underutilized.

US LNG exports are not inexhaustible. Projects under construction or already operating moved ahead based on the assumption of a large and cheap resource base and a significant price gap between the USA and Asia. While the first assumption still holds true, the second ceased to reflect reality in 2015. If project sponsors cannot justify additional LNG projects by their economics, they will be increasingly challenged on the domestic market. There are also political limitations to LNG exports, notably a strong industry lobby applying political pressure to limit LNG growth.

The current low-price environment poses a threat to existing capacity holders in US LNG export projects. When they were sanctioned, US LNG looked attractive when compared with oil-linked gas prices in Asia. Full-cycle costs were estimated at around $10–11/MMBtu, compared with Japanese LNG prices at about $16/MMBtu, which provided a comfortable margin to offtakers. Even Europe, with prices at $8–11/MMBtu, could be an outlet for US cargoes. But since early 2016, when spot prices in both Asia and Europe collapsed to $4–5/MMBtu, US LNG projects have had to compete on the basis of their variable costs – typically 115 per cent of Henry Hub (spot gas price) plus shipping and regasification. The liquefaction fee will have to be partly – or even fully – considered as a sunk cost. While it is not unusual for companies to operate on the basis of variable costs, it is unclear how long some capacity holders will be willing to continue paying the full liquefaction tolling fee while having to discount their supplies in the market in order to sell the LNG. Simply put, each $1/MMBtu lost on 1 mtpa means a loss of around $50 million annually.

Another question concerns the cost of US gas. Most experts consider that there is a lot of gas which can be produced at a low cost. Forward curves from the CME Group indicate that US Henry Hub (HH) prices could stay below $4/MMBtu – and in fact often below $3/MMBtu – for another 10 years. Should this assumption be wrong, and supply turns out to be less elastic than currently expected, this would significantly impact the future of US LNG.

A price war with Russia in Europe?

The next uncertainty is how LNG flows will evolve as capacity builds up. Europe has been the swing demand element of the global LNG balance: it allows LNG to go to other destinations if it uses (mainly Russian) pipeline gas. In 2015, the situation was reversed as Asian LNG demand stalled and some LNG returned to Europe. Looking forward, the absorption capacity of Europe may be tested if Asian incremental demand is lower than the additional Australian, US, Indonesian, and Malaysian supply coming on stream. In that case, Middle Eastern (Qatar) LNG supplies will be displaced toward the Atlantic Basin, while incremental US LNG will also be backed off to the Atlantic Basin (Figure 10.3). Only Europe, which offers underutilized regasification capacity, transparent markets, and trading hubs, can absorb these large LNG quantities. Depending on the volumes at stake, these LNG supplies could threaten Russia's market share in Europe. Our Demand Cases 3 and 4 point to a scenario where massive LNG volumes (above 100 mtpa) head back to Europe by 2020, not because Europe wants them, but because they have nowhere else to go.

Russia is the stabilizing factor in the global gas market through its flexible pipeline gas supplies to Europe. While some may perceive its role as similar to that of Saudi Arabia in the oil market, there are major differences. Oil is a global commodity while gas is not, or at least not yet. Russia is almost entirely dependent on exports to Europe until 2020, while Saudi Arabia has a variety of outlets for its oil. Russia's relationship with Europe is tense, prompting the latter to seek diversification of supply sources. Russia has traditionally accommodated the swings of European supply and demand, but recent declarations indicate that Russia is now ready to fight for its market share. At early 2016 exchange rates, Russian gas could be delivered to Europe at prices as low as $3.5/MMBtu.[3] Gazprom could decide to dump large volumes of gas on the spot markets to keep US LNG at bay when the threat due to the build-up of LNG supply in 2017–18 becomes serious, but this would be a massive departure from the company's

---

[3] One of the key parameters determining the Russian gas price is the US dollar/ruble exchange rate.

current strategy of preserving price over market share. If large additional volumes of spot gas were delivered to Europe, such dumping would also change the role of Gazprom's long-term contracts as its main export focus.

Against that backdrop, European political decision making on supply diversification will be crucial. The European Commission may want to favour LNG against Russian pipeline gas, but that could mean European customers having to pay higher LNG prices. Besides, some European countries depend heavily on Russian gas, making it difficult for LNG to fully replace it in the absence of adequate infrastructure. One effective way of limiting Russian gas supplies would be to delay any capacity additions for Russian pipeline gas (forcing Russia to rely on Ukrainian transit until the contract expires in 2019), while cross-Europe gas pipeline linkages were improved to enable LNG to access eastern and south-eastern European markets. But such changes carry the risk that when the LNG market tightens, with declining European production and problems with North African pipeline suppliers, Europe would need pipeline capacity for more Russian gas.

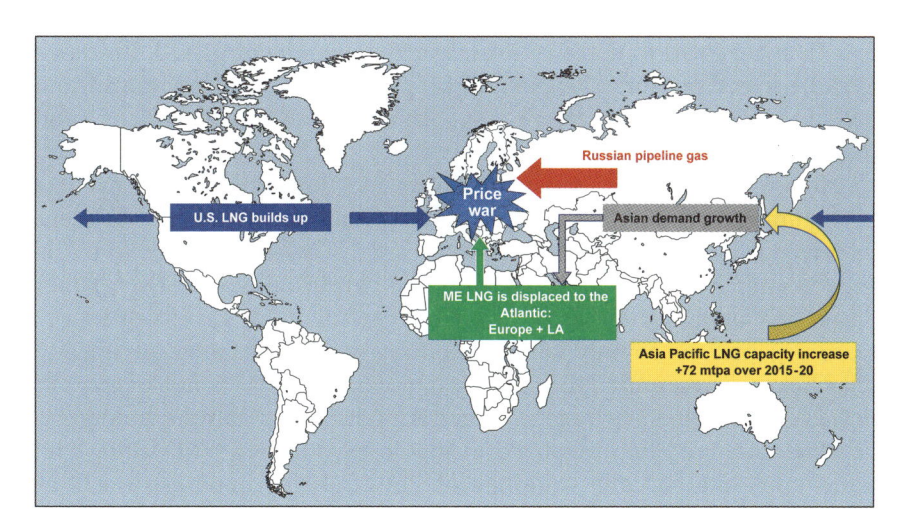

Figure 10.3: The steps towards a price war in Europe between US LNG and Russian pipeline gas
Source: KAPSARC research.

If US Henry Hub prices are significantly above $2/MMBtu, US LNG projects would have to price their gas *below* their variable costs to compete against Russian gas at $3.50/MMBtu. Those companies with LNG capacity may choose not to use it and lose $150 million per mtpa contracted. It remains to be seen whether this move could trigger defaults among these capacity holders and offtakers. Should one company decide that it cannot afford to pay a liquefaction fee of $3–3.50/MMBtu and it consequently negotiates a lower fee, US LNG contracts could all collapse like a house of cards. This would be a huge legal headache, given the absence of any renegotiation or price review clause in those LNG capacity contracts that are currently in the public domain, and the low credit position of US LNG export project developers. This said, the already constructed US liquefaction capacity would still exist and be available for use by project developers (at variable cost) and new offtakers at a lower (bid) tolling fee.

Pricing is key for gas to be competitive ... and for projects to be sanctioned

Prices and costs are two sides of the same coin. They will both determine at what pace future LNG supply comes to markets, and will influence demand developments. Prices – or expectations – have to be high enough for investors to convince lenders that their project is viable, in relation to cost estimates, and to make returns over the investment period. To move ahead, project sponsors will want market prices to cover their costs over the investment cycle, whether the pricing formula is based on oil, HH, or some regional European or Asian hub price.

High prices will deter potential buyers and threaten the attractiveness of natural gas (Chapter 8). Obviously various buyers have a different tolerance to price levels. The period 2011–14 showed that price levels of $15/MMBtu or above are considered too high by all buyers. Even Japan and Korea are not ready to pay such a high premium for security of supply reasons: Japan did so only because shutting down all its nuclear capacity after Fukushima required the country to use more gas. Wholesale prices in new LNG importers (such as the United Arab Emirates, Kuwait, Indonesia, or Malaysia), are often regulated at low levels (below $4/MMBtu). The same applies to a large number of future LNG importers such as Bangladesh, the Philippines, and Vietnam. Even though these regulated prices are being progressively increased, the long-term impact on natural gas demand is still unknown, and the extent to which these countries can absorb 'expensive' LNG will be tested (Corbeau et al., 2016). As of 2016, the low-price era is expected to continue for a few years and could incentivize developing countries to turn to LNG, and potentially some demand side recovery could take place in existing LNG importing countries.

Beyond price levels, the main issue is that of pricing mechanisms, notably in Asian oil-linked LNG contracts. Asian buyers have been pushing for a move away from oil indexation since 2011. The current low oil price environment could have diminished the momentum, but Asian buyers are still promoting a change, for reasons of portfolio diversification and flexibility. One key element is missing: Asia does not have its own spot price, like HH in North America, the UK's NBP, and the Dutch TTF in Europe. Among the key obstacles to establishing such a trading hub are the state of liberalization of Asian markets (apart from Singapore), the high level of dependency on a relatively illiquid LNG market, the lack of maturity of gas markets (unlike North America and Europe where hubs were created in markets with significant infrastructure in place, notably storage), and the existence of oil-linked long-term contracts representing the basis of future LNG supply for at least the coming decade. In the absence of effective price review clauses, it will be complicated to change the pricing mechanism in these contracts to hub pricing, unless a significant gap emerges between spot and term prices – for example, if oil prices were to recover and the LNG glut continues. Buyers' financial distress could be a powerful reason for a change similar to the one that took place in Europe.

It is likely that the coming five to 10 year period will see the coexistence of different pricing mechanisms – oil linkage, HH, spot indices (Platts' JKM, or those from Argus, RIM, and ICIS), and average import prices (JLC for Japan) – until a regional trading price emerges. The emergence of US spot-based LNG as a key source of supply could impact pricing mechanisms in Asia to include an HH cost-plus price, or an NBP cost-plus price for cargoes diverted from the flexible European markets, but this means that the region's gas price would be primarily dependent on that of another region. It also possible that an LNG FOB trading hub could be developed in the Gulf of Mexico, as US LNG volumes build up over 2016–20 or, as some in Eastern Australia are promoting, a hub based on exports from the three Gladstone LNG export projects. The Gulf of Mexico has the advantage of a relatively homogeneous gas quality and multiple players from various regions. The coal and the oil sectors have similar FOB indices which are widely used by each industry.

It is plausible that there will be more than one Asian hub, a position similar to that in Europe where different hubs coexist. Two of them (NBP and TTF) are recognized as the leading benchmarks and they are used in short- and long-term contracts. Asian players need to decide what kind of hub they want: an LNG hub, where the main product is LNG cargoes, or a gas hub, and whether such a hub would be virtual like the NBP or physical like Henry Hub. LNG sellers are confident in using HH prices; these represent a transparent benchmark with a long forward curve, but the equivalent in Asia, in terms of traded volumes and price transparency, could take five or even 10 years to achieve. A significant build-up of spot and short-term trade, becoming sufficiently liquid, will support the creation of national trading hubs. The momentum is building and once markets are engaged in that direction, there will be no turning back.

As of 2016, three leaders have emerged for the creation of a trading hub in Asia:

- Singapore: the country has a liberalized gas market, third-party access to infrastructure, and the backing of the regulatory authorities. Although Singapore is a relatively small market compared to Japan or China, it will be increasingly dependent on LNG. The SLInG LNG spot index, partly an initiative of the Singapore Exchange, was created in late 2015, based on LNG delivery offshore the country.
- China: the development of a hub depends on liberalization processes. There have been advances towards making Shanghai a reliable price benchmark. The Shanghai Energy Exchange is working on establishing trading based on LNG, with a view to including natural gas (domestic and pipeline gas) once the market is liberalized.
- Japan: the development of a hub will also depend on the liberalization process and to what extent effective and transparent access can be achieved. The Japanese government published a new strategy for LNG market development aiming at creating a flexible LNG market and developing an LNG trading hub in Japan.[4]

The rise of flexibility

The LNG industry was born as the 'little brother' of the pipeline business. As of 2016, however, unlike pipeline gas supply, LNG trade is developing greater flexibility. LNG can now routinely be redirected, re-exported, and serve different destinations. Several trends support a further growth in spot and short-term LNG trade: uncontracted capacity in existing and new LNG suppliers, the presence of aggregators using portfolio LNG, the role of the USA and Qatar, and the reluctance of many buyers to bind themselves into 20-year long-term contracts (Chapter 9). Buyers want more flexibility, enabling them to deal with the shocks in the market. Asian buyers are trying to exit/renegotiate contract terms – as highlighted by Petronet's renegotiation with RasGas. They will be opting for more spot and short-term LNG trade at spot prices, and the share of such trades in total trade can be expected to increase from 28 per cent in 2015 to around 43 per cent by 2020. The evolution thereafter will depend on how much and by when

---

[4] 'Strategy for LNG Market Development: Creating flexible LNG Market and Developing an LNG Trading Hub in Japan', METI, 2 May 2016. www.meti.go.jp/english/press/2016/pdf/0502_01b.pdf.

additional LNG export capacity can come on line. A halt to LNG capacity additions is likely to lead to a further growth in spot LNG trade.

Another emerging trend around the theme of flexibility is the growing presence of aggregators. Aggregators used to be project owners, but now they are also US LNG offtakers. They have already contributed to the rise of spot and short-term LNG trade significantly and this trend will continue. They will be increasingly looking to optimize their portfolios based on projects from different regions, and also to optimize shipping. The current pressure on margins is likely to drive more creativity on how to swap cargoes on a large scale, not just within one seller's portfolio, but also between suppliers.

There is currently enough shipping capacity to support the growth of the spot market, and optimizing shipping will also free up LNG carrier capacity. Often, the ships may be ready before the rest of a project is completed, so they would be free to be used in the short-term market until the dedicated liquefaction starts up. Meanwhile, the rise of spot markets triggered by portfolio sellers and buyers with destination flexibility (supported by contractually destination-free US LNG) means that neither party is interested in predictable tanker routes any more. Shorter-term and voyage charters are becoming more common, while the combination of spot charter rates and spot cargo prices has proved to be effective in rebalancing supply and demand – by enabling LNG cargoes to flow to the market that provides the best netback.

Is there a tipping point?

As of 2016 and with current prices and market conditions, it seems impossible that LNG projects could move ahead without the support of long-term contracts, which remain the pillar of the LNG industry. But some things have already changed: though US LNG projects are still underpinned by long-term capacity agreements, they have moved forward on the basis of market-based pricing, as did the Qatari trains in 2005. Some LNG has been contracted based on spot pricing – like Qatar's sales to the UK or Cheniere's to EDF. If some credible and transparent spot pricing alternatives emerge – either as DES or FOB references – long-term contracts may move to include such price references more widely.

Does the rise of spot and short-term mean the end of long-term (20-year) contracts? Not definitely and certainly not immediately. Lending institutions are still more comfortable with long-term contracts covering their investments. But buyers' needs are changing. Incumbents with a dominant position in their home market – the formerly predominant type of buyer – will progressively disappear and with them will go demand certainty. Buyers facing competition from other fuels and other players will become the norm. Lower investment grade buyers and traders will take on a greater role. Buyers are consequently asking for 'long-term' contracts to be of shorter duration (10–15 years). But as they obtain more flexibility in their portfolio by having a mix of long-term, short-term, and spot LNG and turn towards spot indexation in long-term contracts, there might be a tipping point where LNG markets move towards a greater commoditization (Chapter 9). If so, there would be no turning back for long-term contracts. Existing long-term contracts will not (or only partially) be extended; this will not threaten their economics as they have already been amortized.

The question of whether new projects proceed with a lower contract coverage will require four key conditions to be fulfilled:

- Spot and short-term (contracts of less than four years) LNG trade becomes the norm;

- Reliable spot price benchmarks emerge, evolve into deep liquid markets, and eventually turn into hubs;

- LNG costs drop substantially (or smaller-scale LNG becomes the norm);

- Banks and other lenders become comfortable with the fact that a long-term contract selling at a spot price, and a customary long-term contract, are almost equivalent when markets are sufficiently liquid.

The great reconfiguration of the LNG business, toppling 50 years of business practice, will take place when the first LNG project moves ahead with shorter, flexible, and spot indexed long-term contracts. Even prior to that, the next wave of LNG projects may move forward on the basis of sales and purchase contracts of no longer than 10 years; especially if they are lower cost expansion or conversion FLNG projects, this would indicate a significant departure from the traditional 20-year long-term contracts. Cameroon FLNG moved ahead supported by an eight-year contract with Gazprom Marketing and Trading. Up to 2020, however, the industry is set to embark on a period of phenomenal change, growing in size by half, adapting to new ways of operations, and trading, pricing, and contracting with new companies; all of these changes will continue to challenge the industry's traditional standard practices. The future, post-2025, is more uncertain, but growth is expected, although whether it will be smooth or will follow a boom–bust cycle is not clear.

But the great reconfiguration should enhance the role of LNG in the development of flexible international gas trade and hence make a major contribution to the increasing globalization of the gas business.

BIBLIOGRAPHY

Corbeau, A., Shabaneh, R., and Six, S. (2016). *The Impact of Low Oil and Gas Prices on Gas Markets: A Retrospective Look at 2014–15*, KS-1634-DP028, KAPSARC, May 2016.

ExxonMobil (2015). *The Outlook for Energy: A View to 2040*, http://corporate.exxonmobil.com/en/energy/energy-outlook.

GIIGNL (2016). *The LNG Industry in 2015*, International Group of Liquefied Natural Gas Importers, GIIGNL (Groupe International des Importateurs de Gaz Naturel Liquéfié) Annual Report 2016. www.giignl.org/publications.

TECHNICAL APPENDIX

INTRODUCTION TO LNG AND LNG TECHNOLOGIES

Christopher Caswell

Introduction

Natural gas can be transported across long distances (over 3,000 kilometres, which is further than the distances served by onshore or offshore pipelines) economically in the form of Liquefied Natural Gas (LNG). Liquefying natural gas is thus an effective way of enabling a large quantity of natural gas to be transported in a storage container suitable for shipping. Therefore, as pipelines become uneconomic due to volume or length, or when moving gas across multiple countries becomes a political challenge, LNG becomes viable.

At atmospheric pressure and temperature, the conversion of natural gas to LNG requires a drop in temperature to minus 161 °C (−258 °F). Once liquid, LNG can be transported in bulk, by ship or truck, to locations thousands of kilometres away. In fact, once natural gas is converted to LNG, the product destination is only limited by the location of a facility capable of accepting, storing, and vaporizing the LNG.

Since LNG is cold, it requires special infrastructure to create, store, ship, and handle the product. This Appendix will address the technical aspects of this infrastructure, which is often referred to as the LNG value chain (see Chapter 3). The elements of this chain include upstream reservoir or gas supply facilities, liquefaction plant, LNG storage tanks, LNG shipping, and the storage and regasification terminal. In addition to the traditional value chain, this Appendix will address issues related to offshore LNG. While this Appendix is not intended to be a complete narrative of every aspect of the LNG value chain, it will provide a solid foundation to each element of infrastructure in this rapidly growing industry.

Introduction to refrigeration

Before discussing the building blocks of a liquefaction plant, this section will give a basic introduction to a refrigeration cycle. Although there are many textbooks which describe a basic refrigeration cycle (Van Wylen, 1985), the goal of a simple vapour compression refrigeration cycle is to reduce the temperature of a process fluid (vapour or liquid) such as natural gas. This operation requires work to be put in to extract energy (heat) from the process fluid to the refrigerant. An example refrigeration cycle, with a single refrigerant, is shown in Figure A.1.

The gas to be cooled enters and exits the main heat exchanger between points 5 and 6 of Figure A.1. The refrigerant (the fluid cooling the process stream) circulates clockwise around the flow diagram. At point 1, the refrigerant is a low-pressure medium-temperature vapour. Work (by a gas turbine, steam turbine, or electric motor) is put into the system to drive the compressor, and after compression the refrigerant, still a vapour, is at high pressure and high temperature (point 2 in the diagram). The heat from compression is removed from the system in the condenser, between points 2 and 3.

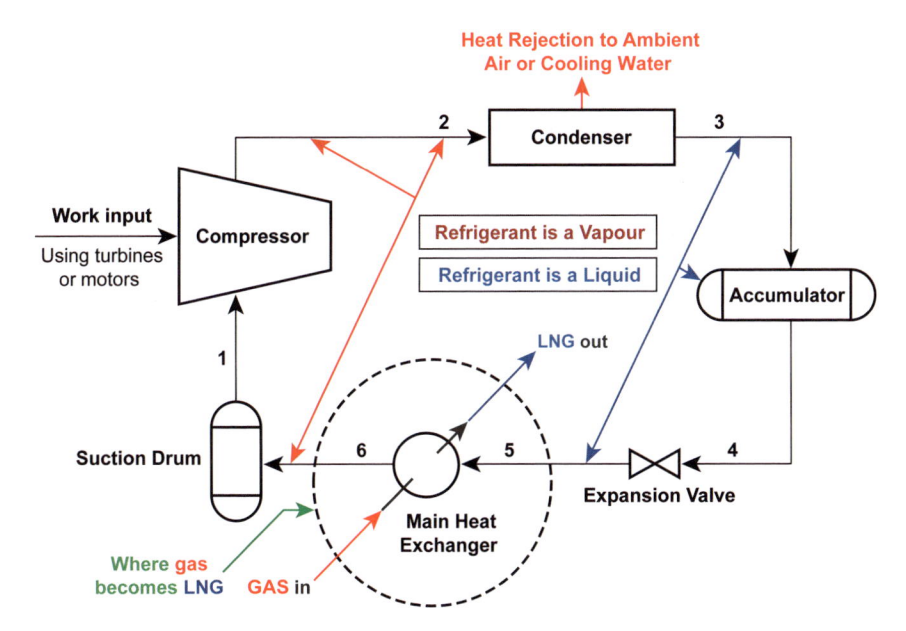

Figure A.1: Example of a refrigeration cycle used for natural gas liquefaction
Source: Caswell, 2014.

The condenser is a set of heat exchangers which cool and condense the refrigerant using ambient air or cooling water. At point 3, the refrigerant is liquid, at high pressure and medium temperature. At stage 4, the pressure of the refrigerant is reduced, which cools it. At stage 5, the refrigerant is liquid, at medium pressure and low temperature, and is ready to enter the main exchanger. After the refrigerant absorbs the heat from the process fluid, the refrigerant becomes a vapour at low pressure, and retraces the refrigeration cycle.

Liquefaction plants

The process of liquefaction is different from what takes place in other hydrocarbon process plants in that the product, LNG, is made by physical conversion from vapour to liquid by refrigeration. While primarily methane, the natural gas feed to a liquefaction plant (often called feed gas) is a mixture of many components with unique properties; only some of these feed gas components are converted to LNG. A representation of these feed gas components and product streams is shown in Figure A.2. The composition of LNG is a mixture of nitrogen, methane, ethane, propane, and butane.

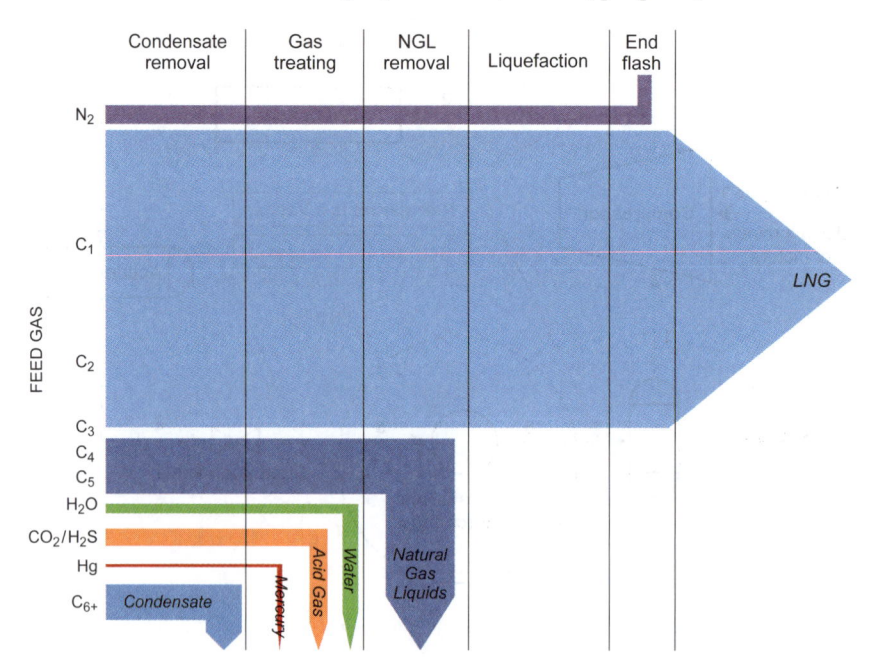

Figure A.2: LNG as one of many products from natural gas
Source: KBR Inc.

Liquefaction projects consume a tremendous amount of energy in order to convert large quantities of gas to a liquid at such low temperatures.

This energy is provided either from external sources (such as imported electric power) or by using a portion of the feed gas as fuel. Liquefaction is performed at high pressure; this pressure is then reduced when the LNG is sent to storage. While we are familiar with the refrigeration systems used to cool the air inside a refrigerator, an automobile, or a building, LNG plants are massively bigger, requiring an incredibly large amount of refrigeration to cool hundreds of millions of cubic feet of gas per day to cryogenic temperatures. This scale of refrigeration requires some of the largest equipment available in the oil, gas, and power industries.

Liquefaction projects are large facilities, often located in remote locations, which require huge capital investment; they utilize proprietary technologies, state of the art equipment, and exotic metallurgy. The elements of a liquefaction facility can be grouped into three general sections: gas processing, liquefaction, and storage and loading. A block diagram for an LNG export plant is shown in Figure A.3. Using this diagram, gas processing is covered by blocks 1, 2, and 3 (pink); liquefaction by 4, 5, and 6 (orange); and rundown and storage by block 7 (blue).

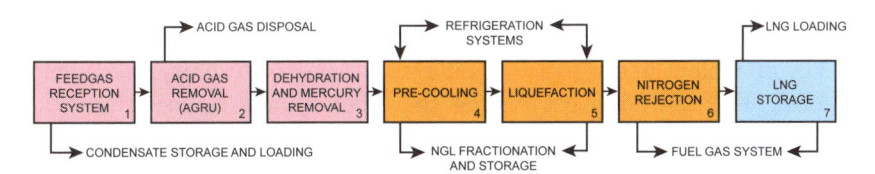

Figure A.3: Simplified block flow diagram for a liquefaction plant
Source: Caswell et al. (2009).

Gas processing

The purpose of gas processing is to remove liquid heavy hydrocarbons (HHCs), as well as unwanted contaminants from the feed gas that are not desirable in the LNG product.

Regardless of the source or composition of gas, these process blocks prepare the natural gas for physical conversion to LNG. For plants in remote locations, the feed gas to the plant may arrive directly from the source reservoir; therefore, the gas may require a significant amount of processing prior to liquefaction and export. For plants in industrial locations, gas processing is still necessary to remove trace components that may be part of shared pipeline networks but which would either damage cryogenic equipment in the liquefaction plant or be undesirable in the LNG product. Although feed gas from pipeline networks has been treated to certain specifications, it is always necessary to treat the feed gas destined for liquefaction.

The first step in gas processing for LNG is a feed gas reception system. This system separates out the HHCs (also known as condensate), to prevent them contaminating the subsequent gas treatment section. This section includes additional distillation equipment to further process the HHCs for export, as the product has a high value.

The next step in gas processing is the acid gas removal unit (AGRU). Acid gases are components of the natural gas that are either undesirable in the LNG product, or could freeze in the liquefaction unit, damaging the cryogenic equipment. These components include carbon dioxide (CO_2), hydrogen sulphide (H_2S), and other trace components like carbonyl sulphide (COS) and mercaptans (RSH).

Most natural gas contains CO_2 in some quantities, but concentrations of the other acid gas components will vary greatly. The most common method of removing acid gases is by using chemical solvents called amines. The gas interacts with the liquid amine to strip the undesirable components from the gas. The concentration of CO_2 remaining in the treated gas must be well below the solubility limit in the LNG. Following the use of amine solvents, the treated gas has less than 50 ppm of CO_2, but it is saturated with water. This water must be removed prior to liquefaction.

The final block in the gas processing section is dehydration and mercury removal. The saturated gas exiting the AGRU must be dried to strict specifications so that water does not freeze in downstream equipment. This unit is typically composed of three large dehydration vessels. The vessels are filled with special material known as molecular sieve (also called a mol sieve), that adsorbs particles of a certain size, but allows larger particles to pass. In this case, the water is adsorbed while the gas passes through. At any time, two vessels are operating while one is regenerating. This batch cyclic process ensures that water is removed from the mol sieve to allow the plant to operate continuously. The gas exiting the dehydration unit contains less than 1 ppm of water.

The final gas processing system is mercury removal. The purpose of this unit is to protect cryogenic equipment downstream in the liquefaction system. Mercury, often present in natural gas in varying concentrations, is harmful to equipment manufactured from aluminium. (Aluminium, due to its thermal properties and weight, is commonly used in cryogenic heat exchangers; mercury will corrode aluminium equipment by accumulating at low points in the system and attacking the alloys found in aluminium welds.) In order to protect aluminium equipment from this type of corrosion, nearly every liquefaction project will have a mercury removal unit regardless of the expected concentration of mercury in the source gas.

The mercury removal system is often a single vessel that treats the entire flow of gas. The mercury is absorbed by a bed of sulphur-impregnated catalyst which is not regenerated. The bed must be replaced every few years as part of routine maintenance. The location of the mercury removal unit may vary from that shown in Figure A.3. The traditional location of this unit is downstream of dehydration, but mercury removal may also be located early in the gas processing sequence, or in combination with the dehydration system. Each location has its benefits, but in a new trend, this unit is located earlier in the overall block flow scheme.

Pre-cooling and liquefaction

In liquefaction, the temperature of the feed exiting the gas processing units is reduced in stages to the desired temperature of LNG. The major steps in transitioning the gas to LNG are pre-cooling and liquefaction, as shown in blocks 4 and 5 in Figure A.3. Prior to liquefaction, the feed gas is pre-cooled; its temperature is reduced in stages, or pressure steps, to improve the energy efficiency of the liquefaction process and to extract additional components such as natural gas liquids (NGLs). These components include liquid petroleum gases (LPGs) and benzene. A graphical representation of the components of LNG, NGL, and LPG from natural gas is shown in Figure A.4. The most commonly used refrigerant for pre-cooling is propane.

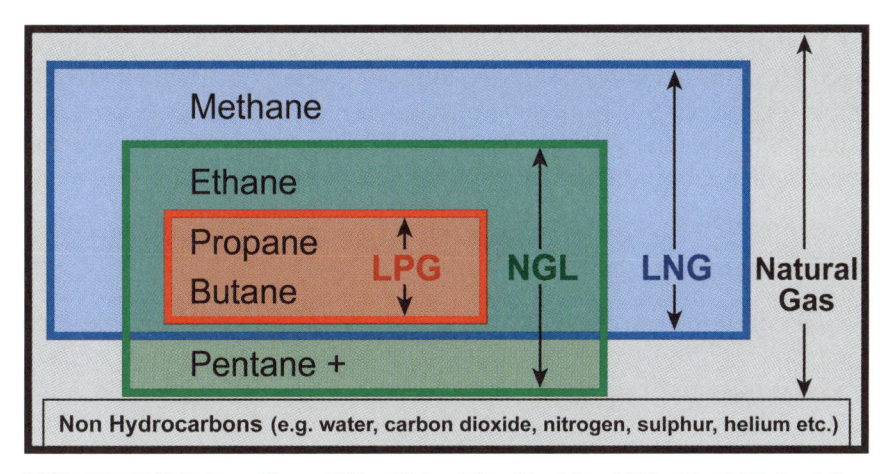

LPG – Liquid Petroleum Gas   NGL – Natural Gas Liquids   LNG – Liquid Natural Gas

Figure A.4: Defining LPG, NGL, and LNG from natural gas
Source: KBR Inc.

Propane is a widely available refrigerant and has a boiling point close to −40 °C. The process of pre-cooling covers the change in temperature from that of the gas exiting the gas treatment plant to that which can be achieved using propane. Coincidentally, this temperature range allows the use of carbon steel in the pre-cooling section, which is less expensive than high alloy materials. Using three or four pressure stages of propane, the feed gas is cooled in a series of heat exchangers to reach the final pre-cooling temperature. At the final precooling level, LPG and benzene can be extracted (block 4 in Figure A.3).

LPG is another term for liquid propane and/or butane. LPG has several areas of value in the LNG industry. If present in large quantities, LPG is profitable as a separate export product and can positively influence the economics of an LNG facility. LPG is also a source of refrigerant, which is continuously needed within the plant. Lastly, the LPG can be added back into the LNG to increase its heating value, or when the export quantity of LPG is not economical.

Benzene belongs to the family of aromatic hydrocarbons and is highly carcinogenic. It will freeze at cryogenic temperatures, so it must be removed upstream of the liquefaction process. Benzene is removed along with LPG and other heavy components (C_5+). Benzene removal often controls the pre-cooling temperature and pressure, especially for a lean feed gas.

After pre-cooling, the feed gas is further cooled to complete the liquefaction process. This liquefaction section may use one or more refrigerant loops to remove the heat necessary to make LNG. The number of cooling stages, the types of refrigerants, and the types of heat exchangers used for liquefaction will be reviewed in the section covering liquefaction process technology. No matter what liquefaction technology is used, the product exiting the liquefaction unit is LNG, intended for storage and export. Before the product is sent to storage, one more level of conditioning is often required.

Rundown and storage

LNG exiting the liquefaction unit is at very low temperature and high pressure. The transfer from the liquefaction unit to the storage tanks is called rundown. At this point, the LNG may include nitrogen, which has the lowest boiling point of any of the components in natural gas. Since nitrogen is an inert component (it does not burn), there is a limit on how much nitrogen is allowed in LNG. The desired concentration is roughly 1 per cent or less, in order to limit the uneconomical transport of this inert component. If the concentration of nitrogen in LNG is higher than 1 per cent, the most usual way of reducing it is by an end-flash system. For higher concentrations of nitrogen, a simple column, or a nitrogen rejection system, is required.

End flash is simply a way of reducing the pressure in the LNG tank or in a dedicated separation drum. During this process, the lightest component, nitrogen, will preferentially boil off from the LNG. The resulting vapour stream is heavily concentrated in both nitrogen and methane and is a source of fuel for the LNG plant. This fuel can be used for power generation, process heating, or to feed the gas turbines driving the refrigerant compressors.

LNG exiting the end-flash or nitrogen rejection area is then sent to the storage tanks. The storage tanks are filled with LNG entering from the roof in such a way that the rundown lines do not penetrate the tank below the liquid level. When LNG enters the tank at the top, an additional amount of flashing occurs due to the pump energy and to the final reduction in pressure of the storage tank. A broad discussion about the different types of storage tanks is included in a separate section of this Appendix.

LNG is exported from the liquefaction plant by intermittent ship loading. Cargo is transferred in batches of 120,000 to 265,000 m^3 based on the size of ship berthing at the jetty. LNG is transferred to the ship by several pumps that are located in each storage tank. The nominal loading rate to the ship is 10,000 to 12,000 m^3/hr, which requires several pumps running in parallel. The loading interface is a set of cryogenic loading arms that allow the transfer of LNG between the fixed jetty and the floating LNG carrier. Most terminals have four loading arms; two arms are for LNG transfer, one is for vapour return, and a fourth arm is a hybrid that can function in either service. There are multiple manufacturers of loading arms for LNG service, but the market is dominated by FMC Technologies.[5] The typical turnaround time for an average-sized LNG carrier to arrive, load LNG, and depart is 24 hours.

Liquefaction process technology

The previous section on liquefaction covered the progress of feed gas to LNG. As in any journey, several paths may lead to the same destination. Liquefaction process technologies are essentially the different paths along the cooling journey, each defining the type of equipment and refrigerants, and also the temperature progression followed in turning gas to LNG (blocks 4 and 5 of the flow diagram, Figure A.3). Each path has certain benefits when determining which road an LNG project should take. While the detailed evaluation of liquefaction process technology is beyond the scope of this Appendix, this section will review the well known categories of technologies, and will also give an overview of the two most dominant process technologies. Simplistically, liquefaction process technologies are

---

[5] Author research and 'Loading Systems' (page on FMC Technologies website): www.fmctechnologies.com/LoadingSystems.aspx.

categorized by the types of refrigerants used and the number of refrigerant loops.

Two types of refrigerants are used in LNG: pure refrigerants and mixed refrigerants. Examples of pure refrigerants are components such as nitrogen, methane, ethane, ethylene, propane, butane, pentane, and ammonia. The benefit of using pure refrigerants lies in the predictability of the thermodynamic properties within the refrigeration loop when a single refrigerant is used. Another benefit is the ability to either produce or import a known pure refrigerant as needed. Mixed refrigerants are a unique combination of the previously mentioned pure components. Commonly called MRs, the composition of mixed refrigerants is tailored to the thermal properties of the natural gas to be liquefied. In another view, pure components offer predictability, while an MR provides customization and efficiency. Common liquefaction process technologies are based on pure refrigerants, mixed refrigerants, or a combination of both.

When discussing the refrigeration system, the choices are one, two, or three loops. In theory, an infinite number of refrigeration loops may be the most thermodynamically efficient cycle, but the capital cost of such a configuration would be exorbitant. Considering the balance of capital cost (CAPEX) and operational cost (OPEX), liquefaction plants are configured with one, two, or three loops.

Single loop refrigeration is accomplished with either nitrogen or a single mixed refrigerant (SMR). This method of cooling is similar to that used in household refrigeration using a single refrigerant. These cycles are the least complicated of those available, but they are not as efficient as those with two or three loops. The CAPEX involved in single loop processes is regarded as being low, due to the simplicity of the process and the low equipment count; however, the OPEX will be higher due to the low process efficiency of these cycles. In order to improve the efficiency of single loop cycles, the refrigerant is often used at multiple pressure levels to provide different stages of cooling. In fact, all liquefaction process technologies use multiple pressure levels in order to improve process efficiency.

Cycles with two refrigeration loops will provide improved process efficiency by balancing the overall cooling duty between two different refrigerants. A warm refrigerant does the pre-cooling while the colder refrigerant does the liquefaction. The refrigerants may be pure components, MRs, or a combination of both. One well-known liquefaction process technology – AP-C3MR™ by Air Products and Chemicals, Inc. (APCI) (Pillarella et al., 2007) – is a combination of a pure component (warm) with a mixed refrigerant (cold). Another two loop MR cycle is the Dual Mixed Refrigerant Process (DMR) offered by both APCI and Shell.

Lastly, three loop liquefaction cycles obtain similar process efficiency to that of the two loop cycles, while adding flexibility in the stages of cooling and the use of refrigerants. Similar to two loop cycles, the refrigerants used can be pure components, MRs, or a combination of both. Another well-known liquefaction process technology, the Optimized Cascade® process by ConocoPhillips, uses three refrigerants that are pure components.[6] Another three loop cycle is the MFC® Process by Linde which uses three MR loops.[7]

In summary, cycles using two and three refrigerant loops provide a balance between CAPEX and OPEX and provide high process efficiency. A simplified table representing these technology categories is shown in Table A.1.

Table A.1: Simplified process technology matrix

		Refrigerants		
		MR	Pure	Both
Loops	One	SMR	N2 Expander	n.a.
	Two	DMR	C1-N2	C3MR
	Three	TMR (MFC®)	Optimized Cascade®	AP-X™

Source: Author research.

The two dominant liquefaction process technologies in LNG are the AP-C3MR™ process by APCI and the Optimized Cascade® process by ConocoPhillips LNG Technology and Licensing. Together, these cycles represent over 70 per cent of the world's annual LNG production. These process technologies are shown in Figure A.5[8] and Figure A.7.[9]

The APCI AP-C3MR™ process

The AP-C3MR™ process has the highest market share in terms of both number of projects and nameplate capacity. The cycle uses two refrigeration loops; one loop is a pure refrigerant and the other is an MR. The pure refrigerant is propane, or 'C3' (shown in the box labelled 'C3 precooling' in

---

[6] *Liquefied Natural Gas, Optimized Cascade® Process*, ConocoPhillips Company Brochure, CSH 15-1106, 2015.
[7] *LNG Technology*, Linde Brochure, LNG/1.1.e, 2008.
[8] The APCI 'AP-C3MR™' process diagram is provided by Air Products and Chemicals, Inc.
[9] The ConocoPhillips 'Optimized Cascade®' process diagram is provided by ConocoPhillips Company and printed with permission.

Figure A.5); it is used for pre-cooling (reducing the temperature of the feed gas to about −35 °C) (Pillarella et al., 2007) and for removing the heat from compression of the MR. MR is used for liquefaction and is customized for the properties of the feed gas to be liquefied. As shown in Figure A.5, the MR is divided into a separate vapour and liquid stream (yellow and orange) for different levels of cooling with the same refrigerant. While pre-cooling is performed in a shell and tube heat exchanger, liquefaction is performed in a coil-wound heat exchanger (CWHE).

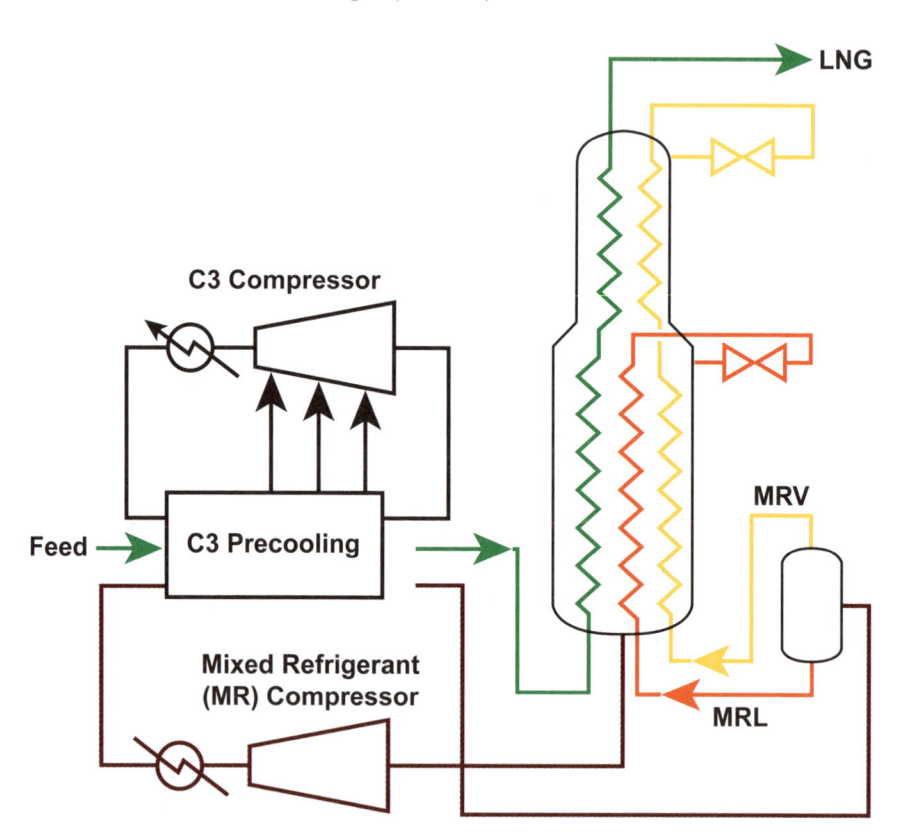

Figure A.5: The AP-C3MR™ liquefaction process
Source: Provided by Air Products and Chemicals, Inc. and printed with permission.

A completed CWHE, ready for shipment, is shown in Figure A.6. From the outside, the CWHE looks like an ordinary tower, as seen in many process plants. On the inside, however, the tubes for all process services are helically wound, in order to provide a large amount of heat transfer area (tube count and length) for a certain diameter and height of heat exchanger. Simplistically, the configuration is similar to a shell and tube heat exchanger, but as it has tubes helically wound around the longitudinal axis, it allows a great deal of refrigeration to occur in a single piece of equipment. Although the CWHE looks commonplace from the outside, very few companies can fabricate a CWHE. For the AP-C3MR™ process, APCI designs and supplies the CWHE as part of its licensor package and process guarantee.

Figure A.6: Coil-wound heat exchanger by APCI
Source: Image courtesy of Air Products and Chemicals, Inc.

The ConocoPhillips Optimized Cascade® process

In terms of market share and worldwide capacity, the ConocoPhillips Optimized Cascade® process is the other dominant liquefaction process in the LNG industry. The process was initially developed in the 1960s for Kenai Alaska; it was then utilized in the 1990s for Atlantic LNG in Trinidad, and has been gaining market share steadily over time.

In the ConocoPhillips process, the feed gas is cooled by three pure component refrigerants: propane, ethylene, and methane. Simplistically, the duty of the propane cycle is similar in both the C3MR and Cascade processes, while the ethylene and methane cycles perform the cooling duty, rather like an MR. Unlike C3MR, but in common with many other processes and technologies, plate fin heat exchangers (PFHE) are used as the main heat exchange equipment for Optimized Cascade®.

An example of a PFHE is shown in Figure A.8. A PFHE allows close temperature approaches between the refrigerant and the feed gas in a compact manufactured volume. Flow paths are alternated among the plates, which contain grooves for channelling the flows through the exchanger. As an analogy, a PFHE could be envisioned as many layers of corrugated cardboard stacked together where the refrigerant and feed gas alternate through the corrugations in each layer. The close proximity of each plate (or layer) allows the fluid temperatures to closely approach each other and provide significantly more heat exchange area per unit volume than a coil wound heat exchanger.

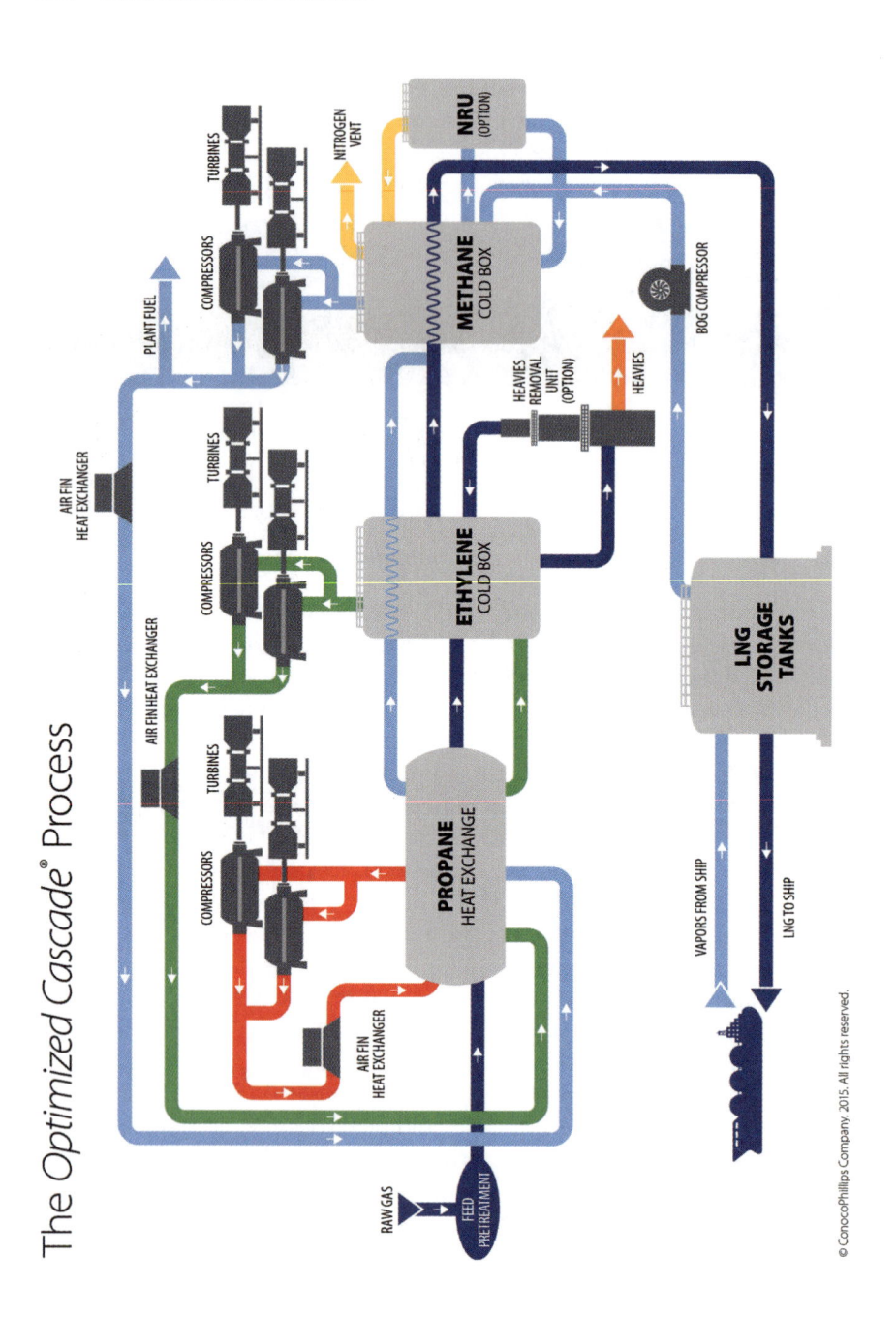

Figure A.7: The ConocoPhillips Optimized Cascade© liquefaction process
Source: Provided by ConocoPhillips Company and printed with permission.

Many PFHEs can be joined in series and in parallel to increase the capacity of the plant. These compact units are arranged in a structure called a cold box (represented in the flow diagram in Figure A.7 and also shown in Figure A.8[10]). The cold box contains the PFHEs, piping, and insulation within a protected structure, but with limited external access. The PFHEs are mounted vertically in this structure. Although appearing simple from the outside, the cold box contains a complex system of cryogenic process equipment and makes efficient use of the space.

Figure A.8: Examples of a cold box and a plate fin heat exchanger from Chart Industries

Source: ©2015 Chart Energy & Chemicals, Inc.

Evolution of process technology and the size of LNG trains

Since the beginning of the baseload LNG industry in the 1960s, process technology has evolved to enable manufacturers to design and supply equipment to support the processes. Initial trains were less than 1 mtpa but once the technology and equipment was proven, new plants chased economies of scale to develop greater LNG capacity using a fixed number of equipment items (compressors, drivers, and heat exchangers). The sizes of process piping and valves were also limited by manufacturing capabilities for LNG plant flow, pressure, and temperature.

---

[10] Images from Figure A.8 used with permission of Chart Energy & Chemicals, Inc. All rights reserved.

592   *LNG Markets in Transition*

A chart showing the growth of LNG train capacity over time, based on EPC award date, is shown in Figure A.9. Train sizes surpassed 2 mtpa in 1979, 3 mtpa in 1993, and the first 5 mtpa train was awarded in 2001. At the time, the ability to go above 5 mtpa in one train did not provide the economic advantage achieved by the previous plants. Parallel equipment and piping could be installed in one train to increase capacity, but parallel equipment, piping, and the increase in plot space can counteract the economic benefits expected from the economies of scale associated with large trains.

Around 2005, the AP-X™ liquefaction process by Air Products was commercialized to increase the limits of a single train by over 50 per cent (from the previous 5 mtpa benchmark). This process 'extended' the AP-C3MR™ cycle by adding a third refrigerant loop using nitrogen (Roberts et al., 2002); six trains of 7.8 mtpa, based on the AP-X™ process, were built in Qatar. After those trains were built, however, no further plants using this large-scale technology have been proposed. In retrospect, the added refrigeration loop added CAPEX without improving the process efficiency for that level of CAPEX and increased train capacity. New large greenfield proposals, with the prospect of 15 mtpa or more of capacity, now often consider three trains of 5 mtpa rather than the installation of two larger trains.

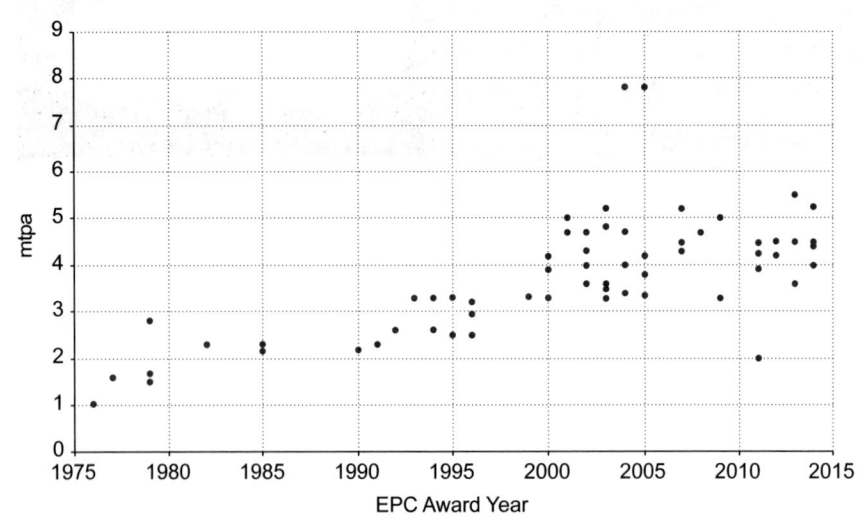

Figure A.9. Growth in LNG train size over time
Source: KBR Inc.

Recently, there have been advancements in manufactured equipment that allow train sizes of over 6 mtpa, using incremental improvements in equipment design and traditional liquefaction technology. Although these large trains are technically feasible and may be built in the future, many prospects continue to prefer train sizes in the range of 4 to 5 mtpa rather than the largest technically feasible trains.

Small-scale LNG

In contrast to the growing trend of larger train sizes, displayed in Figure A.9, there has also been progress in the development of small-scale plants and in large-scale plants based on multiple small-scale trains. There are two concepts that support small-scale LNG:

- small trains and small plants are able to capture a small market – such as LNG for transportation (bunker fuel, for example),
- large facilities based on small trains can test the economics of small-scale LNG.

A small train size, and a potentially lower overall facility cost, is also expected to support an easier path to obtain project financing. While the idea of LNG for transportation is discussed in Chapter 7, the value of small-scale trains for large-scale facilities is discussed in this section.

Since 2005, the CAPEX required to build large greenfield LNG projects in remote locations has risen extensively. One reason for this has been the rise in material and equipment prices during this period. However, the dominant reason for the rise in CAPEX has been the number of challenges facing the execution of complex projects in remote locations; such projects are disconnected from skilled labour markets (leading to high labour costs) and from established power and marine infrastructure. However, even though recent projects appear to be high in CAPEX, it is extremely difficult to compare one greenfield project to another, especially on the basis of $ per unit capacity (Kotzot et al., 2007).

In looking at new prospects on the horizon, some developers pursue the philosophy of building large projects with small-scale trains. The idea behind this concept is that the total facility CAPEX can be reduced on the basis of the simplicity in execution of a small train size; therefore, building a facility with multiple small trains will result in a lower $ per ton of LNG production than the present benchmark. For example, a facility considering 8–10 mtpa may propose 8–10 trains of 1 mtpa or 16–20 trains of 0.5 mtpa. This configuration is a huge shift from the common and proven concept of two large trains of 4–5 mtpa.

The potential cost benefits of building large-scale facilities with small LNG trains lie in project execution, fabrication, and installation. If the design, manufacture, delivery, and installation of LNG trains can be streamlined for small-scale LNG (many units are built in an identical and efficient manner), there could be a CAPEX benefit in selecting small trains for large facilities. While the focus of small-scale LNG is on the train size, the civil engineering and infrastructure costs associated with a large LNG facility are commonly overlooked. However, like the projects based on large trains, these infrastructure costs often dominate the project CAPEX and diminish the net benefit in reconfiguring the design and execution of the trains.

One other point to consider is the parallel nature of multiple small trains versus fewer large trains. Multiple smaller trains normally translate to more equipment, instrumentation, bulk material, plot, and maintenance compared to a smaller number of large trains. The fabrication and delivery of the small-scale solution must overcome this increase in equipment, plot, and bulk material for small trains.

One other area of interest for small-scale LNG is process efficiency. Small-scale trains are often configured using process technology with single loop cycles, such as SMR. The SMR process has a lower process efficiency than pre-cooled cycles such as C3MR, DMR, and Cascade. While the CAPEX to build a given capacity using small-scale LNG may be lower, the OPEX for small scale could be higher than that of the large scale, due to the difference in process efficiency. A less efficient process will use more power (work input to the refrigeration cycle) to make a given quantity of LNG, which will then cost more on the basis of the price of the source gas used as fuel (or the cost of imported power) to generate that power. In regions where the feed gas cost is high, the life cycle cost (CAPEX and OPEX) must be included in the evaluation.

The economics of choosing either small or large trains for large LNG facilities is yet to be proven. Many publications will focus on CAPEX, but the total solution should consider OPEX as well as CAPEX. Whatever the perception, it is extremely difficult to compare one greenfield project to another, due to the site-specific differences among plants around the world or even within a region. Small-scale LNG will continue to be developed for small markets in spite of the economics, while the economics of small-scale LNG for large-scale plants will be tested in the coming years.

LNG shipping

Without cryogenic shipping, there would be no LNG industry. In 1959, the *Methane Pioneer* was the first ship to demonstrate the feasibility of transporting

LNG across the Atlantic Ocean (SIGTTO/GIIGNL, 2014). While the transportation of liquids and liquid fuels is commonplace, the transportation of cryogenic liquids that have a propensity to become vapour is a unique segment of this industry. One of the great accomplishments of the LNG shipping industry is balancing the design of containment systems to safely transport LNG and control the boil off of LNG to natural gas, while streamlining the manufacturing process to control shipping costs.

There are three main types of LNG ships, and they are categorized by the type of cryogenic containment system used. These three ship types are Moss, Membrane, and Prismatic; a cross section of each type is shown in Figure A.10.[11] For each type of containment system, there may be variations among the available designs such that each shipbuilder has a well-known, but proprietary, type of vessel. These ships are often called 'double wall' or 'double hull', but it should be noted that while the external ship hull is not designed for the storage of LNG, a puncture of the external hull will not result in the spillage of LNG. A common ship size is in the range of 135,000 m^3 to 170,000 m^3 and the maximum size is 265,000 m^3.[12] There are over 400 LNG carriers in the current fleet.

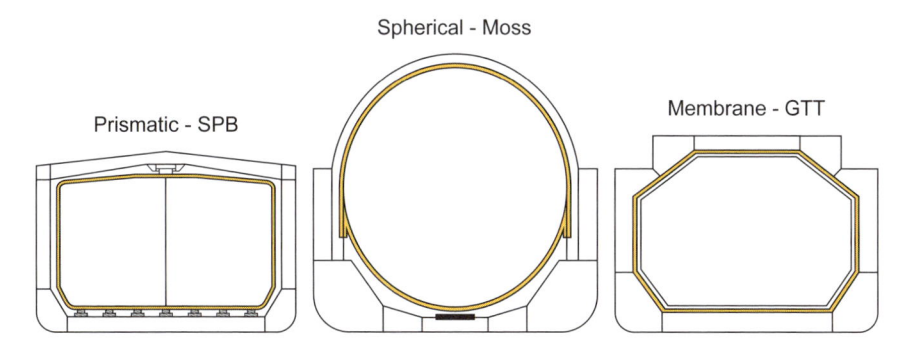

Figure A.10: Cross-section of LNG ship types
Source: Gas Technology Institute.

A photograph of a Moss ship is shown in Figure A.11. The Moss design is named for the company which introduced the system in 1973[13] and it is easily recognized by the spherical tanks which protrude above the main deck. The benefit of the Moss design is the structural integrity of the sphere

---

[11] Gas Technology Institute (GTI): *Fundamentals of Baseload LNG: Markets, Technology, and Economics*.

[12] 'Q-max LNG tankers' (page on website of Maritime Connector): http://maritime-connector.com/wiki/q-max/.

[13] *A Leader in Maritime Technology*, Moss Maritime General Brochure, 2.

and resistance to sloshing forces of the cargo during transport; the simplicity of the sphere is inherently its benefit. In addition, the cargo is not located close to the exterior hull, which gives it the benefit of collision resistance.

Figure A.11: Example of a Moss LNG carrier and a membrane LNG carrier
Source: Images courtesy of Moss Maritime, Norway, and Excelerate Energy.

On the other hand, the construction of the sphere requires a significant amount of welded steel which can affect the total ship cost. At the beginning of the LNG industry, the Moss design dominated the market. While the number of Moss ships is still significant today, the membrane design is now the most commonly built vessel.

A photo of a membrane LNG carrier is also shown in Figure A.11. Gaztransport et Technigaz, also known as GTT,[14] undertakes the engineering design and licensing of membrane containment systems. The membrane system gets its name from the configuration of the primary containment barrier, which is made from very thin alloy steel with an engineered corrugation pattern to account for thermal shrinkage. The membrane is made from either 1.2 mm stainless steel or 0.7 mm 36 per cent nickel steel, and is directly supported by the ship's external hull via the insulation system. The membrane, the insulation, and the hull are physically and mechanically connected; this allows a maximum cargo volume for a minimum amount of hull space. In addition, the cargo volume is almost entirely below the hull deck, allowing for a generous amount of space on the deck (unlike Moss ships which have protruding spheres above deck). The easiest way to recognize a membrane LNG carrier is to look for the 'trunk deck' or trapezoidal protrusion above the main deck, which is the uppermost section of the membrane tank. Many shipbuilders offer the membrane containment system and it has become the most popular containment vessel due to its cost per unit volume of storage and commercial competition among shipbuilders. Membrane ships also incur a relatively

---

[14] Website of Gaztransport & Technigaz: www.gtt.fr/.

low fee through the Suez Canal and are quicker to cool down when empty than Moss ships.

The last type of carrier for discussion is the prismatic-type carrier. Technically, the containment system is called the self-supported prismatic shape International Maritime Organization (IMO) type-B carrier, or commonly, SPB.[15] An easy way to identify this carrier is by the appearance of a nearly flat deck. One of the key characteristics of the SPB containment system is that it is independent of the ship's hull and is therefore a self-supported tank. If there was a leak in the containment system, it could be detected and collected, as there is a designated space between the tank and the ship's hull.

To date, there are only two SPB LNG carriers in operation, both commissioned in 1993.[16] The geometry of the prismatic containment system makes it highly resistant to sloshing loads, but at a higher capital cost versus the membrane-type carrier. The combination of the sloshing resistance and the almost fully below-deck tank profile initially makes SPB storage a popular choice for floating LNG (FLNG) systems, where deck space for process modules is at a premium. However, newbuild FLNG projects in construction have selected a reinforced membrane containment system, based on capital cost.

A graph of the LNG carrier market share by containment type is shown in Figure A.12. Although all containment systems are viable, most of the current fleet employ the membrane containment system, and this system continues to be selected for new vessels (IGU, 2015, 39). As vessels age, they may be converted to offshore regasification terminals in lieu of retirement. No matter what type of containment system, the nominal boil-off rate for the cargo is 0.15 per cent of the storage volume per day. While this boil-off rate is standard for LNG shipping, the rate is three times the design rate for onshore LNG storage. Boil-off rates lower than the nominal rate of 0.15 per cent of storage volume per day can be obtained simply by adding to the insulation system.

Analogous to the changes in size of LNG trains, the size of LNG carriers steadily increased over time. As the LNG industry grew, it was believed that larger carriers were needed to move significant volumes of LNG from Qatar to the exceptionally large regas terminals being built in the UK and the USA. Peak newbuild deliveries took place in the 2000s (IGU, 2015, 37), and some of these deliveries included the Q-Flex and Q-Max membrane carriers (developed for the substantial volume of LNG that was being

---

[15] For a detailed description of the SPB tank see page on website of Ishikawajima-Harima Heavy Industries (IHI): www.ihi.co.jp/offshore/whatisspb_e.htm.

[16] 'Tank Support for the LNG Revolution', *Surveyor*, A Quarterly Magazine by ABS, Fall/Winter 2013, 18.

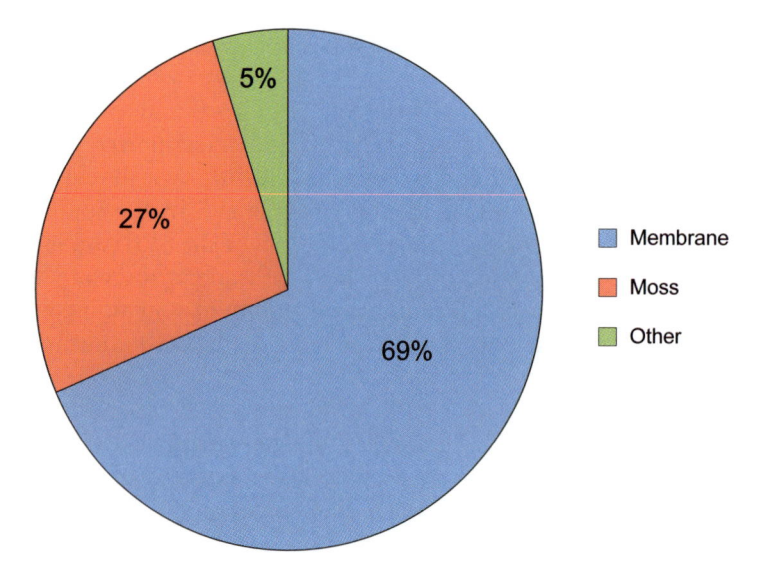

Figure A.12: Percentage of LNG carrier fleet by containment type
Source: Data from GIIGNL.

exported from Qatar) with capacities of approximately 215,000 m³ and 265,000 m³. While these larger LNG carriers were too large to berth at some older receiving terminals, over time, many older receiving terminals were modified, so that they could berth and receive shipments from these larger carriers.

Although Qatar remains the largest exporting country, new export projects from Australia and North America, together with new import terminals, have not continued the trend of shipping with these Q-class carriers. Instead of chasing the limits of manufacturing capability and economies of scale, the desired carrier size is currently one that is not too large to traverse the Panama Canal (170,000 m³ to 180,000 m³). Since the last Q-class vessel was delivered in 2010 (GIIGNL, 2014), there have been no further orders of this type of vessel.

Regasification

The LNG regasification plant, also called a receiving terminal or import terminal, is the smaller cousin of the liquefaction plant; it has many of the familiar features of a liquefaction plant, namely the marine infrastructure and LNG storage. The process plant for the terminal is designed to turn a low-pressure low-temperature cryogenic fluid into a high-pressure ambient-

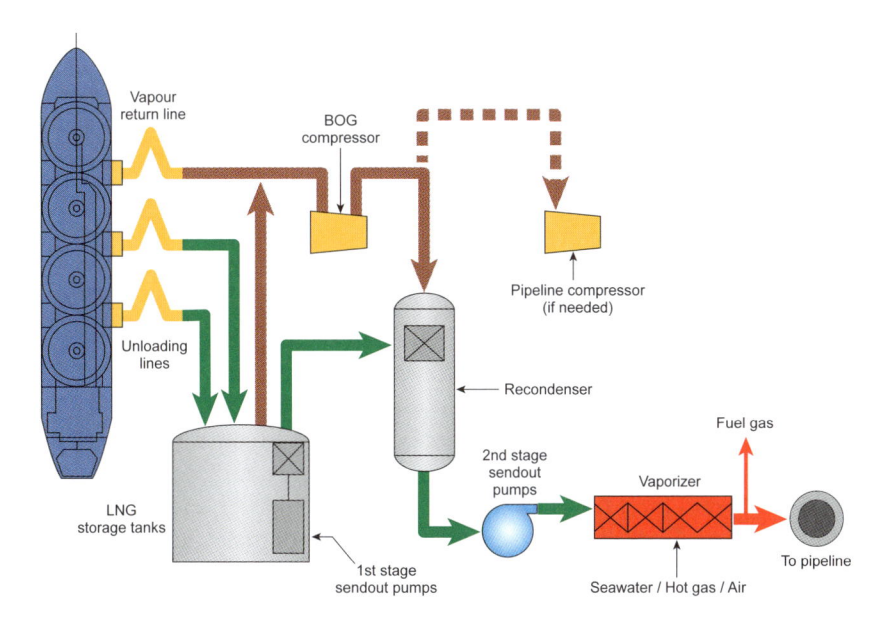

Figure A.13: Process flow diagram for an LNG regasification terminal
Source KBR Inc.

temperature vapour, through the addition of heat (see 'Vaporizer selection' on page 601). In addition, the terminal may operate in a continuous mode, an intermittent mode, or in a shut-in or idle mode. A basic schematic for a regasification terminal is shown in Figure A.13. LNG flows are shown in green, vapour flows are shown in brown, and high pressure natural gas is shown in red.

LNG is transferred from the LNG carrier to the onshore storage tanks of the receiving terminal via the cargo pumps located on the ship. This transfer is done through loading arms similar to those used at the liquefaction plant. Most terminals have four loading arms; two arms are for LNG transfer, one is for vapour return, and a fourth arm is a hybrid that can function in either service. The terminal can be configured with only three arms to reduce cost.

The LNG tanks are also similar to those at the liquefaction plant, although they operate in storage and draw down mode, as opposed to the continuous filling mode of a production plant. Although a receiving terminal could technically operate with one tank, multiple storage tanks are preferred due to their intermittent operation, the possibility of receiving LNG from multiple sources, and the flexibility to operate on the rare occurrence that an LNG tank is out of service.

When the LNG enters the tanks, the volume displaced by the liquid, in addition to the vapour generated as a result of heat gain, is sent to two places: first, back to the ship to keep the cargo tanks in balance from pumping out LNG, and second to a boil-off gas (BOG) compressor, which compresses the low-pressure gas to approximately 8 to 10 bar. This midpressure BOG is often sent to a vessel called a Recondenser when the terminal is in operation.

Recondenser

At first glance, the Recondenser appears counterintuitive to the purpose of the terminal, but it actually improves the terminal's efficiency. The Recondenser combines the BOG with the subcooled LNG exiting the first stage in-tank pumps. The Recondenser vessel is essentially a mixer, and the mixing is done with either co-current or counter-current flow. The BOG is fully absorbed in the LNG; this liquid then passes through the second stage send out pumps, which use a significant amount of mechanical power to increase the pressure to export pipeline pressure, typically 90–100 bar. In essence, it takes less energy to pump the exiting liquid to the send out pressure than to handle the BOG and the LNG separately to the same pressure.

LNG enters the vaporizer at the pressure required for downstream users of the terminal. The fluid is often in the supercritical region of its phase envelope; in this case, the addition of heat to the fluid changes its phase from liquid to vapour. Leaving the vaporizer, some of the gas may be taken for fuel, while the balance is sent to the customer. The end user for the terminal may be a pipeline, a power plant, or another natural gas consumer.

The last part of the process schematic includes the dotted lines connected to a pipeline compressor. These lines illustrate the operational mode called 'zero send-out' where the terminal is not in use; the terminal stores LNG, but is not vaporizing LNG. In this scenario, BOG is still generated by heat gain to the tanks and loading lines. This BOG can be used as fuel or it can be routed to a small pipeline compressor to send the minimum amount of natural gas from the terminal to maintain stable operations. In the 1980s and 1990s, most US terminals operated in either a zero send-out mode (where LNG may have been stored for years) or were shut down.

Other operational modes for terminals include re-export functionality. When gas from the terminal is not in high demand, but LNG is routinely scheduled for delivery, the terminal may re-export its LNG to a new destination. One of the design issues associated with re-export is the capability of the in-tank pumps; for older terminals, the pumps may not have been designed to send LNG at high volumetric rates back to the jetty for re-export.

Similar to re-export functionality, certain import terminals can use imported LNG to support smaller satellite terminals located inland from the primary terminal. In this scenario, LNG is transported by truck, using equipment similar to a vehicular fuelling station. If added to Figure A.13, truck loading would occur directly from the LNG storage tank or a holding drum, at modest pressure. In some countries, LNG can be re-loaded from the main terminal via small LNG carriers.

The concept of peak shaving should also be addressed with terminals. A peak shaver is normally defined as a terminal that operates seasonally, with great shifts in natural gas demand. A peak shaver may also be a self-sustaining inland facility, either with a small volume of liquefaction capacity or the ability to import by road or rail. Lastly, some may call a very small terminal, regardless of its use or seasonal demand, a peak shaver. The peak shaver either imports or liquefies natural gas in a season of low demand, thereby accumulating LNG when prices are low. The peak shaver vaporizes LNG during periods of high demand and when prices are high.

Vaporizer selection

A vaporizer is simply a piece of equipment used to transfer heat to pressurized LNG for conversion to pressurized natural gas. However, if heat were simply added to LNG as stored, the low-pressure vapour would need to be highly compressed before being sent to a distribution pipeline. As mentioned in the section on the Recondenser (page 600), the compression of a low-pressure vapour requires significant mechanical power. As designed, the high-pressure vaporizer is the most efficient way to turn LNG into high-pressure natural gas.

There are two distinctions among vaporizers: those that use ambient heat and those that use above-ambient heat. Ambient heating implies the use of seawater or air to vaporize the LNG, while above-ambient heating requires burning the natural gas to increase the heating rate. The two most common vaporizer types are the Open Rack Vaporizer (ORV) and the Submerged Combustion Vaporizer (SCV).

The ORV is the most common vaporizer that uses an ambient heating medium and it is the preferred method of vaporizing LNG in countries such as Japan, Korea, and Spain. LNG is heated within a series of tube panels connected together in a steel or concrete structure (Egashira, 2013, 65). Seawater, flowing down the exterior of the panels under gravity, heats the LNG (at a rate where the temperature of the seawater leaving the vaporizer is reduced by 5 to 10 °C) while the LNG flows upward, to promote counter current heat transfer. An ORV structure comprising the panels and a seawater handling system can vaporize 200 to 250 million standard cubic feet per day (MMSCFD) of gas flow. Several ORVs are required for a typical receiving terminal. From a cost standpoint, the ORV is high CAPEX and low OPEX (the structure involves high CAPEX but access to warm seawater as a heating medium, and the energy to circulate the seawater, is low OPEX). When selecting an ORV, a backup fired heater is often necessary when operating during periods of cold seawater temperatures.

The SCV is the most common vaporizer that uses an above-ambient heating medium. In addition, it can be used as a backup solution for a terminal using ORVs in the place of a separate fired heater. Water is used to heat the LNG in a continuously heated bath. The SCV is designed to burn natural gas to keep the temperature of the water bath constant. The unit is designed in increments of 150 MMSCFD; this means that multiple units have to be integrated together for a large receiving terminal. The water reservoir enables the SCV to handle large variations in load and it can be turned on and off to meet variations in demand. The SCV is low CAPEX and high OPEX (the unit is simple to construct and low cost, but the OPEX is high because natural gas is burned to operate the unit). Approximately 1.5 per cent of the natural gas vaporized is burned in an SCV (Egashira, 2013, 67). In addition, emissions, both to the air and water as products of combustion, must be accounted for in an SCV.

Both the ORV and SCV are acceptable choices for an LNG vaporizer. Both options have benefits in their use. While the ORV may be preferable due to low OPEX, projects must consider the implications of using seawater as a heating medium, particularly given the environmental impact of the reduced temperature of seawater discharged from the unit. In contrast the SCV, although high OPEX, is low CAPEX and can be easily permitted even with known products of combustion.

Other types of vaporizers are also in use. Two options include the use of air as a heating medium, either with fin-fans or by natural draught. In addition, shell and tube vaporizers may be designed using a variety of heating fluids. Shell and tube vaporizers are ideal choices for floating LNG terminals. The proper choice for a given project will balance CAPEX, OPEX, plot space, and the ease of permitting in the jurisdiction of the terminal.

LNG storage

In addition to shipping, the ability to store large volumes of cryogenic liquids at near-atmospheric pressure was necessary in establishing the global LNG industry. Manufacturing and construction improvements have led to a growth in tank sizes over the years; currently the largest storage tanks will store over 200,000 m^3 of LNG. Nearly every liquefaction plant and receiving terminal allocates plot space for at least two storage tanks; more tanks can be added over time with the expansion of plant facilities.

For liquefaction plants, the number and size of tanks is determined by analysing the cost of storage versus LNG production rate, average LNG carrier size, number of carriers, berthing availability, and the distance to regasification terminals. For regasification terminals, similar parameters apply when aiming to optimize the storage volume, with LNG vaporization rate replacing the production rate. All models incorporate statistical analysis of weather delays and shipping maintenance. Both liquefaction and regasification plants are normally designed for three to five days of spare storage capacity, to accommodate for unforeseen events.

There are three tank configurations which are defined by their containment systems: single, double, and full-containment. API Standard 625 is the US industry standard for the design of onshore LNG storage tanks.[17] EN 1473 is the corresponding industry standard for Europe. Figures depicting the details of the three tank types are included in these standards.

Although the relative cost of each tank configuration is mentioned below, these costs cannot be tabulated with absolute numbers or metrics of cost per cubic metre. While the tank, piping, concrete, and insulation costs of each tank type can be quantified, the accompanying civil engineering and foundation costs will vary significantly from site to site for each tank type. As the civil engineering work is such a large component of the tank cost, the tank costs are simply ranked from low to high.

A single-containment tank is the simplest and lowest-cost option for LNG storage. The LNG is stored in a cylindrical cryogenic cup which is open at the top. The primary container is usually made from 9 per cent nickel steel, but pre-stressed concrete can also be used. There is an outer steel tank and roof, but the outer container is not an LNG containment barrier; this steel shell is used to provide support for the side insulation, containment for vapour, protection from external moisture, and as a means to detect leaks. Underneath the tank, there is load-bearing foam block insulation, while the annular space is filled with perlite insulation.

If there is a failure in the primary containment system, the LNG is not contained by the external steel shell but within a concrete or earthen dyke wall; this wall is designed for more than the volume of LNG stored and is at some distance from the outer tank wall. Due to the simplistic nature of the secondary containment system, the single-containment tank is the lowest cost of the three systems, but it occupies the largest plot space.

A double-containment tank is an improvement on the dyke concept. A double-containment tank has the secondary containment in close proximity to the primary LNG container. The configuration is as if the dyke were moved closer and closer to the primary tank wall, and as the

---

[17] *Tank Systems for Refrigerated Liquefied Gas Storage*, American Petroleum Institute, API STD 625, August 2010.

dyke moves closer to the tank, its height increases to retain the same volume of LNG. From afar, the secondary containment has the appearance of a strong tank wall – a reinforced concrete wall which can withstand the temperature and pressure of LNG in close proximity to the primary container. If there is a failure in a double-containment tank, the LNG is contained within the concrete outer wall, reducing the surface area exposed to the atmosphere.

A full-containment tank is an improvement upon the double-containment concept. In this option, the primary and secondary containment systems work together to contain LNG and to mitigate vapour release if the inner tank fails. If the primary containment fails, the LNG and vapour generated are all contained within the secondary containment system and vapour is not immediately released to the atmosphere. As the roof is integrated into the concrete outer shell, a full-containment tank can be designed for a higher pressure than the single or double-containment tanks. Due to the added strength and vapour containment system, the full-containment tank is the highest cost among the three systems.

Two subsets of the full-containment tank include the membrane tank and the all-concrete tank. The membrane tank utilizes the thin membrane design utilized in LNG shipping (see page 596). The membrane tank uses load-bearing insulation and a reinforced concrete outer wall in order to develop a full-containment solution (Ezzarhouni, 2013). The all-concrete tank utilizes pre-stressed concrete for the primary containment vessel, instead of 9 per cent nickel steel. Certain design provisions are made to allow for concrete as the primary container; this system allows the construction of a full-containment tank without using rare and expensive alloy steel (Hoyle, 2013).

Although all LNG tank options are considered safe, the full-containment tank will allow closer spacing between tanks and will contain the liquid and vapour if there is ever a failure of the primary containment system. While most of the LNG tanks in the world are the single-containment type, the majority of new tanks being built are of the full-containment type. The basis of the shift to full containment is the belief that it gives added safety and security, as well as the ability to reduce the size of the total plot required for multiple tanks.

Offshore LNG – the technical challenges

Moving the LNG value chain offshore requires the combination of several plant systems into fewer pieces of infrastructure. Elements of the value chain (introduced in Chapter 3) are not deleted, but merged, as shown in Figure A.14. Although floating LNG is most often discussed in relation to

Technical Appendix 605

offshore, discussion of 'offshore LNG' does not exclusively imply that the infrastructure is floating. Offshore LNG options include gravity-based structures (GBS) and fixed platforms which are technically acceptable in shallow water.

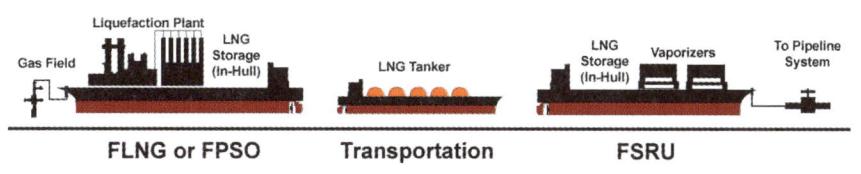

Figure A.14: The full floating LNG value chain
Source: KBR Inc.

While the fully dedicated offshore LNG value chain (where offshore production is dedicated for offshore regasification) is still in the future, floating regasification is already well proven and the first floating liquefaction projects are in construction. For the purpose of this Appendix, a floating regasification unit will be designated as an FSRU (this stands for a Floating Storage and Regasification Unit). Floating liquefaction will be called FLNG. An FLNG unit can also be called an LNG FPSO, which stands for a Floating Production Storage and Offloading unit, which is a common term offshore.

When looking to move liquefaction or regasification projects offshore, the key technical challenges are the marinization of equipment and the inclusion of all the processes and systems in a limited amount of space. Based on the relative simplicity of the regasification process, FSRUs were the first offshore LNG projects to be developed; FSRUs are now well proven and have been in service since 2005.[18] For floating liquefaction, the marinization of equipment requires detailed analysis of the forces imparted to each piece of equipment, as well as an estimation of the effect of a variety of motions on the operation of the plant itself.

With regard to floating LNG structures, there are several motions to consider. Motion occurs in three translational directions (X, Y, and Z axis) as well as three rotational directions (pitch, heave, and yaw). These motions are a function of wind, wave, and current forces; they must be determined on the basis of statistical data and be applied for the operational life of the facility. Rare weather events must also be considered and the equipment, modules, and hull structure must be designed to withstand these combinations of forces. In addition, permanent tilt, or list, needs to be considered as an operating case.

---
[18] 'World's first offshore LNG receiving facility and the birthplace of the FSRU', Gulf Gateway Deepwater Port. http://excelerateenergy.com/project/gulf-gateway-deepwater-port-2/.

Technical issues for an LNG FSRU

Adapting the regasification process for an FSRU may require modest modifications to traditional LNG carriers, significant modifications to larger ships, or purpose-built regasification barges. Nearshore FSRUs may be attached (moored) to an existing jetty while deepwater FSRUs will require more complex mooring systems. The most common FSRUs are converted membrane LNG carriers, but Moss ships can also be considered.[19] Regardless of the choice of FSRU hull structure, the most significant technical modifications are in mooring, LNG transfer, and vaporization.

The mooring system, specifically the turret and swivel, is the mechanical connection between the floating structure and the fixed infrastructure on the sea floor. Although an FSRU may be moored at an onshore facility, an FSRU in open water must have the capability to send high pressure gas to shore. This turret and swivel, whether internal (through the hull), external (in front of the hull), or submerged (fully below the waterline), is a highly engineered element of the FSRU, and it affects the design, operation, and project cost. For FSRUs, the turret is the link to connect vaporized gas to the area of demand, while for FLNG (other aspects of which are considered below), the turret is the connection from the gas reservoir to the production vessel (also, in the case of liquefaction, flow often occurs in two directions as offshore gas processing fluids may be returned to the subsea infrastructure through the turret). Companies involved in turret design for FLNG and FSRU projects include SBM, FMC, and NOV.

Unless moored to a jetty, LNG transfer systems must also be adapted for offshore LNG. While traditional loading arms may be used in benign waters, there are limitations in their use based on expected sea states (wind, wave, and current). In addition, two large LNG vessels connected by mechanical loading arms require close observation and monitoring to maintain the safe and reliable transfer of LNG offshore. To improve upon traditional loading arms, systems such as flexible hoses and tandem (bow to stern) loading are under development; such modifications allow for more variability in sea conditions and increased spacing between the vessels.[20]

Vaporizer selection is also another technical issue for FSRUs. While ORVs and SCVs are the most common vaporizers onshore, this equipment does not perform well in an environment subject to motion. The most adaptable vaporizer for offshore use is the shell and tube vaporizer, which also has the benefit of using shipboard steam as a heating medium.

---

[19] Website of Offshore LNG Toscana (OTL): www.oltoffshore.it/en/.
[20] *Chiksan® ATOL Articulated Tandem Offshore Loader*, FMC Brochure, 2012.

Technical issues for an FLNG (LNG FPSO)

In addition to the mooring and LNG transfer issues offshore, there are other technical elements to consider for FLNG. For liquefaction, much more processing occurs on the topside than on an LNG FSRU or an oil and gas FPSO; therefore more equipment, processes, and structures must be adapted for offshore operations. In addition, there are other issues to consider; these include accommodations, material handling, and operations and maintenance. From a technical perspective, process design, modularization, and process hazard analysis are closely interwoven in the design; developing an FLNG project is an iterative process when balancing these technical, safety, and operational issues.

Although all the technical categories of LNG that are affected by motion are important, one area that is critical to the daily functionality and availability of FLNG is the process design. Traditional methods of process separation and distillation, such as tray columns, will not work offshore because liquids cannot remain level offshore. As a result, mixing, separation, distillation, and heat transfer systems must all be adapted for a marine environment. Offshore process solutions are well known for these services, but they must be tested to the site-specific marine conditions of the facility. While many workable processes exist offshore, LNG processing has a higher level of complexity than offshore oil and gas separation, which only requires the separation of oil, water, and natural gas. The added complexity is due to the process systems required to separate components from natural gas to prevent freezing.

Modularization is another area of great importance for FLNG. While oil and gas FPSOs are fully modularized, the equipment density and weight of the modules is higher for FLNG than for an FPSO (Caswell et al., 2009). In addition to equipment differences, LNG process piping diameters are large, alloy steels are widely used, and insulation is thick and heavy. The iterative design method of modularization requires a keen awareness of weight management, module interfaces, and plant layout, as well as of operational and transportation loading.

Process hazard analysis is another technical area to be taken into consideration for FLNG. Unfortunately, process hazard analysis is a complex subject that is well beyond the scope of this Appendix. However, the propagation and severity of process hazards are magnified in an environment where module density is high and open space to dissipate hazards is minimal. Liquefaction can be safely designed for offshore LNG service, but the design and analysis must be carefully planned. The results of process hazard analysis can affect plant layout, module design, and asset integrity.

Gravity based structure (GBS) LNG

As already discussed, offshore LNG does not exclusively imply floating structures. In shallow water, a GBS provides an opportunity to move LNG offshore while mitigating the issue of motion on the process design. A GBS is a custom-built concrete structure that sits on the ocean floor in shallow water; there are many locations in which a GBS may be constructed and they do not have the size limitations of ship-based systems. A single GBS, or multiple structures, can be integrated together and since the structure is fixed, no motion is imparted to process equipment during operation. Although a GBS is not subject to motion during operation, the facility is constructed and integrated offsite and towed to its final location; therefore, the topsides must be designed to withstand transportation loads. There is one GBS regasification terminal in operation in Italy (see below), and GBS liquefaction has been proposed for areas with shallow water access to large amounts of natural gas.

The Adriatic LNG Terminal is a GBS located offshore Italy and it has been operating since 2009 (GIIGNL, 2014). This GBS utilizes all the process systems and utilities of a regasification terminal, including loading arms, power generation, ORVs, flare, and safety systems. The LNG storage tanks utilized proprietary technology that was specially designed for the GBS, and are not the standard membrane variety seen in LNG ships. Although the terminal may be considered high CAPEX, the GBS concept allowed the permitting of a project in an area that was resistant to onshore LNG development. In the future, CAPEX improvement can be obtained in the areas of project execution, GBS construction, and LNG storage.

The use of GBS is also considered for liquefaction projects. A GBS may have some advantages over ship-shaped structures in certain environments. For large-capacity facilities, an FLNG will be limited by the space available for liquefaction. Large plants would require multiple FLNG units; a facility based on multiple units is high CAPEX because of the high cost of building the hull, which is limited in its maximum size. In certain cases, the construction of multiple large GBS structures will have a cost advantage over multiple floating units.

Another factor that may favour the selection of a GBS is the project location. A GBS, like an FLNG, moves construction workhours from a remote greenfield site to a highly efficient fabrication facility. Some site locations may have weather issues where traditional construction methods are challenging, because of known factors or the uncertainty of weather. While not applicable in all cases, GBS solutions should be considered for unique environments where traditional construction methods are not practical and the advantages of GBS construction methods and facility size can be realized.

LNG technical resources: companies involved in liquefaction and regasification projects

As already discussed in this Technical Appendix, liquefaction, shipping, storage, and regasification projects are technically complex and capital intensive. Due to the size and scale of LNG projects in the twenty-first century, the companies involved may specialize in LNG, but they are also well diversified to handle many other business segments serving the oil and gas industry. While some companies may take on a specific area or scope (for example cryogenic equipment, tanks, or ships), many of the projects are built by a group of companies, commonly in a joint venture.

The capital cost of greenfield LNG projects is often far beyond the financial capabilities of a single company. By spreading the technical and commercial risk among a joint venture, the scope of a large capital project can be shared among many capable companies, united for a common goal. While projects in previous decades were often taken on by one company, the high cost of LNG civil engineering works and infrastructure requires spreading the risk among many partners, both on the owner side and contractor side. This model is likely to be here to stay, except for either the smallest of LNG projects, or for the largest of companies, who can handle the entire risk portfolio.

Lists of companies involved in liquefaction and regasification projects, grouped by technical expertise and listed alphabetically, are provided below.

LNG process technology providers (licensors): The list of liquefaction process technology providers covers over 90 per cent of the current operating market for onshore liquefaction, plus some licensors that may commercialize their technologies in the coming years. Many other companies own technology and/or patents in liquefaction. Some of the listed companies provide more than one liquefaction process technology.

Table A.2: LNG process technology providers/licensors

Air Products and Chemicals, Inc. (APCI)
Black and Veatch Corporation
Chart Industries
ConocoPhillips LNG Licensing and Technology
The Linde Group
Liquefied Natural Gas Limited
Shell Global Solutions

AGRU process technology providers: The current market for acid gas removal technology is dominated by BASF, but other options are available for these systems.

Table A.3: AGRU process technology providers / licensors

BASF	Prosernat
Honeywell UOP	Shell Global Solutions
Huntsman Corporation	

Liquefaction: engineering, procurement, and construction (EPC) companies: The following list of EPC companies includes those that have either completed works for LNG export projects or are currently executing projects in construction. Companies that specialize in construction-only are not included in this list. Companies supporting only offshore LNG are shown in italics.

Table A.4: Liquefaction engineering, procurement, and construction (EPC)

AMEC Foster Wheeler	JGC
Bechtel	KBR
Black and Veatch	Linde
CB&I	Technip
Chiyoda	Saipem
Clough	Samsung Heavy Industries
Hyundai Heavy Industries	WorleyParsons
IHI	

Regasification terminal: engineering, procurement, and construction companies: Due to the size, scope, and complexity of liquefaction projects, more companies are involved in providing services for import terminals than for export plants. Regional engineering and construction companies can also participate in this engineering and construction market, and they should be considered in addition to the following list.

Table A.5: Regasification terminal EPC companies

AMEC Foster Wheeler	Technip
Bechtel	Saipem
Black and Veatch	Samsung C&T
CB&I	Sener
Chiyoda	SK E&C
Deawoo E&C	Sofregaz
Fluor	Techint
IHI	Technimont
JGC	Technicas Reunidas
KBR	Toyo

LNG storage tank technology providers and constructors: For LNG tanks, the companies involved can either self-perform the entire tank construction process or licence their technology to another company to do the construction. Many firms, who are able to construct LNG tanks based on a licensed tank design, are not listed in the group below.

Table A.6: LNG storage tank technology providers and constructors

CB&I
Entrepose-Vinci
Gaztransport & Technigaz (GTT)
Ishikawajima-Harima Heavy Industries (IHI)
Kawasaki Heavy Industries (KHI)
Matrix PDM Engineering
Toyo Kanetsu (TKK)

Offshore classification societies: Classification societies are charged with the development of rules and standards regarding the construction of offshore structures in order to ensure a high level of safety and integrity. Most importantly, they are objective inspectors who guarantee adherence to both international codes and standards and to those of the class itself. Classification societies work closely with the shipyards and engineering companies that design and build offshore LNG facilities.

Table A.7: Offshore classification societies

American Bureau of Shipping	ABS
Bureau Veritas	BV
Det Norske Veritas	DNV
Lloyds Register	LR

BIBLIOGRAPHY

Caswell, C., Durr, C., Rost, E., and Kilcran, M. (2009). 'FLNG – History Does Not Repeat Itself, but It Does Rhyme', KBR, Presented at GasTech 2009, (Abu Dhabi, UAE, 25–28 May 2009).

Ffooks, R. (1993). *Natural Gas by Sea, the Development of a New Technology*, 2nd Edition, Witherby & Co. Ltd.

Hoyle, K. (2013). 'Composite Concrete Cryogenic Tank (C3T): A Precast Concrete Alternative For LNG Storage', Chevron, conference session at LNG 17,(17th International Conference & Exhibition on Liquefied Natural Gas Houston, Texas, USA, 16–19 April 2013).

Ezzarhouni, A. (2013). 'What Drivers Bring a Revival of Interest in the Membrane System for Land Storage LNG Tanks?', GTT, poster session at LNG 17, (17th International Conference & Exhibition on Liquefied Natural Gas Houston, Texas, USA, 16–19 April 2013).

Egashira, S. (2013). 'LNG Vaporizer for LNG Re-gasification Terminal', *KOBELCO Technology Review*, No.32, December 2013,

GIIGNL (2014). *The LNG Industry in 2014*, International Group of Liquefied Natural Gas Importers. (GIIGNL Annual Report)

IGU (2015). *World LNG Report – 2015 Edition*, International Gas Union.

Kotzot, H., Durr, C., Coyle, D., and Caswell, C. (2007). 'LNG Liquefaction – Not All Plants Are Created Equal', KBR, LNG 15, (15th International Conference & Exhibition on Liquefied Natural Gas Barcelona, Spain, 24–27 April 2007). https://kbr.com/Documents/LNG%20White%20Papers/2007%20LNG%2015%20-%20Not%20All%20Plants%20Are%20Created%20Equal%20%5BPaper%5D.pdf.

SIGTTO/GIIGNL (2014). *LNG Shipping at 50 (SIGTTO at 35 and GIIGNL at 43)*, SIGTTO (The Society of International Gas Tanker and Terminal Operators): London, GIIGNL: Neuilly Sur Seine. www.giignl.org/sites/default/files/PUBLIC_AREA/Publications/lng-shipping-at-50compressed.pdf.

Pillarella, M., Liu, Y.-N., Petrowski, J., and Bower, R. (2007). 'The C3MR Liquefaction Cycle: Versatility for a Fast Growing, Ever Changing LNG Industry', LNG 15, 24–27 April 2007.

Roberts, M. J., Petrowski, J. M., Liu, Y.-N., and Bronfenbrenner, J.C. (2002). 'Large Capacity Single Train AP-X™ Hybrid LNG Process', APCI, Presented at Gastech 2002, (Doha, Qatar, 13–16 October 2002).

Van Wylen, G. (1985). *Fundamentals of Classical Thermodynamics*, 3rd Edition, John Wiley & Sons.

Data Appendix

CONTENTS

Table D.1	LNG export data by year and by country (mtpa)	614
Table D.2	LNG import data by year and by country (mtpa)	616
Table D.3	Liquefaction plants	620
Table D.4	Regasification terminals	627

Table D.1: LNG export data by year and by country (mtpa)

	Algeria	United States	Libya	Brunei	Abu Dhabi	Indonesia	Malaysia	Australia	Qatar	Nigeria	Trinidad	Oman	Egypt	Eq. Guinea	Norway	Russia	Yemen	Peru	Angola	PNG	Other	TOTAL
1964	0.08																					0.08
1965	0.68																					0.68
1966	0.82																					0.82
1967	0.98																					0.98
1968	1.13																					1.13
1969	1.21	0.05																				1.26
1970	1.12	0.86	0.05																			2.02
1971	1.11	0.97	0.26																			2.35
1972	1.24	0.93	1.58	0.05																		3.80
1973	1.95	0.94	2.14	1.15																		6.18
1974	2.20	0.92	1.89	2.53																		7.54
1975	2.83	1.06	2.35	3.56																		9.81
1976	3.76	0.97	2.65	4.91																		12.29
1977	3.17	1.01	2.72	5.47	0.39	0.50																13.26
1978	4.89	0.95	2.59	5.35	1.28	3.83																18.89
1979	8.67	0.99	2.26	5.56	1.32	6.26																25.06
1980	5.02	0.87	1.46	5.63	1.95	8.63																23.56
1981	5.36	1.09	0.56	5.30	1.99	8.83																23.14
1982	7.46	0.97	0.62	5.20	2.24	9.33																25.82
1983	11.78	1.06	0.58	5.29	1.81	9.64	1.11															31.28
1984	9.14	1.03	0.83	5.22	2.12	14.21	3.54															36.09
1985	9.50	1.03	0.78	5.16	2.34	14.99	4.45															38.26
1986	9.02	0.98	0.65	5.25	2.20	15.24	5.16															38.50
1987	10.54	0.95	0.60	5.27	2.16	16.63	6.02															42.17
1988	11.15	0.98	0.80	5.45	2.39	18.48	6.21															45.46
1989	12.80	1.00	1.08	5.33	2.34	18.70	6.57	0.68														48.49
1990	14.32	1.02	0.93	5.42	2.41	20.70	6.47	2.96														54.24

Data Appendix

	Algeria	United States	Libya	Brunei	Abu Dhabi	Indonesia	Malaysia	Australia	Qatar	Nigeria	Trinidad	Oman	Egypt	Eq. Guinea	Norway	Russia	Yemen	Peru	Angola	PNG	Other	TOTAL
1991	14.39	1.00	1.19	5.26	2.59	22.34	7.18	3.92														57.87
1992	14.68	1.05	1.38	5.36	2.57	23.78	7.34	4.65														60.83
1993	15.23	1.06	1.20	5.62	2.52	23.91	7.87	5.03														62.44
1994	13.60	1.18	1.11	5.80	3.20	26.43	8.26	6.53														66.11
1995	13.47	1.24	1.12	6.30	5.29	25.05	10.26	7.38														70.11
1996	14.62	1.32	0.90	6.34	5.38	26.53	13.08	7.42														75.59
1997	18.19	1.32	0.84	6.24	5.87	26.53	15.20	7.17	2.15													83.51
1998	18.71	1.41	0.68	6.11	5.39	27.11	14.58	7.55	3.60													85.14
1999	19.18	1.30	0.69	6.09	5.10	28.55	14.80	7.25	6.33	0.16	1.54											91.01
2000	19.75	1.34	0.58	6.58	5.00	26.73	15.03	7.18	10.24	4.43	2.90	2.04										101.81
2001	19.37	1.37	0.59	6.69	5.22	24.01	15.42	7.40	12.55	5.73	2.83	5.48										106.65
2002	20.53	1.33	0.50	6.82	5.11	26.45	14.95	7.37	13.73	5.84	3.99	6.33										112.94
2003	21.29	1.29	0.56	7.10	5.26	26.54	16.84	7.64	14.31	8.74	8.84	6.79										125.19
2004	18.02	1.24	0.49	7.13	5.76	24.84	20.13	8.83	18.22	9.49	9.71	6.94	5.01								0.43	131.22
2005	18.66	1.26	0.72	6.94	5.57	23.49	21.85	11.41	20.72	9.25	9.87	6.79	10.55								0.21	141.74
2006	17.50	1.17	0.51	7.40	5.55	22.05	21.29	14.04	24.80	13.41	11.84	8.69	10.00	1.10	0.13						0.14	158.94
2007	17.87	0.90	0.59	7.07	5.84	20.52	22.63	15.18	29.30	16.67	13.51	9.50	9.98	3.34	1.63							170.80
2008	16.02	0.73	0.41	7.02	5.77	20.14	22.39	15.41	30.27	16.80	13.00	8.91	9.63	3.36	2.33	4.96	0.31				0.27	172.09
2009	15.68	0.56	0.58	6.60	5.39	19.32	22.60	18.40	37.29	11.67	14.46	8.41	6.72	3.63	3.50	9.72	3.99	1.21			0.19	181.74
2010	14.22	0.57	0.28	6.65	6.06	23.50	23.49	19.28	56.71	18.00	13.77	8.91	6.33	3.95	2.51	10.57	6.36	3.70				220.21
2011	12.48	0.32	0.06	7.09	5.82	21.88	24.90	19.52	75.36	18.91	12.98	8.09	4.74	3.62	3.31	10.86	4.89	3.86				240.83
2012	11.21	0.17	0.00	6.82	5.66	18.97	23.72	20.88	76.39	19.58	13.48	8.15	2.66	3.77	3.05	10.69	6.82	4.25	0.33			236.31
2013	10.81	0.00	0.00	7.01	5.08	18.36	25.14	22.41	78.02	16.47	13.67	8.35	0.31	3.38	3.55	10.58	6.27	4.03	0.33	3.38		236.89
2014	12.72	0.25	0.00	6.12	6.08	17.38	24.83	23.60	76.37	19.14	13.09	7.73	0.31	3.38	3.55	10.58	6.27	4.03	0.33	3.38		239.14
2015	12.13	0.32	0.00	6.48	5.70	18.03	24.99	29.45	78.40	19.50	11.81	7.56	0.00	3.65	4.33	10.57	1.52	3.57	0.00	7.18		245.19

Source: GIIGNL.

Table D.2: LNG import data by year and by country (mtpa)

(a) 1964–1998

	United Kingdom	France	Japan	Spain	United States	Italy	Belgium	Germany	South Korea	Taiwan	Turkey	TOTAL
1964	0.08											**0.08**
1965	0.54	0.14										**0.68**
1966	0.53	0.29										**0.82**
1967	0.63	0.35										**0.98**
1968	0.82	0.31										**1.13**
1969	0.86	0.35	0.05									**1.26**
1970	0.69	0.41	0.86	0.05	0.02							**2.02**
1971	0.68	0.37	0.97	0.23	0.06	0.03						**2.35**
1972	0.63	0.56	0.98	0.49	0.05	1.09						**3.80**
1973	0.61	1.26	2.09	0.64	0.08	1.50						**6.18**
1974	0.50	1.56	3.44	0.69	0.00	1.34						**7.54**
1975	0.69	1.93	4.62	0.77	0.11	1.68						**9.81**
1976	0.80	2.38	5.88	1.07	0.22	1.95						**12.29**
1977	0.66	2.06	7.37	0.96	0.24	1.96						**13.26**
1978	0.55	2.27	11.41	1.01	1.80	1.86						**18.89**
1979	0.49	2.31	14.13	1.19	5.38	1.57						**25.06**
1980	0.63	1.59	17.09	1.41	1.83	1.02						**23.56**
1981	0.31	3.22	17.22	1.61	0.78	1.02						**23.14**
1982	0.02	4.95	17.74	1.68	1.17	0.02	0.24					**25.82**
1983	0.00	6.59	18.92	1.80	2.79	0.02	1.17					**31.28**

Data Appendix 617

	United Kingdom	France	Japan	Spain	United States	Italy	Belgium	Germany	South Korea	Taiwan	Turkey	TOTAL
1984	0.00	6.12	26.12	1.57	0.77	0.26	1.25					36.09
1985	0.00	5.91	27.97	1.83	0.53	0.21	1.80					38.26
1986	0.00	5.77	28.68	1.86	0.04	0.00	1.95	0.09	0.11			38.50
1987	0.00	7.04	29.56	1.87	0.00	0.00	2.14	0.09	1.47			42.17
1988	0.04	6.73	31.50	2.44	0.43	0.14	2.17	0.00	2.01			45.46
1989	0.08	6.80	32.84	2.90	0.89	0.21	2.77	0.00	2.00			48.49
1990	0.04	7.00	36.02	3.34	1.86	0.02	2.93	0.00	2.32	0.72		54.24
1991	0.00	6.89	38.08	4.11	1.45	0.11	3.03	0.00	2.73	1.49		57.87
1992	0.00	2.41	39.63	4.35	0.92	0.44	3.44	0.00	3.44	1.68		56.32
1993	0.00	6.77	39.87	4.50	1.74	0.22	3.23	0.00	4.36	1.74		62.44
1994	0.00	6.05	42.71	4.67	1.08	0.16	2.99	0.00	5.94	2.30	0.22	66.11
1995	0.00	6.08	44.34	5.33	0.45	0.04	3.29	0.00	7.17	2.50	0.91	70.11
1996	0.00	5.66	46.57	5.25	0.86	0.00	3.02	0.00	9.74	2.65	1.84	75.59
1997	0.00	6.95	47.93	4.77	1.66	1.43	3.42	0.00	11.81	3.28	2.26	83.51
1998	0.00	7.35	49.79	4.46	1.83	1.50	3.23	0.00	10.76	3.50	2.73	85.14

Source: GIIGNL.

(b) 1999–2015. The '*TOTAL*' column gives the total import figure for each year calculated from both parts of this table for each year.

	United Kingdom	France	Japan	Spain	United States	Italy	Belgium	Germany	Korea	Taiwan	Turkey	Puerto Rico	Greece	Portugal	Dominican Republic	India	Mexico	China
1999	0	7.41	50.80	5.43	3.45	2.07	2.93	0	12.80	3.94	2.18							
2000	0	8.58	53.32	6.82	4.82	2.63	3.11	0	14.31	4.37	3.21	0.26	0.38					
2001	0	8.95	54.99	7.87	5.10	2.66	1.72	0	16.12	4.75	3.68	0.41	0.40					
2002	0	10.57	54.25	10.26	4.83	2.55	2.73	0	17.84	5.36	3.70	0.47	0.38					
2003	0	9.21	58.51	12.11	10.54	2.49	2.52	0	19.41	5.59	3.45	0.54	0.42	0.18	0.24			
2004	0	7.87	56.84	13.81	12.93	1.49	2.28	0	22.29	6.89	2.92	0.46	0.35	1.025	0.10	1.97		
2005	0.38	9.70	58.11	17.03	12.72	1.80	1.99	0	22.49	7.19	3.40	0.47	0.33	1.32	0.19	4.60		
2006	2.48	10.69	62.65	18.77	11.36	2.26	3.11	0	25.48	7.79	3.77	0.50	0.45	1.63	0.23	6.18	0.83	0.75
2007	1.02	9.61	66.98	18.63	15.65	1.73	2.08	0	26.24	8.33	4.10	0.50	0.67	2.11	0.42	7.90	1.85	2.99
2008	0.79	9.35	69.15	21.99	6.96	1.10	2.31	0	29.05	9.15	3.91	0.57	0.74	2.05	0.35	8.30	2.65	3.37
2009	7.99	9.60	65.20	20.23	9.11	2.17	5.00	0	25.22	8.94	4.05	0.53	0.61	2.06	0.40	9.28	2.73	5.74
2010	14.19	10.40	70.87	20.60	8.19	6.66	4.40	0	32.64	11.18	5.62	0.54	0.73	2.16	0.62	8.97	4.28	9.60
2011	18.42	10.53	79.09	17.25	6.14	6.27	4.08	0	35.55	12.20	4.80	0.65	0.91	2.14	0.69	12.33	2.84	13.06
2012	10.38	7.17	88.08	14.46	3.09	5.16	1.82	0.00	36.77	12.67	5.63	0.97	0.76	1.52	0.92	13.27	3.52	14.65
2013	6.91	5.94	87.98	9.13	1.90	4.05	1.19	0.00	40.39	12.72	4.40	1.16	0.45	1.49	0.84	13.05	5.67	18.60
2014	8.40	4.58	89.20	7.90	1.16	3.27	0.97	0.00	37.62	13.45	5.45	1.25	0.38	0.97	0.83	14.54	6.58	18.98
2015	10.08	4.35	85.05	8.82	1.70	4.32	1.87	0.00	33.42	14.45	5.35	1.15	0.45	1.09	0.87	14.60	4.94	20.02

Data Appendix

	Argentina	Brazil	Chile	Canada	Kuwait	Dubai	Thailand	Netherlands	Indonesia	Israel	Malaysia	Singapore	Lithuania	Pakistan	Jordan	Egypt	Sweden	Poland	TOTAL
1999																			91.01
2000																			101.81
2001																			106.65
2002																			112.94
2003																			125.19
2004																			131.22
2005																			141.74
2006																			158.94
2007																			170.80
2008	0.31																		172.09
2009	0.63	0.35	0.47	0.71	0.72														181.74
2010	1.27	2.10	2.17	0.92	1.99	0.10													220.20
2011	2.93	0.61	2.78	2.45	2.60	1.08	0.80	0.58											240.78
2012	3.36	2.70	2.77	1.30	1.99	1.05	1.02	0.56	0.72										236.31
2013	4.72	4.15	2.61	0.76	1.15	1.59	1.45	0.36	1.43	0.40	1.50	0.91							236.90
2014	4.42	5.33	2.57	0.40	2.68	1.34	1.40	0.42	1.56	0.08	1.65	1.68	0.11						239.17
2015	4.08	4.78	2.74	0.49	3.04	2.21	2.70	0.63	2.18	0.12	1.53	2.08	0.32	1.05	1.85	2.60	0.29		245.22

Source: GIIGNL.

Table D.3: Liquefaction plants

Basin	Region	Country	Plant	Location	Capacity bcm/year	Capacity mtpa	Status	Online date	Owners	Operator
Atlantic	Africa	Algeria	Arzew-Bethioua GL 1Z	Arzew	10.7	7.9	Operation	1978	Sonatrach	Sonatrach
		Algeria	Arzew-Bethioua GL 2Z	Arzew	11.2	8.2	Operation	1981	Sonatrach	Sonatrach
		Algeria	Arzew-Bethioua GL 3Z	Arzew	6.4	4.7	Operation	2014	Sonatrach	Sonatrach
		Algeria	Skikda GL1K/GL2K	Skikda	4.4	3.2	Operation	1972	Sonatrach	Sonatrach
		Algeria	Skikda GL1K	Skikda	6.1	4.5	Operation	2013	Sonatrach	Sonatrach
		Angola	Angola LNG	Soyo	7.1	5.2	Stopped	2013	Angola LNG: Chevron (36.4%); Sonangol (22.8%); BP (13.6%); Eni (13.6%); Total (13.6%)	Chevron
		Egypt	Segas	Damietta	6.8	5.0	Stopped	2005	Union Fenosa Gas (80%); EGPC (10%); EGAS (10%)	SEGAS
		Egypt	Egyptian LNG T1	Idku	4.9	3.6	Stopped	2005	BG (35.5%); Petronas (35.5%); EGAS (12%); EGPC (12%); Engie (5%)	ELNG
		Egypt	Egyptian LNG T2	Idku	4.9	3.6	Stopped	2005	BG (38%); Petronas (38%); EGAS (12%); EGPC (12%)	ELNG
		Equatorial Guinea	EG LNG	Bioko Island	5.0	3.7	Operation	2007	Marathon (60%), Sonagas (25%), Mitsui (8.5%), Marubeni (6.5%)	EG LNG
		Libya	Marsa El Brega	Marsa El Brega	4.4	3.2	Stopped	1970	LNOC	LNOC

Data Appendix

Basin	Region	Country	Plant	Location	Capacity bcm/year	Capacity mtpa	Status	Online date	Owners	Operator
Atlantic	Africa	Nigeria*	NLNG T2	Bonny Island	13.1	9.6	Operation	1999	Nigerian National Petroleum Corporation (NNPC) (49%); Shell (25.6%), Total (15%); Eni (10.4%)	Shell
		Nigeria*	NLNG T1	Bonny Island			Operation	2000	Nigerian National Petroleum Corporation (NNPC) (49%); Shell (25.6%), Total (15%); Eni (10.4%)	Shell
		Nigeria*	NLNG T3	Bonny Island			Operation	2002	Nigerian National Petroleum Corporation (NNPC) (49%); Shell (25.6%), Total (15%); Eni (10.4%)	Shell
		Nigeria*	NLNGPlus	Bonny Island	5.5	4.1	Operation	2005	Nigerian National Petroleum Corporation (NNPC) (49%); Shell (25.6%), Total (15%); Eni (10.4%)	Shell
		Nigeria*	NLNGPlus	Bonny Island	5.5	4.1	Operation	2006	Nigerian National Petroleum Corporation (NNPC) (49%); Shell (25.6%), Total (15%); Eni (10.4%)	Shell
		Nigeria	NLNGSix	Bonny Island	5.6	4.1	Operation	2007†	Nigerian National Petroleum Corporation (NNPC) (49%); Shell (25.6%), Total (15%); Eni (10.4%)	Shell
	Europe	Norway	Snøvhit	Melkøya Island	5.9	4.3	Operation	2007	Statoil (36.79%); Petoro (30.0%), Total (18.4%); Engie (12.0%); RWE Dea (2.81%)	Statoil
	Latin America	Trinidad & Tobago	Atlantic LNG T1	Point Fortin	4.5	3.3	Operation	1999	BP (34%); BG (26%); Shell (20%); CIC (10%); National Gas Co. (NGC Trinidad) (10%)	Atlantic LNG
		Trinidad & Tobago	Atlantic LNG T2	Point Fortin	4.8	3.5	Operation	2002	BP (42.5%); BG (32.5%); Shell (25%)	Atlantic LNG

Basin	Region	Country	Plant	Location	Capacity bcm/year	Capacity mtpa	Status	Online date	Owners	Operator
Atlantic	*Latin America*	Trinidad & Tobago	Atlantic LNG T3	Point Fortin	4.8	3.5	Operation	2003	BP (42.5%); BG (32.5%); Shell (25%)	Atlantic LNG
		Trinidad & Tobago	Atlantic LNG T4	Point Fortin	7.1	5.2	Operation	2007†	BP (37.78%); BG (28.89%); Shell (22.22%); NGC Trinidad (11.11%)	Atlantic LNG
		Peru	Peru LNG	Pampa Melchorita	6.1	4.5	Operation	2010	Hunt Oil (50%); SK Energy (20%); Shell (20%); Marubeni(10%)	Hunt Oil
Pacific	*Asia*	Indonesia	Bontang A–B Trains	East Kalimantan	30.3	22.3	Operation	1977	Pertamina (55%); Vico (BP, ENI) (20%); Total (10%); JILCO (15%)	PT Badak LNG
		Indonesia	Bontang C–D Trains	East Kalimantan			Operation	1983	Pertamina (55%); Vico (BP, ENI) (20%); Total (10%); JILCO (15%)	PT Badak LNG
		Indonesia	Bontang E Train	East Kalimantan			Operation	1990	Pertamina (55%); Vico (BP, ENI) (20%); Total (10%); JILCO (15%)	PT Badak LNG
		Indonesia	Bontang F Train	East Kalimantan			Operation	1994	Pertamina (55%); Vico (BP, ENI) (20%); Total (10%); JILCO (15%)	PT Badak LNG
		Indonesia	Bontang G Train	East Kalimantan			Operation	1998	Pertamina (55%); Vico (BP, ENI) (20%); Total (10%); JILCO (15%)	PT Badak LNG
		Indonesia	Bontang H Train	East Kalimantan			Operation	1998	Pertamina (55%); Vico (BP, ENI) (20%); Total (10%); JILCO (15%)	PT Badak LNG
		Indonesia	Tangguh LNG	Bintuni Bay, Papua	10.3	7.6	Operation	2009	Tangguh LNG (BP (37.16%); CNOOC (13.9%); JX Nippon (13.5%); Mitsubishi (9.9%); INPEX (7.8%); KG Berau (5%); LNG Japan (7.35%); Talisman (3.06%); Mitsui (2.3%))	Tangguh LNG
		Indonesia	Donggi-Senoro	Donggi-Senoro	2.7	2.0	Operation	2015	Mitsubishi (45%); Pertamina (29%); KOGAS (15%); MEDCO (11%)	†

Basin	Region	Country	Plant	Location	Capacity bcm/year	Capacity mtpa	Status	Online date	Owners	Operator
Pacific	Asia	Malaysia	MLNG Satu (I)	Bintulu, Sarawak	11.0	8.1	Operation	1983	Petronas (90%); Mitsubishi (5%); Sarawak Government (5%)	Petronas
		Malaysia	MLNG Dua (II)	Bintulu, Sarawak	10.6	7.8	Operation	1995	Petronas (60%); Mitsubishi (15%); Shell (15%); Sarawak Gov. (10%)	MLNG Dua
		Malaysia	debottlenecking	Bintulu, Sarawak	2.0	1.5	Operation	2010	Petronas (60%); Mitsubishi (15%); Shell (15%); Sarawak Gov. (10%)	MLNG Dua
		Malaysia	MLNG Tiga (III)	Bintulu, Sarawak	9.3	6.8	Operation	2003	Petronas (60%); Shell (15%); JX Nippon Oil (10%); Sarawak Gov. (10%); Mitsubishi (Diamond Gas) (5%)	MLNG Tiga
		Brunei	Brunei LNG	Lumut	9.7	7.1	Operation	1972†	Brunei Gov. (50%); Shell (25%); Mitsubishi (25%)	Brunei LNG
		Australia	North West Shelf 1	Burrup Peninsula	3.4	2.5	Operation	1989	Woodside (16.67%); BHP (16.67%); BP (16.67%); Chevron (16.67%); Mimi (16.67%); Shell (16.67%)	Woodside
		Australia	North West Shelf 2	Burrup Peninsula	3.4	2.5	Operation	1989	Woodside (16.67%); BHP (16.67%); BP (16.67%); Chevron (16.67%); Mimi (16.67%); Shell (16.67%)	Woodside
		Australia	North West Shelf 3	Burrup Peninsula	3.4	2.5	Operation	1992	Woodside (16.67%); BHP (16.67%); BP (16.67%); Chevron (16.67%); Mimi (16.67%); Shell (16.67%)	Woodside
		Australia	North West Shelf 4	Burrup Peninsula	6.0	4.4	Operation	2004	Woodside (16.67%); BHP (16.67%); BP (16.67%); Chevron (16.67%); Mimi (16.67%); Shell (16.67%)	Woodside
		Australia	North West Shelf 5	Burrup Peninsula	5.9	4.3	Operation	2008	Woodside (16.67%); BHP (16.67%); BP (16.67%); Chevron (16.67%); Mimi (16.67%); Shell (16.67%)	Woodside

Basin	Region	Country	Plant	Location	Capacity bcm/year	Capacity mtpa	Status	Online date	Owners	Operator
Pacific	Asia	Australia	Darwin LNG	Point Wickham	4.6	3.4	Operation	2006	ConocoPhillips (56.72%); Santos (10.64%); Inpex (10.52%); Eni (12.04%); Tepco (6.72%); Tokyo Gas (3.36%)	Conoco Philips
		Australia	Pluto T1	Burrup Peninsula	5.9	4.3	Operation	2012	Woodside (90%) Tokyo Gas (5%); Kansai (5%)	Woodside
		Australia	Queensland Curtis LNG T1	Gladstone	5.8	4.3	Operation	2014	BG (50%); CNOOC (50%)	BG
		Australia	Queensland Curtis LNG T2	Gladstone	5.8	4.3	Operation	2015	BG (97.5%); Tokyo Gas (2.5%)	BG
		Australia	GLNG T1	Gladstone	5.8	3.9	Operation	2015	Santos (30%); Total (27.5%); KOGAS (15%); Petronas (27.5%)	
		Papua New Guinea	PNG LNG T1&2	Port Moresby	9.4	6.9	Operation	2014	ExxonMobil (33.2%), Oil Search (29%), Indep Public business corp (16.6%), Santos (13.5%), JX Nippon (3.7%); Marubeni (1%); MRDC (2.8%); Petromin PNG (0.1%)	PNG LNG
	Former Soviet Union	Russia	Sakhalin 2 T1	Sakhalin	6.5	4.8	Operation	2009	Sakhalin Energy Invest Co (Gazprom (50% +1), Shell (27.5%-1); Mitsui (12.5%); Mitsubishi (10%)	Sakhalin Energy Invest
		Russia	Sakhalin 2 T2	Sakhalin	6.5	4.8	Operation	2009	Sakhalin Energy Invest Co (Gazprom (50% +1), Shell (27.5%-1); Mitsui (12.5%); Mitsubishi (10%)	Sakhalin Energy Invest

Basin	Region	Country	Plant	Location	Capacity bcm/year	Capacity mtpa	Status	Online date	Owners	Operator
Pacific	North America	USA	Kenai	Nikiski (Alaska)	0.5	0.4	Operation	1969	ConocoPhillips	Conoco Philips
Middle East	Middle East	Qatar	Qatargas I T1&2	Ras Laffan	8.7	6.4	Operation	1996–97†	Qatar Petroleum (QP) (65%); Total (10%); ExxonMobil (10%); Mitsui (7.5%); Marubeni (7.5%)	Qatargas I
		Qatar	Qatargas I T3	Ras Laffan	4.2	3.1	Operation	1999	Qatar Petroleum (QP) (65%); Total (10%); ExxonMobil (10%); Mitsui (7.5%); Marubeni (7.5%)	Qatargas I
		Qatar	RasGas I	Ras Laffan	9.0	6.6	Operation	1999–2000	QP (63%); ExxonMobil (25%); KOGAS (5%); Itochu (4%); LNG Japan (3%)	Rasgas I
		Qatar	RasGas II T1	Ras Laffan	6.4	4.7	Operation	2004	QP (70%); ExxonMobil (30%)	Rasgas II
		Qatar	RasGas II T2	Ras Laffan	6.4	4.7	Operation	2005	QP (70%); ExxonMobil (30%)	Rasgas II
		Qatar	RasGas II T3	Ras Laffan	6.4	4.7	Operation	2007	QP (70%); ExxonMobil (30%)	Rasgas II
		Qatar	Qatargas II T1	Ras Laffan	10.6	7.8	Operation	2009	QP (70%); ExxonMobil (30%)	Qatargas II
		Qatar	Qatargas II T2	Ras Laffan	10.6	7.8	Operation	2009	QP (65%); ExxonMobil (18.3%); Total (16.7%)	Qatargas II
		Qatar	Qatargas III T1	Ras Laffan	10.6	7.8	Operation	2010	QP (68.5%); ConocoPhillips (30%); Mitsui (1.5%)	Qatargas III
		Qatar	Qatargas IV T1	Ras Laffan	10.6	7.8	Operation	2011	QP (70%); Shell (30%)	Qatargas IV
		Qatar	RasGas III T1	Ras Laffan	10.6	7.8	Operation	2009	QP (70%); ExxonMobil (30%)	Rasgas III
		Qatar	RasGas III T2	Ras Laffan	10.6	7.8	Operation	2010	QP (70%); ExxonMobil (30%)	Rasgas III
		Oman	Oman LNG	Qalhat	9.7	7.1	Operation	2000	Oman Gov. (51%); Shell (30%); Total (5.5%); Korea LNG (5%); Partex (2%); Mitsubishi (2.8%); Mitsui (2.8%); Itochu (0.9%)	Oman LNG

Basin	Region	Country	Plant	Location	Capacity bcm/year	Capacity mtpa	Status	Online date	Owners	Operator
Middle East	Middle East	Oman	Qalhat LNG	Qalhat	4.9	3.6	Operation	2006	Oman Gov. (46.8%); Oman LNG (36.8%); Union Fenosa (7.4%), Itochu (3%), Mitsubishi (3%), Osaka Gas (3%)	Qalhat LNG
		Abu Dhabi	Adgas	Das Island	7.9	5.8	Operation	1977	Abu Dhabi National Oil Co (70%); Adgas Mitsui (15%); Total (5%); BP (10%)	
		Yemen*	Yemen LNG T1	Bal Haf	4.6	3.4	Operation	2009	Total (39.62%), Hunt Oil (17.22%), Yemen Gas (16.73%), SK (9.55%), KOGAS (6%), Hyundai (5.88%), GASSP (5%)	Yemen LNG
		Yemen*	Yemen LNG T2	Bal Haf	4.6	3.4	Operation	2010	Total (39.62%), Hunt Oil (17.22%), Yemen Gas (16.73%), SK (9.55%), KOGAS (6%), Hyundai (5.88%), GASSP (5%)	Yemen LNG

* More details on individual trains.

† Editor's corrections based on operator's data.

Source: GIIGNL except where noted.

Table D.4: Regasification terminals

Region	Basin	Country	Terminal	FSRU	Capacity bcm/year	Capacity mtpa	Storage (m³)	Start year	Owners	Operator
Europe	Atlantic	France	Fos Tonkin		3.0	2.2	150,000	1972	Elengy	Elengy
		France	Montoir de Bretagne		10.0	7.4	360,000	1980	Elengy	Elengy
		France	Fos Cavaou		8.3	6.1	330,000	2010	Foxmax LNG (Elengy 72.5%, Total 27.5%)	Elengy
		Spain*	Barcelona		14.5	10.6	390,000	1969	Enagás	Enagás
		Spain*	Barcelona expansion		2.7	2.0		2008	Enagás	Enagás
		Spain*	Barcelona expansion (No. 6)				150,000	2010	Enagás	Enagás
		Spain*	Barcelona expansion (No. 7)				150,000	2011	Enagás	Enagás
		Spain	Huelva		11.8	8.7	619,500	1988	Enagás	Enagás
		Spain*	Cartagena		10.5	7.7	437,000	1989	Enagás	Enagás
		Spain*	Cartagena expansion		1.3	1.0	150,000	2008	Enagás	Enagás
		Spain	Bilbao		7.0	5.2	450,000	2003	EVE (50%), Enagás (50%)	Bahía de Bizkaia gas (BBG)
		Spain*	Sagunto		6.0	4.4	300,000	2006	Union Fenosa, Oman Oil Company, Enagas, Osaka Gas	Saggas
		Spain*	Sagunto expansion		2.8	2.0		2008	Union Fenosa, Oman Oil Company, Enagas, Osaka Gas	Saggas

Region	Basin	Country	Terminal	FSRU	Capacity bcm/year	Capacity mtpa	Storage (m³)	Start year	Owners	Operator
Europe	Atlantic	Spain*	Sagunto expansion		-		300,000	2009	Union Fenosa, Oman Oil Company, Enagas, Osaka Gas	Saggas
		Spain	Mugardos (El Ferrol)		3.6	2.6	300,000	2007	Gas Natural Fenosa, Endesa, Xunta Galicia, Sonatrach, Tojeiro Group, Galicia gov., Caixa Galicia, pastor, Caixanova	Reganosa
		Spain**	El Musel		7.1	5.2	300,000	2013	Enagás	Enagás
		Portugal	Sines		7.6	5.6	390,000	2004	REN Atlantico	REN Atlantico
		Italy	Panigaglia		3.3	2.4	100,000	1971	GNL Italia	GNL Italia
		Italy	Rovigo offshore (Adriatic LNG)		8.0	5.9	250,000	2009	Qatar Petroleum (22%), ExxonMobil (70.7%), Edison (7.3%)	Adriatic LNG (Qatar Petroleum, Edison, Exxon)
		Italy	OLT LNG Toscana	Yes	3.8	2.8	137,500	2013	OLT (Uniper 48.24%, IREN Group 49.07%, other 2.69%)	OLT Offshore LNG Toscana
		Belgium*	Zeebrugge		4.5	3.3	260,000	1987	Fluxys LNG	Fluxys LNG
		Belgium*	Zeebrugge expansion		4.5	3.3	140,000	2008	Fluxys LNG	Fluxys LNG
		Netherlands	Rotterdam (GATE)		12.0	8.8	540,000	2011	Vopak (50%); Gasunie (50%)	GATE Terminal
		United Kingdom*	Isle of Grain		4.6	3.3	200,000	2005†	NGT	Grain LNG
		United Kingdom*	Isle of Grain expansion I		9.1	6.6	570,000	2008†	NGT	Grain LNG

Region	Basin	Country	Terminal	FSRU	Capacity bcm/year	Capacity mtpa	Storage (m³)	Start year	Owners	Operator
Europe	**Atlantic**	United Kingdom*	Isle of Grain expansion II		6.8	5.0	200,000	2010†	NGT	Grain LNG
		United Kingdom**	Teesside	Yes	4.2	3.1	138,000	2007†	Excelerate Energy	Excelerate Energy
		United Kingdom*	South Hook I		10.7	7.8	465,000	2009†	Qatar Petroleum International (67.50%), Exxon Mobil (24.15%), Total (8.35%)	South Hook LNG Terminal Company Ltd
		United Kingdom*	South Hook II		10.7	7.8	310,000	2010†	Qatar Petroleum International (67.50%), Exxon Mobil (24.15%), Total (8.35%)	South Hook LNG Terminal Company Ltd
		Turkey	Marmara Ereglisi		6.2	4.6	255,000	1994	Botas	Botas
		Turkey	Aliaga, Izmir		6.0	4.4	280,000	2006	Egegaz	Egegaz
		Lithuania	Klaipeda	Yes	4.0	2.9	173,000	2014	Charterer: Klaipedos Nafta/ Owner: Höegh LNG	Höegh LNG
		Greece*	Revithoussa		1.4	1.0	130,000	2000	DESFA	DESFA
		Greece*	Revithoussa expansion		3.6	2.6		2007	DESFA	DESFA
		Poland†	Świnoujście		5.0	3.7	320,000	2015	PGNIG	PGNIG
Middle East-Africa	**Atlantic**	Israel	Hadera Gateway	Yes	4.8	3.5	138,000	2013	INGL	Excelerate Energy

Region	Basin	Country	Terminal	FSRU	Capacity bcm/year	Capacity mtpa	Storage (m³)	Start year	Owners	Operator
Middle East–Africa	Atlantic	Egypt	Ain-Sokhna	Yes	7.8	5.7	170,000	2015	Charterer: Egas/Owner: BW	Golar
		Egypt	Ain-Sokhna	Yes	5.2	3.8	170,000	2015	Charterer: Egas/Owner: Höegh LNG	Vopak (60%); Enagas (40%)
		Jordan	Aqaba LNG	Yes	5.2	3.8	160,000	2015	Charterer: MEMR/Owner: Golar	Sempra Energy
	Pacific	UAE (Dubai)	Jebel Ali	Yes	8.2	6.0	125,850	2010	Charterer: Dubai Supply Authority (DUSUP)/Owner: Excelerate	BW
		Kuwait	Mina Al Ahmadi	Yes	7.9	5.8	150,000	2009	Kuwait National Petroleum Corp.	Höegh LNG
North America	Atlantic	USA	Everett		6.9	5.1	155,000	1971	Engie	Engie
		USA	Lake Charles		24.3	17.9	425,000	1982	Trunkline LNG	Trunkline LNG
		USA	Elba Island		16.3	12.0	345,000	1978	Southern LNG (Kinder Morgan)	Southern LNG
		USA*	Elba expansion				190,000	2010	Southern LNG (Kinder Morgan)	Southern LNG
		USA	Cove Point		10.7	7.9	380,000	1978	Dominion Cove Point LNG	Dominion Cove Point LNG
		USA	Cove Point expansion		8.0	5.9	320,000	2008	Dominion Cove Point LNG	Dominion Cove Point LNG
		USA**	Gulf Gateway	Yes	4.9	3.6		2005	Excelerate Energy	Excelerate Energy
		USA	Northeast Gateway	Yes	4.1	3.0	151,000	2008	Excelerate Energy	Excelerate Energy

Data Appendix

Region	Basin	Country	Terminal	FSRU	Capacity bcm/year	Capacity mtpa	Storage (m³)	Start year	Owners	Operator
North America	Atlantic	USA	Cameron LNG		15.5	11.4	480,000	2009	Sempra Energy	Sempra Energy
		USA	Freeport LNG		18.0	13.2	320,000	2008	Freeport LNG	Freeport LNG
		USA	Sabine Pass		26.0	19.1	480,000	2008	Cheniere Energy	Cheniere Energy
		USA*	Sabine Pass expansion		15.3	11.2	320,000	2009	Cheniere Energy	Cheniere Energy
		USA	Golden Pass		21.4	15.7	775,000	2010	Qatar Petroleum (70%), ExxonMobil (17.6%), ConocoPhillips (12.4%)	Golden Pass LNG
		USA**	Neptune	Yes	5.2	3.8		2010	Engie	Engie
		USA	Gulf LNG Energy		12.0	8.8	320,000	2011	Kinder Morgan (50%), GE (40%), AES (10%)	Gulf LNG Energy
		Puerto Rico	Penuelas		3.8	2.8	160,000	2000	Engie (35%); Mitsui (15%); Gas Natural Fenosa (47.5%), GE Capital (2.5%)	Kogas
		Canada	Canaport LNG		10.0	7.4	160,000	2009	Repsol (75%), Irving Oil (25%)	Eco Electrica
		Mexico	Altamira		7.8	5.7	300,000	2006	Vopak (60%); Enagas (40%)	Repsol
	Pacific	Mexico	Energia Costa Azul		10.3	7.6	320,000	2008	Sempra Energy	Golar
		Mexico	Manzanillo		5.2	3.8	300,000	2012	Kogas (25%), Mitsui (37.5%), Samsung (37.5%)	Golar

Region	Basin	Country	Terminal	FSRU	Capacity bcm/year	Capacity mtpa	Storage (m³)	Start year	Owners	Operator
Latin America	**Atlantic**	Dominican Republic	Punta Caucedo		2.3	1.7	160,000	2003	AES	AES
		Argentina	Bahia Blanca GasPort	Yes	5.1	3.7	151,000	2008	YPF	YPF
		Argentina	GNL Escobar	Yes	5.1	3.7	151,000	2011	Enarsa (50%), YPF (50%)	YPF
		Brazil	Pecém	Yes	2.5	1.8	129,000	2009	Charterer: Petrobras/ Owner: Golar	Petrobras
		Brazil	Guanabara Bay	Yes	8.1	6.0	173,400	2009	Charterer: : Petrobras/ Owner: Excelerate	Excelerate Energy
		Brazil	Bahia Escobar	Yes	5.2	3.8	137,000	2013	Charterer: Petrobras/ Owner: Golar	Petrobras
	Pacific	Chile	Quintero		3.7	2.7	334,000	2009	Terminal de Valparaiso (Enagas) (51%), Oman Oil Company (40%); (ENAP (20%); Metrogas (20%); Endesa Chile (20%) (41%)	GNL Quintero
		Chile	Mejillones		2.0	1.5	175,000	2010	Codelco (37%), Engie (63%)	GNLM
Asia	**Pacific**	Japan	Chita Kyodo		9.9	7.3	300,000	1978	Chubu Electric Power, Toho Gas	Toho Gas
		Japan	Chita		14.8	10.9	640,000	1983	Chita LNG	Chita LNG
		Japan	Chita-Midorihama Works		10.5	7.7	200,000	2001	Toho Gas	Toho Gas
		Japan	Chita-Midorihama expansion 1			-	200,000	2009	Toho Gas	Toho Gas
		Japan	Fukuoka†		1.1	0.8	70,000	1993	Saibu Gas	Saibu Gas

Data Appendix 633

Region	Basin	Country	Terminal	FSRU	Capacity bcm/year	Capacity mtpa	Storage (m³)	Start year	Owners	Operator
Asia	Pacific	Japan	Futtsu		26.0	19.1	1,100,000	1985	Tokyo Electric Power	Tokyo Electric Power
		Japan	Hachinohe		1.4	1.0	280,000	2015	JX Nippon Oil and Energy	JX Nippon LNG Service
		Japan	Hatsukaichi		1.2	0.9	170,000	1996	Hiroshima Gas	Hiroshima Gas
		Japan	Hibiki		2.9	2.1	360,000	2014	Saibu gas (90%), Kyushu Elec (10%)	Hibiki LNG
		Japan	Higashi-Ohgishima		18.0	13.2	540,000	1984	Tokyo Electric Power	Tokyo Electric Power
		Japan	Himeji		6.4	4.7	740,000	1984	Osaka Gas	Osaka Gas
		Japan	Himeji LNG		11.0	8.1	520,000	1979	Kansai Electric Power	Kansai Electric Power
		Japan	Ishikari		3.7	2.7	180,000	2012	Hokkaido Gas (70%), TG (20%), JAPEX (5%), Six gas companies in Hokkaido (5%)	Hokkaido Gas
		Japan	Joetsu		3.2	2.4	540,000	2011	Chubu Electric Power	Chubu Electric Power
		Japan	Kagoshima		0.3	0.2	86,000	1996	Nippon Gas	Nippon Gas
		Japan	Kawagoe		6.7	4.9	840,000	1997	Chubu Electric Power	Chubu Electric Power
		Japan	Mizushima		5.8	4.3	320,000	2006	Mizushima LNG	Mizushima LNG
		Japan	Nagasaki		0.2	0.1	35,000	2003	Saibu Gas	Saibu Gas
		Japan	Naoetsu		2.0	1.5	360,000	2013	Inpex	Inpex
		Japan	Negishi		15.1	11.1	1,180,000	1969	Tokyo Gas, Tokyo Electric Power	Tokyo Gas, Tokyo Electric Power
		Japan	Niigata		11.6	8.5	720,000	1984	Nihonkai LNG (Tohoku Electric Power, Japex, others)	Nihonkai LNG

634 LNG Markets in Transition

Region	Basin	Country	Terminal	FSRU	Capacity bcm/year	mtpa	Storage (m^3)	Start year	Owners	Operator
Asia	Pacific	Japan	Ohgishima		13.4	9.8	850,000	1998	Tokyo Gas	Tokyo Gas
		Japan	Oita		7.3	5.4	460,000	1990	Oita LNG	Oita LNG
		Japan	Sakai		8.7	6.4	420,000	2006	Kansai Electric Power	Kansai Electric Power
		Japan	Sakaide		1.6	1.2	180,000	2010	Sakaide LNG	Sakaide LNG
		Japan	Senboku I		2.9	2.1	320,000	1972	Osaka Gas	Osaka Gas
		Japan	Senboku II		15.7	11.5	1,585,000	1977	Osaka Gas	Osaka Gas
		Japan	Shin-Minato		0.4	0.3	80,000	1997	Gas Bureau, City of Sendai	Gas Bureau, City of Sendai
		Japan	Shin-Sendai		1.1	0.8	160,000	2015	Tohoku Electric	Tohoku Electric
		Japan	Sodegaura		40.4	29.7	2,660,000	1973	Tokyo Gas, Tokyo Electric Power	Tokyo Gas, Tokyo Electric Power
		Japan	Sodeshi		3.9	2.9	337,200	1996	Shizuoka Gas (65%), TonenGeneral Sekiyu (35%)	Shizuoka Gas, TonenGeneral Sekiyu
		Japan	Tobata		10.3	7.6	480,000	1977	Kita Kyushu LNG	Kita Kyushu LNG
		Japan	Yanai		3.1	2.3	480,000	1990	Chugoku Electric Power	Chugoku Electric Power
		Japan	Yokkaichi LNG Centre		8.7	6.4	320,000	1987	Chubu Electric	Chubu Electric
		Japan	Yokkaichi Works		2.9	2.1	160,000	1991	Toho Gas	Toho Gas
		Japan	Yoshinoura†		0.5	0.4	280,000	2012	Okinawa Electric Power	Okinawa Electric Power
		Korea	Pyeong-Taek		51.5	37.9	3,360,000	1986	KOGAS	KOGAS
		Korea	Incheon		56.4	41.5	2,880,000	1996	KOGAS	KOGAS
		Korea	Tong-Yeong		33.7	24.8	2,620,000	2002	KOGAS	KOGAS
		Korea	Gwangyang		2.3	1.7	530,000	2005	Pohan Steel (Posco)	Posco

Region	Basin	Country	Terminal	FSRU	Capacity bcm/year	Capacity mtpa	Storage (m³)	Start year	Owners	Operator
Asia	Pacific	Korea	Samcheok		9.0	6.6	600,000	2014	KOGAS	KOGAS
		Taiwan	Yung-An		18.0	13.2	690,000	1990	CPC	CPC
		Taiwan	Taichung		8.0	5.9	480,000	2009	CPC	CPC
		China	Dalian, Liaoning		4.1	3.0	480,000	2011	PetroChina (75%), Dalian Port (20%), Dalian Construction Investment (5%)	PetroChina
		China*	Guangdong Dapeng		5.1	3.7	160,000	2006	CNOOC 33%, BP 30%, others	GDLNG
		China*	Guangdong Dapeng expansion 1			-	160,000	2007	CNOOC 33%, BP 30%, others	GDLNG
		China*	Guangdong Dapeng expansion 2		4.1	3.0	160,000	2010	CNOOC 33%, BP 30%, others	GDLNG
		China	Fujian		6.9	5.1	640,000	2008	CNOOC 60%, Fujian Development and Investment Corporation 40%	CNOOC
		China	Dongguan (Guangdong)		1.4	1.0	160,000	2013	JOVO Group	
		China	Hainan		4.1	3.0	480,000	2014	CNOOC (65%), other companies	CNOOC
		China	Quingdao		4.2	3.1	480,000	2014	Sinopec	Sinopec
		China	Rudong, Jiangsu		4.8	3.5	320,000	2011	Kunlun(PetroChina affiliate) 55%, Pacific Oil and Gas 35%, Jiangsu Guoxin Investment 10%	PetroChina
		China	Shanghai LNG Mengtougou		0.2	0.1	120,000	2008	Shanghai Gas Group	Shanghai Gas Group

Region	Basin	Country	Terminal	FSRU	Capacity bcm/year	Capacity mtpa	Storage (m³)	Start year	Owners	Operator
Asia	Pacific	China	Shanghai LNG Yangshan		4.1	3.0	495,000	2009	CNOOC 45%, Shanghai Shenergy Group 55%	CNOOC
		China	Tangshan, Hebei		4.8	3.5	480,000	2013	Charterer: Engie/Owner: Höegh LNG, MOL, Tokyo Gas	Höegh LNG
		China	Tianjin	Yes	3.0	2.2	60,000	2013	CNOOC	CNOOC
		China	Zhejiang, Ningbo		4.1	3.0	480,000	2012	CNOOC 51%, Zhejiang Energy Company 29%, Ningbo Power 20%	CNOOC
		China	Zhuhai, Guangdong		4.8	3.5	480,000	2013	CNOOC 30%, other companies	CNOOC
		India*	Dahej		8.5	6.2	320,000	2004	Petronet LNG	Petronet LNG
		India*	Dahej expansion		4.0	2.9	272,000	2009	Petronet LNG	Petronet LNG
		India*	Hazira		3.7	2.7	320,000	2005	Shell 74%, Total 26%	Hazira LNG
		India*	Hazira debottlenecking		3.2	2.4	320,000	2008	Shell 74%, Total 26%	Hazira LNG
		India	Dabhol		2.4	1.8		2013	Ratnagiri Gas & Power Private Ltd (National Thermal Power Corp. (NTPC), GAIL)	GAIL
		India	Kochi		6.3	4.6	368,000	2013	Petronet LNG	Petronet LNG
		Singapore	Jurong Island		7.8	5.7	540,000	2013	Singapore LNG Corporation	SLNG
		Thailand	Map Ta Phut		7.3	5.4	320,000	2011	PTT	PTT
		Indonesia	Lampung	Yes	2.4	1.8	173,000	2014	Charterer: PGN LNG/Owner: Höegh LNG	Höegh

Region	Basin	Country	Terminal	FSRU	Capacity bcm/year	Capacity mtpa	Storage (m³)	Start year	Owners	Operator
Asia	*Pacific*	Indonesia	Nusantara Regas Satu	Yes	4.1	3.0	125,016	2012	Charterer: Pertamina (60%), Perushaan Gas Negara (PGN, 40%)/Owner: Golar LNG	PT Nusantara (JV Pertamina, PGN)
		Indonesia	Arun Regas		na	na	220,000	2015	PT Perta Arun Gas	PT Perta Arun Gas
		Pakistan	Port Qasim	Yes	5.2	3.8	150,900	2015	Charterer: Engro Group/ Owner: Excelerate Energy	Excelerate Energy
		Malaysia	Melaka	Yes	5.2	3.8	260,000	2013	Petronas	Petronas

* More details on individual trains.

** Terminal decommissioned or mothballed.

† Editor's corrections based on operator's data.

Source: GIIGNL except where noted.

INDEX

Abadi 148, 149
Abu Dhabi 11, 13, 34, 61, 113, 427, 529
   LNG production prospects 293
acid gas removal unit (AGRU) 582
acid gases 582
ADGAS project 13, 37
administrative price mechanism, India 57
Adriatic LNG terminal 78, 608
Africa 4, 46, 210–12, 273–91, 425, 558, 568
   LNG demand potential 422–6, 428–31, 546, 547, 562
   LNG production prospects 294–6
aggregator 5, 86, 92, 190, 239, 241, 246, 303, 510n, 512–16, 544, 575
   and LNG project structure 121–2
   and shipping 168, 170, 179, 479
AGRU process technology providers 609–10
air pollution, advantage of LNG 23
Alaska 11, 13, 20, 34, 36, 38, 116, 236, 568
Alaska LNG 186, 235–7, 240
Algeria 3, 11–12, 19, 38, 63, 117–19, 422, 423
   LNG exports 17, 18–19
   LNG production prospects 295
   pipeline exports 49, 313
   spot and short-term trade 508–9, 512
Altai pipeline 355
Altamira terminal 55, 418
Alternative Fuel Infrastructure Directive (EC) 459–60
America's Energy Advantage 238, 250
Amoco, and Trinidad 53
Anadarko Petroleum 274–5, 278–9, 281, 287, 289
Andean Region 387, 409–11
Andrés terminal 415
ANEA (North East Asia) spot price index 482
Angola 6, 45, 63, 64, 83
   LNG production prospects 291, 295–6
   and spot market 512, 529–30
Angola LNG 67, 106, 113, 556–7
AP-C3MR™ liquefaction process 143, 586, 587–9
APCI 586, 587
Aphrodite field 294
'applicable range', JCC 36
AP-X™ liquefaction process 592
arbitrage 45, 188

Arctic LNG 268–9, 272
Argentina 16, 60–61, 94–9, 386, 394–9, 408
   FSRUs 91, 421
   gas demand 389, 391, 392, 394, 398, 399
   gas production 388, 394–5
   gas reserves 388
   LNG imports 60–61, 395–6, 398–9, 408, 422, 510
   pipeline exports 89–90, 392, 401, 406, 407
   pipeline imports 398, 399, 402
   regasification terminals 390–91
   shale gas 396–7, 432, 433
Arun plant 13, 71, 86, 110, 370
Asia
   demand 307, 525, 526–9
   LNG imports 382–5
   LNG markets, emerging 349, 382–4
   LNG markets, mature 327–8, 348–9
   LNG production prospects 298–9
   long-term contracts 23, 35, 496
   see also Asian pricing, and entries for specific Asian countries
Asia–Europe price differentials 80–82
Asian Development Bank 56, 203
Asian investment, LNG projects 34, 218–19, 282
Asian pricing 124, 473–92
   Asian premium 211, 230, 478, 484
   Henry Hub, influence of 478–81
   hub pricing proposed 484–5
   and impact on demand 478
   JCC pricing 36, 57, 341, 343, 347, 473–5, 479–81, 493–5
   market pricing, challenges to 494–7
   netback market value 475
   and North American projects 247–51
   spot-indexed prices 482–4
   spot prices 7, 8, 84, 128, 177, 222, 476, 482–4
Atlantic Basin LNG market 16–17, 19–20, 37–8
Atlantic LNG 109, 297
Australia 14, 34, 63, 139, 209–15, 227
   domestic supply concern 220, 225–6
   and FLNG 147, 148, 159, 215, 221
   fracking ban, state 227
   gas market 217
   gas resources 216

LNG exports 11, 13, 14, 22, 31, 60, 100, 557
  see also LNG supply outlook *below*
LNG projects 7, 67, 216–19, 228–9
  potential 214, 224–5, 228–9
  Asian investment in 59, 218–19
  breakeven price 222
  cost escalation 159–60, 215, 220–1, 223, 566
  liquefaction plant costs 137, 141, 143–4
  oil price impact 221–2, 224, 225
  project structures 113–14
LNG supply outlook 209–14, 215–29, 291, 300–301
  capacity growth 209–12, 222–7, 568
  contracted gas 225–6
  spot and short-term trade 509–10, 512–13, 529, 530, 532
Australian dollar weakness 223
Australia–Pacific LNG (APLNG) 102, 216, 217, 221, 226, 526
Azerbaijan 49, 313, 323, 326

BAFA 472
Bahrain 423, 426, 427–8, 433, 561
Baia de San Vicente terminal 407
Baja California terminal 55
Baltic LNG 257, 260, 261, 264–5, 271, 272
Bangladesh 379–80, 382, 383–4, 385, 432, 561
banks, and LNG business 123
Barents Sea 256
Bear Head plant 144
Bechtel 143
Belgium 15, 18, 19, 20, 47, 81, 82, 283, 309–10, 317, 538
Benin 430
BG 51, 53, 65, 66, 67, 87, 102, 122, 125, 190, 214, 275, 277, 280, 295, 296, 479, 543, 544
  purchase by Shell 222, 224, 239, 279, 280, 544, 549, 559
Bilbao terminal 190
Bintulu plant 13, 86, 298
biogas 312
Black & Veatch 143, 147
Blue Corridors 459, 460
boil off 543, 595, 597
boil-off gas (BOG) 600
Bolivia 61, 68, 386, 388–9, 391, 392, 394, 396, 398–9, 400, 402, 404
Bontang plant 13, 86, 110, 370
BOTAS 52
BP 51, 52, 57, 65, 88, 100, 122, 240, 279, 292, 547
  and Qatar 69–71, 74

Brazil 297, 298, 386, 399–406
  energy mix 399–400
  FSRUs 91, 400–401, 402
  gas consumption 389, 400
  gas production 388, 400, 401, 402
  hydroelectricity, fluctuation in 399–400, 403, 404, 433, 563
  LNG demand potential 392, 394, 401–5, 421, 422
  LNG imports 60–61, 283, 391, 392, 401
  LNG production prospects 298
  pipeline imports from Bolivia 398, 400, 402
  regasification requirements 390–91, 400, 401–2, 405–6
Brega plant, Libya 12–13
British Columbia 104, 215, 241–3
brownfield LNG projects 135–6, 229, 567
Browse LNG 146, 148, 224
Brunei 11, 12, 13, 22, 31, 34, 36, 38, 114, 187, 291, 299, 513, 558, 564
Brunei LNG 25, 101
Bumi Armada 153
buyers 104, 211, 524, 559–60
BW Group 91, 153

Cabot 53
calorific value, LNG 26–7
Camel liquefaction plant 3
Cameron LNG 116, 117, 126–7, 143, 239, 479, 555
Cameroon 16, 110–11, 114, 296, 555
Canada 139, 143, 209–15, 251, 302, 458
  British Columbia projects 104, 215, 237, 241–3
  Eastern Canada projects 237, 244–6
  First Nations 211, 241, 243–4
  LNG imports 55, 56
  LNG production 54, 230, 302
  LNG projects 38, 104, 139, 159, 160, 214, 236, 241–6, 568
    impact of US shale gas 83, 245–6
    outlook 254–5
    portfolio aggregators 241–2
  LNG supply outlook 209–14, 230, 241–7, 251, 255
  LNG as transport fuel 456–9
  regasification terminals 181
  regulatory framework 232–3
  tax policy 232–3, 569
Canaport terminal 56
Canvey Island regasification plant 3, 10
carbon dioxide emissions 22, 29, 32, 331, 337, 339, 344–5, 351, 353, 374, 555, 562
  LNG as transport fuel 443–4, 448, 456

carbon dioxide in natural gas 582
carbon dioxide sequestration 215
carbon intensity, LNG 29
carbon price 317, 318
cargo swaps 543
Caribbean FLNG project 147, 149, 150, 152, 154, 156, 158, 411
Caribbean, LNG demand 386, 389, 411–20
Cartagena terminal 410, 411
CB&I 143
Centrica 125
certificate of convenience and necessity 231–2
Chart Industries 143
charter contracts 166–8
charter length, tankers 166–9, 180
charterparty 165–6
Cheniere 67, 83, 86, 125–6, 188, 238, 239, 407
   LNG pricing formula 478–9
   and spot market 537–8, 542
Chevron 188, 223, 295–6
Chile 16, 60–61, 65, 190, 386, 389, 390–91, 399, 406–7, 422
China 4, 46, 57–9, 349–59, 382–5, 555
   coal bed methane 351, 354
   energy mix 349–50
   energy policy 351–2
   gas consumption 350
   gas demand 351, 352–3
      decline 45, 526, 528–9, 557, 562
      potential 432, 356–9
   gas production 354–5
   gas supply 351, 354–9
   liquefaction plant investment 59
   LNG imports 17, 57–60, 80, 267, 351, 355–9, 382–5
   LNG prices 57, 59, 80, 252–3, 473–7, 485–6, 494, 574
   LNG as transport fuel 453, 454, 461, 560
   pipeline imports 57, 59, 264, 351, 355
   regasification terminals 57–9, 91, 181–2
   shale gas 351, 354
   spot market 517, 534
   synthetic natural gas 351, 354
Chiyoda 143
Chubu Electric 13, 33, 103, 219, 527, 566
   and Qatar 70, 71, 72, 73
city gas 26–7
Clean Air Act (1956) 3
Cleveland disaster 10, 37
climate change and LNG 21–2, 29, 30, 555, 562
CNOOC 57, 59, 68, 102, 187, 218, 219, 242, 518, 526, 529, 560

CNPC 57, 68, 218, 219, 263, 266, 280, 355
coal, and Asian markets 328–31, 338–40, 344, 345, 347, 348
coal price 316–18, 348, 561
coal seam gas (CSG) 215, 219–20
coal-to-gas switching 317–18
coil-wound heat exchanger (CWHE) 588–9
Cold Gas Trading 25
Colombia 16, 386, 409–11
   gas demand 389, 410
   gas production 297, 388, 409
   LNG imports 87, 89, 90, 410–11, 422
   regasification terminals 390–91, 410–11
combined cycle gas turbines (CCGT) 25
commercial agreements, LNG projects 118–21
competitive tendering, project contractor 145
compressed natural gas (CNG) 442, 461
'Conch' containment system 161
condenser 579
ConocoPhillips 78, 143, 228–9, 240, 312n, 512, 587, 589
construction contracting strategy 104, 145
construction costs, liquefaction plant 134, 136–8, 566
containment system, LNG ships 595–8
containment tanks, LNG storage 603–4
contract extensions 502–3, 530–32
contract length 168, 539–40, 548, 575–6
contract renegotiations 530–32
contractors, liquefaction plants 143–4
COP21 328, 348, 351, 555
Corpus Christi plant 127, 143, 238, 239
cost reduction, and market change 541
Costa Azul terminal 56, 202, 298, 419
Costa Rica 386, 413
Côte d'Ivoire 430
Cove Point 53, 143, 239, 555
CPC 32, 65, 75–6, 103
Cuba 386, 389, 411, 413
Curtis Island 219, 224
Cyprus 274, 294, 302, 313

Dabhol terminal 56
Dahej terminal 56, 203
Damietta plant 66, 295
Darwin LNG 216, 217
debottlenecking 74, 530, 567
dehydration, natural gas 582
demand shocks, and LNG trade 517–18
Department of Energy (USA) 54, 231, 479
destination clause 23, 166, 168, 175, 238, 490, 491, 520–24, 526, 548–9

destination flexibility 54, 120, 520–22, 575
displacement offer, LNG shipping 254
Distrigas 19, 189–90
diversification and supply growth 211
DKRW 298
Dolphin Gas 61, 63
Domestic Market Obligation 220, 287
Dominican Republic 17, 386, 389, 413, 415–16
Donggi-Senoro plant 67, 86, 102, 299, 370
double hull 595
downward quality tolerance 526
Dragon LNG terminal 51, 102, 185, 514
DSME 147, 152
Dual Mixed Refrigerant Process 586
Dubai 60–63, 79, 424, 426–7

Eastern Africa, LNG outlook 273–91, 294–6
EAX (East Asia Index) 482
Ecoeléctrica 414
economic growth, and energy demand 348
Ecuador 386, 389
EDF Trading 76
Edison 75
Egypt 6, 66, 91, 114, 313, 423, 529
    LNG demand potential 418–9
    LNG exports 22, 45–6, 64
        end of 63, 66, 427, 428
    LNG imports 87–8, 185, 197, 307, 424, 556
    LNG production 66, 291, 294–5
    spot and short-term trade 509–10, 512
El Paso Natural Gas 11, 164, 171, 196
El Salvador 386, 391, 413, 417
Elba Island 53, 239
Elf, and Qatar 70–71
Elk-Antelope 299
ELNG project 109
EmiratesLNG 427
Emission Control Areas (IMO) 447, 448, 449–50
Empresa Nacional de Hidrocarbonetos (ENH) 117–18
Enagas 11, 190
ENAP 407
end flash 584–5
Endesa 52, 76
ENEL 191
'Energy Bridge' concept 164, 174, 196
energy efficiency 316, 319
energy security 20–21, 24, 29, 31, 33, 324
Engie 51, 56, 67, 126, 198, 254
ENI 66, 214, 275, 278, 279, 281, 287, 289

Equatorial Guinea 45–6, 65, 114, 296, 505, 509–10, 512
equilibrium commodity pricing 249–51
equipment supply, liquefaction plant 133–4, 144
Eskom 429, 430
Esso, and Libya 13
Estimated Ultimate Recovery (USA) 250–51
EU ETS 316–18
EU LNG Strategy 324
Europe
    and Asian LNG market 80–82, 325–6
    future gas supply, role of LNG 322–5
    gas demand 314–27, 525
    gas market liberalization 46, 51–2, 469, 484, 519–20
    gas production 48, 311–12, 320–22
    gas supply diversification 48–50, 322–5
    green gas production 312
    hub pricing 470, 472, 484
    see also NBP, TFF
    imports 18–20, 45–53
    LNG demand potential 308–27
    LNG diverted to Asia 80–82, 325–6, 557
    LNG prices vs pipeline prices 472–3, 570–72
    LNG re-exporting 81–2, 310, 325, 514, 542
    as LNG residual market 309–11
    LNG supply 322–5
    as LNG swing market 308
    LNG terminals 50, 199–200, 310–11, 322
    LNG as transport fuel 320, 458–60
    natural gas, position of 308–9, 314, 325–6
    pipeline gas 49–50, 313–14, 321–6
    power sector 47–8, 315–19
    regasification plants 181–2
    security of gas supply 324, 326
    unconventional gas 312
    see also entries for individual countries
European Commission 50, 200, 317, 520, 571
European Gas Directive 199
European Investment Bank 203
Europe–Asia price differentials 80–82
Everett terminal 53
Excelerate Energy 52, 61, 91, 151, 152, 173, 174, 196–7, 415, 426
exchange-based pricing, oil 507
EXMAR 147, 151–2, 154, 158, 297
ExxonMobil 51, 65, 75, 77–8, 102, 214, 239, 242, 254, 281, 289, 299, 514

Far East LNG 260, 269, 270, 272
Federal Energy Regulatory Commission (FERC) 54, 121–3, 231–2
final destination clauses, and spot market 520–24
financing requirements 104–5, 116–18
First Nations 211, 241, 243–4
fiscal incentives, government 103–104
fiscal terms, and LNG projects 103–4
FLNG 92, 110–11, 129, 131, 143, 146–59, 181, 221, 296, 298, 567, 605
  capital costs 153–5
  conversion from LNG tankers 150–51, 152
  market opportunities 147–51
  operating costs 155–7
  production costs 157–8
  project structures 154–5
  SWOT analysis 148–51
  technical issues 149, 150, 151, 607
  value chain 157–8
floating liquefaction unit see FLNG
floating production, storage and offloading unit see FPSO
floating storage and regasification unit see FSRU
FLSO 152
Fortune FLNG project 111, 146, 147
Fos Tonkin terminal 186–7, 205
FPSO 151, 152–3, 605, 607
fracking 227, 232, 251, 312, 397
France 18, 20, 47, 50, 181, 309–10, 317, 472, 531
Freeport LNG 99, 117, 126, 239, 555
FSRU 52, 131, 146, 147, 151, 164, 181, 196–8, 206, 307, 432, 605
  conversion from tankers 197–8
  mooring buoy concept 196–7
  and seasonal demand 424
  and small LNG markets 87–91, 92
  technical issues 606
Fujairah terminal 61, 427
Fukushima crisis 92, 329, 330, 348
  impact of 78, 80, 84–5
  and LNG prices 473, 476, 493
  and spot market 517–18, 533
  and spot tanker rates 176–80
full cost recovery 480–81
futures contracts 123

GAIL 56, 68, 125, 257, 537, 544
gas futures contract 469
gas market liberalization 484, 548
  Europe 46, 51–2, 469, 484, 519–20

Far East 35, 494–7, 504, 526–7, 573, 574
  and spot market 519–20
  USA 17, 53, 540, 556
Gas Natural Fenosa 74, 122, 126, 414
gas price see price, pricing
gas processing 581–3
Gas Sayago 407
Gas Supply Agreement (GSA) 120
gas turbines 144
gas types, cost of liquefaction 135
GasAtacame 407
gasification, efficiency of 27
Gassi Touil 502, 505
Gasunie 11, 188
GATE terminal 52, 185, 188, 204
Gaz Transport system 161, 596
Gazprom 57, 64, 89, 111, 255, 258, 259, 260, 271–2, 297, 301, 322, 462, 570–71
  and Baltic LNG 257, 264–5
  and China 264, 355
  and Far East LNG 270
  market share in Europe 324, 326
  and Sakhalin 2 256, 262–3, 270
  and Shtokman 257, 272
  and Vladivostok LNG 263–4
Gazprom Marketing and Trading 257
GDF Suez see Engie
GE 144
Genpower 402
Germany 312, 320
Ghana 87, 90, 429, 430
Gladstone LNG 67, 86, 216, 218–19, 226
Glencore 516
'global gas price' 7, 92, 492, 497
global warming potential 443, 444
GME pipeline 19
Golar LNG 61, 63, 91, 111, 147, 151, 152, 154, 158, 174, 197, 296, 426
Golden Pass terminal 77, 167, 168, 239, 242, 254
Gorgon LNG 67, 106, 117, 144, 216, 217, 221, 225, 226, 529, 541
Grain LNG 200–201, 205
gravity-based structure (GBS) 608
Great Smog 3
Greater Caribbean 411–18
Greece 19, 20, 309–10
Green Stream pipeline 19
greenfield site, liquefaction plant 135–6
greenhouse gases 22, 32, 443–4
Groningen principle 469
Grupo Bolognesi 402
GTT 161, 596

Guangdong Dapeng terminal 187, 518
Guangdong LNG 57, 100
Guatemala 413
Gulf Gateway project 152, 196
Gulf LNG 239
Gunvor Group 516

Hackberry Decision 122–3, 198
Haiti 386, 413, 416
Hazira terminal 56, 102, 190
heavy hydrocarbons (HHCs) 581, 582
heat exchanger 579
heavy goods vehicles, and LNG 452–3, 461
Henry Hub 7, 53, 66, 67, 83, 126, 127, 249, 300, 469, 472
　and Asia 230, 478–81, 494
Hides field 65
Höegh LNG 91, 151, 152, 154, 197
Honduras 386, 413, 416
hub pricing 451, 469, 470, 472, 484–5, 520, 573–4
hub-plus pricing 450
Hunt Oil 66
hybrid pricing 488, 496
Hydrocarbons Law, 2015 (Argentina) 397
Hyproc Shipping 172

Ichthys 117, 141, 144, 149, 216, 217, 218, 219, 225, 226
Idku plant 66
IHI 143
Incheon 31
India 46, 57, 359–64
　energy mix 359–60, 363
　energy policy 362–3
　gas consumption 360, 361
　gas production 361, 362
　liquefaction plant investment 59
　LNG imports 17, 56–7, 360, 361–4, 383–5
　LNG prices 57, 360, 361, 473, 476–7, 486
　regasification terminals 181–2, 364
Indonesia 11, 13, 32, 34, 38, 63, 114, 368–72
　energy mix 369
　gas consumption and supply 369
　gas demand potential 370–71
　gas production 299, 369–71
　LNG exports 370
　LNG imports 85–6, 371–2
　spot and short-term trade 508–9, 513
Industrial Emissions Directive 319
infrastructure, and spot market 519–22
INPEX 218, 219
integrated project structure 105–6, 129

International Maritime Organization 444, 447
investment and supply growth 212–13
Iran 15–16, 38, 49, 56, 302, 377, 423, 425
　LNG production prospects 292, 293–4
　LNG projects 67–8, 566, 567
Iran Pipeline Project 377
Iraq 423, 425
Iraqi Kurdistan 314, 323, 326
Isle of Grain terminal 51, 185, 200–201, 543
Israel 66, 87, 88–9, 91, 149, 159, 294, 302, 313, 427
Italy 12, 13, 19, 47, 52, 309–10, 470
Itochu 74
Izmir terminal 52

Jamaica 413, 416
Japan 3–4, 13, 328–37
　energy efficiency 331
　energy mix 328–9
　energy security 20–21, 23, 26, 33–5
　gas consumption by sector 329–30
　　city gas sector 26–9
　　industrial sector 27
　　power sector 22–6, 28–9, 330–34
　gas demand 329–36, 526–8
　gas production 335
　gas supply 335–6
　Fukushima, impact of 78, 80, 84–5, 176–80
　government financial support 24–5, 28
　LNG as clean fuel 21–2, 23, 26
　LNG imports 17, 20–29, 33–7, 38, 335–8
　LNG potential demand 336–8
　LNG prices 36, 80, 84–5, 92, 473, 474, 476–8, 485
　see also JCC
　market liberalization 484–5, 495, 526–8
　nuclear generation 329, 330–34, 336, 337
　portfolio LNG 515
　regasification terminals 181–2, 185, 336
　renewable energy 331, 337
　tanker owners 173
　trading houses, role of 25
Japan Bank for International Cooperation 117
Japan Crude Cocktail see JCC
JCC 36, 57, 341, 343, 347, 473–5, 479–81, 493–5
JERA 8, 527, 560
JGC 143, 147
JKM (Japan/Korea Marker) 482–4
JLC prices 488
JOE forward trading platform 482
JOE spot price 482–3
Jordan 87, 88, 89, 427

Jordon Cove 240
JOVO Group 57, 535
Jules Verne 11
Jurong Island terminal 87

Kaliningrad 265
Kanowit (PFLNG-1) 147, 153–4, 155, 158
Kazakhstan 355
KBR 143, 144
Kenai plant 13
Kenya 273
KEPCO 30
Keppel 147, 153
Khazzan gas field 292
Kinder 239
Kitimat terminal 56
Kochi terminal 56
KOGAS 30, 33, 67, 68, 74, 100, 102, 103, 219, 280, 342, 486, 528, 529
KORAS 74
Korea Electric Power *see* KEPCO
Korea Gas Corporation *see* KOGAS
Korea (South Korea) 338–43
   energy mix 338, 342
   energy policy 340
   energy security 33–5
   gas consumption 338–9
   gas demand potential 340–41, 526, 528
   gas supply 339–40
   LNG demand potential 341–3
   LNG imports 17, 29–31, 38
   LNG prices 473, 474, 476–8, 486
   power sector 339, 340
   regasification terminals 181–2
Korean Consortium 102
Kribi project 146, 147
Krishna Godavari K6-D6 field 56
Kuwait 60–63, 63, 91, 197, 423, 424, 426, 433
Kuwait Oil Company 426
Kvaerner Moss 161
Kyoto Protocol 22, 337
Kyushu Electric 219

Lake Charles 53, 239, 514
Large Combustion Plant Directive 319
Latin America
   gas demand 388–90
   gas reserves 388
   LNG demand perspectives 385–94, 420–21, 433
   LNG exports 392, 393
   LNG imports 60–61
   LNG production prospects 297–8

   LNG supply 389–92
   regasification plants 389–91, 393
Leviathan field 294
LiBro 153
Libya 11, 12–13, 19, 38, 45, 49, 291, 295, 313, 424, 556, 558
Linde 143
liquefaction 10, 44–5, 291, 519, 558–9
liquefaction capacity, global 291
liquefaction plant 64–7, 99
   financing structure 117–18
   floating 146–58, 607
   full listing 620–26
   and long-term contracts 502–3, 504–5
   modularization 67, 144–5, 607
   processes 580–93
   and Qatar 73–8
   share of value chain 131
   small-scale 593–4
   technical resources 609–11
   train size 591–4
liquefaction plant costs 130–43
   bulk material supply 134
   contractor competition 143–4
   construction costs 134, 136–8
   cost comparisons 138–9
   cost components 133–40
   cost escalation 141–3, 159–60
   costs over time 132–3
   cost reduction strategies 143–6
   engineering and project management 133
   equipment supply and logistics 133–4, 144
   labour costs, local 137, 141
   operating costs 139–40
   owner's costs 133
   processing capacity 135
Liquefied Natural Gas Limited 143–4
liquid petroleum gases (LPG) 583, 584
lithium bromide 153
Lithuania 50, 87, 89, 309–10, 324
LNG
   calorific value 26–7
   as city gas feedstock 26–7
   as clean fuel 21–2, 29
   energy density 1
   history 1–4
   properties 578, 580
   quality specifications 523
LNG demand potential
   Africa 422–6, 428–31
   Argentina 398–9
   Asian emerging markets 348–84, 432, 433
   Asian markets, mature 327–8, 348–9, 432

Brazil 403–5
Bangladesh 379–80
Caribbean 411–20
Chile 406–7
China 349–59
Colombia 410–11
Europe 308–27, 332–6, 432–3
global 307–8, 431–3, 561–4
India 359–64
Indonesia 368–72
Japan 328–37, 383–4
Latin America 385–94, 420–22, 433
Malaysia 372–6
Mexico 419–20
Middle East 433
Middle East and Africa 422–31, 433
Pakistan 376–8
Singapore 364–6
South Korea 338–43, 383–4
Taiwan 343–8
Thailand 366–8
Uruguay 408
Vietnam 380–82
LNG exports
  data, by year and by country 614–15
  growth 45
  history 11–16
  re-exporting 81–2
  see also individual countries
LNG-fuelled vehicles
  cost implications 454–5
  environmental benefits 455–6
  fuel-price advantage 454–5, 460, 462
  manufacturers 456
  refuelling infrastructure 455, 459–60, 461
LNG imports
  Asian imports, outlook 382–5
  data by year and by country 616–19
  history 16–37
  importers, small 87–90
  and pipeline supply 19
  see also individual countries
LNG Index base, proposed 481
LNG market
  changes in 92–3
  different from oil and coal 503–7
  flexibility 574–5
  growth in 44–6, 558–61
  inflexion point 539
  maturing market 44–6
  oversupply 547
  reconfiguration 547–9, 554–76
LNG pricing see pricing

LNG process technology 591, 609
LNG production prospects, global 299–304
LNG projects
  capital costs 505–6
  commercial agreements 118–21
  financing 116–18, 282
  and governments 104, 568–9
  outlook 567–9
  planned 214
LNG Sales & Purchase Agreement (SPA) 120
LNG, security of supply 324, 326
LNG storage 602–4, 611
LNG structures, floating 605
LNG suppliers 63–93
LNG supply and demand balance 556–8, 564–5, 570
LNG technical resources 609–11
LNG tenders 518–19
LNG terminals see regasification terminals
LNG, as transport fuel 442–63
  bunkering 451–2
  consumption by vessel and vehicle type 445
  cost advantage 449–51
  demand 443–4
  emissions 443–4, 448–9
  growth 442–3
  and marine transport 446–52, 463
  and road vehicles 452–6
  supply 444–6
  technical advantages 442
local content, and supply growth 211
long-term contracts 105, 475, 502–7, 513, 539–40, 547, 549
  and Qatar 535–6
Lumut plant 13
Lunskoye gas field 64

Magnolia LNG 144
Malaysia 11, 63, 81, 103, 115, 147, 372–6, 382–5
  energy mix 372
  gas consumption 300, 373
  gas demand prospects 374–6
  gas production 373, 374, 529
  LNG exports 12, 13, 22, 32, 34, 36, 335, 344, 351, 373, 374
  LNG imports 78, 85–6, 373, 375–6, 383–5
  LNG production prospects 291, 298–9
  spot and short-term trade 509, 513, 530
Malaysia LNG 101, 504, 518, 529
  see also MLNG Satu
Mamba project 279
Manzanillo terminal 55, 419

Index   647

Map Ta Phut terminal 86, 367
Marathon 65
Marcellus shale 56, 232, 245
marine transport, emission by fuel type 448–9
market flexibility 517–22
market pricing 468–70, 493, 575
   in Asia, challenges to 494–7
market transition, drivers 541–2
market uncertainty 525–9
markets, and value chain 100–101
MARPOL VI 444, 446, 447, 462
Marubeni 65, 66, 69, 72
Master Sales Agreement (MSA) 120–21
mega-train 76
Mejillones terminal 406, 407
membrane containment system 161–2, 595
membrane ship 596–7
MENA 422–5, 431
mercury removal 582–3
Methane Pioneer 10, 11, 161
Methane Princess 3, 5, 11, 594
Methane Progress 11
METI 331, 482
Mexico 83, 386, 412, 418–20
   gas demand 389, 418, 419
   gas production 388, 418, 419
   impact of shale gas 83, 298
   LNG production prospects 298
   LNG imports 17, 55, 77, 418–19, 420, 422, 433
   pipeline imports 416, 418, 419, 420
   regasification converted to liquefaction 298, 419
   regasification terminals 55–6, 181, 389, 390–91, 418–19
Middle East 422–8, 431
   LNG demand potential 426–8, 431
   LNG imports 60–63
   LNG production prospects 291–4
   pipeline trade 425
Middle East and Africa 422–31
Mina Al-Ahmadi terminal 197
MISC 172
Misubishi Corporation 25, 64, 102, 126, 256
Mitsui 25, 55, 64, 65, 126, 173, 256, 280
   and Qatar 69–70, 72, 78
MLNG Satu 103
Mobil, and Qatar 71–2, 74, 75
MODEC 153
modified tolling price structure 479
modularization, liquefaction plants 67, 144–5, 607
Morocco 425, 429, 433, 561

Moss containment system 595
Moss Rosenberg design 161
Moss tanker 161–2, 595–6
   for FLNG 150, 153
Mozambique 138, 139, 209–15, 273–90, 425, 430
   Asian investment in 59, 280–82
   costs 282–3
   fiscal terms 285, 286
   FLNG development 158, 159, 277, 279
   gas resources 274–7
   global competitiveness 282–3
   LNG prospects 273–90, 301
   local expectations 285–9
   project development 160, 277–9
   regulatory framework 284–5
Mozambique LNG 118
Myanmar 56, 59, 68, 351, 355–7, 367, 379, 561

Nakilat 168, 172, 173
National Balancing Point *see* NBP
National Development and Reform Commission (China) 59
National Energy Board (Canada) 232
National Environmental Policy Act (NEPA) 231–2
National Grid (UK) 51, 188
Natural Gas Act (1938) 231
Natural Gas Act (2005) 54
natural gas liquids 97, 99, 583
Natural Gas Policy Act 17
natural gas, public image 561
NBP 67, 77, 80, 81, 449, 450, 454, 469, 471, 472, 482–3, 520, 573
Negishi terminal 186, 187
netback 77, 177–9, 249, 469, 475
Netherlands 52–3, 309–12
NEWC Index 542
Nicaragua 413
Niche liquefaction 152
Nigeria 15, 38, 115, 423, 452, 504
   LNG exports 12, 45–6, 49, 64, 211, 214, 424, 425
   Fukushima, impact of 177–9
   gas reserves 273, 422
   LNG production 137, 291, 295, 504, 556
   spot and short-term trade 508–10, 512, 518, 519, 529
nitrogen 21, 134, 580, 584–5
nitrogen oxides 21, 443, 448, 449, 456
non-open access, LNG terminals 122–3
North America
   LNG exports 230–55

LNG imports 53–6
price disequilibrium with Asia 230
shipping LNG to markets 251–4
see also Canada, USA
North America projects
Asian premium 248, 249
contractual commitments 246–7
domestic price issues 250–51
European market 248–9
financial feasibility 247–51
outlook 245–5
Panama Canal enlargement 252–4
see also Canada, USA
North Field 14, 61, 68–9
North Sea gas 48
North West Shelf (NWS) 14, 100, 144, 216, 217, 220, 532
Northern Sea Route 164–5, 266
Norway 19, 45–6, 48, 64, 66–7, 115, 291, 310–11, 460, 509, 512
Novatek 258, 259, 265–9, 271–3
nuclear power 24, 25, 319, 328, 348, 432
see also Fukushima
NYMEX 469

offshore classification societies 611
offshore LNG 604–8
offtaker 479, 569
oil crisis 1973, and impact on LNG 21, 24, 27
oil indexation 7, 573
oil-linked contracts 512–3
oil-linked pricing 7, 36, 59, 70, 75, 85, 92, 241, 248, 468–9, 470, 472, 475, 476
oil prices, low, impact of 209, 213, 221–2, 270, 277, 283, 295, 300, 420
oil pricing 478, 493, 494, 506–7, 561
oil product minus pricing 450
oil-related price formula 36
Oil Search 65
Oman 12, 14, 22, 34, 45, 49, 64, 66, 115, 291–4, 431, 509, 512, 540, 564, 567
Oman LNG 14, 99, 100, 108, 282, 502, 504
ONGC 68
OPEC 61, 63, 506–7
Open Rack Vaporizer (ORV) 601–2
Ophir 146, 147, 149, 275, 277, 280, 296
Optimized Cascade® liquefaction process 143, 587, 589–91
Oregon projects 235, 236, 237, 240
Origin Energy 221, 222
Osaka Gas 27, 33, 65, 102, 103, 173, 187, 219
OSMR process 144
ownership structures 101–4

Pacific Basin LNG market 16–17, 389
Pacific Northwest project 86, 243–4
Pacific Rubiales Energy 297
Pakistan 79, 87, 88, 91, 376–8, 382–5, 535, 536
Pampa Melchorita 66
Panama 413, 416
Panama Canal 163, 180, 251–4
Papua New Guinea 22, 45, 64, 65, 79, 115, 117, 299, 473, 513
Pavilion Energy 87
peak shaver 601
Pechora LNG 260, 261, 271, 272
Perenco 146
Pertamina 86, 110, 111, 115
Peru 45, 61, 66, 297, 388–9, 509–10, 513
Petrobras 400, 401
PetroChina 59, 226, 242, 535
Petronas 51, 68, 86, 102, 103, 151, 158, 218–19, 298, 518, 529
Petronet LNG 56, 75, 362
PetroVietnam 381
PEW 219
Philippines 87, 89, 90
Piltun-Astokhskoye oil field 64
pipeline supply, Europe 48–50
pipeline technology, maritime 12, 19
pipeline vs LNG 2
plate fin heat exchangers (PFHE) 589, 591
plateau volume 504
PNG LNG 65–6, 299
Poland 50, 309–10, 312
portfolio aggregators 230, 599
see also aggregators
portfolio LNG 510n, 514–16
portfolio trading, and tanker capacity 170
Portugal 19, 309–10
Power of Siberia project 355
power sector, Europe, gas demand 315–19
pre-cooling 583
Prelude FLNG project 110, 146, 147, 148, 149, 153, 158, 216, 217, 221, 226
price, citygate 486n
price, domestic gas
and investment 382, 424
subsidized 61, 299, 300, 360, 363, 395, 397, 398,
price, LNG 7, 80, 82, 222
decline 494
historical 11–12, 18
and new investment 128, 141, 209, 221, 228, 247–8, 260
regional 80–81, 92, 204, 492–4
see also country entries

Index 649

price, wholesale gas 7, 48, 87, 89, 361, 363, 425, 454, 486, 572
price benchmarks, and market change 541–2
price competition, LNG and Russian gas 322–3, 325, 570–72
price convergence 92, 254, 300
price deregulation, wellhead 240
price formula, US LNG 478–9
price incentive, and US LNG exports to Asia 230
price premiums 211, 478, 484
price review
    arbitration 489, 490
    long-term contracts 488–91
price risk 503
pricing
    Asian 473–92
    and coal pricing 316–18, 348, 561
    'global price' 7, 92, 492, 497
    hub 451, 469, 470, 472, 484–5, 520, 573–4
    see also Henry Hub, NBP, SLInG, TTF
    hub-plus 450
    hybrid 488, 496
    market 468, 469–70
    mechanisms 213
    netback 77, 177–9, 249, 469, 475
    oil-linked 7, 36, 59, 70, 75, 85, 92, 241, 248, 468–9, 470, 472, 475, 476
    see also JCC
    outlook 572–4
    and security of supply 491–2
    spot 6, 45, 66, 92, 93, 117, 473
    and subsidies 28, 413n, 425
pricing, oil 506–7
PRICO process 143
prismatic containment system 595, 597
process hazard analysis 607
processing capacity, liquefaction plant 135
production sharing contractors (PSC) 110
profit optimization 543–4
project finance 126, 542, 565–6
project structure 105–18
    aggregator model 121–2
    FLNG 110–11
    integrated 105–6
    regasification 122–3
    throughput 108–11
    tolling 108–11
    transfer pricing 107–8
    US LNG exporters 124–7
propane 583–4
Prudhoe Bay field 240

PTT 86
Puerto Rico 414–15
Punta Sayago project 407–8
Pyeongtaek terminal 30, 31

Qatar 14, 16, 34, 38, 45–6, 61, 63, 68–79, 111, 115
    and Asia 536–7
    dominance of 63–4
    and Europe 534–5
    gas reserves 422
    and India 57, 362
    LNG exports by region 78–9
    LNG production 68, 291–3, 300
    LNG tankers 162–3, 168–9, 180
    long-term contracts 535–6
    marketing strategy 69–70, 78–9
    spot and short-term trade 508–10, 512, 533–7
    and USA 534
Qatargas 69–74, 102
Qatargas 1 77, 107, 282
Qatargas 2 76–7, 106
Qatargas 3 77–8
Qatargas 4 77–8
Qatar Petroleum (QP) 51, 69, 70, 75, 76–7, 102, 254, 514
Q-Class tankers 162, 163, 168, 180
Q-Flex tankers 77, 163, 168, 180, 523, 597
Q-Max tankers 77, 163, 168, 180, 523, 597–8
Queensland Curtis (QCLNG) 67, 141, 216–19, 221–2, 224, 226, 526
Quintero terminal 190, 406

ramp-up period 504
ramp-up volumes 513–14
Ras Laffan Industrial City and Port 72
RasGas 72, 74–8, 99
RasGas 1 74–5
RasGas 2 75–6
RasGas 3 77
receiving terminal 598
recondenser 600–601
redirection, LNG cargoes 514
re-export functionality 600
re-exports 81–3, 204, 310, 417, 514, 517, 521, 542, 557,
refrigerants 586
refrigeration 578–80, 585–7
regasification process 598–602
regasification project structure 122–3
    capacity allocation 193–5
    dependent rights 193–5

FSRU 196–8
  independent rights 193–5
  scheduling 195–6
  user agreements 192–3
regasification terminals 50, 53, 56, 57–9, 181–206, 610
  business models 186–98
  capacity 310–11, 322, 324, 519
  conversion to liquefaction 124, 125, 135, 204
  costs 184
  financing 202–4
  full listing 627–37
  growth of 181–6
  integrated 186–7
  merchant 189–91, 203
  regulation of 198–202
  tolling 187–9, 202–3, 206
  utilization 184–5, 204, 205–6
  and value chain 100–101
regulatory framework and supply growth 214–15
'relationship culture' 39
renewable energy 6, 312, 316, 318, 331
Repsol 52, 66
RIM spot price index 482–4
Rolls Royce 144
Rosneft 258, 259, 262, 263, 269–71, 272
Rotan 147, 158
Ruhrgas 11
rundown 584
Russia 15, 45, 115, 209–15, 570–72
  government and LNG 256, 265, 266, 267
  impact of low prices 259
  impact of US and EU sanctions 259, 263–4, 267
  LNG background 255–9
  LNG outlook 255–73
  LNG projects 259–73
  LNG production prospects 301
  LNG supply competition 258, 259
  market liberalization 258
  pipeline exports 49, 313, 314, 321–3, 325–6
  spot and short-term trade 509, 513

Sabine Pass 67, 124, 125–6, 138, 143, 144, 188, 238, 239, 478–9, 538
Sagunto terminal 190
Sakhalin 1 260, 261, 262, 269, 270
Sakhalin 2 64–5, 117, 255, 256, 260, 261, 262–3, 270–71, 272,
Sakhalin 3 262–3

Sakhalin Energy Investment Company 64
sales and purchase agreement (SPA) 503
Samsung 147
Santos 67, 221, 222
SBM Offshore 153
'S-curve', and JCC 36
Second Gas Directive 199
security of supply 324, 326, 524–5
Segas 66, 102, 109, 114
Sempra 126–7, 298
Senboku terminal 187
Senegal 430
Sengkang 299, 370
Senoro plant 13
shale gas 53, 56, 124, 230, 251, 492
  and impact on LNG 82–3, 92, 472
Shanghai hub 485–6, 487, 495
Shanghai Petroleum Exchange 486
shareholder interests, and LNG projects 103
Shell 25, 55, 64, 66, 78, 102, 111, 122, 161, 214, 223, 239, 256, 279, 289, 544, 559
  and FLNG 146, 147, 151, 158
shipping 99–100, 105, 160–81, 254, 505–6, 514, 519, 559, 594–8
  Arctic icebreaker design 164–5, 181
  capacity 169–70
  charter length 166–9
  charterparty 165–6
  charters, price and volume clauses 166–8
  conversion to FLNG 150–51, 152
  finance 174
  life-cycle 170–72
  loading 585
  optimization 542–7, 549, 575
  ownership 172–4
  propulsion systems 162
  and short-term market 174–5
  size 162–3
  spot charter rates 179, 180
  transportation costs 163
  and terminal access 523, 524
short-term contracts 495, 507–11
short-term market, and tanker capacity 174–5, 180
Shtokman 49, 83, 257, 260, 261, 272
Siberia, and China 355–7
Siemens 144
Singapore 85, 86–7, 204–5, 364–6, 486–7
Singapore terminal 190, 191
single loop refrigeration 586
single mixed refrigerant (SMR) 586, 594
Sinopec 65, 102, 219, 526
SK Corporation 66

Index

Skikda 505
SLInG price 487, 495
slope, JCC 36
SNH 146
Snøvhit 66–7, 164, 221n
Sodegaura terminal 187
sole-sourced contractor 145
Sonagas 65
Sonatrach 51, 89, 111, 295
Sonoma 298
South Africa 429–30
South Hook terminal 51, 77, 78, 102, 167, 168, 185, 187, 203, 239, 533
South Kirinskoye field 262, 263
South Korea *see* Korea
South Pars field 292, 294
south-east Asia, LNG imports 85–7
Southern Cone, LNG demand potential 392–408
Southern Gas Corridor 314, 326
Spain 47, 50, 52, 177–9, 246, 460, 470, 492, 531
　LNG imports 12, 18, 19, 20, 46, 309–10, 489, 520
　LNG terminals 51, 52, 181–2, 311, 459, 472
　re-exports 81, 82, 204, 514, 521, 557
SPB, and FLNG 597–8
spot and short-term trade 508–25, 538–48
　challenges 523–5
　market flexibility 517–22
　potential evolution 538–47
　supplier flexibility 511–17
spot cargo rates 177, 180, 511, 512–13
spot charter rates, tankers 175–9, 180
spot contracts 524
spot indices 573
spot LNG imports 517–18
spot market
　buyers' factors 519–22
　contractual constraints 523
　contract extensions and renegotiations 530–32
　future developments 525–38
　market uncertainty 525–9
　and Qatar 533–7
　shipping constraints 523–4
　uncommitted supply 529–30
　and US LNG 537–8
Statoil 89, 257, 275, 282, 287
step-by-step contracting 145
stockpiling, challenge of 35
storage tanks 585

Submerged Combustion Vaporizer (SCV) 601, 602
Suez Canal 162
sulphur dioxide 21, 23, 443, 447, 448, 462, 560
Sumitomo Corporation 25
supplier flexibility 35, 511–17
supply growth 209–15
supply shocks, and LNG trade 517–18
Świnoujście terminal 191

Taichung 32
Taiwan 29, 31–5, 38, 343–8
　LNG demand potential 346–8
　LNG prices 473, 474, 476–7
　power generation 33, 344, 345–6
Taiwan Power Company 32
'take-or-pay' clause 23, 25, 101n, 503, 518
Tamar field 88
Tangguh plant 13, 106, 138, 169, 370
Tanzania 138, 139, 209–15, 273–90, 301
　domestic gas price 287–8
　fiscal terms 285, 286
　gas resources 274–7, 301
　global competitiveness 282–3
　infrastructure for domestic use 287–9
　IOC investment 280, 281–2
　LNG prospects 273–90, 301
　local expectations 285–7
　projects 159, 160, 277, 279–80
　regulatory framework 285
TAPI pipeline project 377
Technigaz 161
Technip 147
Teesside GasPort terminal 52
TEPCO 13, 20, 21, 33, 36, 65, 102, 173, 219, 518, 527, 560
terminals 181–203
　dedicated 188
　integrated 188
　merchant 189–91, 203
　tolling 187–9, 191, 192, 203
Terminal Use Agreement (TUA) 121
Thailand 85, 86, 366–8
third-party access (TPA) 96, 485, 503, 548–9
　and regasification terminals 122, 199–200, 401n, 527
　and spot market 522
three loop refrigeration 586–7
throughput project structure 108–11
Tianjin FSRU 57
Toho Gas 27, 219

Tokyo Electric Power Company *see* TEPCO
Tokyo Gas 20, 21, 27, 33, 36, 102, 103, 173, 186, 187, 219
tolling fee 66, 157, 202, 265, 479, 480, 569, 572
tolling structure, LNG projects 108–11, 123–7, 128–9, 233
tolling terminal 187–9, 191, 192, 202, 203
Total 55, 67, 68, 69, 72, 77, 102, 122, 125, 188, 214, 266, 299
trading houses, and spot market 541
trading hubs, and spot market 520
Trafigura 516
transfer pricing, project structure 107–8
transfer pricing structure 129
Trans-Mediterranean pipeline 19
transport fuel, emissions 448–9
Trinidad and Tobago 14, 45, 49, 53, 111–13, 116, 297, 388–9, 413, 509–10, 513
Trunkline 11
TTF hub price 248, 249, 472n, 494, 520, 538, 573
Turkey 19, 20, 47, 52, 309–10
Turkmenistan 59, 88, 355–7
two loop refrigeration 586

UAE *see* United Arab Emirates
UK 47, 48, 51, 174, 200, 317, 454
   gas production 311–12, 556
   LNG imports 3, 10–11, 18–19, 46, 161, 309–11, 523
   LNG pricing 77, 469, 492, 520
   LNG terminals 51–2, 77, 78, 91, 102, 181, 185, 197, 311
uncommitted cargoes 549
uncommitted volumes 511–13
Union Fenosa Gas 52, 102
Union Stock Yard and Transit Company 3, 10, 161
United Arab Emirates 61, 427
upstream facilities 97–9
Uruguay 87, 89–90, 389, 407–8
USA 209–15
   aggregator investment 233
   Alaska LNG project 235, 236, 237, 240
   Atlantic coast projects 234–6, 238–40
   domestic gas price issues 250–51
   Estimated Ultimate Recovery 250–51
   fracking, state regulations 232
   Gulf Coast projects 234–6, 338–40
   LNG as transport fuel 456–9
   Oregon projects 235, 236, 237, 240
   regulatory framework 231–2
   regasification to liquefaction plant conversions 233
   shale gas production 78, 82–3
US LNG 7, 83, 111, 537–8
   export prices 82, 124, 248–50, 478–81
   export projects 116, 230–55, 337–40
      structure 124–7, 129
   imports 17–18, 53–6, 82
   liquefaction plants 124
   offtake agreement 479
   outlook 569–70
   production, growth of 230
   re-exports 517–18
   and Russian gas 570–72
   terminals 53–5, 181–2
Uzbekistan, and China 355

Vaca Muerta 396, 397
value chain, liquefaction costs 140–41
vaporizer 601–2
Venezuela 15–16, 68, 297–8, 388, 389
Vietnam 380–82
Vitol 517
Vladivostok LNG 260, 261, 263–4, 272
volume risk 503

Wheatstone project 216, 217, 225, 226, 529
Wison 147
Wood-Prince, William 3, 10

Yamal LNG project 104, 164–5, 181, 213, 258, 260, 261, 265–8, 272
   funding 267–8
Yamal Peninsula 49, 256
Yemen 6, 22, 45, 63, 66, 116, 138, 283, 291, 293, 424, 508n, 509, 512, 556, 558
Yemen LNG 67, 102, 108
Yung-An terminal 32

Zeebrugge terminal 76, 78, 185, 204
zero send-out 600
Zohr gas field 66, 87, 289, 294, 295, 428